FEB - - 2006

THE
SAMURAI
FILM

THE
SAMURAI
FILM

EXPANDED AND REVISED EDITION

ALAIN SILVER

THE OVERLOOK PRESS
Woodstock & New York

For Linda
and in memory of Hideo Gosha

First published in the United States in 2005 by
The Overlook Press, Peter Mayer Publishers, Inc.
Woodstock & New York

WOODSTOCK:
One Overlook Drive
Woodstock, NY 12498
www.overlookpress.com
[for individual orders, bulk and special sales, contact our Woodstock office]

NEW YORK:
141 Wooster Street
New York, NY 10012

∞ The paper used in this book meets the requirements for paper
permanence as described in the ANSI Z39.48-1992 standard.

Cataloging-in-Publication Data is available from the Library of Congress

Book design and type formatting by Bernard Schleifer
Manufactured in China
ISBN 1-58567-596-2 (HC)
ISBN 1-58567-780-9 (PB)
1 3 5 7 9 10 8 6 4 2

CONTENTS

ACKNOWLEDGMENTS

Since the first edition of this book was published in 1977, interest and information about the samurai film available outside Japan and to non-Japanese speakers has increased significantly: from almost nothing to a small amount. Given that this book has always been aimed at cinéastes outside of Japan, the emphasis was and is to provide as much useful filmographic information as possible but at the same time to focus on the films themselves. Beyond a core group of twenty titles or so, many key examples of the samurai film, despite the efforts of some dedicated video producers and distributors, remain very hard to find. In revising this book for the first time in twenty years, the hope is to spark an interest in a new generation of filmgoers and urge them to use resources now available through the Internet to expand their experience of a genre that has produced and continues to produce some of the finest motion pictures in the brief history of the art.

For her assistance and support in all phases of the original edition, I must still thank, first of all, Elaine Cardenas. Jim Paris provided research materials, cited the trenchant quote from Lao-Tse, and proofread the initial chapters. My frequent collaborator, James Ursini, offered many suggestions and references beyond the requirements of pure filmography, which he helped create in the first edition. Thanks also to Lowell Peterson and Lee Sanders for giving me titles I could find nowhere else; my late father, Elmer Silver, for assembling the manuscript; Henry Kaiser; Janey Place; the UCLA Film Commission; Stan Berkowitz, Evelyn Renold, and Leigh Charlton at the UCLA *Daily Bruin*, where some of this writing was first published; Franklin Urbach; David Bradley; Bruce Brown and Steven Epstein; and Mort Wexler, then of Toei Los Angeles, for arranging several special screenings. *The Samurai Film* was my third book and thanks to its original editor, Peter Cowie, it was the first to be designed, illustrated, and appear in print in a manner very close to what I had envisioned.

Peter Mayer at The Overlook Press was interested in this book before its publication by A.S. Barnes and, after that company's demise, commissioned a second edition. Elizabeth Ward, who took time off from our work on *Film Noir* for Overlook and made the the final phases of the first edition much easier, also helped on the second edition research and, in that pre-computer era, retyping. Some of the material in this edition is based on articles we wrote together for the magazine *Martial Arts Movies* (please see the Bibliography for details). Others who provided updated notes or *errata* for the second edition were Jessica Amanda Salmonson, Sandra Segal, and Susan Graves.

For this third edition, Tracy Carns and David Mulrooney at The Overlook Press provided editorial support. The initial new research was done by Darren Gross. More extensive filmographic additions and revisions using Japanese language databases as well as details of variant spellings of Japanese proper names in English were completed by Dan Richard. Darrell Davis and Stuart Galbraith IV also kindly reviewed material. Numerous copies of newer releases on DVD and VHS as well as background information on various productions were generously provided by Merlin David at Samurai Video of Suffern, New York. Assistance with other titles came from Gordon Spragg at Celluloid Dreams, Stephen Kang at DvdAsian.com, Spencer Savage at Image Entertainment, Glenn Erickson of DVDSavant, Alexander Jaboby, and Ric Menello. Filmographic information updated and compiled by the author came from the Academy of Motion Picture Arts and Sciences Library in Beverly Hills, California, and from various online sources, most notably the websites of Matsuda Film Productions, Mainseek, and the Internet Movie Database [see more detailed note in the introductory comments to the Filmography]. Lastly, very special thanks go to Linda and India Brookover for tedious hours spent scanning and collating my pre-computer-era manuscript and for moral support on a daily basis.

SAMURAI ASSASSIN (*Samurai*, 1965). Directed by Kihachi Okamato from a screenplay by Shinobu Hashimoto, and starring Toshiro Mifune as Tsuruchiyo Niiro (pictured center). [Extensively discussed in Chapter 6]

INTRODUCTION

Fire leaps from their swords,
The sparks of their own anger
fall upon them like rain,
—SEAMI, *Tsunemasa*[1]

A S A GENRE, THE SAMURAI FILM SHARES ATTRIBUTES WITH THE warrior tales of Western tradition, with the Greek and Roman heroes in the epics of Homer and Virgil, with the Arthurian chronicles, and most recently with the American movies focused on gunfighters and lawmen living in its 19th-century frontier. Like the ancient Greeks besieging Troy, samurais such as the "Loyal 47 *Ronin*," who in late 1702 avenged their dead lord in defiance of the law, are figures grounded in historical fact but elevated through repeated representations in art to the level of myth. This combination of mythic and historical record is like that of Achilles and Aeneas, Roland and Arthur, or Jesse James and Wyatt Earp. The fictional representations of Japan's heroic *bushi* ("warriors") are filled with personas who are larger than life. The combination of real and fabled events which underlie the myriad dramatizations of a character such as Miyamoto Musashi, whether refined or unrefined, whether folktale or epic, whether *Kabuki* or puppet theater, whether primitive mask or painted narrative scroll—all are rooted in a homogenous and unbroken cultural tradition built up over more than a millennium.

The socio-political and ethico-religious stasis of feudal Japan, which endured longer than anything like it in the West, underlies any samurai drama, both as art in general and film in particular. To understand better the samurai as a character in a particular type of film and the other aspects of the samurai as an institution, the facts and perceptions of and about the samurai in past Japanese society which color the contemporary depictions should be briefly considered.

I. The Samurai in History

Evil customs of the past shall be broken off and
everything shall be based on the just law of nature.
—"The Charter Oaths"

Historically, the first *bushi* emerged from the Japanese aristocracy just as the
first occidental knights. In Japan, however, knighthood was never a quest for
grails or glory in the manner of Arthur and Beowulf and was never viewed with
a cavalier attitude. In the foundation legends of Japan, heroes such as Yamato,
the first of the imperial lineage, were princes and dragon slayers. When political intrigues and usurpations began to undermine the absolute authority of
the *mikado*—or emperor—as invested by the *Shinto* goddess of the sun
Amaterasu Omikami, the power base shifted to the aristocracy. The various
baronial clans and families united under provincial overlords called *daimyos*
and began to vie for control of what was formerly public land.

As the possession of land and the ability to tax the serfs who farmed it
were the economic mainstays of an unproductive ruling class, the mode of
government which evolved during the Nara (650-793 C.E.) and Heian (794-
1185) eras was one of classical feudalism. Each armed knight—the original
meaning of the word "samurai" is "servant" or "retainer"—was invested by and
pledged allegiance to his immediate lord in a system of fiefdoms. In exchange
for service in a *daimyo*'s personal guard a warrior was quartered and provi-
sioned. The *karoku* or stipend of the first samurai was paid not in gold but in
rations of rice and usually expressed as a number of *koku*, each of which
equaled one and a half barrels, five bushels, or 180 liters of rice. As sons
replaced fathers in a *daimyo*'s retinue, attachments between a family and a
feudal lord became a valued inheritance. While many of the earliest samurai
labored as mercenary knights under the principle of *issho kemmei*—a desperate striving even unto death for a place in the world—the second and third
generations worked primarily to fortify and secure the acquisitions of their

fathers. All this was translated, quite pragmatically, into a need for an intense loyalty to both family and clan. The lord referred to his vassals as "men of the house" (*kenin* or *gokenin*), and those chosen to be trained to defend it were conditioned to place the welfare of the household over any personal ambitions, even gladly to forfeit their lives for it.

While the Japanese code of honor may have been conceived like the Spartan ideals, early fighting was marked more by ritual than by ferocity. As with the knightly heritage in the medieval West, single combat was held to be the surest way to bring honor and renown to the family name; and an exchange of litanies of their respective lineages by the prospective combatants as they squared-off in the field of battle was the accepted way to proclaim a valiant and distinguished ancestry. A confrontation between rival armies was, as a whole, a highly structured affair with opposing forces lining up to display their standards in orderly fashion at a site negotiated in advance by delegates from each faction. After an exchange of arrows, the mounted samurai advanced, each seeking an opponent of fairly equal stature with whom to duel. Despite all the tournament-like formalities, the unwieldiness of the armor made each horseman concentrate on dismounting rather than dismembering his antagonist, so that once this was accomplished the fallen man might be more easily pierced fatally by a sword, lance, or *naginata*—a halberd-like device best described as a long sword blade mounted in a three to four foot handle. The final task was the collection of heads, which were then hoisted in the air atop banner poles or lances as grisly proof of a warrior's prowess.

Most of the records as well as the literature and art concerned with the earliest samurai paint a fairly uniform portrait, which perpetuates the analogy to the Homeric hero or the Knight of the Round Table. Armed and mounted as awesomely as any Western warrior and guided by an ideal of chivalry called *bushido*—literally the "way of the soldier-knight," an unwritten code of ethical conduct which will be examined further in the next section—as selfless and righteous as Galahad or as furious as Orlando, this first samurai was gradually constrained in his beliefs and actions by a ruling class seeking to preserve their control over the small amount of arable land available to a growing population in a mountainous island nation. As the tiers of a ruling oligarchy solidified, the samurai became less like a hoplite, the individual "man at arms" or Greek citizen-soldier who put down his plow and put on his armor when duty called, and more like a Roman legionnaire. The end of the Heian period was marked by two major civil wars fought for control of this nation. Both the Fujiwara/Minamoto and the Minamoto/Taira feuds were inspired by an erosion of imperial power and the beginning of a system under the Fujiwara of de facto rule by clan lords who maintained the emperor as a mere figurehead. The legendary samurai of this period are not the armed bands of clan retainers who terrorized the streets of Kyoto, but the aristocratic warriors—Kiyomori, Tsunemasa, Tametomo, Yoshitsune, Kumagai and Atsumori—who participated in the courtly battles.

With respect to a change in the nature of the samurai perhaps the most significant result of the victory by the Minamoto or Genji clan was the formal establishment in 1192 of a "shogunate" or military government, a "shogun" being the equivalent of a field marshal or *generalissimo*. Although the concept of nation itself was still centuries from fruition and the idea of acting "for the good of all Japan" was not yet born, continuous fighting between the *daimyos* produced a constant demand for men-at-arms. To answer the needs of this comparatively modern type of warfare, of larger armies with improved weapons, the *ashigaru*—or foot-soldiers, who previously had functioned as a kind of squire to the mounted knight—evolved into the low-caste samurai, a light infantryman who fought not in single combat but with companies of his fellows.

Japan's medieval years, the Kamakura (1186-1336) and Ashikaga (1337-1573) eras, are not purely analogous to any in the West. This span of centuries culminates in an Eastern Hundred Years War (the Senkuko wars, 1467 to 1574) and was marked by the emergence of the *ikko-ikki*—or warrior monks—who at one point controlled the entire province of Kaga and who actually defeated a young Ieyasu Tokugawa at Kaniwada in 1564. In terms of the events depicted in motion pictures, it is as infrequently used as a background as the European "Dark Age." These eras mark the refinement of the methods of war: (1) the organization of quasi-nationalistic armies both to repel successfully two incursions by the Mongols and to launch unsuccessfully an invasion of Korea; and (2) a swelling undertide of identification with the nation rather than the *han* or province overseen by a clan lord, which equated in Japan with a movement to restore full privileges to the emperor. But the most familiar image of the samurai, the archetypal man of action disenfranchised by time, is almost always associated with the long national peace of the socially and politically repressive Tokugawa Era from 1600 to 1868.

The reasons why this era is the most usual setting for the samurai film are as complex and varied as both the dramatic literature and the dramatic history which antedate and underlie the genre. To begin with, the virtuous, unworldly heroes celebrated in the epic sagas and scrolls of the Minamoto/Taira wars of the 11th and 12th centuries were displaced and elevated in succeeding periods to mythic status. Their idealized position became, in light of the bloody realities of unabating internecine warfare, as functionally irrelevant to everyday life as Don Quixote's. After Yoshitsune successfully led the Minamoto against the Taira at Dan-no-ura in 1185, it was still possible to believe that, in a confrontation between two courageous foes, fate had rewarded the greater valor. When Ieyasu Tokugawa carried the field against the slightly larger forces of Mitsunari Ishida and the six-year-old Toyotomi heir at the battle of Sekigahara in October of 1600, his victory was the product of statesmanship, reconnaissance, betrayal, and, ultimately, superior tactics. A mere display of courage did not guarantee victory.

The most renowned survivor of Sekigahara was Miyamoto Musashi. While he will be treated in more detail later, the aspect of his character most pertinent to this discussion is the fact that, although he fought on the losing side in 1600, he renounced all allegiances to make a reputation and a fortune solely by means of his strength and cunning. Provincial economies had devoted fortunes to waging wars. As they adjusted to Tokugawa rule, Musashi gained both notoriety and wealth in a series of ruthlessly fought duels with master swordsmen. Under the Tokugawa repeated famines were tolerated as the shoguns attempted to inculcate the notion of caste privilege in the minds of the war-bled "have-nots." This inspired numerous low-ranking samurai and masterless swordsman to adopt a view as mercenary as Musashi's.

In terms of *chambara* or *ken-geki* (literally "sword-theater"—both terms refer to fighting with weapons on stage) or the genotype of fiction which is the central concern of this book, the Tokugawa shogun is the ultimate autocrat, and his *bakufu*—or military government—is a monolith of class investiture, the last stand of an entrenched feudalism before the modern era. The pragmatic national response to a changing, less predictable style of warfare—in this regard perhaps of almost equal significance to Sekigahara is the Battle of Takeda (1575) in which shogun Oda Nobunaga used a line of marksmen armed with muskets to repel the charges of mounted warriors—led not only to the enforced peace of Tokugawa but to a highly symbolic codification of class privilege. Whether a man was classed among the samurai, the peasant farmers, the artisans, or the mercantile, the *shi-no-ko-sho*—or four major categories in descending order—would have a determining influence on practically every aspect of his material life, from the type of dwelling he could inhabit to the color of clothing he could wear. An injunction against "perambulation" prevented the *heimin* or commoner (that is, a non-samurai) from legally traveling more than a few miles from the place of his birth; and unless he was a doctor or teacher he did not even have the right to a family name. Musashi is reputedly the first "two-sword" man, referring to the method of fighting in which two blades are drawn and wielded simultaneously. In 1588, just before the Tokugawa regime, the shogunate of Hideyoshi Toyotomi ordained that only a samurai could be literally a "two-sword" man by forbidding members of the lower classes to carry more than one weapon, and that only of a limited blade length. Perhaps the most awesome prerogative of the samurai was *kirisutogomen*. Under this sanction, the swordsman had the right to kill instantaneously and without warning any low-caste person he thought had given him insult, a right which needless to say alienated him further from those below him in the pecking order of Japanese society. The resemblance to the military society of Sparta was now even more pronounced. Like the *homoioi*, the Spartan upper class, the samurai was empowered to kill any of those lower castes, whose very function was to support the military hierarchy. Under the Tokugawa, a final analog to the extreme isolationism of that Greek city-state would shortly be put into place.

As the law-making and highly systematized class privileges of the shogunate inspired resistance, the government instituted increasingly prohibitive measures to maintain its oligarchic power. For fear of a recurrence of *gekoku-jo* ("overthrow by underlings"), the concept which had sustained the pre-Tokugawa civil wars, unruly nobles, particularly *tozama*, or "outside" *daimyos* of the outlying, Western *han*, were bound by the doctrine of *sankin-kotai*—or "alternate duty." As refined by the Tokugawa from the policies of earlier shoguns, a lord had to spend every other year in attendance at Edo (Tokyo), the locus of the Tokugawa castle to which the shogunate had shifted the seat of national rule from the imperial city of Kyoto. Cut off from their supporters at home, closely scrutinized for long periods of time, sometimes compelled to leave their wives and children permanently in the capital, and required to spend substantial sums to maintain a second residence and retinue of servants as befitted their station, potential rebel warlords were effectively proscribed physically and fiscally from plotting revolution. To protect against *kikenshiso*—or "dangerous notions"—taking root in any part of the populace, the shogunate developed a complex network of *metsuke* (spies) and informants who functioned as a thought police over all its subjects. Further to prevent any influx of ideas which might threaten the status quo, the Tokugawa gradually closed the door of the island state to all outsiders, inaugurating a persecution of all those converted to Christianity by Jesuit missionaries in the 16th century, culminating with the suppression of an armed Christian force and the Shimabara uprising in 1637-38, and preventing any trade or contact with foreigners through a proscriptive and coercive doctrine of xenophobia. Article Ten of the 1636 revision of the *buke-sho-hatto* ("rules for martial families") read simply: "The Christian sect is to be strictly prohibited in all the provinces and in all places."

The only exception were trading outposts for the Chinese, Vietnamese, and Dutch in the outlying port city of Nagasaki at the southern tip of the country. This policy lasted for more than two hundred years, until 1853, when the seven "Black Ships" of American Commodore Perry forced their way into Edo harbor. The following year, under the terms of the Treaty of Kanagawa, Shimoda Harbor at the isolated tip of the Izu Peninisula, more than 100 miles southeast of Edo, was opened to American trading vessels, and Townsend

Harris established the first American consulate in Japan. Before year's end, the Russians had done likewise. This was the beginning of the end for two centuries of rigorous isolationism and for the shogunate itself.

The Tokugawa regime spent two hundred and fifty years degenerating into a stagnant but self-perpetuating bureaucracy, which attempted to preserve its hegemony by bringing the progress of social time to a standstill; but in the end it was unable to eradicate the need for upward mobility, even in a country with more than a millennium of feudal tradition. At best, the samurai of this period occupied an uncertain or neutral political position. For while the hereditary options toward leisure and the lack of constructive input on the part of the five to ten percent of the population which 2,000,000 samurai constituted was in many ways unconscionable, *kirisutogomen* and attendant abuses were seldom invoked. Consequently the elevation in class of the samurai was tolerated by the *akindo*—or men of commerce—as long as they too prospered. As the loss of foreign exchange and the restrictions on internal movement took their economic toll, as taxes rose and the ordinances of the *bakufu* multiplied, the position of the samurai decayed from both within and without. Without, in the face of increasingly polarized group interest and rising class tension, the clan retainer, no matter what his political inclination or his posture in previous eras, could only be identified as an accomplice of the oppressive minority of landed gentry. Forced to be idle warriors, some samurai found occupation in provincial government or with schools of the martial arts; but most lived totally unproductively off a land which was far from fat. Within, the samurai class itself was divided into high and low caste roles: from the *kyunin*—relatives of the *daimyo* and other elders—to the *kachi*, or lowest rank, all of which were fixed not on merit but according to length of family service. Within the clan system the status of a retainer was determined by the amount of the *karoku*—or stipend. Throughout its era, the gold and silver coins devised by the Tokugawa were still based on rice and its value [see *koku* in the glossary for further details]. Rice allotments were reclaimed as ranks were reduced either forcibly, by weeding out low-ranking members who would otherwise overtax a *karoku* not geared to keep pace with the cost of living, or through voluntary resignation from the clan by the most ambitious and power-hungry. Some discharged retainers managed to become *jizamurai*—or land-owning samurai. But most joined the growing number of *ronin* ("man on the wave")—or samurai without masters—a group of wandering "two-sword" men who sustained themselves by mercenary work for wealthy merchants or sometimes by criminality, and who personified for all a strong disaffection for the shogunate.

In *chambara* in general and in the samurai film in particular, the *ronin* occupies an important position. Certainly there are analogies to the Western concept of tragedy, to the dramatic idea of a man cast down by fate or mis-guided ambition; and certainly the change in status of the *ronin* was a highly melodramatic one, a fall from the top rank of the four high castes to that of *chori* (outcast) or *hinin* (non-man), the substrata of untouchables in Japan's system. The allegorical characterization of the *ronin* in fiction as a kind of "stray dog" is an inbred one, deriving from the actual treatment of the *chori* and *hinin* by the *shi-no-ko-sho*, who went so far as to develop special linguistic conventions for them as things rather than human beings, and to count them with words usually reserved for animals. For example, the Japanese title of Hideo Gosha's *Three Outlaw Samurai* (1964) is *Sanbiki no Samurai,* which is literally "three outcast" or "three animals of samurai." This is something of a contradiction, for true samurai were not numbered in the manner of cattle or pigs. The *chori* (gardeners, sandal makers, tanners, grave diggers) organized themselves into ghetto-like settlements and were forbidden from mingling with the higher classes or undertaking any but their hereditary occupation. The *hinin* (beggars, minstrels, panderers, and prostitutes) clustered in the *yukaku* or brothel districts. Killing one of them was not considered murder but merely a misdemeanor punishable by a fine. With most of the facets of their precarious low-caste existence severely regulated, the samurai who was reduced to one of their number but continued to act as if he were still a man of privilege found himself the object of enmity and persecution by all the *shi-no-ko-sho*. An outlaw as well as an outcast, he was often equally scorned by the classless men who could not accept him as one of their own. For all its tragic potential, the plight of a totally ostracized *ronin* also conferred a kind of liberation. Divested of social responsibility, unburdened of the heavy weight of *giri*—the absolute fealty owed to a lord—the former samurai carved out whatever place he could. As a man of rank he had been inhibited by innumerable invisible ties. As a *ronin* who might become a *yakuza* (an "8-9-3" gambler) or *sanzuku* ("bandit"), he was as free as he dared to be; and if, like Musashi, his luck matched his audacity, he was one of the very few with a real opportunity for advancement in the cramped, occupational structure imposed on all by Tokugawa. In post-Tokugawa society becoming a *yakuza* offered a similar opportunity for advancement without benefit of social pedigree. Some *yakuza* regarded themselves as heirs to the samurai tradition. Long having their own code, *ninkyodo*—literally "the way of chivalry" but once meaning an "outlaw code"—the *yakuza* often enacted Mafia-style vengeance in their own turf wars and instituted the severing of a finger in expiation as an alternative to *hara-kiri* or ritual suicide. For a period in the 1960s, *ninkyo eiga*—or "chivalry movies"—dominated the *yakuza* genre.

The modern era in Japanese history begins with the "restoration" to power of the Meiji dynasty, which was in fact the institution of the parliamentary system which governs Japan to this day. The *bakumatsu*, the series of civil conflicts which overthrew the military government, was forged out of growing dissatisfaction with the economic instability and exorbitant taxation of the shogunate and foreign incursions, which engendered the *sonno-joi* movement (*sonno* was to revere the emperor and *joi* to expel the "barbaric" foreigners). For a decade both Edo and Kyoto became the scene of repeated assassinations and bloody encounters between the *ishin shishi*, or "men of noble purpose," young, low-ranking samurai from the outside provinces, and the *shinsengumi* (literally "new group of select men"), the quasi-official police force or vigilantes for the Tokugawa.

When finally accomplished in 1867, the imperial restoration brought an end not only to the fifteen-generation dynasty of Tokugawa shoguns but also to a large number of their feudal institutions, including the samurai. In late 1867, the last shogun resigned and, after a brief conflict known as the Boshin War, the new rulers triumphed and promulgated the Charter Oaths, which abolished social rank and all attendant restrictions of occupation and badges of status. With the emancipation to all classes, the samurai saw their *karoku* reduced by fifty percent in 1869 and lost their immediate overlords two years later when the *han* became prefectures ruled not by hereditary *daimyos* but bureaucrats appointed by the central government. In 1873, a draft law created modern armed forces; and, as if all this had not firmly enough suppressed the need for the continued investiture of feudal warriors, in 1876 the samurai were divested of their stipends altogether. That same year the wearing of two swords was made illegal throughout Japan. Stripped even of the now impotent symbol of their former privileges, these disenfranchised samurai and the *shizoku* (their descendants) carried on some of the ancestral traditions, and continue even to this day. Elements of their *bushido* were incorporated into the codes of behavior of the imperial army; but for all practical purposes, the full-bodied *bushi*, who was born and flourished during Japan's feudal millennium, perished with the shogunate.

The restoration figures not only as the commencement of Japan's modern era but also as the conventional dividing point between the theatrical and filmic genres of *jidai-geki* ("period drama") and *gendai-geki* ("modern drama"). The former is not always *chambara*, but any motion picture associated with the Tokugawa or earlier eras is part of the broad class into which the samurai film falls.

II. BUSHIDO, THE WAY OF THE WARRIOR

> I speak of *Giri*, literally the Right Reason, but which came in time to mean a vague sense of duty which public opinion expects an incumbent to fulfill. In its original and unalloyed sense, it meant duty, pure and simple—hence, we speak of the *Giri* we owe to parents, to superiors, to inferiors, to society at large . . .
>
> —INAZO NITOBE
> *Bushido—The Soul of Japan*

Historical consensus identifies the first written version of *bushido* as "The Way of the Samurai" by Yamago Soko (1622-1685), a Tokugawa-era *ronin* who became a sage. As an unwritten code according to which a warrior should pattern his life, *bushido* had an abstract power. The quasi-paradox of possessing a conception of appropriate lifestyle without the specific organizing principles reflects the complex, centuries-long process by which *bushido* evolved: practically, on the field of battle; ideologically, through the guardians of the culture; aesthetically, among the poets and storytellers; and ethically, with the social and religious philosophers. As these changes were introduced on various levels, the disposition of the samurai himself toward his calling was altered accordingly. For instance, under the *shushi*—the ethics of Japan's indigenous religion, *Shinto* (from the Chinese *shin tao* or "way of the gods")—*bujutsu* ("the martial arts") were merely a reflection, like the mirrors hung in the ancient temples, of human perfection. The practice of *bujutsu* was the noble occupation. Treading the martial path of *budo* would lead the warrior to paradise and true godliness. After the incursion of Confucianism and, more significantly, *Butsudo* ("the way of Buddha") late in the first millennium,[2] when *Dhyana* ("thought") abstracted *Shinto* perfection into the underlying search for *satori*—or enlightenment—and *Zen* ("meditation") provided the key to understanding the unbroken chain of being, a skill such as swordsmanship retained significance as a potentially transcendent activity. For the true believer a tranquil self-reliance made it unnecessary ever to draw the weapon which he had painstakingly mastered; and the assuredness of his bearing was sufficient to discourage challenges to his skill. Before Yamago Soko, Ieyasu Tokugawa himself purportedly wrote the first *buke-sho-hatto*, which was promulgated in 1615.[3] Much of these regulations had to do with controlling the *daimyo*. The rules about samurai behavior, the *shoshi hatto*, appeared in 1632. Article Three of the more detailed 1636 version by Iemitsu Tokugawa reads: "With the exception of military weapons, there must be no indulgence of personal luxury, or fondness for unnecessary utensils or household gear. In everything economy must be practiced."

As with its political institutions, the ethical and religious traditions of Japan are rooted in the *uji* (the "clan" or "family"). The thousands of *Shinto* deities sprang not just from the myths of the *Kojiki* ("the record of ancient matters") and *Nihon-gi* ("the chronicle of Japan") but also from the animistic belief which attached particular spirits and demons to practically all forms of organic and inorganic matter. Their numbers were constantly being increased by an ancestor worship through which the clans apotheosized their forbears. Hence a kind of cult emphasizing familial gods (*ujigama*), not unlike the ancient Roman conception, took root in pre-historical Japan and focused on the family so irrevocably that centuries of religious change have not displaced it as an ethical center. It is in light of this that the simply made and doggedly maintained equation of individual good with familial good, of an *issho-kemmei* aimed not at personal advancement but at the bettering of unborn descendants, can be understood.

Obviously, neither the tenets of *Shinto* nor the various forms which Buddhism assumed in Japan can be summarized adequately in a few paragraphs, for as the Westerner Lafcadio Hearn suggests in *Japan: An Attempt at Interpretation*, "the influence which Buddhism exerted upon Japanese civilization was immense, profound, multiform, incalculable; and the only wonder is that it should not have been able to stifle *Shinto* forever." Why Buddhism failed to stifle *Shinto* is of less interest in terms of the samurai than how the teleology of each system, or rather how the hybrid faith of *Ryobu-Shinto* ("the two ways of the gods"), the merging of philosophies in which Shinto deities became buddhas, was subsumed into *bushido* and became the basis for the conditioning and indoctrination into chivalry of every warrior. *Shinto* saw the world as floating in a primordial sea and its inhabitants as offspring of gods, while *butsudo* deemed it a mere mirage, not matter but illusion sprung from myriad consciousnesses which were trying to return to one consciousness. *Shinto* saw the dead as individual beings with supernatural powers, while Buddhism aspired to an ultimate *nirvana* (literally "annihilation"), where the identities of countless reincarnations were lost in the cosmic mind. The metaphysics of each religion were divided by a chasm of irreconcilable beliefs, yet none of this polarized the ideal of *bushido* into opposing schools of thought.

Perhaps the reason for this lies in the very nature of *bushido*, unwritten but specific, intangible, but ever present in the mind. Structured in this way and reinforced by a class order which elevates the samurai to quasi-aristocracy, *bushido* might be characterized as analogous to the Western notion of *noblesse oblige*. Consequently, a concept such as *bushi ho-ichi gon* ("the word of a warrior") is two-edged. Both persons of lower caste and the samurai's peers are compelled to accept what he says as true on face value; but the speaker is constrained from abusing that socially governed faith or else must suffer loss of that "face" which the convention affords him. There is, in fact, nothing mysterious or unique, in the sense of being unknown to Western history, in the Japanese idea of "face saving" or any aspects of *bushido* concerned with moral rectitude. It is these aspects which have resisted codification, for concepts of "code" and "honor" which are still in play in contemporary armed forces are no more part of formal statutes of military behavior in the West than they are in the East.

Still it would not be accurate to claim that *bushido* aligns itself with one ethic in the sense that European knights from the Arthurian to the Crusader or the Conquistador embraced Christianity. *Shinto*, Confucianism, and Buddhism have contributed quite variously to the tenets of *bushido*. The deterministic or objectivist precepts of Chu Hsi (1130-1200) dominated neo-Confucianism for several centuries. His belief about the purification of material presence or "ch'i" developed from early Taoist principles asserting that a person's fate and ethical disposition were pre-ordained by the sociological circumstances of his or her birth. In Japan this belief, *shushigaku*, was a core construct of the social system. In deviating from Chu Hsi, the Chinese subjectivist Wang Yang Ming (1472-1529) and his Japanese disciples re-emphasized the intellect: the mind was humanity's godlike portion, capable in a way beyond rational thought of insights into questions of both morality and material causation. When these two systems are interfaced with Buddhist anti-materialism or a Shinto ideal like *yamato-damashi*—literally "the soul of Yamato," a hero-god whose qualities were conferred on the morally superior—the results can easily be contradictory. When such contradictions carry over into the ethical conditioning of a samurai, they can create between alternative systems psychological double-binds which may be highly dramatic or even schizophrenogenic.

Giri, often rendered as "right reason," combines aspects of Chinese systems: the right or justice (*gi*), as propounded by Confucius and Mencius, and reason, or the epistemological ideal (*ri*), as defined by the neo-Confucians. In practical terms, in Japan, this notion of duty or fealty which each warrior owes to his master springs from social expectations, from the behavioral demands made on a samurai by lords and others. The action of the forty-seven *ronin* prompted considerable contemporary debate between Confucian ethicists about whether or not their revenge was a proper affirmation of *giri*. The Kimon-school philosopher Sato Naokata believed that *giri* owed by the Ako clan *ronin* to Lord Asano, which compelled them to seek revenge, should have been subsumed by the greater *giri* owed to the Tokugawa overlords, which compelled them not to act. Traditionally, the greatest potential inner conflict facing the samurai, either in fact or in fiction, is between *giri* and *ninjo*. The latter word variously represents instinct, inclination, or natural conscience but can be roughly equated with Wang Yang Ming's subjective faculty for proper judgment. As Miwa Shissai, who disagreed and broke with Naokata over the forty-seven *ronin*, explained Wang's metaphysical construct:

> The Lord of heaven and earth, of all living beings, dwelling in the heart of man, becomes his mind . . . the spiritual light of our essential being is pure, and is not affected by the will of man. Spontaneously springing up in our mind, it shows [us] what is right or wrong: it is then called conscience.

Obviously, if the warrior subscribes to this belief and trusts in his own *ninjo* then a conflict between what he sees as correct action and what *giri* requires him to do—for instance, avenge his lord against the wishes of his overlord—could induce a double-bind. This first type of interior conflict is a dramatic mainstay of in the samurai film. As Nitobe points out, *giri* itself is directed at the individual from a number of external parties: parents, superiors, inferiors, etc. From such a multiplicity of viewpoints a contradiction between one duty and another is easily conceivable. It was not unheard of for a lord to require a retainer to sacrifice his wife and/or children as proof of his loyalty. Thus, disjunction between familial *giri* and feudal *giri* is also a frequent nexus of conflict in fiction. Finally, even when *giri* and *ninjo* agree, the inherent fatalism of *shushigaku*, or the Buddhist disinterest in material affairs, can short out the circuit of required actions. For if station and events are determined from birth, then action or inaction are in any case equally ineffectual in altering them.

Thus, this potential for moral confusion underlies all fictional depictions of the samurai. While examples of sub-types are multiform both in film and older styles of drama in Japan, the essential conflict remains the same: the samurai receives conflicting directions from two sources and struggles to resolve them. Although the "tragedy" in Japan is constructed in a way which is somewhat different and perhaps more rigid than in the West, it is not difficult to perceive that this notion of contradiction is analogous to the time-honored "tragic" form in Aristotelian and numerous other traditions. What may most distinguish or particularize the samurai film is its highly defined ethical ground, the fact that the input of *shushigaku*, or Buddhism, may allow the wandering *ronin* or disillusioned retainer alike to find some philosophical comfort for their oppressed situations, to discover in it experiential proof of the retainer's denial of free will or to escape from it through the *ronin*'s detachment from worldly concerns. Either inner state may be used to dramatize behaviors that range from benevolence to sociopathic nihilism.

Since war and combat are inherently a part of the samurai's calling, death must be part of it also. To a very high degree the concept of and preparation for death is the fulcrum of *bushido*. According to the samurai philosopher Daidoji Yusan in his *Primer of Bushido*:

The idea most vital and essential to the samurai is that of death, which he ought to have before his mind day and night, night and day, from the dawn of the first day of the year till the last minute of the last day of it. When this notion takes firm hold of you, you are able to discharge your duties to their fullest extent: you are loyal to your master, filial to your parents, and naturally can avoid all kinds of disasters. Not only is your life thereby prolonged, but your personal dignity is enhanced. Think what a frail thing life is, especially that of a samurai. This being so, you will come to consider every day of your life your last and dedicate it to the fulfillment of your obligations.[4]

Because *bushido*—which existed, all questions of ethics aside, on a sociological level to support a hierarchical feudal system—values loyalty in the extreme, it willingly recruits anti-animistic and anti-free will philosophies. If these doctrines can in turn breed an indifference toward death in the dedicated samurai, then fear of death ceases to be a threat to any action or, most significantly, to those obligations of loyalty which Yusan cites.

If *bushido* directs the warrior to contemplate, it is precisely so that he may later act without reluctance. Because the warrior code as a moral system is answerable to itself, once it instills a readiness to perish for the sake of loyalty and honor in the samurai, it can never make him willing to act dishonorably, to do what he sees intuitively as unrighteous; so neither *shushigaku* nor *butsudo* could undermine *ninjo*. Ideally, of course, *giri* and the beliefs of *bushido* are never in discord; yet they create a basis for placing the samurai in an ethical dilemma. Consequently the system must provide instruments for rectifying discrepancies should they occur; and the most common of these, in film, are revenge and ritual suicide.

In the society of feudal Japan, the "necessary" death is to some degree self-perpetuating. For even if *otoko no michi* ("the manly way") made a loss of face less tolerable than dying, even if an insult had to be answered with a thrown gauntlet and a duel had to be without quarter, an incident still might end with a single mortal blow. However, under the Japanese formula for exacting vengeance derived from a Confucian model, when a man was killed, whether in a military expedition or a personal encounter, it became the duty of his family, most particularly of his brothers and male heirs, to claim a life in return. As Hearn explains "kindred, as well as parents; teachers, as well as lords, were to be revenged. A considerable portion of the popular romance and drama is devoted to the subject of vengeance . . . women, and even children, sometimes became avengers when there were no men of a wronged family left to perform the duty. Apprentices avenged their masters and even sworn friends were bound to avenge each other." Mikio Naruse's 1952 *jidai-geki* film, *Okuni to Gohei*, for example, concerns a widow who must seek revenge for her husband. A similar concept, the Sicilian version of vendetta, drives the

Chushingura (Hiroshi Inagaki): the *47 Ronin* assemble outside Lord Kira's manor.

adolescent Vito Corleone out of his home in *Godfather II* (1974) to avoid being killed by those who fear he will grow up to avenge his father.

While the rules governing the *kataki-uchi*—or Japanese vendetta—were unwritten, they were not informal. As in the feudal West, an unintended slight between former friends could without warning disrupt the lives of countless others. The plight of Roderigo and Cimene in the Cid legend is a well-known Western example. The alternatives for the designated avenger or avengers were narrow: either seek out the man who had offended the *uji*, place his severed head on the tomb of the one he had caused to die, and expiate that soul, or suffer a loss of face which might well compel self-immolation instead.

Japan's most celebrated vendetta has already been mentioned: *Chushingura*, the saga of the loyal forty-seven *ronin*. The avengers' statement, which they placed on their Lord's grave after killing Lord Kira, the high shogunate official who was responsible for the suicide of their Lord and the divestiture of their clan, reads in part:

> We, who have eaten of your food, could not without blushing repeat the verse, "Thou shalt not live under the same heaven nor tread the same earth with the enemy of thy father or lord," nor could we have dared to leave hell and present ourselves before you in paradise, unless we had carried out the vengeance which you began . . . Having taken counsel together last night, we have escorted [the head of] my Lord Kosuke-no-suke hither to your tomb. This dirk, by which

our honored lord set great store last year, and entrusted to our care, we now bring back. If your noble spirit be now present before this tomb, we pray you, as a sign, to take the dirk, and, striking the head of your enemy with it, to dispel your hatred forever. This is the respectful statement of forty-seven men.[5]

The placement of the severed head by the cemetery marker of the vindicated party and the leaving of a rhetorical, explanatory note (*zankanjo*) at that place and on the site of the assassination are just two aspects of the elaborate ritual of vendetta. In fact, the latter custom was occasionally still followed in political killings of 20th-century Japan. Obviously lacking was a method for bringing the chain of murderous retribution, the *fukushu,* or "blood feud," to an end. In the Saxon epic *Beowulf*, the narrator notes that the monster Grendel must be slain because "he would not make peace with any man of the Danish host . . . nor make a lawful compensation; and none could look for a handsome reparation at the slayer's hands."

Two *Ukiyo-e* prints inspired by the *Kanadehon Chushingura* — Act XI, scene 1: The Raid, the *ronin* in the snow surrounding Lord Moronao (Kira), who has been dragged from the charcoal shed.

RIGHT: Hasegawa Sadanobu (1848-1935)

BELOW: Utagawa Kuniyoshi (1797-1861)

Because *bushido* encompassed neither this Germanic *wergild*, the monetary compensation which Grendel could not be expected to pay, nor any similar method of formal reparation for the unlawful taking of another's life, two other concepts were substituted to break the vicious circle of *kataki-uchi*. The first, *ryo-sebai*—or "dual guilt"—permitted an overlord to declare two aggrieved parties to be equally at fault and subsequently to subject both of them to identical penalties ranging from a fine to capital punishment; and the matter would theoretically end there.

Few if any aspects of Japanese culture have captured Western fancy as strongly as the second concept: ritual suicide, known primarily as *seppuku* or *hara-kiri*. Both terms have the same literal meaning, the difference being that the ideographs "cutting the stomach" (切腹) which form *seppuku* can be reversed to "stomach cut"—or *hara-kiri*. As this order of ideographs is contrary to formal usage, *hara-kiri* is the more colloquial or vulgar expression. The custom of self-immolation itself originates in pre-historic times and is similar to the Roman tradition of running onto the blade of a sword whose hilt was buried in the ground, still remembered in the Western colloquialism "falling on one's sword." As a formal practice of *bushido*, which was reserved for the samurai class, the "stomach-cut," with its particular and intricate ceremonies, evolved during the Kamakura and Ashikaga eras. As the ultimate sentence for misconduct or breach of faith by an armed retainer, one which brought death but not necessarily personal or familial divestiture, it belongs most properly to the Tokugawa period.[6]

In a long era full of repressive regulations, it is not surprising that ritual suicide was the fate not only of the forty-seven *ronin* but of countless thousands of other samurai during Japan's feudal centuries.[7] *Bushido* subdivides the action into several types depending upon motivation. When Buddhism suggested that death was spiritually to be preferred to life and introduced self-control and mortification into the warrior code, it also allowed that the orderly taking of one's life might be the penultimate practice of both these virtues. Perhaps the earliest form of *seppuku* is *chugi-bara* (literally "stomach cut out of loyalty"), which contains two sub-classes. The first, *kanshi*, was performed to admonish an overlord and inspire him by its sacrifice to rectify his errant or injudicious behavior. Thus the inspiration of *kanshi* is not unlike that of contemporary incidents of self-immolation in the West designed to protest war or injustice. Less specific than this was *junshi* or *oibara*, in which the retainer kept faith simply by "following one's master in death." In his book *Hara-kiri*, Jack Seward speculates that "when a period of peace began . . . many of the warriors who fought so valiantly on the battlefield were still alive. Life became rather dull for them; there was something wanting, for there were no means to show loyalty to the lords and distinguish themselves. This situation brought forth many examples of self-immolation on the occasion of the death of a great lord." For whatever reasons, by the beginning of the Tokugawa shogunate, *junshi* had so proliferated that it was officially banned. Violation of the interdiction could mean the confiscation of the family land and titles or, at its most severe, the death penalty for all of the offender's heirs. In his book *Currents in Japanese Cinema,* Tadao Sato recaps the narrative of *The Abe Clan* (*Abe Ichizoku,* 1938): a Lord punishes an entire family for the *junshi* of its elder male. When the sons rise up and fight, the entire clan, with all its retainers, is annihilated. "In this film," Sato remarks, "the absurdity of the feudal institution of self-immolation upon the death of one's lord is exposed, and the barbarity of samurai society is revealed."

Distinct from either of these *chugi-bara* is *funshi* or *munen-bara,* in which the warrior finding himself oppressed or ill-used takes his life in a supreme gesture of righteous indignation. For instance, unlike the sons in *The Abe Clan,* the innocent heirs of a man who had rashly committed *junshi* under the Tokugawas, finding themselves sentenced to death as examples to dissuade further practice might defiantly comply with the edict through *munen-bara.*

The suicide of the forty-seven *ronin* in early 1703 was not *junshi*—although the various adaptations of it clearly stress that it came as a consequence of their intense loyalty—but *sokutsu-shi* or "death in expiation." As men stripped of their high station, who kept faith with their clan and exacted vengeance in defiance of the Shogun's law, they were liable for a death sentence. Because they had acted nobly, according to the warrior code, they were granted the privilege of taking their own lives. In a very real sense, there was no alternative for these masterless samurai (who were hardly impulsive young men, more than a dozen being over fifty-five and the eldest attacker, seventy-seven years old). Having been reduced to *ronin,* if they failed to avenge their clan lord, they could not continue living without shame. Yet without formal status they could not ethically seek revenge. It was a classic double-bind. The popularity of the tale is a cultural reaffirmation that courage and loyalty should be honored. Many contemporaries believe that the *seppuku* of the forty-seven men was a genuine and painful disembowelment. In sharp contrast to the degraded style, dubbed "empty" by purists, of the early 19th century, in which the *kaishaku*—or second—beheaded a man after his hand merely touched his sword, the ethics of *Shinto* and *butsudo* alike could embrace this legendary equation of honor maintained or retrieved through suffering. More importantly, because the saga contains the classic conflicts of *giri* and *ninjo,* because there is an irreconcilable contradiction of past and present duties, because circumstances beyond their control conspire to place the forty-seven *ronin* in a situation where they must follow through an action through to perish *isagi-yoku* ("without regrets"), all the dramatizations of that action from Chikamatsu's plays to epic films to a recent movie-of-the week continue to epitomize both the tragedy and the glory of *bushido*.[8]

III. THE SWORD, "SOUL OF THE SAMURAI"

> In knightly hands the Sword acknowledged no Fate but that of freedom and free-will; and it bred the very spirit of chivalry, a keen personal sentiment of self-respect, of dignity, and of loyalty, with the noble desire to protect weakness against the abuse of strength. The knightly Sword was ever the representative idea, the present and eternal symbol of all that man most prized— courage and freedom.
>
> —SIR RICHARD BURTON, *The Book of the Sword*

The history of the sword in Japan falls roughly into three periods. In the first, which ranges from pre-historical times to the middle of the Heian era, the sword was a straight-bladed, single-edged but poorly tempered weapon fashioned in the manner of Chinese sabers. Extremely sharp but slightly curved at best and unresilient, the blades broke easily when striking a hard object and consequently were used principally to thrust at and pierce an opponent.

The large scale civil wars beginning under the Fujiwara not only crystallized the concept of the samurai as a professional, full-time soldier but helped to standardize the sword as well. Inspired by the Chinese horse saber, an apocryphal artisan of the 10th century perfected a process for tempering a long blade of curved steel. The swordsmiths of this middle period are still reputed the finest in Japan's history. Most of the weapons used by the samurai during these six centuries were produced by five provincial schools of artisans who instituted the tradition of inscribing the maker's name on the *nakago*—or tang—of each sword and who by the end of the pre-Tokugawa era—the *koto* or "old saber" period of sword making—were providing three-fourths of all the country's swords.

Used by both mounted warriors and *ashigaru* (foot soldiers) the single, basic blade of this period (*shinogi-zukuri*, or tempered with a ridge line) served both cavalry and infantry, possessing a hardness and tensile strength unmatched in the West, which allowed an able swordsman to cut through armor without damaging the blade or, depending on the power of his arm, to bisect the trunk of a tree or a human body with a single blow.

The relative peace of the Tokugawa period began the new saber period (*shinto*). Many provincial craftsmen moved their forges to castles, where individual *daimyos* became their patrons, or to metropolitan areas, with Edo becoming the new center of sword production. From around the middle of the 15th century, most smiths no longer refined their own iron ore but relied on steel from mills, which further standardized quality and appearance. Three types or sizes of weapons continued to be made: (1) the long sword (*ken* or *to*—"saber") was known variously as a *daito* (literally "long saber"), *katana*, or *tachi* and measured an average of two and one-half feet in length (although some could exceed three feet) and were officially classified as "over two *shaku*" (one *shaku* is almost exactly one Western foot); (2) the medium or short sword (*shoto*—"short saber"—or *wakizashi*), which measured between one and two *shaku*; and (3) the short sword or dagger (*tanto*), which was less than one *shaku* long. The *tachi* was a *koto*-era long sword with a slightly accented curve to the blade and was usually carried with a hanging scabbard or slung over the back by mounted samurai.

Before the Edo or Tokugawa period, it was the sole privilege of the samurai, or "two-sword man," to wear not only more than one sword but also to possess a blade more than two feet long. Although the Tokugawa tolerated non-samurais carrying a single two-foot blade, two swords for commoners were never permitted. The *daito* or *katana* is the one which is traditionally regarded as *the* samurai sword. Despite the proscription against possession of it by non-samurai, the *daito* was often carried by the *kyokaku*—the designation of a *heimin*, or commoner, who has the privilege of carrying a short sword—and the outlaw *yakuza*. While *kyokaku* might freely carry the *wakizashi* without fear of legal retribution, the classless *chori* and *hinin* were forbidden to possess arms of any sort. The discrete answer to this interdiction was the *shikomi-zue*, a *katana* blade concealed inside a walking cane. This last is the weapon of the blind masseur featured in Daiei studios' Zato-Ichi films, since he would in Tokugawa society have been a non-human being. A final weapon in evidence in numerous motion pictures is the *jitte*—or police baton. Designed to be wielded as sword-breaker by the *doshin*, or constable, who might have to confront a socially superior samurai on a drunken spree, the *jitte* was an eighteen-inch bar of wrought iron to which a side-bar *kage*—or hook—was attached. Trimmed with a colored braid and/or attached to a loop of cord worn over a police officer's shoulder, the *jitte* was not only a defensive arm to catch and snap a sword blade and an offensive club to strike unruly commoners but, when tucked into the *doshin*'s sash, also served as a badge of his office.

Among the samurai proper, there were two types of mountings for their *dai-sho*—matched pair of *daito* and *wakizashi* (or *shoto*). The older *jindachi-*

zukuri featured an unbound, ornamented hilt of lacquered wood and two rings fastened to the scabbard through which a cord was passed. This last was then tied around the waist or diagonally across the back of the warrior, so that the hilt was readily accessible either just over the hip or behind the shoulder. The mounting more familiar to the Westerner is the *buke-zukuri*, a type mainly produced in the Tokugawa era, in which the sword hilt is brocaded in a crosswise pattern. After the former process was superseded by the latter in the New Sword (*shih-ken*) period early in the 16th century, the *jindachi* was viewed as more valuable because it was less common, but it was also less practical because it could not be as firmly gripped as a fabric handle. As a result, this mounting is usually associated with aristocrats and high-ranking samurai, who may have been more concerned with the aesthetic than the functional values of their *dai-sho*. For example, characters in Masahiro Shinoda's *The Assassin* (*Ansatsu*, 1964) remark that it is rather out of the ordinary for that film's itinerant title figure to sport a pair of antique and expensive matched swords. Beginning around 1530, most *dai-sho* were worn *otoshi-zashi*—that is, inserted into the sash that wound tightly around the man's waist—so that the hilts protruded, ready to be drawn, in front of the body on the left side of the abdomen. While both the *buke* and the *jindachi* mountings could be placed between the waist-sash and kimono, the new style scabbard frequently provided small slits in its interior, where the samurai could keep a dart or *kozuka* ("knife") for use in cutting food or throwing at an attacker.

Obviously the most important measure of value for a man whose life depended on his weapon was not its beauty nor its rarity but its strength and utility. The flawless sword of the fables would never lose its edge and could slice through inferior blades without even sustaining a nick. The efforts of all of Japan's smiths, who were the highest ranking of the artisan class and could receive honors normally reserved for *daimyos*, were to come as close as possible to this perfection. Both *Shinto* and *butsudo* regarded swordmaking as a sacred craft; and the process, laborious and painstaking in itself, was complicated by attendant rituals of purification. In the animistic *Shinto* principle, the sword had a life of its own which must be free of taint from its creation. For Buddhism, the material blade symbolized "the One Sword of Reality," the implement which cuts through the false distinction of life and death to truth. Because of all this, not to mention feudalism's real dependency on the sword for survival, the work of the artisan who fashions the sword is somewhat romanticized in fiction. Woodcuts depict the smith toiling at his forge with a guardian deity glancing over his shoulder. The *noh* drama *Kokaji* recounts the story of the tempering of a nearly perfect blade. The film *Saga of Tanegashima* (*Tenpo Denraki*, 1968) recreates actual incidents surrounding the first guns made by a Japanese swordsmith. The characters identifying the maker and imprinted on the tang were of great significance to feudal samurai and *kyokaku* because their lives depended on it. They continue to be significant to present-day collectors because, as in any art, the signature is the primary guarantee of authenticity.

For the low-caste *yojimbo*—or bodyguard—Izo Okada in Hideo Gosha's *Tenchu* (*Hitokiri*, 1969), it is a source of major self-esteem to be the owner of a genuine Masamune, one of the finest and most famous *daito*s in Japanese history. The reason for his pride is not merely the excellence of workmanship which went into its making. One of the film's most subtle ironies is that in the course of an assassination, Okada's Masamune is nicked. Okada's sword epitomizes all the traditions embodied in the epithet which equates "the soul of the samurai" with his sword. For Okada, who is low-born, mastery of any sword represents power and opportunities for advancement. The particular renown of his weapon adds a level of prestige which he lacks as a person, no matter how skilled. Combined, sword and skill give him, literally, a sense of existence. By acquiring the objects and skills society prizes most, Okada, like Miyamoto Musashi, may advance socially without challenging or subverting the system.

The question of why the sword and, more significantly, why swordsmanship is so highly valued by the culture, is more complex. The bow, the halberd, the *yari* (or lance), these and other arms are fundamentally a part of *bujutsu*. All have their adepts and masters whose prowess is universally admired; but only the sword is worshipped. Only the swordsman ever inspires that peculiar combination of fear and adulation, in legend or in fact.

Sir Richard Burton propounds a version of the mystique of the sword in the West; but that is only half the answer to an Easterner. According to D.T. Suzuki in *Zen and Japanese Culture*, "it was necessary for the samurai who carried two swords—the longer one for attack and defense and the shorter one for self destruction when necessary—to train himself with the utmost zeal in the art of swordsmanship. He could never be separated from the weapon which was the supreme symbol of his dignity and honor." In the master syllogism of the samurai's life, *bushido* governed his behavior and he governed his sword. As the latter expressed him, so it must have also expressed the tenets of chivalry. It is no exaggeration for the clan retainers in Masaki Kobayashi's *Hara-Kiri* (*Seppuku*, 1962) to be horror-struck upon learning that a *ronin* has pawned his swords to support his starving family. When he exchanges steel blades for those of bamboo, he reduces himself analogously, as for the retainers the true samurai is only as resilient and unbreakable as his blade: he *is* his sword. In selling it, he forfeits not merely his honor but, in their eyes at least, his very being.

On a more pragmatic level, the ethics of *kendo*—or "the way of the sword"—are answerable in their own abstracted way to the action itself. With few exceptions—such as the legendary "beard cutter" and "knee cutter"[9] of the Minamoto clan—the Japanese did not venerate the sword as a relic, as an object of the past, but as a symbol of potentiality belonging to the present and future. The philosopher/swordsman who tried to construct a metaphysics for this hazardous implement of his livelihood soon confronted a paradox. Because the symbol, which might be conceptually perfect, required an operator, *kendo* asked the swordsman for a complementary perfection. Of course, the more he attempted by sheer force of will to master his weapon, the more the act of concentration impinged on his performance. As the 17th-century sage Takuan theorizes:

> In terms of swordsmanship, the genuine beginner knows nothing about the way of holding and managing the sword, and much less of his concern for himself. When an opponent tries to strike him, he instinctively parries it. This is all he can do. But as soon as the training starts, he is taught how to handle the sword, where to keep the mind, and many other technical tricks which make his mind "stop" at various junctures. For this reason whenever he tries to strike the opponent he feels unusually hampered . . . as soon as there is a moment's "stoppage," your mind is no longer your own, for it is then placed under another's control. When the mind calculates so as to be quick in movement, the very thought makes the mind captive.[10]

For the thinkers of feudal Japan, the chief impediment to perfection in swordplay or any endeavor is *ushin no shin*—or the mind conscious of itself. For the samurai specifically, this over-consciousness is manifest in *suki*—literally, the "space between which something can enter". Figuratively it is the minute hesitation or pause for thought, which can become the unguarded instant when the enemy strikes. For Takuan the acquisition of technique is not sufficient and, initially at least, ironically engenders greater *suki*. As the various moves become more reflexive, Takuan concedes that the tendency may be reversed.

There are two ontologies of the sword which instruct the practitioner against *suki*. The first is *kufu* ("discipline"), a basically Confucian notion of delocalizing the mind. Since in this system the mind is evanescent, some swordsmen practice "stomach thinking" or situating the mind in the corporeal center, so that it may freely and rapidly move from there to an arm or hand or foot or wherever is needed to parry or dodge a blow. To the warrior who follows *butsudo*, this is not enough. Since any thought, no matter where it resides, breeds delay, the second necessary concept is *sunyata* ("emptiness"), voiding the body of all consciousness until a state of *mushin no shin*—or "no-mindedness"—is attained. Clearly, the anti-materialist portion of *bushido*, which has already been discussed, and its breakdown of the dualism embodied in life and death, are the underlying principles of *sunyata*. In practice, the fighter with "no mind" is expected to become one not just with his own weapon but with his assailant and his assailant's weapon as well. Giving himself over entirely to the unconscious, beyond concerns of winning or losing, his actions should be totally spontaneous and directed by something higher than his subjective being. The mental state after any combat is called *zanshin*—or "remaining mind"—a reflex condition inactive but ready to engage again. For some masters of *bujutsu*, *zanshin* is a variant of *sunyata* that occurs whenever one's weapon is sheathed, the mind empty but totally aware.

For a samurai who achieves *sunyata* the moral syllogism is also attained. Provided that his training has been rigorous, *bushido* itself, unaffected by the pettiness of personality or evil purpose, now governs his sword. On a practical level, the swordsmanship purged of any idea of failure lingering in the consciousness can, at worst, be equaled. More often than not, disinterest in either committing a fatal mistake or in dying should make both of these easier to avoid. Finally, in dramatic terms, *sunyata* is the rationalization for the extraordinary abilities of both fictional characters such as Zato Ichi or Akira Kurosawa's *yojimbo*, Sanjuro, and real ones such as Musashi, and for film sequences in which a dozen antagonists are dispatched by what appears a single stroke. As Takuan explains:

> Suppose ten men are opposing you, each in succession ready to strike you with a sword. As soon as one is disposed of, you will move on to another without permitting the mind to "stop" with any. However rapidly one blow may follow another, you leave no time to intervene between the two. Every one of the ten will be successively and successfully dealt with.[11]

There is one final aspect of swordsmanship which often figures in motion pictures and should be briefly introduced here: the sword school or style. Historically, such schools in Japan, unlike the Western fencing academies, taught more than technique or simple physical mastery of a weapon. Because they fulfilled a need of the feudal system, they were culturally assimilated in a manner which is most analogous to Yale or Harvard, Cambridge or Oxford. Like the diploma from such a university, successful completion of training at the best-known schools of the martial arts appealed to a certain class and had a specific social value. It might be expected that, after flourishing during an era of intense civil wars, these preparatories would diminish under the Tokugawa; but since their intra- and inter-school competitions and tournaments provided an outlet for the otherwise unoccupied samurai, they continued to prosper. Moreover, because they had a heritage of association with ethical and religious questions—the gymnasium was known as a *dojo*, a term which also designates a place for religious exercises—teachers of *budo* were sometimes called *oshos*, a title used for revered monks as well. The sword schools were almost as sacrosanct as temples. Eventually, as each institution strove to develop a style or method of its own, the identification and loyalty of the swordsman to a particular school and its *sensei* (literally, "the life before" or teacher who mastered the form before him) became second only to that which he felt for his family or clan.

In film, the boastful samurai may issue a challenge that says essentially, "my style of swordplay is better than yours." Just as there are good and honorable techniques, there is potential for the inverse, for the "evil sword" wielded by the unscrupulous master. There are various adaptations of *Daibosatsu Toge*—literally the "Great Buddha Pass"—a immense novel by Kaizan Nakazato which was serialized in Japanese newspapers over a thirty-year period beginning in 1913. It described the wandering swordsman Ryunosuke Tsukue, who becomes a *shinsengumi*. His sword style is inspired by a real school and its form, *Kogen Itto Ryu*. But Tsukue is "excommunicated" by his father, the *soke sensei*—or founding master of the school—because he perverts or degrades *Kogen Itto Ryu*. This "evil style" is both disparaged and feared. Hence the titles used by the most recent film versions: *Satan's Sword* (directed by Kenji Misumi, 1960-61) with Raizo Ichikawa and *Sword of Doom* (directed by Kihachi Okamoto, 1966) with Tatsuya Nakadai. Ichikawa also appears in most of the Kyoshiro Nemuri films, a serial hero who wields an unorthodox, hypnotic "full-moon cut."

Tatsuya Nakadai as Ryunosuke Tsukue in *Sword of Doom*

How determinant a factor sword style was in historic duels is less clear than it is in fictional encounters. Musashi's successful one-man assault on the sword schools implies that genuine superiority depends on more than style. For what he lacked in formal training, Musashi acquired through *musha-shugyo* ("training in hardship") on the battlefield. But Musashi himself was as contemplative as he was violent and might well have agreed with a verse from the articles of the Shikage-ryu School as translated by Suzuki:

> Victory is for the one,
> Even before the combat,
> Who has no thought of himself.

CHAPTER ONE

THE SAMURAI IN FICTION

Yugen is considered to be the mark of
supreme attainment in all the arts and
accomplishments. . . . Yugen is attained
when all different forms of visual and
aural expression are beautiful.

—SEAMI MOTOKIYO,
On Attaining the Stage of Yugen[1]

I N FICTION, AND MORE SPECIFICALLY ON FILM, THE HISTORY OF THE SAMURAI, *bushido*, and the icon of the sword are subsumed into a genre tradition. Naturally the simplifications introduced in order to mold a fictional character, whether from a generic concept or an authentic personage, distort much of the social and ethical heritage outlined in the first chapter. Yet the fact that the film samurai follows chronologically in the wake of the social reality does not prevent "him" from re-writing the history to fit the need of the fictional persona. Besides the movies inspired by the *Chushingura* or Musashi legends, a considerable number of other samurai films involve actual figures fictionalized to varying degrees. It is not the intent here to use the historical accuracy of any motion picture as a measure of aesthetic merit. The question is rather how a type of film identified with a particular country recruits elements from both that nation's past and its other modes of fiction to constitute a vital genre in its own right.

I. THE SAMURAI IN LEGEND AND ART

In its most recent manifestations, the association of extreme violence and polarized characterizations with *chambara* reinforces analogies to archetypes of expression found in the American Western or in the gangster film. In earlier forms, however, the figure of the samurai is most often rendered in an "epic" style. Arguably the first examples of the *bushi* in art are the *haniwa*, clay

Sword-bearing *haniwa* figure from the 6th century (Kofun Period)

statues of warriors found in tombs, which date from the Nara period. These figurines may have been simply grave decorations or may have served a ritualistic purpose in which they "died" for or otherwise took the place of an actual warrior. Whichever is the case, the *haniwa* suggest that, from pre-historic times, the warrior was the focal figure in a certain type of myth. Specifically, when societal dilemmas or inadequacies could not be remedied in practical terms, they were transferred to the level of folktale to be "answered" or figuratively rectified. Here, the *bushi* functions as both legendary hero and instrument of social correction.

While it may be somewhat oversimplified to claim that this tradition is perpetuated in all of Japan's pre-modern art, such is effectively the case. On one level, the *kodan*—or prose tales—and the *naniwa-bushi*—or poetic recitals of brave exploits in an Homeric manner—are essentially parables which glorify men of righteousness and proper conduct. On a more formal level, that tragic potential in the samurai repeatedly figured in the patrician, semi-religious *noh* drama, the more popular theater of *kabuki*, and the *bunraku* or *joruri* puppet plays. None of these forms are free or open. The mixture of speech, chant, and dance and attendant actor performance depend on highly stylized and non-natural expressions. The dramatic conflicts, whether between one character and another or between one character and his own conscience, are specific and reflect the cultural prejudices of feudalism. Generalizations are constrained from reaching the point where they might be perceived to be between characters and existing institutions. In primitive myth, Prince Yamato Take is half god and half man. Possessing the "soul of Yamato" is subsequently inscribed as a positive cultural value. The warrior-heroes and villains of Japan's classic drama and literature follow in this tradition by being less human beings than models or personifications of virtues and aberrations. Complicating this is the unusual evolution of theatrical performing styles. *Kabuki*, which originated early in the Tokugawa era, changed from being all-female casts (*yujo kabuki*, usually performed by prostitutes) to all-male casts (*wakushu* and then *yaro kabuki*). In the 18th century, *kabuki* developed further by region. In imperial Kyoto, the plays often depicted young samurai smitten of geishas. The actor prototype was the handsome and sensitive Tojuro Sakata, who helped define the refined—or *wagoto*—style of acting. In Edo, the *aragoto*—or rough—style (an abbreviation of *aramushogato* or "reckless warrior matter"), which used fierce looks and menacing poses to typify aggressive masculine characters, was more popular. Danjuro Ichikawa founded a lineage of *kabuki* performers that specializes in this form, which stretches to the present day. In some plays the *aragoto* style might be reserved for the antagonist, a *jitsuaku*—or villainous samurai—featured in the more realistic *kabuki* preferred outside of Kyoto.

Neither myth nor drama could deconstruct or impartially examine codes of behavior imposed by the culture. As a consequence, the pre-modern *higeki*—or stage tragedy—is not an action-drama but develops its catharsis in a more contemplative mode. Although the samurai film combines this tradition with that of *ken-geki*, "sword theater" spectacles in which fights and other action were more realistically performed, the tendency from the silent era well into the 1950s was more toward set pieces and dialogue scenes than action sequences, and toward a formalized rather than naturalistic context whether in dialogue, wardrobe, make-up, or action.

Japanese aesthetics during the Tokugawa era developed through the *kokugaku*—the study of the nation or national ideals. Using the *kojiki, nihonji,* and the *manyoshu* ("countless leaves," a collection of the earliest Japanese poetry), scholars called *kokugakushu* attempted to remove all foreign influences and distill the essence of Japanese culture. The preeminent *kokugakushu,* Motori Norinaga, is credited with inventing *mono no aware,* which is usually rendered as the "sadness of things." From the *manyoshu* and *Shinto* precepts, Norinaga devised his concept of the touching or tragic aspects of *mono,* everyday matters. According to *mono no aware,* the naturalness and impermanence of these things are analogs for all human vicissitude.

In feudal art as well as in feudal life, the classic, melodramatic dichotomy was between dutiful action and impulsive action. As *giri* was often characterized by a repression of violent inclination, it is not unusual for *ninjo* to have been associated with an outburst of violence. And yet visualization of any such outburst in the art of pre-modern Japan was infrequent. The scroll painting of the battle of Dan-no-ura, which is used as an insert in Kobayashi's *Kwaidan* (*Kaidan,* 1964), illustrates the contrast between painterly and filmic stylizations of violence. The former with its masses of armed men frozen in opposing poses even incorporates, in a manner reminiscent of the Bayeux tapestry's treatment of the Norman invasion, the debris of warfare into its scheme of historical depiction by gradually reducing those mounted warriors to piles of naked, headless corpses

Toshiro Mifune used the *aragoto* style as Kurosawa's *ronin* Sanjuro.

stripped of armor and pierced by arrows. Ultimately, however, not even this kind of detailing can narrow the stylized distance between viewer and object and must remain more in the convention of the *kabuki* "sword dances" than in one of realism.

II. THE SAMURAI ON FILM

If the post-War samurai film does employ an expressive equation (which its predecessors in motion pictures, art, and legend did not possess) for bridging that distance between mythic object and spectator, then violence is its key exponent. In fact, with increasing frequency and graphic detail, the contemplation of violence has long been a major factor in all motion pictures, both Eastern and Western. The reel-long interlude at the conclusion of *The Wild Bunch*, punctuated by scores of stylized, slow-motion shootings, has become an archetype for screen massacre; yet much of Peckinpah's orientation toward killing as an integral part of human affairs and his visualization of it derives from the work of Akira Kurosawa, with the most obvious analog to *The Wild Bunch* being the latter's *Seven Samurai* (*Shichinin No Samurai*, 1957). In Japanese cinema, as in Japanese metaphysics, the qualities of death and violence have always been essential to understanding life, to its transcendence and its annihilation. Ultimately this study will trace various and specific manifestations of that ethic in a few examples of *chambara* motion pictures produced in post-War Japan. It may be useful to begin with a brief catalogue of some of the samurai film's distinctive features.

Narrative and Character Conventions. The primary genre expectation of *chambara* is quite obviously the swordsman. Whether this character is developed as a hero or an anti-hero, his physical introduction into the scene and the viewer's apprehension of him as the potential dramatic center are basic to all samurai films. While this character does not need to be a true samurai—the principals of *Seven Samurai*, for instance, are not clan retainers but *ronin*—he must, even if a *kyokaku*, be armed. In this manner, the sword may be seen as *chambara*'s fundamental icon, and the whole genre as a manifestation of the ideal which regarded the swordsman and his weapon as one. In a very real sense, the mere sight of the man with a sword in his sash, even standing with his back to the camera against an undefined landscape—as in, for example, the first shot of Kurosawa's *Yojimbo* or Gosha's *Three Outlaw Samurai*—is enough to identify the film generically. It is conceivable that, for many viewers, merely a shot of the sword could convey the anticipation that a samurai film was to follow.

There are, of course, a range of subsidiary expectations which such initial images engender. The main elements are simple and might be explained by analogy to the American Western. The second half of the 19th century in Japan was, as in the United States, a post-Civil War period of social and political flux. In the post-Tokugawa reassessment of governing principles and the transition from isolationism into imperialism in the modern sense, the feudal *daimyo* and their clansmen tried unsuccessfully—like the anachronistic "cattle barons"—to keep the Japanese equivalent of the homesteader at bay with the threat of violent death. Like the bounty hunter or hired gun, the swordsman, whether a true samurai or wandering mercenary, may align himself with either of these factions; he may be either good or evil or a figure of moral ambivalence depending more on individual characterization than genre typing, because, like the Western's scruples against never drawing first or back-shooting, *bushido* is not always unswervingly adhered to by either hero or villain. Like the gunfight, an encounter between master swordsmen frequently serves as the climax of the film, the event toward which most of the early narrative and character development is genotypically directed. Just as six-shooters may be tied down or cross-drawn, fanned or cocked and fired, the samurai has, as previously described, a variety of fighting styles with which to wield his sword. In most films there is a considerable amount of preliminary swordplay in which protagonist and antagonist may display prowess by defeating a number of non-principals as preludes to the final duel. There, two opponents whose skills have been established as roughly equal meet to settle the question of who is best. Whether they meet behind the corral or behind the temple, the generic set-up is the same.

Since the *daito* or *katana* is a slashing as well as piercing weapon, and since most fighting methods incorporated downward cuts at the head or shoulders and forward thrusts to puncture the chest or stomach, the climactic duel between masters often receives a very particular and highly stylized visual treatment. Unusual lenses and lighting, slow-motion, optical printing, and all manner of other special effects often become part of the precise choreography of a deadly ballet. The analogy to the Western is not perfect; but beyond being an analytical device, it has been a remake strategy for Western filmmakers. Three of Kurosawa's samurai films have been transposed to the American West: *Seven Samurai* as *The Magnificent Seven* (1960, directed by John Sturges), *Rashomon* (1950) as *The Outrage* (1964, directed by Martin Ritt), and *Yojimbo* as *A Fistful of Dollars* (1965, directed by Sergio Leone). It is even applicable to the concept of serialized characters, with recurring personalities such as the Three Musketeers, the Lone Ranger, or Hopalong Cassidy in the U.S. productions of the 1930s and 40s finding their equivalents over time and space in the Crimson Bat, the

Three Outlaw Samurai, Zato-Ichi, and Kyoshiro Nemuri in Japan in the 1960s.

As with the Western, certain historical figures and events have been a recurring subject for films since the silent era. Just as the views on American events from the Civil War to the gunfight at the OK Corral may have changed from *Birth of a Nation* (1915) to *Glory* (1989) or from *My Darling Clementine* (1946) to *Tombstone* (1993) and *Wyatt Earp* (1994), the portrayal of the *Chushingura* saga or the events of the *bakumatsu* have also evolved with *chambara.* Since World War II, the samurai film has undergone significant stylistic and thematic changes, moving away from the sometimes actionless *jidai-geki,* or simple period film. The use of tangential violence only is exemplified in certain pictures of Kenji Mizoguchi: civil war is a disruptive but marginal consideration in *Ugetsu* (1953); the few battles in *Tales of the Taira Clan* (*Shin Heike Monogatari,* 1955) end quickly and almost bloodlessly; and the only swordplay in his two-part *Chushingura* (1941-42) is over in the first scene.

Although completed and released as Japan entered World War II, Mizoguchi's *Chushingura* is remarkably unbellicose in that it is practically bloodless: aside from the initial brief attack, two scenes hinge on the discovery of a person dying from suicide. This oblique approach to the suicides and killings at the heart of the forty-seven *ronin* saga is very different from the scores of other retellings in plays, motion pictures, and television programs, as it relies entirely on moving camera, staging in depth, nuanced performances, and details of costuming and set decoration to convey a sense of fatality and resignation. While the violent events and behaviors depicted in many later samurai films effectively externalize the emotions of their troubled protagonist, Mizoguchi's restrained but telling staging underlines the despair, the existential angst, of his characters.

Mizoguchi began by presuming that the audience would be quite familiar with the subject. He also abandoned the tradition stretching back to the early 18th century and the *Kanadehon Chushingura*—various early *kabuki* and puppet plays in which the names and places were transposed to the Kamakura era so as not to embarrass the shogunate—in favor of the contemporary *kabuki, Genroku Chushingura,* by Seika Mayama, who restored the historical names, dates, and places.

After a static shot of assembled dignitaries, Mizoguchi's sustained opening both belies and anticipates the contemplative tone that will follow. During a slow traveling to the right along one of four corridors that surrounds a freshly raked open courtyard, dark posts pass through the foreground like mile markers of doom. After a full minute, an off-screen voice is heard and seems to compel the moving camera to quicken its pace as a pan reveals two men, Lord Kira and an attendant. As Kira disparages "Lord Asano," he faces away from the attendant, with the back of his head to camera. Finally, more than two minutes into the shot, the two men turn and exit the frame on the left, revealing another figure, presumably Lord Asano, who has been kneeling in the background but blocked from view by the attendant's body. Asano springs up, contemplates for a moment, then hurries in pursuit. The camera dollies back quickly, leading him to the corner, then pans as he draws his sword, catches up to Kira, and strikes. The cut comes on the slash of the blade, as Asano cries out, "Vengeance!" Men appear from all sides of the previously empty area and pull him off.

Much has been made of Mizoguchi's statement at the time of *Chushingura's* release about Japanese visual style, of using planes and perspectives different than those of Western painting and film. Certainly the long and "pensive" takes throughout *Chushingura* use moving camera to reveal different planes. The depth of field when the clan's Edo retainers arrive to report events permits the chamberlain Oishi to move dramatically from rear ground to foreground. This use of staging in depth is also quite different from the previous shot, a wide view of the room with the chamberlain at the back, his figure increasingly obscured as more and more kneeling samurai edge forward to hear the report.

The long take and moving camera are extensively used by such diverse Mizoguchi contemporaries as Max Ophuls and John Farrow. What separates Mizoguchi's work is his use of viewer expectation to create visual metaphor within the drama. The slow move down the "Pine Corridor," where the audience knows what will happen, becomes a trope for the inevitable pull of fate. The momentary hesitation by Asano, barely two seconds in a shot that lasts two and half minutes, is even more telling: the briefest but profoundly existential pause where free will comes into play.

The high angle shot in the Palm Room, where Asano awaits the official investigators, is also rich in figurative values. The "omniscient" perspective looks down on Asano hemmed by screens but sees only his head and torso. Around the edges of the room guards kneel with their backs to Asano (and camera). While the screen that is visible behind the lord has pastoral drawings of clouds, mountains, and vegetation, the one in the foreground is not lit, so that its top edge cuts like a jagged blade through the shot and bisects the doomed man's body. The interrogation is another long take, after an opening move that pulls back from the lead official and cranes down to a three shot with the figures of the two shogunate men higher than Asano's. Both the sustained camera and the men's darker forms constrict the frame and refuse to permit Asano any "breathing room." As the lord surrenders emotionally to his fate, he bows so that the visual dominance of the others is even more pronounced. For one instant, as he invites them to laugh at his lack of sword skill, he leans back, becoming as tall as they are in the shot and pressing against the left edge. Again, the existential display is fleeting: Asano bows low again and Mizoguchi cuts away. Mizoguchi's later *jidai-geki*, from *Five Woman around Utamaro* (1946) to *Sansho the Bailiff* (1954), stress the personal story as the dramatic core and emphasize the pathos of the individual fate over any sense of epic tragedy. But the concept of *mono no aware*, which figures prominently in most of Mizoguchi's work, is seldom expressed in *Chushingura,* the preeminent moment being chamberlain Oishi repeating the last poem of Asano: "More frail than petals scattered by the wind, I bid a last farewell and leave spring behind."

The straightforward adaptation in Hiroshi Inagaki's 1962 *Chushingura* returns to the *Kanadehon* structures but retains the real names. Inagaki also attempts an epic sweep while embodying the classic *giri-ninjo* dilemma. Unlike Mizoguchi's version, the exposition of what could be considered a prologue— that is, everything leading up to Lord Asano's *seppuku*—is fully detailed and consumes a major portion of the narrative. Certainly Asano's prideful behavior up to his interrogation and the shogun's clipped comment ("The rules are clear. Keep to the rules.") serve as ironic undertone. Asano's celebrated refusal to bribe Lord Kira because such action is forbidden by the *Kemmu Shikimoku*, the legal code established by the Muromachi shogunate in 1336, becomes more an act of anachronistic stubbornness than existential revolt against Tokugawa policy in 1701. Kira pointedly taunts Asano about the fate his retainers will suffer should he dare to draw his sword in the shogun castle; and yet Asano draws it. Compared to the vigorous stagings of Kurosawa's early 1960s *chambara*, Inagaki's stately style is somewhat detached. The use of sound-stage "exteriors," such as chamberlain Kuranosuke's farm, where he and his eldest son must formally separate themselves from his wife and younger children, reinforces this effect. On the other hand, the forced perspective set in Horibe's half-hearted attack on the *ronin* Tawaraboshi effectively externalizes the almost counterfeit nature of Horibe's position. Perhaps the most telling moment in this version of the forty-seven *ronin* saga is an indirect questioning of cultural value: when Kuranosuke and his son are at an inn visited by several periwigged men in Western garb. "If those Dutchmen knew," the son asks, "would they think we were doing the right thing?"

Those working in the genre after Mizoguchi initiated a genuine exploration of the social aberrations of Japan's long feudal history. The warriors of the *kabuki* drama were also white-powdered and periwigged, and the pastel full-lit sets where action was more often discussed than portrayed gave way to a large number of dark, nihilistic motion pictures which repaint Japan's past in blacker hues. Although Western audiences remain most familiar with the films of Akira Kurosawa, many other directors in that same span of over fifty

Kikuchiyo (Toshiro Mifune) slips in the mud during the final battle in *Seven Samurai*.

years have continued to extend the limits of the samurai film.

Their new genre heroes are physically or psychologically scarred, ostracized and stigmatized by their society. Aware of the intransigent nature of societal judgments, their violent responses are invariable and understandable both as generic constructions and simple, desperate acts. In Kurosawa's case, whether it is a body falling in slow motion or bandits writhing in mud as a score of villagers descend upon them with bamboo spears in *Seven Samurai*, or the fountain of blood that gushes from the chest of the losing duelist at the end of *Sanjuro* (1962), the visualization of death is manipulated so as to be beyond strict conventions of realism. Nonetheless in these pictures and in *Yojimbo*, Kurosawa helped to bring the genre to maturity not merely by injecting it with wry humor but also by fashioning heroes more intent on anonymity than vainglory, more concerned with concealing their martial abilities than displaying them.

In the same vein, Masaki Kobayashi's *Hara-Kiri* and *Rebellion* (*Joi-Uchi*, 1967) are manifestations of developing anti-feudal themes. The extreme cynicism of both films is focused on the oppressive concept of clan loyalty, to the point where the *bushido* ideal of a noble—or, in Western terms, tragic—death is rendered contextually impossible. All lives and deaths in an impersonal and meaningless social order become inevitably impersonal and meaningless as well. The reward for obeisance or rebellion is ultimately the same, indistinguishable annihilation. The hopelessness of the title action in *Rebellion* does not negate the ethical "rightness" which motivates it; but Kobayashi's bleak, overriding determinism will not permit the "rebellion" to assume more than a personal significance, will not allow his characters genuinely to threaten the established order.

Kobayashi, like Kurosawa, remains traditional in the sense that he stages his action relative to thematic constants. They derive from and outline a consistent world view. Characters who reject the feudal values of Tokugawa implicitly reject the principle of *mono no aware* as well, and instincts of sensitivity and sadness are replaced by the more fundamental concept of survival. In the years just following *Yojimbo* and *Hara-Kiri*, directors such as Masahiro Shinoda, Hideo Gosha, and Kihachi Okamoto made action (i.e., violence) into a more purely expressive component in their films. As their characters are estranged from their environment, violence functions as both existential definition of their being and the most direct method for expressing their oppressed relationship to that environment. Okamoto's *Samurai Assassin* (*Samurai*, 1964) and *Sword of Doom*, Gosha's *Sword of the Beast* (*Kedemono No Ken*, 1965), *Goyokin* (1969), and *Tenchu*, and Shinoda's *Assassin* and *Samurai Spy* (*Ibun Sarutobi Sasuke*, 1965) all possess the same "anarchic" qualities. Through unnervingly orchestrated sound effects of steel ripping into flesh and images of spurting blood which stains clothing or—as in both the murderous battle which closes *Samurai Assassin* and the final duel of *Goyokin*—which leaves dark, red blotches in freshly fallen snow, a new type of samurai is defined: pitiless, obsessive, perhaps more alienated than any other genre hero. The *ninja* sub-genre—which features exponents of *ninjutsu*, a Heian-era martial art that originated in the Koga and Iga regions late in the first millennium—often features the exploits of Iga clan spies, who became an essential part of the Tokugawa espionage system, and individual practitioners, from the first Iga follower of Tokugawa, the legendary Hanzo Hattori Masashige, onward. A unique aspect of these films in terms of *chambara* is the *kunoichi*—or female *ninja*; for, while no female could become a samurai, a significant number of *ninjutsu* practitioners were young women. In the late 1970s, and long before *Teenage Mutant Ninja Turtles* (1987), the hooded, dark-clad, and semi-magical spies crossed over to the mainstream partly via Hong Kong-made pictures and became martial arts icons in the West.

With the identification of this new breed of fictional samurai who are somewhat less than noble and may have flecks of rust on their formerly untarnished weapons, of *ronin* less stalwart than the legendary forty-seven, the classical limitations of the genre have been expanded but not entirely superseded. Both independently and as a whole, the post-War samurai films may make a disturbing impression on the Western viewer. This is not merely because of their violent content and visceral style but also because their directness runs counter to those clichés of ambiguity and understatement

Toshiro Mifune as
Tsuruchiyo in the final
battle in *Samurai
Assassin* (1964)

which the West has formulated for the East, because the consistent display and ultimate impotence of the violence in these films are as difficult to accept as the idea of contemplative men being cold-blooded killers.

Visual Conventions. Visual style in the samurai film, as has already been suggested through a number of examples, contributes to and reinforces narrative and character development. It does not constitute a genre convention in the same sense as these others. Certain motifs which may reoccur in the work of various filmmakers—such as the use of slow motion or elaborate special effects in the sequences of combat—are heavily predetermined by an iconic typing with no visual specificity. As the sword, for instance, is an icon, its treatment in film is associated with both *kendo* style and the sword-dances of classical theater. Any film's visualization of swordplay is highly derivative from these or primarily an elaboration of previous usages, both social and artistic. A second set of conventions influencing film is rooted in earlier visual arts. For example, the assumption of the Eastern landscape painter that the spectator is not standing in an ideal spot merely observing the work but is actually *within* its topography contributes, via a heritage of visual expression, to the manner in which a filmmaker inscribes his frame. The pen-and-ink simplicity of terrain, a fondness for mists, and line drawings which emphasize the interfacing of earth, sky, and sea are other qualities of traditional Japanese landscapes that often find equivalents in filmic images.

The best-known artists of the Tokugawa era were viewed from the isolationist principle of *ukiyo-e*—or "images of the floating world." In a literal sense, the "floating world" is the island of the Japan, removed from all outside

Early version of the great wave by Katsushika Hokusai (1760-1849)

ABOVE, AND RIGHT:
Ukiyo-e prints by Utagawa
Kunisada (1786-1864) inspired by
the *Kanadehon Chushingura*

influences by the Tokugawa policy. In a figurative sense, it is the organizing principle behind material reality. As such, it permeates art as diverse as the landscapes of Katsushika Hokusai and the theater posters of Kitagawa Utamaro, it underlies the wave or tea plantation painted by Hokusai and the geishas of Utamaro alike. Utamaro, Hokusai, and scores of other artists, such as Utagawa Kuniyoshi and Utagawa Kunisada (Toyokuni III), produced numerous *ukiyo-e* prints centered around the *Chushingura* legend.

Hokusai is credited with creating the term *manga* (literally "funny pictures"), which was retroactively applied to many captioned wood-block prints of the 18th century. Since World War II, the term *manga* has been associated with the long-form comic books immensely popular with consumers of all ages. One of the earliest samurai *manga* was a version of "Tange Sazen" drawn by modern *manga* pioneer Osamu Tezuka and published in book form in

1954. Sazen, a one-armed, one-eyed samurai created in the 1920s by novelist Fubo Hayashi (a pen name of Umitaro Hasegawa) was first adapted into a film by Daisuke Ito in 1928 and more than a score of other movies and television versions have followed, most notably Gosha's *The Secret of the Urn* (*Tange Sazen Hien Iai-giri*, 1966). Tezuka wrote about his approach that:

> Most *manga* were drawn from a two-dimensional perspective like a stage play. Actor's entrances from stage left and right focused on the audience. I came to realize there was no way to produce power or psychological impact with this approach, so I began to introduce cinematic techniques from the German and French movies of my student days. I manipulated close-ups and angles and tried using many panels or many pages to faithfully capture movements and facial expressions that previously would have been a single panel.[2]

It did not take long for *chambara-manga* to proliferate. *Anime*—or Japanese animation for features and television—soon sprang from *manga*, and scores of animated samurai stories have been produced. Just as the movies he watched as a medical student during World War II help to shape Tezuka's style, *manga* and *anime* techniques have influenced many post-War, live-action filmmakers.

Finally, there are a number of principles of aesthetic perception which antedate *mono no aware*. Besides Seami's notion of *yugen* (literally "mystery" or "obscurity") cited at the beginning of this chapter, there are *wabi* (melancholy or desolation), *sabi* (weathered or antique), and *shibui* (silent or understated). Seami's classic examples of these qualities—*sabi* found in a tarnished silver bowl full of snow, *yugen* in the moon partially hidden by rain clouds—suggest how a motion picture can be grounded in forms antecedent to its invention, as part of an organic conception of art and a belief that, within the introspective and experiential totality of a work, style may be "mysteriously" transformed into viewer emotion.

None of this is to say that the samurai film, particularly since World War II, has been shackled by a host of aesthetic prescriptions, that any filmmaker has mistaken his method of expression for the scroll landscapes of Sesshu or the *noh* drama of Seami. As should become apparent in succeeding chapters, most of these extrinsic, formal prejudices have been, under the shadow of Western film production and as

1834 *manga* of men in a spider's web by Hokusai

Pen-and-ink landscape by Sesshu Toyo (1420-1506)

part of the indigenous evolution of the Japanese motion picture, thoroughly transmuted or entirely discarded over the last few decades. The same is true of factors which intrinsically affect the basic images of any motion picture, usages such as wide screen aspect ratios and color film stock, to which all but a handful of Japanese productions have conformed since the 1960s, or the preeminence of long-focal-length lenses. Both pre-modern aesthetics and post-War technology contribute to the genre's imagistic conventions, but neither does so in a dominant way.

If, in fact, the samurai film possesses a genotypical visual style, it may be related as much to the ideographic nature of the Japanese language as it is to aesthetics or technology. All of these are involved in the complex question of how film generates figurative meanings. The development of color, wide-screen, and lenses of greater focal range control in an obvious way the production of any given film image. A step further along, aesthetic considerations may be overlaid, and a filmmaker's fondness for the primary colors of Kitagawa Utamaro may relate to the actual colors employed. But the conceptual thought which supports that production is intricately bound up with certain perceptual dispositions.

On a literal level, the conventions of "squaring" written characters— which are themselves patterned after a rough sketch of the object represented (for example, the ideograph for "sun" was originally drawn ⊙ and was squared off to become 🟦)—produces in most Japanese films an emphasis on straight lines and angular compositions over curves and circular forms. The fact that words are read from left to right and top to bottom means that an image is scanned similarly. As a consequence, if persons or objects are "stacked" from foreground to background in a CinemaScope frame, the stage line linking them will most often recede from right front to left rear or top front to bottom rear.

On a figurative level, the sometimes metaphorical way in which the ideographs themselves are constructed may have implications for the creation of visual metaphors in Japanese film. Sergei Eisenstein argues in his essay "The Cinematic Principle and the Ideogram" that the ideograph is a linguistic analog to the process of montage, since each combines sub-units or sub-images to produce a higher meaning. Perhaps a clearer understanding of the relation of the ideograph to perception can be found in Ernest Fenollosa's study of Chinese poetry.[3]

MOTHER   SEES   SUNRISE

The first level of metaphor is internal, pertaining to the construction of each symbolic word. While the structural addition of 🝣 (woman) plus ⟨ (breast) to equal mother seems mainly physiological, 𝄞 (sun) plus ⌣ (horizon) is a pictorial compound in which each element adds to a visual understanding of the other through context, i.e., it is metaphoric in the sense of elucidation through contrast. Finally, 𝄞 (eye) plus 〜 (legs) is almost purely figurative, as it derives the notion of vision itself from a metaphysical image of the eye running toward a perceived object. On an external or interactive level, even when the ideograms are placed vertically, Fenellosa distinguishes a complex of a dynamic, metaphorical syntax in which the eye seems to run from the mother toward the rising sun. The problem with the analyses of both Eisenstein and Fenellosa is that, in actual usage, the "montage" or synthetic stage is eliminated. An ideograph such as 𝄞 is not read metaphorically by adding the sub-units of 𝄞 and 〜 or by relating to any graphic signification grounded in perception. Simply put, Japanese is a phonetic language, and the ideographs symbolize the sounds already in the language, not their concepts. Many words in Japanese require two or more ideographs, each representing a phoneme and/or syllable. Consequently most words are apprehended in a purely arbitrary manner, that is, just as an English speaker would associate the letters in "sunrise" by rote with a memory image of an actual event.

Can Japanese film, then, as Fenellosa suggests of ideographs, "bear its metaphor on its face"? Clearly, any film viewer, Eastern or Western, whether from a phonetic or hieroglyphic linguistic background, has a choice when searching for visual meaning. One can first search interiorly, in mise-en-scène or the interaction of figures within the shot, or exteriorly, in montage or the interaction of separate shots. But if Japanese filmmakers have a greater general tendency toward conditioning their audience to the interior method than their Western counterparts, it is not apparent from their films. It remains then for figurative usage as well as the other stylistic and narrative questions to be further examined at the level of the individual motion picture.

CHAPTER TWO

AKIRA KUROSAWA

I dare do all that may become a man;
Who dares do more is none.

—*Macbeth*

A T THE FOOT OF A CLOUD-ENSHROUDED MOUNTAIN ARE AN ARRAY of wooden markers. The camera scans the horizon and in a succession of cuts moves in closer to them. Voices chant solemnly in the background: "Behold, within this place, long ago, there stood a mighty fortress where lived a strong warrior murdered by ambition." As a vertical panning shot moves down the scarred ideographic record cut into the face of the largest marker, traces of mist creep in at the edge of the frame and finally obscure the ground all around it.

After this elegiac prologue, the story of Taketoki Washizu, the "warrior murdered by ambition," unfolds. If the narration of his brief tenure on Kurosawa's *Throne of Blood* (*Kumonosu-Jo*, 1957) seems vaguely familiar, it may be because it is adapted from *Macbeth* or simply because it conforms to structural patterns common to all moral tales in any era of culture. As it

ABOVE: Toshiro Mifune as Taketoki Washizu in *Throne of Blood*

LEFT: Traces of mist creep in at the edge of the frame

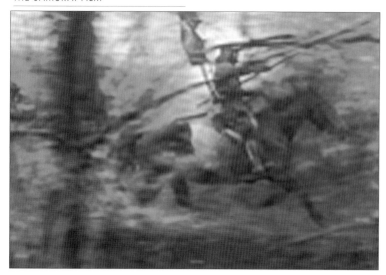

The camera pans to follow the two men riding through on horseback

Opposite page
TOP: An almost phosphorescently white presence who sits winding thread in a crude hut

CENTER: Miki's specter at the banquet

BOTTOM: Washizu's reaction

happens, Celtic Scotland, like Japan of the Ashikaga period, was peopled by contending warlords and usurping vassals and, just as Macbeth's initial shrinking from daring more than "may become a man" implies, was only restrained from political chaos by an ethic of honorable actions. While the social backgrounds and the main story elements—from the hag-given prophecies and "Duncan's" murder to Lady Asaji's blood-stained hands and "Birnam" wood come to Kumonosu-Jo ("the Castle of the Spider's Web")—are identical in many respects, they are transposed and reconstituted by Kurosawa to appear as classically Japanese as they were Elizabethan. It is in the visual specifics of this transposition—that is, in Kurosawa's imagery and figurative devices—that the unique qualities of *Throne of Blood* are most apparent.

For the first view of Washizu and his companion Miki ("Banquo"), Kurosawa chooses a dense forest of tall, dark trees. It is "so foul and fair a day" that although it is raining heavily, the thick branches filter out most of the light and moisture. Sunbeams glint off the isolated drops of water and the forest floor is a maze of light and shadow, wet and dry. When the camera pans to follow the two men riding through on horseback, long lenses create a textured gray of blurred leaves and tree limbs, which obscures their outlines and separates them both literally and associatively from the open ground they are desperately seeking. Up to this point in the film everything has occurred on a natural level. All the incidents have been both reportable and explicable on that level: the victories of Washizu and Miki are not seen on screen but related to their overlord by a series of messengers, the first of whom had ridden literally out of the mists of the prologue. But now, the two lost men conclude that the forest is enchanted. They pronounce a formula over their weapons and gallop through, Washizu firing arrows and Miki thrusting his spear furiously, as if to kill the demons of the woods. Instead they plunge deeper into its mysteries.

In this manner, Kurosawa erects a dynamic historical distance around his characters, as he shifts from a convention of realistic action to a much more ritualized one, from the "present" perspective of the *kabuki*-like chant of the first scene to the "long ago" past time of the main narrative, without a cut, as the first messenger's horse parts the mists. The subsequent encounter of Washizu and Miki with an androgynous old sorcerer or spirit, an almost phosphorescently white presence who sits winding thread in a crude hut, may not seem so different from Macbeth's meeting with the three weird sisters mumbling over a cauldron on the moors. But the particular mise-en-scène here defines the calculated effect Kurosawa is seeking. The old man's "preternaturalness," like that of the forest itself or of the banks of fog in and out of which Washizu and Miki must ride for so long after leaving the forest, is deceptively simple. Since their meeting with the seer takes place in the scheme of events between the two highly stylized wanderings, it is as if the hut, like the gate of Dante's hell, can only be found by "losing the straight path" or being left behind in the same circuitous fashion.

The menace of the ghostly or parapsychic in *Throne of Blood*, like the actual motivations of the characters, is suggested rather than stated explicitly, seen rather than discussed. The appearance of Miki's specter at the banquet illustrates this, as the irony of the disturbed Washizu surrounded by guests who are oblivious to the apparition is sufficiently clear from the visuals to make the dramatic declamations of the play unnecessary. Throughout the film Kurosawa's realization of the extraordinary events the original describes is a subdued one. There are few close shots and little action. The battles are either not witnessed or brought to issue within a few moments. Even the celebrated conclusion in which Washizu's own men destroy him with a torrent of arrows is actually but a series of slow movements, as he stumbles around the platform of a watchtower, which build to a climactic jump-cut the instant a shaft pierces his neck. Mifune's interpretation of Washizu is full of repressed energy and unusually so. Only in the scene with

Miki's ghost does he approach the histrionics frequently associated with the personage of Macbeth; so that he moves somnambulantly through many scenes and seems more genuinely to be driven to action by his scheming wife. Kurosawa may even force the audience's view away from him at dramatically crucial moments, such as the scene in which Washizu is convinced by his wife of the Lord's ingratitude. They begin their dialogue sitting opposite each other in a balanced medium-close shot and, as he responds to her words, Washizu stands, implying a momentary dominance as the camera tilts up to hold him in frame. But as he paces back and forth, she begins her most telling argument; and when he moves quickly back to her, the camera reframes on her figure, so that he is visible only from the waist down. The audience cannot see his change of expression as her icy rhetoric sways him. Not until he is convinced and his expression is altered into one of submission does he slump down onto the floor and back into the shot.

This understatement in both acting and action is maintained in the imagery and symbolism. Superficially, certain traditional animal metaphors—such as the crows which invade the castle before Washizu's downfall, and conversely the rats which leave it "before it burns"—support the narrative mixture of "real" and "metaphysical" phenomena. To underscore this dichotomy more directly, Kurosawa alternates between montage sequences and others photographed in one shot, as, for example, the discussion between Washizu and his wife cited above. The intrinsic formal values in a usage like the sequence shot[1] may be combined with a symbol, so that the effectiveness of each is enhanced. For instance, in the intense conversation between Washizu and his wife regarding the prophecy that Miki's son, rather than his own, will succeed him, the camera moves first from left to right and then tightens on the figures, until a shrill pipe sounds on the track. Washizu drops to his knees, as his wife tells him that she is pregnant. The sequence itself is one shot; the cut which follows—and which breaks the tension of both the sustained camera work and Washizu's doubts over the prophecy—is to a horse rearing in the courtyard of Miki's manor. This image not only discharges the pent-up energy of the preceding scene through the violent movements of the frightened animal but also acts as an emblem of the "rising" destiny of Miki's son and a chilling portent that the divination against Washizu's heirs will be fulfilled.

Beyond the presence or absence of montage, Kurosawa organizes other elements into a recurring expression of the inevitable and quasi-tragic consequences of Washizu's ambition—the ominous, mask-like, white visage of Lady Washizu, the fateful traveling shots which seem to stalk after the Lord, the blood-stained walls of the forbidden room, and the courtyard, visible behind an open screen, which burns with an overexposed intensity on either side of Washizu as he sits within planning the assassination—all of these reinforce imagistically the notion of some exterior force guiding the thoughts and actions of the characters. Other devices in the staging—such as the swish of Lady Washizu's kimono across the polished floors sounding like wings flapping, or the design of uneven lines on the wall of Washizu's great hall, which seem to close on him like the fingers of misshapen hands when he is framed against them—continue to reassert this sense of doom both aurally and visually.

In a way, *Throne of Blood* is patterned after Macbeth's "tangled web": the blurred forest branches which cling graphically to the riders; the old ghost winding a silken thread like a spider while he warns that "man is vain and death is long"; the very name of the castle of the spider's web (which is the title of the film in Japanese);

Opposite page
TOP: Washizu's enemies storm his castle in *Throne of Blood*

CENTER AND BOTTOM: Washizu drops to his knees, as his wife tells him that she is pregnant. The cut which breaks the tension is to a horse rearing in the courtyard.

This page
BELOW: The ominous, mask-like, white visage of Lady Washizu as she contemplates the blood on her hands

BOTTOM: The courtyard, visible behind an open screen, burns with an overexposed intensity on either side of Washizu.

The final annihilating mesh of arrows

and the final annihilating mesh of arrows. Each scene and each image is spun more tightly around the central notion of a man brought down by ambition. Accordingly, the closing images are of the same markers which open the film. The wisps of fog float silently around them, as the camera moves back and the chanting begins anew:

> His spirit walks. His fame is known.
> For that which was once so is still true.
> Murderous ambition will pursue
> Beyond the grave to give its due.

I. PICTORIALISM, GENRE TYPING, AND SOCIAL CONSCIOUSNESS

The distinctive visual interpretation Kurosawa attaches to the tragedy of noble personages in *Throne of Blood* is grounded in his earlier films of *jidai-geki* and *chambara*. From the visual simplicity and the eminently theatrical mannerisms—still in evidence in *Throne of Blood* via the choral chanting and the make-up of certain characters—of his first "martial arts" film *Judo Saga* (*Sanshiro Sugata*, Parts I and II, 1943-44) and the end-of-war *Walkers on Tiger's Tails* (*Tora No O Wo Fumo Otokatachi*, 1945), Kurosawa's directorial approach to the genre quickly encompassed an elaborate pictorialism.

In *Rashomon* (1950, photographed by Kazuo Miyagawa), as it would be in the forest and moors of *Throne of Blood*, the principal determinant of visual tonalities is weather. Huddled under the Rashomon gate, seeking shelter from the wind and rain, are the priest, the woodcutter, and the thief whose conversation initiates the multiple flashbacks to the main story. The random cutting from medium to close shots, the meandering pans across and down the weather-worn fixtures of the gate, and the cacophony of creaking signboards and bursting rain spouts combine with the muted gray light of a simulated overcast to create a sense of nervous instability. This sense complements the manifest anxiety of the priest ("I can't understand it") over the hidden cause of the events he relates to the thief. The staging of those events, which center around the assault of the bandit Tajomaru on the samurai Takehiro and his wife, is in marked contrast to the framing material at the gate. In the initial transition back in time, as the viewer follows the woodcutter, the editing scheme develops from straightforward composition and angles of the prologue through numerous panning shots and a traveling camera. There is a powerful kinetic quality in the blur of lines as a long lens pursues the terrified woodcutter running from the samurai's corpse. Then a wipe moving in the same direction seems to concentrate that energy into the shackled figure of Tajomaru, who squats in the magistrate's courtyard. That implication of power channeled into the audience's first sight of Tajomaru is reinforced by the sunlit background, which forms a white rectangle of overexposure behind the bandit. The play between light and dark introduced here is not only distinct from the pervasive grayness of the scenes at the gate but is carried over throughout all the flashbacks. The mottled hue thrown across the forest clearings by the sun, the shadows curving through deeply composed shots, the frequent silhouetting of characters and objects against a bright sky become part of an expressive pattern in *Rashomon*, a pictorialism which functions as ironic background not merely to Tajomaru's animal behavior but, as it is ultimately revealed, to that of the samurai and his wife as well.

Kurosawa's richly textured frames are a first level of meaning, which he compounds to express abstract relationships. His placement of a placid or balanced frame over the surface of a chaotic and violent narrative is an occasionally paradoxical inscription which underscores Kurosawa's world view. The geometry which he imposes on a scene such as the funeral of Heihachi in *Seven Samurai* equates the six remaining who stand on the windswept cemetery ridge with the cloth banner they had devised as their emblem. Planted on the rooftop by Kikuchiyo, the banner is itself a defiant symbol that mocks the *hatamoto*—or "banner men"—the highest rank of clan samurai, from which these *ronin* could not be further removed. The repeated panning movement down the length of the banner is accompanied by the martial theme of the *ronin* on the soundtrack. The visual implies, on the one hand, that the human figures on the hill are pawns with no more free will than the

The banner maker Heihachi, who will be the first to die in *Seven Samurai*, points out that Kikuchiyo is the odd shape or triangle.

crudely inked circles and triangle on the cloth, which supplant them in the frame; on the other hand, the cut back to the characters themselves and the surge of martial music on the soundtrack counterindicates that the men are the flesh which fills in those empty geometric figures. This in turn infuses the entire concept of social interaction symbolized by the flag (banding together or nation forming) with a dynamic immediacy.

This ambivalence over roles and, at times, over the very nature of reality is also reflected in the specifics of Kurosawa's expository techniques in *Seven Samurai*. Explicitly, it may be in the verbal self-realization apparent in Kanbei's tactic of appealing to reckless chivalry in the men he recruits: "I'm preparing a tough war that will bring us neither money nor fame. Want to join?" Or it may be implicit in the visual usage—in the side-light falling on the face of someone pondering indecisively or in a figure made graphically indeterminate by a blurring movement or silhouetting. The bamboo spears of the villagers in *Seven Samurai* are held so that they lean expectantly toward their approaching enemies. A traveling shot around the ravished wife in *Rashomon* reveals her husband's sneer of disgust. A pull back from a close shot of the woman includes the sword blades of Tajomaru and her husband touching in the foreground of the shot. Images such as these elaborate visually on relationships by gradually disclosing to or anticipating for the viewer facts which the characters already possess. This establishes a sort of inverse, dramatic irony in which the audience must experience an uncertainty of its own, analogous to the emotions of the personages on screen.

Finally, Kurosawa uses formal values to create metaphorical significance. The series of three traveling shots—which trace a 180-degree arc from a medium close-up of the village elder to a two shot with Kanbei, then pull back to link all the samurai and farmers in the hut—link all the figures. This equation is reinforced by the unbroken movement rather than simple cuts between Kanbei to the elder, so that when he explains that "farmers are scared a lot," it is

Farmers are scared a lot.

ABOVE: The elder explains that "farmers are scared a lot."

clear that the *ronin* are also fearful of the task ahead. The final shot of the film is a justifiably classic and essentially figurative statement on the tragedy of the "wave men." As they stand exhausted after the final rain-drenched battle, Kanbei observes dispassionately to Gorobei that "again we've survived." The scene shifts to the villagers, singing as they methodically replant the rice paddies on a sunny morning. As the three survivors stand watching them at the foot of the hill, below the four mounds and four swords which mark the graves of the fallen *ronin*, the third man, Sekichi, leaves the frame to follow the peasant girl, Shino. A cut shifts the angle ninety degrees and reinstates the three-shot, but with Sekichi in the foreground and Kanbei and Gorobei behind him. With this cut, Kurosawa defines the invisible ties which bind Sekichi, after his baptism of blood, firmly to the other two. Caught in the grip of tradition or *shushigaku* or whatever one chooses to name the impulse to fulfill the samurai role, Sekichi stands undecided. Sekichi remains torn between the two worlds, as Kurosawa cuts "inside" of him back to a two-shot of Kanbei and Gorobei, as the former quietly replies: "Again we're defeated. The winners are those farmers. Not us."

This realization does not diminish the irony, and Kurosawa embellishes it with a pan up to the two center graves, irrevocably linking Kanbei and Gorobei not with the farmers but with their dead comrades. This time the martial notes of the score sound the final irony as the last image—the graves rather than the three survivors—fades.

The fatalism over the role of the samurai, *ronin*, and bandit alike, which Kurosawa

BELOW: "The four mounds and four swords which mark the graves of the fallen *ronin*."

Left, Kanbei proclaims, "Again we've survived."

The winners are the farmers.

"Invisible ties which bind Sekichi"—the final shots of *Seven Samurai.*

evidences in *Rashomon, Seven Samurai*, and *Throne of Blood*, is a specific one. It is directed at individuals or small groups rather than large social units. While these films may suggest that the fate of the various individuals is grounded in a kind of social determinism—that Washizu, Tajomaru, and the seven *ronin* are equally victims of the feudal system—the dramatic or first level of meaning with which the audience is asked to involve itself is focused on personal rather than institutional conflicts: that is, Tajomaru versus the samurai; the *ronin* and farmers versus the bandits; Washizu versus first his wife, then Miki and those loyal to the murdered Lord. In short, Kurosawa does not compel the viewer, as Kobayashi and other directors may, to regard institutions as the villainous figures or even as major antagonists.

In Kenji Mizoguchi's *Tales of the Taira Clan*, the young clansman Kiyomori Taira is portrayed by Raizo Ichikawa. Ichikawa's image, as a then youthful star coupled with the particulars of costuming and make-up, make it easy for the viewer to empathize with the ambitious, high-ranking samurai he portrays simply because he has an attractive aspect. In this, Mizoguchi initially relies on a male performance derived from the *wagoto* style of *kabuki* acting. In the silent era, Japanese filmmakers often used heavy theatrical make-up to coarsen the aspect of *jitsuaku*—or villainous figures—or to create a softer *bidanshi* ("handsome man") character. In his later portrayals, Ichikawa's relatively short-lived career would ultimately combine aspects of these two types, culminating with aspects of both *aragoto* and *wagoto* in *Kyoshiro Nemuri*.

While Mizoguchi's sympathies may not lie with either of the factions that participated in the Taira/Minamoto wars or in the conflict between the Tairas and the clergy, as described in *Tales of the Taira Clan*, the viewer is clearly directed by the film's formal values to identify with Kiyomori and his cause. Eventually, Mizoguchi's mutely tinted frames and stately moving camera make the energetic figure of Kiyomori the film's incontestable center visually as well as narratively. In the course of that formal detailing, the historical reality of the 12th century itself is transformed, and Kiyomori's struggle is characterized in such a way that it appears he supports democratic ideals or the advancement of the general or clan cause as opposed to the clergy's elitism. Unquestionably it is the prerogative of filmmakers to distort the past or to use it as a ground for a stylized dramatization of ideological conflicts it did not actually contain: in this case, a fictional encounter between ostensibly democratic and oligarchic factions. In terms of Japanese film history, *Tales of the Taira Clan* is one of the last illustrations of a pre-War genre typing at work in the samurai film. Kiyomori is not alienated by the institutions or feudalism itself but by the monastic attempt to suborn those constructs to their own purposes. The iconoclasm he demonstrates in "defiling" the sacred Buddhist palanquins with his arrows is not aimed, literally or

ABOVE, TOP: Toshiro Mifune (right) in *Sanjuro*

CENER: Yuzo Kayama as Hiro (right) and Toshiro Mifune as the title character in *Sanjuro*

BOTTOM: *Yojimbo*

figuratively, at the whole structure of government but at only a symbol of special interests which he believes imperil that structure.

From the first, Kurosawa's performances are skewed towards the *aragoto*, or rough, style. Still the aspect and the performances of Takashi Shimura as Kanbei, Isao Kimura as Katsuchiro, and Toshiro Mifune as Kikuchiyo in *Seven Samurai* are very different. Shimura's Kanbei is the patient anchor that holds together such diverse types as the dour master Katsuchiro and the bumbling braggart Kikuchiyo. Yet all three are "rough" and eminently masculine. Even the handsome and youthful Sekichi aspires to become a man like these. By the time of *Yojimbo* and *Sanjuro*, the sardonic *ronin*, as incarnated by Toshiro Mifune, is the graphic opposite of Kiyomori. The costuming and make-up—soiled kimono, unkempt hair, unshaven face—do not immediately encourage the spectator to identify; but the fact that *Yojimbo* opens with this character alone in the shot restricts the audience's choice considerably. More significantly, an expository title even before he appears places the narrative stress squarely on historical events: "The time is 1860. The emergence of a middle-class was brought about by an end to the power of the Tokugawa dynasty." The generic invocation of the film is bifocal: the central character is defined in terms of audience expectation. He is, despite his physical unattractiveness, alone in the frame and the star of the film. The narrative core is defined in terms of historical reality. Finally, the notion of fated or predestined action is brought into play when the unidentified swordsman pauses at a fork in the road and throws a stick to decide which path he will follow.

Unlike Kiyomori, this figure has neither a history nor a cause. He is decentered to the extent that he fashions his surname from whatever he happens to be gazing at when asked to identify himself. ("Sanjuro" means "thirty," "Kuwabatake" in *Yojimbo* means "mulberry fields," and "Tsubaki" in *Sanjuro* means "camellias.") Lacking allegiances, again unlike Kiyomori, he has no inbred enemies or any reason to seek quarrels. Instead, conflict finds him. The arbitrary choice of path in *Yojimbo* leads him to a town disrupted by warring gangs. The hut in which he seeks shelter before *Sanjuro* even begins turns out to be the meeting place for a group of rebellious young samurai. What identity "Sanjuro" does possess consequently depends entirely on genre typing. This is not the typing of a figure such as Kiyomori, which derives, as do other forms of fiction, on a reading or exposition of character rather than context. Rather it develops from an interplay of character and environment, of figure and ground. Because the ground is inscribed first in *Yojimbo* through the expository title, the figure is distinguished against it. In other words, because Sanjuro is to be a reactant rather than an initiator in the unfolding narrative, the historical context must be invoked first, so that the hero without a name or a past may be defined in relation to it.

What Kurosawa also makes clear—in the stark gray visual of the isolated figure on a windswept road with his arms tucked protectively inside his sleeves, or in the grim verbal aside when he is greeted at the edge of town by a dog with a human hand in its jaws ("The smell of blood brings the hungry dogs")—is that his title character is strongly alienated. As man and animal cross paths there is an identification of one with the other. The swordsman is typed as a "stray dog"; but becoming a *yojimbo* ("bodyguard") in no way re-integrates him. In a sense, the *ronin* spends the entirety of *Yojimbo* perched mentally on the watchtower he climbs to sneer at the tremulous gang men facing off in the street below. The immediacy of his contempt is carried through the film not because of his frequent sardonic exchanges of dialogue with the other characters, but because it is a symptom of the role of indifference into which he has retreated and which, for his own peace of mind, cannot be violated. The sincerity of the role is never resolved, but clearly Sanjuro is not a Zen-man. His angry threat to the family he assists in *Yojimbo* (that he will kill them if they cry because he detests pathos) or his parting words to his would-be disciples in *Sanjuro* ("Don't follow me, or I'll kill you") elucidate his own emotional insecurity. If he is a fallen romantic, he is still not a complete fatalist. As he tells the ambitious peasant's son he sees fleeing home at the film's beginning and whose life he spares near its end: "A long life eating mush is best."

BELOW, TOP: Isolated figure on a windswept road with his arms tucked protectively inside his sleeves

CENTER: A dog with a human hand in its jaws ("The smell of blood brings the hungry dogs")

BOTTOM: "A long life eating mush is best"

Sanjuro is caught between the lack of awareness which would allow him to be content eating mush and the Buddhist conviction to disengage himself mentally, which might make him equally content to eat mush. He kills the rival master at the conclusion of *Sanjuro* knowing that the duel has lost all "real" or political meaning but unable and, to some degree, unwilling to avoid it. He cannot follow the Zen-like advice which he gives the young samurai explaining that a skilled rival is "exactly like me: a drawn sword . . . really good swords stay in their scabbards."

What differentiates such an ending generically from that of *Seven Samurai* is that the central character in *Yojimbo* and *Sanjuro* enters the film profoundly alienated. Unlike Kanbei, whose realization that he cannot win comes at the end of the earlier motion picture, Sanjuro is acutely aware of his own alienation and likewise of his inability to resolve it. In either case the principal dramatic statement—given that the viewer, standing outside the film's genre structures, possesses an added level of awareness—is grimly ironic. The beaten figure smuggled out of town in a coffin in *Yojimbo* must return to settle the score, half out of indifference to escaping and half out of the unstated fear that what minimal identity he does have through action, through swordsmanship, will disappear unless he returns. What becomes the pervasive irony of the entire genre is, of course, that the hero cannot find satisfaction in that action or any action. Where Tajomaru the bandit did not perceive the complex fabric of personal and social exchange which restricted his freedom of choice and action, and where Kanbei the *ronin* saw that fabric but resigned himself to surviving and assisting others even without fulfillment, Sanjuro cuts through it with his sharp wit and his sword only to find that he is still entangled in it and no freer.

What this means iconically is that a symbol like the gun which fells the four *ronin* in *Seven Samurai* and which liberates the central figure in a film such as *The Ambitious* (discussed in Chapter Four) is parried indifferently by the *ronin* in *Yojimbo*. There is an element of parody, of mock *wagoto*, in Sanjuro's antagonist, Unosuke, who adopts an effeminate manner to confuse his enemies. He stands with his hips thrust out, a contorted smile flashing through dark lips, an arm sometimes creeping out of his striped kimono sleeve to display his pearl-handled pistol. It is the fey Unosuke who manages to capture and torture Sanjuro, but whose pistol is defeated by a dagger. For Sanjuro, defeating a man such as Unosuke, who is a lampoon of a samurai, is an empty victory indeed.

A pessimistic reading of Kurosawa's genre typing might conclude that the alienated figure must overcome his opponents and survive—and to some extent the audience does expect just that—because death would be a genuine release. But if his genre identity is primarily a social one, then death annihilates the awareness of social ills, which potentially might be communicated to others, permanently. This is the question Kobayashi and others take up; but for Kurosawa, the final dramatic moment, however stylized, remains more direct. The *ronin* says "So long, old man" to the innkeeper and walks away in *Yojimbo*, his back to the camera and flattened against the empty street by a long lens. In *Sanjuro*, the closing image reduces the whole conflict of the narrative into an abstract one of lines of force: the young samurai stand backlit against bright windows, and another long lens reduces the title figure to little more than an intermittent shadow which moves through the foreground of the frame.

To a large extent, Kurosawa's genre typing derives from a socially conscious view of the human condition shared by most of Japan's post-War filmmakers. While Kurosawa's work may not be as pointedly anti-feudal as that of Kobayashi or others, it relies on much the same ironic hindsight. The vigor of *Seven Samurai*, *Yojimbo*, and *Sanjuro* derives primarily from Kurosawa's visual usage; and that usage is grounded in the social consciousness of Kurosawa's earlier work. From *Judo Saga*, his directorial debut, through the contemporary dramas of the 1950s, Kurosawa incorporated action scenes, humor, and an aggressive pictorialism into the standard and stable narrative formats of *jidai-geki* and melodrama. With *Yojimbo*, for the second time in his career Kurosawa tested the limits of style and content possible in a commercial Japanese motion picture. Judo is not the cause of dramatic conflicts in *Judo Saga,* the characters are; but scenes of judo prowess are the emotional focal points of the film. In *Judo Saga* and *Seven Samurai* and, by opposing equation, in *Rashomon* and *Throne of Blood*, Kurosawa's characters survive or perish based in large part on their respect for the ethical values of society. *Bushido* and its interactive structure of moral and martial discipline is not portrayed as an empty form. Perhaps the most direct example of this outlook is *The Hidden Fortress (Kakushi Toride No San-Akunin,* 1958). As that film develops, the behavior of the noble fugitives, General Makabe and Princess Yukihime, is at once sophisticated and

ABOVE: The *ronin* walks away in *Yojimbo*, his back to the camera and flattened against the empty street by a long lens.

BELOW: *Yojimbo* depicts the supremely confident and sardonic swordsman.

CENTER: Depth of field, as Sanjuro peeks out at Unosuke and his henchmen.

BOTTOM" "High Noon," as Sanjuro returns to confront Unosuke and his cronies in *Yojimbo*.

Two coffins...maybe three.

naive. Sophisticated, in that it derives from a thousand years of martial tradition; naive, in that it ignores the need for or the actuality of social change.

The *ronin* Sanjuro is in many ways the antithesis of General Makabe. Being low-born, ill-bred, and self-serving, Sanjuro shares nothing and has no genre identity in common with a character like Makabe except for fighting ability. For all of his underlying sentimentality, Sanjuro is a break with the themes and social outlook of Kurosawa's earlier characters. Sugata of *Juda Saga* and his immediate successors, even Kanbei in *Seven Samurai,* are sustained by their idealism. Sanjuro and his sardonic descendants survive by their wits and their fatalistic disregard for social mores.

Kurosawa's penultimate *chambara* drama, *The Shadow Warrior* (*Kagemusha,* 1980), is surprisingly retrogressive. It does contain striking examples of Kurosawa's evocative images and dynamic staging. As with *Dodes-Ka-Den* (1970), in which Kurosawa revisited the locus of his earlier *Lower Depths* (*Donzoko,* 1957), *Kagemusha* explores genre constructions from a more stylized perspective. While this may not be anticipated from Kurosawa's prior film, the muted and understatedly elegiac *Derzu Usula* (1975), many of the visual usages, from whip pans and long focal-length lenses to scenes staged in sustained shots, are typical of his earlier work. Like *Yojimbo* or *Sanjuro, Kagemusha's* narrative depends on an underlying ironic situation: a "shadow warrior," a condemned thief, must stand in for a dead warlord. The characters caught in this situation, while grounded in genre identities and realistically drawn, lack the resilience of Kanbei, Sanjuro, or even General Makabe. The protagonists, Shingen Takeda and his double, are older, which may account for some of the film's languorous pacing; but, from the first, Kurosawa obliquely plays off genre constructions. In his lead actor, Tatsuya Nakadai, Kurosawa has one of *chambara's* prime figures, the star of *Hara-Kiri, Sword of Doom,* and *Goyokin* brings a potent iconic presence to any role. Even in Kurosawa's own earlier work, Nakadai's facile progression—from the role of Unosuke, the flamboyant gun-toting punk in *Yojimbo,* to the honorable master swordsman Hanbei in *Sanjuro*—demonstrates his range as a performer. Perhaps the best example of Nakadai's dramatic intensity is in the non-*chambara* role as Kaji in Masaki Kobayashi's monumental *The Human Condition* (*Ningen no Joken,* 1959-61); but as a genre figure nothing surpasses his brief appearance as a powerful and predatory Miyamoto Musashi in Hiroshi Inagaki's *Kojiro* (*Sasaki Kojiro,* 1967): earnest, fearless, and deadly. As a consequence, with Nakadai in a dual role, the audience automatically invests both the warlord Takeda and his shadow with similar genre expectations.

The opening scene is a sustained three-shot: Shingen, his brother, and the *kagemusha* are all dressed identically. As the lord's brother, who has also

Tatsuya Nakadai in *Kagemusha*

served as his double, explains how he discovered Shingen's "twin," he remarks that "He's a tough one—he wouldn't talk under torture." Since Kurosawa's choice is to play the entire scene, which runs several minutes, in an unbroken three-shot, there can be no close-up. Consequently, while the viewer may suspect, from the dramatic context and from the brother's words, that the new double does have some quality, does fulfill the genre expectations reserved for the central character, there is no visual confirmation. As the "shadow warrior" sits slumped at the edge of the frame and the expository dialogue between the noblemen continues, there is nothing to convince the viewer that he is actually "tougher" than he appears. Nothing, that is, except Nakadai's genre presence. When he finally speaks, in response to Shingen's observation of his criminal past, the *kagemusha* seems indignant: "You've killed hundreds and robbed whole domains. Who is wicked? You or

BELOW: Tatsuya Nakadai as the "Shadow Warrior" holds Kota Yui as the grandson in *Kagemusha*.

BOTTOM: Kenichi Hagiwara (right) as Shingen's son plots a takeover.

I?" Again the staging—he turns his back to camera to deliver these lines—does nothing to prevent his protest from sounding feeble and ill-advised. The wide shot itself works against the dramatic concept. From a distance, all three men resemble each other, so much so that the more marked physical similarity of Shingen and the "shadow warrior" is undercut.

A dichotomy between illusion and reality is suggested in the basic premise of *Kagemusha*; but, excepting a dream sequence, Kurosawa refrains from employing any variations on the highly symbolic usages contained in *Throne of Blood*. Kurosawa's pictorialism is readily apparent and remarkably expressive. A long lens flattens a rider coming straight at the camera. Troops besieging a fortress give way to a massive wall as the camera pans up to survey their objective. Both graphically suggest the impotence of the siege. After Shingen is wounded, his army retreats. An endless line of soldiers walk across a dusty ridge diffracting the light from the setting sun. Silhouettes come over a slope under a red sky. Both reinforce the sense of peril and loss of identity of these troops without a leader. Yet neither example has the range or power of a sustained scene such as Washizu's fateful discussion with his wife in *Throne of Blood*. In instances where the opportunity for such a dramatic revelation may be present, Kurosawa may choose to not exploit it. When the wounded Shingen gathers his retainers, there is a high-angle wide shot of the entire assembly. The key light on his white arm-sling makes Shingen the visual center, draws all eyes to him as the dramatic context itself does. But only a few moments of the scene are played from this angle; most of it is intercut between a close shot of Shingen and a reverse view of his men.

There are stagings which do develop into forceful, nonverbal statements in *Kagemusha*. A pan across a line of Takeda's troops; a side angle as they curve across a field of view; and a long lens shot of marching *ashigaru*, all cede to a red sun cut by gray clouds. This image accompanied by wistful music adds a visual irony that belies a soldier's pride in "the invincible Takeda army" and effectively presages its doom with a tinge of *mono no aware*. But such figurative asides too often remain just that: asides never fully integrated in the flow of the narrative. What is perhaps the most moving scene in *Kagemusha* does not depend on either pictorial values or visual metaphor. Three attendants and two valets, who know that the real Shingen is dead, have been introduced to the "shadow warrior" they must help to impersonate their lord. One of them tells the *kagemusha* not to be "too proud" and chides him for not behaving as the lord would. The "shadow warrior" asks ingenuously, "How is this?" as he moves an armrest into place, leans forward, and casually strokes his beard. The illusion is so compelling that it supersedes the retainers' awareness of who this man really is; and they instinctively stiffen into a formal pose, as they would in the true lord's presence.

Moments such as this, and the general thrust of Kurosawa's earlier dramatizations of feudal society, do not anticipate the conclusion of *Kagemusha*. Certainly the self-destruction of the Takeda army, annihilated as it prosecutes a hopeless battle, has seemed inevitable under the press of social and historical forces. But the "shadow warrior" himself becomes a conscript to their outmoded viewpoint. As the repressive Tokugawa era dawns, the "shadow warrior" performs his own sort of ritual suicide. As his body floats past the submerged Takeda banner, the only emotion evoked is pathos, the emotion Sanjuro and the *ronin* who follow that character's expressive lead in the *genre* so pointedly shun.

II. DRAMATIZATION AND VISUAL STYLE

As if we were villains on necessity; fools by heavenly compulsion.

—*King Lear*

Kurosawa's *Ran* (1985), his second transposition of Shakespeare into *chambara*, is a stylistic tour-de-force combining various conventions of theater and film, both Eastern and Western. As tragedy, Kurosawa blunts the remorseless measure of Shakespeare with an epic sweep. As epic, he defines anti-Homeric proportions and constrains the action by limiting the direct participation of most of his protagonists.

The introductory moments of *Ran*—Kurosawa's "Lear" (the warlord Hidetora, has three sons rather than daughters)—are at an encampment on a plain. There Hidetora attempts to divide his domain, but in a fit of pique banishes his outspoken youngest son, Saburo. Kurosawa uses unnatural make-up, accenting Hidetora's sallow cheeks and blood-shot eyes, which are surrounded by tufts of white hair, so that when he awakens from a dream his face is like a *kabuki* mask. To bracket these opening scenes, Kurosawa cuts away to shots of billowing clouds. These shapes, boiling against a blue sky, are portents of a troubled future for all the characters.

In the early establishing scenes, Kurosawa's staging is entirely naturalistic. While there are subtle visual metaphors, from the bracketing shots of clouds to when the banished Tango rides off over a ridge so that the earth seems to swallow him, nothing in Tatsuya Nakadai's performance as Hidetora is excessively mannered. Only Kyoami, the fool, behaves somewhat outlandishly, but that is his charge. If anything, Hidetora's description of how he acquired his domain and his plans for living out his old age, his own "unburdened crawl toward death," are remarkably benign in light of his savage career.

The first long take Kurosawa employs is a discussion between his eldest son and

BELOW: When he awakens from a dream his face is like a *kabuki* mask.

BOTTOM: Kurosawa cuts away to shots of billowing clouds. These shapes, boiling against a blue sky, are portents of a troubled future for all the characters.

heir, Taro, and daughter-in-law Kaede at the "first" castle. Lady Kaede rebukes her husband for permitting Hidetora to take the banner belonging to the clan chief. Taro is effectively hemmed in by his wife, who reminds him of the fate of her own family ("Hidetora murdered them"), an emotional position which the long take (100 seconds) reinforces. When Hidetora is summoned and asked to sign a formal renunciation of his status in blood, Kurosawa primarily cuts between angles on him and his antagonists, Taro and Kaede. While they are posed against a bright background, Hidetora is framed by dark word posts and dimly-lit *shoji* panels. In this context of power shift, Hidetora's exasperation is natural enough. But moments later, as Kyoma is menaced by a Taro retainer he has mocked, Hidetora cuts the man down with an arrow shot. With this action Hidetora, firing from a cramped position in a castle tower, has now set his inexorable fate in motion.

As with *Kagemusha,* Kurosawa has the resources to create an epic backdrop for the tragic end of Hidetora and his family. Again, he punctuates the panoramic battle scenes with selected long takes. When Hidetora and his retinue move to the castle of Jiro, his second son, he meets his daughter-in-law Lady Sue as she prays at sunset on a parapet. In a shot sustained for well over three minutes, Kurosawa's camera tilts and pans several times but holds longest on a two shot of Hidetora and Sue. While both are posed against the red horizon, as Lady Sue kneels before him, Hidetora chides her to "Look upon me with hatred." Now realizing the full import of his voluntary transfer of power, Hidetora desires that hatred as validation of a life spent ruthlessly subjugating others. The pious Sue refuses to comply.

Shortly after this encounter, the destruction of Hidetora's world is complete. Spurning Jiro, Hidetora takes refuge in the castle abandoned by the banished Saburo, where his two eldest sons attack him. As Hidetora's mind reels from this event, Kurosawa adds a subjective element to the lengthy montage of the battle by

ABOVE, TOP The first long take Kurosawa employs is a discussion between his eldest son and heir, Taro (Akira Terao), and daughter-in-law Kaede (Mieko Harada)

BOTTOM: Hidetora (Tatsuya Nakadai) meets his daughter-in-law Lady Sue (Yoshiko Miyazaki) as she prays at sunset on a parapet in a shot sustained for well over three minutes.

BELOW: Hidetora retreats to an upper room and sits oblivious to the action outside, to the bullets and burning arrows whizzing by his body.

removing all the natural sounds. Men charge down a mist-swept hill without battle cries, hoof beats, or gunshots. Only a rhythmic, dirge-like score is heard on the soundtrack. As Hidetora's retainers are systematically killed, as his women commit suicide, Hidetora retreats to an upper room and sits oblivious to the action outside, to the bullets and burning arrows whizzing by his body. Having broken his sword on an opponent's armor, Hidetora has no weapon with which to commit *seppuku*. Finally, as flames consume the keep, Hidetora's white-clad figure emerges from the thick smoke like a ghost.

From this point in the narrative, the traumatized Hidetora is reduced, even more than Shakespeare's character, to a remnant of a man, wandering the plains with Tango and his fool. The underlying violence of *Ran* (which translates roughly as "disorder") begins with Hidetora's back-story. While Lady Kaede and Lady Sue regard Hidetora's quite differently, the slaughter of families is not part of the history of Lear. While Lear's eldest daughter, Goneril, complains because her father dares to "strike my gentleman for chiding his fool," Hidetora puts an arrow in the back of Taro's retainer as casually as he would into a that of a boar. While Goneril may find "gross crimes" in trifles, Lady Kaede has legitimate reasons for her hatred. Lear storms out of his second daughter Regan's household because she questions his need for five and twenty men, which he deems "worse than murder, to do upon respect such violent outrage." Hidetora stumbles away from scores of dead bodies. In this context of literal slaughter, and unlike Lear, who remains vocal if not completely rational while wandering the stormy heath with Kent and his fool, Hidetora is more than ever silent, his face a mask of pain. At one point, Nakadai even strikes a pose that

TOP: Having broken his sword on an opponent's armor, Hidetora has no weapon with which to commit *seppuku*.

CENTER: As flames consume the keep, Hidetora's white-clad figure emerges from the thick smoke like a ghost.

LEFT: Hidetora is reduced to a remnant of a man, wandering the plains with his fool.

vividly recalls Edvard Munch's *The Scream*. On the windy plain, the fool makes a reed helmet for Hidetora and draws a manic smile from the fallen lord, whose hair hangs over his yellow eyes like a veil. Moments later, as Hidetora watches Tango kill Jiro's banished generals, another ghostly pose is struck when the shock of white hair catches in the breeze.

Having invented Hidetora's backstory, Kurosawa and his co-screenwriters use it to put a different spin on Shakespeare's sub-plots. A minor variation is the discovery of Lady Sue's brother, Tsurumaru, living in a hermit's hut and blind, like Shakespeare's Gloucester, but because Hidetora put out his eyes. The most notable "new" character is Lady Kaede. She has the ruthlessness of Goneril; and, when she goads Taro into action against his father, she vividly recalls the portrayal of Asaji, Kurosawa's Lady Macbeth, in *Throne of Blood*. At the same time, Kaede is driven by the righteous anger of a Medea. As they overwhelm Hidetora's men, Jiro has Taro killed, and his widow Kaede seizes the opportunity to wreak final destruction on Hidetora and his kin. After seducing Jiro, she commands that Lady Sue be killed and her head brought back. Jiro's general, Kurogane, first asserts that "the order is unreasonable, I must refuse," then brings back the head of a stone fox. In the end, as the castle that was once her family's burns, Kaede coldly confesses before Kurogane's sword slashes her that "I wanted to avenge my family. I have done all I set out to do."

It is in the character of Kyoami that Kurosawa comes closest to a Shakespearean personage. Both fools are permitted by their positions to give free rein to sardonic observations. Both are compelled to reverse roles with their maddened masters. As Hidetora is more profoundly unhinged, Kyoami is more burdened. While it may paraphrase Thomas Gray rather than Shakespeare, Kyoami's observation that "ignorance is bliss, indeed" ruefully confirms that, although caught in a chain of events not of his making, he must, like Lear's fool, "stay, and let the wise man fly. The knave turns fool that runs away." As Hidetora deteriorates, Kyoami is compelled to spout rational aphorisms, such as "If the rock you sit on starts to roll, jump clear." As they remain in the ruins of a castle Hidetora burned down long before, Kyoami verbalizes acceptance of his new role: "You speak nonsense. I'll speak truth."

TOP AND CENTER: At one point, Nakadai even strikes a pose that vividly recalls Edvard Munch's *The Scream*.

BOTTOM: On the windy plain, the fool places a reed helmet for Hidetora and draws a manic smile from the fallen lord, whose hair hangs over his yellow eyes like a veil.

As in *Throne of Blood*, Kurosawa's integration of stylized performance and striking imagery derives from many traditions, from Shakespeare and

BELOW: Kyoami (Peter [Shinosuke Ikehata]) verbalizes acceptance of his new role: "You speak nonsense. I'll speak truth."

CENTER: "I wanted to avenge my family. I have done all I set out to do."

BOTTOM: Kurosawa adds delicate nuance by selective framing: while Hidetora smiles, Tsurumaru's figure in the foreground permits only the right eye of Tango and the left eye of Kyoami to be visible.

RIGHT: A long take as Hidetora (Tatsuya Nakadai) dismounts to cradle his slain son in *Ran*.

kabuki, from *chambara* and classical form. To the narrative irony of the encounter with Tsurumaru, Kurosawa adds delicate nuance by selective framing to create a singular moment in which Hidetora smiles wanly at the fire, while his companions regard the pitiful blind man, posed in such a way that Tsurumaru's figure in the foreground permits only the right eye of Tango and the left eye of Kyoami to be visible.

Kurosawa reserves the last long take for the death of his protagonists. Unlike Cordelia's forces, Saburo's troops are victorious. Nonetheless, as he rides back with Hidetora behind him on the horse, Saburo is shot. Without a cut, Kurosawa stages Saburo falling dead and Hidetora jumping down from the horse. As others move off to pursue the assailants, Kyoami and Saburo's lieutenant join Hidetora by the body. "He is dead," the warlord laments, "is this justice?" As with Lear, this last event leaves Hidetora unable to continue, and he himself expires. In the epilogue, Jiro is defeated by Saburo's allies and Kaede joylessly savors her revenge before the last remnants of Hidetora's household are immolated. In the chaos it has been revealed that another retainer has killed Lady Sue before she could escape with Tsurumaru.

After a funeral procession carries off the bodies of Hidetora and Saburo, Kurosawa's ending is enigmatic. Unaware of Sue's fate Tsurumaru continues to wait in the castle ruins. As he nearly totters off the edge of a wall, he drops the scroll with the image of Amida Buddha, which Sue has left to reassure him. It unfurls at the base of the ruin. At Hidetora's death, Saburo's general has repudiated the observation (taken from *Lear*) that "The gods are just, and of our pleasant vices make instruments to plague us." He asserts rather, "It is the gods who weep to see us killing each other since the world began." The image of the Amida Buddha represents a third belief, preempting the others. In the Shin Buddhist belief of Lady Sue, the realization of past evil and egocentricism is a liberating act. Sue would see herself, Hidetora, Lady Kaede, young and old, good and evil, freed from blind passion and abiding in the pure land. Whether Kurosawa sees his characters there as well is unclear.

CHAPTER THREE

GENRE TYPES

For among all peoples it is only
through those actions which merit
praise that a man may prosper.
—*Beowulf*[1]

I. *THE AMBITIOUS*

SUPERFICIALLY *THE AMBITIOUS* (*BAKUMATSU*, DIRECTED BY DAISUKE Ito, 1970) may seem closer to *jidai-geki* than *chambara*, closer to Mizoguchi than to Kurosawa. Although the Japanese title is the term which designates the end of the Tokugawa shogunate, the film's action sequences are few and interspersed throughout a complicated narrative which blends historical fact and fiction in the manner of *Tales of the Taira Clan*. The film's character focus, however, is on a prototypical figure in an era of socio-political change; and it is in the definition of this character, although he resembles Kiyomori Taira in many respects, that the *chambara* constructs of *The Ambitious* are most evident. Egocentric and possessing a monomaniacal energy, the central figure is Ryunosuke (Ryoma) Sakamoto.[2] A vassal of the dissatisfied *tozama* of Tosa, this character moves, as in *Tales of the Taira Clan,* from political ineffectualness to a position of power, in this instance, to being one of the drafters of the Meiji constitution, through sheer force of will. Even within the context of the Restoration era's peculiar opportunism and cultural upheaval, Sakamoto is portrayed in *The Ambitious* as an extremely flamboyant

BELOW: The Ambitious, main title

BELOW: Kinnosuke Nakamura as Ryoma Sakamoto uses a gun to fight off would-be assassins.

BOTTOM: An assassin emerges from behind a screen to kill Nakaoka (Tatsuya Nakadai) in *The Ambitious*.

revolutionary. He is similar to the Western political man sometimes typified by Sam Houston: a man of vaguely idealistic goals tinged with a ruthless pragmatism, a man impatient for both social change and self-advancement—in short a mixture of cynic and populist caught up in a political climate where only the ambitious could acquire power.

Sakamoto's particular history starts out rather conventionally. He begins as a reactionary xenophobe and loyal subject of the shogunate who schools himself in the art of swordsmanship. He becomes a supporter of the Restoration and the head of trading company who reads tracts by Enlightenment philosophers. Here the generic inscription posits a change in lifestyle and cultural attitudes from the physicalness and feudalism of the sword, as in the early scenes where Ryoma still adheres to clannish dictates and the first shot of him with his sword propped against his shoulder. It moves through the rationality of industrialism with his founding of the trading company; to the the discovery of power outside the traditional structures in the form of the gun he uses to fight off the shogunate assassins; and ends in a position of reflective, almost sedate *puissance* in the final scene in his somber chambers. In the successive "liberations" of sword, gun, industry, and finally mind, Sakamoto moves through almost all the potential levels of awareness the film samurai may attain. Underscoring all of it is Sakamoto's stature, his self-image as a "figure" in history, which keeps him generically in flux.

In terms of the samurai film, the narrative movement from violence to non-violence, from the sword to the pen, can only be progressive if accompanied by a parallel mental evolution. As the title suggests, Sakamoto's ambition never allows him, no matter how great his achievement, to reach a state of serenity or dispassion. His long-standing associate Shintaro remarks on this

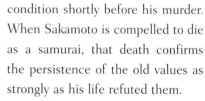

condition shortly before his murder. When Sakamoto is compelled to die as a samurai, that death confirms the persistence of the old values as strongly as his life refuted them.

What makes *The Ambitious* most instructive as an illustration of genre typing is that the motion picture explicitly questions not merely the ethics of the samurai class but also the fundamental assumptions of the repressive feudalism which supports it. Few other samurai films do so with as much detail at either the narrative or expressive level as *The*

Ambitious. The final scene is a confirmation of the literally maddening effect entailed in a samurai's challenge to those very traditions which identify him, a historical paradox discussed in Chapter One. As such, it merits a detailed recapitulation:

SHINTARO NAKAOKA, *a comrade of* SAKAMOTO *since their investiture as squires, has come to the latter's chambers to discuss his draft for a constitution.*

NAKAOKA
(reading)
"Article Two, the establishment of a legislative system for decision by vote. Representatives will be elected by vote of the samurai, craftsmen, farmers, and merchants," that's the sore point. Why must you include samurai with these others? You're putting us on the same level as them, those illiterates.
(short pause)
A samurai belongs to a higher class than the others. A samurai is something special. That's how it was and that's how it must be. I'm not saying your parliamentary government is wrong.

SAKAMOTO
The samurai class must go, unless it's abolished Japan cannot live. You know that.

NAKAOKA
No. I don't.

SAKAMOTO
We were all squires from the same clan, me, you, we left the clan to give our lives for this great ideal; but this came from our deep hatred of the samurai.

NAKAOKA
Don't say that.

SAKAMOTO
I have to.
Nakaoka gets up and walks to the window.
They are all dead. Takeichi, Masaki, Yoshimura, Nasu, Kitazoe, Mochizuki.
Reverse cut to CLOSE SHOT *of* NAKAOKA.
The twenty-three of Noneyama . . . they all died without knowing of the great restoration. . . . Everyone is human. There are no samurai or farmers or merchants. We are all human—everyone is equal. That's the basis of parliamentary government.

NAKAOKA
(interrupting)
Equality of mankind, yes; but there are kings in the world.

SAKAMOTO

Yes, and they're the root of all trouble. That is the cause of all class struggle. An emperor is entirely useless. . . . We call ourselves a divine state, and foreigners, barbarians. This would only prevent ties with other nations. Our closed-door policy has at long last been lifted to bring in the world culture. The Mikado must first become a human being like everyone.

NAKAOKA
(shuddering)

You say fearful things. Is that what you learned from those Western books? It's good you're talking to me because no one else would understand what you're saying. They'd behead you as a traitor or madman.

SAKAMOTO

Put me in a prison. Blindfold me and gag me and imprison me.

From a MEDIUM CLOSE TWO SHOT *the camera has tightened on a* MEDIUM CLOSE SHOT *of* SAKAMOTO. *He ends by burying his head in his hands. [Intermediate action: a servant comes up to clear away dishes and places a screen in front of the door.]*

SAKAMOTO

I'm afraid of myself. If I keep on they'll think I'm mad.

NAKAOKA

Certainly, if your extreme views should become known, someone from our group might try to kill you.

CLOSE SHOT *of* SAKAMOTO.

SAKAMOTO

I can't afford to die at a crucial time like this.

He looks up. There is a LOW ANGLE, MEDIUM CLOSE SHOT *of* NAKAOKA, *then back to a* CLOSE SHOT *of* SAKAMOTO.

SAKAMOTO

What if I should really become insane?

NAKAOKA

I'll be here.

SAKAMOTO

If the time comes when I'm considered insane, when I must be killed, Shita, you must be the one to kill me.

This sequence of approximately of two minutes' duration, having begun with a medium two-shot then tightened on Sakamoto, now pans over as he picks up and examines the calling card brought up by the servant, then pans back and widens as he walks and sits by the lamp to study it. On the cut, one of the assassins emerges from behind the screen. Sakamoto is killed before he can fully resolve the issue of his madness but, in a sense, he perishes as much a victim of his own apprehension as of his enemies. The fact that he sits reading Rousseau and drafting egalitarian articles for a new government does not make him entirely immune to the Shintaro's arguments. The actual staging of the assassination does not resolve the ambiguity of the dialogue. Bleeding from a grievous head wound, Sakamoto examines it by drawing his sword and looking at his reflection in the polished blade; his last words are "My brains are spilling out. It's no use."

What the visual and aural specifics suggest is that, in the moment of his death, Sakamoto again "sees" himself in his sword,

TOP: Sakamoto, bleeding from a head wound, wards off a *coup dé grâce* and, BOTTOM, gazes at his reflection in a sword blade

regresses to the traditional identification of man and weapon which he had thought an oppressive, feudal conceit. His brains spill out, literally, because his skull has been split open; but, metaphorically, his fear of incipient insanity and the latent schizophrenia in which the feudal or samurai identity recoils at the thought of its destruction: "I'm afraid of myself." His own revolutionary ideals have overwhelmed his samurai heritage and short-circuited his ability to act decisively. His mental vacillation cedes, then, to the muscular spasm and finally the torpor of death. The camera pulls back so far from the scene that it vignettes the set, revealing empty, black space at the top and bottom of the frame.

Certain formal usages in the concluding sequence are part of a visual pattern for the entire film, which stresses a direct dramatization of conflict. While sustaining the shot at a critical moment may imply the sensation of Sakamoto's mental tension, which is broken by the entry of the hired killers, most of the shots simply underscore the dialogue and move in for reactions. The reflection of Sakamoto's face in the blade and the traveling camera which seems to freeze him in an historical tableau pertain to a different scheme of expression. Much as the dialogue contains overt discussion of the ideological issues which support the historical action, many of the particulars of image throughout *The Ambitious*—from lighting, framing, and color to superimpositions and even irises—delineate and elaborate on critical relationships.

Color, for instance, has a major role in clarifying the events of several sequences. During a party of the members of Sakamoto's trading company, all

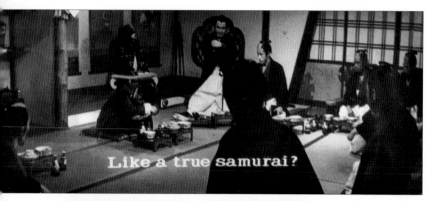

Tosa clansmen and lower-caste samurai by birth, the shots frame them into groups of three or four. They are dressed in brown and white, which blends with the cream-colored panels of the room. All except one, Chojiro Konda, a former baker and unofficial protege of Ryoma. He is in a Western suit of gray tweed and is isolated in three close shots. The party is interrupted; the members array themselves around him in a circle and demand his suicide for violating a rule of the company. The ceremonial knife and table are placed in front of him. He takes them, screaming that he is as much a man as they, and runs out smashing the wooden tray. At this point, there is a subjective traveling shot moving forward through some colored beads hanging in a doorway and through to a dark back room, suggesting a passage into spiritual as well as physical darkness. Konda falls to his knees and, outlined against the multicolors of lanterns out of focus in the background—again the association is of colors being the exclusive privilege of the elite in Japan—plunges the blade in. Metaphorically, the color supports the idea of his death being forced upon him by the proponents of traditional values. Konda's position has already been established as that of a "liberated" proletarian. In a black-and-white photo of the company members, which Ryoma has sent his sister, all the faces are colorlessly "equal," and Ryoma and Konda are posed next to

each other. A long lens subjectively scans the picture and isolates them in a flat, front-face two shot, which stresses their physical resemblance, a resemblance accentuated by the fact that the actors playing Ryoma and Konda are actually brothers. Simultaneously a voiceover of Ryoma tells his sister of Konda's diligence and promise as a businessman. Hence on a number of correlative levels, Konda and Ryoma are equated or made to seem similar, and when Konda is situated politically in the suicide scene—his costume clashing with the drab, orderly decor and the traditional garb of the other clansmen; his flight through the glittering beads toward the colored lights going contrary to their codes of color *and* conduct, violating the social order, and ending in death—his identification with Ryoma foreshadows the latter's eventual death at the hands of the same order.

Konda's position as a martyr to social prejudice is discussed directly in the closing dialogue; but it is most acutely depicted in that black-and-white two-shot. That shot linked him not only with Ryoma but also with the "twenty-three of Noneyama," whom Sakamoto mentions in his last speech, political criminals who are seen executed in a black-and-white flashback. That sequence opened, in Ryoma's memory, with a close shot of a moistened sword blade, the symbol of his past and the old order. The last element of these complex character associations is tied in to the suicide scene by Nakaoka's arrival. Torn between clan allegiance and personal attraction to Ryoma, he is dressed exactly as the others but for one detail, wearing blue rather than brown, which conveys quite simply the sense of his middle-ground stance. His arrival disrupts the emotional solidarity of the others, just as his figure in the doorway breaks the geometric pattern of the screen doors.

Such mise-en-scène creates an overall visual geometry in *The Ambitious* as specific as Kurosawa's. This is most evident in scenes such as the confrontation of the *ishin shishi* rivals from Tosa and Choshu. An iris in and pan reveal a line of negotiators seated before a wall. On it are painted the huge symbols of their clan. Then a medium long shot discloses another line of men sitting opposite with a similar array of painted screens behind them. Framed dead center between them, in the immediate foreground, is a lamp. On top of it is another clan symbol. This symbol of the individual clan, of the feudal concept which divides them abstractly by its

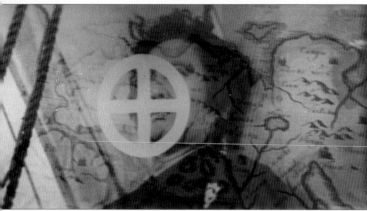

very "clannishness," now divides them concretely as well; or so the two-dimensions of the frame make it appear. This chamber is in marked contrast to Ryoma's own room, the *shoji* of which are decorated with dozens of different clan ensigns, externalizing his desire to unite all the clans into one nationalistic consciousness. The icons themselves, particularly the monstrously large ones, are a sort of natural iris. Accordingly, in the sequence where Ryoma pleads the reasonableness of an alliance to a clan representative, the camera iris over the lens never opens fully. Its presence throughout the discussion becomes a direct representation of Ryoma fighting the enclosing grip of both those symbols and the feudal ideals for which they stand.

The axioms of this geometry are not rigid. They flow out of the narrative situation, with symbol and personage each informing the other, much as did the *ronin* in *Seven Samurai* and the seven figures painted on their handmade banner. When Ryoma consults with Admiral Goto, they position themselves in profile, each framed by half of a global map affixed to the bulkhead behind them. The iconic reference is to an earlier scene of Ryoma's movement and conversion to nationalism, when the naval minister pointed to a globe and told him "you need a magnifying glass to find Japan on a world map." In this later scene, Sakamoto is liberated from isolationism and clan loyalty alike. Free from the constriction graphically contained in the earlier iris shots and from the even more overt superimposition of the feudal design emblazoned on a map over his figure standing at the helm of a vessel, Sakamoto becomes an emblem himself. His corporeality represents the new Japan and, by superimposition, looms over the hemisphere.

Daisuke Ito's career as a director began in the silent era. While much of that work is lost, fragments suggest an early facility at integrating the elements of *jidai-geki* décor and costume for dramatic and ironic effect. Even as his face and the map of the world merge in the two dimensions of the frame, Sakamoto is less "free" than he was at the film's beginning. Certainly for the viewer familiar with the facts of the real person, Sakamoto's fate is no mystery. Still the visual constrictions created by Ito continuously foreshadow the protagonist's fate.

Sakamoto is not even present in the opening scene, which sets the course of his life in motion. A drunken samurai exercises the right of *kirusu-togomen* on the commoner he catches arrogating a privilege of the higher classes: wearing *geta* or wooden clogs. The samurai is then killed by the commoner's brother, a young squire like Sakamoto. When the clan retainers enter the squires' quarters to arrest the offender, Sakamoto defies them. Tight close-ups of him are intercut with group shots of the clansmen outraged by this "lowly squire's" arrogance. When they are framed together, Sakamoto is the visual center. Generically, there is only one way for the viewer to read this. Sakamoto's *hubris* manifests the ambitiousness of the title, which has led to rejection of the clan and its values. But as Sakamoto rises and kneels at will in defiance of protocol, he has been clearly identified as protagonist and as free agent, as liberated and doomed.

Despite his initial rebellion, Sakamoto does not immediately reject all the trappings of the past. Given the viewer's expectation based on genre and on history, his isolationism, his lingering elitism, and his belief in the sword are prerequisite starting points. When he surveys the coastline to ponder who will stop the influx of foreigners, his defiant, staccato shout ("I . . . this Ryoma . . . will!") is punctuated by three cuts to increasingly tighter close shots. When he prepares to assassinate the naval minister who is planning to reopen trade with the "barbarians," he is framed in an act of personal isolationism. He is alone in a empty room, thrusting his sword through a narrow aperture in the screen which encircles and conceals him. In the last shot of the sequence, he reaffirms his faith in the weapon he brandishes, saying, "This [sword] will tell us what we must do." The close-up is framed so that the blade bisects the shot horizontally and right in front of his face. It is to this pose that Sakamoto will revert before his death, when he glances at his reflection in the blade.

Even after Sakamoto and his followers embrace the Meiji cause, many of the planes of interaction and opposition defined in the editing continue to build from the most simple of wide-screen two-shots. With characters carefully placed in foreground and background so that the stageline is at a forty-five degree angle from

BELOW: The tip Sakamoto's sword protrudes over the screen.

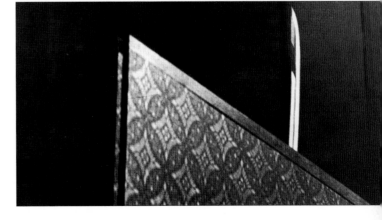

the lens, the shifting alliances of the *bakumatsu* become graphically apparent. This usage forms an axiomatic core Deviation from it, as in the meeting with Goto aboard ship or, more obviously, the earlier staggered cut-ins to Sakamoto on the mountaintop, acquires an added significance, as an editing pattern which is not oblique but which bespeaks an emotional intensity and sincerity. Ultimately, what most distinguishes *The Ambitious* from the less dynamic constructs of a *jidai-geki* melodrama or a film such as *Tales of the Taira Clan* is this manipulation of both image and narrative. Whether or not a drama maintains, as Nakaoka does, that "a samurai is something special," the formal definition of aggressive personal action and historical contexts in *The Ambitious* are prototypes of the generic inscription in the samurai film.

II. *HARA-KIRI* AND *REBELLION*

The ironic or tragic cause of Sakamoto's death in *The Ambitious* is manifest in the film's English title. His epitaph, like that of the Saxon hero Beowulf, might recall that he was "most eager for fame" and that, as a consequence, like Washizu/Macbeth he was "brought down by ambition." An inversion of this prideful and aggressive character type is found in the *chambara* films of Masaki Kobayashi and demonstrates that the plight of the unambitious samurai in feudal Japan might through the contrivance of circumstances be equally tragic and ironic.

Hara-Kiri opens with a close shot of a mask-like visor reposing atop a display of knightly armor. A wider shot discloses more of this empty shell of a warrior, as dissonant notes punctuate the soundtrack. The camera pans down over the matte black surface of the armor; vapors cling to it. A slow travel back reveals the white-paper walls and polished floor of the otherwise empty chamber. A disembodied voice reads what sounds like a logbook entry: "Date, 13th day of May, 1630. Weather, fair. The heat of the day rises hourly." With a lighting shift the vapors dissipate to reveal a normal room. A shot of the book itself follows. As the voice continues, a hand fills the page with a column of black characters: "No incident worthy of note." A cut to an exterior scene focuses on the gate of a manor house, apparently that of a local *daimyo*. The harsh sun falling on the dusty roadway intercut with the somber interior light of the initial shots suddenly illuminates the screen and strikes the viewer's eye in a way which removes the gray tones from the black-and-white image and viscerally suggests "the heat of the day." As the eye adjusts to the light and the narrator intones "However," a dark-robed figure enters the frame, back to camera, pauses momentarily, then strides quietly toward the massive wooden doors of the manor house.

The inscription is simple, somewhat detached, and visually direct. With a few shots, sounds, and dispassionate words by a voiceover narrator, Kobayashi and screenwriter Shinobu Hashimoto—whose remarkable career also includes the script of *Rebellion* for Kobayashi, as well as *Rashomon, Seven Samurai, Throne of Blood,* and *Hidden Fortress* for Kurosawa; *Under the Banner of the Samurai* for Inagaki; *Tenchu* for Gosha; and *Samurai Assassin* and *Sword of Doom* for Okamoto—quickly establish the generic conflicts. The voice identifies itself as belonging to the early Tokugawa period ("1630"). Its lack of emotion appropriately reflects the orderliness and precision which marked the temporal height of samurai influence over Japanese culture and society. More than that, it is the voice of a scribe, a recorder. Superimposed by Kobayashi, it resonates over the soundtrack, as if out of the bowels of the empty armor. Like the armor, it manifests the unassailable traditions of feudalism. But in the "heat of the day," a dark-clad swordsman also "rises" to answer the viewer's genre expectations. Like the visor, his visage is grim and silent. Unlike it, he fits uneasily into the same frame with the manor and its fixtures, charged by the mise-en-scène, by the manner of his entrance and an aspect recalling that of Mifune in *Yojimbo*, with an elemental power that conflicts graphically with the placid facade.

The characters and objects delineated here aurally and visually constitute a stylized expression of conflict, which Kobayashi maintains throughout the film. The narrative structure of *Hara-Kiri* is, on the one hand, an equally stylized element intricately constructed from a series of shifts between present and past time; but is also, on the other hand, as simple, detached, and direct as the film's genre typing. Explaining that he has been reduced to poverty because of the divestiture of his clan, the black-robed *ronin*, Hanchiro Tsugumo, asks the chamberlain of the Iyi clan for help in committing *seppuku*. Consistent with the thrust of the genre typing, Kobayashi and Hashimoto immediately exploit the historical and cultural context for dramatic effect. In the first portion of the film, Tsugumo remains a mysterious figure. Flashbacks from the chamberlain's point of view, designed to test Tsugumo's firmness of purpose, relate the story of an

BELOW: A tight close-up of Tsugumo, intercut with medium close shots of the chamberlain, subtly establishes his dominance.

"unfortunate" *ronin* who had earlier begged the same boon from the Iyi clan. Eventually, the clansmen discovered that the young man had been inspired by a story circulating among the samurai made masterless by the crushing power of Tokugawa: that a northern clan, touched by the similar request for assistance in ritual suicide, had taken the supplicant on as a retainer. This young *ronin* was insincere and expected to be sent away from the manor house with a cash gift. Throughout this flashback, Hashimoto's dialogue confronts and characterizes the social issues quite directly: "They will pour forth like ants," observes the master swordsman of the clan, Hikokuro Sawagata, of the local *ronin*, "to a land of sweet sugar." The central concern of chamberlain Kageyu and the clan "insiders" is preserving the sanctity of their institutions. Accordingly, after the Iyi men find that the young *ronin*'s sword blades are of bamboo, they decide not merely to grant his petition but actively to compel his self-immolation. Afterward Kageyu's first act is to apologize to the armor which "houses" the ancestral spirits for "the *ronin* blood which defiles our sacred garden." Sawagata, acting as the *kaishaku*, assures the young man that his *seppuku* will be no "shallow imitation or idle formalism." The young *ronin* is horror-struck when he opens his short sword and sees his fragile bamboo blade is still there. "A samurai's blade is his soul," Sawagata coldly continues, "What blade could be more appropriate?" The chamberlain's flashback concludes with the young *ronin*'s literal and painful "stomach-cut" using this bamboo sword; and Tsugumo answers simply that "neither of my blades are of bamboo."

This prologue sets in motion one of the most explicitly tragic narratives in samurai film. For what the disillusioned Tsugumo reveals in his own series of flashbacks, as he sits on the white mat of *hara-kiri* in the Iyi courtyard, is that he has come to the manor not to kill himself but to confront the inexorable fate which seems to have him in its grip. More flashbacks begin to fill in the life story which Tsugumo offers his hosts "to pass the time" until the *kaishaku* he has requested arrive. As those prospective seconds fail to appear and send their excuses instead, it becomes clear to Kageyu, and confirms the viewer's suspicions, that the man on the mat before him is no ordinary *ronin*. In another sense, for the ironic underpinnings Kobayashi and Hashimoto give Tsugumo's story to retain dramatic impact, this hero must at some level remain an ordinary man. That Tsugumo is a genre hero in the film's present tense is certain when he first steps into the frame, from every detail of his rough appearance and his calm demeanor. What the succession of flashbacks makes clear is his genuine reluctance, in the film's past tense, to view his own plight as tragic or to become a melodramatic hero.

The key events Tsugumo recalls for the chamberlain verge on the pathetic: the dissolution of his clan for rebuilding a fortress against Tokugawa wishes; the suicide of his best friend and marriage of that man's son to his own daughter; the bare subsistence of his family on his earnings as a parasol maker and his son-in-law's occupation as a tutor to merchant-class children; and finally, his grandson's illness and his son-in-law's desperate attempt to extort money from the Iyi by threatening *hara-kiri* before their gate. Similar incidents taint the life of Isaburo Sasahara and are depicted by Kobayashi/Hashimoto in *Rebellion*, produced five years later; and they

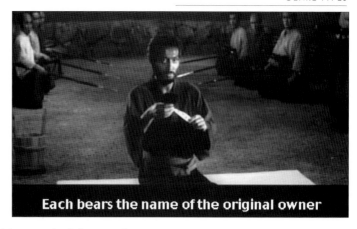

Each bears the name of the original owner

ABOVE: Tsugumo displays the top-knots.

lead to the same violent conclusion. In *Hara-Kiri* Tsugumo's elaborate plan is to expose the Iyi clan's murder of his son-in-law by challenging and cutting off the top-knots of the seconds at the earlier *hara-kiri*. As expected this causes them to decline serving as his seconds and to lose face. Ths plan fails because Tsugumo cannot overcome the clan's control of its own history as easily as he can the weapons of its retainers. After the climactic gesture in which Tsugumo flings the samurai top-knots at his feet, the chamberlain has no alternative but to order the *ronin*'s death. Although he holds off the Iyi spearmen for several minutes and finally penetrates to the inner chamber where he demolishes the display of sacred armor, Tsugumo is shot down by musketeers. In the film's epilogue, the chamberlain orders the suicide of his own, dishonored swordsmen; and the retainers cut down by Tsugumo are listed as "victims of illness" by the scribe. The closing shots mirror those of the opening. Men rake over the blood-spattered courtyard, and a close shot records the symbolic top-knots being unceremoniously dumped in a wash bucket. A voiceover relates that the shogunate has approved the Iyi's reported action, that is, permitting two *ronin* to commit *seppuku* in their manor. The logbook is closed. A traveling shot moves back from the armor which has been cleaned of Tsugumo's blood and restored to its original position. Over a close shot of the unchanging, eyeless gaze of the visor, the end title is superimposed.

BELOW: Clan retainers surround Yoko Tsukasa as Ichi the daimyo's former concubine in *Rebellion*.

The conflict in *Rebellion* turns even more pointedly on a quirk of fact. It begins with the forced marriage of a *daimyo*'s discarded concubine to the son of the retired samurai Sasahara, who initially resists but is compelled to agree. When the child she bore earlier becomes the clan's heir apparent, officials attempt to take her from Sasahara's family. In a feudal milieu recreated by Kobayashi and

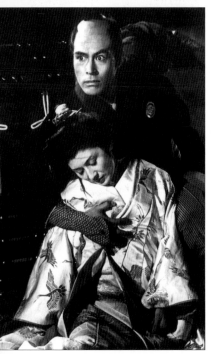

Hashimoto, Sasahara resists, and the consequences are predictably similar to those in *Hara-Kiri*. After his son and daughter-in-law are killed, Sasahara attempts to reach Edo, taking his infant granddaughter with him to "tell their story"; but he also is shot down. Dying at the frontier of the clan's domain, his final words to the infant—"We cannot go to Edo. No one will ever know the story of your mother and father"—echo the irony of Tsugumo's rebellion. Neither of their defiant gestures are entered in the histories of the affected clans.

Obviously the tension between the fictional "record," in which the viewer does witness the ultimate ineffectualness of the rebellion in each film, and the suggestion of a "historical" fact, from which all actions such as these have been erased, is the core element for the filmmakers. The literal annihilation of its heroes comes without the elaborate background detail. Personal dramas are played out in *Hara-Kiri* and *Rebellion* without protagonists who are visionaries like Ryoma Sakamoto. As ordinary men, loyal men who want merely to do what is best for their own families, the tragic fates of Tsugumo and Sasahara resonate more powerfully than in a film such as *The Ambitious*. The title card which opens *Rebellion*, like the voiceover beginning *Hara-Kiri*, invokes the feudal era directly in terms of its repressed relationships: "During the Tokugawa period, there were 264 feudal lords and *daimyos*. These people ruled their clans with absolute authority. Our story takes place in 1725." There is an unbridged distance between the expository generalization of this title card or the narration in *Hara-Kiri* and the specific characterizations of each narrative, which permits each film to retain a significant degree of universality. Initially, both Sasahara and Tsugumo are passive participants in the repressive, "absolute authority" of the period. They are obscure low-caste samurai, members in good standing of their clan and class in a way Ryoma Sakamoto never is. Even after their retirement and divestiture respectively, Kobayashi and Hashimoto stress their characters' initial acceptance of their fates and continued involvement in their own roles as samurai. Neither's initial response is to repudiate the social order which has governed his life.

The unoccupied Sasahara becomes restless and irritable because he has lost his sense of participation in that role. Toshiro Mifune's performance even hints at a certain sense of satisfaction as he girds himself for the final combat, because he is "getting back into harness." Tsugumo confesses his own horror on discovering that his dead son-in-law had pawned his swords to buy medicine for his grandchild. "Yet I never parted with mine," he continues, "I would never have dared. In my ignorance I clung to these useless symbols." His angry rhetoric reveals the depth of his inculcation into the warrior's way. He cannot deny that he clung to his swords out of his own oppressed need to retain some sense of identity through these "symbols" or adherence to *bushido*. Neither can he deny that there is still more than a trace of warrior's pride in his voice when he relates how his practical knowledge of terrain and wind allowed him to defeat the highly skilled but inexperienced Sawagata: "Swordsmanship untested in battle is like swimming on land." At some level of consciousness, Tsugumo must know that while some men may die or be dishonored, in the end, the clan will merely kill him. The Iyi will endure, while he will be erased. All sense of honor, righteous anger, vengeance will be snuffed out with his life.

As the narratives of *Hara-Kiri* and *Rebellion* invoke a notion of personal, destructive *shushigaku* and focus on "ordinary" samurai as genre heroes, both films go beyond *The Ambitious* as deterministic and tragic depictions of historical Japan. On one level, both Tsugumo and Sasahara perish expressing a naive belief that *bushido* is not an empty ideal, that there is an inherent justice somewhere in their society which will vindicate them. This is a belief Kobayashi and Hashimoto systematically deny, and which a character such as Sakamoto seems to have risen above. On another level, both Tsugumo and Sasahara experience some realization of the meaninglessness of their rebellion but possess the strength of character to persevere. Sakamoto, despite his higher consciousness of feudal structures, is driven mad by his own doubts. Tsugumo and Sasahara are simply destroyed by those structures.

In terms of visual style, the spare, black-and-white images and wide-angle framing Kobayashi employs in *Hara-Kiri* and *Rebellion* contrast markedly with the pictorialism and long focal-length lenses of Kurosawa. For that

ABOVE: Tsuyoshi Kato as Yogoro and Yoko Tsukasa as Ichi in *Rebellion*

Left: Toshiro Mifune in action as Sasahara in *Rebellion*

From the "Snow Maiden" episode of *Kwaidan*

matter, they also differ from the rich colorations or low-key black-and-white night photography of Kobayashi's own *Kwaidan* and *Inn of Evil* (*Inochi Bonifuro*, 1971). The expressive values Kobayashi stresses in *Hara-Kiri* and *Rebellion* are those of angle, montage, and moving camera. For instance, in the first flashback to Tsugumo's son-in-law, Motome, Kobayashi cuts from a close shot of the older Tsugumo saying to the chamberlain, "I am listening," to a view of young Motome standing in the same place in the same room. This juxtaposition implies a cross-identification between the two and anticipates the revelation of their actual relationship. The lighting beginning with that scene and continuing intermittently throughout the flashbacks also places Motome in a position where ominous shadows falls over his face. The mise-en-scène places him in a room full of screens painted with trees, clouds, and half-moons in a night sky—in short, amidst stylized, artificial landscapes—as he awaits word of the clan's action on his request. All this reinforces the sense of something unnatural impending. At the same time, there are severe shifts in camera placement. A low-angle medium-close shot of Motome alone shifts to a high-angle medium two shot as a clansman enters with news. Then sudden, rapid cross-traveling shots move first into a medium-close shot of the young man's back then into a close shot of his face reacting to their unexpected decision to assist him in suicide. The cross-cut moving shots dynamically externalize the emotional instability and panic he experiences. At this point, as Motome is handed his white death robes, the narrative superstructure intervenes and returns the scene to present time, creating a tense pause for the viewer whose interest is now engaged in the story the chamberlain is recounting. When the flashback resumes, Kobayashi forces the spectator even more fully into Motome's point of view. In the courtyard, as Sawagata announces that "this unworthy will be your second, exponent of the Shindo-Munen school," the camera moves quickly from medium-close back into medium-long shot, as if recoiling with Motomo from the prospect of death. As Motome prepares to pierce himself with the bamboo blade, Kobayashi cuts from a point-of-view shot of the sword in his hand and zooms in with a sudden, mad determination to a choker close shot of the actor grimacing in pain. Abruptly the camera tilts off from horizontal as if tipped by the intensity of his anguish. As Motome's agony is prolonged, there are inserts of the various witnesses and of the young *ronin* putting his whole weight on the flimsy blade to get it to penetrate his abdomen. A final restatement uses a traveling shot that tilts first left then right to convey the sensation of *hara-kiri* itself as a deadly visual spasm.

Once the flashback of Motome's death has ended, Kobayashi alters the visuals to accompany the shift in character interaction between Tsugumo and Chamberlain Kageyu. When Kobayashi cuts to the courtyard where Tsugumo is now to commit *seppuku* after assuring the chamberlain that his swords are of steel, the fixtures are revealed: the *ronin* is sitting cross-legged on the ceremonial mat in the center of the gravel surface and Chamberlain Kageyu is on an elevated wooden porch facing him. The natural geography of the setting would normally allow Kageyu to dominate the scene visually from his higher position. However, the texture of the respective medium-close shots, which alternately frame the men, undermines that effect. The contrast of the darkly clothed Tsugumo against the white mat and gravel rivets the eye of the viewer more firmly than the image of the chamberlain in his brocaded robes against a neutral background. Kobayashi intercuts eye-level close-ups of Kageyu with low angles and traveling shots into the face of Tsugumo, as each of the seconds he has requested sends an excuse. This editing scheme affirms Tsugumo's high degree of hidden control over the events unfolding in the enclosed yard and ends in a decisive low angle as Tsugumo rejects Kageyu's impatient urging that he accept a *kaishaku* designated by the Iyi: "I do not die a criminal. I am free to choose a second."

Much is made in the Hashimoto script of the empty "tokenism" of feudal society; but while Tsugumo may assert that he has come to regard his swords as such "useless tokens," he skillfully exploits the much more impractical symbolism of the samurai top-knots and the ritual aspects, such as choosing a second, of the *seppuku* itself. As a *ronin*, Tsugumo himself is free of the necessary affectation of the shaved crown and braided knot of hair. Still his decision to dishonor rather than to kill the clan's master swordsmen by literally cutting that emblem of superiority from their heads again suggests that he himself remains caught in the coded and impersonal behavior patterns of the retainers. Accordingly, Kobayashi stages his confrontation with the representatives of order on two levels: first, as a ritual, and subsequently as a more expansive, sensory experience.

The end point of the initial type of staging is the sequence that culminates with Tsugumo throwing the top-knots onto the gravel. In the eighth flashback segment of his life story, Tsugumo had explained that "Motome returned at the hour of the dog, accompanied by an escort." When Sawagata and the two other arrogant swordsmen delivered the decapitated body of his son-in-law, Tsugumo had appeared momentarily to cower before them. Haunted by the image of the leering faces of the Iyi men standing illuminated by a sinister low light, the frustrated Tsugumo relates that he sat silently for a long time. The ninth flashback reveals him contemplating the bamboo-bladed weapons the clan samurai had pointedly returned to him and striking his own scabbard against the floor in impotent rage. That image strongly reinforces the self-control and premeditation of Tsugumo's behavior when Kobayashi cuts back to the present time. As a medium long shot frames Tsugumo from a slight high angle, he remarks aloud on the circumstances of Motome's death: "For a member of the samurai class to extort by threatening *hara-kiri* is an abominable act and cannot be forgiven; yet. . . ." Kageyu begins to pace nervously back and forth during the ominous pause. Kobayashi cuts to a low-angle close shot which reemphasizes the forcefulness of his words as Tsugumo continues, "Even the vaunted samurai is a mere human being. He cannot live on air alone." The sidelight falling on his face gives Tsugumo the same sinister aspect as the Iyi samurai who delivered Motome's body. A high-angle medium-long shot pans suddenly to Kageyu, who motions to his men, then back to a medium-close shot of the *ronin* framed center as he is quickly surrounded by the leveled lances of the Iyi attendants. "After all," Tusgumo calmly continues, "our samurai honor merely glosses the surface." Feeling more confident now that Tsugumo is surrounded, the chamberlain begins to defend the honorableness of the clan's decision. His attempt to overwhelm the man on the ceremonial mat before him with rhetoric is partially supported by a traveling medium-close shot which moves in tighter on the Chamberlain's back. Then Tsugumo laughs at his empty sentiments, and a shot of the *ronin*'s face, tighter and from a lower angle, reasserts his emotional dominance of the scene. Again there is a pan to Kageyu, which links the antagonists, as he denounces "hot-headed" behavior. Again there is a cut to Tsugumo as he produces the top-knots to prove the clan's "sham of honor."

In terms of visual conventions, Kobayashi's editing of this sequence develops the confrontation of the two men along fairly literal lines. At first, the conflict between them is contained within a single frame. The abashed Kageyu competes for viewer attention by his pacing in the foreground, which distracts from Tsugumo's speech. The countereffect is in the shot selection. Not only are the shots of him close but the low camera placement externalizes Tsugumo's own sense of "looking-down" on or controlling the surrounding scene. The high angle and panning shots suggest the continued existence of an "objective" perspective, that there may be, by extension, an overriding, deterministic viewpoint actually governing the two men's actions. This may be the unseen force that joins the figures in a single frame or with a fluid, unbroken motion. This repeated scheme of linkage using moving camera and wider angle and rupture by cutting to isolated views of Tsugumo, parallels the *ronin*'s ongoing struggle both to break from and to overthrow the structures the chamberlain supports. Visually, the dynamic interplay of composition and cutting reduces the contest of wills to a formal, even ritualized event by making it an unnatural dance of shifting angles and sight lines.

In contrast, the staging of Tsugumo's duel with Sawagata, which is related incompletely on the screen via interrupted flashback, creates a physical interaction between antagonists which seems more natural and direct for being manipulated in a less obvious way. In a standard narrative, this confrontation would be the climax of the viewer's genre expectations. In *Hara-Kiri*, it begins with Sawagata's shadow falling on the door of Tsugumo's hut, an ominous apparition accompanied by a rush of wind on the soundtrack. Inside Tsugumo crouches behind the ribs of a parasol, a skeletal reminder of his debasement. That prop remains in the foreground as the businesslike Sawagata, lifting the brim of his straw hat to survey the scene and concluding that his sword thrusts might be hampered by the cramped quarters, makes the *beau geste* and invites the *ronin* to join him on the plain of Goyu-In. The animism of the mise-en-scène inside Tsugumo's hut, which includes the parasol,

BELOW: Omadaka (Tetsuro Tamba, left) and Tsugumo (Tatsuya Nakadai) pass through a graveyard on their way to Goyu-In in *Hara-Kiri*.

Bottom: Omadaka (Tetsuro Tamba, left) assumes a fighting stance.

the wedges of hard light which strike both the figures, and the constricting wooden supports, is even more exaggerated in the exteriors which follow. First, long shots from above travel with the two men as they walk through a misty cemetery overcrowded with headstones. Then the plains themselves come into view, dim in the morning overcast, with black clouds clinging to the horizon as wind stirs the tall grass and billows in the men's kimonos. Against this background, the swordsmen begin their own deadly ballet: lashing down their sleeves, drawing their weapons, locking grips, side-stepping, rotating sword blades, and finally making contact. The only visual artifice Kobayashi includes in this sequence is a tilted shot of the resolute Tsugumo re-extending his weapon after his garment has been cut in the first parry. This device underscores through a partial point of view the overwhelming emotion of Tsugumo's will to conquer. Its tilted angle also succinctly equates him again, as did the cut to begin the chamberlain's flashback, with his son-in-law's final moments. The real imbalance, however, is in the physical details of the action. The slow precision with which the opponents circle each other, the unstable weather, the dissonant

Top: Tilted angles evoke the overwhelming emotion of Tsugumo's will to conquer as he prepares to vanquish Sawagata.

Bottom: "Swordsmanship untested in battle is like swimming on land." Sawagata falters.

score and sound effects—all these create a tone of eerie fatality that hangs over the entire encounter and elicits a suspenseful viewer participation. None of this is attenuated by Kobayashi's cutting back to the present for Tsugumo's after-the-fact comments on Sawagata's "untested" swordplay. That is, even though the viewer realizes on some level—either by genre convention or, more specifically by the very fact that Tusgumo is narrating the events—that the *ronin* had survived the mortal combat with Sawagata, there is nonetheless an impatience to learn the specifics of how he accomplished what he did. Playing conspicuously against this expectation, Kobayashi and Hashimoto refuse to reveal those specifics. Instead there is a cut from a moment of apparently extreme peril for Tsugumo in the flashback, after he has begun the duel with Sawagata, to the present time for a zoom-in to Kageyu's face and his reaction. In a sense the filmmakers conspire here with the character to keep both the chamberlain and the audience in suspense for a moment longer. Then Tsugumo jeeringly observes that "taking only his top-knot was doubly hard" and drops the lock of hair onto the gravel with the other two.

This montage alienates the viewer from Tsugumo's viewpoint, both by withholding visualization of the climactic duel in its entirety and by impelling a momentary identification with the chamberlain—visually through the zoom-in to his reaction and narratively through the shared desire to know what happened. All this sets up an objective, that is, a third person or authorial statement at *Hara-Kiri*'s conclusion. For at the moment that the third top-knot is produced, the Iyi men attack Tsugumo. The ensuing battle becomes a sort of pathetic substitute for the missing resolution of the single combat on the plains of Goyu-In. Before, during, and after the brutal fight in the courtyard and inside the manor itself between the hopelessly outnumbered *ronin* and the Iyi retainers, the filmmakers elucidate how in systematically stripping away the "sham" of samurai honor Tsugumo has compelled his own merciless annihilation. Ironically, while Sawagata was in a position to make a grand gesture, to tell Tsugumo, "make ready. I suggest you leave a note," the ineluctable social reality of what Tsugumo has done leaves the Iyi no option but to obliterate him. Not only is Tsugumo permitted no note left behind, no record of what he has done, but like Sasahara at the close of *Rebellion*, he is not spared the realization that his actions are meaningless, that his suffering and death have no effect. His frantic, wide-eyed stare into the muzzles of the Iyi guns, a stare which is at once Western in its subjective tragedy and Eastern in its objective nihilism, affirms that he comprehends the futility of his attack on the ancestral spirits housed in the armor. In the instant before his death, he realizes that the Iyi will merely piece it together again, that the very insincerity and deception which he has uncovered in the traditions of the samurai, in *bushido* and *seppuku*, are precisely what permit them to survive. Tsugumo's final action is a crazed reversion to the training of his samurai youth. Again a warrior, he plunges his own blade into his stomach and performs the ritual cut in a desperate attempt at redemption of honor before the fatal rifle volley is discharged. Like the loyal retainer Sawagata, who immolates himself voluntarily without need of orders from the chamberlain, out of reflex Tsugumo lapses back into that very sham of honor which he abhorred, negates the impact of his rebellion and personal tragedy, and leaves the alienated viewer with nothing but the somber and lifeless restoration of order in the epilogue.

ABOVE: Tsugumo (Tatsuya Nakadai) is surrounded by the Iyi as he attacks their ancestral armor in *Hara-Kiri*.

LEFT: Tsugumo's frantic, wide-eyed stare into the muzzles of the Iyi guns, a stare which is at once Western in its subjective tragedy and Eastern in its objective nihilism

CHAPTER FOUR

THE ALIEN HERO

Heaven and Earth are ruthless

To them the Ten Thousand Things are but as straw dogs

The Sage too is ruthless

To him the people are but as straw dogs

Yet Heaven and Earth and all that lies between

Is like a billows

In that it is empty but gives a supply that never fails

Work it and more comes out

Whereas the forces of words is soon spent

Far better is it to keep what is in the heart

—Lao-Tse[1]

I. The Blind Swordfighters: Zato Ichi and the Crimson Bat

I N THE PROLOGUE OF *Zato Ichi and a Chest of Gold* (*Zatoichi Senryo Kubi*, 1964), a solitary figure crouches in the artificial blackness of a studio forest. Suddenly an assailant detaches himself from the shadows and rushes at him with an upraised long sword. A second blade flashes for a split second. A man twists and crumples. More attackers pour into the circular spot of light, and the crouching man stands and performs a silent, deadly dance, pivoting in the midst of them, dodging their sword thrusts, and executing a single, elaborate cut of his own, until the entire group freezes and falls to the ground as if one. There is a low rasping as the victor's weapon slowly re-enters its scabbard and the collar clicks into place. Then the figure turns and walks into the surrounding darkness.

This prologue suggests a number of possible readings, with its stylized violence and mood of quiet, low-key menace; but a simple description fails to reveal the extremely unusual premise underlying the series of films typified by *Zato Ichi and a Chest of Gold*. The title character, the "hero" of these motion pictures, is Zato Ichi, a burly, crew-cut masseur. Dressed in a short, wrinkled kimono of plain gray cloth and walking on straw sandals, or sometimes perched unsteadily on forbidden wooden clogs, he picks his way slowly through towns and across country with the help of a wooden cane, because he is also a blind man. Nevertheless, as over two dozen productions have amply demonstrated, he is also one of the deadliest sword fighters in *chambara*.

Zato Ichi wields his weapon quite literally by ear. He is armed only with a cane sword and survives by his combination of instinct for danger and incredibly acute aural perception, often indicated on screen by a zoom-in to

Three scenes with Shintaro Katsu as Zato Ichi in *The Blind Swordman's Cane Sword*.

LEFT: *Zato Ichi Challenged*

tight shot of an ear, which Ichi can swivel around like an antenna. He can fend off unannounced blows, bisect various objects from a canteloupe to a gold coin to a sapling, or even cleave an arrow in half in mid-flight. In his showier moments, he may astonish festival-goers by using a bow and arrow himself to win a prize at a shooting gallery. He "sees" the targets by having a frightened attendant tap them. Still more extraordinarily, he may punctuate an after-dinner conversation by skewering a moth in mid-flight with a toothpick.

Clearly these exploits of Zato Ichi require that the viewer suspend a considerable amount of disbelief. Consider for a moment, a similar pretext for a series of Westerns featuring a blind gunfighter. In fact, in the tradition of *The Magnificent Seven* and *Fistful of Dollars*, there is a Spaghetti Western entitled *Il Pistolero Cieco* (directed by Ferdinando Baldi, 1971), literally "The Blind Gunfighter" (released in the U.S. as *Blindman*). The American film *Blind Fury* (directed by Phillip Noyce, 1989) is actually loosely adapted from *Blind Swordsman's Cane Sword* and *Zato Ichi Challenged* (both 1967) and stars Rutger Hauer as a blind Vietnam vet who carries a cane sword. An earlier analog is *Eyes in the Night* (directed by Fred Zinnemann, 1942), in which Edward Arnold as police Captain Maclain uses a seeing-eye dog to assist his detecting. In one sequence, Maclain actually has a shoot-out in his den; but first he levels the playing field by turning out the lights.

Zato Ichi does not require that the lights be out; but, once his unique talents have been accepted, his subsequent actions are not all that fantastic. Zato Ichi operates with a very particular context, the last decade or so of Tokugawa rule, when masseurs—a common occupation for blind men of the era—were at the bottom of the caste ladder. As a *hinin*, Zato Ichi is equally subject to scorn from peasants, merchants, and small-time criminals, not to mention arrogant samurai. Despite these intense physical and social handicaps, Zato Ichi manages to subsist; but his humors are irregular. At times, he summons up sufficient Buddhist stoicism to witness injustice or endure a personal wrong silently and inactively without retaliating. As that could make for a rather inactive plot as well. A frequent device in films of the series uses an opening scene in which person or persons unknown launches an unprovoked attack against Zato Ichi when he is alone and vulnerable, on the road or in a hostel room. When he can, Ichi tries to escape from such confrontations out of principle, meekly turning tail if there is an opportunity, warning men of his ability when cornered, or trying to discover what quarrel the unidentified assailant has with him. As this opponent often is or represents a friend or relative of someone whom Ichi has killed previously, he seldom manages to avoid dealing out more death.

When genuinely provoked, when a gambling boss or petty official has betrayed his trust, Zato Ichi can display an indomitable ruthlessness of his own. The massacre of Boss Asagoro and his followers, in which the leader is decapitated after all his retainers have been systematically mown down, at the end of *The Blind Swordman's Rescue* (*Zatoichi Ro Yaburi*, 1967), exemplifies his tenacity and wrath when he is avenging those incapable of self-defense, in this instance, the local farmers. There is also a bitter, sardonic streak in the blind masseur which occasionally surfaces. When he severs the right arm of an arrogant pickpocket in *Zato Ichi's Pilgrimage* (*Zatoichi Umio Tataro*, 1966) he admonishes him to "use the remaining arm to mend your ways." As he philosophizes before killing the moth with a toothpick in *Rescue*: "It should have been a pretty butterfly. . . . A lot of people are hated like moths. I hate people who don't work for good in this world. Things I hate, I kill."

There are many things and persons Zato Ichi does not hate. Despite being blind and frequently ill-used, his alienation is not total. He retains certain scruples and a sense of justice and judges his own behavior in relation to those. He has an obvious soft spot for widows and orphans, for anyone he regards, like himself, as a victim of *shushigaku*, feudal class structure, or some unspecified quirk of fate. Shintaro Katsu, who portrayed Ichi for more than twenty-five years, from 1962 through 1989, also has a way of making wistful, young women fall in love with him that adds melodramatic poignancy to the inevitable parting at a film's conclusion. Zato Ichi is not above a quasi-Victorian self-recrimination for being tempted to ruin some young woman's life by abusing her trust and reliance on him as a kind of knight-protector. More seriously, his adherence to *butsudo* compels his ongoing repentance for his violent life. When an unknown pursuer chases him through a grassy field in the beginning of *Zato Ichi Meets Yojimbo* (*Zatoichi To Yojinbo*, 1970) it triggers a reflex of self defense and the discovery that "once more my hands are stained with blood." Zato Ichi retires to a secluded village in search of a respite from killing.

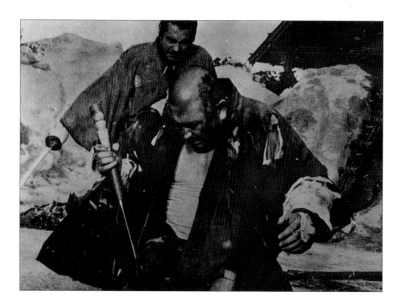

Zato Ichi Meets Yojimbo: Toshiro Mifune and Shintaro Katsu as the title characters in their final duel.

Naturally, the genre dictates that his good intentions be shattered, and he discovers the quiet town is now filled with rival factions and professional killers. While the exact number of men he has killed in the span of his film career has never been tallied, in *Zato Ichi's Pilgrimage* Ichi resolves to expiate his sins by visiting eighty-eight Buddhist shrines or one for each victim of his deadly cane sword.

Aside from this trail of blood in his wake, Zato Ichi's past is rather ill-defined. A flashback dream in *Pilgrimage* shows him as a sighted child of five playing by the shore of a lake. In Katsu's final *Zato Ichi* (which he also directed, 1989), while in a large wooden bathtub preliminary to a carnal encounter with Boss Ohan, a female gambler, he tells her that the only woman he has ever seen naked was his mother when he was a child. "I became blind when I was two. My mother was eighteen at the time. She hasn't aged since." In *Zato Ichi's Rescue* he offers cursory explanations of both his condition ("I've been blind since I can remember—so I don't wish to see") and his swordsmanship ("When I was small I didn't want to be looked down on"), which indicates that he is not immune to pride. As a *hinin*, Zato Ichi can act free of the ethical restraints which beset a samurai, of conflicts which involve *giri*. Still the moral exposition of the blind masseur is rooted in feudal values, so that the narrative structure of the series as a whole depends on his belief in certain of those values, if not in *bushido* or *ninkyodo* then in a fundamental *ninjo*-like sense of what is right. While he may oppose some of the arbitrary tenets of Tokugawa life, Zato Ichi mostly encounters ruffians, gamblers, and thieves whose political beliefs are irrelevant and who give him no option but to defend himself or die.

Shintaro Katsu and Rentaro Mikuni (left) as Asagoro in *The Blind Swordsman's Rescue*.

Zato Ichi's peculiar condition allows the various writers and directors of the series to develop the same satirical undertone found in Kurosawa's *chambara* without undercutting a film's seriousness of intent. *Zato Ichi's Rescue* illustrates this interplay of comic and dramatic elements. First, stereotyped figures are erected on either side of an ambivalent Zato Ichi. There is a self-righteous, non-violent, former samurai named Shusui who has rejected the sword in order to aid the overtaxed local farmers. Zato Ichi: "A samurai. Why no sword?" Shusui: "Even blind men have them now. . . . I'd be sorry to kill and taint the earth with blood." Alternatively there is boss Asagoro, who oppresses the farmers further by tempting them to gamble away their meager earnings. After wandering into this situation, Ichi questions each set of values in turn. He is puzzled by Shusui's asceticism and wonders facetiously how he can be "sorry for the earth" or over his conversion of the peasants: "No gambling, no drinking or fighting. I've come to a strange village." His predisposition toward surface values and motives causes Zato Ichi to be initially deceived by Asagoro ("Chivalry isn't dead yet. Boss Asagoro's a fine man") and to trust him more than the inexplicably altruistic Shusui. Once that poor choice is made, the film shifts in tone. There is a stylized staging of Zato Ichi's attack on Asagoro's unreformed rivals in the midst of a thunderstorm, and then the image of a dying profiteer clutching at a shattered and bloody money chest. What follows is a comic sequence of a momentarily reformed Ichi working with six other masseurs, four being blind and another having one good eye. Ironically, his preference for the *ninkyo*, or chivalry, represented by Asagoro over the selflessness of Shusui, for traditional values over revolutionary ones, compels Ichi to return to his "proper" station as a "non-human being," where the one-eyed man can bully and torment him.

Obviously the viewer cannot accept Zato Ichi's reform in *Rescue* or *Pilgrimage* or any other film as permanent, no matter how sincerely he may claim that "violence makes me shudder." As the overall formula for the series is fairly rigid, the masseur never manages to keep his cane sword closed for very long. The secluded village in *Zato Ichi Meets Yojimbo* turns out to be the center for an intrigue to steal shogunate gold. The pilgrimage of repentance ends with at least another score of men dead. Asagoro is revealed to be unchivalrous. In some ways the Zato Ichi films epitomize the formulaic aspects of the genre because many standard elements are in play, such as the build-up in nearly all the titles toward a climactic duel with an extremely skillful opponent. Perhaps the epitome of this is *The Blind Swordsman Meets His Equal* (*Zatoichi "Yabure! Tojin-ken,"* 1972), a Sino-Japanese co-production in which the opponent is the serialized Chinese hero Wang Kong, who is actually skillful enough to defeat Zato Ichi, but only in the Chinese version.

Recurring plot elements, such as Zato Ichi winning over the sister of a man he has reluctantly killed not just in *Pilgrimage* but in two other titles, or his proclivity in a half dozen others for assuming the guardianship of orphans, are only minor variations on the essentially antagonistic structure of the series, which repeatedly poses a basically valorous Ichi against forces of "evil." In both exterior/mythic and interior/character terms, Ichi must accept his role as both instrument and scapegoat of the violence of other figures and institutions. Any element which may question the underlying social assumptions of the genre usually enters the film at a satirical level. The comic image of the ambushed Ichi in *Rescue*—masquerading as a scarecrow, feigning death in the rainslick roadway, or spurting out a jet of water like a beached whale—allows the audience to distance itself from the guilt and makes the inevitable destruction of the villains by a blind, stumbling, comedian-turned-wraith all the more unsettling. The use of such a formula and repetitious situations has not prevented the Zato Ichi series from becoming the most popular in Japanese motion picture history. The standardization came to reflect the producers' unwillingness to tamper with a profitable product.

The last three titles of the original series, *Zato Ichi at Large, Zato Ichi in Desperation,* and *Zato Ichi's Conspiracy*, were the twenty-third through twenty-fifth features and were released by Toho after the character outlived its original company, Daiei. *Zato Ichi in Desperation* was also the first directed by the Shintaro Katsu.[2]

The narrative of *Zato Ichi in Desperation* is freely constructed from stock scenes and encounters. The central premise is a familiar one: in the first sequence Ichi inadvertently causes the death of a samisen player journeying to redeem her daughter from a brothel. Feeling guilty, he buys the girl's freedom himself and assumes responsibility for her welfare. Around this relationship are arrayed the predictable elaborations: a slit-voiced, white-kimonoed master swordsman lurking in wait to test his skill against Ichi's; a demonstration of prowess in which Ichi flings a gold coin onto the tip of a sword blade; the massacre of four thugs who are first advised to "lose face and live long"; some ironic repartee (Master: "I want to see the color of your blood." Ichi: "I couldn't see my blood whether it was red or black"); some moralizing by the masseur ("Gamblers should live humbly in the shadows of honest people—we shouldn't try for a place in the sun"); and a scene of comic relief during a dice game, which is repeated almost intact from an earlier film. Most of Katsu's attempts at innovation are on the level of style, and some of these are fairly imaginative. There are the point-of-view soundtracks: a volume drop when Ichi covers his ears or amplified footsteps when he is on his guard. There is a "flash forward" when Ichi tries to visualize how his attackers will come at him. Other moments, like the montage of short shots to depict the samisen player's fatal fall from the footbridge, seem less inspired. Katsu also handles a sub-plot involving an orphaned brother and sister with disinterest. *Zato Ichi in Desperation* is also slightly retrograde in terms of the character development already attained in the series with *Zato Ichi's Rescue* (#16) and *Zato Ichi Meets Yojimbo* (#20). However, the twist added in *Zato Ichi in Desperation*'s conclusion, in which Zato Ichi's hands are pierced so that he cannot hold a sword, is one of the most intriguing since *Zato Ichi and the Doomed Man* (*Zato Ichi Sakata Giri*, 1965), in which the blind masseur's enemies beat large festival drums to mask the sound of their approach. In the last image of *Zato Ichi in Desperation*—an extra long shot as Ichi slowly picks his way down a beach while the roar of the waves forms a final aural point of view—Katsu effectively recapitulates the physical estrangement and insecurity of the genre hero.

Katsu returned to Zato Ichi one last time as star and director in the 1989 *Zato Ichi*. It opens with some disconnected, quasi-flashbacks and a stay at a

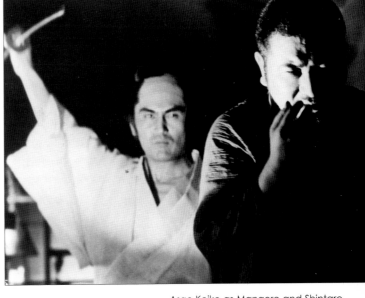

Asao Koike as Mangoro and Shintaro Katsu as the Blind Swordsman in *Zato Ichi in Desperation*.

hut near the beach. While some time passes until Ichi's first deadly encounter with a handful of gamblers on a dark path, by the time of the final battle the number of men killed by the blind masseur in this last feature is well over a hundred. Among the odd encounters is a starving *ronin* who sketches by the roadside and is ultimately hired by the Tenjin gamblers who are pursuing Ichi. In this first conversation, the sketching samurai talks to Ichi about colors, trying to explain "red" to the blind man. While he tries to avoid the encounter, once employed by the Tenjin, he must go after Ichi. When they meet again at an inn, the samurai tries to get Ichi drunk, discusses his sleeplessness, and is shown the mirror given to Ichi by his mother. He draws his sword, is poised, but does not attack. At the next meeting, Ichi has learned that the samurai inscribed his water flask with the epithet: "The fallen leaves don't resent the wind." Realizing the sub-textual warning which has been left to him, Ichi parts with the samurai by remarking that "the fallen leaves do resent the wind." In the final scene, on a misty hill against a blue sky, Ichi meets and dispatches the sleepless *ronin* with the remark: "Mr. Samurai, at last you can sleep."

This Ichi is as much a rescuer as his twenty-five predecessors, saving a bird's egg that has fallen from a tree and a young woman from a lascivious shogunate inspector. But in more than a half dozen encounters, bodies pile up all around him as never before. In one combat scene inside an inn with a group

TOP: Takeshi Kitano as the title character in *Zato Ichi* (2003).

BOTTOM: Takeshi Kitano as Zato Ichi attacks the gambler's den.

of chanting, killer monks, Ichi's blade slices off a nose which splatters against a wood beam, as in a parody of his sensory limitations. A moment later, he uses an antagonist's hat to shield himself from the torrent of blood gushing from a severed artery. While the unnamed samurai is reminiscent of such sympathetic antagonists as the afflicted (by tuberculosis) Hirate or the one-armed Nagisa in the first two Zato Ichi films, by the end of the picture Ichi himself seems a bit worn out. After slaughtering the entire Tenjin gang, Ichi hits the road again. The last credits roll over a freeze frame to the accompaniment of a pop ballad, English-language theme song, "The Loner," which laments about such things as "making my way through a place full of strangers."

While Katsu's embodiment of Zato Ichi ends on this note of mock alienation, a new *Zato Ichi* feature was completed in 2003 directed by and starring Takeshi "Beat" Kitano. The Ichi of Kitano, who previously directed his own portrayals of modern *yakuza* and rogue cops in such films as *Violent Cop* (1989), *Sonatine* (1993), *Fireworks* (1997), and *Brother* (2000), is older, blonder, but certainly as bloody as Katsu's. Kitano's measured performance takes

Zato Ichi irrevocably into middle-age, which Katsu never confronted, although he was a year older in 1989 than Kitano was in 2003. Much has been made of the "deadpan" Kitano has brought to roles since a near fatal motorcycle accident in 1994 left his face partially paralyzed. Ichi's blindness makes this "mask" into something else: a subtly appropriate lack of expression from a character who has never seen it on the faces of others.

Kitano opens with his Zato Ichi alone at the edge of the roadway. A lone man peeks over an incline, goes back, reappears with seven equally scruffy companions. A boy with a stick approaches. "Bring us the cane," one of the men says while proffering a coin. The boy actually gets the deadly *shikomi-zue* away from Ichi, but the head man refuses to pay as promised. Instead he yells a challenge: "Ichi!"; and all of them approach the lone blind man. They mock him, and, of course, he exploits their inattention to retrieve his sword and bring them all down.

As in the prologue of *Zato Ichi and a Chest of Gold*, Kitano invokes the legend with an immediacy as graphic as the main title: it splashes across the screen in red like a spray of blood. Kitano then establishes that there is more than one killer on the road. In a montage of shots at a crossroads, a masterless samurai is walking with his wife and his thoughts are revealed in a flashback to a killing. Two geishas rest by the roadside and another flashback reveals them murdering a clerk. With a rhythmic visual style, Kitano sets not one but three stories in motion: Ichi, the *ronin*, and the geishas, whose fates, genre expectation suggests, will soon intertwine.

In the town Ichi shortly reaches, the "Ginzo gang makes life hell." Kitano creates a counterpoint with an almost surreal scene of farm hands tilling the soil while keeping time to music like a line of drummers. Ichi takes shelter with Oume, a farmwoman whose nephew Shinichi is a gambling addict. Gennosuke the *ronin* tells his wife, who is ill, that, while he may be offered a clan post again someday, in this town he must seek work as a *yojimbo*. Another flashback reveals how he lost his retainership: he was beaten in combat with a brash, *bokken*-wielding *ronin*. He is soon hired by one of the rival local gambling factions. Two final flash backs complete the personal histories: Ichi recalls a fight in some rain-swept sand dunes where he kills another eight men. The geishas flash back to the death of their entire family at the hands of masked thieves.

Top: The Ginzo gang makes life hell.

Center: Tadanobu Asano as the *ronin* Gennosuke

Bottom: Takeshi Kitano as Zato Ichi flashes back to a fight in the rain.

Opposite page:
TOP: *Watch Out, Crimson Bat*:
Oichi (Yoko Matsuyama) and
the two orphans

CENTER: Yoko Matsuyama in *Crimson Bat, the Blind Swordswoman* (1969)

BOTTOM: Junko Miyazono as Quick
Draw" Okatsu

Having set up the three backstories, Kitano throws the characters together. Shinichi takes his aunt's houseguest to a local gambling house, and, as with Katsu's final incarnation, Kitano's Ichi has an uncanny ability to sense whether the dice are odd or even. After a night of winning, Zato Ichi and Shinichi meet the geishas. Before they can attack, Zato Ichi's keen sense of smell tells him that one "geisha" is actually a man. Disarmed at being unmasked, the geishas confess that they are the only survivors of the Naruto family and living by their wits as they search for the killers who orphaned them. Shortly thereafter, Ichi encounters Gennosuke at a local inn. Although Ichi quickly demonstrates that he is faster on the draw, Gennosuke still presumes that he can vanquish the blind man.

Of course, he cannot. Kitano adheres to the genre expectations regarding Ichi's prowess and adds a dimension of parody similar to many of the Katsu series. At one point, Shinichi paints eyes on Ichi's lids, which anticipates the sustained final sequence in which Ichi pretends to be sighted. While the farmers dance in the rain, Ichi overcomes Gennosuke and all the other minions of the local gambling chiefs. Ultimately he unmasks the old man who, while serving as a busboy at the inn, is really the criminal mastermind and killer of the Narutos. Kitano's stylized ending visually recalls the ironic aftermath of Gosha's *Goyokin* with an elaborate festival of masked dancers and drummers. With anachronistic choreography, all the principals join the chorus line of dancers on a stage in front of a lantern-lit pagoda. Through a computer-graphic effect, as they dance the Narutos momentarily become children again.

Kitano's feature makes Zato Ichi a 21st-century enigma. In some ways, he is a Zen-like figure, at peace with his existence, less tortured than Katsu sometimes was over his murderous past. His fights are focused, measured, never as frenzied as Katsu's often were. Despite his introduction of musical and visual anomalies, as with Katsu's incarnation, Kitano makes this ritual of combat an almost automatic behavior, as stylized as a ballet. In ending with the farm festival, Kitano reasserts this. But unlike the Narutos, Ichi can never recapture his lost innocence.

Shochiku Studios' answer to the popularity of Daiei's blind masseur was the Crimson Bat, a short-lived (four films) series based on a *manga* and featuring a blind swordswoman named Oichi. The parallels to Zato Ichi are too numerous to catalog completely, but the conventional stress in the Shochiku productions is on an estranged and mercenary character. In *Watch Out, Crimson Bat!* (*Mekura No Oichi Midaregasa*, 1969), Oichi describes herself as "a drifter; I usually work for money," who is melodramatized through romance and moments of broad comedy. While that narrative disequilibrium is sometimes apparent in the Zato Ichi titles as well,

Yoko Matsuyama as Oichi in *Crimson Bat: Oichi, Wanted, Dead or Alive.*

the creators of the Crimson Bat envision her prowess with a sword as potentially hampered not merely by her physical loss of sight but also by a tendency toward a "feminine" emotionalism. In the complex narrative and sexist assumptions of the series, love is Oichi's severest handicap. Under its influence in *Watch Out, Crimson Bat!* she forgets that "I'd become so that I could only believe in my cane sword." First, her sentimentality leads her to accept a commission to deliver a parcel from a dying man, then she adopts two orphans, and finally she falls for the masterless samurai who has been hired to take the parcel from her. The film shifts from scenes involving Oichi's emotional commitments to these characters to others directed toward action and comedy.

Like Zato Ichi, the Crimson Bat is capable of vanquishing a host of assailants. Occasionally, as when she dispatches two ruffians who stumble across her while she is bathing, the "anomaly" of martial abilities combined with female sexuality is played for comedy. But when Oichi is forced to kill a master swordsman to whom she had been attracted, she loses self-control. In *Watch Out, Crimson Bat!* she forgets her promise to the dying man and the orphans and takes disconsolately to drink, so that it requires the death of one of the children and a lascivious challenge from an unemployed bodyguard to jolt her out of her inaction.

In one sense Oichi does belong to that tradition of low-born genre heroes who sardonically reject social values: "Samurai are fools, aren't they?" In another sense her actions, like those of Zato Ichi, eventually belie her words. Unlike Zato Ichi the fact that she is woman not only makes her the target of frequent offers of "love duels" from rival swordsman but permits her a more overt satisfaction in her generic role. "Just so someone's happy, it's enough for me," is the kind of statement which also depersonalizes her at a film's conclusion. After the last battle in *Watch Out, Crimson Bat!*, she walks off not alone but in a medium shot which encloses five figures, coyly rejecting at the same time another pass by the bodyguard. By sharing the frame with others at this point, Oichi is effectively reintegrated. Oichi's failure as a complete genre "hero" stems from her lack of self-reliance rather than from her sexual identity. In the Toei releases featuring "Quick Draw" Okatsu (*Hitokiri*

Okatsu, 1969), the sword-wielding heroine is also treated as a sexual object. A scene in which the physically attractive star is stripped or raped is not only *de rigueur* but staged in a prurient manner. Her character is delineated with a simplistic Freudianism: she is one of many literally castrating female sword-fighters in productions of the 1960s and 1970s, long before the *bishoji* ("pretty girl") tradition engendered a *manga* character such as Azumi (the film version of which is discussed in Chapter 8). Nonetheless, Okatsu is a genuinely driven and alienated figure, who can walk off alone at the end of a film. Oichi not only has a tendency to become enamored of her antagonists—which may also happen to a male figure, as for example in *Sword of Vengeance IV* (*Kozure Ohkami IV*, 1973)—but more significantly, she is unable to strike the genre's classic pose and stand isolated in the film's closing image.

11. KYOSHIRO NEMORI, "SON OF THE BLACK MASS"

"Samurai or not . . . life is a battle."

Those words spoken by the title figure in *The Adventures of Kyoshiro Nemuri, Swordsman* (*Nemuri Kyoshiro Shobu*, 1962) could be taken as the prototypical response to why any alienated swordsman, samurai or *ronin*, *yakuza* or *hinin*, must fight. For Kyoshiro, the hero of a series of twelve films starring Raizo Ichikawa[3] made by Daiei studios from 1963 to 1969, the question seems more inextricably caught up with the pessimistic belief in *shushigaku* than it is for most other film personages. With a backstory adapted from the serial novel by Renzaburo Shibata and as disclosed by flashbacks and by Kyoshiro's own words in various of the series productions, the red-haired, black-kimonoed vagabond is a Eurasian, the offspring of an illicit union between a Portuguese missionary and a lady-in-waiting. "Son of the Black Mass" is an epithet Kyoshiro chooses for himself, an epithet which is appropriate to his quasi-existential brooding over the quirk of his birth. For although he may feign a Zen-like disdain for such concerns as birthright and cultural heritage, his actual obsession with such things is soon apparent. As with Zato Ichi, Nemuri's dreams are often visualized by the series' filmmakers. What they reveal is a recurring nightmare of a black ritual in which sacrificial blood is poured over the body of his mother and a caped, white-haired figure bends to violate her on an altar.

These "dream" prologues to several films may be either real or imaginary, since the use of dream images never distinguishes between objective and subjective viewpoint to indicate whether these scenes are hallucinated or recollected. In narrative terms, the circumstances of Kyoshiro's conception functions, like Zato Ichi's blindness, as the primary factor in the character's psychological estrangement from the normal values of Tokugawa society. In a much more deliberate way than Zato Ichi, Kyoshiro actively seeks revenge for the injustices of his personal, classless situation. Thus he actively hates Christians, and in titles such as *Kyoshiro Nemuri at Bay* (*Nemuri Kyoshiro Joyokin*, 1964) and *Castle Menagerie* (*Nemuri Kyoshiro Akujo-Gari*, 1969, both directed by Kazuo Ikehiro), he kills dozens of converts along with a number of shogunate officials conspiring to massacre them. Nemuri's love/hate relationship with Christianity, as manifest in these two films, contributes to a general negativism and misogyny and, at times, to a self-image which glories in its own ruthlessness.

In a film such as *Kyoshiro Nemuri at Bay*, this particular aspect of Nemuri's character is easily subsumed into a wry version of the genre stereotype. The film opens with the by-now standard usages of a title giving the year and a long shot of a manor house. Inside, director Ikehiro's visual choices are more stylized: the shadow of a Tokugawa princess on a wall becomes a grotesque gargoyle as she laughingly slaughters one of her female attendants. After an expository sequence shot in which the deadly situation at the castle is discussed by her doctor and a retainer, the stage is set for Kyoshiro. A long shot of the exterior with the tiled roof of the castle constricting the frame is balanced by his sudden appearance in the right foreground. As with Tsugumo in *Hara-Kiri*, Nemuri's stance and facial expression convey a mixture of disinterest and untapped energy. The tight close shot of a spilled sake bottle which follows is both a sardonic, phallic symbol and a confirmation for the viewer of an imbalanced (upset) and sinister potential in the dark figure. The film goes on to involve Kyoshiro in a search for a woman who is rumored to be the object of Madonna-like worship among the Christians and the illegitimate daughter of the same priest who fathered him. In the course of his search, the *ronin* effortlessly vanquishes several assailants, pausing as he wipes the blood from his sword to make cynical observations about "divine judgment" descending on the dead men. The conclusion is even more telling, as it dramatizes Kyoshiro's confrontation with the woman, whom he has discovered is neither his half-sister nor a Christian but a shogunate informant. Pursuing her into the hold of an abandoned ship, they exchange dialogue which explicitly delineates his position as alienated hero. "Inferno is a Christian word for hell," he replies to her threat of shogunate reprisal should he kill her: "It's too late to warn me. I'm already in it." After seduction also fails, she inadvertently plays directly on his own martyr complex and his twisted relationship to the Christian faith: "You look like him . . . the man on the cross." Ultimately, in defiance of her belief that he cannot be so merciless as to murder a defenseless woman—a belief supported for the viewer, on another logical level, by the simple fact that he is the protagonist of the film—Kyoshiro draws his sword and pierces her. "I'm a villain to be sure. So I can kill you in cold blood . . . I can destroy, as I'm a villain." The iconic inscription is completed as he walks off in an extra long shot and a stray dog crosses his path.

As with Shintaro Katsu's interpretation of Zato Ichi, the visceral impression made on the viewer by the re-introduction of the character of Nemuri in film after film depends heavily on the acting of Raizo Ichikawa. As noted before, Ichikawa's performance as Kiyomori Taira in *Tales of the Taira Clan* and a host of other more traditional, *bidanshi* heroes in a score of films throughout the 1950s contributed heavily to the samurai archetype against which Kurosawa and Toshiro Mifune played in *Yojimbo*. Ichikawa himself changed from a *wagoto*-style in pictures with titles such as *The Gay Masquerade* (*Benten Kozo*, 1958) and *The Swishing Sword* (*Hitohada Kujaku*, 1958). Over the course of a decade he became the villainous Ryunosuke in the *Daibosatsu Toge* series, Goemon and Saizo in the *Shinobi no Mono* or *Band of Assassins* series (1962-1966), and the quasi-*jitsuaku* Kyoshiro Nemuri, characters who were darker, more cynical, and in stark contrast to the roles of his youth.

The character in the first *Satan's Sword* feature (*Daibosatsu Toge*, 1960, directed by Kenji Misumi) anticipates many aspects of Nemuri. In the opening scene in Daibosatsu Pass, a black-kimonoed figure cuts down an old man, then casually wipes the blood from his sword and tosses the paper over a cliff edge. Shortly thereafter, Ichikawa as Ryunosuke Tsukue tells a woman who has come to plead for her "brother" (actually her husband) that "for a samurai *bushido* is sacred, like chastity to a woman." Ryunosuke rapes her, fathers a child, and eventually kills her. After becoming a *shinsengumi*, Ryunosuke watches a master swordsman defeat a band of his comrades and remark over the fallen that "the sword is the soul. If the soul is evil so is the sword." While cast as an essentially heroic character in *Shinobi no Mono*, Ichikawa's portrayal of Goemon, a farmer/*ninja* caught in the civil wars of the late 16th century, is both rough-hewn and remorseless in seeking revenge on those who killed his family. In a grotesque killing at the end of *Band of Assassins Continued* (*Zoku Shinobi no Mono*, 1963), Goemon hacks off the right arm and left leg of the object of his vengeance, then laughs coarsely at the prospect of having him bleed to death.

Like Katsu, Ichikawa's portrayal of the title figure gives the entire series a specific and evolving identity. Despite Nemuri's many unappealing and distinctly anti-heroic traits, despite him even typing himself as a "villain," Ichikawa's approach to the part resembles Mifune's in *Yojimbo* and *Sanjuro*. Tadao Sato suggests that the appearance of a character such as Ryunosuke Tsukue during the lengthy serialization of Nakazato's novel influenced the portrayal of recurring characters such as Chuji Kunisada, a "Robin Hood" figure, beginning with *chambara* in the silent era. The moral righteousness of the *tateyaku*, or male hero in the *kabuki* tradition, was undermined by the nihilistic outlook of figures such as Tsukue.[4]

Certainly the outlooks of Ichikawa as Nemuri and Mifune as Sanjuro can be deemed nihilistic; but even as alien heroes their performances incorporate a considerable residue of human sentiment. For example there is Nemuri's outraged cry at the princess's amusement when he is forced to cut down a number of her guards in *Kyoshiro Nemuri at Bay*: "Does she think it's a show?" To some extent, Ichikawa's portrayal is developed from a character he played in *Destiny's Son* (*Kiru*, 1962), a mixture of

Raizo Ichikawa in *Destiny's Son*

traditional and anti-heroic elements and a complex narrative in which Ichikawa starred as the offspring of a former lady-in-waiting and a low-caste samurai who eventually had to prove his loyalty by executing the mother of his own child. One of the sequences is a flashback to that execution which, in some ways, visually anticipates Nemuri's recurrent dream of the black mass. The similarity ends there, however, for the hero of *Destiny's Son* uses his martial skills to secure a position as *yojimbo* to a clan chamberlain. He is so fully reintegrated into an acceptance of feudal values that he follows his assassinated master in death by allowing himself to be killed in a kind of passive performance of *junshi*. The early Kyoshiro in *Adventures of Kyoshiro Nemuri, Swordsman* is not as arrogant and unfeeling as the protagonist of *Kyoshiro Nemuri at Bay*, *Castle Menagerie*, or the aptly titled *Human Tarantula* (*Nemuri Kyoshiro Hitohadagumo*, 1968). In fact, the story line of *Adventures of Kyoshiro Nemuri, Swordsman* opens as he avenges the death of the father of a street urchin at the hands of a sword-school master. Shortly thereafter, he assumes the role of unofficial bodyguard to a pro-reform shogunate official. But even this early characterization has Nemuri fully rejecting the ideals of *bushido* as he openly professes that "swordsmanship is nothing but murder."

As for the "evil sword," Nemuri's own is wielded in the "Engetsu" style, or what he terms the "full-moon cut." As an opponent in *Adventures of Kyoshiro Nemuri, Swordsman* describes it: "He circles his sword and kills before he completes the circle . . . he has a blind spot when it passes in front of his eyes." The visualization of the Engetsu style is accomplished by means of step-printing, so that as he slowly rotates the weapon a dozen swords seem to flash and spread out before him like the blades of a fan. The multiple reflections off the polished steel in the "full-moon cut" are reminiscent of a secret "no-minded" (*mushin*) swordsmanship known among the Zen masters as "The Moon in Water" and exemplified in the following verse of the Shinkage-ryu school:

> The eye sees it,
> But no hands can take hold of it
> The moon in the stream:
> That is the secret of my school.

As the single moon and the water of a hundred streams interact unconsciously, the one reflected in the others, so Nemuri's obsessive style possesses what he calls a "fatal inward draw," which interacts subliminally with the countless swordsmen who test it. That fatality, rather than a blind spot, is what the observant opponent of *Adventures of Kyoshiro Nemuri, Swordsman* discovers in the final duel.

Sexual arrogance is the final component of Nemuri's make-up, and his peculiar magnetism appeals most strongly to the aristocratic and even princely among women. The princesses, for example, who figure in *Adventures of Kyoshiro Nemuri, Swordsman, Kyoshiro Nemuri at Bay*, and *Castle Menagerie*, all have a perverse desire to enjoy Kyoshiro's "favors" before thugs they have hired to dispose of him do their job. Nemuri gives satisfaction to none of them. Occasionally, he even assumes an indignant posture when he discovers that yet another seduction is merely a trap to separate him from his sword. For instance, there are his melodramatic remarks after such an attempt in *Castle Menagerie*: "How dare you touch my clean body, woman of sodom." While the Kyoshiro of *Adventures* has a teasing, platonic relationship with a noodle-shop girl, the later Nemuri is infrequently susceptible to virginal charms and seldom has use for women except as sexual objects or, as in the end of *Kyoshiro Nemuri at Bay*, victims of his sword.

As a consequence of all this, it may seem a stretch to contemplate the ruthlessness of Nemuri's swordplay and sexuality with the sage words of Lao-Tse. Nemuri's emblem is a variant of the *manji*, or fylfot (). In Japanese the Western cross saltire or a swastika ideogram (卍) equals the number "ten thousand" and connotes the same infinity or wholeness as the Chinese "Wan-wu" in Lao-Tse's epigram; and Nemuri could be said to pattern his life after that of the sage to whom both the ten thousand things and the people are "but as straw dogs." Perhaps the best illustration films of the enigma of Nemuri's status as a hero among all the series is found in the 1967 production *Trail of Traps* (*Nemuri Kyoshiro Masha No Hada*, also directed by Kazuo Ikehiro). As the English title implies, the narrative core of the

Raizo Ichikawa as Kyoshiro Nemuri sports a fylfot emblem on his black kimono in *Trail of Traps*.

film is a perilous journey Nemuri undertakes for a number of ambitious reasons. He may be doing it for money—he is approached by a shogunate official to guard a golden statue his daughter is transporting to Kyoto; for love— he is attracted to the virginal daughter, Chisei; for revenge—he is opposed by the Black Finger group, renegade Christians who want to restore the statue as a religious icon; or simply in defiance of fate as the following dialogue with a fortune-telling geisha suggests:

GEISHA

Bad time for trips.

NEMURI

Then I'll go.

GEISHA

Where to?

NEMURI

To Kyoto—to see some things for myself.

While Kyoshiro's motives are never really clarified through all the twists of the plot, *Trail of Traps* uses that uncertainty to explore, visually and narratively, other aspects of the "hero's" personality.

The introduction of Nemuri as central character is both unmistakably and sensorially direct: red title cards are followed by a re-enactment of the black mass, where the blood-stain on his mother's kimono fills the shot. Ichikawa draws his sword as the sound of an infant crying is heard over both scenes to act as a transition. Yet for all the implicit violence of this opening, Nemuri refrains from fulfilling the easy generic role and actually kills no one in the entire first half of the film. In a stylized encounter early in the plot, he

Raizo Ichikawa in *Trail of Traps*

finds his path blocked by four masked men who announce their intention to slay him. While an overhead shot arrays the figures in a way which suggests an inevitable combat—the roadway bisects the frame and Nemuri stands in the center of it in geometric opposition to a wedge of men on the right—the black-robed Nemuri dismisses their challenge: "Who'd want to punish me, a *ronin*?" He simply steps through them as they move to attack. This literal detachment might be interpreted generically as the mark of a supremely confident swordsman, of a Zen-man who fears neither for his life nor his reputation in telling his assailants to "punish me later." Yet this lack of trepidation, as a later scene in which Kyoshiro is captured by the Black Finger group confirms, stems not from any ethical or religious conviction. Nemuri's reply to the fanatic who offers to spare his life if he will "accept the baptism of Yahweh, he is our almighty god greater than Buddha or Christ," is unequivocal. He recites a variant of the atheist's creed: "There is no Buddha or Christ. Yahweh does not exist. . . . Fools. God didn't make Man. Man made God." Despite his disbelief in a higher power, Nemuri's composure in the face of imminent annihilation—"You'll be blown to pieces and fade unknown to others from this world"—reaffirms his Zen-like inability to feel fear.

In terms of character typing, this creates an ongoing paradox. For while the traps which are set for him on the trail may threaten him physically, Nemuri's emotions remain unassailable. On the one hand, Kyoshiro identifies with nothing except the material reality embodied in his weapon. Often repeated in many films of the series is a scene in which he meticulously cleans and dusts his sword. In *Trail of Traps*, Ikehiro uses a rack-focus from the blade to his face to graphically assert that identification. Nemuri continues to portray himself to others as an unscrupulous killer. "I'm sorry," he informs the shogunate official when initially refusing his request to accompany Chisei, "but you're asking the wrong man. I'm a man your daughter should be on guard against." On the other hand, Nemuri's behavior repeatedly types such statements as false candor, for not only does he eventually agree to safeguard the girl, for whom he develops if not love, at least, a genuine, fraternal affection, but he continues to act under the direction of some unorthodox but moral sensibility. When he severs the arm of a pimp who attacks him without provocation at an inn, Nemuri tells him, "You can't kill or gamble now, but you can make love." This last admonition is strongly reminiscent of Sanjuro's words to the man he spares at the conclusion of *Yojimbo* and adds an erogenous element to Zato Ichi's remark after a similar amputation in *Pilgrimage*. Nemuri in *Trail of Traps* is much less passive than either Sanjuro or Zato Ichi. His response to events marks him as more single-mindedly ("I'm going to Kyoto to find out what's on people's minds") and more sardonically ("Welcoming me with guns instead of crystal rosaries?") in control than any of Kurosawa's heroes.

The last battle by the lake in *Trail of Traps*

Perhaps the ultimate irony of Nemuri's alienation is that in all of the films he does retain control, but more out of reflex than conscious desire. He might well die without regrets, but he is too perfect a swordsman to lose. What the ending of *Trail of Traps* clarifies is that Nemuri also has a residue of human feeling. In this film, at least, if not throughout the series, this gives his final situation a tragic potential. Driven to murderous rage by Chisei's death, he rushes after the Black Finger group, and "for the first time in his life, Kyoshiro Nemuri challenges." Amidst a display of festival banners by a lake shore—a scene which he would normally find "too beautiful for bloodshed"—he methodically slaughters them, until only the leader is left. He pauses for that man to reflect on his fate:

NEMURI

Look at the corpses of men who believed in god's help. You still think there is a god?

LEADER

Be quiet! Obsessed by an evil sword, God will determine who is right.

NEMURI

I will kill you. . . . Watch my Engetsu style as a present for your god.

The opponent is drawn in to Nemuri's circling blade. It flashes up and blood spurts over his now complacent brow; but revenge affords no satisfaction. "It is," Nemuri muses by Chisei's pyre, "the only path a child born under an unlucky star can follow." A panning shot tracks him as he walks away bearing the burden of his *shushigaku*; then a long shot, with the pyre smoking and flaming in the foreground, reduces him to a dark, barely distinguishable figure at the frame's center.

What effect does a low-budget or serial format in a *chambara* film have on the central character of the swordsman? *Yojimbo* functions in critical practice as a dividing point between the traditional *jidai-geki*, with its clear-cut heroes and villains, and the fusion of those opposites into the single, enigmatic mold from which Zato Ichi and Kyoshiro Nemuri are cast. Prior to that a low-budget "costumer" in Japan could be a wordy and overwrought melodrama. To some extent that sort of motion picture continued to exist well into the 1960s in the most cheaply made of the various studios' *chambara*. For instance, Toei's "Crescent Scar Samurai," Mondonosuko Saotomi, who describes himself as "a direct descendant of the Shogun, generally known in Edo as the weary man," is a weary filmgoer's Kyoshiro Nemuri. Sporting a flowery print kimono, a pot-belly, and Nemuri-esque bangs parted over his forehead to reveal a scarlet-colored, moon-shaped scar, Saotomi is accompanied by a pair of bumbling, bespectacled merchants. Saotomi tackles an assortment of villains with an un-Nemuri-like relish that frequently makes the comic relief of his companions seem rather extraneous. However unconvincing his weariness, even the Crescent Scar Samurai reflects a post-War, quasi-mythic disenchantment among heroes of serial and "serious" samurai films alike that permeates all the genre's basic structures and expressions. And neither the technological improvements which added sound effects and spurting blood to the previously silent sword strokes of an angry Raizo Ichikawa nor the apparent change in sensibility brought on by those who write and direct the actions of the film samurai can fully account for this striking evolution of the genre hero in the 1960s and 1970s. Nor do studio economics explain the simultaneous evolution of narrative themes that stress a protagonist's nihilism during that time in films as diverse as *Hara-Kiri* and *Trail of Traps*.

Obviously serial films tread a fine line between the fantasy of motion pictures like Shiro Toyoda's *Illusion of Blood* (*Yotsuya Kaidan,* 1965) or Daiei's golem-like "samurai-monster," Majin, who debuted in *Daimajin,* 1966, and reappeared in *Return of Majin* (*Daimajin Ikaru,* 1966) and *Majin Strikes Again* (*Edaimajin Gyakushu,* 1967). Under the supervision of three of Daiei's stable of stylish action directors, Kimiyoshi Yasuda, Kenji Misumi, and Kazuo [Issei] Mori, respectively, the Majin series manages to imbue its title character, who lumbers around like a giant *haniwa,* with a genuine sense of alienation. The essential realism of the *chambara* of Kurosawa or Kobayashi and the characters portrayed by Toshiro Mifune or Tatsuya Nakadai quickly carried over in the heroes and anti-heroes of other filmmakers and performers. Despite such elements as the surreal Engetsu style of Nemuri and the sightless swordsmanship of Zato Ichi, their serial features rely heavily on the tone of nihilism and estrangement sounded in *Yojimbo* and *Hara-Kiri.*

The 1960s versions of the *ninja* or spy films also relied heavily on visual style. These early film *ninja* were black-robed and hooded figures who possess legendary magical powers far greater than any of the historical *metsuke.* Beyond all the gimmicks of animated ropes, exploding darts, or incredible leaping abilities, the heroes of films such as Mori's elegiac *Mission: Iron Castle*

Chiaroscuro in Mission: Iron Castle.

(*Shinobi No Shu,* 1970) are far more akin to Nemuri and Hanchiro Tsugumo in their sense of displacement and estrangement than the neo-*ninja* who made a flashy transition to the West. Running through all of these films, from Toyoda's haunted samurai, unable to shake off the literal ghosts of his victims, to the figurative specters which plague the embittered stray dogs like Sanjuro or Nemuri, and even to the latently schizophrenic Sakamoto of *The Ambitious* is the same anti-traditionalism, the same dramatic deconstruction in one way or another of the older, unreflective archetype of the samurai ethos.

III. MIYAMOTO MUSASHI

Unlike Zato Ichi or Kyoshiro Nemuri, Musashi Miyamoto is neither a fictional nor a formally serialized characterization. Although the number of motion pictures produced which feature Musashi as a character may rival the number of episodes in the two Daiei series combined, the historical Musashi, like his analogs in the warriors of Medieval Europe and more recently the gunfighter of the American West, is difficult to separate from the exaggerations and embellishments of legend. Musashi was born around 1584 in either Mimasako or Harima province but took his surname from the birthplace of his father. He began his career at the age of thirteen. After the battle of Sekigahara, he devoted himself to the perfection of two sword styles, the Enmyo-ryu and Niten-ryu, in the course of over sixty lifetime duels. He died in the service of Lord Tadotoshi Hosokawa in 1645 and is buried in Kyushu.

A possible self-portrait of Miyamoto Musashi.

Those are the facts of Musashi's life; but for all the violence and pragmatism associated with his rise to fame in the early years of Tokugawa Japan, his reputation in many quarters rests less with his stature as a swordsman than as an artist and follower of Zen. The other side of Musashi is found in the *Gorin no Sho*, a five-volume, autobiographical treatise on swordsmanship and philosophy originally published in 1693, wherein his conflicting inclinations—contemplation and action—are revealed, and in the numerous samples of his pen-and-ink drawings. Many of the *chambara* about Musashi are based on the lengthy novel by Eiji Yoshikawa known simply as *Musashi*. It originally appeared from 1935 to 1939 in serialized newspaper installments and covers the early years of Musashi's life from the ages of sixteen to twenty-nine. The novel gained a certain amount of notoriety in the West when former U.S. Ambassador Edwin Reischauer dubbed it the *Gone with the Wind* of Japan.

The relationship of either the historical or fictional writings of Musashi to the various film portraits is an inconsistent one at best. Unlike the genre types represented by Ryomo Sakamoto in *The Ambitious* or Hanchiro Tsugumo in *Hara-Kiri*, the real Musashi seems never to have been bound to the concept of a warrior code as either a complete way of life or an institution against which one should react. Rather he tempered and shaped his own ambitions in relation to those social realities, against which some film samurai may rebel. His *kataki-uchi* against the Yoshiaka, whom he held responsible for his father's dishonor and death, was also an opportunity to acquire notoriety as a swordsman, something needed by anyone who hoped to establish a successful fencing school.

Because of the influence of Zen, ethical questions for Musashi required a more fundamental response than the potentially empty form of *bushido*. Educated

TOP: Rentaro Mikuni (left) and Toshiro Mifune as Musashi (right) in the three-part *Samurai*

BOTTOM: Mifune's Musashi captures the fancy of the millkeeper and her daughter in *Samurai*.

Opposite page:
TOP: Kinnosuke Nakamura (left) as Musashi in the Tomu Uchida-directed series

CENTER: Kinnosuke Nakamura (right) as Musashi

BOTTOM: Kinnosuke Nakamura (left) as Musashi in *Swords of Death*

by his uncle, a monk who mastered the martial arts, Musashi never saw himself in the ostracized role of either *hinin* or "wave man" and could not in life accept the alternative of sardonic resignation to *shushigaku* evinced by Zato Ichi or Sanjuro. Most film versions of Musashi's life were produced during the standardization of the enigmatic hero-type in the 1950s and 1960s and demonstrate that Musashi on screen need not be confined to fulfilling any single role.

Accordingly the motion picture image of Musashi over those two decades may vary considerably. He is a noble hero seeking the true way as in the Toho three-part version directed by Hiroshi Inagaki and entitled simply *Samurai* (*Miyamoto Musashi*, 1954; *Ichijoji No Ketto*, 1955; and *Ketto Ganryujima*, 1955). He is a confused, rebellious youth without a cause in Tomu Uchida's five-parter for Toei.[5] A different novel—by Ryotaro Shiba—whose other fiction has been adapted to a range of *chambara* from *The Ambitious* to *Mission: Iron Castle*—was used in another Toei adaptation (also *Miyamoto Musashi*, 1968) starring Rentaro Mikuni as more of an amoral, opportunistic Musashi.

Even free of the restraints of *bushido*, samurai heroes may be guided by the concept of upright behavior contained in *otoko no michi*. For the very different Musashis, acting in the "manly way" has radically divergent implications. For instance, one of the first incidents in the Yoshikawa story has Musashi and a companion seeking shelter at a mill after escaping from the battlefield at Sekigahara. In the Toho production, Musashi is righteously interpreted by a youthful Toshiro Mifune and captures, quite without trying, the fancy of the millkeeper and her daughter. They attempt, each in turn, to seduce him, are rebuffed by the scrupulous youth, and conspire to get revenge by accusing him of rape. In the Toei adaptation of Ryotaro Shiba's novel, Musashi also makes his way to a mill after fleeing the fight; but this scruffy, lecherous figure repays the millkeeper for her food and lodging by raping and robbing her. In the course of all three films, the Mifune Musashi spends a good part of the time in monastic retreat and tortured introspection—not merely over the injustice of the rape charge, which has caused him to be ostracized, but also over deadly duels which he has hotheadedly fought—and even worrying over whether it had been inconsiderate of him to refuse the advances of the women at the mill. The Mikuni Musashi has no such scruples but ruthlessly pursues his announced goal of self-advancement, while he exults unabashedly in his triumphs in an almost childish manner. In fact, the final shot of that *Miyamoto Musashi* is a half-comic, half-chilling freeze-frame as Mikuni runs from a field which he has littered with corpses, leaps joyously in the air, and shouts, "Look, Ma, I won!"

What may be most interesting about this version of Musashi's story, which is more freely scripted than the expansive Inagaki and Uchida adaptations of Yoshikawa's novel, is that its earthiness, amorality, and sardonic humor ties the legendary figure to the seminal film characterization in *Yojimbo* and not to the historical perception of the real Musashi. Merely the physical aspect of Rentaro Mikuni's Musashi is very difficult to reconcile with the clean-shaven, naive-looking portrayals by Toshiro Mifune and Kinnosuke Nakamura in the Inagaki and Uchida productions. Mikuni, with his stockier build and rough-hewn features, was infrequently cast in the heroic role. As it happens, Mikuni plays Musashi's companion from Sekigahara in *Samurai* and an opponent of Musashi in the last three parts of the Uchida version. His lethargic movements, his brow beaded with sweat, his hair in disarray, all suggest an unusually world-weary and even slow-witted Musashi. When Mikuni scratches the stubble on his face or the unruly locks on top of his head, he echoes the almost identical, insouciant gesture Mifune used repeatedly in the films of Kurosawa to express his disdain for the tiresome formalities of samurai manners and grooming. Neither the Mifune of *Samurai* nor Kinnosuke Nakamura of *Zen and Sword* had yet become that unwholesome as heroes; and they convey nothing resembling the somber, slouching, almost bestial presence of Mikuni.

As if this departure from the ongoing conventions of how a heroic samurai should look and carry himself were insufficient, director Yasuo (Kohata) Furuhata's initial staging is equally anti-heroic. Musashi is first seen at the battle of Sekigahara dodging the bullets of the Tokugawa riflemen and shouting insults at them for not daring to fight like men. After strangling an enemy general with his bare hands like a common thug, he mocks the samurai custom of naming illustrious forbears by first yelling out, "I'm a *ronin* from Sasshu," pondering an instant, and then

Top: A trussed-up Musashi
(Toshiro Mifune) in Hiroshi Inagaki's
Samurai series.

Bottom: Kinnosuke Nakamura as
Musashi in *Zen and Sword*.

correcting himself: "That's not right. I'm Musashi Miyamoto from Banshu."
After this he spits on his hands and re-enters the fray. The film's version of
Musashi's discovery of the "two-sword" style (*niten-ryu*) comes shortly after he
has made a Falstaff-like exit from Sekigahara bearing off the body of a comrade and seems also to thumb its nose at the legend. There is a comical point-
of-view shot as Musashi buries his friend, taken upside-down to simulate
Musashi's perception of three men approaching him as he looks through his
legs. In the course of tricking the enemy soldiers into picking up the swords
he has put down out of reach before digging the grave, Musashi spontaneously
grabs both hilts. After using the two weapons to quickly kill all three men, a
medium-close shot taken from below, and again mocking the convention of an
heroic angle, captures a bemused look on Mikuni's face as he considers the
potential of this serendipitous discovery.

Up to this point, the viewer may well be uncertain whether to take this
roughneck Musashi seriously. After the crude fighting style at Sekigahara and
the off-handed formulation of *niten-ryu*, Mikuni's wry remarks over the dead
and his adoption of a stray dog as he walks off perpetuate a satirical tone. The
first indication that this characterization of Musashi possesses any psychological depth occurs in the following scene, when he
seeks to evade the sweep of the victorious Tokugawa
forces in an isolated mill house. That evening a somewhat mellower Musashi ponders over his past in the
presence of the woman millkeeper. "All men are
alone anyway," he concludes with more resignation
than complaint; then he turns to the subject of his
"old man," recounting how his father tried to kill him:
"He was crazy . . . I called him an old has-been."
After throwing down his food knife and drawing his
sword to examine the blade, he continues, "I was
eight then." This revelation of Musashi's quasi-
Oedipal relationship to his father is the first clue to
the motives of his subsequent quest for fame. "I
stamped on his grave," he shouts as he strikes the floorboards with his foot,
"so he wouldn't get out."

The memory of what he believed was his father's failure is the factor
which precipitates the confusion of impulses entangling Mikuni's Musashi.
After the preliminary scenes conclude with Musashi's rape of Ei, the millkeeper, four years pass, during which time Musashi determines on a course of note-
worthy action and posts a written challenge to a duel on the gate of the Yoshiaka
fencing school in Kyoto. What Musashi expects to gain from the duel, whether
he wants more than fame at its purest, is less clear. When he is accused of being

Depth of field: Musashi tests a *bokken*.

High angle: Musashi and Ei, and the wall which separates them

Musashi and Ei

High angle: open ground in Musashi's first duel

Top: Rentaro Mikuni as Musashi carves a figure to pay for his son's grave marker.

Center: Musashi and his banner

Bottom: Ei (Jitsuko Yoshimura) stares at Musashi's banner.

"still a hick, like your old man," he recoils violently from the thought of reliving his father's insignificant life. "Today I'm famous for being crazy," he replies, "tomorrow I'll be famous as a swordsman." For a while, Musashi considers using his father's swordbreaker in his duel but discards the iron truncheon, after he melodramatically announces that "I can give up my life—but not my name." Paradoxically, the filmmakers play on the fact that Musashi had already given up one name, changing it from what was originally Shinmen Takezo. They also introduce an ironic twist into the narrative when Ei reappears seeking revenge and informs Musashi that the son borne of his rape, whom he never knew existed, has died. At this juncture, Musashi's disturbed psychology refocuses his ambivalent, guilty feelings onto this unknown child, alternately spurning Ei and any further information about him ("The hell with it! You won't soften me up") and offering to "fix up the kid's grave."

Compounding all this is the issue of Musashi's art, which he has been using to support himself while perfecting his swordsmanship. For it becomes increasingly apparent that the filmmakers regard Musashi's quest for a reputation and his residue of concern for his dead son as examples of transference of more basic needs. First, Musashi is neurotically driven to secure parental approval, which is manifest in the shout addressed to his mother in the film's final image. Second, he is compelled to perpetuate his own uncertain identity, as in his words when he exultantly flings his sword away after his first victory: "Shinmen Miyamoto Musashi. Today Kyoto. Tomorrow Osaka. In five days, they'll hear of me in Edo. How about that!" But the filmmakers' withhold from their character any apprehension of the fact that his most enduring fame may lie in his simple pen-and-ink drawings. By making explicit Musashi's own underestimation of his art—he assesses it in making a gift of a drawing to an admiring serving girl, merely as something which "pays the rent"—the ironies of his relentless ambition are multiplied. Not only does he offer a carved figure to Ei to pay for his son's grave marker but he cradles the statuette, like the more significant object that it is with a greater chance of immortalizing his name than any human offspring, without comprehending its real value. Thus one of the film's most subtle ironies is the large banner reading "Miyamoto Musashi, Swordsman," which Musashi hangs outside his quarters. By framing the banner in medium shot with Musashi or in the foreground during a close-up of Ei peering in at him, viewer awareness of it is heightened. Knowing Musashi's ultimate fame, the banner is an art work which might well be prized retrospectively, for the formal beauty of its calligraphy, but in which the artist himself takes pride only for its message.

Musashi's art also figures in the question of his personal morality. "A warrior lives for his sword," is the quote which opens *Miyamoto Musashi*; but this version, unlike *Samurai* or *Zen and Sword*, confronts that statement mainly in terms of societal context. On one level, the interaction of Musashi the gruff opportunist and Musashi the introspective artist creates a situation for vaguely philosophical dialogue, as when he gives the serving girl a drawing of a shrike before departing for the climactic duel at Ichijoji:

> MUSASHI
>
> A bird's lucky. It can go where it wants.
>
> GIRL
>
> Are you going alone?
>
> MUSASHI
>
> Like a bird.

Musashi's identification with the subject of his drawing reflects his belief that the power to go where one wants is not automatically granted to any man. Lacking wings, in Musashi's view man must claw for self-determination without reservation or scruple. Whereas the heroes of *Samurai* or *Zen and Sword* do not regard the social order as particularly oppressive, Mikuni's Musashi realizes that to act "like a bird" challenges that order. The effective rationalization of that action—that is, what extenuates his aggression and ruthlessness so that he remains an acceptable vehicle for viewer empathy—is neither his obsession with swordsmanship nor an understanding of the psychology behind his single-minded pursuit of a "name," as much as it is the even greater ruthlessness of the times. At Sekigahara, where the film's events are set in motion, "Shinmen Takezo" and his enemies are equally loutish and brutal. Four years later, a sword school, which is an emblem of the times changed under Tokugawa, becomes the target of the violent campaign of the man who has become Miyamoto Musashi. If Musashi still, as Ei remarks, "smells of blood," it connotes a different, less mindless brutality than that of Sekigahara. For part of Musashi's metamorphosis is the acquisition of a sense of destiny—"No one can kill me"—aimed not coincidentally at the Yoshiaka school. No matter how

TOP: Musashi paints the "Shrike on a Dead Branch."

BOTTOM: "Shrike on a Dead Branch," ink drawing by Musashi

TOP: The wooden statuette mutilated by the Yoshiaka

CENTER: Tatsuya Nakadai appears as Musashi in *Kojiro*, chiseling a tiger from a block of wood.

BOTTOM: Musashi in rim-lit profile

much the viewer is put off by Musashi's brusqueness, it is of a natural sort. The Yoshiakas deal rather in artificial behavior. When Musashi succeeds in defeating both the fencing master and his brother, the school elders have no qualms about planning to "use guns" to kill him and to conceal this "dishonorable" recourse afterwards. Even Hanshichiro, the eight-year old son of the former master, who must according to *bushido* and the rules of vendetta become Musashi's last opponent, is caught up in the system and stripped of his innocence. As it happens, it is Hanshichiro's sword which mutilates Musashi's statuette after Ei has sold it to the school. This suggests a relationship between him and Musashi's responsibility for his son's death, a relationship which is fatally confirmed at the film's conclusion when Hanshichiro himself is cut down by Musashi.

Although it is unlikely that the historical Musashi regarded his victim at Ichijoji as a surrogate son whom he killed a second time, the film does not restrict itself to psychologizing about the personage but deals as well with the record of Musashi's ethical and martial beliefs. D.T. Suzuki describes the following verse as corresponding to the principle of "emptiness" which Musashi taught:

> Into a soul absolutely free from thoughts and emotions
> Even the tiger finds no room to insert its fierce claws.[6]

In one of the three scenes in which Tatsuya Nakadai appears as Musashi in *Kojiro*, he is seen chiseling a tiger from a block of wood. Although Nakadai's Musashi asserts that sculpting is "only a pastime," his choice of subject matter for the carving is singularly appropriate. Not only does Nakadai's portrayal, from the alert flash of his eyes to the growl of his voice, suggest the same bestial instincts as Mikuni's, but in the other two sequences which include him he stalks his opponents with the silent, concentrated, and deadly tread of a tiger. Like Nakadai, Mikuni's Musashi is still struggling with those "thoughts and emotions" and may resemble the tiger more than the man. Where he partakes most fully in *sunyata* is at a metaphysical level. It is at that level, the film's narrator explains, that Musashi suspects the Yoshiaka school of treachery and that "Musashi knew what they were doing. He calls this perceptive ability 'thrusting eyes.'" On a more practical level, Mikuni, like the historical Musashi, wants to rid himself of *suki*, the unguarded moment in which the tiger inserts his claws: "I want my arms to live separately—block then strike." In a sense the composite personality the film constructs reflects the underlying oxymoron of Musashi's life: how to reconcile self-effacement and Zen with self-aggrandizement and the sword. Oddly enough, certain images in this *Miyamoto Musashi*, most specifically the boy's identification of the carving with Musashi, could almost be modeled after a principle of the Tokugawa *osho* and the *sensei* of the Yagyu school, Munemori:

> Turn yourself into a doll made of wood: it has no ego, it thinks nothing; and let the body and limbs work themselves out in accordance with the discipline they have undergone. This is the way to win.

The "way to win" may seem less thoughtful or "enlightened" for Mikuni's Musashi than it is for the more ostentatiously Zen-minded figures in the Inagaki and Uchida films, if only because Furuhata directs his narrative from action to reflection and not the reverse. His Musashi, frozen between action and reflection, as he is between ground and sky in the closing shot, is no less a hero for being multifaceted, but perhaps closer to flesh and blood than to legend.

Whatever the differences in characterization between Furuhata's *Miyamoto Musashi* and other versions, certainly no aspect of it makes a greater impression on a sensory level than its visual style. In obvious comparison with Inagaki's full-lit, softly-focused color "epic," this black-and-white *Miyamoto Musashi* is by any standards more visually imaginative. Admittedly, some of its technologically limited optical effects, specifically crude dissolves and freeze-frames, are of poor quality compared to other productions. *Miyamoto Musashi* demonstrates more of an affinity with the chiaroscuro, fluid camera, and precise compositions of a film like Mori's *Mission: Iron Castle*. Its distinctive and highly developed formal values are often more striking than in the high-budget productions such as *Samurai* or *Zen and Sword*.

The overall visual scheme of Furuhata's film is keyed not only to the notion of Musashi's dynamic, elemental frame of mind but also to the subject/object split between his and the viewer's understanding of the reasons behind that dynamism. In some sequences tight close shots are employed for seventy to eighty percent of the screen time. Such a staging compels the audience not merely to scrutinize Musashi's expression for whatever index of behavior or meaning they may carry, but quickly instills in them an impression of constriction which is mildly claustrophobic. Such a sequence, coupled with the repeated use of deeply textured compositions—which inspire additional viewer tension as foreground and rearground details—compete for attention and do much to externalize Musashi's own sense of being on the edge.

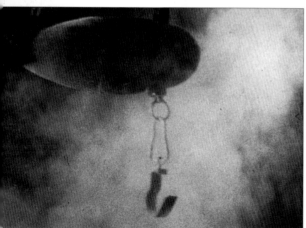

Top: Ei watches while Musashi carves the warrior deity Fudo Myoo.

Center: Ei with the Fudo Myoo in left foreground

Bottom: The counterweight over the fire pit

Because Mikuni's Musashi represses so many of his genuine feelings, simple deviations from normal staging, such as lighting a close shot from the side or choosing a profile angle, inform the spectator graphically that only half of Musashi, man or personality, is visible or on the surface. At the same time, long lenses which reduce the spatial distance between objects and persons suggest that the heightened immediacy of interaction which occurs in the frame's two dimensions is affording the viewer a more accurate, albeit figurative, "view" of the dramatic situation, which the characters in their alienated states may not appreciate.

This is particularly true when Furuhata's inscription charges an object with some additional value. For instance, throughout the scene in which Musashi discusses his dead son and his own ambitions with Ei, the very presence of the carved figure is rich in the symbolic associations already mentioned. Then, by selecting a shot such as the medium close-up of Ei with the statuette in the left foreground, the specific psychology of her love-hate relationship with Musashi is distilled and clarified. She despises not the man but the formal posture of the warrior, which, like the statue, he has assumed. The relationship defined in this scene carries over into the following one and creates a second level of meaning as Ei caresses the carving before selling it to the Yoshiaka school. The Yoshiakas themselves subsequently discern the equation of Musashi and the figurine, which Ei and the viewer have already made. They, too, interact with it. The isolated shot of the damaged carving ending the scene in which the school members discuss ways to kill Musashi might appear unmotivated to the viewer, but the associative pattern previously established makes it an appropriate and natural usage.

The typical effect of Furuhata's stylization is a shifting level of viewer involvement with the film. His rapid transitions—the whip pans from person to person in the crowd as they read Musashi's first public challenge, the foreground clutter, and the unusual lighting—are all elements of distraction. These break up both the narrative as a whole and individual sequences and force the viewer momentarily to stand outside the motion picture. Rather than being facile, these devices help to maintain a balance in the audience's mixed apprehension of Musashi as both hero and villain. Thus Furuhata may perhaps cut away from Musashi's rape of Ei to a shot of a counterweight swaying over a smoldering fire pit to suggest iconically the animal or hellish aspects of Musashi represented by the primordial graphics of the hulking mass of metal and the steam. Equally, if not more significantly, the cutaway diminishes the degree of audience revulsion over Musashi's brutish behavior, at a point just after the semi-buffoonery of the opening scenes when a direct visualization of such action might irremediably distance them from the central character. There are other manipulations of image toward a similar end, such as the slow motion and aural distortion used in Musashi's second duel with the Yoshiaka school. Furuhata is normally content to exploit both the genre convention and the Musashi legend and refrain from inordinate special effects to add "reality" to his swordsmanship. The severest test of verisimilitude in the film is when Musashi amazes an audience of would-be disciples by bisecting a kernel of rice, an extraordinary but less showy display than the scene in *Duel at Ganryu Island* in which Mifune picks flies out of the air with his chopsticks.

TOP: Musashi in the tall grass during the second duel's slow motion sequence

CENTER: Musashi after bisecting the kernel of rice

BOTTOM: Musashi scouts the terrain.

The artificiality of the second duel is a clear exception to that procedure. Its distended movements not only prolong the violence but make it seem more cold-bloodedly destructive, while the inhuman growling noise on the soundtrack adds a bestial aura. Both serve to invert the effect of the cutaway during the rape. By giving the audience a more alienating perception of the combat than they could have in reality, Furuhata undercuts both their acceptance of Musashi's rationale for the duel and viewer empathy for him as a character. Perhaps most unusual and alienating are the shots Furuhata elects to photograph from Musashi's point of view. The upside-down angle near the film's beginning has previously been described. The increased time and effort a viewer requires just to read such a shot or to remain oriented during the numerous hand-held POVs which occur throughout the picture, most of them panning or running, make it repeatedly as difficult physically to assume Musashi's viewpoint as it is to do so emotionally.

Occasionally the meaningful quality of the images in *Miyamoto Musashi* may alter dramatically within a single shot. For instance, a sustained shot when Musashi examines the terrain at Ichijoji the day before the duel opens with a choker close-up in which the audience initially shares Musashi's "blindness" to the vantage he must discover in the landscape to overcome the Yoshiaka trap. When he moves forward, the

camera travels back, circling a large tree on the side opposite him and stopping in a medium shot. The result, even as Musashi tells himself, "Don't be afraid," is that the camera's movement to a more objective or distant position has figuratively diminished his stature. It reduces the area of the image which his body now occupies and frames him against the massive tree which physically dwarfs him, thus externalizing his loss of confidence. Even more understated is the perceptual change in the extreme low-angle, medium-close shot of the Hanshichiro, the Yoshiaka boy, sitting under that tree the following morning. Such an angle may initially imply that his position is one of exaggerated dominance over the scene of imminent battle between Musashi and a hundred of his men. Only after the shot has been held long enough for the viewer to scan the tree looming up above him and to discern Musashi crouched in its branches, does the actual "meaning" of the choice of angle become apparent.

Finally, beyond any question of affecting viewer empathy or reading of a shot, many of Furuhata's images could be said to function under the same aesthetic as the spare, reflective style of the historical Musashi's line drawings. Mikuni's watchful stance and "thrusting eyes" are drawn from Musashi's actual writings. Going further, a comparison of the author's "Shrike on a Dead Branch" with a close shot of Mikuni's Musashi framed against a similarly shaped twig reveals that Furuhata has also drawn from the real Musashi's painted record of his perceptions. The synthesis on film of Musashi's two "world-views" mentioned at the beginning of this section produce such images as the long lens of Mikuni racing out of the sun toward an opponent. When silhouetted against the flat disc of light or a tight close shot of him in the trance of combat, his eyes are highlighted perhaps with transcendent emptiness, perhaps with demonic energy. This literally fiery presence and the calmly analytical Musashi, who goes over the duel in subjective flashbacks, freezing critical moments as he tells himself to "bend the leg more at the beginning" or "I held back too long," are metaphorically significant in Furuhata's visual conception of the character.

Perhaps the most telling aspect of Furuhata's visualization is that it can recruit the traditional pictorialism of directors such as Kenji Mizoguchi but still derive a figurative

meaning of a variant or even opposing nature. Mizoguchi's own dramatization of Musashi's life, *Miyamoto Musashi* (1944), was produced under the constraining social realities of a country at war. Nevertheless, its ethical values are consistent with Mizoguchi's humanistic viewpoint and colored by a serene resignation, akin to *shushigaku*. Mizoguchi's Musashi is neither boisterous nor bumptious but a soft-spoken and pious Buddhist. When he carves a statue of the warrior deity Fudo Myoo, it is out of religious as much as martial inspiration. It is certainly not, as for Furuhata's Musashi, an activity by which to earn some money and buy food. Despite his scruples, Mizoguchi's character never resembles the guilt-ridden youth of the Inagaki trilogy/Yoshikawa novel. In fact, he is far from youthful. If he has any failing, it is the pride evident in his pronouncements on martial techniques: "The art can be mastered by seeking truth and casting away illusion." Mizoguchi's staging of the Yoshiaka duel is fully as powerful as Furuhata's but underscores an entirely different character emotion. An unbroken traveling shot follows Musashi as he moves sideways across a shadowy hillside, fighting his way down to a well-lit farm field, moving like an avenging angel. The victory accomplished, Mizoguchi suspends the moment of triumph, backs away from the very emotion which sustains Furuhata's Musashi, and merely dissolves away from a frozen tableau.

A wedge of light creates the "demonic" figure

Mizoguchi's moral outlook, like his character's "seeking truth," is tinged with Gnosticism and with the opposition of good and evil, the latter being Kojiro Sasaki, whom Mizoguchi portrays as unabashedly villainous in *jitsuaku* style. Whereas Furuhata's figure exults in combat and killing, Mizoguchi's hero is chastened by it. His final renunciation of human gratification is consistent with his rigid ethics: "I was deluded. My art is not perfect. I must continue to train." It is these very ethics and the valorization of form above all that Furuhata's Musashi and the other major figures of post-War *chambara* challenge.

The real Musashi closed his book of five rings with a discussion of the void that echoes the Heart Sutra (see Chapter Eight):

> In the Way of strategy also those who study as warriors think that whatever they cannot understand in their craft is the void. This is not the true void . . . taking the void as the Way, you will see the Way as Void. In the void is virtue, and no evil.

Opposite page:
TOP: The Yoshiaka heir and Musashi in the tree above him

CENTER, TOP: Musashi and the dead branch

CENTER BOTTOM: Musashi silhouetted against the sun as he charges

BOTTOM: A close shot as Musashi runs out of the sun

CHAPTER FIVE

HIDEO GOSHA

For the samurai to learn
There is only one thing,
One last thing—
To face death unflinchingly.
—Tsukahara Bokuden[1]

Generally speaking the Way of the warrior is
the resolute acceptance of death.
—Miyamoto Musashi[2]

FROM THE INSTABILITY AND PERSONAL ANNIHILATION OF KOBAYASHI to the violent and anarchic constructs of Hideo Gosha, Masahiro Shinoda, and Kihachi Okamoto is a short way in terms of literal progression and passage of years. The emergence of new archetypes in the films of Kurosawa and Kobayashi created a basic definition of the wandering, alienated *ronin* who soon developed into a serial hero. This hero, fused or synthesized from rough-hewn antecedents, is both serious and sardonic, both honor-bound and unscrupulous, both a survivor and self-destructive, even as or perhaps because he searches for personal freedom. The problem for the directors who emerged in the late 1960s is bifocal. First they came to grips with the immediate tradition, both thematic and stylistic, of the previous ten years, in the genre itself and also in concurrent, analogous genres developing outside Japan. They did so while remaining faithful to their own notions of what the historical situation was. In short, they established a new emphasis without completely rupturing the generic expectations of the general audience. Second, they discovered the expressive values to convey not just the enigmatic and subversive position of an actively alienated character in a feudal context but also the interior conflicts of such characters: conditioned to accept the mores of their time and residually dependent upon them for their own sense of identity, but nevertheless rejecting them as void of meaning. In an ironic way, these directors occupy a position similar to their characters relative to the genre itself. On the one hand they are presented with a closed or pre-established generic identity with which to work, an identity substantially defined by and reinforcing, if not glorifying, a feudal system. On the other hand, there is a possibility for breaking away from that system, an open generic potential, grounded in both the post-War evolution of the samurai character and their own appreciation of the genre as a medium for serious expression.

1. GENRE TYPING

The particular methods of Hideo Gosha in relating to his material as "genre" are evident even from his early work in the television version of *Three Outlaw Samurai (Sambiki No Samurai).*[3] Many of the episodes in the series are thematically divided between an almost nostalgic adherence to the notions of chivalry by the three principals, the "outlaw" samurai or *ronin*, and a cynical distrust of institutions. As in the film version of 1964 and in almost all of Gosha's subsequent work, the lives of his characters or how they became "outlaw" is scantily detailed but is implicitly connected to some disillusionment with the codes of the past. These contrary inclinations find expression not just in the opposition of personal valor or honor with objective, social brutality but also in the juxtaposition of heroic introspection with semi-parody, as in *Yojimbo.*

A typical episode of the televised *Three Outlaw Samurai* focused on an appeal for help made to the title characters by persons in need. In the feature an orphaned brother and sister are under threat of death from local gangsters. Early in the course of the narrative, Gosha details a massacre of townspeople by this latter group, so that the question for the outlaw samurai, the usual question for any ostracized heroes, is crystallized. Will they re-involve themselves with everyday society? Will their disdain for biased, contemporary interpretations of justice be overcome by their intrinsic sense of fair play, which disallows the oppression of the weak? For Gosha the contending emotions are distilled by inserts of wide-angle medium close-ups of the attackers from the victims' points of view. Such a shot selection makes the action both more real, when it "subjectifies" or makes it more directly experiential, and less real, for the audience has no equivalent in perception of the actual world of the distorted depth of the wide-angle lens. This visual ambiguity also externalizes the indecisive posture of the principals: empathetic yet detached from the physical effect of the action. What ultimately determines their commitment to assist the imperiled brother and sister is reflex, as exemplified in the "mechanistic" staging of the concluding scene, which is partially a satire of a Western gunfight.

A high-angle long shot opens the sequence and reveals an empty street, windswept and dusty as any in the American West. Three men are stationed in the right foreground (the outlaw samurai) and three more in the left background (the best swordsmen of the local gang). As they move toward each other, they are picked up first by panning medium-close shots that set up an opposing dynamic line of counterdirectional pans. The concentration of the conflict is broken by inserts of the onlooking townsmen represented only by a face half-visible through a torn wall or an eye straining at a knothole. This and the succeeding shots of the men's feet striding in opposite screen directions visually degrade the encounter. The montage of opposing lines is diminished by non-dynamic inserts, and the shots of bulging eyes and bare feet in lock-step are made comic through context. Medium-close shots of the antagonists walking individually toward the camera partially re-establish the sense of imminent violence, as there is an implication of threat whenever someone strides directly at the camera. Instead of photographing the fight itself, Gosha goes back to reaction shots supported by amplified sound effects. Up to this point, the visual usage has both downplayed or undercut the heroic aspects of the combat. It has not lingered on the stylized or ritual conventions of battle. It has kept the viewer spatially distant through the use of long shots and/or long lenses.

When the participants are seen again, it is first in a brief medium-long shot at eye level, then in a series of tight, off angles, tilted and/or low views of individuals frozen in their final lunging or parrying positions. There is an immediate dichotomy between an objective view of the conflict in the distant, eye-level shot and a more revealing, ironic one in close on the figures in contorted positions, made to look grotesque or ridiculous and anti-heroic. Finally, another high-angle long shot re-asserts conventional usage. As the three samurai return their weapons to their scabbards, their opponents fall lifelessly to the ground.

As a narrative event this sequence allows for variable interpretations, if only because the combatants and onlookers are equally mute, silently and effi-ciently fulfilling their generic roles as if according to program. While there are no plot "surprises"—the heroes win and the villains fall—the actual staging is unexpected. The graphic progression from long shot to close shot while main-taining spatial distance, from set-ups which are essentially heroic (high-angle long shot) to neutral (eye-level medium shot) to anti-heroic (off-angle close shot), clarifies and restricts the narrative statement. Violence becomes action of a lower order, not in the sense of a debased act but because it lacks emo-tional engagement or is reflex. As such it is neither exonerated as ritual nor condemned as unnatural. This mechanistic undertone creates an implied pres-ence in Gosha's staging of an unimpeachable, conditioned response which is capable of taking control. Being derived from social structure, this reflex counteracts or short circuits any conscious, anti-social, or even asocial rejec-tion of values. However indirectly stated it may be, it is an awareness of this reflex, knowing that at some level of consciousness they have been condi-tioned by their society, that distinguishes Gosha's heroes.

Tetsuro Tanba as Sakon in
Three Outlaw Samurai

II. VISUAL EXPOSITION: *SECRET OF THE URN* AND *SAMURAI WOLF*

Although *The Secret of the Urn* (*Tange Sazen Hien Iai-Giri*, 1966) and two-part *Samurai Wolf* (*Kiba Okaminosuke*, 1966 and *Kiba Okaminosuke Jikokugari*, *1967*) are Gosha's third through fifth samurai features, they are the best choice for initial consideration because of their thematic simplicity and narrative directness. Unlike *Goyokin* or *Tenchu* or the earlier *Sword of the Beast* (*Kedamono No Ken*, 1965), they are "undated," lacking in typical expository titles which establish day, month, or even year. There is a clue to their focus in their Japanese titles, all of which allude to specific characters by their names, Tange Sazen and Okaminosuke, rather than abstract or purely figurative concepts. Before the movie even starts, the titles anticipate a clearly defined central character and a dramatic conflict based more on personalities than ideologies. "Directness" is used in the two films' sub-plots. Their complications are self-contained, remaining relatively uncolored by the social history of the time and requiring only the broadest genre knowledge. This provides an opportunity to isolate in these films certain interior structures of Gosha's work that are primarily visual or dependent on a visually oriented sensory response. Being both actively and passively expressive, these structures contribute to or compound the viewer's narrative understanding.

The prologue of *The Secret of the Urn* begins in darkness. A door swings open letting in light and disclosing the bare walls of a dungeon. The visual perception of thick stone glistening under the shaft of light is coupled with a slight reverberation on the soundtrack to create the impression of an impacted subterranean chamber. Compositional instability is then added to the ominous connotations of this obscurity. A three shot frames Samanosuke (later to become Tange Sazen) and two others, as they enter the chamber. It is disrupted by the presence of pillars in the foreground, fracturing the composition. As a captured woman spy is tortured for information, there are cuts which move directly from high-angle to low-angle medium-close shots, an alternation which, reinforced by shifts in lighting from side light to back light to front light, fractures any sense of visual consistency. In other words the audience must constantly reorient itself to angle and lighting. At the same time, recurrent inserts of Samanosuke, both close and medium close, isolate the main character and at least partially subjectify the scene. Its disequilibrium, which in the organization of shots both "surrounds" Samanosuke and derives from him, is associated by the viewer with the isolated figure.

The notion of equilibrium becomes even more central in the next scene, when Samanosuke rides out with Kojuro, his fiancée's brother and the man whom he has been instructed to kill. Under the establishing exterior view of the men on horseback, the camera is traveling sideways, which again tends to disallow stability, even in long shot. The two men dismount and their verbal confrontation is staged with intercut medium-close shots from an extreme low angle. These suggest an equality between the two men, as neither is permitted to dominate the other through exclusive framing in low angle and being more proximate to the lens. There is also a persistent off-angled or unbalanced undercurrent. The usage is subtly unconventional. Whereas eye-level medium-close shots might oppose the men within one plane or, at least, create a stronger sense of a stage line rather than disorienting the viewer, the intercut low angles will not permit a sense of normality.

Added to the informing values in this use of the low angle is the general context of instability held over from the previous scene. At this point, the audience must begin causally to relate this effect to Samanosuke. Not only is such an association common in the genre, but it is expressively reinforced when Kojuro, the most immediate antagonist, backs off. Normally, the camera would tilt down with the action in order to keep his head in the upper part of the frame and would narrow the angle off from horizontal—that is, it would reset closer to a normal or eye-level set-up. In this instance there is no tilting, so that Kojuro appears to sink lower and lower in the frame. His attempt to "level off" by backing away coincides expressively with an attempt to avoid the precarious and chaotic fight with Samanosuke. But he fails on both literal and figurative levels.

All this again identifies Samanosuke as either the cause of disruption or its expressive cipher. In terms of genre conventions, this is not an unnatural or unusual reading of the character for an audience to be asked to make. The associations are far from absolute, and the visual usage is not all that extraordinary. If anything, the most violent disorientation of the prologue is yet to come, and it is not primarily affected by visual means. A group of six men suddenly appear and attack Samanosuke, after he has been wounded killing Kojuro. This event is not narratively anticipated but surprises both Samanosuke and the viewer. The implication is that his own Nakamura clansmen are the assailants. Gosha uses a long lens to photograph the dark figures coming over a low hill, making their strides seem slower, more deliberate. The actual fight is a mixture of perspectives. A traveling shot from the attackers' point of view stalks Samanosuke relentlessly. A quick reverse is followed by a closer shot of his slashed eye. The sequence concludes with a slow-motion view of his severed arm flying from his body and a POV of the sky from the bottom of the ditch, into which the presumably dead samurai has been thrown.

So ends the prologue on a note that is subjective in the midst of abundant visual confusion. In this way, Gosha economically sets up the audience's genre expectations for the entire film that is to follow. These events, a reluctant assasination on clan orders and a personal betrayal, adhere to an easily discerned archetypal scheme. They serve to alienate if not destroy the hero; but the formal surprise in this opening plot twist is perfectly acceptable in the frame of genre convention. There is little if anything that is original or distinctive in the events of the prologue. What is distinctive are, first of all, Gosha's staging as examined above and, second, the subsidiary expectations which taken together this staging and the events themselves engender.

The visual confusion of the attack on Samanosuke, the shifting points of view and violent special effects, serve as a final, irrevocable focus of viewer attention. The "fact" of his death is obviously false, even though he does not immediately reappear and no specific images offer proof of his survival. If anything, the color change and fade-out from his last POV in the ditch conventionally suggest the opposite: that he is dead. These shots cannot alter the viewer's generic dependence upon Samanosuke's presence as "hero." Obviously, Samanosuke is the star part portrayed by the film's principal actor, so the audience must realize from that and/or from advance publicity that he has merely undergone the physical transformation required if he is to return as Tange Sazen. His "resurrection" is generically preordained. Beyond that, Gosha has imagistically forged a link between Samanosuke/Tange Sazen and the chaotic/disruptive forces which drive the narrative forward.

The introduction of the dilemma of the Yagyu clan, which is trying to find their lost urn with its secret inscription, and the other expository sequences after the prologue, form a narrative pause after the climactic attack on Samanosuke. There is a title superimposed over the fade-in: "One year after that . . . Chiyoda Castle in Edo," which gives the first suggestion of time as a narrative dimension, time which the audience knows a still-living Samanosuke would require to recover from his injury. It also introduces the first tranquil images in the film: the opening shot is a placid, day-lit panorama of the castle gardens, ringed with blossoming trees and a pond with waterfowl, all the connotations of a vernal rebirth. This shift offers the viewer what might be termed a "breather," a few moments to assimilate and interpret the events of the prologue. The visual scheme during this pause is also altered. Unusual angles and contrasting lighting do not disappear entirely but are at least partially subsumed into a less energetic, plot-developing mise-en-scène. Rather than from the images, dramatic tension is built on ironic, narrative revelations: the fact that one of the shogunate ministers enjoying the Yagyus' confidence is secretly working against them and the narrow escape of the unidentified intruder who overhears this minister conferring with his accomplices.

What is most significant is that, although Samanosuke/Tange Sazen is literally absent from the scene, no strong, antagonistic figure other than the minister, who is clearly destined to be a mental rather than physical participant in any later fights, emerges. In fact, except for the *ronin* who calls himself the "God of Death" (a villainous conceit carried over from *Three Outlaw Samurai*—see below) and has a minimal role, Tange Sazen's major competition for the urn will come not from among the minister's co-conspirators but from Genzaburo, the chief retainer of the Yagyus, who acts out of fealty rather than self-interest.

Appropriately, given the sardonic tone of *Secret of the Urn,* when the ill-used and understandably alienated Samanosuke re-appears as Tange Sazen, he situates himself in a moral middle-ground. His first exchange with Genzaburo comes after he strides suddenly out of a fisherman's hut among the contending forces and places his sandal down on the wayward urns. "Folks seem to have died for a useless pot," he proclaims, not swayed by Genzaburo's entreaties, "I'll take it, so there won't be any more trouble after this." As might be expected, there has been a significant change in Sazen's attitude as well as in his physical aspects: he is no longer a samurai, a loyal retainer, in mind or body. This physical and

spiritual alteration places Sazen in a position familiar to any *ronin* or outlaw cast out by feudal society. The viewer must presume that he dragged himself half-dead out of the ditch and put on the mantle of a *ronin* such as Sanjuro. In this role, he must return to question the tradition of *giri* and offer sarcastic observations on empty codes of honor.

Most of Tange Sazen's remarks bluster with self-assurance. He confidently advises a dozen assailants to "attack me, if you want to die" and defends the urn simply because "I'm beginning to like it." it is also obvious that, beneath the transformation, Samanosuke is still trying to reconcile both his disfigurement and his disillusionment to his old beliefs. "Listen," he counsels the boy who first ran into his hut with the urn, "a samurai isn't as strong as you think. He just has a sword. A samurai isn't strong at all." His response to Genzaburo, when this still faithful samurai has rescued him from Gunraku and asks mockingly if Sazen is "going to commit *hara-kiri,* according to bushido" is more sober. After laughing hoarsely Sazen concedes that "until I became a monster, I didn't realize how foolish it was." The entire thematic thrust of *Secret of the Urn* is contained within that line. A man must become a monster to comprehend the monstrosities which surround him, but it remains much simpler to key plot and dialogue to such a theme than to develop images which are expressive of "monstrousness."

Top: Kinnosuke Nakamura as Tange Sazen in *Secret of the Urn*

Center: Tange Sazen and the Yagyu urn

Bottom: Tange Sazen's challenge— "Attack me, if you want to die"

Tange Sazen (Kinnosuke Najamura) and Fuji (Keiko Owaji)

Tange Sazen (1982) TOP: Sazen (Tatsuya Nakadai) holds the "urn worth a million ryo." which casts a fateful, noose-like shadow over his back; BOTTOM, a much older Szaen laughs at the concept of a "God of Death"

Opposite page:
TOP: Okaminosuke (Isao Natsuyagi) brings a dead highwayman into town.

CENTER, TOP: Okaminosuke and the blind girl

CENTER, BOTTOM: Okaminosuke trims his beard.

BOTTOM: Okaminosuke under attack

The problem is that the surfeit of both generic and visual violence creates an emphatic, almost overheated, context. The incidents of violence move toward a saturation point where the mere fact of their occurence is no longer sufficient to be shocking or disruptive to the audience. Accordingly, it becomes increasingly difficult to underscore a thematically pertinent scene through conventional staging. Because of this emphatic context, the underplaying in Sazen's remark on *hara-kiri* echoes his earlier meeting with Gunraku, Ultimately the core issue for Sazen is now simple: "I don't want to be anyone's kept dog."

All the dialogue is as strongly expressive of Sazen's personal rebellion against monstrousness. There is a clear visual equivalent to this in the duel with Gunraku's henchmen. The surface calm and reflection of the words and the visual simplicity of the editing scheme contrasts markedly with the chaos of the surrounding sequences. The notion of disequilibrium in the visual exposition of *Secret of the Urn* is thus extended or externalized. In Gosha's television remake, *Tange Sazen: Ken fu! Hyakuman ryo no Tsubo* (1982), he adapts the earlier script and, a decade and a half later, occasionally mirrors the visual style of Secret of the Urn; but the casting of Tatsuya Makadai as Sazen changes the emotional dynamic. Nakadai's older and somewhat languorous Sazen is a wearier figure that Kinnosuke Nakamura's earlier incarnation. Nakadai's initial encounter with Genzaburo is more disinterested that defiant. His primary antagonist Taiken (Isao Natsuyage, the star of *Samurai Wolf*) is more menacing and more thoughtful than Gunraku. Gosha's extended use of humor, night scenes, and constricted staging, create a darker variant on the same story. Although the viewer knows Sazen must prevail in the final duel, Taiken's remake ("I'm a wild dog without any owner now") is aclear reflection of Sazen's own attitude. In both versions, the flux between scenes of violence and reflection engender and sustain an underlying emotional tension. Even where the shot or shots in a sequence are not intrinsically dynamic or imbalanced, a simple deviation from what is expected in genre context may still allow them to contribute their own form of emphasis.

Samurai Wolf contains an even clearer, almost "classic" example of tension through a montage of contrasting textures—specifically Okaminosuke's duel while the blind girl, who has appealed to him for help, plays the harp. The intercutting of these events creates two sets of polarities. There is dramatic discord between the girl's frenzied hand and body movements, between the highly agitated motions as she depresses the strings and the jerk of her wrist captured in a close shot as she rapidly plucks the notes, and the lack of peril in her position secure in a rear room. The reverse is true of the stance and expression of Okaminosuke, who is calmly shielding his eyes from the sun despite the vulnerability of his position, in the open road, in danger of attack by several opponents waiting all around for the moment to strike. After the fight has begun, the constant intercutting from the road—where Okaminosuke is dueling for his life and where viewer apprehension is focused—to the harp playing inside is a conventional way of protracting the dramatic tension.

What distinguishes this montage is Gosha's zoom scheme or zoom editing.[4] Repeatedly Gosha moves from a shot that encompasses the entirety of a scene's action into a detail which runs expressively counter to the whole: into a close shot of the girl's fingers moving violently over the strings or into a close-up of Okaminosuke passing effortlessly through a crowd of enemies and easily cutting them down. The usage in both instances is so "inappropriate" that it makes the reflective action seem, upon closer inspection, excessively violent and the violent act seem almost reflective. The parallel editing as a whole becomes disquieting and subversive, running counter to the audience's normal expectations and ultimately creating a visual irony in *Samurai Wolf* analogous to the sardonic thrust of Tange Sazen's spoken remarks in *Secret of the Urn*.

It cannot be asserted that all or even most of the images in *Samurai Wolf* are used as unconventionally or imaginatively. The film opens with formula scenes of a wandering *ronin* crossing open country and entering a dusty, ramshackle town much like that in *Yojimbo*. Gosha does add a few quirks, for example the nervous habit Okaminosuke has of stroking his beard or idly trimming it with the pair of iron scissors he carries in his sash—scissors that, inevitably, end up planted in an assailant's chest. Most of *Samurai Wolf*'s characters and situations are taken from stock. While it may be a bit simplistic, it could be said that Gosha assembles these clichés in the manner of a Sergio Leone Western, using violence, if not nonchalantly, at least non-dramatically. Gosha plays a spate of expendable, villainous gargoyles off against a preoccupied hero, all to anticipate and add counterpoint to the ineluctable final duel.

In that duel Okaminosuke must face an opponent of more clearly equal talents than any of Tange Sazen's. His combat with the blind girl's former fiancée, who up to that point has acted as Okaminosuke's ally under an unspoken truce, constitutes a compromise to the generic norm. This

may make *Secret of the Urn* the more consistently unconventional of the two films. Nonetheless, Gosha builds effectively to that confrontation in *Samurai Wolf*, working from an established pattern of balanced intercutting between the two men in earlier scenes, where their commensurate abilities as swordsman were suggested, and sustaining that suggestion through the shot selection of the closing sequence. Low-angle zooms into medium-close shot, on both of them and long-lens, profile two-shots, which flatten perspective and downplay physical distinctions, help to make their near identical fighting stances mirror images of each other.

Such a visual equation of protagonist and antagonist is never really made in *Secret of the Urn*. Sazen dispatches Ikkaku, the gargantuan "kept dog" of Gunraku, with inordinate facility. Although there are intercut low-angle shots of both men and a balanced two shot from the side, which creates a momentary tension of image, given its position near the center of the film, the outcome of this encounter cannot be in doubt. The viewer knows that Sazen must emerge victorious and continue on to the conclusion of the movie. Since this tension of image is somewhat at odds with genre expectation it becomes, like the disruptive and deceptive editing scheme described earlier, visually ironic. The viewer appreciates what the narrative outcome must be, yet that does not nullify a sensory response to such tensing devices. The opponent who intercepts Sazen at the conclusion on the highway outside of town is no real threat either. For although this challenger is the self-christened "death-god"—a man whose name has unmistakeable implications and who successfully impersonated Sazen in assaults on the Yagyu retainers—the simple low-angle shot of Sazen striding confidently into the frame moments before the "death-god" steps from hiding vigorously re-states the former's dominance and accurately predicts his ultimate triumph. In the television remake, where an actor of generic statute portrays the "death god," Gosha's staging is more conventional and opens with tight, balanced close-ups which undercut Sazen's dominance.

Triumph, of course, is relative in *Secret of the Urn*, for killing this last man neither restores Samanosuke/Tange Sazen's lost limb nor alleviates his quasi-schizophrenic mental disturbance. Tange Sazen lacks the purgative resolution of a genuine test of his skills. He lacks political inhibitions, as evidenced by his real and symbolic anti-social acts. When cornered in the imperial gardens, Sazen doesn't hesitate to shout from a high tower so that all can hear: "Do you know, Mr. Shogun, you aren't so bright! You've been Gunraku's puppet." Even though he is formally pardoned and survives all the attacks on his person, the generic elements are arranged to form a conspicuously ironic finale, in which the "death-god" is dispatched almost as an afterthought by a grimly smiling one-armed hero. So Samanosuke remains

Tange Sazen, remains ostracized, and—in the film's characteristic closing long shot, silhouetted against a red sky and partially concealed by reeds in the foreground—he walks off alone until his figure melts from sight.

III. THE OUTSIDERS: *THREE OUTLAW SAMURAI*

Although it may be chronologically inexact to turn back at this point and consider Gosha's first feature, *Three Outlaw Samurai* is an appropriate work through which to explore Gosha's thematic preoccupations. The film opens with a view of a roadway, wet and slimy after a rainfall. A straw sandal comes down into the frame, sinks slightly into the mud, and pushes free. After a few more steps the whole man is visible, arms akimbo beneath a tattered kimono, swords positioned for a quick draw. While the main titles roll over the shot, the lone figure wanders idly across the countryside, the image of a stray dog searching for shelter under a still overcast sky. Finally, he sights an abandoned mill and quickens his pace in its direction.

Such an opening, constructed entirely of dismal grays and silent once the title music has faded, is neither unusual nor wholly unexpected in generic terms. The audience realizes that something is in the offing, possibly in the

TOP: Low-key lighting captures Tetsuro Tanba as Sakon Shiba and Mikijiro Hira (right) as Einosuke Kikyo.

BOTTOM: Low-key lighting and staging in depth in *Three Outlaw Samurai*

mill, but as the man seems more apprehensive about the weather than about highwaymen demanding his probably empty purse, the viewer has an immediate confidence in the resilience of this somewhat shabby "hero." What he discovers in the mill is a bit more out of the ordinary, neither a band of brigands waiting to be killed nor a helpless young farmwoman to be violated, but three cringing peasants and the kidnapped daughter of their over-taxing magistrate. Shiba, the *ronin*, assesses their chances of success with a shrug and assumes the convenient attitude of non-involvement. Beneath his fatalistic jibes at the farmers, a thematic pattern is already being suggested: the outsider stumbling into a pre-existing social turmoil and discovering in it an opportunity to be re-enfranchised. Specifically, Shiba enters the film as a complete alien, a dirty, sandalled foot and featureless back intruding without identity into the frame. He shortly becomes a spectator, as he remarks while propped up on his elbow in a crude bunk, "I'll enjoy the show." Before too many minutes more have passed, he has prevented a group of armed men from rescuing the local magistrate's daughter and is wondering aloud why he has been foolish enough to get mixed up in someone else's quarrel.

After this initial characterization has been sketched in and the narrative situation economically thrown into motion, the second and third of the three figures promised by the title are introduced simultaneously in the dungeon of the magistrate's manor house. Kikyo, the arrogant black-kimonoed bodyguard, looks on while a prisoner is tested as a potential recruit. Sakura, a scruffy, corpulent spear carrier asleep on some soiled matting, repels the unwarranted assault on his slumber and mutters a protest against execution without trial. These two, the simple-minded, earthy street brawler and the silent, aloof mercenary, form a familiar composite with the world-weary but honor-defending Shiba—for, if not a sense of honor, what else precipitates his decision to aid the peasants? Compare, for example, the roughly analogous characterizations of Kikuchiyo and Kyuzo in *The Seven Samurai*, who find themselves in the similar plot position of helping defenseless farmers. Yet for all the archetypal resemblances that might be cited, Gosha's expansion of narrative within the first third of his *Three Outlaw Samurai* differs markedly from the method of Kurosawa. While Kurosawa from *Seven Samurai* through *Yojimbo* and *Sanjuro* is inventing situations to satirize genre stereotypes and, more importantly, to develop character, Gosha seems to operate from an inverse formula: using a

TOP: Gosha's variation on *Yojimbo*—Shiba tosses a hatpin in the air to determine which direction the three scruffy *ronin* will take at the end of *Three Outlaw Samurai*.

BOTTOM: A cloud of dust will completely obscure the protagonists as they walk off in the final shot of *Three Outlaw Samurai*.

kind of "pre-set" character to develop situation. Obviously, the work of the two men does not fall into any absolute opposition but, as an operative generalization, Kurosawa's films might be said to possess a narrative drive based on plot twists and unforeseen incidents, an emphasis which makes it easier to establish the stress conditions through which Kurosawa's heroes define themselves. Dealing more frequently with the literally unexpected makes it more difficult for Kurosawa to manipulate genre expectation and its frustration/fulfillment.

Gosha's approach is both more genre-integrated and more "natural," not because it is "truer-to-life" but because situations do not spring full-blown or unanticipated into the midst of the narrative. They derive instead from character interaction which the audience has witnessed. In a very real sense, Kurosawa in a film like *Yojimbo* did not—perhaps could not, because of the then shifting state of the genre—take full advantage of generic typing but spent much of the narrative time filling in Yojimbo's personality, even indulging in a certain redundancy of image and dialogue to do so. Gosha on the other hand exploits the audience's knowledge of the genre in that first silent sequence which follows Shiba to the mill, directing them with visual clues toward a fairly accurate notion of who this unnamed man in gray may be and what he may become. It is Gosha's characters who spring fully or at least partially drawn into the scene, as Gosha pencils them in with a generic shorthand that the viewer knows how to read.

The most obvious example of information which the spectator receives without "knowing" it in *Three Outlaw Samurai* is the identity of the three principals. There are no bits of expository dialogue, nothing certainly like the Leone device in *The Good, the Bad, and the Ugly* of freezing the action to superimpose the appropriate title over a character's face and so indicate which of the title figures he is. Yet by the end of *Three Outlaw Samurai*'s second sequence the audience realizes that all of the "outlaws" have been introduced to them and that, even though they may be on opposing sides of the dispute at that moment, Shiba, Sakura, and Kikyo will eventually end up together.

How the viewer assimilates genre information is an essential question and merits a brief digression. Genre types are identified by a variety of indicators. How much of this does the viewer take from the film itself, that is from the sounds and images irrespective of their genre identity? How much comes from generic constructions? Finally how much is from expectations which are nongeneric, for instance, the designation of "three" in the title and the viewer's familiarity with the actors or stars and assignment of each role's importance through billing in the main titles or on the posters in the theater lobby? Filmmakers understand how to incorporate these expected viewer responses into their work. In fact, what distinguishes many genre filmmakers, what is evident in their individual films, is this very awareness of how to manipulate exposition, staging, and genre expectation for maximum dramatic impact. If Gosha does depend more heavily on the average spectator's *a priori* knowledge of the genre, if he assumes a base level of understanding for that spectator and builds significantly on it, using it like points on a graph from which to extrapolate a dramatic character curve, then a film by Gosha relies on that genre expectation for viewer engagement. That is not to say that a viewer who does not speak the national language of a given film or does not appreciate the idiosyncrasies of the culture which produced it cannot perceive the genre manipulations. Genre, beyond all that may have been claimed of or for it in this study or any other, is something quite distinct from language or culture or any "reality." It is distilled from all of the above in an ongoing process but most heavily dependent on the content of other fiction of its own type. The simple designation of the protagonists in *Three Outlaw Samurai* trancends *chambara*, because Western—both geographically Western and generically Western—film is another expressive reality which the filmmaker has incorporated into his own catalog of values. Perhaps the best and probably only proof of this transcendent if ill-defined faculty of genre is that the English-speaking viewer unfamiliar with even the most rudimentary of samurai film conventions may still with no less accuracy than a Japanese viewer read the indicators and pick out the three outlaw samurai.

This elaborate process of building from pre-conceived types allows Gosha specifically to fill in the details of character with considerable economy. He is not required to use expository time to explain actions *or* attitudes. Gosha establishes a scheme of situation from character, so, in turn, thematic statements appear to be less imposed on the narrative by an outside personality than emanating from the figures actually caught up in the film's events. It is this second capability in a motion picture like *Three Outlaw Samurai* which makes it possible for a character such as Shiba to offer observations from both sides, from within and without the film. In one sense, Shiba is a fully-formed personality with a full and presumably eventful generic past who happens onto an existing situation, interacts with it for the course of the film, and leaves it at the end. In another, more literal sense, Shiba and the others have no existence beyond the film. What the first sense makes possible is for the viewer to regard the entire movie as but a few days of indeterminate significance in the whole span of Shiba's generic identity or "life." His reflections and remarks emerge not only from the film's reality, from the various sequences which actually appear on screen, but also from the unspecified, generic reality which creates him and constitutes his "history." In short, when Shiba says, "the farmers acted bravely—a samurai can do no less" he draws a conclusion based both on the actions of the farmers, which the audience has witnessed along with him, and also based his conception of himself as an honor-bound individual, which antedates any of the film's actions. It is precisely at those points, when Shiba's (or any character's) consciousness synthesizes the realities of film and genre, that Gosha makes the most direct thematic statements.

Of course, such a method of thematic statement is hardly unique to Gosha. But to return to an earlier comparison, what distinguishes Shiba's above remark from that of a typical Kurosawa character is the investiture of a solid generic identity before the statement is made and the lack of character revelation contained in it. Although there is general information in the expository title at the beginning of *Yojimbo,* neither Sanjuro nor Shiba ever tell their back story to another character; and yet the viewer knows it. When Sanjuro shouts at the peasant family he has just rescued—"If you cry, I'll kill you—I hate pathetic people!"—he says something surprising, something poignant and revealing about himself first, and about social institutions which create the atmosphere for his antipathetic sentiments second or not at all. Shiba's belief that "a samurai can do no less" confirms nothing about his attitude which the audience did not, at minimum, strongly suspect. What the words and the circumstances in which they are spoken elucidate is the "larger picture," encompassing in a single, terse line implications of the repressive structures which affect samurai and peasant alike. As regards individual viewer response, the specific effect of word choice and intonation are difficult to analyze precisely. Nonetheless, there are often telling distinctions in word choice in the work of Kurosawa and Gosha. There are strongly active verbs ("cry," "hate," "kill") and first-person pronouns in Sanjuro's statement. The stress is on self. Shiba's substantive "a samurai" may situationally refer to himself and his own feelings, but it is a general noun and in the third person. The verb structure, "can do no less," is negative and auxiliary, so that the stress is on indirectness, on the objective rather than the personal. Again it would be far from accurate to claim that all such statements in Gosha's work are dramatic generalizations or that none are in Kurosawa's. What is accurate is that Gosha lays a groundwork which makes it easier and sometimes unavaoidable for the viewer to move from the narratively specific to the thematically general.

At this point, it may be anticlimactic to assert that the thematic statements of *Three Outlaw Samurai* are fairly conventional; and yet they are. All the notions of rebellion, unity, betrayal, and social despair are generated through narrative and pinpointed or elaborated by the personages—a rather straightforward procedure. The genre itself generates a wide but not necessarily infinite range of potential themes. What separates a film directed by Gosha from that by Kurosawa or anyone else is the mode of expression, quite often ironic or foreshadowing, as much as any particular expression itself.

With respect to dialogue, a few examples may clarify the process. Sakura's off-handed killing of one of the farmers who attacks him while he is relieving himself by the roadside is bitterly ironic, as he muses, "What made him do that? Reckless fellow!" The farmer's death is reduced to a brief pause in the flow of Sakura's urine. It also foreshadows Sakura's later moral dilemma: first, whether to confess this murder, committed while he was still part of the magistrate's faction, to the wife of his victim; and eventually whether to abandon his comrades and run off with her. When Sakura returns from a momentary flight with the farmer's wife to help Shiba and Kikyo combat the clan forces sent in to quell the rebellion, he shouts, even as he cuts down several men, "Shiba, I've done you wrong. I deserve to die. Kill me." Shiba's reply is "too busy," not so much out of sarcasm as to reorient his friend to the priorities.

TOP: Shiba (Tetsuro Tamba, left) and Kikyo (Mikijiro Hira) exhausted by the final battle

CENTER: A dark composition of Kikyo (Mikijiro Hira) in his room

BOTTOM: Shadow play as Kikyo fights the "death God."

The primary reading of the first example depends rather heavily on the viewer's appreciation of Sakura's brash but basically good nature from genre type. Otherwise his words must seem callous or cruelly sardonic. Beyond that, the line of dialogue also functions as an ironic portent, tying in directly with the subsequent thematic suggestion that deception and betrayal are not the exclusive province of villains. Sakura's self-deprecation near the end of the film is equally brash and ironic. Superficially it makes him a kind of straight man, setting up Shiba's curt, somewhat mocking response; but that simple "too busy" also affirms that deception and betrayal are redeemable through action. Taken independently these examples have diverse narrative functions. Thematically they share a common ground. Taken independently the characters express only themselves. Thematically they manifest a consistent general attitude.

A final example of this sense of "exterior" constructions or meanings, even in characters of very limited typing or depth, are the remarks of the two killers dispatched to eliminate the gang of roughnecks the local magistrate had conscripted to meet the emergency. Their exchange—"What did the magistrate say?" "Kill!" "Who are you?" "Gods of Death"—first introduces the conceit of Gunraku's henchman in *Secret of the Urn* and is so conspicuously figurative as to seem slightly unreal. The emotionless words are spoken with a kind of savage facetiousness, as the two men draw their weapons with a deadly, thoroughly composed precision. The words then assume a bloody and literal reality as the men methodically annihilate the score of discarded hirelings. Gosha takes them at their words, making them inhuman, making them perhaps more like soulless engines of destruction than "gods of death," but certainly not like men.

The distinctions between figurative and thematic expressions in Gosha are occasionally hazy, possibly because many of the thematic generalities in his films are inferred through figurative usage. The "gods of death" conceit is, at first, purely figurative and personal—that is, meaningful only to the speakers. Its translation into literal action and the grisly absorption of its meaning by the killers' victims imply the recurring Gosha theme of mechanical or conditioned violence. Although reinforced by the composition and staging, which has the two killers moving silently among the trees while their prey try clumsily to flee, never wasting a stroke or misstepping, moving with the flow of the pans and from rearground to foreground several times, a complex trope such as this is constructed principally from plot and dialogue. More purely visual is the combat between Kikyo and the "death gods" later in the film. Here Gosha tranforms the antagonists into shadows on a wall screen, depersonifies them through a manipulation of image alone, which admits all the metaphorical implications of "shadow play." It also equates Kikyu with his opponents via a two-dimensional reduction similar to the mirror-image near the conclusion of *Samurai Wolf.*

This scene among numerous others takes place within the broadest and most pervasive metaphor of the entire film, that of darkness, for fully half of the action is set at night, much of it in moonlit exteriors. This succession of night sequences permits a variety of figurative readings from an overhanging, political "unenlightenedness" to the personal despair of a dark night of the soul. The more immediate metaphor comes via dramatic lighting or the visual "loss of identity," which a figure literally undergoes upon stepping into the shadows.

In general, Gosha's imagery in this first feature film is less concentrated on adding metaphorical value than in controlled dynamism and a visual expression of sensation. For instance, there is a long-lens panning shot, a favorite Kurosawa technique, which follows Shiba after his escape from the manor house dungeon. The nature of the optics, foreshortening and reducing the background to blurred streaks, makes his flight seem faster than it "really" is. When he hides under a building, even a static long lens can inject visual instability by causing figures and objects to flash by the foreground, breaking up the shot's concentration as a cacophony of shouts and alarms punctuate the soundtrack. During the final battle with the clan retainers, long lenses alternately accelerate the crossing action, while views of men rushing directly toward the camera render the same slowing effect, as in the attack on Samanosuke at the beginning of *Secret of the Urn*. Combined with traveling and panning, the lens selection gives the audience the sense of a closing circle around the three protagonists.

The use of foreground clutter is not as extensive in *Three Outlaw Samurai* as in later Gosha films; but it does appear as an externalization of emotion. There is, for example, a medium-close shot of Aya through the bars of a side-gate after she has said good-bye to Shiba and is watching his escape. The realization that she is now separated from him both physically and by all the standards of the caste system is translated into a visual construction by the foreground objects. This last usage also implies a kind of subjectification of image, a clear attempt to convey character sentiment or sensation by visual methods. When the cook Omitsu rescues Shiba, there are sudden tilting movements of the camera, which are timed to the stabbing of the guard and her own fatal wound as if to convey the physical shock of being

BELOW: Scene stills from
Three Outlaw Samurai

pierced by a dagger. These are obvious subjective images which compare with those of Motome's death in *Hara-Kiri*. More complex are the two zoom shots, into the manor door and down an interior corridor, when Shiba comes back to kill the magistrate. The fact that they are intercut with close shots of Shiba, exhausted from the fighting but driven on by his outrage at the magistrate's treachery, make them unmistakeably subjective images or substantives for what Shiba is seeing. The rapid zoom effect, however, is not to be taken as some preternatural faculty of his eye, but as an expression of his intense desire to find and kill a man, so that his "mind's eye" rushes forward through the manor searching for his prey. This kind of manipulation of image causes the viewer to coexperience not merely what a character is seeing but also what he may be feeling, physically and/or emotionally.

One final usage which should be examined before moving on to Gosha's later samurai films is the development of visual tension, principally through sustained camera and depth of field. The former effect, as noted earlier in the chapter on Kurosawa, depends on viewer anticipation that a cut will normally be made after so many seconds have passed. When that cut is withheld, it can, in conjunction with the actual content of the shots, create a strong dramatic impact when the cut finally occurs. Perhaps the best illustration of both sustained camera and depth of field in Gosha's early films is in *Secret of the Urn*, specifically in the escape of Sazen and Fuji with the urn early in the film. As they try to elude their pursuers across the rooftops, Gosha combines the spatial tension of repeated movement from foreground to rearground with that of shot duration. The climactic set-up in this elaborately staged sequence begins with Fuji jumping from a balcony in the near ground. The camera is set at an oblique angle to the wall behind her, so that it forms a receding diagonal in the frame. The shot is held while she maintains her position in the left foreground, turning and firing at the men behind her, a staging which runs counter to the eye's natural inclination to follow the line of the wall toward the vanishing point. Finally, Sazen enters the background at that precise point, and the camera rack focuses to the darker area in the rear where Sazen exchanges blows with several black-clad figures. He remains the new center of attraction in his white-colored garments amid a flurry of sparks which literally fly from the clashing sword blades. After some seconds more, Sazen extricates himself and runs forward to rejoin Fuji. Since there is no cut, the shot must record his entire movement. They exit together. The viewer, expecting the tension of the sustained camera is about to be broken by a cut and surveying the emptied frame in anticipation, may begin to relax. But the shot is held; and as the eye again moves down the diagonal of the wall, there is another rack focus to the rearground plane as more pursuers appear and rush forward after Sazen and Fuji. This single shot, which itself is taken from a complicated sequence, contains in its usages and effects a multiplicity of expressive values. The concerted action of sustained camera, depth of field, angle, and lighting does create a definite and complex emotional response in the viewer. Since the viewer never really expects that Sazen will perish, suspense may well depend more heavily on staging than on content for its impact. By forcing the audience to reorient its focus, to reread the continuing shot while waiting for a more typical cut to another angle, Gosha compels suspense even in that viewer who is confident that Sazen will not die.

IV. PERSONAL REBELLION AND SOCIAL IDENTITY: *SWORD OF THE BEAST* AND *GOYOKIN*

Sword of the Beast:
TOP: Mikijiro Hira as Gennosuke

BOTTOM: Go Kato as Yamane and Shima Iwashita as Taka

Personal rebellion in one form or another is the central concern of all of Gosha's *chambara.* It is the principal, human force in contention with Gosha's conception of depersonalized, feudal society. What distinguishes *Sword of the Beast* and *Goyokin* in this regard is the explicitness of that personal rebellion. Yuki Gennosuke in *Sword of the Beast* and Magobei Wakizaka in *Goyokin* are clan retainers—although Magobei is older and of higher rank—who pride themselves in having risen above the traditional status of their families. Magobei is from a low-caste family but has attained a more elevated station through a judicious marriage and unimpeachable reputation. Gennosuke is not born of a samurai family at all. More importantly, both are men of strong conscience, individual in their interpretations of honor and too proud to accept compromise. Following the genotype, this *hubris* is what precipitates a crisis situation for both, what divides them between personal ideals and duty to clan in classic *giri/ninjo* conflict, and what ultimately compels them to abandon their fealty and their fellows. In superficial character terms, Gennosuke and Magobei are closer to Tange Sazen than any of the three outlaw samurai or Okaminosuke in that they are former clansmen and possess a specifc past relationship with feudal institutions. Among the latter characters, not even Kikyo in *Three Outlaw Samurai* is a retainer in the sense of being part of a family or tradition of samurai, having been hired on the strength of his swordplay not his clan connections. Very unlike Tange Sazen,

the alienation of Gennosuke and Magobei is not thrust upon them by any tangible exterior forces. They suffer neither personal treachery nor physical attack but initiate the action themselves. From the clan's viewpoint, they are the traitors and not the betrayed, most particularly Gennosuke. In this regard, both men bear a closer resemblance to Shiba, outwardly mistrustful of the institutions of government but retaining an implicit standard of conduct, never approaching the outspoken bitterness of Tange Sazen.

Inasmuch as all of Gosha's heroes are anti-social, they define a range of individual morality which is fairly broad. Both Magobei and Gennosuke are at the top end of that range. Reflective, aware of feudal decay, made somewhat cynical by official hypocrises, the violence and rebellion which they represent is selfless. Their figurative cry of outrage is thematically much louder than Tange Sazen's because it is not motivated by personal revenge. At the same time, the specific events which precipitate the rupture prey on these characters' thoughts and actions much more forcefully than the vague generic pasts of Shiba or Okaminosuke.

In *Sword of the Beast* and *Goyokin*, the fact that the causal scenes are not presented chronologically underscores the suggestions that the sense of rupture is greater than for other Gosha heroes. Unlike the "past time" prologue of *Secret of the Urn*, seen in flashback, the key events are automatically filtered through Gennosuke's and Magobei's viewpoint. By detailing the precise moments of the protagonist's break with society from a subjective vantage, imagistically the past becomes the present in *Sword of the Beast* and *Goyokin*. When it displaces the frames containing present time, the past impinges more tangibly than through Tange Sazen's empty sleeve. The past defines and focuses the present action.

"The year was 1857." The written characters are the simplest possible, uncluttered by any adjectives or other qualifiers. The fact that it is 1857, that particular year, means nothing to the plot. However, the notion that what follows is "case history," rather than the exploits of any legendary figure such as Tange Sazen, is significant. The title superimposed over the opening frame of *Sword of the Beast* is added for its sense of real time, of actuality. Unlike Shiba or Okaminosuke, who are in motion across a landscape when first seen, Gennosuke Yuki is discovered reclining in some tall grass. A woman stumbles onto the scene, her clothes in disarray; and Gennosuke's thoughts immediately take a lecherous turn. This instantaneous inscription of Gennosuke's baser instincts, the non-heroism of his immediate posture and action, reinforce the aura of actuality, of a plausible character in an authentic situation. That Gennosuke, before this first sequence is over, is able to sense a trap and recover the sword the woman steals from him reassures the audience that he is not without some skill as a samurai and some potential as a hero. That his weapon is taken from him at all and that he is compelled to steal a horse to evade capture by unknown attackers, who mockingly shout after him "Where is your pride as a samurai?" and dare him to stand and fight, make it equally clear that he is not brimming over with *zanshin*.

The staging of this introductory sequence further undercuts any implicit, generic promise of a strong protagonist. Through frenzied whip-pans, handheld running shots through the thick grass, quick cuts and radical lens changes, all accompanied by an incoherent clamor on the soundtrack, the viewer's perceptions are thrown into an expressive chaos. This aptly underscores the manifold implications—fatigue, confusion, peril—of the events of the first few minutes which end in an abrupt freeze-frame, a static image saturated with repressed energy.

What the audience cannot guess about Gennosuke from this opening, Gosha reveals expositionally. The dialogue between his assailants soon clarifies that Gennosuke is being hunted for killing a clan minister as part of a conspiracy to bring reform. It also establishes the ruthless determination of the official avenger: "A vendetta is not like a duel. You can have anybody's help. So says the warrior code." Moreover, as the flashbacks emphasize, Gennosuke's action was not thoughtless: "Japan is changing-since Perry's ships. The minister cannot suppress the tendency." Neither was it purely idealistic: "My sword is the only way I can avoid misery," he confides to Daizaburo, who is now one of his pursuers, in the flashback. That belief leads him to become the dupe of an ambitious clan officer. Superficially, the flashbacks seem a facile way to fill in needed information. Expressively, this visual recreation permits the viewer not only to relive those crucial past incidents with Gennosuke but to do so from his bitter, present perspective that this past was full of misconceptions. In short, Gennosuke is a lost man, a felon without hope of pardon from society, and a fugitive estranged from his own former self.

Sword of the Beast:
TOP: Gennosuke (Mikijiro Hira)

BOTTOM: A moment's respite for Gennosuke (Mikijiro Hira)

This idea of being lost or beyond redemption, coupled with that of reflexive action, receives unusual treatment in the first part of *Sword of the Beast*. The narrative line continues to focus on Gennosuke's flight. It alternates from Gennosuke's exhausted efforts to stay alive to the arrangements made by Daizaburo, Misa (his fiancée and the daughter of the murdered minister), and their followers to trap him by hiring extra men or going over the floor plan of the inn where he is staying before attacking. As he pauses to check the low beams in his rented room as a possible impairment for his sword before slumping wearily into a corner for a few hours rest, Gennosuke's emotional state is to go on fighting through habit, through reflex, or some lingering indignation at the thought of being hunted and

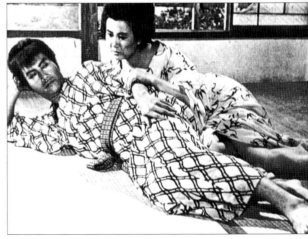

cut down like a beast. When ambushed again, he seems even more like an animal at bay, summoning strength to escape through a mixture of outrage and desperation. When Daizaburo admonishes him, "Gennosuke, die like a samurai," he screams back, "How can I? This is butchery."

In the first half of *Sword of the Beast*, Gennosuke is short-circuited by the crossed wires of individual conscience and societal duty. He cannot die like a samurai nor, conditioned as he is to accept the code of the warrior, can he live like a beast. In an image of isolation at the film's turning point, he ponders going upriver to search for gold with Tanji, the gambler who has helped him evade capture. "If you want to keep running the rest of your life, you'll have to get money first," Tanji observes. Still trying vainly to account for the nightmarish disruption of his previous existence, for the crushing consequences of a single rash act, Gennosuke asks himself a question aloud—"To keep running?" Sitting rim-lit with his features barely discernible in an obscure close shot, he receives no answer.

At this moment in the film, with the full context of Gennosuke's position defined and the actual threat restated in a subsequent violent confrontation, Gosha has significantly developed the interior conflicts merely implied in that climactic freeze-frame at the beginning. Despite his shortcomings the audience's empathy has been fixed on Gennosuke. He is the hero; but what hope is there for his salvation? That full daylit frame, held against sky and field for enough seconds to burn his visage into the viewer's brain, has changed to the interior close shot, overhung by dark rafters, in which his expression is shaded by backlight. This could well suggest that a figurative obliteration is in progress.

Upriver the promise is not just of gold or the safety of a geographical seclusion, putting miles of empty, rugged lanscape between him and his relentless trackers. "Upriver" has Edenic, archetypal connotations: a return to the source, to clean waters, renewal and refreshment as well as isolation. As

Gennosuke (Mikijiro Hira) considers whether or not "to keep running" by going upriver.

the film relocates to this new ground, both new characters and new metaphoric images emerge and assume major roles. The characters are Jurata Yamane and his wife, Taka, who have been mining in the canyons, not for their own gain but to remedy their clan's financial difficulties. The imagery is explicitly bestial: in this alien locus of bleak, rocky riverbanks backed by canyon walls covered with black brush, the characters themselves speak of the animalistic nature hidden within men. The first words between Gennosuke and Yamane, as they meet, circle, and eye each other are:

GENNOSUKE

How many have you killed?

YAMANE

All who came.
(*raising his sword*)
To protect my gold from wolves like you, I must use this.

GENNOSUKE
(*backing off*)
If I'm a wolf, I have sharper fangs than most. I'll show you later.

Prior to this scene the audience observed Yamane just twice, when he quickly dispatched four shogunate officers patrolling the river for "gold poachers" and in a later expository sequence with his wife, which outlined his rea-

TOP: "To protect my gold from wolves like you, I must use this"; Go Kato as Yamane.

CENTER AND BOTTOM: "I'll tear out with my hand what I long for"; Gennosuke's exclamation is followed by a cut to Yamane as he measures out his day's takings.

son for being there: "a 200 *koku* stipend and promotion from squire to samurai." Given even that limited information the viewer cannot, as does Tanji, immediately construct a mental picture of Yamane as the terrifying unseen force that sends bodies floating down the river. To reinforce the genre identities of his characters, Gosha had previously intercut scenes over time and place. Gennosuke tells the woman spy at the inn "I'll tear out with my hand what I long for" in medium-close shot frame right. The cut is to Yamane in medium-close shot frame left as he measures the day's yield of gold dust. When the men first confront each other Gosha uses balanced wide-angle close shots. This confirms what has already been implied about the two characters: they are equal and photographed in the same size in their respective frames. They are also opposed, positioned on opposite sides of those frames as one hoards what the other wants to "tear of with his hand." The very fact of the unanticipated or unmotivated cut over time and space from the face of Gennosuke to that of Yamane confirms that their respective fates are somehow interlocked. When Gennosuke does journey upriver, he approaches the house of Yamane and his wife with renewed confi-

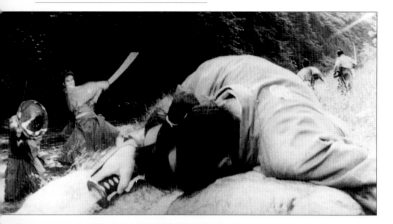

TOP: Depth of focus: Yamane cuts down three shogunate men.

CENTER and BOTTOM: Gennosuke resists an attack by three claim jumpers.

dence in his sword. That confidence is visually reinforced by a low-angle close shot of him as he strides up to the dwelling. The audience has already been primed for a combat between equals, for a duel to the death of uncertain outcome. That Gennosuke backs off from the fight is a bit surprising. At the same time, the viewer understands that it is still too early for any irrevocable test of skills between the two protagonists. In fact, much of the preceding narrative, despite Yamane's limited amount of screen time, has been subtly geared to suggest a potential transference relationship. Besides the cut described above, there is another, earlier shift from Gennosuke in flashback killing the minister to Yamane killing the officers. The editing scheme and the composition have forged a specific link between the two before they ever meet.

This interaction expands as the background changes to an isolated terrain and the metaphor of the beast is discussed again and again. Tanji and Gennosuke pick it up the evening after the near fight with Yamane and the rescue of his wife from three rival gold hunters: Tanji argues that Gennosuke is not a beast because such a being "doesn't warn his victims." After Gennosuke had saved Yamane's wife, his conclusion is that "many beasts live here, [so] I'll turn into a wolf." Still later that same night, Taka will confide to him, "I wish I could be a beast. I can't stand living for a mission." But which is the beast? Is it the hunter? Yamane says, "I killed everyone who approached. Everyone of them." Or is it the hunted? Misa says, "Gennosuke is a beast. He should be drawn and quartered." Is it the man or the samurai?

Beasts, wolves, unnatural creatures—is the real question how unnatural these people are or whether they are unnatural at all? What this motif actually brings into focus are the social circumstances that have compelled the atavism, the primitive behavior. "I've experienced the loneliness and frustration of an underling," Gennosuke answers Taka, "I understand how your husband feels." Appropriately, it is as he speaks with her that two final flashbacks reveal the last details of Gennosuke's personal rebellion. After this juxtaposition he begins to imagine the possibility of a similar betrayal of Yamane by his clan. Gennusuke transfers his guilt and reassumes some notion of social responsibility by correcting that possible evil. On his own part, Yamane acquires a portion of Gennosuke's doubts. His resolve to kill Taka when she returns, not for wronging him but for breaking faith with their clan by revealing the mission, falters.

Gennosuke tells Taka (Shima Iwashita), "I understand how your husband feels."

In simple terms the transference between the two men is one of despair, despair conferred on Yamane by undermining his belief in his clan and its institutions, and despair shaken off by Gennosuke through a restoration of his righteous indignation and his will to fight. The transference transcends that, as both men discover the real beasts, and it becomes necessary for Yamane and Taka to perish so that Gennosuke may be saved. He is not saved in the sense of being reintegrated into society, for after their death his alienation is more profound than ever. Rather Gennosuke is saved from those regrets and residual uncertainties about the justice of his rebellion which have oppressed him, which have driven themselves into his consciousness as forcefully as the flashbacks to those events have intruded into the flow of the film's time. Yamane, the squire, faces death because, he tells Taka, "I have my pride as a samurai." He also dies because Gennosuke has lost *his* pride as a samurai, his status, his efforts for personal advancement, because only in the ultimate fulfillment of the transference can Gennosuke come to see that such pride and status were always valueless.

The dramatic irony of *Sword of the Beast*, drawn from this dualistic treatment of Gennosuke and Yamane, stands on its own as narrative statement. What Gosha adds are compositional touches of counterpoint and atonality. Subjectification of image is again an expressive value in several scenes, perhaps most strikingly in the confrontation between Yamane and his wife after she returns from her talk with Gennosuke. At that moment, the breech between them is an emotional chasm. She had gone out to release her sexual tensions with Gennosuke but had not done so. Enraged that she may have betrayed him and their mission, he plans to kill her. When she returns there is a cut to a high-angle two shot with the figures in balance at either side of it. Framed dead center between them is a wooden pillar, which in the two dimensions of the image literally separates them and acts as a tangible externalization of a barrier in their minds. That barrier disappears with the next

Top: Ominous low angle as three claim jumpers accost Gennosuke at the inn.

Center: Medium shot as Gennosuke and his co-conspirators wait to kill the minister.

Bottom: Closer shot of the conspirators

cut, when Yamane drops his sword and embraces her.

The flashbacks to Gennosuke's rebellion constitute another level. They are not substantively subjective, not like the explicit point-of-view traveling shot when the camera "became" Gennosuke fighting his way out of the trap at the inn. The only thing that identifies them as emerging from Gennosuke's memory is the narrative context. The first flashback is not from Gennosuke's point of view at all but is brought to mind by Daizaburo. That scene from the past, as it happens, is the only one which is daylit or exterior or shot from a high angle. Gennosuke's memory images proper are all night interiors with strong side light and considerable movement in the frame. The assassination of the minister, in particular, is composed of tight three shots of Gennosuke and his coconspirators aligned diagonally in the viewing plane and lit so that only a portion of their faces are visible, giving the whole sequence a nightmarish quality in stark contrast to Daizaburo's recollection. Thus the expressive components of the respective sequences—the detached angle and "neutral" lighting of the former versus the low-key and engaged camera of the succeeding flashbacks—are arranged to correspond to the interior states of those recollecting. For that matter, the use of side light throughout the film is at least partially subjective: a rendering of Gennosuke's vacillation between life and death, between acceptance and resistance of his preordained fate, as a division of his face into dark and light halves. A similar but slightly more explicit indecision is expressed in the sharply side-lit close shot of Yamane, which throws half his visage into shadow as he stands on a bridge and hesitates between ransoming his wife and preserving the gold.

The sustained camera functions independently as a tensing device in a scene such as Gennosuke's killing of the other gold hunters, the shot being held until the last one is cut down. In *Sword of the Beast* it is also used to subjectify. Gennosuke's discussion with Tanji at the inn, for example, is a long

Sword of the Beast: Gennosuke reports to the minister who will betray him.

RIGHT, AND BELOW: Yamane in strong side light, as he watches his wife being terrorized from a vantage on a bridge.

Matching close shot of Gennosuke that indicates equality (same size) and opposition (counter-placement in the frame).

Traveling back with the figures on a narrow porch, as Gennosuke speaks with Tanji (Kunie Tanaka).

traveling shot which follows them around a narrow porch. Since Gennosuke still believes that "my destiny depends on the gold," his way out is like the narrow passage constricted and unidirectional. He is compelled emotionally by a resolve that finds plastic expression in the unbroken line of the shot.

Finally Gosha makes use of a variety of shots to clarify interpersonal relationships. The visual scheme linking Gennosuke and Yamane has already been discussed, as has the divided two shot of Yamane and his wife, which falls as much into this category as any other. One last, intriguing example, which retains considerable ambiguity, is the panning and rack focus in the conversation of Gennosuke and Taka. The staging simultaneously joins them via the sustained shot and separates them via the different planes of focus. It shifts emphasis to capture neither and both viewpoints. Through this "plural" perspective, compounded by the factor of sexual attraction between strangers, the sequence's visual usage forms an objective correlative, an expansion and a restriction of ordinary, singular subjectification.

Like *Sword of the Beast*, *Goyokin* is concerned with gold. Over the opening shot of a sun-bleached island centered in an azure sea, a narrator informs the viewer that "from the 17th to the later 18th centuries, the gold and silver island of Sato produced shogunate gold." Under the titles which follow, a procession is seen in slow motion along the shoreline, keeping time to a festival air in the score and silhouetted against the greenish-gold hues of the solarized

TOP: A succession of shots charged with the near constant motion of panning, tracking, and zooming. Gosha "reverses" typical Kurosawa by panning with a figure (Oriha) as she walks backwards.

BOTTOM: The first obscured glimpse of Magobei as his head blocks the sun and his sword returns to the scabbard.

water. A long lens from the front reveals a white-robed bride on horseback. Then another cut comes around to an extra-long shot of a snowscape, as the solarization process is reversed and the greens and golds are drained from the frame. Without explanation, the scene shifts to a fishing village; and the literally dazzling imagery of the initial shots reverts to a more primordial type. A title reads, "The year 1831, In Sabai Country." A girl, Oriha, watches the procession from a ridge and, taking it as a beneficent sign for her homecoming, enters the village. There, a succession of disquieting, quasi-subjective shots isolate her only welcomers, a flock of ravens. A black bird suddenly emerges in unnatural slow-motion from a torn wall panel. Another raven floats dead in the tide. After a blurring pan, a third is revealed hanging lifelessly from a string in a doorway. Gosha compounds the shock cut and dizzying pan with a distorted cawing on the soundtrack, which increases in volume as the girl searches frenziedly for the inhabitants. As she enters a hut, a bird falls into the lens and blacks out the screen. A bloody carcass is visible for a few frames, and as a door sways open a blue sunflare streaks through the shot, bisecting it horizontally. Finally, as Oriha stumbles and falls, the viewer is fully immersed into her point of view. The frame tilts violently and the soundtrack drops to a slight rustling. She hallucinates the discovery of a corpse, and the camera rocks back and forth then steadies when she realizes it is only an abandoned slab of raw meat. "Kamikakushi," she whispers to herself, "the Gods hid them." As she flees, the flock of birds flies up. A shot freezes them against the sky, where their bodies melt, bleed together, and reform into the ideographs for "October, 1831."

Methodically Gosha uses a succession of shots charged with the near constant motion of panning, tracking, and zooming, all geared to the girl's growing apprehension to impart the sensation of her shock and recoil directly to the viewer. The result, as in the opening of *Sword of the Beast*, is a kind of formal chaos. While the earlier film began with a scene of a swordsman under attack and indicated to the audience through its generic inscription that this figure was to be the film's central character, all of this action in *Goyokin* comes before any introduction of a hero. While Gosha exploited the unsettling potential of editing and mise-en-scène in *Sword of the Beast* to cause the viewer to associate the still unnamed Gennosuke, isolated in a climactic freeze-frame, with a suspension of disorienting motion, that optical device is re-used in *Goyokin* for strikingly different effect. In *Goyokin*, at the analogous moment of a forced pause, as the bodies of the ravens are frozen in mid-flight, the viewer has not yet received sufficient information with which to form any expectations of how the narrative will develop. The various expository titles, ending with "October, 1831," metamorphosized from the birds, recall the words superimposed over the first shot of *Sword of the Beast*. As in that film, the relationship between the given specifics of time and place and the events of the plot, either already seen or to come, has not yet been established.

From this abundant visual and narrative confusion, Gosha moves not toward rapid clarification but to an image of maximum disequilibrium: a shot of a street bazaar tilted ninety degrees from horizontal. For a spectator the Panavision frame turned completely vertical or halfway between normal and upside-down views is an almost impossible composition to read. Impelled to turn their heads and scan the image repeatedly to comprehend what they are seeing, the audience's physical discomfiture intensifies the need for some object or character on which to fix their attention. But even after the frame has slowly rotated back to a normal position, Gosha continues to delay the appearance that character, the swordsman. As a barker touts an exhibition of

A rack focus using a long lens moves from a candle flame in the foreground to the blade of a sword to a close shot of the performer's face, now fully visible.

"lightning swordplay" and a samisen girl provides a monotonous musical accompaniment, three toughs detach themselves from a milling crowd and, echoing the film viewer's impatience, demand the start of the show. Undismayed, the barker carefully parts the samisen player's kimono and places a fish over her thighs. A man appears on the makeshift stage, his face concealed by straw hat. After lifting the brim for an instant, he cuts the fish in two. One of the three men steps forward, draws his own weapon, and severs each string of the samisen in turn. For a few seconds, the terrified woman continues to strike the plectrum against the soundbox. "I want to test my powers against you," the challenger calls after the performer, who is retreating. "Running?" He slices

away the hat brim. The generic reading of this scene is still ambiguous. Clearly, the performer has some of the traits of a genre hero—a calm bearing evident in his silent entry onto the scene, a desire to conceal his identity, even by a curious inversion his reluctance to fight—all type him as a possible protagonist. Of course, the most direct and decisive typing is the fact that this character is portrayed by the star of the film, Tatsuya Nakadai, whose dark eyes and gaunt features are easily recognizable once the hat brim has been cut away. Later a rack focus using a long lens moves from a candle flame in the foreground to the blade of a sword to a close shot of the performer's face, now fully visible. This rack focus which reveals those features emphatically to the viewer also, in the unbroken flow of the shot, figuratively equates him with a flame and a sword. But why, if this bearded and mute figure is the long anticipated central character whose presence will explain and stabilize a thus far chaotic narrative, does he back down from a duel? Gosha elucidates neither his literal position, slicing fish in a side-show, nor his metaphorical one, entering the film after the visual kinesis, after the odd angles and tilted frames have subsided. There are many satirical elements in this initial encounter—the image of the fish on the woman's thighs, the comic plucking of strings which are no longer there—which have already undercut Nakadai's heroic aspect. Rather than giving the viewer any background information, Gosha further reduces his tenuous claim to audience attention by cutting to a scene which introduces a second swordsman. When this man is attacked by the toughs of the previous sequence, who have mistaken him for the unnamed performer portrayed by Nakadai, he does not back down. Instead he effortlessly dispatches two of them, then smilingly asks the survivor to pay for a vase broken in the scuffle. Now the audience has an alternative hero—reinforced by the fact that this second man is also portrayed by a starring actor, Kinnosuke Nakamura—as a glib, good-natured killer who is in some ways more appealing than Nakadai.

At this point, after manipulating the narrative inscription to lead the viewer away from any stereotypical set of expectations, Gosha restores a sense of generic equilibrium with two "standard" sequences. Unlike the "degraded" encounters full of semi-parody and compositional fracturing, which Gosha employs in earlier films and in the first scenes of *Goyokin* to distance the spectators and make them more aware of the genre's expressive limits, what comes next reverses the process. While distinct from each other in texture and tone, both invoke a knowledge of the samurai ethos which the audience should have acquired from any number of previously seen motion pictures. First, the performer, Magobei Wakizaka, speaks to the barker inside a tent and offers to sell him his sword. The latter's comments as he examines the weapon—"A real Sukehiro. A fine sword, a fine swordsman. The sum total of your worth now"—go unacknowledged by Magobei, whose distracted gaze is barely discernible in the soft, brownish half-light of an oil lamp. "What will you do," the Barker continues, "A samurai can't become a farmer." Finally the barker's questioning receives a response: "Is being a samurai so great?"

Outside, hard light cuts a manor wall into deep blue wedges of color, and gold lanterns throw uneven patches onto an open field around a watchtower. Magobei approaches the tower and pauses tensely. A voice calls his name from the surrounding darkness and advises him to "die quietly without

"A samurai can't become a farmer."

"Is being a samurai so great?"

a fuss." He moistens and wraps the hilt of his weapon and moves forward into the blue light to answer: "Come out, if you want me." As the battle is joined, Gosha shifts from a low-angle close shot of Magobei to a high-angle long shot, as four figures converge on him out of the shadows. Almost in a single motion he kills them all then backs a fifth man up against the ladder of the tower. As Magobei interrogates him, a thin red line appears on his forehead, and their rapid breathing frosts in the air

Tatewaki clicks his sword guard against his scabbard in a gesture of *bushi no-ichi gon*, the solemn word of a warrior.

before their faces. Then images of an earlier scene of cold and violence flash simultaneously into Magobei's mind and across the screen. In a staccato flashback, the wedding procession is massacred in the snow. The villagers had taken shogunate gold from a shipwreck, and the bankrupt Sabai clan slaughtered them to keep the spoils for themselves. Having ridden to protest the action, Magobei finds a *fait accompli*. Now he confronts another mounted man, clan Chamberlain Tatewaki. As their animals shift position nervously on a snow-covered ridge, Magobei denounces the other's crime. "Does loyalty take priority in all things? No! No!" Magobei rejects the rhetorical reply—"A few worthless fishermen had to be sacrificed for our six hundred clansmen"—and announces his decision to leave the Sabai: "I'm tired of the samurai way." Gosha concludes the flashback with an extra-close shot: after the mounted clansman has promised never to repeat the slaughter, Tatewaki clicks his sword guard against his scabbard in a gesture of *bushi no-ichi gon*, the solemn word of a warrior. From there, he cuts directly to a traveling shot as Magobei walks away from the tower in present time. Slowly, the camera cranes down to a low-angle view: he draws, stops, and runs through his last assailant without looking behind his back.

This last shot crystallizes Magobei's position as the dramatic center of the film, as both the action which it captures and its expressive components remove all doubts about the elemental power of the character. Not only does Magobei's stride "draw" the camera after him, but the sheer emotion of his indignation upon realizing that the Sabai plan to murder for gold again seems to force it down to an angle which both highlights his angry expression and externalizes his dominance even more incontrovertably than the low-angle close shot before the fight began. In fact, Tatsuya Nakadai's interpretation of Magobei has an immediacy and impact in the two scenes just described which transcend any residual confusion of the previous sequences. Not only does Magobei's presence in current time and flashback link all the events, but it is the primary factor in resolving the viewer's distance. Identification with Magobei is not only much easier than it was in the festival scene but is actively encouraged. For what the acting, the brief combat, and the flashback make clear is that this character lacks the self-serving motives of Rentaro Mikuni's Musashi. He is even more unflinching in his resolve than Nakadai's own portrayal of Hanshiro Tsugumo in *Hara-Kiri*. All of which creates one of the most indomitable figures in post-War *chambara*. What Gosha directs the viewer to perceive beneath the shuddering violence of Magobei's martial abilities and the death of the villagers, beneath the synthesis of past and present, is that precise moment when the last constraints of feudal mentality are sloughed off.

While Magobei may already have vocally questioned and even quit "the samurai way," every new thrust of his blade testifies to his outrage at the emptiness of that path. While Tange Sazen merely laughed at the retainer who inquired if he would commit *hara-kiri* according to *bushido*, or while Gennosuke could only scream out a protest and flee the attackers who requested that he "die like a samurai" in *Sword of the Beast*, Magobei's refusal to "die quietly" is much more active. His literally murderous response speaks louder than any laughter or vocal protest, not just of denial but of a direct assault on the foundations of *bushido*.

The crucial difference between that assault and the ones mounted by Tsugumo and Sasahara in Kobayashi's films resides in the sensibility of the personage. Even at their most disillusioned, the heroes of *Hara-Kiri* and *Rebellion* retained some measure of belief in justice and some measure of loyalty to the "samurai way," as their final actions confirmed. Sasahara's notion, in particular, of carrying word of clan iniquities to Edo seems remarkably idealist and unaware of what the whole structure of feudalism, from its governing institutions to its codes of behavior, have done to him and his family. Because neither Tsugumo nor Sasahara understand until it is too late the extent to which their conditioning and the conditioning of others controls their lives, their acts are subsumed into the same pattern of "useless tokenism" they are protesting.

In *Rebellion*, Tatsuya Nakadai's portrayal of Tatewaki Asano, Sasahara's friend and unwilling opponent in the film's final duel, typifies the inbred restraint which goes too far in one direction. Because he defines himself totally in terms of the samurai way and its code, that character is criticized by the clan for his refusal to bend it slightly: "You go too far, Asano. You're too scrupulous." Ultimately he is killed by Sasahara for not allowing him to pass his sentry post at the frontier, telling his friend that "to carry out my duty and to uphold my honor as a samurai, I forbid it." On the surface, it may seem that Asano is a completely misguided character. Mifune's Sasahara moves from a passive and repressed way of life, as exemplified by the analysis of Sasahara sword style which Asano offers early in the film: "Push and you step back. Push and you step back further. But at the last moment, you change from defense to offense. You wait until your opponent tires and then you strike." Asano never lives for "the last moment." Asano could never observe as Sasahara does, once his rebellion has irrevocably begun, that "for the first time in my life I feel really alive," because Asano's unassailable sense of duty safeguards his psychological well-being and avoids the desperate ends of Tsugumo and Sasahara, torn schizophrenically between *giri* and *ninjo*. Whether Tsugumo's self-immolation is pure reflex or Sasahara's refusal to lose faith in Edo is just a gesture in the face of total hopelessness, neither character survives the maddening consequences of the *giri/ninjo* double bind. Neither does more than approach the kind of break with society and his own past which Magobei effects in *Goyokin*. For Nakadai as Asano, there is only *giri*; for Nakadai at the other extreme as Magobei, there is only *ninjo*. Given the controlled chaos of the opening, there is no need for Gosha to fill in expository detail to the extent he does in *Sword of the Beast*, no need for dialogue like Sazen's about learning to be a "monster" or Gennosuke's comments on why he is a "beast." Midway through *Goyokin*, Magobei does speak to his wife about his motives for returning to Sabai country, and why he fails to fear the threats of her brother, the clan chamberlain: "He can't kill me. I'm dead already. Ever since I closed my eyes, I forfeited my worth as a man. I forgot that samurai are supported by weak masses. I learned that living in the gutter for three years. What was the use of a sword then? I lost hope and even tried to sell my sword. . . . I must stop Tatewaki so that I can regain my worth as a man, so that I, too, can live again."

Chamberlain Tatewaki, like the chamberlain and steward in *Rebellion*, is a compromiser who fears overly "scrupulous" men. Like the clan officials in *Secret of the Urn* and *Sword of the Beast*, he exploits the idealistic loyalty of men such as Samanosuke and Gennosuke before their departure from the clan. If Magobei has an advantage over the genotypical protagonists of these other films and over the usual pattern of *giri/ninjo* narratives as well, it is because, as he says, his rebellion is at once intensely personal and passionately selfless. Unlike Sasahara, the act of rebellion itself cannot make him "feel alive." Although Magobei does imagine himself "already dead," he also regards the whole, long history of his loyal service as a mistake which requires more than a mere change of heart to be redeemed. Like Tsugumo, his swords, the supreme symbols of his rank, are not sold; but for different reasons: because they still have utility and not out of any attachment to them as objects. While the actions of Kobayashi's heroes continue to be governed by ironic and symbolic values, Magobei's "devotion" to the cause of the weak masses is founded on his own newly acquired identification not with any caste status, but with simple manhood and his need to reassert his forfeited worth "as a man," not as a samurai. Consequently, he cannot move from this realization of his common humanity into either a Zen-like self-effacement or a pessimistic resignation to *shushigaku*. Free of the cynicism of Mifune's Sanjuro or Ichikawa's Nemuri and the ambitions of a Musashi or Sakamoto, Nakadai's Magobei becomes a defiant and potentially tragic antagonist to the forces of oppression.

In one sense, Magobei's successful prevention of another shipwreck and massacre by the Sabai samurai is a more optimistic conclusion than that of *Rebellion* or *Hara-Kiri* or Gosha's own *Sword of the Beast*. In another sense, the destruction or alienation which the central characters of those films experience is not spared Magobei. Although he survives the battle with his former clan, and although the last image of him walking off in the snow followed by Shino, his wife, is more hopeful that the analogous closing shots of Samanosuke/Tange Sazen, Gennosuke, or the three outlaw samurai, the dilemma of his continuing position as a disenfranchised member of the samurai class is not resolved.

Gosha uses the character of Chamberlain Tatewaki, who is still a samurai in "good standing," to place Magobei's feelings in perspective. In a medium two shot, Tatewaki and Samon, the shogmate spy who took Magobei's place in the sideshow and later permitted his escape from a Sabai ambush, discuss the latter's possible employment to stop Magobei. Samon becomes embarrassed after slurping his tea and receiving a surprised glance from the chamberlain. "A masterless samurai since father's time," he explains, "I don't know how to drink tea." Tatewaki ponders an instant then replies, "Since father's time? I envy you." On a conscious level Tatewaki's profession of weariness with his position corresponds to Magobei's wish to be freed from duties, from the burden of a privileged ancestry. On an unconscious level, however, the mise-en-scène suggests the critical difference between the two retainers. Unlike his brother-in-law, Magobei, the chamberlain is not free from even the minutest of the samurai rituals and still reacts with unnatural puzzlement when the proper form is not observed.

Some scenes later Magobei is captured by Tatewaki and bound to a tree, where he listens to the chamberlain's final rationalization: "I'll break promises any number of times, whenever the necessity arises. The world's made so that samurai can't get along without dirtying our hands. You ran away to keep your hands clean." Gosha cuts to a shot of the helpless Magobei as he answers, "You're right. I'm a coward." Again, in his haste to blame himself for his apparent failure to correct injustice, Magobei seems unknowingly to accept Tatewaki's deterministic logic that "the way of the world" compels dishonorable actions. It is not until Magobei's last talk with Samon after the defeat of the Sabai that he seems to have discovered the real meaning behind Tatewaki's claim of "necessity." "I'm returning to Edo. I quit being a spy," Samon confides unemotionally and, while observing the fishermen performing a masked dance, asks if it is a "life-saving festival?" Magobei responds with equanimity: "No. It's a funeral. A funeral for the samurai."

"A masterless samurai since father's time. . . ."; Samon (Kinnosuke Nakamura) meets with Chamberlain Tatewaki (Tetsuro Tamba, right).

That statement and the situation itself, masterless samurai having saved a village from destruction, is strongly reminiscent of the conversation between Gorobei and Kanbei at the close of *Seven Samurai*. But while the final irony of Kanbei's position was in his impotent realization that the samurai were always the losers in the end, Magobei perceives the samurai as, like him, already dead. He also understands the "funeral for the samurai" is a result of the political context, that "while we small worms kill one another, the shogunate grows bigger and fatter." Consequently, not only is Magobei's personal rebellion a resolution of the ambivalence over their roles as samurai or *ronin* felt by Kurosawa's characters, but it is also more aware than Gennosuke's in *Sword of the Beast*. In that film, Gosha restricted his observations on the nature of the rebellion to the ironic mode: while those stalking Gennosuke enlisted the aid of mercenary and unscrupulous characters in tracking him down and justified such action as allowable under the rules for a vendetta ("So says the warrior code"), Gennosuke agonized over his own position and suffered mental anguish for failing to accept his punishment under *bushido*. In the end, Gennosuke can appreciate the hypocrisy of the code without necessarily being rid of his inbred sense of guilt. Whereas Gennosuke may always have a lingering belief that he is a beast and coward for not recouping his honor through self-immolation, Magobei's ultimate realization is that his cowardice was in not violating the notion of honor and clan loyalty earlier than he did. Gosha underscores that in *Goyokin*, by subjectifying this realization, by compelling the viewer to experience it simultaneously with Magobei rather than in the light of such third person scenes as the conferences of Gennosuke's pursuers in *Sword of the Beast*. If Magobei is emotionally estranged from his fellow men at the film's conclusion, it is a condition subtly different from the genre stereotype, a condition of alienation not from the empty and meaningless institutions (the "small worms") of feudalism, some of which he has violently destroyed, but from the oppressive reality behind those institutions and from himself as a former unwitting functionary of that oppression. Because he breaks free of the perception of himself as "lost beyond redemption" which plagues Gennosuke, the depth of Magobei's estrangement, or how fully redeemed he may think himself after killing Tatewaki and ruining the Sabai plans, is unprobed. When Magobei leaves Samon and the villagers behind he also abandons his sword at the edge of an icy plain. As he walks off in long shot toward the shadowy aspect of a distant mountain, leaving behind the symbol of his rank and fealty, both his wife and his past follow in his track. Whether he will ever be able to escape the psychological scarring of this past, which figuratively envelops him as ominously as the cold mists that obscure the outline of his receding figure, is undetermined.

From the solarized shots of its prologue to the extensive night photography of the battle between Magobei and Samon and the Sabai men at the fishing village and the bright snowscapes of the final duel, *Goyokin* may contain a greater variety of visual usage than any earlier Gosha film. Rather than undermining the narrative unity, the various devices Gosha brings to bear expositionally and metaphorically create a fluidity of expression that drives that narrative forward, at times with calculated abruptness but never with misdirection. It is characteristic of Gosha to open on the note of disequilibrium already described. That he does so by cutting without cueing viewer expectation from one scene to another or from one angle to another—the high/low scheme of Magobei's first duel is typical here—is not only expressively economical but instills a sense of growing tension in the audience without being overstated.

The pattern of intercutting in the concluding combat of Tatewaki and Magobei from figure to figure *and* intermittently to the masked dancers in the village operates in the same way. The cutaways from the critical action serve to increase viewer anxiety over the outcome and prolong suspense despite the fact that Magobei's victory is the clear genre expectation. Moreover, because the audience is repeatedly frustrated in their desire to witness the climax of the encounter, Gosha compels them partially to co-experience the intense frustration felt by both participants in the duel *and* to intellectualize about the masked faces of the dancers and their ritual aspects, which they are being shown instead of the principal event. The narrative *over*statement being made through this montage, which makes the combatants and the dancers interact over time and space, establishes a simple equation between the actions and suggests that the swordfight is itself at some level a masked ritual. On another level, Gosha is still most interested in a visualization which is sensory before it is figurative. The sound of the dancers' drums and shouts and the sight of their grotesque and brightly painted masks, alternately motionless and blurred as a long lens captures them pausing and then jumping in the air, impart anxiety and chaos to those scenes which carry over into the shots of Magobei and Tatewaki. This in turn externalizes an aspect of the men's inner sensations that is repressed and inapparent as they implacably circle and approach each other.

As in prior films Gosha uses sustained camera and a competition between foreground and background objects or characters as an alternate tensing device. The long take when Magobei and Samon are surrounded and attacked in a mill is an example of withholding a cut, which is particularly contrary to the more normal practice of editing heavily to isolate individual blows and parries in a fight scene and which heightens viewer uneasiness during an appropriately perilous scene. Color is another expressive factor in *Goyokin*, and not just in the

TOP: The final duel between Magobei (Tatsuya Nakadai, left) and Chamberlain Tatewaki (Tetsuro Tamba) in *Goyokin*

BOTTOM: Magobei (Tatsuya Nakadai) and Samon (Kinnosukle Nakamura) in *Goyokin*

Top: A red blotch begins to spread out on the snow behind Tatewaki.

Bottom: Grotesque and brightly painted masks, alternately motionless and blurred as a long lens captures them pausing and then jumping in the air

unnaturally intense hues of the first sequence. The contrast between an emotionally bright past, such as the flashback to Magobei and Shino's wedding, and a somber present consistently finds reinforcement in the color scheme. At the climax of the duel between Tatewaki and Magobei, Gosha relies simply on imaginative and unobtrusive mise-en-scène. From a side view as the antagonists make their last charge and lock weapons and fall together, Gosha shifts to an overhead shot of them lying on the snow. For several instants neither moves, and the viewer may begin to wonder if the expected outcome, Magobei's triumph, has indeed come to pass. Then a red blotch begins to spread out on the snow behind Tatewaki, growing slowly until it covers an area larger than his body. Magobei painfully extricates himself from the dying man's grasp and from the passive yet violent imagery of this shot. This action, taken along with Tatewaki's last words—"What of the Sabai clan? What will become of it?"—is in ironic contrast to the murderous energy of many preceding scenes.

The visual emphasis in *Goyokin* is not only on disjunctive editing and broken shots as already detailed but also on the panning and zoom-editing which generates the "energy" in those scenes. Such usage complements both the general vigor of the narrative statement itself and also the disturbed and disturbing individual characters and events to which it is often keyed. Thus the panning, tilting, and zooming previously analyzed in Oriha's return to the village subjectifies the sequence not just at the level of seeing what the personage sees but more significantly at the level of feeling what she feels. Subjectification is not, however, the only result of such manipulation. For instance, in the staging of the battle between Magobei and the Sabai retainers in the deserted village at the frontier of the clan's territory, Gosha first uses a pan and zoom as an alternate to montage. Opening on a marker which reads "Sabai country begins here," the camera pans down and Magobei steps into the frame in front of it. Then, rather than cutting to an establishing shot, Gosha zooms back rapidly as he crosses the borderline and enters the town. The arrangement of formal elements—pan down sign; entry of figure into foreground; rapid zoom back—is in order of increasing unexpectedness. Combined with an iconic reading of the crossing of an inimical frontier and the silence of the empty buildings, which already suggest ambush or peril, the abruptness of the zoom has a shock value which accentuates viewer apprehension. As the sequence continues and Magobei is challenged by the waiting Sabai men, who again ask that he "die here for the peace of our clan," Gosha cross zooms from right to left, into the Sabai spokesman, and from left to right, out from Magobei in the roadway. Not only does this set up conflicting vectors in the geography of the scene, which underscores the antagonism of those present, but the effect of tightening and loosening also sustains the tension engendered in the shot which began the sequence.

Some of the figurative statements in *Goyokin*, such as the rack focus which associates Magobei with a flame and a sword, have already been treated in other contexts. Gosha recruits the metaphorical values already present in various natural elements: the scavenger birds which follow the scavenger Sabai clansmen; the cold, snowy climate which besieges the country of the calculating Sabai. He also takes established ritual elements such as the masked dance. Still others are fashioned on Gosha's own from purely cinematographic elements. A trope in motion pictures is, of course, a matter of particularized perception. A viewer either sees it or does not see it. Gosha inserts a hazy long lens of the relentless Magobei trudging back to Sabai with his legs obscured by grass in the foreground, so that he seems to float preternaturally in the artificial shallowness of the frame. This image is used before and after a discussion between Tatewaki and an aide over the dangers of Magobei's return. In this shot, his presence becomes almost ghostly. His posture as a self-appointed champion of the fishermen is transformed by the visualization into that of an avenging angel. Yet the image is sufficiently disturbing that it is not necessary for a viewer to completely penetrate the metaphor in order to experience at least a portion of its sensory effect. In another shot Oriha is visible on the left edge of a shot, three-quarters of which is blocked off by Magobei's figure in the foreground. While he interrogates her after rescuing her from ruffians, it is much more difficult to misread the abstract implication of her constriction or sense of being hemmed in.

Whether the trope suggests that Magobei is a flame, a beast, an elemental force, or anything else, he clearly functions as the center around which these visual and figurative usages are arrayed. The multiplicity of metaphors focused on him color the entire narrative. Thus the image of Magobei as a metaphysical avenger is recalled when it is he who happens

TOP: Magobei (Tatsuya Nakadai) saves "Kamikakushi" Oriha (Ruriko Asaoka).

BOTTOM: Magobei tries to warm his hands as he waits with his wife, Shino (Yuko Tsukasa), for the inevitable duel with her brother Tatewaki.

TOP: Oriha is visible on the left edge of a shot of which three-quarters is blocked off by Magobei's figure in the foreground.

BOTTOM: Leaving behind merely his footsteps as emblems of what he has accomplished, his small mark in "history," Magobei disappears from the scene.

to save the life of "kamikakushi" Oriha, who has become a gambler after the Sabai's massacre of her family. The same connotation is in play with the dancers' demon-like spirit masks seen during his duel with Tatewaki.

Analyzed in terms of metaphorical values, the final scene becomes something quite different than the traditional solitary departure of the genre hero. To begin with, he is not alone. His wife has already represented a certain abandonment of ritualized and institutionalized actions, as when she uses the natural warmth of her body to warm his frostbitten hands before the fight with her own brother; and now she follows him. The early shot at the festival which linked him with the sword-blade supports the traditional identification of the sword with the "soul of the samurai," so the weapon which Magobei plants in the ground in the frame's foreground is a part of himself also abandoned. The swirling mist from an impending storm is a many-faceted trope. It announces the approaching political tempest which will overthrow the warrior class even as it forms a white shroud to serve as winding sheet in the "funeral of the samurai." It enshrouds Magobei as well, but in a way which supports the narrative ambiguity already discussed. For the consciousness of good and evil which Magobei cannot abandon is a continuing anomaly in the historical context which is the film's reality. Leaving behind merely his footsteps as emblems of what he has accomplished, his small mark in "history," which the swirling wind will soon obliterate. Magobei simply disappears from the scene.

V. SOCIAL REBELLION AND PERSONAL IDENTITY: *TENCHU*

Tenchu may, with some justice, be cited as one of the most accomplished examples of the samurai genre since World War II. It is equally, with Kobayashi's *Hara-Kiri* and his *gendai-geki* epic *The Human Condition*, one of the most penetrating and intense films Japan or any nation has produced in the past forty years. More than twenty-five years after the first edition of this book, this may still seem a large claim to put forward for a motion picture directed by a man who, despite a special re-release of *Goyokin* in the United

States and renewed interest in *chambara* outside Japan, remains almost unknown as a director.[5] No doubt some large measure of the accomplishment of *Tenchu* is due to screenwriter Shinobu Hashimoto, who is ironically almost as anonymous in world cinema as Gosha. Yet Gosha's own preoccupation with the ambitious or conscience-bound swordsman as a social force in feudal Japan antedates any association with Hashimoto, just as the Hashimoto scripts for *Hara-Kiri*, *Samurai Assassin*, and *Seven Samurai* are fatalistic antecedents to the narrative of *Tenchu*. Unlike that of Kobayashi/Hashimoto in *Hara-Kiri* and *Rebellion*, the synthesis of the Gosha/Hashimoto viewpoints transcends any cynical or socially conscious lapses in dramatic expression of which both men may be independently guilty in past work. The result is both more and less than a total genre piece. More because it uses the codes of generic and visual expression already constituted as a straightforward system of mythic transformation; then it explores social questions through this dramatic cipher. Less because, as with much of Gosha's genre work, *Tenchu* uses those stereotypical emblems, the shorthand of the samurai film, without fully deconstructing them at a formal level.

> The world's turning upside-down soon, I'll kill one hundred even two hundred men, then I'll have done the most to turn the world upside-down.

Hashimoto adapts these words from *geku-kujo*, and midway through *Tenchu* the fictionalized Izo Okada speaks them. Superficially, the boastful tone of his declarations ("I'll have done the most") might type Izo with the simple-minded bravura of a character like Sakura in *Three Outlaw Samurai*. Although Shintaro Katsu's interpretation of Okada is that of a scraggly, good-natured, oafish-looking man who physically resembles Isamu Nagato in Gosha's earlier production, the narrative context the filmmakers have already established permits a fuller understanding of these words and adds considerably to this overall portrait of the itinerant swordsman.

To begin with, unlike Sakura in *Three Outlaw Samurai*, Izo is an authentic assassin,[6] an adept of the titled *hitokiri* or "man killing." The real Hampeita Takechi, or Zuizan *sensei* as he was called by the devotes of his sword-school, formed the Tosa Loyalist Party in 1861. Among his actual recruits to join his own *ishin shishi* group were Shimbei Tanaka and Izo Okada. While some viewers might be aware of the minor historical personnage, *Tenchu*'s Izo Okada is generically designated as the central figure. The film opens with a tight close shot of an old man, moving his body from side to side and softly chanting. A cut to medium shot reveals that he is one of several monks carrying water up a slope, and a title is superimposed: "Tosa Country—1862. Tanizato Village." As with *Sword of the Beast* and *Goyokin* or Hashimoto's script for *Samurai Assassin*, the specifics of time and place are less important than the general sense of actuality or documented event they subconsciously convey. Unlike *Goyokin*, Gosha cuts immediately to the swordsman. He inserts a shot of Izo resting his foot on an empty water jug and gazing out the window of an abandoned house. The inscription is fairly direct: a desolate scene; a man with a sword whose frustration becomes apparent when he steps outside, draws his weapon, and proceeds to cut through branches and bamboo stalks growing around the house; and finally, when they are depleted, to slash at the empty air for another half minute.

As in *Yojimbo*, the inscription is also bifocal, including both the historical ground and the figure of the samurai posed against it. Whereas Kurosawa's hero was a detached figure guided by chance across an alien landscape, Gosha and Hashimoto quickly define their character in terms of personal violence and social status. Izo's inclination toward violence is clear from his opening statement. Equally clear is the disturbing sustained shot of him hacking away at invisible foes. A cut to a long shot reveals a discarded suit of armor in the foreground of the frame inside the house. In a moment, Izo sees it also and comes over excitedly to blow off the veil of dust and cobwebs which cover it. As an icon of the chivalrous past, the interplay of the armor and the lumbering Izo may have certain ironic overtones relating to the degradation of the genre itself through its heroes. After a jump cut to a pawnshop, where Izo attempts to bully the owner into purchasing the worn suit as a family heirloom only to be told that "it's worthless," it becomes apparent that the primary purpose for its introduction into the film is to clarify Izo's economic position. At this point, Izo seeks out Hampeita Takechi, a petty official of the Tosa clan. "I'm up against the wall," Izo explains as he offers his services; "I'm up to my ears in debt." Takechi is persuaded to hire him as a *yojimbo*.

The genre typing of these opening scenes places Izo in a familiar position. The "heirloom" he presents the pawnbroker strongly implies that he has no family, no history of participation in the samurai tradition, that he is not even a *ronin* with former allegiances to color his present behavior. His

In their first scene together Takechi's figure dominates and hems in Izo's.

Today we rise to kill Yoshida Toyo.

impoverished free agency, impatient tendency toward violence, the fact that he is "up against the wall," any or all lead the viewer to formulate expectations. Still, the Izo of the film's beginning is not inordinately ambitious. In the final shot before the titles, after Izo has witnessed a killing, presumably for the first time, Gosha zooms in to a tight close shot of his rain-drenched features, glistening unnaturally as he snarls, "I'd do it better. I'll kill!" Even this ambition is directionless, part of a spontaneous burst of emotion which makes no connection between killing and self-advancement. As such it is still some distance from his stated intention to do "the most to turn the world upside-down."

The method by which Gosha and Hashimoto bridge the narrative gap between these moments involves a process of polarization. Principal among them is Izo himself and his inability to formulate an identity, compounded in the final stages by his imprisonment and literal loss of his name. In a simplistic way, it is possible to characterize Izo's development in *Tenchu* as a movement from *id*, demonstrated by his brusque, primitive behavior in the film's beginning, to *super-ego*, evidenced by his monomaniac obsession to free himself from Takechi's dominance at the film's end. Izo's recruitment by the Tosa loyalists is designed to make him perceive himself as an impersonal agent of some divine or historical imperative. "*Tenchu*," the word he and other loyalist assassins are instructed to say when murdering a political opponent, means "heaven's punishment," as if the assassins were instruments of God. Izo's "mirror-phase," where self-reflection forms his *ego*, clearly depends on Takechi as the representative of the "other." Thus, there is some justice to Takechi's assertion that "Izo's a dog I trained." He, after all, indoctrinated Izo in the confusion of idealism and pragmatism which guides the Tosa cause. At the same time, Takechi's description of Izo as a beast, however domesticated, is imagery Gosha has used numerous times before.

For Hashimoto as well as Gosha, the question of bestiality has a profundity which is located in social rather than psychological context. Takechi's relationship to Izo and the latter's ultimate assertion of his own alienated and animal nature ("Izo Okada . . . no, Torazo [Tiger], Torazo the vagrant . . . with men it's always each for himself") is governed from the first by social rather than psychological realities. In the feudal tradition, for a samurai let alone a masterless swordsman to place his own ambition above those of honor and loyalty is morally anathema. Because the initial hope of the hero of *Tenchu* is merely to rise to a caste position in that society, where he would be free from indebtedness or insecurity over his next meal, he subscribes indirectly to the codes of conduct which the likes of Sanjuro, Musashi, Nemuri, Tange Sazen, and Magobei have already cast off. Like Niino in *Samurai Assassin* Izo is a pawn to ambition. Ironically, Izo's declaration about the world turning upside-down is directed at the ambitions of Ryoma Sakamoto. Although the protagonist of *The Ambitious* plays a smaller role in *Tenchu*, Izo's position as he speaks is a dramatic inversion of Sakamoto's in that earlier film. Where Sakamoto in *The Ambitious* was torn between an inbred sense of identity as a samurai and a political stance designed to strip that class of its privileges, Izo is caught between an active role in the *bakumatsu* and a desire to achieve standing in the very system he is helping to destroy. When Sakamoto tells him that there

You fight like a wild animal.

More constricted framing in the opening discussion between Takechi and Izo

will be "no *daimyo* when the new era comes," Izo's hasty reply is, "Nonsense. You're dreaming." Because Izo does not consciously perceive this bind, he falls into its psychological trap. The resultant interior conflict is a kind of upside-down *giri/ninjo* struggle, which is eerily appropriate to Izo's hazy visions of what's coming for the "world."

As he searches for social position and psychological wholeness, the exterior form which Izo Okada's struggle for identity assumes in *Tenchu* is a series of narrative and imagistic oppositions. The old order versus the new, the sophisticated versus the primitive, the megalomaniac versus the subservient, and simply the human versus the bestial—all these figure in *Tenchu*'s particularized restatement of traditional conflicts. Takechi the power-hungry, ruthless, well-educated conspirator and Izo, his guileless, illiterate "right arm," are two exaggerated halves of the revolutionary personality. Still, their peculiar relationship is more accurately a violent symbiosis of two types of opportunist with grand designs. The vastly different scales of their personal ambition complicate the relationship, which has permutations of transfer of guilt and obsessive behavior. That Takechi and Izo are antagonistic characters thrown together under the same political banner is evident almost from the first scene between them. Unlike the principals in *Samurai Wolf* or *Goyokin*, however, any truce or temporary cooperation between them is not based on a mutual respect for the other as mental or physical equal. Takechi's lack of regard for Izo as a man let alone as an equal is such that, in the introductory scene when he accepts Izo as a participant in the Tosa cause, he does not even look at him while he speaks of their goals. As he keeps his eyes fixed on some point down the beach and away from the rough-mannered swordsman he has just taken into his service, Takechi's expression and manner emphasize the spiritual distance he believes will always separate him from this scraggly buffoon. The effect of his continuing aloofness not only gives the viewer a direct impression of Takechi's unstated but enlarged notion of a personal destiny but constantly discomfits Izo, since it could block his own plans to gain recognition for "doing the most." Although Izo never hears Takechi's deprecating remarks about him being a trained animal—or "a wolf, but he's alive and human so he worries and thinks sometimes"—he is stung by Takechi's condescending attitude. Conditioned as he is into a belief that social superiors may demand obeisance, Izo is usually willing to submit to it. On the one hand, this posture gives Izo the freedom to act, to kill, without bothering to rationalize or justify his behavior, as a discussion with Sakamoto at the inn confirms:

IZO

I kill for my country's sake.

SAKAMOTO

Why is killing me for the country's sake?

IZO

It's too complicated for me. Leader Takechi says so. . . . He's always right.

On the other hand, Izo cannot accept all the implications of Takechi being "always right." In allowing the leader to assume the responsibility for his violence, Izo must confront the realization that he has become a puppet. Early on, he can still laugh at the two-edged fable Sakamoto tells him—"You mean Leader Takechi's the hunter, and I'm the dog?"—and counsel his overly scrupulous friend to "worry about yourself." Eventually Izo's fear of being subsumed into another persona precipitates an emotional crisis and a rebellious confrontation:

TAKECHI
(shouting)

Dissatisfied? You are? Then go home! At once, if you don't want to do what I order you to.

IZO
(aroused)

I'm not your dog! Don't talk big!

If there is a tragedy in Izo's dilemma, it is in these confrontations that Gosha and Hashimoto elucidate it. Unable to find employment with any of the other pro-*bakumatsu* clans, he is compelled to come to grips not merely with the nature of his indenture to Takechi but also with the assumptions supporting it: "I know I'm a fool. He urged me on saying to kill this one and that

Izo's answer to Takechi's bluster.

I'm not your dog!
Don't talk big!

one. He said it was for the good of the country." Without Takechi's protection, payment for Izo's crimes falls due; so he goes back to the leader and begs to be pardoned. Takechi himself seals the rupture by denying that Izo is a Tosa retainer and abandoning him in prison after an arrest for drunkenness. At this point Izo is fully enmeshed by the consequences of his bestiality. Not only does Takechi refuse to recognize Izo, but his words attack him through that of which he had felt most secure, his own legend: "Izo is a famous swords-

TOP: Izo is branded and becomes "Torazo."

BOTTOM: Izo is crucified.

man. He would not get drunk, or go to brothels, or fight officials and get caught. He's not like that." Stripped of his identity, Izo's response—which the film's narrative structure implies is the only one he can make—is to give himself over completely to being a *hinin*. As a "non-human being" Izo Okada is branded a felon by the prison guards and rechristens himself Torazo or "Tiger." Liberated from the insupportable weight of his own ambitions and a confusion of identity, Izo is now in a position where he has nothing further to lose. He acquires the freedom of action he has misguidedly sought as a hired killer. Made somehow preternaturally resilient by becoming "Torazo, the vagrant," Izo is able to reject Takechi's offer of reinstatement: "Get this clear, I'm not becoming his dog." He survives the attempt to poison him and betrays the assassinations to unsympathetic clan officials.

If Izo's resultant execution is less pessimistic a conclusion than that of *Hara-Kiri* or *Rebellion*, it certainly does not make any positive statement about personal re-enfranchisement as in *Goyokin*. Izo is neither saved nor destroyed by the social events, by the *bakumatsu* itself. The fact of his participation in that historical action has little influence on his fate. His inability to perceive until too late the constraining power of the social realities he sought vainly to master, a plight Magobei overcame, is what dooms Izo. He does eventually comprehend the full dimensions of that monolith of tradition which crushes him, so Izo's virtual self-immolation seems neither as bleak nor as terrifying as the deaths of Hanchiro Tsugumo or Isaburo Sasahara in Hashimoto's earlier scripts. It is also less direct that the admittedly impassive, "duty-bound" *hara-kiri*, in *Tenchu* itself, of Shimbei Tanaka, after he has been falsely implicated in one of Izo's killings. Learning that Takechi will, because of his rank, commit *seppuku* for treason rather than be executed for murder, Izo's dying words are a defiant affirmation of some existentialist triumph even as he hangs on a cross:

OFFICIAL
Any last words?

IZO
One question: what will happen to Takechi?

OFFICIAL
His are political crimes. Yours are a ruffian's crimes. Different deaths to differentiate them. He will be allowed to commit suicide. You die in this way.

IZO

I see. It went better than I thought. I'm free at last!

OFFICIAL

Free?

IZO

I cut my ties with Takechi in this world. So he will be nothing to me in the next. Pierce me!

Obviously, the context of social determinism the filmmakers evoke throughout *Tenchu* is in conflict with Izo's sense of victory. The same forces which drove him to kill for self-advancement drive him to die for "freedom." Since he is not, like Magobei, "already dead" nor, like Tsugumo or Sasahara, disillusioned at the very moment of physical release, Izo could be freed from personal alienation as he perished. Freed also from the quandary of being both beast and man—the burdensome thought of which Magobei and Gennosuke must carry away at the conclusions of *Goyokin* and *Sword of the Beast*—Izo's tragedy is that he finds annihilation in place of fame. As the tight-close shot frames him as he expires freezes and then bleeds to white, Izo descends literally and figuratively into oblivion.

As in previous films, Gosha uses sustained camera both to intensify the action being recorded and to underscore character emotions. The first usage is exemplified by the pre-title assassination of a Tosa minister who opposes the Meiji restoration faction. It is bifocal in that it is also a rough point-of-view shot photographed from Izo's vantage as he observes, under orders from Takechi, to "learn to the full what is done." Gosha begins the long take after the minister has been attacked. Initially the frame becomes an abstract of incomprehensible motions as a thicket obscures Izo's view. Presumably he moves sideways, which is rendered via a short pan, just in time to see an assailant cut the minister's neck. For nearly two minutes, as the unbroken shot continues, the assassins are unable to administer the *coup de grace* to their wounded victim. The tension and uneasiness generated by the sustained camera matches the concurrent viewer perception that the slow death of the minister has an agonizing basis in real time. The sustained camera gives the sequence much more impact than a comparable but heavily-edited scene such as the murder of Gromek in Hitchcock's *Torn Curtain*. The sense of unease is futher compounded by other disquieting elements: the night setting; the heavy rain, which drenches the combatants and adds a persistent drone to the soundtrack; the deliberate motions of the actors, which suggest a kind of grotesque dance; and the harsh side light. The killing establishes an ominous tonality for the entire film. Moreover, the revulsion a viewer may experience in response to this disturbing violence is irrevocably attached to Izo by way of being photographed from his viewpoint.

Gosha also employs sustained camera in the "third person." The narrative suspense which underlies the first meeting of Shimbei and Sakamoto at the inn is visually stated with a prolonged close shot of an empty *sake* bottle rolling back and forth at the edge of a table. The denouement of the sequence is simply the bottle crashing to the floor, as Gosha cuts to a serving girl frightened by the unexpected sound. Her response and the broken container itself externalize a release of tension appropriate to the two men's unstated decision not to fight each other. While the anxiety level here depends as much or more on the objects (bottle/girl) and mise-en-scène as it does on the visualization, other usages are more precisely keyed to shot construction. For instance, in the discussion between Izo and Minakawa, after both have drunk from a poisoned jar of liquor sent by Takechi, Gosha compounds the effect of a long take with panning and zooming. As they wait with obvious apprehension for the poison to take effect, the camera moves from one man to the other. Several seconds pass and Minakawa begins to think that the drink may not have been adulterated after all. As Izo discourages his hopeful expression by remarking that Takechi "hasn't any kindness," Gosha zooms back. For an instant de-intensifying the shot implies that Minakawa may be right. Then suddenly, after momentarily encouraging the viewer to misread the scene, the younger man starts to gag and vomit. Gosha zooms back in rapidly to Minakawa's horrified face and frothing mouth then whip-pans to Izo as he touches his fingers to his lips and discovers the same white fluid on them. With the question of the poison graphically resolved, a cut is finally introduced, and the combined tension of narrative uncertainty and unbroken visual are simultaneously relieved. This sequence might be taken as partially subjective, because the vacillation of the side-to-side and in-and-out movement of the frame line accompanies an emotional vacillation on the part of the characters; but whatever subjectivity may be inferred is divided between Izo and Minakawa and further deconcentrated. More significantly, Gosha's temporary misdirection of the audience distances them from the scene as a whole and heightens their awareness of its formal manipulations. That sentiment is carried over in the following sequence, which introduces hallucinatory flashbacks from Izo's point of view. The opening overhead medium-close shot is of a partially conscious Izo collapsed near a cistern. Because the angle and his position upside-down in the frame make the shot difficult to read, the multi-colored (red, yellow, and blue) and slow-motion inserts which depict Izo's visions of his victims lead the viewer more toward an ironic analysis of his phantasms than a subjective co-experiencing of them. More specifically, the viewer may conclude that the "life" Izo reconstructs in his mind as he lies near death is rooted in the spectral personalities of those he has dispatched rather than in his notion of personal identity.

As Izo's sense of identity and free will is thematically central to *Tenchu*, those of Gosha's visual usages which support a feeling of constriction or closure may be of greater relevance than more purely suspenseful ones. The strongest example with regard to sustained camera is Izo's visit to his woman, Omino, after being dismissed by Takechi and failing to be hired by any other clan. In a fit of powerless resentment and depression, he rocks back and forth with his head in her lap as she strokes his hair and calmly observes that "We're the same: bound. I'm bound by money; you by Tosa and the man named Takechi. You can't break away." Those lines of dialogue are fairly explicit: Izo's will and even personality have been subsumed into Takechi's. Gosha underscores them by constructing a sequence-shot, which zooms in and out as Izo indecisively ponders his lack of alternatives. Gosha's unbroken shot holds Izo with an implacable and precise grip. It even pans to "recapture" him when he slumps out of the frame for an instant.

The constriction which is translated into a long take in this scene is part of a complex scheme of similar expressions throughout *Tenchu*. Traveling shots down a dark alleyway when the viewer first witnesses Izo stalking a victim are not strictly subjective. What is on one level visual claustrophobia is on another level a descent into the maze-like trap where both Izo and his prey play out their roles unconsciously. Even after Izo's awareness of having no options is established in the narrative, the visual usage continues to anticipate and support that development. The montage of Izo out in the rain trying to find a job after arguing with Takechi is a multifaceted example. In a high-angle medium shot, a standing figure listens to Izo's petition. At this point he is not merely displaced from the visual center but, kneeling just out of the rain in the right of the shot, obscured and boxed into that corner by a wooden post which cuts through the frame vertically. Izo's first rejection comes as he is photographed alone in medium shot, back-lit and with his body hidden from view by a chair and table in the foreground. At Kumamoto, Izo is revealed in medium close-up, front-lit by a flame in the shot's foreground, which seems momentarily a more hopeful image, until a man steps in front, blocking off the light with his lower body and throwing Izo's face into darkness. Finally, as an official tells him in voiceover why it is impossible for any of the other clans to hire him, Izo's body is not even in the shot. Instead he is seen dimly mirrored in a puddle rippled by raindrops.

The graphic progression of this sequence of shots effectively diminishes Izo's physical presence even as he is being emotionally destroyed by his inability to break away from Takechi. As he is successively removed from center screen, hemmed in by the fixtures of the room, thrown into shadow, and finally taken out of the shot entirely and reduced to mere reflection, the viewer is subconsciously reminded of his deteriorating position and primed for his literal breakdown in the scene with Omino, which follows. Similarly, in the scene in jail where Takechi denies knowing Izo, Gosha uses just three shots to tie together Izo's psychological regression. First, a tight close shot captures Izo's uncomprehending look as he hears Takechi explain that the real Izo would not "fight officials or get drunk." Simultaneously, one of the thick wooden bars of the cell blocks the viewer off from a part of Izo's face. At this instant, with his character thoroughly undercut not only in his boasts to the other prisoners but in his own sense of who he really is, Gosha inserts a reverse close two-shot or rather what becomes a two-shot as Izo starts to fall to his knees and reveals Takechi standing on the other side of the bars. The fluid geometry of this second shot isolates the two men within and without the cell. The placement of one of the wooden bars also separates them in two dimensions, which reinforces the smiling Takechi's total dominance over the exchange. Finally, Gosha cuts back to the original angle as Izo, in shock, his name gone without hope of appeal, sinks completely out of the frame. Visible behind him in the shadowy enclsoure are the sparks from a coal fire, over which the guards will shortly heat the iron to brand him. With only a few seconds of screen time and a marked economy of shots, Gosha ties together the critical relationships and prepares the audience for Izo's subsequent rebirth as Torazo.

In *Goyokin*, Gosha keyed his broken compositions and disjunctive editing to a conflict which was essentially external: Magobei against the Sabai. What exploration there was of Magobei's interior make-up interplayed with standard elements of the samurai film. Deconstructing both hero and narrative gave the audience a more distanced appreciation of Magobei's role as figure in a genre piece. The development of Izo's personality on the other hand depends less on his actual role than on his misperception of what that role is. Because he is less enlightened than Magobei in that regard, Izo operates at a disadvantage as a hero with whom the viewer may identify throughout most of the film. Because the central conflict is an internal and ironic one, between Izo's desire to "make a name" for himself and to preserve his psychological identity, the audience is distanced from him as a character. There is no need in *Tenchu* for the formal manipulations and extreme disequilibrium of *Goyokin*. Instead Gosha visualizes the interior violence and compulsion of his personage with the understated indicators of composition or texture. From the strong diagonal of a slashed bamboo shade framed beside the man Izo kills in the alley to that of a roof line pointing at Izo as he confesses his crimes in the courtyard of a Tosa manor, Gosha's expressive vectors remain within the limits of the frame. Occasional foreground clutter, such as the dark, glistening tabletops at the inn or the slatted screen in Omino's room, separates the audience from Izo and other characters without the overt tilting or other compositional fracturing of *Goyokin*. Side light and an overlay of shadows compound and confuse the stage-lines in a variety of deep-focus two-shots. Screens and pieces of furniture divide the wide anamorphic frames into smaller, isolated units.

Below:
TOP: Izo is seen dimly morrored in a puddle rippled by raindrops.

CENTER: "I've never seen this man before now."

BOTTOM: "He's only pretending to be Izo Okada. An imposter."

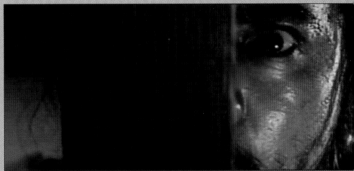

Above:
TOP: Izo Okada and Ryoma Sakamoto are both hemmed in by fate.

CENTER: But Izo's position is even more fractured and obscured.

BOTTOM: Izo is not merely displaced from the visual center but, kneeling just out of the rain in the right of the shot, obscured and boxed into that corner by a wooden post which cuts through the frame vertically.

The pattern of external manipulation in *Goyokin* was sometimes focused on clarifying particular emotions or relationships. The more contained effects of *Tenchu* accomplish the same. Two shots of Izo exemplify the way Gosha externalizes the character's sense of detachment from reality. In the first, after he has quarreled with Takechi, a medium close-up using a long lens flattens Izo against the gray shingles of roof covered with a myriad rivulets of rainwater. As he hesitates, turns to go back, then strides defiantly off, the long lens and the distorted background of the roof destroy any sense of visual geography. The viewer is disoriented physically while Izo vacillates mentally. In the second shot, a high-angle wide which captures him reclining in a field of tall grass view after his release from prison, Izo is photographed as if he were floating in a green sea. Not only does this show him cast adrift as "Torazo the vagrant" but it also anticipates the narrative revelation of Izo's decision to "cut his ties."

A similar, dynamic usage is geared to Takechi, as he raves after his arrest by the more conservative Tosa clansmen. As he begins to prophesy his release and his future accomplishments, Gosha zooms from a medium-long shot through the bars of his cell, so that they disappear from the frame. Figuratively liberated—the viewer can no longer see the prison Takechi has already left in his mind—he speaks of moving "from small destructions to large ones, then decisive destruction . . . only then will a new dawn appear over Japan." So powerful is Takechi's flight of fancy that Gosha cuts away before he finishes, and his final words and his laughter sounds over an aerial shot of a sunrise.

This aura of progressive physical and mental violence, of small then large then decisive destructions, permeates *Tenchu* at a variety of levels. Whether the viewer is dsigusted or fascinated at the sight of flesh being punctured and life-blood spurting out via graphic special effects, Gosha formally redirects those sentiments. In *Goyokin*, where identification with Magobei and his growing distaste for killing helps to predispose the viewer, a heavily edited but straightforward staging accomplished this redirection. In *Tenchu*, the characterization of Izo demands uninterrupted combat peppered with elements of brutal satire and unexpected detail. Just as he uses zooming and voiceover to ridicule Takechi's undiminished visions of the coming destruction, Gosha precedes Izo's slaughter of a score of anti-Restoration men at an inn outside Kyoto with a sequence of overtly comic events. Unaware of an agreement between Tosa and Choshu that forces his to not participate in this mass assassination, Izo learns of the plan at the last minute and undertakes to run the twenty-seven miles to the inn. In this parody of a marathon, Izo is photographed with a variety of lenses, crossing large expanses of open country, jumping over children, brushing past pilgrims on the highway, framed against a golden sunset, and even running in place when he pauses to read a road sign so as not to break pace. Reaching his destination caked from head to foot with white dust, Izo finds that the battle has begun. He pours two buckets of water over himself, draws his sword, and rushes into the inn yelling that Izo Okada of Tosa has arrived. Despite the intense violence that follows, in which Izo's long sword seems to cut indiscriminately through wall panels, bodies, and even rafters, the verisimilitude of the encounter is severely diminished before it begins by the mock-heroism of Izo's race to the inn. Also significant in this sequence is the fact that Izo violates the established ritual, shouting out his name and clan in his excitement and not just *"Tenchu!"*

The question of ritual itself is less important than that of betraying his clan's involvement. That is the point of the reprimand Takechi delivers in the following scene. From his initial, vicarious participation in the pre-title murder, *"Tenchu,"* the simple, two-syllable epithet, has had a magical or totemic meaning for Izo. Not only is he genuinely dismayed when he omits the word during an otherwise successful murder ("I made a mistake yesterday," he reports guiltily to an amused Takechi, "I forgot to say '*tenchu.*'"), he ascribes a supportive faculty to the term. As he explains in an early scene, relating to his own endeavors:

MINAKAWA
Teach me how to kill men like that.

IZO
Say *"tenchu."* There's no other knack to it. *Tenchu.*

Protected and sustained by the notion of meting out "heaven's punishment" Izo fights without fear, an experience no other Gosha hero from the bitter Tange Sazen to the indignant Magobei is permitted. As they did in the ending of *Goyokin*, ritual and satire diminish the intensity and impact of staged events that might otherwise be unacceptably or distractively violent.

The inverse of this visual scheme is the use of formal elements to accentuate situations and events that are not inherently dramatic. Color and angle, for example, add a sensory impact to Izo's phantasm after being poisoned. The overhead shot of Prince Anenojoji's body and the red trail of his blood spreading down a sewer is a repellent image through which the viewer co-experiences Izo's horror over what he has done. Because much of *Tenchu* is painted in drab browns and blues, the mere use of these deeper colorations subtly intensifies the scenes which contain them. The bright expanse of water, transmuted by a long lens into soft highlights in the background as Izo tells Sakamoto of his dream of future great deeds, comments on the unreal and detached quality of Izo's reverie. Similarly, the festival banners littering the shore across which Izo stumbles the morning after the attempt to poison him act as sadly evocative remnants of that bright dream. The point of this imagery is not to romanticize Izo's life or his death, no more than the last shots of *Goyokin* romaticize Magobei's survival.

Although Gosha rejects many of the shock values and jarring effects of that previous film in *Tenchu*, he substitutes a stylistic overview with similar implications. Certain unsettling moments may confuse rather than surprise the viewer: Sakamoto's premonition that there are assailants lurking in the surrounding darkness of the frame or the cross-like portion of Takechi's easel in the foreground of a close-up of Izo which foreshadows his crucifixion. As in past films, Gosha may prefer to convey sensory impressions over symbolic meanings. In *Tenchu* even those impressions are less overt. The result is a continuity of expression which no other Gosha film possesses quite as fully. Undoubtedly, this is to some extent due to the participation of Hashimoto and his more organic approach to filmmaking. To some extent only, as Gosha's powerful visualizations can easily override verbal expressions. Perhaps the best example of this begins with the first shot after the titles. An extremely long-focal-length lens is trained on a cobbled street flanked by two buildings in the distance. For a moment, there is nothing but the clatter of wooden clogs on the soundtrack. Then men begin to appear, and the lack of depth in the lens makes them seem to rise head first out of the street. As they come forward, the voices of onlooking townsmen are heard, explaining who they are and singling out Takechi, "the black dragon of Tosa," at the head of the band. Izo is just behind him, "a wolf under the black dragon." Even before the dialogue has made the expository point in words, the shot itself has placed Izo "under" Takechi. Through the unnatural geometry of the unusual lens, Izo is held in that position for a considerable amount of time. This visual usage, which addresses the critical relationship between Izo and Takechi, may seem like a throwaway; yet it is significant enough for Gosha to reconstruct some of its elements and to reverse its statement at the film's conclusion. As he decides what to do, Izo stands unsteadily among some smooth gray stones by the ocean shore, the background the same color as his kimono, so that he blends into it. Gosha then cuts and uses another extremely long lens to photograph Izo on the steps of the Tosa manor. As Izo opens the gate, Gosha zooms back from him into a wide angle, radically unflattening the image. He repeats this effect again in the courtyard, then the scene of Izo's confession proceeds with normal focal length lenses. Whatever the figurative implications of the Tosa men rising out of the cobblestones or of Izo among the rocks on the beach, for Izo to be spiritually free of Takechi, to summon the will to confess his crimes, the constriction of that long lens must be loosened. The zooming back liberates him before the moment of truth.

Although neither as diverse nor as frequent as in *Goyokin*, some primarily metaphorical visuals are also contained in *Tenchu*: the bamboo water pipe, which is used as a kind of punctuation between scenes, or Takechi's *sumi* painting, which is often seen in the back-

The bamboo water pipe, which is used as a kind of punctuation between scenes

ground and seems to progress side-by-side with his plans for the Tosa loyalists. These are perhaps as significant as mere props, which add sensory impact or texture, as they are as symbols. Other usages generally address the question of how to take the measure of a man. Izo's "bestiality" has already been examined, as has Takechi's attitude toward it. As it happens, Takechi's first words to Izo (and in the film) contain the more traditional equation of man with sword: "Yours is an evil sword. It's wild." The townsmen who describe Izo as "a wolf" also remark that his sword "looks more like a pole." Izo's relationship to his well-crafted "Masamune," as with Magobei's "Sukehiro" in *Goyokin*, is both practical and symbolic. As a *ronin*, it is the only residue of self-esteem he possesses. Izo is first seen in a wordless expression of this fact slashing the air, wielding his sword against spectral enemies. As a Tosa retainer, he expects that those who ask if Shimbei Tanaka is greater than he will seek an answer by reckoning who has killed the most men with his sword. Finally, as one who knows of the samurai belief that the sword is his soul, Izo is encouraged to regard his own excellence as commensurate with that of the legendary blade he possesses. After his weapons are stolen and used to assassinate Anenojoji, Shimbei Tanaka kills himself because of that belief. Izo himself is inordinately upset when his blade is nicked and demurs at the thought of carrying out any assignment with a borrowed weapon while his is being repaired.

There are, of course, other measures of manhood suggested. Sakamoto tries to explain one with his fable of the dog who bit the liver and this spoiled the taste of the rabbit his master has shot: "the point of the story is not to hurry too much." But temperance is not a standard of conduct Izo can comprehend either in life or in death. If Izo is an "evil sword," he is not like the killer in the adaptations of *Daibosatsu Toge*, obsessed with cold-blooded mastery of his weapons. Nor is he like Nemuri, who uses his Engetsu style as a means to an end, which is revenge. Izo's own words repeatedly define his ambition. He is an assassin of a different order than the dispassionate and precise Shimbei Tanaka. Tanaka's *seppuku* is a meaningless proof of his faith in an old and expiring order, and the audience cannot help but recoil when it sees him confronted with the stolen sword which killed Anenojoji, reflect for only an instant, then draw, and finally expose and pierce his abdomen in one deliberate motion. This staging is made all the more chilling by the fact that Yukio Mishima's performance of *hara-kiri* as the character Tanaka was repeated in real life a few months later. Izo's end, while just as fatal, is of a different order. The social rebellion is accom-

Izo Okada (Shintaro Katsu, right) attacks Ryoma Sakamoto in *Tenchu*.

plished without either Izo or Takechi seeing it through. The world turns upside-down by itself, destroying the Tanakas, glorifying the Sakamotos, and indifferent to the Izo Okadas. For him, as for all of Gosha's heroes, Bokuden's words are inapplicable. The "last thing" for the samurai is to die in ignorance or despair. Only the common man "dies unflinchingly." The crucifixion of Izo, who has been called "evil" and a "beast," is not merely a personal redemption or a cry of existential anguish but an affirmation of simple, perishable humanity.

VI. THE LOWER DEPTHS: *KUMOKIRI NAZAEMON*, *HUNTER IN THE DARK* AND *DEATH SHADOWS*

Both *Bandit vs. Samurai Squad* (*Kumikiri Nizaemon*, 1978) and *Hunter in the Dark* (*Yami No Kariudo,* 1979) mark a thematic return for Gosha to the outlook of *Sanurai Wolf* and *Secret of the Urn*. Although neither "Fog" Nizaemon nor Gomyo, the title characters, have the pre-existing genre identity of a figure such as Tange Sazen, their attitudes, without being overtly sardonic, and their social positions, are similar. Like Sazen, neither has any trust in or respect for the era's formal institutions. To survive, they inhabit an underworld full of nocturnal activity and populated by burnt-out drifters. While Nizaemon and Gomyo both possess some status within that world, neither seems to have the opportunity, or even the inclination, to rise above it. Magobei, the side-show barker, and Gennosuke, the fugitive, were both men driven to restore their lost honor and were never a part of the universe of outcasts through which they were forced to pass. Certainly they never had a position of leadership in that underworld's informal association of outlaws, gamblers, and prostitutes, as do the gang bosses Nizaemon and Gomyo.

As gang bosses, neither Nizaemon nor Gomyo are lone wolves. In fact, although Tatsuya Nakadai essays both roles, Gosha devotes a considerable portion of the narrative of both *Bandit vs. Samurai Squad* and *Hunter in the Dark* to the activities and motivations of other figures. Having diffracted the dramatic focus of the films by giving equal weight to other than the title characters, Gosha eschews the concentrated visual exposition of *Secret of the Urn* and *Samurai Wolf I* and *II*. The frenetic montages and zoom schemes of the three earlier features would also be hard to sustain over a much longer running time (*Secret of the Urn* is 91 minutes long; *Bandit vs. Samurai Squad* runs 163 minutes). More pertinently, except perhaps for the tortured Tanigawa in *Hunter in the Dark,* none of the characters has the emotional intensity appropriate to an energetic visualization.

That is not to imply that the visual style or the narrative action are restrained. On the level of violence, the opening sequence of *Bandit vs. Samurai* Squad matches anything in Gosha's earlier work. Dark clad figures grapple up a wall and break into a manor in the middle of the night. They are interrupted first by other thieves and then by the police. In the fighting and chaos that ensue, action which rivals the combat in the inn in *Tenchu,* Gosha's camera moves repeatedly over the scene as if searching for a figure on which to focus. Unlike the violent openings of *Secret of the Urn* or even *Tenchu,* in which the central character is easily identified by both visualization and genre typing, the title sequence of *Bandit vs. Samurai Squad* is a general introduction to a violent and unstable night world, a world of masked robbers and lantern-carrying policemen in constant conflict, a kind of samurai noir.

Uncharacteristic nostaligia: the bandit Nizaemon (Tatsuya Nakadai) announces his final job.

As *Bandit vs. Samurai Squad* develops, the only motivation revealed for the master robber, "Fog" Nizaemon, and his cohorts is greed. The activities of the gang are directed towards a single "big score," the theft of a sum of money sufficient to permit them all to retire from criminality. Obviously this is not a novel storyline; but it is a marked change of subject for Gosha. Some of his previous *chambara* characters may have been avaricious—but for power, not money. Honor, ambition, revenge—all the standard motivations of the genre figure—have driven Gosha's heroes, both good and bad, to action. In Gosha's earlier samurai films, the desire for money, for gold or treasure, even, in *Sword of the Beast* (which is also known as *Samurai Gold Seekers),* is always a secondary motive, a means to a higher end. The conflict between Nizaemon and the representative of Tokugawa repression, the chief constable, does not derive from either personal or social rebelliousness. While it may not be completely apolitical, their antagonism is more accurately a professional attitude, based on the natural opposition of thief and policeman. Early in the film, details of Nizaemon's ten years as an *oyabun*—or boss—are filled in. The fact that he was once a samurai in a Lord's household is also revealed. Unlike *Goyokin or Sword of the Beast,* where the present situations of Magobei and Gennosuke anticipate and contrast starkly with the flashbacks to their break with their clans, Gosha includes no extended exposition of Nizaemon's disenfranchisement in *Bandit vs. Samurai Squad.* To a degree, this reinforces a variant genre typing. For the robber, a man who lives by his wits and his daring, is not bound by the genre expectations attached to the samurai or the *ronin.* The plot revelation that Nizaemon was once a samurai is subsumed by his present activity as a leader of thieves. Gosha's visualization does not compromise

Nizaemon's apparent disinterest in his lost honor. Dark frames enmesh robbers and constables alike. Zooms fail to penetrate enigmatic visages. Cuts accent the instability of the milieu. Objects become motifs, like the bamboo water pipe in *Tenchu*; but the characters themselves move through this universe like emblems, like personifications rather than persons.

What Gosha may be suggesting is that the robber's mask is more than just a dark cloth drawn over his face. While Izo Okada may want to "turn the world upside-down," Nizaemon wants to avoid tumult, wants to pass through his underworld like a fog and to succeed through stealth. Nizaemon and his fellows are, to the outside observer, dark-clad fugitives; but within the gang structure, they re-acquire an identity, the very identity Izo despaired of finding as long as he was Takechi's "kept dog." This freedom of choice for its protagonists gives *Bandit vs. Samurai Squad* the singular, quasi-existential tone of hope and despair which sustains many American "caper films," such as *The Asphalt Jungle* or *The Killing*. If *Bandit vs. Samurai Squad* is, at times, more reminiscent of film noir than of *chambara*, that also is part of its mask. The ultimate destruction of the gang and Nizaemon's self-realization that he has been driven all along by a desire for revenge are certainly plot twists worthy of noir. Their impact, however, can only lead to a confrontation that is pure *chambara*.

By ritualizing Nizaemon's final attack on his former clan, by making him an armor-clad figure waging single combat in a thunderstorm, Gosha and Nakadai recapture some of the tragic futility of Tsugumo in *Hara-Kiri*. But Gosha's thematic conclusion more closely resembles the last films of John Ford, such as *The Man Who Shot Liberty Valance* or *Sergeant Rutledge*, than any of Masaki Kobayashi. In the end, as the constructs of the genre reveal a more detached and pessimistic view of the human condition, for "Fog" Nizaemon there is neither the possibility of a triumph, like Magobei's, nor of a release from suffering, like Izo's.

Hunter in the Dark continues in the black vein of *Bandit vs. Samurai Squad*. The opening scene is ungrounded action: an attack on a sedan chair as it crosses a bridge. Gosha records the action, like the first ambush in *Tenchu*, not from a particular person's point of view but from a perspective that any passerby might have, detached but fascinated. The attacker is a one-eyed assassin, Yataro Tanigawa, and his action leads to an offer of employment as a bodyguard for Gomyo, one of two local bosses engaged in a territorial dispute. The new-found position as Gomyo's *yojimbo* gives Tanigawa his first real glimpse of the highly regimented *yakuza* underworld. It also quickly presents him with the opportunity for money and advancement if he will join in a conspiracy with Gomyo's mistress, her lover, and a rival boss to eliminate Gomyo.

The figure of Gomyo, to which Tatsuya Nakadai brings elements of the fanaticism of Takechi in *Tenchu* and the honorable thievery of Nizaemon in *Bandit vs. Samurai Squad,* is not driven by any surface emotion. Gosha gives Tanigawa the more dramatic characteristics of several earlier heroes from Gennosuke to Izo Okada. He is plagued by memories of an unspecified but traumatic past event. He is seeking some thing, a cause or a leader, a new direction for his troubled mind to follow. Given this mental state and Gomyo's insouciance, Tanigawa chooses to remain loyal to the gang boss. In so doing he sets in motion a chain of events that precipitate the destruction of both the gang and a local clan. For like his one-eyed antecedent, Tange Sazen, Tanigawa seems content to be led by chance from encounter to encounter, from killing to killing. Unlike Tange Sazen, who assumes a new identity not because he has forgotten his first one but because it has imperiled him, Tanigawa is genuinely unable to probe his past and discover a key to his present malaise. His attitude and the inadvertent parricide which haunts him recall the plight of Niino in the Hashimoto/Okamoto *Samurai Assassin* more strongly than anyone in Gosha's work.

ABOVE: Yoshio Harada as Yataro Tanigawa in *Hunter in the Dark.*

Gosha's last *chambara* film is *Death Shadows* (*Jittemai,* 1987). While it does feature Tokugawa-era *yakuza*, it does not form a trilogy with *Bandit vs. Samurai Squad* and *Hunter in the Dark.* The "shadows" of the title are assassins recruited and rendered mute with a deft slice across their throats by shogunate magistrate Utsumi. Twenty years later, Shadow Yasuke encounters Ocho, a daughter he was forced to abandon—but before any reconciliation can be affected, he is killed and Ocho forcefully recruited into the shadows in his stead. Working on a limited budget, Gosha's mise-en-scène is an unusual melange. In the titles, Ocho performs a dance routine with a twirling ribbon, which becomes like the water pipe in *Tenchu,* a recurring motif as either unmotivated cutaway or transition between scenes. Gosha adds cutaways of Oren, Ocho's antagonist, also dancing, but much more lasciviously, in front of an array of colored lights and fog.

It is through art direction that *Death Shadows* is often stylized to the point of phantasmagoria. The film is shot almost entirely on sound stages with all but a few scenes set at night. Many of the studio "exteriors" feature exag-

ABOVE: Each actor poses as if for a mug shot, while a narrator reads their crimes.

TOP: In the titles, Ocho performs a dance routine with a twirling ribbon, which becomes a recurring motif, like the water pipe in Tenchu.

RIGHT: Many of the studio "exteriors" feature exaggerated use of colors, such as a blood red sky for a slaughter by a stream.

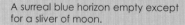

A surreal blue horizon empty except for a sliver of moon.

The stylized execution features upraised blades against a plain gray background.

gerated use of colors, such as a blood red sky for a slaughter by a stream or a surreal blue horizon empty except for a sliver of moon when Utsumi tells Yasuke to leave his family. Gosha juxtaposes strange but realistic sets with these quasi-operatic backdrops. The introduction of the shadows is almost a parody, with each actor posed as if for a mug shot while a narrator reads their crimes. Their sentences, of course, are all the same: death. Their stylized execution features upraised blades against a plain gray background and sliced pieces from their bloodstained paper hoods floating in the air. It is possible to read this as an appropriate staging for a "fake" execution, just as the saturated colors in Yasuke's flashbacks could be a histrionic extension of his pathetic self-image as a literal and figurative shadow. There is even an overtly symbolic moment when one flashback segment opens with a spider web against an indiscernible background followed by a rack focus revealing the "enmeshed" Yasuke and his wife.

When Ocho "listens" to her father's story, they stand in a dimly lit warehouse full of small statues of Buddha. The awkward sign language used by the mute Yasuke is like exaggerated theatrical movement, almost as unreal as the flashback scenes he conjures up for Ocho. How much of that story she "hears" is questionable, since much of the time that her father is gesturing to her in arcane sign language she is looking away. As the film progresses, it becomes clear that almost any plot twist and any staging are possible in the shadow world. There is a tour-de-force fight scene near the conclusion. Ocho saves the disgraced clan operative Kanoya from three clan samurai who then are confronted by Utsumi. The entire sequence plays out in obscurity, with only an occasional glint of a blade or darkly lit close-up, as the figures move back and forth through a swamp, gliding over a fog amid bare black tree branches.

Ocho is certainly the most vulnerable of Gosha's *chambara* "heroes." While she has a certain aptitude with her *jitte*, or truncheon inside of which a short blade is sheathed, she is repeatedly captured and struggles to overcome every opponent. Her use of the twirling ribbon as a second weapon is extremely curious, as if there were a hynoptic effect to the movement of the colored fabric that prevents those holding swords from merely slashing through it. Her duel with Kakizaki, the corrupt officer who calls himself the "devil," is curious on several levels. The mannered performance of the actor who portrays Kakizaki becomes a Bruce Lee parody when he fights. He survives his first encounter with Kanoya, but mesmerized by Ocho's ribbon, he is fatally wounded and dies cackling in disbelief. By now the viewer realizes from genre expectations that, whatever perils she may encounter, Ocho will survive to the end of the film. Nonetheless, coldly dispatching a comic figure is unusual behavior for a genre hero.

When Ocho "listens" to her father's story, they stand in a dimly lit warehouse full of small statues of Buddha.

As odd as *Death Shadows* may be, Gosha does use sustained camera and zoom editing for telling dramatic effect. Ocho's fake execution features a parade through the streets and a crucifixion before a cheering crowd. Afterwards she meets with Utsumi in a dark chamber lit by a single candle, where the walls are barely visible. When the magistrate stands he picks up the candle. As he walks around Ocho, the light moves behind her turning her literally into a shadow even before she has agreed to accept the role. At the same time, Gosha zooms in, slowly tightening to a medium-close two shot. When Utsumi puts the candle down again and circles back to the right, another zoom moves in more rapidly to a tight two shot. Ocho refuses to look at Utsumi, but her decision is clear. Even as the narrative situation permits her little choice, Gosha's visual schema of sustained camera, precise lighting, and zooming reinforces the sense of entrapment and metamorphosis and confirm that she has no option.

In *Hunter in the Dark* Gosha paces his visual usage to a narrative which develops slowly and conservatively but with precision. Like *Bandit vs. Samurai Squad*, *Hunter in the Dark* runs well over two hours. Pans and tracking shots replace the more immediate impact of zooms and cuts. The chiaroscuro of *Bandit vs. Samurai Squad* is carried over and even amplified. The "hunter in the dark" becomes literally that, a dark figure skirting the pools of light in a succession of shadow-filled frames. Gosha creates this dark environment in a way that evokes the familiar readings: constriction, peril, struggle against unseen forces. At the same time, the underworld promises freedom from detection and, for Tanigawa, from the unsettling past.

Ultimately Tanigawa takes his place with Magobei and Gennosuke as an irresistible avenger. In an orgy of death, he singlehandedly destroys the Kitama clan and seeks release in *shinju*—double suicide—with his lover, Oriwa. Even with this action, he cannot entirely fulfill the genre expectations of the viewer. The final duel between Gomyo and the local lord, Shimokuni, comes closer, but having built the narrative around Tanigawa, Gosha pulls back from a last, direct genre statement. Darkness and constriction give way to daylight and open fields as Gomyo and Shimokuni meet and murder each other in a farmyard. Gosha's staging may seem an anti-climax or even a parody, but it subtly reaffirms a thematic conclusion akin to *Goyokin* and *Sword of the Beast*. Skill, valor, right reason—all have their limits. The only indefatigable trait of the genre hero is his mortality.

TOP AND CENTER: As he walks around Ocho, the light moves behind her, turning her literally into a shadow even before she has agreed to accept the role. At the same time, Gosha zooms in, slowly tightening to a medium-close two shot.

BOTTOM: An eye peers through a carved panel in *Death Shadows*.

CHAPTER SIX

THE SLAYERS

If the red slayer think he slays
Or if the slain think he is slain,
They know not well the subtle ways
I keep, and pass, and turn again.
—RALPH WALDO EMERSON, "Brahma"

I. KIHACHI OKAMOTO

Yuzo Kayama in *Warring Clans* (1964)

ERHAPS MORE THAN ANY OTHER DIRECTOR TO emerge in the 1960s, the very titles of Kihachi Okamoto's films suggest a predisposition toward violent men and events: *Warring Clans, Samurai Assassin, Sword of Doom, Kill!, Red Lion*. This is coincidence, of course, because the Japanese titles are not the same, but appropriate nonetheless. For while the "beasts" and outcasts who populate Gosha's cinema may take a few moments to deliberate their position, Okamoto's heroes are already in action. This is not to say that they are all brash men. In fact, it would be difficult to argue a more cold-blooded and calculating killer than Tsukue in *Sword of Doom*, Okamoto's adaptation of *Daibosatsu Toge*. Where Gosha's protagonists transform the reflective *giri/ninjo* struggles of Kobayashi's figures into active ones and, in a few instances, even manage to free themselves from the double bind of duty and conscience, the men of Okamoto's films are altogether unconcerned with such questions. Those of them who are born with certain loyalties—as in *Red Lion* (*Akage*, 1969) and *Warring Clans* (*Sengoku Yaro*, 1962)—try to redirect them toward the personal and away from the institutionalized. Those without loyalties do not seek to establish any. *Bushido*, with its plethora of codes, hardly matters. Even a simple sense of honor is not a crucial issue in Okamoto's *chambara* narratives. Violence, then, is not an

attempt at resolution of an ethical conflict, as much as it is a depersonalized manifestation of power and discontent. The attack on an aged pilgrim which opens *Sword of Doom* is a purposeless and irrational act of cruelty that crystallizes the essential question of the film: why must the swordsman use his sword? Why must the "red slayer" slay? The answer may come through the psychopathic frenzy of Okamoto's version of Tsukue in *Sword of Doom*—for whom killing becomes such a necessary function that after his real adversaries are exhausted his mind creates phantoms to oppose him in an unending battle—or through the misguided ambition of Niino in *Samurai Assassin*. Neither answer is a simple one. The freeze frame which closes *Sword of Doom* continues, by extrapolation, to hold the film's central character in the grip of a timeless combat even after the image has faded from the screen. The nature of violence, by whomever it is initiated, places an autonomous and self-perpetuating process in motion. The reel-long battle—which leaves scores of dead in a snow-covered street and in which all the "victors" inadvertently defeat their own purposes at the end of *Samurai Assassin*—further suggests that such violence may also be entirely ineffectual.

Samurai Assassin opens with a shot of a manor house somewhere in Edo. A title card sets the date: "February 11, 1857." A man watching the gates of the building reports that "Lord Ii did not enter the castle today." The scene shifts to a conference of anti-shogunate conspirators as they discuss the possibility of a betrayer existing among them. The shot is held for some moments, broken all the while by a sword in the foreground center. The cut is to a close shot of a man (played by Toshiro Mifune) in the rear of the room. As the titles appear, he picks his nose. With this rather undynamic beginning and simple bit of stage business, the assassin of the film's title is introduced. The genre indicators are clear enough. The fact of Mifune starring in the film and the shot selection which isolates him in the first close-up leave no doubt that he is the central character. At the same time, the very casualness of the staging provides additional information. To begin with, his boredom at the bickering of what one may assume are his employers or co-conspirators separates him from the brash, simple-minded swordsman he later depicted in *Red Lion*. If he is not the unwitting pawn of these men, neither—reading from his rude gesture and the lack of self-consciousness which it implies—is it certain that he is attempting, like the psychopathic killer of *Sword of Doom*, to exploit their cause for his own ends.

"Loyalists. The shogunate side. What's the difference? The point is are you really going to kill Lord Ii? If such a plan's afoot, I'll join you." Tsuruchiyo Niino cannot, like Tsugumo or Sasahara or heroes of other Shinobu Hashimoto scripts, afford the luxury of personal honor. The pragmatism of one of his early remarks in *Samurai Assassin* dispels any viewer expectation that conscience or guilt will figure strongly in the characterization. And yet, as Hashimoto's flashbacks gradually reveal, Niino is not a prototype of *Tenchu*'s Izo Okada, not an ambitious vagabond caught up in the confusing tide of social upheaval. As in all Hashimoto scripts, the social context is present. Both Niino ("It's either make money like you, a merchant, or become a respectable samurai, living haughtily and in comfort.") and the target of his murderous ambition, Lord Ii ("Killing me to reform the Shogunate is a fool's dream. If I die the three-hundred-year-old Tokugawa Shogunate dies with me. That will mean the end of the samurai in Japan."), are aware of the limited alternatives for advancement and reform that their society allows.

Under Okamato's direction in *Samurai Assassin* that context is subsumed into an overriding and distancing style, into a complex scheme of flashbacks and expository titles that interweave past and present with an alienating precision. The audience appreciates from the initial stages that Niino's real enemy in *Samurai Assassin* is neither Lord Ii nor his companions, nor even the press of historical events, but rather that exterior and antagonistic force which seems to direct those characters and events. On a narrative level, that conflict is already firmly established in Hashimoto's script. The use of a scribe, as in *Hara-Kiri*, to provide a detached, third-person commentary, as well as the disjunction entailed in the constant shifting back and forth between past and present, erect an intangible but potent barrier between Niino's defiant determination to succeed ("A sword does not make a samurai. . . . The world is unpredictable today. I'll live as I please.") and any uninterrupted viewer empathy with that goal. On that level also, Hashimoto injects the threat of annihilation. In an act reminiscent of Chamberlain Kageyu in *Hara-Kiri*, at one point the head of the conspirators orders the scribe to "delete everything on Kurihara and Masui. We need no record on betrayers." As with Izo Okada, the complicating factors of Niino's illegitimate birth and the emotional distur-

ABOVE, TOP: Niino (Toshiro Mifune) indicates disinterest by sprawling and picking his nose in *Samurai Assassin*.

BOTTOM: Toshiro Mifune in *Red Lion*

Opposite page:
Tatsuya Nakadai in *Kill!* (1968)

CENTER: Tatsuya Nakadai as Ryunosuke Tsukue and Michiyo Aratama as Ohama in *Sword of Doom*

BOTTOM STILLS: Tatsuya Nakadai as Ryunosuke Tsukue in the final combat sequence in *Sword of Doom*

bance he suffered when discovering that illegitimacy have caused him to equate winning fame with assertion of identity. On a formal level, as it did in *Tenchu*, Hashimoto's screenplay provides the ground for that search that is governed by an underlying existentialism rather than *shushigaku*, and by social rather than individual action. It is Okamoto's visualization which gives this literate and ironic script a visceral and tragic impact.

Realizing he has no legitimate claim to hereditary rank as a true samurai, Niino leaves his fencing school and voluntarily seeks employment as a slayer of men. Doing so, he conforms to genre type. The viewer familiar with the narrative patterns of samurai film appreciates from convention the depth of Niino's dilemma and identifies to some degree with his response. Still, as the first shot of him and the initial flashbacks suggest, Niino is ambivalent about that decision. Okamoto accommodates that character emotion with a particular visual style. Side-lit, deep-focus, wide-screen compositions which divide viewer attention between foreground and rearground objects, and intercutting between high and low angles all inject a subtle but ongoing instability into the film's images. This supports Niino's vacillation in determining a course of action by keeping half of his face literally in shadow and uncertainty, for instance, in the shot of Niino waiting to kill his friend Kurihara because the other conspirators suspect he has betrayed them. By breaking up audience concentration with formal manipulations, Okamoto underscores the narrative

Top: Side-lit, deep-focus, wide-screen composition: the Leader contemplates his blood-stained hand while Niino (right) looks on.

Bottom: "I'll live as I please;" Niino defies his guardian.

disjunction caused by the numerous flashbacks and cutaways. The rack focusing between objects or persons and the shock cutting, both to begin sequences and as a transition between them, take on a stylistic connotation in terms of the entire film: not randomness but premeditation, a continuous counterbalancing of effects to involve and then to distance the viewer, as if introduced into *Samurai Assassin* by some controlling, exterior force. Obviously, the viewer cannot simultaneously respond emotionally to the images and intellectualize about their narrative import. A visual usage which creates or intensifies associations between otherwise unconnected persons and objects makes a direct statement that need not be further analyzed to be understood. One simple example is the cut from Niino, who has returned to his dwelling in an old mill after declaring he will live as he pleases, to a close-up of the mask of a

Noh actor performing inside the shogunate manor. The implication is unmistakable from the juxtaposition of his figure with the theatrical mask: even as he declares his freedom to do as he pleases, Niino is unconsciously playing a predetermined role. Such an interpretation is reinforced by the sound dissolve which places the Noh actor's chanting on the track while Niino is still on the screen and, more importantly, by the shock cut to the mask itself. The very unexpectedness of the shot—which the viewer must assimilate without the contextual information of a performance in the manor— compels the audience to refer back to the last, fully comprehensible image (that is, the shot of Niino) to search for meaning. At that point, because the audience cannot know the narrative explanation for the mask's tangible presence (a performance is under way in the manor), the only reading possible is that Niino is also a performer in a drama but does not realize his own position.

The scribe accomplishes the "deletion" of references to Kurihara in the conspirators' records by burning several pages of the document. Just in terms of Hashimoto's narrative invention this action is disturbing because it destroys the identity of character with whom the viewer has been encouraged to empathize. Okamoto's staging compounds that effect. As the scribe moves away from the window through which he has witnessed the killing of the real traitor, Masui, a side-traveling follows him and reveals Niino standing and watching sullenly in the foreground. A reverse shot concentrates on the pages themselves, in the left rearground, while the right of the frame is filled by the lower portion of the scribe's kimono as he holds the paper over a coal fire. Niino is visible in the background, but his face and part of his body are blocked from view by the pages. When these are ignited, the flames and heat further obscure Niino and distort the outlines of his figure. This ominous overlay of the burning pages and the character's body in the unbroken depth of the shot creates a marked foreshadowing. In fact, a similar treatment of Niino's "documentary identity" will be ordered by the leader at the end of the film. In the context of

Top: The *Noh* mask.

Center: Niino (left foreground) watches the scribe prepare to delete Kurihara's name.

Bottom: Niino (center background) watches as the records mentioning Kurihara are burned.

TOP: Tight close shots of Niino as he delivers Hashimoto's most explicit lines: "I do not know who my father is."

CENTER: "If samurai blood runs in me, whose is it?"

BOTTOM: Depth of focus and foreground object bisecting the frame: Niino sleeps drunkenly in the company of Okiku (Michiyo Aratama).

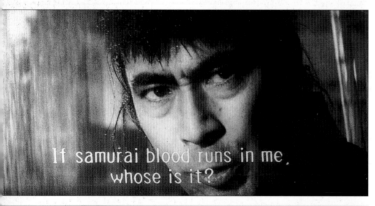

that final deletion, Niino's understated participation in the earlier scene becomes part of a pattern of visual determinism with which Okamoto elucidates the fatalistic overtones of Hashimoto's story.

Many of these overtones in *Samurai Assassin* are, as they were in *Tenchu*, focused on the question of personal identity. The tight close shots Okamoto trains on Niino as he delivers Hashimoto's most explicit lines ("I do not know who my father is" and "If samurai blood runs in me, whose is it?") reassert that question on a visual level. The viewer is distanced from Niino's obsession not merely by the achronology with which his life story is recounted or the distracting elements in Okamoto's staging but also by the very nature of what Niino does and how he looks. Unlike the performance of Shintaru Katsu in the role of Izo Okada, Mifune's moments of self-pity and occasional drunkenness are slightly out of sync with the basic character strength he projects. Certainly a scruffy appearance or cynical posing are a part of the genre typing Mifune created in *Yojimbo*. There is a combination of traits in *Samurai Assassin*, using the flashback structure, in which a scene of the unkempt, impoverished Niino in present time may either precede or follow one of him dressed in expensive clothes and wearing a samurai tonsure. This intercutting is particularly disquieting. This graphic contrast may alternately involve or disassociate the audience from Niino. If he is constrained by some exterior force or, as in the shot of him reclining drunkenly on the floor of an inn, figuratively imprisoned by a wooden bar which bisects the frame in the foreground, Niino's indecision and his intoxication put him in collusion with that force. If the interaction between Niino and the burning pages is a visual trope which helps link Hashimoto's chain of tragic events stretching out beyond the character's knowledge or control, his sullen passivity in that shot and at moments during the entire film indicates that the tragedy is somewhat of his own making.

The film's conclusion avoids the issue of responsibility and the making of moral judgments. The assassination of Lord Ii begins as present rather than flashback action and contains several dramatic ironies. First, the con-

Depth of field: a hungover Niino complains to the geisha Okiku in *Samurai Assassin*.

A shaft of light cuts the frame diagonally as Niino and Okiku sit before a doll shrine.

Balanced long shot: Niino challenges Kurihara before his sword-school pupils.

Niino drunk on the floor of the mill

Visual dominance: A blood-spattered Niino walks towards the camera as his co-conspirators try to kill him.

TOP: Long shot creating a confusion of activity during the final battle in the snow storm in *Samurai Assassin*

CENTER: Camera travels with Niino as he strikes out frenziedly in the final battle.

BOTTOM: Before the battle, a grim-faced Niino awaits Lord Ii's palanquin

spirators who had decided that the unruly Niino should not participate in the assault and dispatched several men to deal with him are surprised to discover him still alive. "Neither friend nor foe can stop me now" is his declaration to them, which is, of course, doubly ironic in that those who pass for his friends have tried to kill him and the object of the impending attack is not a real foe but his father. Lord Ii himself utters the final irony as Niino's sword pierces him: "Fools! It's the end of the samurai in Japan." After a single establishing long shot, the visual intensity of the actual combat is photographed entirely in medium and close shots. The panning to follow Lord Ii's sedan chair is inter-cut with a traveling shot to follow Niino, as the narrative structure which linked personal destinies comes together in an inevitable and fatal collision.

Niino's triumphant departure from the field carrying Lord Ii's head upraised on his sword blade occurs, however, in a different context, namely as an event in the scribe's memory. As a shot of the scribe carrying a bundle of records out of the conspirators' house sets up the new time frame, he reports through voiceover narration that "Niino severed chief man Ii's head without knowing it to be his father's." As he slips and drops several pages into a garden stream, Okamoto cuts to Niino in what is now past time and travels back with him as he parades. The voiceover continues: "But Leader Hehachi orders the record of Niino to be stricken off. So Tsuruchiyo Niino's name cannot be found on our list of members [a traveling medium-close shot follows Niino from the rear], but it was the chief man's own son who cut off his head." The shot changes again to a front view of Niino, and the scribe's voice is replaced by sounds of snow-fall on the track, so that the film slips fully into flashback for Niino's proclamation of victory: "Look! This head! It's not for 200 *koku*! Cheap even at 300 *koku*. Look! I, Niino, have distinguished myself. I have the chief minister's head." Even as Niino makes this most vociferous claim for distinction and for simple identity, the viewer is aware that he has merely been allowed to erase himself. Even more decisively than with Tsugumo's protest in *Hara-Kiri*, it is known from the voiceover that Niino's action is already "stricken off." The "end of the samurai in Japan" is also the end of Niino—there is no real triumph, not even an existentialist one. Not only is the portent created by the burning report after Kurihara's death fulfilled, but the scribe's voiceover returns to assert the implacable anonymity of history. In a sense, Niino has doomed himself with his own words: "A sword does not make a samurai." Neither does it distinguish a man. Accordingly, as the voiceover resumes, the image must become one of literal obliteration. "The day is March 3rd, 1860. It happened on Doll's Festival day at the Sakurada gate of Edo castle," the scribe observes dispassionately; then, as Niino strides off until his figure is completely hidden from view by a white haze of swirling flakes, the shot and voiceover fade simultaneously with the closing remark: "Snow rarely falls in March."

After a two-and-a-half-decade absence, Okamoto returned to *chambara* with the mixed genre film *East Meets West* (*Iisuto Miitsu Uesuto*, 1995). This picture does not take itself as seriously as the similarly plotted *Red Sun* (1970), in which an ambassador's dishonored retainer played by Toshiro Mifune postpones self-immolation to team with a train-robber (Charles Bronson), catch his double-crossing partner (Alain Delon, no less), and retrieve a stolen sword; and the film as a whole could embrace neither the Western nor the samurai genre. In *East Meets West*, Okamoto's humor creates an uneven tone. As in *Red Sun*, Japanese envoys are robbed and then team up with a American to track the thieves. But besides a pursuing samurai (Hiroyuki "Henry" Sanada), Okamoto's narrative includes a bumbling sidekick whose relationship with an Indian woman verges on tasteless stereotyping. Lacking the eccenticity of Okamoto's own *Dixieland Daimyo* (1986)—in which four emancipated slaves take a wrong turn on their way to Africa, end up in Japan, and anachronisitcally instruct a *daimyo* how to play jazz licks—*East Meets West* unfolds somewhere in between the genre expectations of Western and *chambara* but fails to deliver a new riff on either.

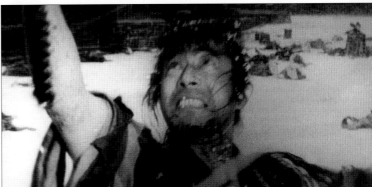

TOP: Lord Ii's sedan chair in *Samurai Assassin*

CENTER: Niino raises Lord Ii's head aloft and shouts, "Look! I, Niino, have distinguished myself. I have the chief minister's head."

BOTTOM: Niino disappears into the storm carrying the head.

Most recently, Okamota again cast Hiroyuki Sanada as the title figure in *Vengeance for Sale* (*Sukedachiya Sukeroku*, 2001), a long-form remake of the 1960s television series. Initially Sukeroka tries to avoid deadly encounters, as he brandishes a *bokken* and sells his services exacting vengence for petty offenses. In a plot turn that again recalls the American Western, Sukeroku returns to his home province to discover that an old sword fighter, Katahiro (Tatsuya Nakadai), is the target of an official vendatta. Sukeroku confronts Katahiro, whom he does not realize is his own father, but the samurai knocks him out and is killed by four gun-toting assassins. While this might seem like a plot twist on *Samurai Assassin*, the dynamic of *Vengeance for Sale* is quite different. The youthful, handsome Sukeroku is more than just thirty-five years removed from Mifune's scruffy, impetuous Niino. In what may be a paean to old-school *chambara* while putting a different face on the samurai film at the millennium, Katahiro perishes but Sukeroku's fate is much more benign.

II. MASAHIRO SHINODA

Masahiro Shinoda's films are distinguished from those of his contemporaries, including Gosha and Okamoto, by his stress on pictorialism and theatricality. When he emerged on the international scene in the late 1960s and early 1970s, these qualities rapidly enhanced Shinoda's reputation. As Shinoda himself has said in essays on various of his motion pictures, he considers film a form with potential for expressive continuity with the traditional arts of Japan. Regarding *Double Suicide* (*Shinju Ten No Amijima*, 1969), he wrote that "the idea that truth can be approached through deformation and abstraction is essential to all forms of contemporary art." This belief in turn inspires Shinoda—like Chikamatsu, on whose *bunraku* play *Double Suicide*[1] is based—to seek "the thin line between truth and falsehoods."

For Shinoda, that material distinction is analogous to the equally thin line between reality or verisimilitude and fantasy in art. Pictorialism and theatricality are the alternately deforming and abstracting qualities in film which define that line. Extrapolating from this aesthetic assumption, Shinoda retains the *kurogo* in *Double Suicide*. These black-clothed figures act "invisibly" to change the scenery in Japanese theater, but their appearance on screen in another medium of expression automatically transforms the conventional surface reality. In *The Scandalous Adventures of Buraikan* (*Buraikan*, 1970), a semi-comedy about a band of traveling players in the early 19th century, Shinoda uses both set decoration and lighting to imbue his shots with a Fauve-like color scheme and provide a surrealistic background for the naturalistic performances of his actors. For Shinoda this mise-en-scène is not paradoxical.

Rather it is just one subtext creating tension through a mixture of expressive styles. Even filmic devices—long takes with their intensified sense of real time, low-key lighting, or unusual framing, all of which occur in *The Assassin* and *Samurai Spy*—become formal transliterations and analogs to the deformation and abstraction Shinoda perceived to be at work in painterly and theatrical traditions.

In most examples of post-War *chambara*, the central character brings to his actions a degree of awareness of playing out a generic role—that is, fulfilling or frustrating the expectations both of other figures in the fiction and of the audience watching it. The same is true of Shinoda's motion pictures but at a more abstract level, not that of character consciousness but of actor consciousness. *Double Suicide* and *Buraikan*—which are *gendai-geki* but marginal samurai films—provide the clearest examples, from the retention of Chikamatsu's scene structure in the former to the fact that the principals in the latter are designated as professional actors by the film's storyline. This same sense of characters and events being "acted out" is carried over to the stricter *chambara* contexts of *The Assassin* and *Samurai Spy*.

Tetsuro Tamba's interpretation of Kiyokawa, the title figure in *The Assassin*, is typically enigmatic. At the level of characterization, the development of the plot (which in set in the pre-*bakumatsu* year of 1863) calls for Kiyokawa to change sides from the loyalist to the shogunate factions and then back again. Because the viewer in not aware, at first, of Kiyokawa's true intentions, this shifting of allegiances creates an uncertainty about his position as hero. In other words, unable to discern whether he is "good" or "evil," the viewer cannot perceive the "line between truth and falsehood" that Shinoda draws. At the level of performance, Tamba keeps this line in focus. Between scenes in which Kiyokawa participates dispassionately in the conflicting conspiracies and those in which he addresses public gatherings with an aroused rhetoric, Tamba's portrayal is emotionally polarized. Because the viewer lacks the narrative information to distinguish which of Kiyokawa's behaviors is natural and which affected, there is a confusion or deformation of the usual logic of theatrical conventions, specifically between the moments in which the actor (Tamba) has become a character (Kiyokawa) and those in which the character (a loyalist) has become an actor (an anti-loyalist). This ambivalence is left unresolved when Kiyokawa is murdered at the film's conclusion.

Like Gosha and Okamoto, Shinoda exploits genre typing in his samurai films as both an expository shorthand and a source of viewer expectation

Buraikan;
Top: Tatsuya Nakadai (right)
Center: Tetsuro Tamba (center)
Bottom: Shima Iwashita

Samurai Spy
TOP: Sasuke is attacked by a band of men on the highway.

CENTER AND BOTTOM: Koji Takehashi as Sasuke

against which he may play dramatically. In *The Assassin*, Shinoda first controverts then confirms the audience's initial perception of Kiyokawa as a hero by manipulating character conventions which are essentially theatrical. In *Samurai Spy*, Shinoda accomplishes his deformation at the structural and stylistic levels. The narrative, which centers on the pursuit of a man named Nojiri, an agent of the defeated Toyotomi faction, by a legendary figure named Sarutobi Sasuke, is a maze of assumed identities and false trails. Like Tamba's Kiyokawa, Koji Takahashi's interpretation of Sasuke is somewhat detached. Wandering through a countryside where he regularly encounters the residual violence of a recently ended civil war, Shinoda's personage moves with the guileless self-assurance of a Dante passing through an insubstantial but murderous inferno. As a result, Sasuke often appears to be more of a spectator than a participant in the film's events, while serving as a catalyst for other characters to begin "acting" in all senses of the word. Because Sasuke's pursuit is so often passive—that is, constructed of many individual scenes in which he literally waits for something to happen —a number of the audience's normal expectations are diminished and redirected toward the less predictable supporting figures in the film, most notably the mysterious, white-hooded Sakon and his band of spies who are stalking Nojiri for reasons of their own. The result is a narrative tone which strongly supports an observation made by Sasuke early in the film: "I believe nothing is certain these days."

The visual usage which precedes that remark is equally charged with the unexpected and uncertain. Over a montage of stock footage of war banners and battle scenes, the titles begin. Shortly, a disembodied voice establishes the time: "1614. Fourteen years after Sekigahara." Suddenly a whip-pan scans a rooftop and centers on a dark figure who leaps from it. An overhead shot reveals more men clambering silently over the rafters of a portico. An interrogation scene follows in which a figure whose features are hidden in shadow questions a captured spy, who is possibly one of the men from the preceding shots. Before this can be clarified, another cutaway occurs, and reverse pans using long-focal-length lenses track a black-garbed man as he runs through a mist, while a voiceover laments: "I am pursued. I am always pursued by something."

The effect of this prologue to Sasuke's appearance is less expository than it is evocative. The setting in the early years of the Tokugawa is slightly atypical but well within the normal viewer's genre familiarity. What information the audience does receive—there are spies involved; someone is being pursued—is subsumed into the dissociative impression of the graphics. As if to restrict identification, Sasuke is often in shadows, masked, or seen from the rear. Dizzying effects from whip-pans to unanticipated cutaways create a visual confusion which immediately displaces the placidity of the opening narration and the scrolls seen under the titles. In this context the dark form moving against the textured background of roof tiles becomes less a figure than an object and is abstracted into the kind of neutral component—or point in that line "in between"—Shinoda is seeking. It is in this context also that the viewer can sensorially embrace Sasuke's assertion that "nothing is certain." Such visual deformations are a motif of Shinoda's work and continue to evolve until, by the time of *Owl's Castle* (*Fukuro no Shiro*) in 1999, they incorporate use of expressive CGI ("computer generated images").

TOP: Texture, as a pursued spy jumps to the ground in *Samurai Spy*

CENTER: Sasuke (Koji Takahashi) as an anonymous figure flanked by trees

BOTTOM: A dark figure climbing through the rafters of a portico

According to Shinoda, the *kurogo* in *Double Suicide* "sometimes represent the eye of the camera, sometimes the desire of the audience to force their way deeper into the story, the minds of the characters, and possibly even into the mind of the author himself." In *Samurai Spy*, the surface realities of the film function in the same enigmatic way. Like Gosha, Shinoda uses broken shots: images full of angular and conflicting lines of force or with actors partially blocked from the audience's sight by foreground clutter. Such usage compositionally sustains the visual kinesis of the opening sequence throughout the film. While Shinoda may occasionally revert to a device such as a long lens or a long take in order to concentrate or intensify an image and draw the audience "deeper in the story," he is most intent on rupturing any prolonged suspension of disbelief and in compelling the viewer to accept the film as a deformation and not emulation of reality. By intercutting choker close-ups with group shots, by using frequent rack-focus set-ups, whip-pans and long-lens framing, Shinoda not only restricts what the audience can see but imbues the very act of watching the film with a distinct feeling of instability.

Like Gosha and Okamoto, Shinoda is often less interested in a striking visualization for its own sake or its potential figurative meaning than for its sharp sensory impact. If there is a metaphorical value to the dark alleyways down which his figure must repeatedly

Samurai Spy: A figure stalks down a dark alleyway.

move or a cyclical implication to the closing shot of Sasuke disappearing into the mountain mists, recalling the pursued man of the opening, there is also a prevailing sense of peril or mystery to which all tropes are subsidiary. Above all there is a constant undertone which says that the apparent is reliable. "Who are your enemies or friends?" Sasuke must ask because gestures, faces, and words are no longer trustworthy indices. Nor for that matter are rituals and roles. Ironically, it is his participation in a ritual act, a festival dance, which finally betrays Nojiri's identity.

Despite his profession of greater interest in the aesthetic than in the social context of his films, Shinoda's probing for that division between truth and falsehood often creates the same ironies as Kurosawa, Gosha, or Okamoto. There is an enforced anonymity in *Samurai Spy*'s conclusion: Sasuke disappears into the "mist" while a voiceover relates that "six months later the winter war took place in Osaka. The Sanada fought the Toyotomi, but there is no record that Sarutobi Sasuke fought in Sanada's army." This is reminiscent in tone and effect of *Samurai Assassin*. The hero slays the man he had set out after and then fades from view; but Sasuke, the legendary figure, seems even more anachronistic in his leave-taking than Niino, the legend-seeker. The audience is left with no real information about the nature of the title character, no exploration of his actions or inactions, nothing more than Sakon's remark just before he dies: "Sasuke, you are an odd person. You really are."

More than twenty years after *Samurai Spy* and *Double Suicide*, Shinoda brought many of the same techniques to bear when he revisited the sub-genres in *Owl's Castle* and *Gonza the Spearman* (*Yari no Gonza*, 1986). The latter is again an adaptation of a Chikamatsu play and again features a doomed romance; but in this film doom descends on many because of the need for perfection at a tea ceremony. Osai, portrayed by the now middle-aged star of *Double Suicide*, Shima Iwashita (Shinoda's wife), is the spouse of a samurai forced to be absent for *sankin-kotai*. In the opening, the lovesick young Oyaku pursues the remarkably handsome Gonza. Despite the disapproval of her brother and his colleague, Bonnojo, Oyaku succeeds in seducing him. Later, as an indolent group of samurai practice *chanoyu*, the tea ceremony, Osai comments (presumably with no pun intended) that with "no more wars, no battle now, samurai must serve differently." When a new heir is born to the *daimyo* and with Osai's husband Ichinoshin, the master of the tea ceremony, still away at Edo, Gonza and Bonnojo are in competition to perform it in his absence. They also realize that failure to be perfect may harm their careers with the clan. Each now wants desperately to see Ichinoshin's family scrolls on how best to carry out the ceremony; and each devises a different plan.

Gonza visits Osai with a straightforward request. As the methods are a family secret, she suggests an engagement to her daughter Okiku, which would make Gonza a future family member and remove any constraints on her. Gonza accepts the deal. Bonnojo, who has already boldly offered to provide masculine company to Osai while her husband is away and been flatly rejected, plans to break in during the night and steal a look at the scrolls. When Osai accidentally discovers that Gonza is already secretly engaged to Oyaku, she waits until Gonza comes to her home in the middle of the night and confronts him. Realizing that Gonza's sash bears the intertwined emblems of his family and Oyaku's, Osai histrionically tears it off him then sardonically removes and offers her own sash as a substitute. Just as Gonza throws both into the courtyard, Bonnojo appears, grabs them, and runs off promising to report them as adulterers.

From such a narrative base, Shinoda easily fashions a monumental ironic structure. Dishonored Osai's brother kills Bonnojo. Ichinoshin is compelled to return, track down, and kill both Gonza and Osai. In peacetime, dead and orphans spring from a tea ceremony. Visually, Shinoda is restrained and lets the heavy irony carry the expressive load. There are moments, such as Gonza practicing spear thrusts in a dark, red-tinged room at sunset, that add to the sense of doom; but for the most part Shinoda relies on Iwashita's performance and the physical beauty of Hiromi Go as Gonza to advance his story toward its grim end. Osai's repressed, romantic yearnings are briefly fulfilled at the cost of her life. When they become fugitives, Gonza pawns his sword blades and has no chance against Ichinoshin with wooden blades. The high-angle shot of Osai's pitiful attempt to say a few words to Ichinoshin, who cuts her down in midsentence, reaffirms the overweening grimness. The last sequence, as Osai's father and daughter watch her son practice the tea ceremony, compounds the irony in which feudal society restores its version of order.

Owl's Castle opens in a forest grove, where a band of *ninja*s from Iga prefecture conceal a girl in a shallow trench. A troop of cavalry gallops over a hill, then long lens pans in the style of Kurosawa watch them marauding through a village, where all the inhabitants are slaughtered. A digital effect shows a woman's head spinning through the frame as the horsemen ride past.

While Shinoda uses step-printing, freeze frames, and other computer-generated effects, his most effective compositions do not require such devices. After the death of shogun Hideoyoshi's heir, a static shot from inside the palace bisected by a dark wall panel captured a bustle of retainers filing past. In the distance, the tiered portico of the main gate is visible. While the shuffling movement of the men suggests the emotional depression of the court, the two panels of the shot foreshadow the strategic bifurcation the heir's death will cause among Hideoyoshi's enemies. Another example of visual foreshadowing is a later scene in which Sokyu, a plotter against Hideoyoshi, is poisoned. The other figure in the shot has his back to camera. He shifts to the left, cutting off the view of Sokyu moments before he chokes and expires, visually obliterating the character an instant before his death.

In an introductory scene, the main character, Juzo, a surviving Iga *ninja*, was commissioned to kill Hideoyoshi. When first seen, Juzo is facing away. When he turns, his face is obscured behind a hanging cloth. Then Shinoda uses a storm, with the flashes of light not synchronized but realistically preceding the thunderclaps by several seconds, to powerfully externalize Juzo's emotional position. The hot flashes of lightning are animal impulse, the desire for revenge on the successor of the military ruler who ordered the murder of his family. The low rumble of thunder is the pull of reason that confirms the uselessness of such an act: "Kill Hideoyoshi and someone else will merely take his place." Juzo vacillates between these emotions for most of the film. His samurai garb and his *ninja* costume further underscore the sense of two

BELOW: *Owl's Castle*

characters in one body. Shortly before Juzo enters Hideoyoshi's chamber, Shinoda uses a long lens to flatten an interior, so that when Juzo rounds a corner he seems to spring out of the wall next to a painted lion. In that moment, typical of Shinoda's style, the abstraction of Juzo's *ninja* persona is revealed; in this garb he is merely a figure, not a person. When Juzo sees that Hideoyoshi is nothing more than a feeble old man, he realizes that his initial assumption—that such an assassination would be pointless—is correct, so he renounces it and leaves.

The narrative irony of *Owl's Castle* is that Gohei, Juzo's former Iga colleague who has become a retainer of the castle's marshal and Juzo's antagonists, is mistakenly taken for the would-be assassin and imprisoned. Although Juzo lowered his mask and revealed his face to him, Hideoyoshi also realizes that it makes no difference who is executed, so he identifies Gohei. Infuriated by the fact that ambitions have led him to die under an assumed name for a crime he did not commit, Gohei is boiled in oil. Juzo and the mysterious woman who tried several times to have him killed retire to a modest hut in the forest. As in *Tenchu,* the world turns upside down but turns out to be same on the other side.

III. THE RED SLAYERS

"Swords are useless tokens."
　　—Hanshiro Tsugumo in *Hara-Kiri*

"Swordsmanship is murder."
　　—NEMURI in *Adventures of Kyoshiro Nemuri, Swordsman*

"He just has a sword. He isn't strong at all."
　　—TANGO SAZEN in *Secret of the Urn*

Given that the samurai film is a living genre, its "sociology" is in flux. If there is a core question which poses itself repeatedly to anyone who watches these films, it would likely be the relationship of their cynicism and violence to the society which created them. Somewhat simplistically, earlier cultural historians in the West postulated that an acceptance of social conditions was inbred in the Eastern mentality. No less an authority than Edwin Reischauer asserted that during the Tokugawa era "adventurous Japanese of the 16th century became by the 19th century a docile people looking meekly to their rulers for all leadership and following without question all orders from above." As if to affirm that the samurai was merely a high-level institutionalization of the mercenary concept, Maurice Collis in *The Land of the Great Image* recounts that a group of samurai refuges, who had fled their homeland because they were liable to persecution as Christians, established themselves in India in the early 19th century; and yet their conversion to Western religious belief had affected neither their identity nor their skill as fighting men, so they found new occupation in the palace guard of a rajah.

Whatever his ethics, many samurai may indeed have been warriors first and men second; but that contingency where and when it existed was as necessary to duty and survival as the training and discipline of any Western knight. To generalize from the reality of Tokugawa Japan to the mindset of its citizenry reveals a mid-20th century prejudice about social conditioning that has lost much of its cachet. What Japanese feudalism gave its men-at-arms was rank; and for a class of men to exchange personal choice for privilege is certainly not a uniquely Eastern phenomenon. The underlying ideology for the feudal fighter was the same in the East and West. If, as a cog in a rigid caste system there was no personal freedom of choice, then the need for codes of chivalry would have been obviated and *giri/ninjo* conflicts would have been infrequent at best. In that era, political belief that could be termed self-consciously reactionary or revolutionary may, indeed, have been rare. Yet many samurai, such as Ryoma Sakamoto and the others who fueled the *baku-matsu*, freely relinquished their privileges and their lives for the ideal of a modern Japan. That fervor could easily equal that of such diverse modern groups as Yukio Mishima's Shield Society, martial devotees trying to restore *bushido*, or the militants of the Japanese Red Army. Even though the samurai may often have paid for status with his life, in taking up his occupation the warrior made a simple social exchange.

Is then the filmic archetype of the *bushi*, however historically accurate, a cipher for the purging of repressed social anxiety, a catharsis for an alienated audience? Or does the unrelenting image of the "red slayer" in motion pictures merely derive from a dramatic tradition stretching back into pre-history? Both hypotheses are true to some extent; yet neither exhausts the issue nor explains the diversity of expression to be found in the samurai film as a whole.

If the manifold changes in the society which produces these films cannot be charted through its cultural product with full precision, it is still possible to discern patterns in the evolution of the motion pictures themselves. If such "classic" productions as Mizoguchi's *Tales of the Taira Clan* or Teinosuke Kinugasa's *Gate of Hell* (*Jigokumon*, 1953) are now part of an "old school" of film-making, if their full-lit, saturated color and understated action give a sense of slow-pace or wordiness or tragedy that is too artificial, it is quite obviously because standards of producing and watching films have altered greatly. Compared to a pitiless "hero" of newer *chambara*, the misguided passion and subsequent contrition of the love-struck Morito in *Gate of Hell* is as anomalous as a lap dissolve would be to current visual style. Nor is it merely a result of new directors imposing their world-views on the genre. Daisuke Ito and Hiroshi Inagaki are men whose careers spanned many decades from the silent period to a final film released in 1970. In his few samurai films, such as *The Ambitious*, Ito's mise-en-scène was anything but

Machiko Kyo as Lady Kesa and Kazuo Hasegawa as Morito in *Gate of Hell*

old-style. Even Inagaki—who in the three-part life of Miyamoto Musashi released in 1955-56 and as late as *Chushingura* in 1962 did perpetuate the stylistic and narrative preferences of the pre-War era—updated his methods of exposition and visualization considerably by the time of *Under the Banner of the Samurai* (*Furin kazan*, 1969) and The *Ambush* (*Machibuse*, 1970). Not only is improved technology evident in the long focal length lenses and rich, metallic colors of the former, but *Under the Banner of the Samurai*'s realistic detailing of a central character whose qualities are less than noble is in marked contrast with the heroes of his *Samurai I* through *Sanurai III* and *Chushingura*. Although, contrary to the most recent tendency in the genre to focus on the disenfranchised samurai, the film does concern itself with the lives of such high-ranking figures as a general and a *daimyo*, the pre-title sequence reveals how the character who is to become a general remedies his masterless status: he persuades another *ronin* to attack a lord then interposes and kills the would-be assassin in order to ingratiate himself with the nobleman.

The degree to which such an undisguised betrayal of a fellow human being taints the central character's honor or alienates the viewer is determined by the generic context. As a result, action which might have seemed at one time grossly evil is perfectly acceptable for the new hero. The protagonists of *Sure Death* are not just killers but cheap ones to boot. They supplement regular jobs making musical instruments or roof tiles by knocking off their neighbors; or as Mondo, the constable who moonlights as an assassin ruefully admits, "We do kill people for petty cash only to end up with wrinkled faces and crooked spines." It is easy for some to conclude that such an increased tolerance for less-than-scrupulous heroes, that the cynicism and violence which imbues much of *chambara* since the mid-1980s, is another symptom of moral

decay; and where a film is uninspired or superficial that argument is difficult to refute. But if Ikehiro's revenge piece, *Trail of Blood*, is a step down from *Trail of Traps*, it is not because his new heroes disagree with Nemuri that "swordsmanship is murder." If the driven, sardonic main character of the *Sword of Vengeance* series also stars in a gorily illustrated *manga*, it need not necessarily imply that his characterization is two-dimensional. It is precisely because the *chambara* filmmakers of the 1960s used the genre to penetrate the prevaricative facade of *bushido* and to expose the sham of honor which shackled the historical samurai that viewer expectation from a samurai film has changed. A new hero must manifest his or her rejection of those false standards not merely with words but with actions. If such a hero is ruthless, it is because survival is the only value he or she has. Accordingly, when Itto Ogami, the *kaishaku* or effective executioner for the shogun, decides to give up his privileged position in *Sword of Vengeance I* (1972), he offers his infant son a choice between a ball and a sword. Ogami plans a "mercy killing" if the boy chooses wrongly. If such a hero is called a "monster" or "beast" it is because the realities of the period have placed that brand on him. From Rentaro Mikuni as Miyamoto Musashi to Toshiro

TOP: Toshiro Mifune (left) as the general and Kinnosuke Nakamura as the *daimyo* in *Under the Banner of the Samurai*.

BOTTOM: Toshiro Mifune in *The Ambush*

TOP, CENTER: The *Sword of Vengeance* comic book or *manga*: "the seagull style."

BOTTOM: *Sword of Vengeance*: Tomisaburo Wakayama as Itto Ogam.

Mifune as Kurosawa's *Yojimbo* to Tatsuya Nakadai in Gosha's films, the directors and actors have created a consistent characterization in this regard. If such a hero cannot lay down his sword, it is because he is locked into a time where to do so is to perish. Itto Ogami does not savor his aimless odyssey but believes rather that he has "entered the road to Hades." Having just killed dozens of men with what he sarcastically terms his "seagull style" of swordplay, in which he may leap high in the air to cut down at the head or even throw his weapon in order to win, Itto turns at the conclusion of *Sword of Vengeance II* (1972) to face a master swordsman whose employer has already perished. "Was dying with him," Itto asks his opponent after delivering the fatal blow, "the way of the samurai?" "Explain it to me, Itto Ogami," the loser questions in turn, "the real way of the samurai?" Convinced like Bokuden that he will continue to prevail precisely because it makes no difference whether he does or not, like Nemuri, like Sanjuro or Tsugumo, like Tange Sazen or Gennosuke, like all the alienated figures that survive or perish in the samurai film, Itto smiles wryly and gives the only possible answer: "To live prepared to die."

CHAPTER SEVEN

EVOLUTION OF THE GENRE

Form is emptiness; emptiness also is form. Emptiness is
no other than form; form is no other than emptiness.
In the same way, feeling, perception, formation, and
consciousness are emptiness.

> —"The Heart Sutra" of the *Prajnaparamita*

The howls of stray dogs and the tramp of clogs pierce
the air.

> —"The Flower of Hell"
> (theme song from *Lady Snowblood*)

I. Violence, East and West: The Last Samurai

OVER THE COURSE OF ITS SIX PARTS, THE *Sword of Vengeance* series tested the limits of the genre and its viewer expectations in the early 1970s. Neither the Lone Wolf with child nor the four-wheeled arsenal which doubles as a baby-cart are that extreme or outlandish in comparison to other samurai films. What distinguishes these films, what causes Itto Ogami to diverge from the road followed by so many antecedents, is the treatment and concentration of violence that surrounds the central figure. Itto presages this in the flashback to his wife's death: "They will pay with rivers of blood." In the course of six episodes, "they" is never really defined. For Itto, as with Kyoshiro Nemuri, killing is an existential expression. No amount of killing can calm Itto's disturbed mind, can erase the image of his dead wife and red fingerprints on his child's cheek. These vestiges of a past life, bloody emblems confusing death and innocence, drive Itto forward like an automaton. But Itto has no destination.

The inhumanity of Itto's attitude does more than color the *Sword of Vengeance* narratives. It reduces them to the black-and-white of the comic book page. A chilling moment, as when Itto throws a *kozuka* back into an antagonist's scabbard, is no longer just a typical genre touch, a demonstration of almost preternatural skill. Nor is it purely parody, but rather a radical deconstruction of what is typical in the genre. All that remains are the constructs, an "empty form" far different from the sense of the oft-quoted passage from the "Heart" sutra.

For two decades from the mid-1970s until the mid-1990s, images of the samurai were often relegated to the small screen or part of mixed-genre productions. While still at work on the Zato Ichi series, Shintaro Katsu began producing and starring in the short-lived *Sword of Justice* (*Goyokiba*) films focusing on the exploits of constable Hanzo "the Razor." The influences are clear from the title sequence of the first *Sword of Justice,* in which a *Starsky-and-Hutch*-like theme plays over a TV-style cop montage of Hanzo's "beat" in Edo. Director Kenji Misumi includes a lot of foreground clutter and careful compositions, but the pointedly off-beat elements—not the least of which are Hanzo's priapism and investigative self-torture—overwhelm any imposition of visual nuance. While acting as executive producer for the *Sword of Vengeance* movies starring his brother Tomisaburo Wakayama, Katsu also produced *Oshi Samurai* (*Silent Samurai*), a television series with Wakayama portraying a mute *shokin kasegi*—or bounty hunter—named Kiichi Hogan. Based on a story by Hideo Gosha about a swordsman whose throat is slit as a child by a renegade Jesuit priest, Katsu employed the feature film technicians from his Daiei productions and directed the first episode himself (and also appeared as the quasi-villain Manji). With violence somewhat sanitized for television and, in Hogan, a lead figure more restrained than the remorseless Itto Ogami, *Oshi Samurai*'s style (its third episode was directed by Kenji Misumi) mirrors that of contemporary features.

Lady Snowblood (*Shurayukihime*, 1973) and its 1974 sequel reflect the various narrative and stylistic influences on the genre at the time the *Sword of Vengeance* pictures were in their initial release. A precursor to Gosha's *Death Shadows* (and even Luc Besson's *La Femme Nikita* [1990]), this film's title character, Yuki, "a child of the netherworlds," is born in prison and raised to avenge the murder of her family during the draft riots of 1873. As a young woman, Yuki embarks on her campaign armed only with a *shikomi-zue* concealed in an umbrella, which is somewhat anachronistic in the gun-toting days of the early Meiji era. Nonetheless, Yuki manages an effective vendetta. Several elements from the episodic plot to the dark glistening interiors of the women's prison and the frequent zooms into tight shots of eyes suggest the influence of Sergio Leone; but *Lady Snowblood* is a world removed from *Once Upon a Time in the West*. During her quest, Yuki encounters a journalist (and would-be novelist) who dies helping her bring the last culprit (coincidentally, the jouralist's father) to justice. Despite being shot and stabbed (by the daughter of an earlier victim) and collapsing in the snow at the end of the first feature, Yuki is miraculously revived for a sequel.

Of the various productions of the 1970s, the original *Last Samurai* (*Okami yo Rakujitsu O kire*, 1974; the last film directed by Kenji Misumi) most clearly anticipates the narratives of the late 1990s to present. Epic in length (over two and a half hours), *Last Samurai* follows Toranosuke Sugi as he is caught up in the violence of the *bakumatsu* but survives it ultimately to exchange his sword for a razor and become a barber in post-restoration Edo. From the furious sword fight at the festival in the title sequence, Misumi, as usual, treats violence as endemic to Tokugawa Japan. Another samurai, Hanjiro Nakamura, readily mixes his sensory experiences: first some killing then some sex with Ohide, a "working girl" Sugi has rescued. Estranged from his family, Sugi is embarrassed to be a low-class or farm samurai and does not take "privileges" for granted in the manner of Hanjiro. Flashbacks reveal the rest: as a disinherited child, Sugi was so oppressed by his uncle that he attempted suicide. When he saw a *ronin* named Ikemoto cut down six men, Sugi adopted him as his *sensei*.

In present time, Sugi is asked by Ikemoto to protect Reiko, a woman being tracked by the Satsuma clan. In Kyoto, Sugi wants to join a faction, but Ikemoto forbids it: "I didn't teach you to use the sword for fighting . . . so don't waste your life." Sugi nearly crosses swords with the *shinsengumi* unit of which Soji Okita is captain. Then a random encounter on the street unites the four principals as Hanjiro gives Sugi money from Ohide, who has become a Buddhist nun. Hanjiro's character—which is based on a actual follower of Takamori Saigo and a prominent figure in the *bakumatsu*—is nostalgic about Satsuma, but now that the clan has firmly aligned themselves in favor of the restoration, he is eager for more combat. Reiko, who is now a geisha, reports back to Ikemoto then meets Sugi in a graveyard to deliver another letter urging that he return to Edo. The argument between Reiko and Sugi, framed so that they are hemmed in by headstones, visually recalls the carving Sugi made when his father died.

When Sugi learns that Ikemoto is the target of an ambush, he rushes to intercede but arrives too late to save him. In a low-budget, albeit stylized, staging of the historic battle of Toba-Fushimi,[1] the sword-wielding shogunate loyalists are mowed down. Sugi has taken Reiko back to Edo, but their domestic bliss is short-lived when she is fatally attacked by army thugs. Although he tracks down the killers and mutilates their leader, Iba, Sugi renounces the sword. The sixth year of Meiji finds all the surviving characters transformed. Ohide is leaving for England, Sugi is a barber, and Hanjiro must shortly return to Satsuma with the disgraced Takamori. When Sugi learns that Hanjiro was responsible for Ikemoto's death, he goes to Satsuma to kill him but stops short. In his last picture, after a score of *chambara* where sword-skill was the only hope for survival, Misumi opts for an ironic twist in *Last Samurai*: characters must either perish or accept, as Sugi proclaims, that "it's no longer the age of the sword."

Also released in 1974, *The Last Swordsman* (*Okita Soshi*) focuses on the actual *shinsengumi* captain and minor character in *Last Samurai*, Soshi or Soji Okita, one of many members of that militia who were appointed by the *daimyo* of the Aizu *han*. The opening sequences reveal the economic difficulties of the members of the Tennen Rishu-ryo school, where Soji is a star pupil. The actual Soji was a *budo* prodigy who joined the *dojo* at age nine and was a master at fifteen. The opening sequence features an extreme long-lens of an as-yet-unidentified Soji running down a road, using step-printing and European music to complicate the genre reading. Soji meets another Tennen disciple and a deadly fight with anonymous assailants ensues. Afterwards an exhausted Soji makes clear that it has been his first real combat: "I haven't even killed a cat before."

The dingy and unappealing interior of the *dojo* suggests why so many of the Tennen adherents leave to join the low-paying *shinsengumi*: it's a step up in pay. Once in Kyoto, they became "the wolves of Mibu," a fearsome epithet from the Kyoto district where they were housed, which they merited from their bloody encounters with Choshu men. Choker close-ups and even step-printing create eerie slow-motion deaths that establish an undertone of fatalism and constriction. Unusual icons such as blood-drenched flowers and black-and-white dream imagery of innnocent children and hanged men create a visual disequilibrium that reflects the narrative situation.

Soji is the one who must track down his friend and pupil from the days at the Shieikan *dojo,* Seisuke Yamanami, who has tired of the violence and deserted. Soji could let Yamanami escape, and no one would know, but *giri* forbids it. Shortly after he serves as the *kaishaku* for Yamanami's compulsory suicide, Soji's health starts to deteriorate. Besides the discovery that he is fatally ill with tuberculosis, the woman he loves is cut down by a cadre of *ishin shishi.* Although he avenges her, Soji's anonymous death in a rural mill is grimly inglorious and ironic. In style and narrative, both *The Last Swordsman* and *Last Samurai* antipate numerous releases of twenty-five years later from *Samurai Fiction* (*SF: Samurai Fiction,* 1998) and *Taboo* (*Gohatto,* 1999) to *When the Last Sword is Drawn* (*Mibu Gishi Den,* 2002) and the American *The Last Samurai* (2003)

It may be that the violence and self-parody of the samurai film of the 1970s did more than deconstruct the genre expectations of the audience. In fact, the evolution of *chambara* as a whole over the end of the millennium was somewhat retrograde. As with the American Western, there were fewer and fewer samurai films made. Of those produced in the 1980s, only a few—such as Gosha's *Bandits Vs. Samurai Squad* and *Hunter in the Dark* or *Kagemusha*— give evidence that the expressive potential of the genre had not been entirely exhausted. Still, it is significant that a filmmaker such as Gosha could carry forward the powerful themes of *Goyokin* and *Tenchu* more effectively in *The Wolves* (*Shussho Iwwai,* 1971), a *yakuza* film, than in his more recent, traditional *chambara.*

Of the few theatrical productions of *chambara* undertaken in the past twenty-five years, even fewer have reached the Western viewer. Most of the directors of the "program" period films for Daiei, Toei, et al, have died or retired. The new generation works in television or in other genres. In 1974, Columbia Pictures released a re-edited and dubbed version of *Sword of Vengeance III* under the title *Lightning Swords of Death*. After the successful television adaptation of the novel *Shogun* in 1980, an independent production company dubbed, re-cut, and re-scored *Sword of Vengeance I* and *II* to create *Shogun Assassin*. The success of both *Shogun and Shogun Assassin* in their respective media caused a minor resurgence of interest in samurai films or, at least, in shoguns. For instance *Shogun's Destiny* and *Death of a Shogun*—the latter, like *Kagemusha*, containing a favorable portrayal of Ieyasu Tokugawa—were released in the United States.

The scarcity and quality of productions in the 1980s evinced a decline in the samurai film as a vital genre. Shintaro Katsu's last appearance in *chambara* was as the hapless, drunken *ronin* "Bull" Goemon in the flaccid remake of *Ronin-gai* (1990). "Times have changed," he observes early on; "Even horse traders like you can be given the chance to hit samurai." It is a far cry from Izo Okada on the cross, when Katsu's "Bull" pierces himself with a broken sword to kill his arrogant samurai employer standing behind him. Directors such as Shinoda and Okamoto moved away from *chambara* entirely. The former's *Under the Blossoming Cherry Trees* (*Sakura No Mori No Mankai No Shita*, 1975), a supernatural fable of a bandit and a witch, has a few *chambara* elements, like *Double Suicide,* but avoids genre typing. With the exception of the second remake of *Judo Saga* (*Sanshiro Sugata*, 1975), Okamoto has made a dozen films outside the *bujutsu* milieu. Masaki Kobayasbi's long-planned epic of the 10th-century Sino-Japanese wars was shelved due to loss of financing. Occasionally, the residual influence of *chambara* was evident in films of other genres. This is not a reference to the spate of martial arts or kung-fu movies from a variety of Asian producers, films whose often contemporary setting and always clear-cut oppositions of good-and-evil never probed an era, a social structure, or an expressive tradition in the manner of the best samurai films.

Perhaps the attitude of *chambara*, like the practice of swordsmanship, does require more than "empty form." Many Western filmmakers incorporated elements of *chambara* source material into their movies from the 1960s on. The first example is even earlier than that: John Huston's *The Barbarian and the Geisha* (1958), shot in Kyoto and starring John Wayne as Townsend Harris, the ambassador forced upon the Tokugawa through gun-boat diplomacy. While filtered through its American star's point of view and focused on his titled, cross-cultural romance with the geisha, many of the film's plot points—from a cholera epidemic and failed attempt by *ninja* assassins which leads to *seppuku* by the chief conspirator—derive from a long-standing Western bias to seek out the "inscrutable" aspects to Asian traditions.

Eventually filmmakers adopted not just the plots—in the manner of *The Magnificent Seven* transposing *Seven Samurai* or *The Outrage* (1964), *Rashomon*—but also, as Sergio Leone had in *Fistful of Dollars*, began looking for style points as well. The most outrageous, of course, is Tom Laughlin's *Master Gunfighter* (1975), in which the creator of "Billy Jack," the successful series about an outcast American Indian martial artist, transposed Gosha's *Goyokin* into the American West but opted to have his gunfighters pack samurai swords as well as six-guns. While Laughlin aimed at reconstructing *Goyokin* shot-for-shot (and kept a portable editing room on location so that he could refer to a print of Gosha's film whenever necessary), most of Gosha's visual tropes and his character Magobei's sense of angst are lost in translation.

Conan the Barbarian (1982) uses period and mythic figures to create a traditional martial arts story. But the similarities to certain samurai films—the epic structure, the chanting narrator, the sword-play, the supernatural interventions, even the insistent drum beating on the music track—are all merely borrowed from Kurosawa of twenty-five years prior. A better example of the samurai ethos, at least, can be found in Walter Hill's *Hard Times* (1975). In the context of the Depression-era South, Charles Bronson portrays a street fighter named Chaney with the same understated intensity as Mifune. Hill's plans to make "The Last Gun," a Western whose man character was named "Ronin," fell through in the late 1970s, so despite more obvious allusions to *chambara* in other films—*The Warriors* (1979) and the *Yojimbo* remake, *Last Man Standing* (1996)—it is Bronson's portrayal that resonates most powerfully with antecedents in the samurai genre.

As actor and director, Clint Eastwood has also repeatedly attempted to recreate that ethos. His portrayal of Leone's gunfighter, known as the "Man with No Name" (despite the fact that had a name in the first two pictures) evolved significantly in Eastwood's later work. In just his second film as a director, *High Plains Drifter* (1972), Eastwood portrayed the mysterious hired gun known only as the Stranger, whose arrogant disdain and sexual rapacity types him as both samurai and devil, a Kyoshiro Nemuri on horseback. Four years later, the merciless but fair-minded title character in *The Outlaw Josey Wales* (1976) reaffirmed Eastwood's character roots in the outlaws of *chambara*, which culminate in his portrayal of the aged gunfighter in *The Unforgiven* (1992). Eastwood even permitted moments of outright parody in *Pale Rider* (1985), where his Sanjuro-esque Preacher has a *bokken*-style combat using ax handles.

Much has also been made of the relationship of the George Lucas *Star Wars* trilogy to samurai film and Kurosawa's *The Hidden Fortress* in particular.

Certainly Lucas' Jedi warriors follow a *bushido*-like code and have the ability to wield light sabers like *daitos* to vanquish dozens of assailants. Darth Vader lacks only a fylfot on his cape to type him as a helmeted variant of Nemuri or the evil swordsmen of the *Daibosatsu Toge* adaptations. Still, the best examples can be found in the earth-bound science fictions of the Australian production *Mad Max* (1979) and its first two sequels, *The Road Warrior* (1981) and *Beyond Thunderdome* (1985). Both contain overt allusions to *chambara*, from character names and hairstyles to asides by a police dispatcher. More substantively than *Mad Max*, *The Road Warrior* borrows heavily from the situations of *Seven Samurai* and *Yojimbo*. It even uses an antiquated optical device, the wipe (as does Lucas in *Star Wars*), also a Kurosawa favorite, for transitions. Ultimately, however, what distinguishes *The Road Warrior* from Conan and Luke Skywalker are the attitudes of the title characters. Mere allusions or stylistic homages to the samurai film have as much dramatic impact as a group of men playing mah-jongg (which is also a reference in *The Road Warrior*). When Mel Gibson as Max Rockatansky enters the narrative, he does so like Mifune in *Yojimbo*, like a stray dog. It is that attitude which types him, although a figure in a science fiction narrative, as a lineal descendant of the *ronin* Sanjuro, and ironically one of the few such to grace the screen in recent years.

The most recent foray into the "samurai homage" sub-genre is Quentin Tarantino's *Kill Bill* (2003), which in some ways outdoes Tom Laughlin. As a *noir* samurai film, *Kill Bill* is burdened by Tarantino's usual fractured narrative and kitchen-sink approach, a grab-bag from *The Killing* to the *Sword of Vengeance* series with a tip of the hat to Vicente Aranda's *La Novia Ensangrentada* (1972)— a whole different genre—thrown in. The parody elements—from the pre-title fake "Shaw Scope" logo and "Feature Presentation Banner," scratched up as if purloined from the projection booth of

TOP & CENTER: The Bride (Uma Thurman) faces a horde of masked assailants and assumes the position.

Bottom: The Bride faces off against Go Go Yubari (Chiaki Kuriyama).

TOP: Hanzo (Sonny Chiba) presents his new creation to the Bride (Uma Thurman).

CENTER: The Bride (Um Thurman) and O-Ren Ishii (Lucy Liu) duel in the snow.

BOTTOM: O-Ren Ishii (Lucy Liu) after beheading a recalcitrant *yakuza*

some drive-in, to the extended *anime* sequence that fills in the back story of O-Ren—are purposefully over the top. The gun in the box of "Kaboom" cereal is about as deft as this movie gets, for Tarantino appears to be reaching for the American-take-on-the-samurai analog of *Last House on the Left* (1972), Wes Craven's modern-day, blood-and-guts variant on Bergman's *Virgin Spring* (1960). The problem is that, while the exploration of a character's revenge for the death of a child has dramatic resonance from Sweden to Japan, the chivalric code that requires and controls vengeance looks different from a 21st-century perspective. Moreover, as far as disjunctive style and narrative is concerned, Japanese filmmakers have already thoroughly deconstructed the genre on their own, directly, through the *ninkyo eiga*, and in all manner of commercials and music videos. The use of Ennio Morricone themes and other allusions on the soundtrack notwithstanding, the saga of "The Bride with No Name"—whatever her name is, in case the audience should fail to notice, is "bleeped" out in the first sequence—is as far from Leone as it is from Gosha; and the pre-existence of *Zoku Kill Bill* does not create an effective link to a series figure, to Nemuri or Zato Ichi or even Crimson Bat Oichi. Any audience understands from genre expectation, if not from the existence of Volume 2, that the Bride who would not die in the flashback cannot die in the extended combat at the end. Possessing the same preternatural sword skills as countless samurai figures, the Bride's unbreakable blade slices through scores of black-suited minions as easily as Itto Ogami disposed of Yagyu-clan *ninja*. Of course, in *Kill Bill* the namesake of the legendary Iga *ninja*, Hanzo Hattori, is an Okinawan swordsmith (portrayed by Sonny Chiba, the star of a long-running 1980s television series about Hanzo and other shadow warriors), who makes the Bride's blade. Given that, even those who did not notice that O-Ren's name was already crossed off the list as the saga began must certainly expect the Bride, newly spattered with the blood of others, to conquer. Hattori's Japanese voice that coaches her at the end of the first sequence, exhorting her to "kill whoever stands in your way," has become a voice inside. But all the elements, the *ninja*-style concealment in the eaves, the long stretches of black-and-white photography, the young combatant spared with a Sanjuro-like admonishment, add up only to the expected result.

While the period martial arts films of Hong Kong and mainland China share many of the attributes of the samurai film, particularly the *ninja* sub-genre, the operatic complications and physical magic of the swordplay movies—as evident in the recent crossover success *Crouching Tiger, Hidden Dragon* (2000)—overwhelm any version of *giri-ninjo* conflict its characters might confront. A contemporary action film like *Kiss of the Dragon* (2001) is actually generically more proximate to *chambara*. Although seeking to clear himself of criminal charges, the protagonist's attack on the headquarters of a crooked police detective self-righteously defies all odds in order to rescue a child. The bare-handed combat after he stumbles into a roomful of Parisian cops in white karate *gis* is closer in staging and tone to such defiant figures as Sanjuro or Itto Ogami than any scene in *Kill Bill.*

There are certainly antecedents to the recently released *The Last Samurai* (2003). Besides Okamoto's *East Meets West* and *Red Sun,* there is *Bushido Blade* (1979), where sailors from Perry's black ships and a shogunate retainer (portrayed by Mifune) search for a stolen sword intended as a gift for Townsend Harris. *Journey of Honor* (*Shogun Mayeda,* 1991) depicts events prior to the battle of Sekigahara and a trip to Spain by the son of Ieyasu Tokugawa to obtain muskets for his father's faction. Guns are also at the crux of *The Last Samurai.* While somewhat at variance with the Kojiki,[2] the narration which opens *The Last Samurai* tells of how Japan was formed when the gods tempered a sword in the sea and the drops which fell from it created the island nation. After this mythic invocation, the scene shifts to 1876 San Francisco, where the former cavalry Captain Nathan Algren gives a drunken demonstration of his proficiency with a Winchester. His back story as a "hero" is parcelled out over several conversations about Custer and the 7th Cavalry and physically intrudes into the narrative in the form of flashbacks to a massacre at an Indian camp. After he is hired to go to Japan with a former Colonel and a single non-com to train the Imperial army, the plot that unfolds might well have been pitched as *Dances with Wolves* meets *Ran* with a bit of *Star Wars* and *They Died with Their Boots On* thrown in.

The antagonist of the emperor is a former minister, a reactionary samurai named Katsumoto who disdains Western arms. The real Katsumoto, Takamori Saigo, who lead the Satsuma Rebellion in 1876-77 and was a minor character in Kenji Misumi's *Last Samurai,* may have been more of a neo-imperialist than a *bujutsu* purist.[3] When untrained troops are, despite Algren's protest, sent out against him they turn and run. In the slaughter, many are killed and a wounded Algren is taken captive. While Taka, Katsumoto's sister and widow of a samurai killed by Algren, tends the captive's wound, there are more flashbacks to Indian camp killings as his recuperation is compounded by the delirium tremens of alcoholic withdrawal. While Algren screams for sake, his journal is being read by Katsumoto. The winter spent in Katsumoto's mountain village is the narrative core of *The Last Samurai.* With scenes and characters all but transposed whole from *Dances with Wolves,* new journal entries provide a voiceover narration. Algren acquiesces to requests for conversation by Katsumoto, who has heard of Custer and the Indian wars; picks up Japanese during meals with Taka and her sons; is chaperoned by an older samurai whom he calls "Bob"; and gets some harsh *bokken* lessons from Ujio, Katsumoto's angry lieutenant. Certainly when the voiceover remarks about being taken in "as if I were a stray dog," there are some telling allusions to the genre traditions of *chambara*; but much of the process of "going native" is generic. Although the circumstances which bring him to the village are clearly different, as with Kevin Costner's portrayal of Lt. Dunbar amongst the Sioux, Tom Cruise's Algren is won over by the noble savagery and sense of tribal community in the samurai enclave. Over the course of several months, Algren's skill with the *bokken* also grows prodigiously. With Taka's sons acting as his *mushin-no-shin* coaches by calling out "no mind," Algren visualizes a series of moves, a bit like Ichi in *Zato Ichi in Desperation*, and remarkably achieves a draw in a practice duel with Ujio.

While the village enjoys a puppet play, as with the sneak attack by the rival Pawnee in *Dances with Wolves*, a squad of *ninja* assassins strike, and Algren joins the defense. In an extended sequence of classic *chambara* Algren first protects Taka and her family then fights side-by-side with Katsumoto until the *ninja* are defeated. At this point, the genre indicators—if not the movie publicity—are clear: there is no turning back for Algren from the path to full investiture as a samurai. Returned to Tokyo when Katsumoto agrees to discuss resuming his position as government minister, Algren is offered direction of the Imperial forces by Minister Omura, who hired him in San Francisco. Before refusing Omura, Algren understates Katsumoto's threat: "He's a tribal leader. I've know many of them." As he packs to leave, Algren learns of Katsumoto's arrest and realizes he cannot abandon him. When confronted by Omura's sinister aid and three henchmen, Algren chooses not to draw his pistols but still kills them all in a frenzied display of *niten-ryu*—or two-sword technique—using blades snatched from the hands of his assailants. After Algren mentally replays the combat in a slow-motion, monochromatic, "no-minded" flashback, Omura's man rises up to say the day of the samurai is over and be beheaded.

TOP: Katsumoto's samurai warriors prepare for battle.

CENTER: Katsumoto (Ken Watanabe) fighting the Meiji soldiers

BOTTOM: Algren and Taka (Koyuki)

Opposite page:
TOP: Katsumoto attacks Algren's Imperial forces by riding out of the mist.

CENTER: Algren and Katsumoto ride out of the village bound for Tokyo.

BOTTOM: Algren (Tom Cruise) and Katsumoto (Ken Watanabe) end up fighting side-by-side when ninja assassins attack.

While the use of genre expectation can be effective dramatic shorthand, the thumbnails that act as mile markers on Algren's path are somewhat disjointed. When Algren talks to Katsumoto about the Spartans at Thermopylae, the conversation is more about myth-making than tactics. The last battle is an extended and bloody affair that is conspicuously epic in scale and seeks to resonate with pictures as diverse as *Ran* and *Lawrence of Arabia* but ends up being mostly *The Charge of the Light Brigade.* Making Katsumoto and his followers, a small band of 300 or so outsiders, defiant to the death is certainly more melodramatic than the thousands who fought (and died) on each side at the historical battle of Tabura-Zakao and it is also in keeping with the *chambara* spirit of hopeless causes typified by the saga of forty-seven *ronin.* Certainly also, Japanese filmmakers from Misumi's *Last Samurai* to *When the Last Sword Is Drawn* have distorted the actual events at Toba-Fushimi to emphasize the hollow triumph of technology over tradition. But the Western viewer is unlikely to perceive a sub-text in which the slaughter of the last of the fierce traditionalists under the withering fire of a Gatling gun could be read as a mass *funshi* to protest the government's policies.

Who, in fact, is to be perceived as the last samurai of the title? Clearly Katsumoto qualifies, whether it's striding into the council of ministers with two swords in his sash in defiance of the 1876 law or riding into battle to embrace "a good death." But Katsumoto's persistent vision, the primordial scene of a white tiger fighting off a slew of warriors which comes to him in a Zen trance during an early sequence, also dies with him. Part of the new myth constructed by the filmmakers of this *Last Samurai* is in the link which Katusmoto saw when Algren fought against his warriors at their first encounter and the banner of the tiger attached to the broken lance with which Algren flailed. The transference of that vision, as Algren helps the defeated

Algren (Tom Cruise) charges with
the Katsumoto band.

Katsumoto perform an impromptu *seppuku* on the field of battle, defines the real last samurai. In terms of narrative, Algren is as unlikely a surviror as Dunbar was at the beginning of *Dances with Wolves*. In terms of genre and myth, the expectations and impact are much the same. While the narration gives the audience alternate possibilities of Algren's fate, the images are of him returning to the village. As last man standing, Algren becomes the unlikely, very Western repository of the samurai spirit embodied by Katsumoto and his men.

II. STYLE AND POLITICAL STATEMENT

In the *jidai-geki* of Kenji Mizoguchi an understated, quasi-humanistic tradition is reflected. Man is a tragic figure predestined towards some obscure fate. The long, elaborate traveling shots both lead and follow Mizoguichi's stately figures down corridors, past shrines, to the edges of the forest and the dark unknown that lurks within. By the time of *Yang Kwei Fei*, decorous colors, wide-angle lenses, and portentous dolly shots all create a mise-en-scène and visual choreography akin to Western-style opera in its stylistic grandeur and artifice. When he traverses familiar narrative ground, Mizoguchi's outlook, from his *47 Ronin*, a legend retold more for its edifying qualities that its irony or horror, to his *Tales of the Taira Clan*, with its implicit validation of the feudal system, is unflinchingly personal. As drama, the results are often extraordinary. While he fully exploits genre expection in *Chushingura* and *Miyamoto Musashi*, in terms of early *chambara*, Mizoguchi's minimalist approach to the energy and social insight of the samurai film is unique.

There is no question that the rise of Akira Kurosawa from the ashes of the Japanese film industry shortly after the Second World War is the seminal event in modern *chambara,* the groundwork which defines the samurai film as most Western viewers know it. *Rashomon* typifies this. Even without widescen or color, many new visual techniques are in play: location work, long-lens panning shots, naturalistic lighting, framing that emphasizes pictorial values. On a narrative level, the elaborate plot conceits of *Rashomon* are significantly affected by these techniques. As the narrative laboriously ponders the moral distinctions between Tajomaro and his victims, Kurosawa's images subtly but forcefully make the same point by equating the bandit and the samurai on a visual level.

Seven Samurai is arguably the first masterwork of post-War *chambara*. Its aesthetic and critical success laid a genre foundation on which most film-makers rely to this day. Its protagonists are not commoners, but not exalted samurai either. If there are days of privilege in a clan manor in any of their pasts, nothing of that is evident or pertinent. Whether they became *ronin* or were born from disenfranchised forebears, they are trapped, unable to find or reacquire status or to affect social intergration with another, lower class such as the farmers, who judge them harshly and eye them with suspicion even as they beg for their help. These samurai are not victims of fate but of a political system. The statement at the end of *Seven Samurai* is straightforward, whether in the dialogue or the simple tilt up from the survivors to their fallen comrades. The manipulations of image through lens selection, framing, and lighting at the end of *Yojimbo* and *Sanjuro* are a natural progression.

The key filmmakers of this era resisted the impulse to deconstruct the archetype. Kurosawa as director repeatedly used Toshiro Mifune as a performer and helped propel him to the status of genre icon. In Kurosawa's movies, *chambara* and otherwise, Mifune is virtually always the same. Even when cast as the patient physician in the *jidai-geki* tale *Red Beard* (*Akahige*, 1965), Mifune's character is permitted a display of martial arts prowess in an intricately choreographed bare-handed fight with a gang of pimps, which underscores that person's physical resilience and ethical superiority. Kurosawa uses stereotypical situations to create a humanistic portrait, and ultimately the personal supersedes the political. Sanjuro is a brash, strong, and fundamentally symmpathetic character; but when he counsels the peasant-swordsman that "a long life eating mush is best," he indulges in a reactionary polemic that belies his own actions.

The year after *Sanjuro* was released in Japan, two series were begun. One was the first feature from Daiei starring Raizo Ichikawa as "Kyoshiro Nemuri." The other was on television: *Three Outlaw Samurai*. As previously detailed, Raizo Ichikawa's unusual transition from early in his career as the handsome hero of Mizoguchi's *Tales of the Taira Clan* to the "rough" look was clearly influenced by the *aragoto* heritage of mannerisms and vulgar poses Mifune had embraced as Kurosawa's Sanjuro. While promoted as a quasi-evil personage, Nemuri is more accurately a sardonic fatalist like Sanjuro. Nemuri's attacks on the feudal institutions are ostensibly because he is the estranged "son of the black mass." In fact, Nemuri's position is one of self-confidence and control, of a man who embraces the possibility of death, not of a man who believes that "a long life eating mush is best." He relishes the killing of the arrogant and overprivileged, the rape of aristocratic women, and giving comeuppance to the sanctimonious.

In Nemuri and in the title characters of *Three Outlaw Samurai* there is a full break with the heroic, self-sacrificing genre figures established in *Seven*

Samurai and further developed, albeit circuitously, in *Yojimbo* and *Sanjuro*. Still, Nemuri's proclamation, as he cuts down an unarmed woman, that he can kill in cold blood because he is a villain, is entirely ingenuous. It is precisely because he follows his own code, because he is not a self-serving villain, that Nemuri's actions have a larger political implication that any of Sanjuro's. Nemuri is not merely alienated or anarchic. He is murderously opposed to any manifestation of repressive authority. Sanjuro impulsively helps the young farmer whose wife has been taken by the gang boss even though he professes to "hate pathetic people." In *Trail of Traps*, Nemuri's journey to Kyoto to "see what's on people's minds" is a reverse of that paradox. Nemuri has no interest in other people's minds, merely in relieving his personal torment through cathartic violence. By the end of the 1960s, such manifest alienation is almost a character constant in the samurai film, but the depiction of this condition covers a wide range. Kurosawa spends much of his narrative time establishing humanistic dilemmas and drawing Sanjuro into positive action. The Nemuri series sets up situations which draw its protagonist into anti-social action. Neither figure manages to exorcise his personal demons.

As has been noted, screenwriter Shinobu Hashimoto is the common link to many of the most notable samurai films ever made. His ten *chambara* scripts for five different directors resulted in four of the finest examples of the genre: *Seven Samurai, Hara-Kiri, Samurai Assassin*, and *Tenchu*. His collaboration with Kobayashi on *Hara-Kiri* certainly begins as a more direct statement on social responsibility than any of Kurosawa's samurai films to that point. Yet the focus on the individual and tragic dilemma of Tsugumo, as he attacks the very core of feudal institutions, undercuts some of the social statement. That the Iyi clan has no compunction about rewriting its own records or reassembling the ancestral armor to conceal its shame is clearly just one element of an the oppressive social hypocrisy in which men whose skills are no longer required are simply discarded.

In the very brief period from 1964 to 1969, Hideo Gosha became the first director working in the genre to define a profound and consistent world view. Using different performers and other collaborators, Gosha's extraordinary creative outburst of seven features in five years easily ranks with the Western series of Peckinpah, Leone, and Anthony Mann or the *noir* films of Robert Siodmak and Fritz Lang. From the modest beginnings of *Three Outlaw Samurai*, spun off from a television series, to the extraordinary *Tenchu*, Gosha picks up the tools of Kurosawa—the pan, the zoom, the long lens, the angular mise-en-scène—and with tremendous visceral impact reinforces both the narrative situations and the character emotions of his *chambara*. Using genre expectations to the fullest, Gosha's films also consistently isolate the true antagonist: the feudal system.

What further distinguishes the work of Gosha and, to a degree, that of Kihachi Okamoto and Masahiro Shinoda, is the equation between personal violence and political repression. For Gosha most of all, it is repression not alienation that breeds violence. In terms of the genre, the progession might be summarized thusly: in Kurosawa and Kobayashi, violence begets irony and tragedy; in the Nemuri and to some extent the Zato Ichi series, violence begets anarchy; in Gosha, violence begets clarity. Unlike *Hara-Kiri*, where violence is swept up and hidden away like the blood-stained sand in the courtyard of the Iyi, in *Sword of the Beast*, *Goyokin*, and *Tenchu* violence unmasks the institutions and compels them to betray themselves.

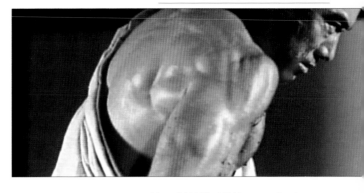

Novelist Yukio Mishima, portraying Shinbei Tanaka, commits *hara-kiri* in *Tenchu*

In Kurosawa's final pictures, wide-ranging narratives span and incorporate many broad themes, from fate and free will or revenge and forgiveness to simply good and evil. The "disorder" in *Ran* is, as in *Lear,* human and personal. In Gosha's work the chaos and disruption are a societal disorder. In *Ran*, the battle montage is elegiac, the fountains of blood that erupt from the back of Lady Kaede or the chest of Hanbei in *Sanjuro* are abstracted and almost surreal. In Gosha, the violence is brutal and ugly and, as when Mishima as Shinbei Tanaka commits *seppuku*, chillingly real.

III. The Samurai at the Millennium

Over the last two decades, there have been less than fifty feature films produced in the samurai genre. Of those a significant number have dealt with the morbidity of the samurai class, often in the context of the *bakumatsu*. The Japanese title of Yasuo Kohata's *Shogun's Shadow* (*Shogun Iemitsu no Ranshin: Gekitotsu*, 1989) translates as the "madness of Shogun Iemitsu," the author of the 1836 *shoshi hatto* regulations. It centers on an attempt by that early Tokugawa ruler to kill his first-born son. While the film relies heavily on oddly-staged fight sequences and a somewhat clichéd narrative in which the band of *ronin* who protect the young price Takechiyo from his demented parent are killed off one by one. Kyogo, the leader, has a personal motive, having been disenfranchised for protesting Iemitsu's order to surrender his wife to concubinage. When his former brother-in-law, Minister Abe, tries to buy Kyogo off, his terse response is "a samurai has the *bushido* code."

For most of the samurai figures portrayed at the turn of the new millennium, the *bushido* code offers little solace. While the ironies confronted by these characters may not be as bitter as the experiences of Hanshiro Tsugumo in *Hara-Kiri* or Izo Okada in *Tenchu*, they share their disillusionment with the very concept of a code of honor. While a disproportionate number are associationed with the *shinsengumi*—the last somewhat perverse expression of samurai honor before the full impact of the *bakumatsu* sent the entire class into oblivion—the contexts of that disillusionment vary widely.

In *Taboo*, the anti-traditionalist director Nagisa Oshima makes a rare foray into *jidai-geki* with a narrative that centers on a "beautiful youth" who has newly been recruited to the *shinsengumi*, where he tantalizes his comrades and commanders alike. Certainly it should not be that shocking to see the *shinsengumi* consciously or subconsciously consider the Spartan warrior ideal. There is an even odder variant rendering in *Bakumatsu Jyunjyoden* (1991), where Ryoma Sakamoto and *shinsengumi* Lt. Commander Hijikata compete for the affections of Soji Okita, who is a really a master swords*woman*. Oshima eschews the subversive lasciviousness he brought to *In the Realm of the Senses* (*Ai no Corrida*, 1976) and opens the picture with furtive glances and darkly saturated color cinematography. Amid the blacks, browns, and grays of the clothing and set decorations only one recruit, Sozaburo Kano, wears white with its virginal connotations. With his long hair pulled back in a ponytail and framing his face, he is a prototypical "beautiful youth," deriving from the *nimaime* or *wagoto*-style actor in *kabuki* or a human rendering of the *bishojo/bishonen* figures, the "pretty" girls and boys whose exaggerated, androgynous good looks are rife in Japanese *manga* and *anime*. If there were any doubt remaining, when the two prospects, Kano and Hyozo Tashiro, come to interview with the *shinsengumi* commanders, Oshima cuts across the stage line to a medium close shot of Kano. After zooming in to a close shot, two extreme close shots of Kano's eye and brow and nose and lips are cut in while Ryuichi Sakamoto's insistent, nine-note, minor key "Taboo" theme plays on the soundtrack. Finally, a cut to a close shot of Hijikata reveals that all this is from his point of view. As if to reaffirm the elemental power of the "Kuleshov effect,"[4] Oshima drains any expression from the semi-paralyzed face of actor Takeshi Kitano. All this, of course, is to hammer home a character point that was already, and unsubtly, made in the opening sequence.

Oshima follows this sequence with a series of white letters on black: "Code of Conduct. Never Betray the Samurai Ways. Never desert the *Shinsengumi*. Never borrow money. Never be involved in civil suits. Never fight for personal motives. . . ." The penalty for any infraction is, as might be expected, *seppuku*. The unwritten rule, Oshima permits the viewer to presume, is "Never seduce your colleague into homosexual activity," which is precisely what Tashiro attempts that evening with Kano. While Oshima never clarifies the exact relationship between Kano and Tashiro, the fulcrum is Hijikata. In addition to the title cards Oshima intercuts at odd intervals, Hijikata is given to interior remarks (delivered in a different voice), as he mulls over and sometimes directly questions the sexual inclinitions of various subordinates

When the two prospects, Kano (Ryuhei Matsuda) and Hyozo Tashiro (Tadanobu Asano), come to interview with the *shinsengumi* commanders ("Beat" Takeshi Kitano, center, and Yoichi Sai), Oshima cuts across the stage line to a medium close shot of Kano. After zooming in to a close shot, two extreme close shots of Kano's eye and brow and nose and lips are cut in. Finally, a cut to a close shot of Hijikata reveals that all this is from his point of view.

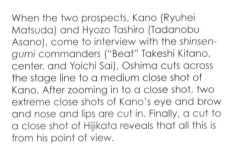

Kano, how old are you?

Eighteen.

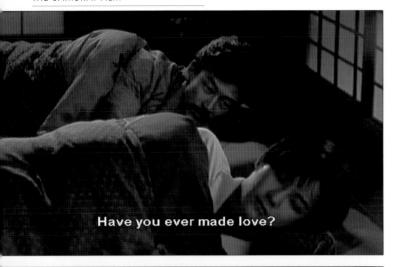

Have you ever made love?

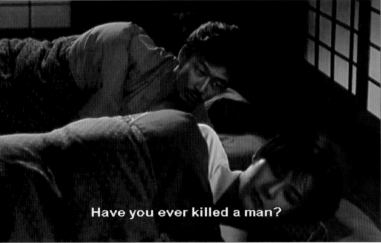

Have you ever killed a man?

ABOVE: Two types of "virginity" for a *shinsengumi* in *Taboo*

Opposite page:
TOP: Hijikata's vision of Kano meeting a phantom lover in a white kimono

CENTER, TOP: A defensive Okita affirms his hatred for homosexuals.

CENTER, BOTTOM: Hijikata's vision of Kano meeting Okita in a red kimono

BOTTOM: Hijikata fells a blossoming cherry tree with a single sword cut.

vis-à-vis Kano. Early on, Hijikata's protégé, Soji Okita, observes that "it takes a madman to know a madman." Against the historical background of the *bakumatsu*, the question of Kano's sexual orientation seems less significant than why the son of a wealty merchant family would join a reactionary militia.

Oshima refuses to the end to stipulate which issues matter. After Yuzawa, a *shinsengumi* man, who the viewer—but not Hijikata—knows has had a sexual liaison with Kano, is reported murdered by a comrade, Tashiro and Kano are prime suspects. In a sort of trial by combat, the *shinsengumi* commanders decide to order Kano to kill Tachiro. As Hijikata and Soji wait to observe the confrontation, the deputy Commander imagines several scenarios and contemplates how "a samurai can be undone by the love of men." Soji's tale of male devotion puts him on the defensive, compels him to assert that he "hates queers" but admires beautiful stories. After visions of Kano meeting phantom lovers in first a white and then a red kimono, Hijikate and Soji watch the fight. Despite the outcome, there is no emotional release for Hijikata. The final, heavily symbolic sequence, in which he fells a blossoming cherry tree with a single sword cut, offers little resolution.

When they were released in the West in 2000, both *Dora Heita* and *After the Rain* (*Ame Agaru*) were marketed as being based on projects developed (and partly scripted) by Akira Kurosawa before his death in 1998. The script of *Dora Heita*, directed by Kon Ichikawa (who was eighty-four when he made this movie), was co-written by the director and originally planned as a co-production with Kurosawa, Masaki Kobayashi, and Keisuke Kinoshita in 1969. The title character of *Dora Heita* (literally "alley cat," figuratively, "playboy") is Koheita Mochizuki, a magistrate who arrives at his new assignment with a letter from the local lord that gives him carte blanche to clean up the province. In order to ferret out rogue officials, Koheita, whose reputation as a playboy precedes him, feigns indolence and disinterest. Ichikawa's framing device, an introductory black-and-white sequence in an unfurnished room where the clan's secretaries record the ongoing failure of the magistrate to report formally to his office, sets up and sustains viewer uncertainty about Koheita's motives. His nocturnal forays into the local town, which he has declared off-limits to all clan retainers because it is rife with gambling and prostitution, contain a lot of comic relief that may further mislead the spectator. In the end, of course, Koheita reveals a singular and unforeseen ability as a swordsman, when he singlehandedly takes on scores of *yakuza*, and as an investigator, when he unmasks his longtime friend as the one on the take from the criminals. The fact that the script originated three decades earlier may contribute to the style of social criticism in the narrative, which has touches of the heavy irony of Kobayashi and the dark humor of Kurosawa but not their overt impact.

Ten years earlier in his *47 Killers* (*Shijushichinin no Shikaku*, 1994), Ichikawa had demonstrated a vigorous revisionist sensibility, using actual exteriors, cramped "practical" sets with blown out overexposures of sunlit windows and characters ducking to avoiding hitting their heads, and deeply-saturated natural colors isolated in a frame of drab earth tones to create an *ukiyo-e*-style version of *Chushingura*. In *Dora Heita*, while the serene compositions and stiff poses of the retainers seen in the clan manor contrast repeatedly with the drab décor and disorderly conduct in the town, the clean lines conceal the contagion and corruption that has infiltrated the clan itself. It is only by attacking and breaking down these structures—and by incurring the enmity of the young clansmen who try to assassinate him for his very unruliness—that Koheita can accomplish his mission.

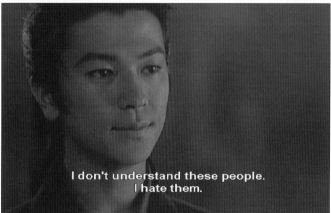

A middle-aged, black-kimonoed samurai walks down a roadway with an umbrella during a heavy storm. At a river, porters confirm what it obvious: no one will be able to cross for some time. The man returns to an nearby inn and gives the news to his wife. A succession of genre indicators take the

viewer from an expectation of a traditional samurai story to something very different, something almost elegiac. Another project developed by Akira Kurosawa, *After the Rain*, was directed by Takashi Koizumi, Kurosawa's longtime assistant, whose approach is clearly reverential. The samurai, Ihei Misawa, is actually a *ronin*, recently "laid off" and unlikely to find work due both to ageism and the relative tranquility of the late Tokugawa era. While waiting to move on, Ihei decides to help his impoverished fellow travellers and has a catered banquet delivered to the inn. Ihei's generosity—demonstrated at this event and staged with allusions to *Donzoku* (1957) and *Dodes'ka-den* (1970), rather than to Kurosawa's *chambara*—touches even the hard-bitten local prostitute.

Returning from practicing alone in the woods, Ihei stumbles upon a group of young samurai on the brink of a sword fight. When he intervenes, they turn on him; but before he must draw to defend himself, the local Lord rides up. Ihei is thanked for preventing possible bloodshed and invited to the local manor, where he tells Lord Shigeaki his story, illustrated in a black-and-white flashback: restless youth causes him to leave his clan and to survive by challenging local sword masters to duels, always conceding quickly, knowing they will likely pay him a honorarium or sparring fee. Ultimately, Ihei meets the famous *sensei* Tsuji Gettan (portrayed by Tatsuya Nakadai), the historical founder of the Mugai style often associated with the Iga *ninja*. Flummoxed by the fact that Ihei's unpolished swordsmanship presents "too many openings," Gettan yields to him. Charmed by Ihei, Shigeaki proposes that he consider becoming the clan's fencing master. When Shigeaki's chamberlains object, Ihei is asked to demonstrate his skills in *bokken* duels. He easily defeats two young clansmen. Then the Lord himself takes up a lance and ends up in the pond. Ihei's apologies are so profuse that they irritate Shigeaki. Ultimately the chamberlains learn from the local *dojo* that Ihei had won enough money to buy the banquet at the inn by prize fighting, something *bushido* forbids, and convince the Lord to rescind his offer. Although his wife Tayo had herself disapproved of such behavior, when she hears her husband being reprimanded, she chastises the chamberlain for being too shortsighted to realize that sometimes "what's important is not what he has done, but why he has done it."

By this point, Ihei has been typed as almost a reverse of Sanjuro. Not only would Sanjuro's harsh admission in *Yojimbo*—"I hate pathetic people! I'll kill you if you cry"—never occur to a man such as Ihei, but the character created by novelist Shugoro Yamamoto shuns killing. In an earlier adaptation of Yamamoto, *Samurai from Nowhere* (1964), Ihei is driven to despair when it cannot be avoided. Ironically, in *After the Rain*, this character now finds that helping others has cost him what is likely his last chance at a good position. The film ends as Ihei and Tayo resume their journey, reconciled to him remaining masterless, while Shigeaki overhauls his court and rides after Ihei. In one sense, it's a long way from Sanjuro's declamation about mush and his brusque departure from the village, a stray dog heading off down a windswept road at the end of *Yojimbo*, to the last shot of Ihei and his wife marvelling at a view in *After the Rain* and remarking that "it brings the strength welling up inside of you." But what Sanjuro says is one thing, what he does is another. Of course, he has no doting wife at his side, no band of riders chasing after him to confer a lucrative post. Having just killed off all his employers has effectively diminished Sanjuro's prospects, but it doesn't matter any more for him than it does for Ihei and Tayo.

If *After the Rain* could be described as steeped in *mono no aware* and overflowing with an optimistic variant of Kurosawa's renowned humanism, *Samurai Fiction*, directed by Hiroyuki Nakano, attacks traditional narrative and style with a scatter-gun approach. There are many powerful images in *Samurai Fiction*, starting with a black-and-white pre-title sequence in which a young samurai rushes into a grove of black bamboo. The first shot is a panning long lens on a running figure, a succinct tribute to Kurosawa and quite different from the black-and-white still images of the "Emperor" at work in the formal dedication that prefaces *After the Rain*. In the next shot, the young samurai draws his *bokken* and attacks the thick bamboo, shouting with every slash and thrust. A jump cut brings him to the foreground, with a side move antcipating his rush out of frame. Finally, a slight low angle captures the last series of jabs and he goes to his knees, and a voiceover says, "This is me three hundred years ago. My name was Heishiro Inukai. It's a good name." The sequence ends on a point-of-view shot up into the trees; all in all a very different invocation of *mono on aware*.

Compared to one of the final scenes in *After the Rain*, in which Ihei stands amid willows in a mossy grove with a waterfall behind him, this invocation of the samurai becoming one with his sword is energetic and atypically staged. But the color title sequence which follows—pans across tempered blue blades; fencing silhouettes revealed behind red screens; flames filling the frame—suggests that the line should have been delivered: "the name's Inukai . . . Heishiro Inukai." After a graphic of digital numerals take us back those three hundred years, a pedal guitar *waa-waa*s under shots of a castle. Inside a snide swordsman named Kazamatsuri crosses words with some petty

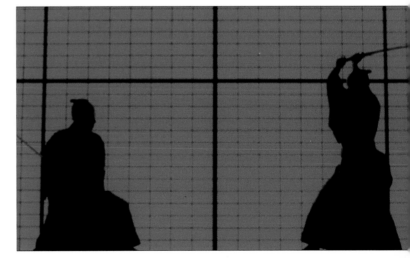

Title sequence from *Samurai Fiction*—fencing silhouettes revealed behind red screens.

samurai. One moment Kazamatsuri is accused of murder and stealing a clan heirloom. The next he's on a beach helping out an old man and young widow on a vendetta against five young thugs.

In many ways, *Samurai Fiction* and Nakano's *ninja* movie, *Red Shadow* (*Aka Kage*, 2001), epitomize how a newer generation of filmmakers embrace *wakon yosai*, a term from the early Meiji era that is usually translated as "Japanese spirit, Western things." The opening of *Red Shadow* is also a visual tour de force, using digital effects, macro photography, and *ninja* POV shots; but it goes on to introduce parody elements from *Star Wars* to baseball (as one *ninja* admonishes a colleague, "Don't play to the stands.") to create more of an aura of video game than *chambara*. Until the picture's end, *Samurai Fiction* continues to combine non-traditional sights and sounds, to confound Japanese and Western styles, and to include a lot of parody and outright comic relief. But mostly there is too much Tarantino-*tai* and not enough Mizoguchi-*damashi*, too much visual Brakhage and not enough virtual Brecht. Or, by way of analogy, as Chamberlain Inukai observes to his son, "You've studied fencing but you've yet to master the samurai spirit."

Both *The Twilight Samurai* (*Tasogare Seibei*, 2002) and *When the Last Sword Is Drawn* are reflections of the new realism and fatalism that 21st-century filmmakers are bringing to *chambara*. Superficially the plots are quite different: the events of *Twilight Samurai* transpire entirely in a provincial *han*, while *When the Last Sword Is Drawn* centers on the *shinsengumi* and the *bakumatsu* in Kyoto. Still, both central narratives do concern the end of the Tokugawa era, and both are framed by flashbacks from a perspective of many years later. Most significantly, both focus on low-ranking samurai driven to desparate action because they have families to support.

The story of Seibei Iguchi, an impoverished, low-ranking widower who has spent all his life working as a clan clerk, is told by his younger daughter, Ito, now an old woman but only five when she opens her recollection with the funeral of her mother, dead of tuberculosis in 1868. As portrayed by Hiroyuki Sanada—a protégé of Sonny Chiba as a juvenile actor and who starred in Kihachi Okamoto's last two *chambara* and as "Ujio" in the American *The Last Samurai*—Seibei Iguchi is a man aged prematurely by the adverse and suffo-cating social strictures of Tokugawa society. The film begins in a sustained shot flashback. A shrouded body lies in the background by a window; a wheel of prayer slips is turned in the foreground; someone cries. As the camera travels sideways, a stoic-faced man is revealed, then two women sobbing, and on through the darkened house as an elderly voiced Ito begins speaking. Finally, the camera reaches Ito as a child, and as it zooms in snow falls from the roof into an open courtyard just behind, startling her. A dissolve to the funeral procession in the snow erases her face.

As the clan clerks are dismissed, the narration and the gossip of Seibei's colleagues complete the back story of the one they call "twilight" Seibei, unkempt and too poor to do anything but trudge home every evening. Seibei walks off in a shot narrowed by dark shapes on both edges of the frame, a visual equivalent of his social constriction. The contrast between the sharp lines and bright room of the accounting office in the manor and the dinghy disorder of Seibei's house reveals the irony of his situation. After the subtle tension of the opening sequence, the pattern of visual usage continues to underscore the protagonist's position,

Seibei (Hiroyuki Sanada) with his two young daughters, Kayana (Miko Ito) and Ito (Erina Hashiguch), in *The Twilight Samurai*

trapped by the rigid structures of the clan, which restrict the options of a petty, "50-*koku*-per-year" samurai and assign him a personal "value" based on this very meager stipend. While Seibei may have scant hope for improving his lot, compared to those whose starved bodies are found floating by during two scenes at the local river, Seibei and his family are at least subsisting.

During a meeting by the rifle range, Seibei's childhood friend and higher-ranking samurai (400 *koku* per year), Michinojo Iinuma, paints a verbal picture of disorder in Kyoto: "Filthy masterless samurai everywhere, cursing in dialects you can't understand, then someone shouts 'Heaven's punishment,' and swords come out. The Kamo River's full of bloated headless corpses." After complaining of the clan's inattention to the *bakumatsu*, which may "snuff out 250 years of the shogunate like a candle in the wind," Michinojo mentions that he has gotten his younger sister Tomoe divorced from her abusive and alcoholic husband. The following day, Tomoe visits Seibei's house to renew their own childhood friendship. As Seibei walks her home that evening, he encounters Tomoe's former husband, Toyotaro Koda, challenging Michinojo. Seibei intervenes and takes the challenge himself. Knowing that dueling is forbidden and that merely injuring a 1,200 *koku* retainer, a man more than twenty times his worth, would be severely punished, Seibei is armed with only a short stick when he goes to meet Koda.

"However the world might change," Seibei has told his ten-year-old daughter Kayana in an earlier scene, "if you have the power to think you'll always survive somehow." When he hears the dire predictions about "times changing" from Michinojo, Seibei presumes that "when they do, I'll give up samurai status and be a farmer. That's what I'm suited for." In another long take, over two minutes without a cut, in the courtyard of Iinuma's house Seibei had been drawn into the duel with Koda. Hardly a newcomer, having directed more than sixty

Top: "Do you apologize?"

Center, bottom: Seibei (Hiroyuki Sanada) uses a short *bokken*-like stick to duel with Koda (Ren Osugi) in *The Twilight Samurai*.

features and best-known for the forty-eight features that constitute the "Tora-san" series of comedies, director Yoji Yamada brings a highly-developed visual scheme to his first *chambara* film. The use of long takes in particular reinforces the deterministic undertone of the narrative. The fulcrum of Seibei's beliefs is the notion of acceptance in both the clan tradition and Buddhist faith.

The shot selection in the duel with Koda is equally telling. Going from close shots on particular lines, such as Seibei's reply that "the apology is yours to make," to long shots without movement cues, Yamada uses montage for tensing effect. The main portion of the duel is a long-take wide shot, just over a minute long, which pans left and right to hold the action within frame until Koda's sword is knocked from his hand and he is thrown out of the shot. In a three shot with Koda foreground right and Michinojo rearground center, Seibei kneels in the left midground by Koda's sword to ask "Do you apologize? Or do you continue?" In a silent, extra-wide high angle, Koda gets up on his knees. The duel ends in a final medium two shot. Koda lunges for his sword and slashes at Seibei's legs, but he leaps over the blade and knocks Koda out with a blow to his head while in mid-air. Although perhaps not much of a duel by Itto Ogami's standards, Yamada constructs Seibei's fight in *The Twilight Samurai* as a mirror of his resilient character. As with the rifle fire in the background during Seibei and Michinojo's first conversation, there is also aural counterpoint: a single cuckoo's ten-note call repeats several times from somewhere nearby.

Do you apologize?

The series of ill-fated mischances seem to turn for Seibei. Even though he presumes "a beaten dog won't bark" and swears Michinojo to silence, word spreads quickly. Already taken with him and his daughters, Tomoe now visits frequently. Zenemon Yogo, master of the watch and a "drinking companion" of Koda, tells Seibei he has been asked to take revenge but will not do it. Finally, while they fish at the river, Michinojo tells Seibei that Tomoe would gladly marry him; but knowing how meager his life is, Seibei refuses. The sequence ends with a second, ominous discovery of floating bodies.

When the young Lord dies unexpectedly, the clan reorganizes itself. A pro-restoration liberal faction is to be purged. For a samurai of the lowest rank such as Seibei, such changes should have little impact; but when Zenemon Yogo refuses to commit *seppuku* and kills the first retainer sent to his home, Seibei is summoned in the middle of the night to meet the chamberlain. They have researched and discovered that he was an instructor in Toda-style short sword, a technique that should be well-suited to a fight inside a small house. Seibei attempts to decline. During his explanatory speech, a close shot slowly tightens and, as Seibei leans forward in a bow, the edges of the frame close in even more. "Your clan orders you to kill Yogo," the chamberlain bellows in response. "Do you understand that? The very thought of refusal is an offense against the clan." Non-acceptance is not an option.

Since he must fight Yogo, Seibei goes home and meticulously sharpens his sword. In the morning he must ask Tomoe to help him prepare his hair and formal dress. Seeing her again, he realizes he was wrong to reject her. The promise of advancement if he kills Yogo and status that would befit Tomoe overwhelms his disinclination to kill pointlessly. Although Tomoe now rejects him because she has accepted another proposal, he leaves to face Yogo.

Yogo has been drinking and wants to talk with Seibei. As flies from the corpse in his courtyard buzz around them, the staging arrays the men in the two dimensions of the frame so that their backs are to each other or separated by the vertical line. Yogo forces Seibei to listen by mocking his claim that he must fight: "You're the clan's errand boy out to claim a reward." Echoing Tsugumo in *Hara-Kiri*, Yogo tells his story: forced to leave his own clan when his overlord is disgraced, Yogo spent seven years as a *ronin*, working for farmers or begging alms to feed his wife and daughter, who both died of tuberculosis. He followed orders of his new Lord, who also fell into disgrace. Why should he have "to cut open his stomach for that?" Why can't he just run away? After he sees the ashes of Yogo's daughter and learns how she died, Seibei falls into Yogo's rhetoric. He admits his own life his been hard. He even reveals that to pay for his wife's funeral, he sold his blade, "a fine sword I'd inherited from my father, but I figured the age of the sword was over." Knowing now that Seibei's *katana* has a bamboo blade, Yogo sees an advantage, decides to fight, and feigns being insulted: "You mean to kill me with some sort of cheap trick? You're not taking me seriously." Despite Seibei's attempts to back away, there is no avoid-

I was desperate, so I finally sold my sword.

The Twilight Samurai:
TOP: Seibei (Hiroyuki Sanada, left) cuts Yogo (Min Tanaka) during the duel inside Yogo's house.

CENTER: Seibei (Hiroyuki Sanada, right) and Yogo (Min Tanaka)—the aftermath to the duel inside Yogo's house.

A dynamic craning shot moves rapidly over the steeply sloped roof tiles all the way down to ground level where various men spar with *bokken* in a courtyard, then pivots and goes up to a terrace where Saito of thirty years ago, historical captain of the third squad of shinsengumi, stands and watches.

ing it. In the end, a doob jamb blocks Yogo's long sword, and Seibei slashes him fatally. While the combat with a live blade in a darkened house is quite different from the duel with Koda, one sustained shot sets the tone, as neither man can escape the dark panels at the frame's edges.

Although Tomoe is waiting for him when he returns and they marry soon after, as Ito recounts, their joy is short-lived. The age of the sword is over, and Seibei is gunned down shortly thereafter during the Boshin War. Despite his daughter's slightly upbeat voiceover, as she stands by his weathered grave, on many levels Seibei's fate is as bleak that of Tsugumo or Magobei or Zenemon Yogo—enmeshed, impoverished, and ultimately destroyed by the vagaries of feudal society in the twilight of the era.

As with other dramatizations of the *shinsengumi*, *When the Last Sword Is Drawn* presumes some familiarity, however slight, with the historical context on the part of the viewer. As with *The Twilight Samurai*, the flashback perspective is immediately invoked. But while *The Twilight Samurai* restricts itself to an audio narration, *When the Last Sword Is Drawn* opens in the "City of Tokyo, Winter, 1899." A middle-aged man, Hajime Saito, limps through the snow carrying a boy. The office where he knocks is in disarray, full of half-packed boxes; but the doctor takes the man's grandson in to his wife, who examines the children. The boy knocks over a photograph, which triggers the remembrance.

As Saito's voice reveals that the man in the picture was his comrade in the "Wolves of Mibu," the flashback begins. A dynamic craning shot moves rapidly over the steeply sloped roof tiles all the way down to ground level, where various men spar with *bokken* in a courtyard, then pivots and goes up to a terrace where Saito of thirty years ago, historical captain of the third squad of *shinsengumi*, stands and watches. Other captains of *shinsengumi*—Konda, Hijikata, Ito, and Okita—are all present as one recruit, Kanichiro Yoshimura, is called forward. First squad captain Soji Okita suggests to his colleague Nagakura of the second squad that real swords be used. In the title sequence, Nagakura and Yoshimura duel to a draw, prompting Kondo to appoint Yoshimura as one of the *kenjutsu* instructors for the group.

Although he remarks during the duel that "he had killed, you could see that in a glance," Saito's instant dislike for Yoshimura is intensified at a group dinner that night. While Saito critiques Kondo for having "a taste for distinguished families and the promotion of glib fools," Yoshimura plays the obsequious bumpkin and irritates Saito to the point that the squad leader decides to kill "this awful country samurai." As Yoshimura walks Saito home in the rain, the left-handed swordsman draws on the newcomer. As in *The Twilight Samurai*, this contest—and all the other swordfights—is no display of intricate skill but a serious struggle between two equally matched opponents. In close quarters Yoshimura is sorely pressed but grunts out "I won't die." When Saito sees that he might not prevail, he relents and pretends it was all just a test. "You don't want to die," he asks, "What kind of samurai is that? I'm only alive because no one will kill me." "I'm different," Yoshimura responds, "I kill because I don't want to die."

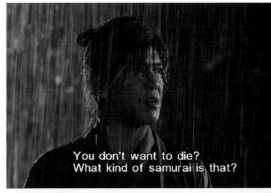

Without the rest of his backstory, Yoshimura's point may not yet be clear to either Saito or the viewer. The next morning, as in *Taboo*, the new recruits are tested by being appointed *kaishakus* for a ritual suicide. When the condemned man tries to bolt, Yoshimura cleanly beheads him. After being offered two *ryo* for his work, Yoshimura complains to Hijikata that his sword was chipped. Noting that "your blade doesn't bear its maker's name," Hijikata offers a few more gold coins; but Yoshimura's long face shames him into doubling the amount.

In taking real personnages and fictionalizing their relationships, *When the Last Sword Is Drawn* adopts a formula that goes back beyond *The Ambitious* to the beginnings of the genre. While all the *bakumatsu*-period scenes are ostensibly flashbacks, the complex, time-layered narrative moves freely using character emotion as a trigger to particular recollections and without stringent concern about point of view. As the first flashback ends, it is clear that Yoshimura is motivated by money. When asked by the aged Saito if the man in the photograph is his father, the doctor, Chiaki Ono, takes up the story. Initially, as with Saito's first recollections, only scenes in which the narrator has been present are depicted. In the next portion of flashback, an omniscient context allows the narrator to picture events he did not see. Soon there are flashbacks within flashbacks, connecting freely between what the narrator might know and other dramatic nexi—as in the second half of the film, when the suicide of Saito's concubine is discovered by Yoshimura. That prompts Yoshimura's interior flashback to when his own family was starving and his wife attempted to drown herself to relieve the burden.

Although the non-linear and multiple perspectives of *When the Last Sword Is Drawn* are quite different from *The Twilight Samurai*—the old Ito is not seen until the end when she kneels at her father's grave—the evocation of the era strongly connects the films. Before she is even seen, Yoshimura tells Saito of his own five-

ABOVE: Koichi Sato (top) as Saito and Kiichi Nakai as Yoshimura.

BELOW: With two swords drawn Yoshimura charges the imperial troops in *When the Last Sword Is Drawn*.

Top: Yoshimura indicates with forensic precision how only a gifted and left-handed swordsman could have inflicted the fatal wounds.

Bottom: With two swords drawn Yoshimura charges the imperial troops in *When the Last Sword Is Drawn*.

Opposite page:
Column 1:
First 3 stills: Gessai and the Priest: The aftermath of Sekigahara features a flashback to a CGI-created battlefield littered with thousands of slain men.

Center: Azumi questions the mission.

Bottom: Azumi is spattered with blood.

Column 2: Azumi assassinates her first victim, a *daimyo* opposed to the Tokugawa.

Bottom: Bijomaru (Jo Odagiri) in full regalia

year-old daughter, Mitsu. His son, Kaichiro, is Chiaki's childhood friend just as Chiaki's father was Yoshimura's, but the difference in their ranks push them into different orbits as it did with Seibei and Michinojo. At one point in *The Twilight Samurai*, Seibei speaks with Kayana about "book learning," assuring her that, while needlework might earn her money, "book learning gives you the power to think and, however much the world might change, if you have the power to think, you'll always survive somehow." Against one wall of Yoshimura's family home in Nanbu, as meager as Seibei's in Unasaka, are piles of books. While Seibei is a clerk, Yoshimura was both grade school teacher and sword instructor. But as the flashback's reveal, while an opportunity was forced upon Seibei, if Yoshimura does not leave his clan to find money for them somewhere, his family will die of hunger like those whose bodies floated down river in *The Twilight Samurai*.

"Sometimes good nature itself," observes a clan retainer in *After the Rain*, "can rub people the wrong way." While that is certainly Saito's first impression, Yoshimura's country-samurai antics are the perfect cover for his real motives. When Kondo announces that the Shogun has appointed the *shinsengumi* as direct retainers—Tokugawa *hatamoto* or "banner men" —Yoshimura rises to ask about the stipend. "Forty bags of rice" is a princely sum for one with starving children back home. As he "humbly thanks" all the group leaders, even Saito cannot see beyond the posturing. When the cowardly Sanjuro Tani is found murdered, Yoshimura is one of the investigators. When Saito walks past the body in the courtyard, Yoshimura indicates with forensic precision how only a gifted and left-handed swordsman could have inflicted the fatal wounds. This blackmail of Saito actually effects a rapprochement between the men. Shortly after visiting Saito's modest quarters and meeting Nui, a "hick" from Osha, Ito recruits Saito and Yoshimura for a splinter group and offers "twice what you get as shogun *hatamoto*." Somewhat to Saito's surprise, despite the monetary inducement Yoshimura demurs, remarking that "in leaving my clan I have already failed one lord, so I will not betray the trust of another." Saito does leave, but as a spy for Kondo. As part of Ito's *ishin shishi* faction, Saito tells of how he killed Ryoma Sakamoto for advocating non-violence. When he must disappear for a while, Nui takes her own life. A chastened Saito returns to the *shinsengumi* to participate in the slaughter of Ito and his followers. In that encounter, Yoshimura pursues Ito's lieutenant down an alleyway. The man excoriates him: "You're going to kill me? A country samurai who doesn't care about anything as long as you get paid. Money-grubber! Mercenary! How much are they paying you?"

The tubercular Okita coughs up blood while the Ito party is massacred. Saito reports that Kondo is killed soon after, so the end is near for a group of "no use in the new era." The depiction of Toba-Fushimi in *When the Last Sword Is Drawn* is as urban combat; and Yoshimura, perhaps chastened by the attack on his motives, is the cheerleader for the doomed enterprise. While Saito is newly infuriated when Yoshimura gives him the last of the rations and takes nothing for himself, he urges Yoshimura to run away, "not to die." Low-ranking origins or not, Yoshimura's pride will not permit that. As the shogun faction is routed by the Imperial army, Saito sustains the leg wound that still hobbles him in 1899 and Yoshimura charges through a cloud of gunsmoke at a line of riflemen and disappears.

While Sugi in Misumi's *Last Samurai* and Seibei both realized that "the age of sword is over," Saito takes it a step further: "The day of the sword was already far in the past." Certainly a key irony of *When the Last Sword Is Drawn* is that Saito, a man "only alive because no one will kill me," does survive while the other principals perish. In an extended coda, Chiaki reveals how Yoshimura manages to die back among his clansmen and how years after the death of his own father and Kaichiro in the Boshin War, Chiaki marries Yoshimura's daughter Mitsu. That she is the doctor treating his grandson permits Saito, when she emerges from a back room, to offer his "humble thanks, Yoshimura-*sensei*," to Mitsu and her father.

While these recent productions have focused on the era of the *bakumatsu*, where the samurai film will go from here is uncertain. *Azumi* (2003), adapted from a popular *manga* as was the *Sword of Vengeance* series, is not only non-stop swordplay but an idealization of the early Tokugawa. Like *Owl's Castle* and *Samurai Fiction*, *Azumi* makes extensive use of computer graphic technology and renders a lot of "comic book" visuals into movie effects. Azumi and her comrades are Tokugawa agents trained from birth by Gessai. His dream of the aftermath of Sekigahara features a flashback to a CGI-created battlefield littered with thousands of slain men, his own son among them. Warning that ambitious warlords will not accept domination by the victorious Tokugawa, a pontificating priest orders Gessai to train an elite corps of assassins. From that point the movie features repeated slaughters, quite often of innocents, beginning with half the youthful assassins when Gessai ruthlessly orders them to turn on each other. Shortly thereafter he forbids them from intervening when they stumble across a group of brigands pillaging a town and murdering all the inhabitants. "Merely killing a hundred bandits will not change this nation," he proclaims, clearly indicating the mode will not be that of *Seven Samurai*.

Azumi's remembrance of her own mother's death and childhood trauma, as she obediently refuses to intervene while a village mother and daughter are

COLUMN 1 & FIRST STILLS IN COLUMN 2: Yae tries to get Azumi to give up violence.

COLUMN 2, BOTTOM TWO STILLS: Azumi remembers her own mother's death and childhood trauma as she watches another mother and child about to be killed.

killed, again leads her to question the "mission." When she refuses to permit the mercy killing of a dying comrade, Gessai tells her that her services are no longer required; the young man she has saved kills himself moments later. She decides to go with Yae, the only survivor of a troupe of performers slaughtered by bumbling killers. Yae makes her put on a kimono, paints her lips, and asserts that "The swords don't suit you." Then, of course, more lecherous brigands appear, and Azumi has to submit to rape or kill them all. In a slow-motion pastiche of the leering men and the struggling Yae, with dialogue and sound effects replaced by the plaintive main theme, Azumi seems to ponder her options. Then she grabs a sword and gets busy. "No matter how much I try to escape, I can't avoid it," Azumi laments after cutting down two of the men. "Even if I don't want to kill, I am forced to kill. I have no choice but this."

The surviving assassins are indeed killing machines, and the body count soon moves from scores to hundreds, the last being Lord Kiyomasa, an outspoken supporter of the Toyotomi heir. When Kiyomasa's chamberlain, Kanbei, recruits Bijomaru—an over-the-top parody of Unosuke in *Yojimbo* who carries an oversized, bejeweled sword and a red rose—the comic book aspects overwhelm the fragile narrative as easily as Azumi conquers a hundred-odd ruffians and retainers and then slices off Bijomaru's head. Before dying, Gessai releases her: "It's all over. . . . from now on, live as you wish." Although she has an open invitation from Yae to enjoy being a girl, Azumi decides to continue her mission and strides away from a pile of bodies that mirrors the Sekigahara dream to kill Kiyomasa and get ready for a sequel.

Azumi 2 was, in fact, released earlier this year. Although not a sequel to *Twilight Samurai*, Yoji Yamada adapted more material from Shuhei Fujisawa into another elegiac story of ordinary samurai caught up in the turbulent wake of the *bakumatsu* in *The Hidden Blade* (*Kakushi ken oni no tsume*, 2004). Still while the *shinsengumi* march on in episodes of a television series and as antagonists for the *manga*, game, and *anime* TV-series versions of *Kenshin the Wandering Samurai* (*Ruruoni Kension*), while movies about *yakuza* are resurgent, and while Chinese martial arts pictures occupy entire sections of video stores, fewer *chambara* features than ever are produced. Films such as *When the Last Sword Is Drawn* and *The Twilight Samurai* and Kitano's *Zato Ichi* (with a *Zato Ichi 2* being prepared) have demonstrated that the genre is still viable. *Azumi* confirms that it can also still be vacuous. While there in scant likelihood of ever having a repeat of the extraordinary group of movies produced in the 1960s, with *Tenchu* now the title of a video game, the series *Samurai Jack* screening regularly on the Cartoon Network, and a resurrected Izo Okada traveling through time and space to mow down scores of new victims in Takeshi Miike's mock *chambara* fantasy *Izo* (2004), anything is possible.

PART TWO

FILMOGRAPHY

Data for the original filmography—which, as noted in the Acknowledgements, was compiled with James Ursini—was assembled from a wide variety of sources: *Uni-Japan Film Quarterlies* and *Film Annuals* (1959-1973); promotional booklets, press kits, and handbills published by the major Japanese distributors; several general film dictionaries and director studies [see Bibliography]; and, where written listings simply were not to be found, by transcription from actual film prints. These various publications were and remain somewhat inconsistent in the range of credits which they provide, so that the availability of release date, major technical credits, characters names, etc. varies considerably. The problem is compounded by the fact that productions which are actually released in the West usually appear in printed lists from several months to several years after their Japanese release. Because Japanese titles and names can be variously rendered in *romaji*, the romanized version of Japanese words, there are often inconsistencies in spelling for the same persons between various sources for the same film and on different productions. Rather than attempt to cross-reference all these, one spelling has been adopted for all listings and significant variants are indicated in brackets.

The intent in this filmographic compilation was and continues to be to include as much information as possible without regard to form. Entries in the director and serial-character filmographies are chronological. Films in the general category are grouped first by year of release and then alphabetically by English-title, if possible, or by Japanese title if no other is available. The video release of many films has multiplied the

number of alternate English titles. Where there are two or more English titles in use for the same film and the discrepancy is between a bibliographic source and the film's actual U.S. distributor precedence has been given to the latter, presuming that is the title which is most likely to appear on prints of the film itself. More prominent alternate titles are listed at the head of the entry in parentheses preceding the Japanese language title. Others are given at the end of the entry.

Numerous errors from the first and second edition have been discovered and corrected using various on-line search engines and databases. It is clear, from the fact that they have replicated many of those errors, that numerous entries on the Internet Movie Database, as well as at Chambara.com and Sengoku.com were created using the filmography from the second edition of this book and hopefully this edition may provide a guide for updating and correcting. There are undoubtedly some errors still present in this version of the filmography, and any suggested corrections and additions which a reader might wish to submit through www.samuraifilm.com would be most welcome.

Some Japanese actors and filmmakers have used different names in their credits and, as noted, Japanese characters are variously and sometimes erroneously Romanized, Dan Richard has compiled a separate list of major "aliases" which appears at the end of the filmography. His ongoing database on samurai /ninja/yakuza films is forthcoming online at www.snydb.com. Finally, information on distributors of video versions has been added and a list of video distributors with contact information (and web sites where applicable) appears at the end of the filmography.

HIDEO GOSHA (1929-1992)

THREE OUTLAW SAMURAI (*Sanbiki no Samurai*, 1964). Producers: Ginichi Kishimoto and Tetsuro Tanba [Tamba] [Samurai Productions]. Screenplay: Keiichi Abe, Eizaburo Shiba, Hideo Gosha, Ginichi Kishimoto. Photography: Tadashi Sakai [Shochiku GrandScope]. Lighting: Hiroyoshi Somekawa. Art Direction: Junichi Osumi. Music: Toshiaki Tsushima. Sound: Kenyo Fukuyasu. Editor: Kazuo Ota. Fencing Choreography: Kentaro Yuasa. Cast: Tetsuro Tanba [Tamba] (Sakon Shiba), Mikijiro Hira (Einosuke Kikyo), Isamu Nagato (Kyojuro Sakura), Miyuki Kuwano (Aya), Toshie Kimura (Oine), Yoko Mihara (Omaki), Kyoko Aoi (Omitsu), Yoshiko Kayama (Oyasu), Tatsuya Ishiguro (Uzaemon Matsushita), Kamatari Fujiwara (Jinbei), Jun Tatara (Yasugoro). Distribution: Shochiku. Release Date: May 13, 1964. 94 minutes (8,563 feet). Video: Samurai Video.

Mikijiro Hira as Gennosuke (right) and Kunie Tanaka as Tanji in *Sword of the Beast.*

SWORD OF THE BEAST (*Kedamono no Ken*, 1965). Producers: Ginichi Kishimoto, Masayuki Sato. Screenplay: Eizaburo Shiba, Hideo Gosha. Photography: Toshitada Tsuchiya [Shochiku GrandScope]. Art Direction: Mamoru Abe. Music: Toshiaki Tsushima. Sound: Toshiyuki Ishikawa. Editor: Masanori Tsujii. Cast: Mikijiro Hira (Gennosuke Yuki), Go Kato (Jurota Yamane), Shima Iwashita (Taka), Toshie Kimura (Misa), Kantaro Suga (Daizaburo Torio), Yoko Mihara (Osen), Kunie Tanaka (Tanji), Eijiro Tono (Minister). Distribution: Shochiku. Release Date: September 18, 1965. 85 minutes (7,573 feet). Video: Samurai Video; Criterion.

THE SECRET OF THE URN (*Tange Sazen Hien Iai-giri*, 1966). Producers: Mikio Ogawa, Norimichi Matsudaira. Screenplay: Kei Tasaka and Hideo Gosha, from the novel by Fubo Hayashi [Umitaro Hasegawa]. Photography: Sadaji [Sadatsugu] [Teiji] Yoshida [ToeiScope, Eastmancolor]. Lighting: Haruo Nakayama. Music: Toshiaki Tsushima. Sound: Yoshio Watabe. Editor: Kozo Horiike. Fight Choreography: Reijiro Adachi. Cast: Kinnosuke Nakamura [Yorozuya] (Samanosuke/Sazen Tange), Keiko Awaji (Ofuji), Tetsuro Tanba [Tamba] (Tsushima Yagyu), Isao Kimura (Genzaburo Yagyu), Wakaba Irie (Hagino). Distribution: Toei. Release date: May 21, 1966. 91 minutes (8,080 feet). Video: Samurai Video.

THE AMBITIOUS (*Bakumatsu*). Directed by Daisuke Ito from his adaptation of a novel by Ryotaro Shiba and starring Kinnosuke Nakamura as Ryunosuke Sakamoto(pictured left center), Toshiro Mifune as Shojiro Goto (pictured top center), Tatsuya Nakadai as Shintaro Nakaoka (pictured top right), Sayuri Yoshinaga as Oryo (pictured right center), and Noboru Nakaya as Hanpeita Takechi (top left).

SAMURAI WOLF (*Kiba Okaminosuke*, 1966). Producers: Enzaburo Honda, Norimichi Matsudaira. Screenplay: Kei Tasaka. Photography: Sadaji [Sadatsugu] [Teiji] Yoshida [ToeiScope]. Lighting: Haruo Nakayama. Art Direction: Akira Yoshimura. Music: Toshiaki Tsushima. Sound: Masayoshi Mizoguchi. Editor: Kozo Horiike. Fight Choreography: Kentaro Yuasa. Cast: Isao Natsuyagi (Okaminosuke), Ryohei Uchida (Sanai Akizuki), Junko Miyazono (Ochise). Distribution: Toei. Release date: November 19, 1966. 75 minutes. Video: Samurai Video.

SAMURAI WOLF II (*Kiba Okaminosuke Jigokugiri*, 1967). Producers: Enzaburo Honda, Norimichi Matsudaira. Screenplay: Noribumi Suzuki, Yasuko Ono. Photography: Sadaji [Sadatsugu] [Teiji] Yoshida [ToeiScope]. Lighting: Haruo Nakayama. Art Direction: Akira Yoshimura. Music: Toshiaki Tsushima. Sound: Masayoshi Mizoguchi. Editor: Kozo Horiike. Fight Choreography: Kentaro Yuasa. Cast: Isao Natsuyagi (Okaminosuke), Ko [Akira] Nishimura (Magobei), Yuko Kusunoki (Oren), Rumiko Fuji (Oteru), Chiyo Aoi (Otatsu) Ichiro Nakatani (Nakaya) (Ikkaku). Distribution: Toei. *Release date: May 13, 1967. 72 minutes.*

GOYOKIN (1969). Producers: Masumi [Sanezumi] Fujimoto, Hideo Fukuda, Hideyuki Shiino, Masayuki Sato [Fuji Telecasting and Tokyo Eiga Companies, Ltd.]. Screenplay: Kei Tasaka, Hideo Gosha. Photography: Kozo Okazaki [Panavision, Eastmancolor]. Lighting: Yosuke Sakakibara. Art Direction: Motoji Kojima. Music: Masaru Sato. Sound: Toshio Harashima. Editor: Michio Suwa. Fencing Choreography: Kentaro Yuasa. Cast: Tatsuya Nakadai (Magobei Wakizaka), Tetsuro Tanba [Tamba] (Rokugo Tatewaki), Kinnosuke Nakamura [Yorozuya] (Samon Fujimaki), Isao Natsuyagi (Kunai), Yoko Tsukasa (Shino), Kunie Tanaka (Hyosuke Nagai), Ruriko Asaoka (Oriha). Distribution: Toho. Release date: May 1, 1969. 124 minutes.(11,183 feet). Alternate English titles: *Official Gold, Steel Edge of Revenge.* Video: Samurai Video.

Goyokin

262

TENCHU (*Hitokiri*, 1969). Producers: Shichiro Murakami, Takashi Hoga [Katsu Productions and Fuji Telecasting Company, Ltd]. Screenplay: Shinobu Hashimoto. Photography: Fujiro Morita [DaieiScope; Eastmancolor]. Lighting: Hiroshi Mima. Art Direction: Yoshinobu Nishioka. Music: Masaru Sato. Sound: Masao Osumi. Editor: Kanji Suganuma. Cast: Shintaro Katsu (Izo Okada), Tatsuya Nakadai (Hanpeita Takechi), Yukio Mishima (Shinbei Tanaka), Yujiro Ishihara (Ryoma Sakamoto), Mitsuko Baisho (Omino), Takumi Shinjo, Noboru Nakaya, Ichiro Nakatani [Nakaya], Jiro Sakagami, Tsutomu Shimomoto, Kunie Tanaka, Kei Yamamoto, Akira Yamauchi. Distribution: Daiei. Release date: August 9, 1969. 140 minutes. Alternate English titles: *Manslaughter*; *Heaven's Punishment*. Video: Samurai Video.

BANDIT VS SAMURAI SQUAD (*Kumokiri Nizaemon*, 1978). Producers: Masayuki Sato, Ginichi Kishimoto, Shigemi Sugisaki. Screenplay: Kaneo Ikegami, from a story by Shotaro Ikenami. Photography: Tadashi Sakai, Masao Kosugi. Lighting: Mitsuo Onishi. Art Direction: Yoshinobu Nishioka. Music: Mitsuaki Kanno. Sound: Wataru Onuma. Editor: Michio Suwa. Fencing Choreography: Kentaro Yuasa, Katsuto Yasukawa. Cast: Tatsuya Nakadai (Kumokiri Nizaemon), Shima Iwashita (Chiyo), Somegoro Ichikawa (Shikibu Abe), Takashi Yamaguchi (Tsugutomo Owari), Koshiro Matsumoto (Kuranosuke Tsuji), Tetsuro Tanba [Tamba] (Kichibei Matsuya), Keiko Matsuzaka (Shino), Teruhiko Aoi (Rokunosuke), Mitsuko Baisho (Omatsu), Shoji Ishibashi (Hyotaro), Takuzo Kawatani (Sanji), Junko Miyashita (Omaki), Hiroyuki Nagato (Kichigoro), Isao Natsuyagi (Kumagoro), Jo Shishido (Tominoichi), Shingo Yamashiro (Jinnosuke). Distribution: Shochiku. Release date: July 1, 1978. 163 minutes. Alternate English title: *Bandits vs Samurai Squadron*. Video: Samurai Video.

HUNTER IN THE DARK (*Yami no Karyudo*, 1979). Produced by Masayuki Sato, Ginichi Kishimoto, Shigemi Sugisaki. Screenplay: Naoto Kitazawa, from the novel by Shotaro Ikenami. Photography: Tadashi Sakai. Lighting: Mitsuo Onishi. Art Direction: Yoshinobu Nishioka. Music: Masaru Sato. Sound: Tetsuya Ohashi. Editor: Michio Suwa. Fencing Choreography: Kentaro Yuasa, Katsuto Yasukawa. Cast: Tatsuya Nakadai (Gomyo no Kiyoemon), Yoshio Harada (Yataro Tanigawa), Ayumi Ishida (Oriwa), Keiko Kishi (Omon), Ai Kanzaki (Osaki), Kayo Matsuo (Oren), Tetsuro Tanba [Tamba] (Okitsugu Tanuma), Hajime Hana (Hanba no Sukegoro), Koji Yakusho (Kuwano no Sadahachi), Hideo Murota (Hino no Sakimatsu), Daisuke Ryu (Someyoshi no Bunkichi), Tatsuo Umemiya (Kawazu no Yaichi), Mikio Narita (Gosun no Toramatsu), Makoto Fujita (Kasuke), Hideji Otaki (Shiba), Yoshi Kato (Zenzaemon Sasao), Eijiro Tono (Shogen), Isao Natsuki (Sharaku), Shinichi "Sonny" Chiba (Samon Shimoguni). Distribution: Shochiku. Release date: June 17, 1969. 137 minutes. Alternate English title: *Hunter in the Darkness*. Video: World Artists.

TANGE SAZEN: KEN FU! HYAKUMAN RYO NO TSUBO (1982) Producers: Ryota Yokojima, Yoshio Tokuda, Takeshi Endo, Yasuhito Katori. Screenplay: Hideo Gosha, Kei Tasaka, based on a story by Fubo Hayashi. Photography: Fujiro Morita. Lighting: Hiroshi Mima. Art Direction: Yoshinobu Nishioka. Music: Mitsuaki Kanno. Editor: Toshio Taniguchi. Fencing Choreography: Eiichi Kusumoto. Cast: Tatsuya Nakadai (Sazen Tange), Kayo Matsuo (Ofuji), Masako Natsume (Hagino), Tsutomu Isobe (Genzaburo Yagyu), Isao Natsuyagi (Taiken), Ko Nishimura (Guraku), Kinzo Sato (Yokichi), Ago Isamu (Game Doro), "Smiley" Ohara (Tsushima Yagyu) Kyoichi Sato (Ikkaku Kazama), Goro Ohashi (Yoshimune Tokugawa), Minoru Sakurai (Chobiyasu), Ichiro Nakatani [Nakaya](Lord Echizen Ooka), Kazuichi Horiuchi, Sumao Ishihara, Susumu Kubota, Junichi Kami, Chiharu Komatsu, Shigeru Kiyota, Yoichi Sasayama, Seizo Fukumoto, Tankuro, Miwako Arita, Katsue Nagano, Satoko Yamamura, Yuki Akane, Mineko Maruhira, Toshiyo Shimomoto, Ryoichi Fujimura, Katsumi Ito, Etsuji Azuma. 96 minutes. English title: *Tange Sazen: The Pot Worth One Million Ryo*.

DEATH SHADOWS (*Jittemai*, 1986). Executive Producers: Kinen Masumoto, Takeshi Endo, Yoshinobu Nishioka, Hideshi [Shuji] [Hideji] Miyajima. Producer: Yoshio Tokuda. Screenplay: Motomu Furuta, from a story by Hideo Gosha, Kotaro Mori. Photography:

Death Shadows

Fujiro Morita. Lighting: Genken Nakaoka. Art Direction: Yoshinobu Nishioka. Music: Masaru Sato. Sound: Iwao Otani. Editor: Isamu Ichida. Cast: Mariko Ishihara (Ocho/Osaki), Masanori Sera (Shipping agent Kanoya), Mari Natsuki (Oren), Takuzo Kawatani (Yasuke), Takeo Chii (Denzo), Naoto Takenaka (police officer), Tsunehiko Watase (Magistrate Utsumi), Eitaro Ozawa [Sakae Ozawa] (Majordomo Umezu). Distribution: Shochiku. Release date: September 20, 1986. 115 minutes (10,372 feet).

MASAKI KOBAYASHI (1916-1996)

HARA-KIRI (*Seppuku*, 1962). Producer: Tatsuo Hosoya. Screenplay: Shinobu Hashimoto, based on a novel by Yasuhiko Takiguchi. Photography: Yoshio Miyajima [Shochiku GrandScope]. Lighting: Shojiro Kamohara. Art Direction: Shigemasa [Jusho] Toda, Junichi Ozumi. Music: Toru Takemitsu. Sound: Hideo Nishizaki. Editor: Hisashi Sagara. Fencing Choreography: Hideki Kato. Cast: Tatsuya Nakadai (Hanshiro Tsugumo), Rentaro Mikuni, (Kageyu Saito), Shima Iwashita (Miho Tsugumo), Akira Ishihama (Motome Chijiiwa), Shichisaburo Amatsu, Yoshiro Aoki (Umenosuke Kawabe), Jo Azumi (Ichiro Shinmen), Hisashi Igawa, Yoshio Inaba (Jinnai Chijiiwa), Masao Mishima (Tango Inaba), Ichiro Nakatani [Nakaya] (Hayato Yazaki), Kei Sato (Masakatsu Fukushima), Toru Takeuchi, Tetsuro Tanba [Tamba] (Hikokuro Sawagata), Akiji Kobayashi. Distribution: Shochiku. Release date: September 16, 1962. 135 minutes.

KWAIDAN (*Kaidan*, 1964). Producer: Shigeru Wakatsuki [The Ninjin Club]. Screenplay: Yoko Mizuki, from short stories by Lafcadio Hearn. Photography: Yoshio Miyajima [Eastmancolor; TohoScope]. Lighting: Akira Aomatsu. Art Direction: Shigemasa [Jusho] Toda. Music: Toru Takemitsu. Sound: Hideo Nishizaki. Editor: Hisashi Sagara. Cast: [*THE BLACK HAIR* (*Kurokami*)] Rentaro Mikuni (husband), Michiyo Aratama (abandoned wife),

Misako Watanabe (second wife); [*THE SNOW MAIDEN* (*Yuki-Onna*)] Keiko Kishi (the Snow Maiden), Tatsuya Nakadai (Minokichi), Yuko Mochizuki (mother); [HOICHI THE EARLESS (*Miminashi Hoichi no Nanashi*)] Katsuo Nakamura (Hoichi), Takashi Shimura. (Priest), Ganjiro Nakamura (assistant), Tetsuro Tanba [Tamba] (warrior in full armor), Yoichi Hayashi (Yoshitsune); [IN A CUP OF TEA (*Chawan no Naka*)] Kanemon Nakamura (Kannai, a warrior), Osamu Takizawa (Author/Narrator), Seiji Miyaguchi (Old man), Ganjiro Nakamura (Publisher), Noboru Nakaya (Heinai Shikibu), Kei Sato (Heinai's Servant), Haruko Sugimura (Madame), Jun Tazaki. Distribution: Toho. 183 minutes. Video: Criterion.

REBELLION (or *SAMURAI REBELLION*; *Joiuchi: Hairyo Tsuma Shimatsu*, 1967). Produced by: Tomoyuki Tanaka [Mifune Productions]. Screenplay: Shinobu Hashimoto, based on a novel by Yasuhiko Takiguchi. Photography: Kazuo Yamada [TohoScope]. Lighting: Yasuo Konishi. Art Direction: Yoshiro Muraki. Music: Toru Takemitsu. Sound: Junosuke Okuyama. Editor: Hisashi Sagara. Fencing Choreography: Ryu Kuze. Cast: Toshiro Mifune (Isaburo Sasahara), Yoko Tsukasa (Ichi Sasahara), Tatsuyoshi Ehara (Bunzo Sasahara), Etsuko Ichihara (Kiku), Isao Yamagata (Shobei Tsuchiya), Tatsuya Nakadai (Tatewaki Asano), Shigeru Koyama [Kamiyama] (Geki Takahashi), Michiko Otsuka (Suga Sasahara), Tatsuo Matsumura (Lord Masakata Matsudaira), Masao Mishima (Sanzaemon Yanase), Jun Hamamura (Hyoemon Shiomi), Emi Yamada (Shiomi's wife), Takamaru Sasaki (Kenmotsu Sasahara), Hideo Fukuhara (Sahei), Noriko Kawajiri (Nui), Tetsuko Kobayashi (Otama), Hisano Yamaoka (Sannojo Kasai's mother), Tomoko Nitto (Yoshino), Yoshiro Aoki (Takazo Komiya), Go Kato (Yogoro Sasahara). Distribution: Toho. Release date: May 27, 1967. 128 minutes. Video: Criterion.

INN OF EVIL (*Inochi Bonifuro*, 1971). Producers: Masayuki Sato, Ginichi Kishimoto, Hideyuki Shiino [Haiyuza/Toho]. Screenplay: Tomoe Ryu [pseudonym for Kyoko Miyazaki], based on the novel "*Fukagawa Anrakutei*" by Shugoro Yamamoto. Photography: Kozo Okazaki [TohoScope]. Lighting: Kazuo Shimomura. Art Direction: Hiroshi Mizutani. Music: Toru Takemitsu. Sound: Hideo Nishizaki. Editor: Hisashi Sagara. Fencing Choreography: Kentaro Yuasa. Cast: Tatsuya Nakadai (Sadahichi), Shintaro Katsu (a drunken wanderer), Shin Kishida (Yunosuke), Yosuke Kondo (Masaji), Shigeru Koyama [Kamiyama] (Officer Kaneko), Komaki Kurihara (Omitsu), Daigo Kusano (Genzo), Shun Ueda (Senkichi), Masao Mishima (Funayado Tokubei), Kanemon Nakamura (Ikuzo the Innkeeper), Ichiro Nakatani [Nakaya] (Officer Okajima), Wakako Sakai (Okiwa), Kei Sato (Yohei), Yusuke Takita (Kohei), Kei Yamamoto (Tomijiro), Hatsuo Yamaya (Bunta). Distribution: Toho. Release date: September 11, 1971. 121 minutes.

AKIRA KUROSAWA (1910-1998)

WALKERS ON THE TIGER'S TAIL (or *THEY WHO STEP ON THE TIGER'S TAIL*; *Tora no o o Fumu Otokotachi*, 1945). Producer: Motohiko Ito. Screenplay: Akira Kurosawa, based on the *Kabuki* play "*Kanjincho*" and the Noh drama "*Ataka*". Photography: Takeo Ito. Lighting: Iwaharu Hiraoka. Art Direction: Kazuo Kubo. Music: Tadashi Hattori. Sound: Keiji Hasebe. Editor: Toshio Goto. Cast: Denjiro Okochi (Benkei), Susumu Fujita (Togashi), Masayuki Mori (Kamei), Takashi Shimura, (Kataoka,), Aritake Kono (Ise), Yoshio Kosugi (Suruga), Dekao Yoko (Hidachibo), Shubo Nishina [Hanshiro Iwai] (Yoshitsune), Kenichi Enomoto, Yasuo Hisamatsu (Kajiwara's messenger), Soji Kiyokawa (Togashi's messenger). Distribution: Toho. Release date: April 24, 1952 [war delayed]. 58 minutes.

RASHOMON (1950). Producer: Jingo Minoura. Screenplay: Shinobu Hashimoto, Akira Kurosawa, based on "*In a Bush*" by Ryunosuke Akutagawa. Photography: Kazuo Miyagawa. Lighting: Kenichi Okamoto. Art Direction: Takashi Matsuyama. Music: Fumio Hayasaka. Sound: Iwao Otani. Editor: Shigeo Nishida. Fight Choreography: Shohei Miyauchi. Cast: Toshiro Mifune (Tajomaru), Masayuki Mori (Takehiro), Machiko Kyo (Masago), Takashi Shimura (firewood dealer), Minoru Chiaki (priest), Kichijiro Ueda (commoner), Daisuke Kato (police-agent), Noriko Honma (the

medium). Distribution: Daiei. Release date: August 26, 1950. 88 minutes. Video: Criterion.

SEVEN SAMURAI (or *THE MAGNIFICENT SEVEN*; *Shichinin no Samurai*, 1954). Producer: Sojiro Motoki. Screenplay: Akira Kurosawa, Hideo Oguni, Shinobu Hashimoto. Photography: Asakazu Nakai. Lighting: Shigeru Mori. Art Direction: Takashi Matsuyama, Kohei Ezaki (consultant). Music: Fumio Hayasaka. Sound: Fumio Yanoguchi. Martial Arts Choreography: Yoshio Sugino, fencing; Ienori Kaneko, Shigeru Endo, archery. Cast: Toshiro Mifune (Kikuchiyo), Takashi Shimura, (Kanbei Shimada), Yoshio Inaba (Gorobei Katayama), Seiji Miyaguchi (Kyuzo), Minoru Chiaki (Heihachi Hayashida), Daisuke Kato (Shichiroji), Isao Kimura (Katsushiro Okamoto), Kokuten Kodo (Gisaku), Bokuzen Hidari (Yohei), Yoshio Kosugi (Mosuke), Kamatari Fujiwara (Manzo), Yoshio Tsuchiya (Rikichi), Keiko Tsushima (Shino), Yukiko Shimazaki (Rikichi's wife), Haruko Toyama (wife of Gisaku's son), Gen Shimizu (ronin), Keiji Sakakida (Gosaku), Jun Tatara (coolie), Atsushi Watanabe (bun vendor), Toranosuke Ogawa (grandfather), Noriko Sengoku (wife), Eijiro Tono (thief), Isao Yamagata (iron fan ronin), Sojin Kamiyama (minstrel), Jun Tazaki (tall samurai), Shinpei Takagi (bandit chief), Jiro Kumagai, Tsuneo Katagiri, Yasuhisa Tsutsumi (peasants), Kichijiro Ueda, Akira Tani, Haruo Nakajima, Takashi Narita, Senkichi Omura, Toshio Takahara, Masanobu Okubo (bandits), Hiroshi Akitsu (husband). Distribution: Toho. Release date: April 26, 1954. 200 minutes (shortened version: 161 minutes). Video: Criterion.

THRONE OF BLOOD (or *THE CASTLE OF THE SPIDER'S WEB*; *Kumonosu-jo*, 1957). Producers: Akira Kurosawa, Sojiro Motoki. Screenplay: Shinobu Hashimoto, Ryuzo Kikushima, Hideo Oguni, Akira Kurosawa, based on the play, "Macbeth" by William Shakespeare. Photography: Asakazu Nakai. Lighting: Kuichiro Kishida. Art Direction: Yoshiro Muraki, Kohei Ezaki. Music: Masaru Sato. Sound: Fumio Yanoguchi. Cast: Toshiro Mifune (Taketoki Washizu), Isuzu Yamada (Lady Asaji Washizu), Minoru Chiaki (Yoshiaki Miki), Akira Kubo (Yoshiteru Miki), Takamaru Sasaki (Kuniharu Tsuzuki), Yoichi Tachikawa (Kuniharu's son), Takashi Shimura (Noriyasu Odagura,), Chieko Naniwa (sorceress). Distribution: Toho. Release date: January 15, 1957. 110 minutes. Alternate English Title: *The Hidden Forest*. Video: Criterion.

THE HIDDEN FORTRESS (*Kakushi Toride no San-Akunin*, 1958). Producers: Masumi [Sanezumi] Fujimoto, Akira Kurosawa. Screenplay: Ryuzo Kikushima, Hideo Oguni, Shinobu Hashimoto, Akira Kurosawa. Photography: Ichio Yamasaki [TohoScope]. Lighting: Ichiro Inohara. Art Direction: Yoshiro Muraki, Kohei Ezaki. Music: Masaru Sato. Sound: Fumio Yanoguchi, Hisashi Shimonaga. Cast: Toshiro Mifune (Rokurota Makabe), Misa Uehara (Princess Yuki), Minoru Chiaki (Tahei), Kamataki Fujiwara (Matashichi), Takashi Shimura (Izumi Nagakura), Susumu Fujita (Hyoei Tadokoro), Eiko Miyoshi (old woman), Toshiko Higuchi (farmer's daughter), Kichijiro Ueda (slave-dealer), Koji Mitsui (soldier). Distribution: Toho. Release date: December 28, 1958. 139 minutes (shortened version 120 minutes). Video: Criterion.

YOJIMBO (*Yojinbo*, 1961). Producers: Tomoyuki Tanaka, Ryuzo Kikushima [Toho/Kurosawa Productions]. Screenplay: Ryuzo Kikushima, Akira Kurosawa. Photography: Kazuo Miyagawa [TohoScope]. Lighting: Choshiro Ishii. Art Direction: Yoshiro Muraki. Music: Masaru Sato. Sound: Choshichiro Mikami, Hisashi Shimonaga. Cast: Toshiro Mifune (Sanjuro Kuwabatake), Tatsuya Nakadai (Unosuke), Yoko Tsukasa (Nui), Eijiro Tono (Gonji), Kamatari Fujiwara (Tazaemon, the silk merchant), Seizaburo Kawazu (Seibei), Isuzu Yamada (Orin), Hiroshi Tachikawa (Yoichiro), Takashi Shimura (Tokuemon, the sake merchant), Kyu Sazanka (Ushitora), Daisuke Kato (Inokichi), Susumu Fujita (Honma), Atsushi Watanabe (coffin-maker), Ikio Sawamura (Hansuke), Ko [Akira] Nishimura (Kuma), Yoshio Tsuchiya (Kohei), Yosuke Natsuki (Kohei's son). Distribution: Toho. Release date: April 25, 1961. 110 minutes. Video: Criterion.

SANJURO (*Tsubaki Sanjuro*, 1962). Producers: Tomoyuki Tanaka, Ryuzo Kikushima [Kurosawa Productions]. Screenplay: Ryuzo Kikushima, Hideo Oguni, Akira Kurosawa, based on a novel by

Shugoro Yamamoto. Photography: Fukuzo Koizumi, Takao Saito [TohoScope]. Lighting: Ichiro Inohara. Art Direction: Yoshiro Muraki. Music: Masaru Sato. Sound: Wataru Onuma, Hisashi Shimonaga. Fencing Choreography: Ryu Kuze. Cast: Toshiro Mifune (Sanjuro Tsubaki), Tatsuya Nakadai (Hanbei Muroto), Yuzo Kayama (Iori Izaka), Akihiko Hirata, Kunie Tanaka, Hiroshi Tachikawa, Tatsuhiko Namisato, Tatsuyoshi Ehara, Kenzo Matsui, Yoshio Tsuchiya, Akira Kubo (young samurai), Takashi Shimura (Kurofuji), Kamatari Fujiwara (Takebayashi), Masao Shimizu (Kikui), Yunosuke Ito (Mutsuta), Takako Irie (Madame Mutsuta), Reiko Dan (Chidori), Keiju Kobayashi (the captive). Distribution: Toho. Release date: January 1, 1962. 96 minutes. Video: Criterion.

KAGEMUSHA, THE SHADOW WARRIOR (*Kagemusha*, 1980). Producers: Akira Kurosawa, Tomoyuki Tanaka [Kurosawa Productions]. Production Advisor: Shinobu Hashimoto. Screenplay: Masato Ide, Akira Kurosawa. Photography: Takao Saito, Shoji [Masaharu] Ueda; Asakazu Nakai, Kazuo Miyagawa (associates) [Deluxe Color; Panavision]. Lighting: Takeji Sano. Art Direction: Yoshiro Muraki. Music: Shinichiro Ikebe. Sound: Fumio Yanoguchi. Cast: Tatsuya Nakadai (Shingen Takeda/Kagemusha), Tsutomu Yamazaki (Nobukado Takeda), Kenichi Hagiwara (Katsuyori Takeda), Jinpachi Nezu (Sohachiro Tsuchiya), Hideji Otaki (Masakage Yamagata), Daisuke Ryu (Nobunaga Oda), Masayuki Yui (Ieyasu Tokugawa), Kaori Momoi (Otsuyanokata), Mitsuko Baisho (Oyunokata), Hideo Murota (Nobuharu Baba), Takayuki Shiho (Masatoyo Naito), Koji Shimizu (Katsusuke Atobe), Noboru Shimizu (Masatane Hara), Sen Yamamoto (Nobushige Oyamada), Shuhei Sugimori (Masanobu Kosaka), Kota Yui (Takemaru), Yasuhito Yamanaka (Ranmaru Mori), Kumeko Otowa (Takemaru's Nurse), Tetsuo Yamashita, Kai Ato, Takashi Ebata (Monk), Yutaka Shimaka, Toshiaki Tanabe, Yoshimitsu Yamaguchi (Salt Vendor), Eiichi Kanakubo, Akihiko Sugisaki (Noda Castle Soldier), Yugo Miyazaki, Masatsugu Kuriyama, Norio Matsui, Jiro Yabuki, Yasushi Doshida, Takashi Watanabe, Noboru Sone, Eihachi Ito, Alexander Kiersch, Senkichi Omura, Takashi Shimura (Gyobu Taguchi), Kamatari Fujiwara (Doctor). Distribution: Toho. Release date: April 26, 1980. 179 minutes. Video: Criterion.

RAN (1985). Producers: Serge Silberman, Masato Hara. Executive Producer: Katsumi Furukawa. Screenplay: Akira Kurosawa, Hideo Oguni, Masato Ide, based on "King Lear" by William Shakespeare. Photography: Takao Saito, Shoji [Masaharu] Ueda; Asakazu Nakai [Deluxe Color]. Lighting: Takeharu Sano. Art Direction: Yoshiro Muraki, Shinobu Muraki. Music: Toru Takemitsu. Fencing Choreography: Ryu Kuze, Hiroshi Kuze. Cast: Tatsuya Nakadai (Lord Hidetora Ichimonji), Akira Terao (Taro Takatora Ichimonji), Jinpachi Nezu (Jiro Masatora Ichimonji), Daisuke Ryu (Saburo Naotora Ichimonji), Mieko Harada (Lady Kaede), Yoshiko Miyazaki (Lady Sue), Takashi Nomura (Tsurumaru), Hisashi Igawa (Kurogane), Peter [Shinnosuke Ikehata] (Kyoami), Masayuki Yui (Tango), Kazuo Kato (Ikoma), Norio Matsui (Ogura), Binpachi [Toshiya] Ito (Naganuma), Kenji Kodama (Shirane), Takashi Watanabe, Takeshi Kato (Koyata Hatakeyama). Production: Greenwich Film/Herald Ace/Nippon Herald Films. Distribution: Toho. Release date: June 1, 1985. 160 minutes. VIDEO: Wellspring.

KIHACHI OKAMOTO (1923-2005)

WARRING CLANS (*Sengoku Yaro*, 1963) Producer: Tomoyuki Tanaka. Screenplay: Ken Sano, Kihachi Okamoto, Shinichi Sekizawa. Photography: Yuzuru Aizawa. Lighting: Shoshichi Kojima. Art Direction: Hiroshi Ueda. Music: Masaru Sato. Sound: Shin Watarai. Editor: Yoshitami Kuroiwa. Fencing Choreography: Ryu Kuze. Cast: Yuzo Kayama, Yuriko Hoshi, Makoto Sato, Kumi Mizuno, Ichiro Nakatani [Nakaya]. Distribution: Toho. Release date: March 24, 1963. 97 minutes.

SAMURAI ASSASSIN (*Samurai*, 1965). Producers: Tomoyuki Tanaka [Mifune Productions]. Screenplay: Shinobu Hashimoto, based on the story "Samurai Nippon" by Jiromasa Gunji. Photography: Hiroshi Murai [TohoScope]. Lighting: Tsuruzo Nishikawa. Art Direction: Iwao Akune. Music: Masaru Sato. Sound: Yoshio Nishikawa. Editor: Yoshitami Kuroiwa. Fencing Choreography: Ryu Kuze. Cast: Toshiro Mifune (Tsuruchiyo Niino), Keiju Kobayashi (Einosuke Kurihara), Michiyo Aratama (Okiku), Yunosuke Ito (Kenmotsu Hoshino), Eijiro Tono (Seigoro Kisoya), Tatsuyoshi Ehara (Ichigoro Hayama), Tadao Nakamaru (Shigezo Inada), Shiro Otsuji (Kaname Kojima), Yoshio Inaba (Keijiro Sumita), Akihiko Hirata (Sobei Masui), Hideyo [Eisei] Amamoto (Matasaburo Hagiwara), Ikio Sawamura (Tatsukichi Bizenya), Chotaro Togin (Seiichi Morikawa), Yasuzo Ogawa (Ronin), Masaya Nihei (Ronin), Toshio Kurosawa (Katsunoshin Itamura), Yoshifumi Tajima (Samurai), Komazo Ichikawa (Shuzen Nakano), Nadao Kirino (Samurai), Junichiro Mukai (Samurai), Koji Iwamoto (Ronin), Naoya Kusakawa, Yasuhisa Tsutsumi (Sumoya manager), Fujio Tokita (Ronin), Hiroshi Hasegawa (Ronin), Mitsugu Terashima (Chuzaemon Nishikawa), Susumu Fujita (Tatewaki Todo), Shikaku Nakamura (Gengobei Nosaka), Kazuo Suzuki (Samurai), Yu Sekita (Ronin). Distribution: Toho. Release date: January 3, 1965. 124 minutes. Video: AnimEigo.

THE SWORD OF DOOM (*Daibosatsu Toge*, 1966). Producers: Masumi [Sanezumi] Fujimoto, Masayuki Sato, Kaneharu Minamizato. Screenplay: Shinobu Hashimoto, based on a novel by Kaizan Nakazato. Photography: Hiroshi Murai [TohoScope]. Lighting: Tsuruzo Nishikawa. Art Direction: Takashi Matsuyama. Music: Masaru Sato. Sound: Shin Watarai. Editor: Yoshitami Kuroiwa. Fencing Choreography: Ryu Kuze. Cast: Tatsuya Nakadai (Ryunosuke Tsukue), Yuzo Kayama (Hyoma Utsuki), Michiyo Aratama (Ohama), Toshiro Mifune (Toranosuke Shimada), Yoko Naito (Omatsu), Tadao Nakamaru (Isami Kondo), Ichiro Nakatani [Nakaya] (Bunnojo Utsuki), Ko [Akira] Nishimura (Shichibei, Omatsu's "uncle"), Kamatari Fujiwara (Omatsu's grandfather), Kei Sato (Kamo Serizawa), Yasuzo Ogawa (Yohachi), Ryosuke Kagawa (Danjo Tsukue), Atsuko Kawaguchi (Okinu), Kunie Tanaka (Senkichi), Takamaru Sasaki (Isshinsai Nakamura), Akio Miyabe (Toshizo Hijikata), Kinnosuke Takamatsu (Old Pilgrim), Hideyo [Eisei] Amamoto. Distribution: Toho. Release date: February 25, 1966. 122 minutes. Video: Criterion.

KILL! (*Kiru*, 1968). Producer: Tomoyuki Tanaka. Screenplay: Kihachi Okamoto, Akira Murao, based on an original story by Shugoro Yamamoto. Photography: Rokuro Nishigaki [TohoScope]. Art Direction: Iwao Akune. Music: Masaru Sato. Sound: Shin Watarai. Editor: Yoshitami Kuroiwa. Fencing Choreography: Ryu Kuze. Cast: Tatsuya Nakadai (Genta), Etsushi Takahashi (Hanji), Atsuo Nakamura (Tetsutaro Oikawa), Shigeru Koyama [Kamiyama] (Tamiya Ayuzawa), Akira Kubo (Monnosuke Takei), Seishiro Kuno (Daijiro Masataka), Nami Tamura, Tadao Nakamaru (Magobei Shoda), Eijiro Tono (Hyogo Moriuchi), Isao Hashimoto (Konosuke Fujii), Yoshio Tsuchiya (Shinroku Matsuo), Hideyo [Eisei] Amamoto (Gendayu Shimada), Yuriko Hoshi (Chino). Distribution: Toho. Release date: June 22, 1968. 115 minutes. Video: Criterion.

Sword of Doom: Yuzo Kayama (left) and Toshiro Mifune as Shimada.

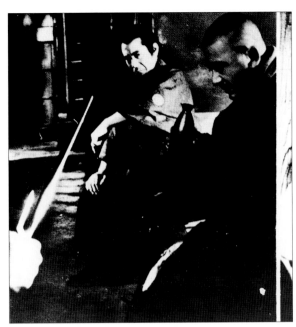

Zato Ichi meets Yojimbo: Toshiro Mifune and Shintaro Katsu.

RED LION (*Akage*, 1969). Producers: Toshiro Mifune, Yoshio Nishikawa [Mifune Productions]. Screenplay: Kihachi Okamoto, Sakae Hirosawa. Photography: Takao Saito [Eastmancolor; TohoScope]. Lighting: Yukio Sato. Art Direction: Hiroshi Ueda. Music: Masaru Sato. Sound: Masamichi Ichikawa. Editor: Yoshihiro Araki. Fencing Choreography: Ryu Kuze. Cast: Toshiro Mifune (Gonzo), Shima Iwashita (Tomi), Minori Terada, (Sanji), Etsushi Takahashi (Hanzo), Jitsuko Yoshimura (Oyo), Yuko Mochizuki (Ume), Takahiro Tamura (Sozo Sagara), Yunosuke Ito (Kamio), Shigeru Koyama [Kamiyama] (Yaiichiro Aragaki), Tokue Hanazawa, Nobuko Otowa, Kawai Okada. Distribution: Toho. Release date: October 10, 1969. 116 minutes.

ZATO ICHI MEETS YOJIMBO (*Zatoichi to Yojinbo*, 1970) — See ZATO ICHI Filmography

DIXIELAND DAIMYO (or *JAZZ DAIMYO*; *Jazu Daimyo*, 1986). Producers: Hiroshi Yamamoto, Masao Kobayashi. Producer: Nobuaki Murooka. Screenplay: Kihachi Okamoto, Toshio Ishido, based on an original story by: Yasutaka Tsutsui. Photography: Yudai Kato. Music by: Yasutaka Tsutsui, Yosuke Yamashita. Art Direction: Kazuo Takenaka. Editor: Yoshitami Kuroiwa. Sound: Nobuyuki Tanaka. Lighting: Kojiro Sato. Cast: Ikko Furuya, Ichiro Zaitsu, Ai Kanzaki, Mami Okamoto, Taiji Tonoyama, Hirotaro Honda, Masao Imafuku, Shinji Ogawa, Go Riju, Mickey Curtis, Juro Kara, Ronald Nelson, Lenny Marsh, George Smith. Distribution: Shochiku. Release date: April 19, 1986. 85 minutes.

EAST MEETS WEST (*Iisuto Miitsu Uesuto*, 1995). Executive Producer: Kazuyoshi Okuyama. Producers: Mineko Okamoto, Yoshihasa Nakagawa. Producer: Simon Tse. Screenplay: Kihachi Okamoto. Photography: Yudai Kato. Lighting: Kojiro Sato. Art Direction: Toby Corbett. Music: Masaru Sato. Sound: Koshiro Jinbo. Editor: Akimasa Kawashima. Fencing Choreography: Kanta Ina. Cast: Hiroyuki Sanada (Kenkichi Kamijo), Scott Bachicha (Sam), Chip Mayer (Gus Taylor), Naoto Takenaka (Tamejiro), Richard Nason (Hatch), Angelique Roehm (Nantai), Etsushi Takahashi (Kimura), Jay Kerr (Hardy), David Midthunder (Chief Red Hair), Jed Curtis (Easy Come Bartender), Bobby Harwell (Preacher), Carlos Moreno Jr. (Charlie), Robyn Reede (Bella), Tatsuya Nakadai (Rintaro Katsu), Ittoku Kishibe. Distribution: Shochiku. Release date: August 12, 1995. 123 Minutes.

VENGEANCE FOR SALE (or *VENGEANCE IS SUCH A GREAT BUSINESS*; *Sukedachiya Sukeroku*, 2002). Executive Producers: Masaya Nakamura, Tadao Toyo. Producers: Shoichiro Ishimaru, Shigeki Nishimura, Hiroshi Fujikura [Nikkatsu/Fuji Television]. Screenplay: Kihachi Okamoto, based on an original story by Daisaku Ikuta. Photography: Yudai Kato. Art Direction: Yoshinobu Nishioka. Music: Yosuke Yamashita. Editor: Akimasa Kawashima. Cast: Hiroyuki Sanada (Sukedachiya Sukeroku), Kyoka Suzuki (Osen), Tatsuya Nakadai (Katakura), Takehiro Murata (Taro), Shingo Tsurumi, Ittoku Kishibe, Kyoko Kishida. Distribution: Toho. Release date: February 16, 2002. 88 Minutes.

MASAHIRO SHINODA (1931-)

THE ASSASSIN (*Ansatsu*, 1964). Producer: Shizuo Yamauchi. Screenplay: Nobuo Yamada, based on a novel by Ryotaro Shiba. Photography: Masao Kosugi [Shochiku GrandScope]. Lighting: Yoichiro Ichinose. Art Direction: Junichi Osumi. Music: Toru Takemitsu. Sound: Kenyo Fukuyasu. Editor: Eiji Amano. Cast: Tetsuro Tanba [Tamba] (Hachiro Kiyokawa), Eiji Okada (Lord Matsudaira), Eitaro Ozawa [Sakae Ozawa] (Premier Itakura), Isao Kimura (Tadasaburo Sasaki), Muga Takewaki (Shingo Miyagawa), Shima Iwashita (Oren, Kiyokawa's sweetheart), Keiji Sada (Ryoma Sakamoto). Distribution: Shochiku. Release date: July 4, 1964. 104 minutes.

SAMURAI SPY (*Ibun Sarutobi Sasuke*, 1965). Producer: Shizuo Yamauchi. Screenplay: Yoshiyuki Fukuda, based on a novel by Koji Nakada. Photography: Masao Kosugi [Shochiku GrandScope]. Lighting: Akira Aomatsu. Art Direction: Junichi Osumi. Music: Toru Takemitsu. Sound: Hideo Nishizaki. Editor: Yoshi Sugihara. Cast: Koji Takahashi (Sasuke Sarutobi), Jitsuko Yoshimura (Omiyo), Misako Watanabe (Okiwa), Eiji Okada, Tetsuro Tanba [Tamba] (Sakon), Rokko [Mutsuhiro] Toura. Distribution: Shochiku. Release date: July 10, 1965. 102 minutes. Video: Criterion.

DOUBLE SUICIDE (*Shinju Ten no Amijima*, 1969). Producer: Masayuki Nakajima, Masahiro Shinoda. Screenplay: Taeko Tomioka, Masahiro Shinoda, Toru Takemitsu, based on a play by Monzaemon Chikamatsu. Photography: Toichiro Narushima. Art Direction: Kiyoshi Awazu. Music: Toru Takemitsu. Sound: Hideo Nishizaki. Cast: Kichiemon Nakamura (Jihei), Shima Iwashita (Osan/Koharu), Hosei Komatsu (Tahei), Yusuke Takita (Magoemon), Kamatari Fujiwara, (owner of Yamatoya), Yoshi Kato (Gozaemon), Shizue Kawarasaki (Osan's mother), Tokie Hidari (Osugi). Production Company: Hyogensha/Nippon Art Theatre Guild. Distribution: Toho. Release date: May 24, 1969. 142 minutes. Video: Criterion.

THE SCANDALOUS ADVENTURES OF BURAIKAN (or *OUT-LAWS*; *Buraikan*, 1970). Producer: Yasushige Wakatsuki [The Ninjin Club]. Screenplay: Shuji Terayama, based on a play by Mokuami Kawatake. Photography: Kozo Okazaki [Eastmancolor; Panavision]. Lighting: Yosuke Sakakibara. Art Direction: Shigemasa [Jusho] Toda. Music: Masaru Sato. Sound: Hideo Nishizaki. Editor: Yoshi Sugihara. Cast: Tatsuya Nakadai (Naojiro Kataoka), Shima Iwashita (Michitose), Tetsuro Tanba [Tamba] (Soshun Kochiyama), Shoichi Ozawa (Ushimatsu), Fumio Watanabe (Seizo Moritaya), Masakane Yonekura, (Ichinojo Kaneko), Hiroshi Akutagawa, (Lord Echizen Mizuno), Suisen Ichikawa (Okuma), Kiwako Taichi (Namiji). Distribution: Toho. Release date: April 18, 1970. 104 minutes.

GONZA THE SPEARMAN (*Yari no Gonza*, 1986). Producers: Kiyoshi Iwashita, Masayuki Motomochi, Masatake Wakita [Hyogensha]. Screenplay: Taeko Tomioka, based on the play by Monzaemon Chikamatsu. Photography: Kazuo Miyagawa. Lighting: Takeharu Sano. Art Direction: Kiyoshi Awazu. Music: Toru Takemitsu. Sound: Shotaro Yoshida. Editor: Sachiko Yamaji. Cast: Hiromi Go (Gonza), Shima Iwashita (Osai), Shohei Hino (Bannojo), Misako Tanaka (Oyuki), Hideji Otaki (Iwaki), Takashi Tsumura (Ichinoshin), Kuniko Miyake, Haruko Kato (Oyuki's nurse), Kaori Mizushima (Okiku), Eiji Shima (Torajiro), Choichiro Kawarazaki, Shoichi Ozawa (ferryman). Distribution: Shochiku/Fuji. Release date: January 15, 1970. 126 Minutes. Video: Kino.

266

OWLS' CASTLE (*Fukuro no Shiro*, 1999). Producers: Masaru Kakutani, Masaru Koibuchi [Hyogensha]. Executive Producer: Shigeaki Hazama. Screenplay: Masahiro Shinoda, Katsuo Naruse, based on the novel by Ryotaro Shiba. Photography: Tatsuo Suzuki. Lighting: Yoshio Unno. Art Direction: Yoshinobu Nishioka. Music: Joji Yuasa. Sound: Tetsuo Segawa. Editor: Hiroshi Yoshida. Fight Choreography: Motosada Mori. Cast: Kiichi Nakai (Juzo), Mayu Tsuruta (Kohagi), Riona Hazuki (Kisaru), Takaya Kamikawa (Gohei), Toshiya Nagasawa, Jinpachi Nezu, Gaku [Manabu] Yamamoto, Mako Iwamatsu (Hideyoshi). Distribution: Toho. Release date: October 30, 1999. 139 Minutes.

"KYOSHIRO NEMURI" SERIES (BEGUN 1956)

KYOSHIRO NEMURI: DIARY OF A RUFFIAN (*Nemuri Kyoshiro: Buraihikae*, 1956). Director: Shigeaki Hidaka. Producer: Tomoyuki Tanaka. Screenplay: Hideo Oguni, based on the novel by Renzaburo Shibata. Photography: Kazuo Yamazaki. Art Direction: Morio [Takeo] Kita, Iwao Akune. Music: Sei [Shigeru] Ikeno. Sound: Masao Fujiyoshi. Lighting: Tsuruzo Nishikawa. Cast: Koji Tsuruta (Kyoshiro Nemuri), Seizaburo Kawazu, Keiko Tsushima, Kyoko Aoyama, Machiko Kitagawa. Distribution: Toho. Release date: December 26, 1956.

KYOSHIRO NEMURI: FULL CIRCLE KILLING METHOD (*Nemuri Kyoshiro Buraihikae Daini-wa: Engetsu Sappo*, 1957). Director: Shigeaki Hidaka. Producer: Tomoyuki Tanaka. Screenplay: Hideo Oguni, Shigeaki Hidaka, based on the novel by Renzaburo Shibata. Photography: Kazuo Yamazaki. Art Direction: Morio [Takeo] Kita, Iwao Akune. Music: Sei [Shigeru] Ikeno. Sound: Wataru Onuma. Lighting: Tsuruzo Nishikawa. Cast: Koji Tsuruta (Kyoshiro Nemuri), Seizaburo Kawazu, Keiko Tsushima, Setsuko Wakayama, Yasuko Nakata, Momoko Kochi, Machiko Kitagawa, Koji Mitsui. Distribution: Toho. Release date: April 2, 1957.

KYOSHIRO NEMURI: EVIL SWORD HELL (or SPELL OF THE HIDDEN GOLD; *Nemuri Kyoshiro: Maken Jigoku*, 1958). Director: Masazumi Kawanishi. Producer: Tomoyuki Tanaka. Screenplay: Masazumi Kawanishi, Takeshi Kimura, based on the novel by Renzaburo Shibata. Photography: Tadashi Iimura. Lighting: Choshiro Ishii. Art Direction: Morio [Takeo] Kita. Music: Ichiro Saito. Sound: Norio Tone. Cast: Koji Tsuruta (Kyoshiro Nemuri), Michiyo Kogure, Yasuko Nakata, Kumi Mizuno, Haruko Sugimura, Isuzu Yamada, Seiji Miyaguchi, Hisaya Morishige, Kichijiro Ueda, Ken Uehara. Distribution: Toho. Release date: October 21, 1958. 91 minutes.

KYOSHIRO NEMURI: THE SCROLL OF SWORDSMANSHIP (or THE ADVENTURES OF KYOSHIRO NEMURI: THE CHINESE JADE; *Nemuri Kyoshiro Sappocho*, 1963) Director: Tokuzo Tanaka. Producer: Kyuichi Tsuji. Screenplay: Seiji [Kiyoshi] Hoshikawa, based on the novel by Renzaburo Shibata [credited as source material for the entire series]. Photography: Chishi Makiura (Eastmancolor, DaieiScope). Lighting: Genken Nakaoka. Art Direction: Akira Naito. Music: Taichiro Kosugi. Sound: Masahiro Okumura. Editor: Hiroshi Yamada. Fight Choreography: Shohei Miyauchi. Cast: Raizo Ichikawa (Kyoshiro Nemuri), Tamao Nakamura, Kenzaburo Jo [Tomisaburo Wakayama], Katsuhiko Kobayashi, Kuniichi Takami. Distribution: Daiei. Release date: November 2, 1963. 81 Minutes. Alternate English Title: *Sleepy Eyes of Death—the Chinese Jade*. Video: AnimEigo.

KYOSHIRO NEMURI: THE DUEL (or THE ADVENTURES OF KYOSHIRO NEMURI, SWORDSMAN; *Nemuri Kyoshiro Shobu*, 1964). Director: Kenji Misumi. Producer: Kyuichi Tsuji. Screenplay: Seiji [Kiyoshi] Hoshikawa. Photography: Chishi Makiura (Eastmancolor, DaieiScope). Lighting: Reijiro Yamashita. Art Direction: Akira Naito. Music: Ichiro Saito. Sound: Masahiro Okumura. Editor: Kanji Suganuma. Fight Choreography: Shohei Miyauchi. Cast: Raizo Ichikawa (Kyoshiro Nemuri), Shiho Fujimura, Miwa Takada, Naoko Kubo, Yoshi Kato, Junichiro Narita. Distribution: Daiei. Release date: January 9, 1964. 83 Minutes.

THE EXPLOITS OF KYOSHIRO NEMURI, SWORDSMAN (*Nemuri Kyoshiro Engetsu* Giri, 1964). Director: Kimiyoshi Yasuda.

Screenplay: Seiji [Kiyoshi] Hoshikawa. Photography: Chishi Makiura [Eastmancolor; DaieiScope]. Lighting: Kenichi Okamoto. Art Direction: Shigeru Kato. Music: Ichiro Saito. Sound: Iwao Otani. Editor: Kanji Suganuma. Fight Choreography: Shohei Miyauchi. Cast: Raizo Ichikawa (Kyoshiro Nemuri), Yuko Hamada, Kyoko Azuma, Taro Marui, Junichiro Narita. Distribution: Daiei. Release date: May 23, 1964. 86 minutes. Alternate English Titles: *Kyoshiro Nemuri: The Full-Moon Cut*; *Sleepy Eyes of Death—Full Circle Killing*. Video: AnimEigo.

KYOSHIRO NEMURI AT BAY (*Nemuri Kyoshiro Joyo Ken*, 1964). Director: Kazuo Ikehiro. Producer: Sadao Zaizen. Screenplay: Seiji [Kiyoshi] Hoshikawa. Photography: Yasukazu Takemura [Eastmancolor; DaieiScope]. Lighting: Hiroya Kato. Art Direction: Yoshinobu Nishioka. Music: Ichiro Saito. Sound: Masao Osumi. Editor: Toshio Taniguchi. Fight Choreography: Shohei Miyauchi. Cast: Raizo Ichikawa (Kyoshiro Nemuri), Shiho Fujimura, Naoko Kubo, Kenzaburo Jo [Tomisaburo Wakayama], Katsuhiko Kobayashi, Masumi Harukawa. Distribution: Daiei. Release date: October 17, 1964. 81 minutes. Alternate English Titles: *Kyoshiro Nemuri 4: Passionate Sword*; *Sleepy Eyes of Death: Sword Of Seduction*. Video: AnimEigo.

KYOSHIRO NEMURI: FLAMING SWORD (*Nemuri Kyoshiro Enjo Ken*, 1965) Director: Kenji Misumi. Producer: Sadao Zaizen. Screenplay: Seiji [Kiyoshi] Hoshikawa. Photography: Fujiro Morita [Eastmancolor; DaieiScope]. Lighting: Kenji Furuya. Art Direction: Akira Naito. Sound: Masao Osumi. Editor: Kanji Suganuma. Music: Ichiro Saito. Cast: Raizo Ichikawa (Kyoshiro Nemuri), Tamao Nakamura, Michiko Sugata, Sanae Nakahara, Ko [Akira] Nishimura. Distribution: Daiei. Release date: January 13, 1965. 83 Minutes. Alternate English Titles: *Kyoshiro Nemuri 5: Fiery Sword*; *Sleepy Eyes of Death: Sword Of Fire*. Video: AnimEigo.

THE MYSTERIOUS SWORD OF KYOSHIRO NEMURI (*Nemuri Kyoshiro Masho Ken*, 1965). Director: Kimiyoshi Yasuda. Screenplay: Seiji [Kiyoshi] Hoshikawa. Photography: Yasukazu Takemura [Eastmancolor; DaieiScope]. Lighting: Reijiro Yamashita. Art Direction: Shigeru Kato. Music: Ichiro Saito. Sound: Masao Osumi. Editor: Mitsuzo Miyata. Cast: Raizo Ichikawa (Kyoshiro Nemuri), Machiko Hasegawa, Kazuko Wakamatsu. Distribution: Daiei. Release date: May 1, 1965. 75 minutes. Alternate English Titles: *Kyoshiro Nemuri 6: Devil's Sword*; *Sleepy Eyes of Death: Sword Of Satan*. Video: AnimEigo.

THE PRINCESS' MASK (*Nemuri Kyoshiro Tajo Ken*, 1966). Director: Akira [Sho] Inoue. Screenplay: Seiji [Kiyoshi] Hoshikawa. Photography: Yasukazu Takemura [Eastmancolor; DaieiScope]. Lighting: Kenji Furuya. Art Direction: Tadao Uesato. Music: Akira Ifukube. Sound: Yukio Kaihara. Editor: Mitsuzo Miyata. Cast: Raizo Ichikawa (Kyoshiro Nemuri), Yoshie Mizutani, Ichiro Nakatani [Nakaya], Keiko Kayama. Distribution: Daiei. Release date: March 12, 1966. 85 minutes.

KYOSHIRO NEMURI: THE VILLAIN'S SWORD (*Nemuri Kyoshiro Burai Ken*, 1966) Director: Kenji Misumi. Screenplay: Daisuke Ito. Photography: Chishi Makiura (Eastmancolor, DaieiScope]. Lighting: Reijiro Yamashita. Art Direction: Shigenori Shimoishizaka. Music: Akira Ifukube. Sound: Tsuchitaro Hayashi. Editor: Kanji Suganuma. Cast: Raizo Ichikawa (Kyoshiro Nemuri), Shigeru Amachi, Shiho Fujimura, Kentaro Kudo, Ryuzo Shimada, Tatsuo Endo. Distribution: Daiei. Release date: November 9, 1966. 79 Minutes. Alternate English Title: *Sleepy Eyes of Death: Sword of Villainy*.

THE TRAIL OF TRAPS (*Nemuri Kyoshiro Burai-Hikae Masho no Hada*, 1967). Director: Kazuo Ikehiro. Screenplay: Hajime Takaiwa. Photography: Yasukazu Takemura [Eastmancolor; DaieiScope]. Lighting: Hiroshi Mima. Art Direction: Shigenori Shimoishizaka. Music: Takeo Watanabe. Sound: Iwao Otani. Editor: Hiroshi Yamada. Cast: Raizo Ichikawa (Kyoshiro Nemuri), Nobuo Kaneko (Shurinosuke Asahina), Toshie Kimura (Sonoe), Haruko Wanibuchi (Chisa), Mikio Narita (Ukon Saegusa), Naoko Kubo (Oen). Distribution: Daiei. Release date: July 15, 1967. 88 minutes.

A RONIN CALLED NEMURI (*Nemuri Kyoshiro Onna Jigoku*, 1968). Director: Tokuzo Tanaka. Screenplay: Hajime Takaiwa. Photography: Fujiro Morita (Eastmancolor, DaieiScope). Lighting: Genken Nakaoka. Art Direction: Akira Naito. Music: Takeo Watanabe. Sound: Yukio Kaihara. Editor: Hiroshi Yamada. Cast: Raizo Ichikawa (Kyoshiro Nemuri), Miwa Takada (Princess Saya), Yoshie Mizutani (Osono), Takahiro Tamura (Tatsuma), Eitaro Ozawa [Sakae Ozawa] (Hori), Toru Abe (Geki), Yunosuke Ito (Jinnai). Distribution: Daiei. Release date: January 13, 1968. 85 minutes. Alternate English Title: *Sleepy Eyes of Death: Hell is a Woman.*

THE HUMAN TARANTULA (*Nemuri Kyoshiro Hitohada Gumo*, 1968). Director: Kimiyoshi Yasuda. Screenplay: Seiji [Kiyoshi] Hoshikawa. Photography: Senkichiro Takeda [Eastmancolor, DaieiScope]. Lighting: Kenji Furuya. Art Direction: Shigenori Shimoishizaka. Music: Chumei [Michiaki] [Hiroaki] Watanabe. Sound: Masahiro Okumura. Editor: Kanji Suganuma. Cast: Raizo Ichikawa, (Kyoshiro Nemuri), Mako Midori (Murasaki), Mako Sanjo (Suma), Yusuke Kawazu (Ietake), Fumio Watanabe (Ikkan), Minori Terada. Distribution: Daiei. Release date: May 1, 1968. 81 minutes. Alternate English Title: *Sleepy Eyes of Death: In the Spider's Lair.*

CASTLE MENAGERIE (*Nemuri Kyoshiro Akujo-Gari*, 1969). Director: Kazuo Ikehiro. Screenplay: Hajime Takaiwa, Ichiro Miyagawa. Photography: Senkichiro Takeda [Eastmancolor, DaieiScope]. Lighting: Reijiro Yamashita. Art Direction: Shigenori Shimoishizaka. Music: Takeo Watanabe. Sound: Iwao Otani. Editor: Kanji Suganuma. Cast: Raizo Ichikawa (Kyoshiro Nemuri), Shiho Fujimura, Naoko Kubo, Kayo Matsuo, Hideko Yoshida, Machiko Hasegawa, Yukiji Asaoka, Shinjiro Ebara, Asao Koike. Distribution: Daiei. Release date: January 11, 1969. 82 minutes. Alternate English Title: *Sleepy Eyes of Death: Hunt for the Wicked Woman.*

KYOSHIRO NEMURI: FULL MOON SWORDSMAN (or *THE FULL MOON SWORDSMAN*; *Nemuri Kyoshiro Engetsu Sappo*, 1969). Director: Kazuo [Issei] Mori. Screenplay: Koji Takada, Minoru Takahashi. Photography: Senkichiro Takeda [Eastmancolor, DaieiScope]. Lighting: Hiroshi Mima. Art Direction: Seiichi Ota. Music: Taichiro Kosugi. Sound: Masao Osumi. Editor: Toshio Taniguchi. Cast: Hiroki Matsukata (Kyoshiro Nemuri), Tomomi Sato, Sanae Nakahara, Machiko Hasegawa, Mikio Narita, Yusuke Kawazu. Distribution: Daiei. Release date: October 4, 1969. 82 minutes.

KYOSHIRO NEMURI: FYLFOT SWORDPLAY (or *SWASTIKA SWORDPLAY*; *Nemuri Kyoshiro Manji Giri*, 1969). Director: Kazuo Ikehiro. Screenplay: Yoshikata Yoda. Photography: Senkichiro Takeda [Eastmancolor, DaieiScope]. Lighting: Kenji

Raizo Ichikawa in *Trail of Traps.*

Furuya. Art Direction: Shigeru Kato. Music: Takeo Watanabe. Sound: Masao Osumi. Editor: Toshio Taniguchi. Cast: Hiroki Matsukata (Kyoshiro Nemuri), Yoko Namikawa, Kikko Matsuoka, Masakazu Tamura, Reiko Kasahara, Shigako Shimegi. Distribution: Daiei. Release date: December 20, 1969. 88 minutes.

KYOSHIRO NEMURI: LOVE'S FULL CIRCLE KILLING METHOD! THE SHOGUN IS CRAZY, KILL HIM! (*Nemuri Kyoshiro: Koishigure Engetsu Sappo! Shogun Ke, Wakagimi Ranshin no Nazo o Kiru!*, 1989). Director: Tokuzo Tanaka. Cast: Masakazu Tamura (Kyoshiro Nemuri), Yumi Takigawa. Release date: June 22, 1989. [TV Movie]

KYOSHIRO NEMURI: A CONSPIRACY SWIRLS IN EDO CASTLE (*Nemuri Kyoshiro: Edo-jo ni Uzumaku Inbo!*, 1993). Director: Akira [Sho] Inoue. Cast: Masakazu Tamura (Nemuri), Keiko Takeshita. Release date: September 30, 1993. [TV Movie]

KYOSHIRO NEMURI: LIVING LIKE THERE'S NO TOMORROW (*Nemuri Kyoshiro: Kyoatte Ashita Naki Inochi o Ikiru Mono!*, 1996). Director: Sadao Nakajima. Cast: Masakazu Tamura (Nemuri), Yuko Natori, Shin Takuma. Release date: September 19, 1996. [TV Movie]

KYOSHIRO NEMURI: MURDER IN THE NIGHT SNOW! KYOSHIRO'S BELOVED WOMAN (*Nemuri Kyoshiro: Yuki no Yoru ni Watakushi o Koroshite! Kyoshiro o Itoshi Tsuzuketa Onna*, 1998). Director: Akira [Sho] Inoue. Cast: Masakazu Tamura (Kyoshiro Nemuri), Hitomi Kuroki, Kimiko Ikegami. Release date: December 28, 1998. [TV Movie]

"ZATO ICHI" SERIES (
WITH SHINTARO KATSU, 1962-1989)

THE LIFE & OPINION OF MASSEUR ICHI (*Zatoichi Monogatari*, 1962). Director: Kenji Misumi. Producer: Ikuo Kubodera. Screenplay: Minoru Inuzuka, based on an original story by Kan Shimozawa [credited as source material for the entire series]. Photography: Chishi Makiura [DaieiScope]. Lighting: Hiroya Kato. Art Direction: Akira Naito. Music: Akira Ifukube. Sound: Iwao Otani. Editor: Kanji Suganuma. Fight Choreography: Shohei Miyauchi. Cast: Shintaro Katsu (Zato Ichi), Masayo Banri (Otane, Tatekichi's sister), Ryuzo Shimada (Shigezo, yakuza boss), Hajime [Gen] Mitamura (Hanji), Shigeru Amachi (Miki Hirate), Chitose Maki (Oyoshi), Ikuko Mori (Otoyo), Michio Minami (Tatekichi), Eijiro Yanagi (Sukegoro), Toshio Chiba (Masakichi), Manabu Morita (Seisuke), Yoichi Funaki (Yogoro), Kinya Ichikawa (Mokichi), Eigoro Onoe (Rihei), Yoshindo Yamaji (Yahei), Yukio Horikita (Kanaji), Ryuji Fukui (Daihachi), Masayoshi Kikuno (coolie), Hajime Koshikawa (farmer), Akira Shiga, Yuji Hamada, Koichi Aihara, Hiroyoshi [Kozen] Nishioka, Shingo Hosoya, Katsuyoshi Baba, Kaname Yuki (yakuzas), Taizo Sengoku (Ishichi), Noboru Taniguchi (Tomozo), Keiko Awanami (Osaki). Distribution: Daiei. Release date: April 18, 1962. 96 minutes. Video: Home Vision Entertainment.

THE RETURN OF MASSEUR ICHI (*Zoku Zatoichi Monogatari*, 1962). Director: Kazuo [Issei] Mori. Producer: Ikuo Kubodera. Screenplay: Minoru Inuzuka. Photography: Shozo Honda [DaieiScope]. Lighting: Sadaichi Ito. Art Direction: Seiichi Ota. Music: Ichiro Saito. Sound: Tsuchitaro Hayashi. Editor: Takashi Taniguchi. Fight Choreography: Shohei Miyauchi. Cast: Shintaro Katsu (Zato Ichi), Yoshie Mizutani (Osetsu), Masayo Banri (Otane), Kenzaburo Jo [Tomisaburo Wakayama] (Nagisa no Yoshiro), Yutaka Nakamura (Kagami no Sanzo), Sonosuke Sawamura (Seki no Kanbei), Shosaku Sugiyama (Tamigoro), Sanemon Arashi (Kai Yoshida), Yoshindo Yamaji (Yahei), Eijiro Yanagi (Sukegoro Iioka), Fujio Harumoto (Lord Kuroda), Koichi Mizuhara (Kanzo), Saburo Date (Morisuke), Shintaro Nanjo (Samon Shiraishi), Shozo Nanbu (Goemon Kashiya). Distribution: Daiei. Release date: October 12, 1962. 72 minutes. Video: Home Vision Entertainment.

MASSEUR ICHI ENTERS AGAIN (*Shin Zatoichi Monogatari*, 1963). Director: Tokuzo Tanaka. Screenplay: Minoru Inuzuka, Kikuo Umebayashi. Photography: Chishi Makiura [Eastmancolor;

DaieiScope]. Lighting: Kenji Furuya. Art Direction: Seiichi Ota. Music: Akira Ifukube. Sound: Masao Osumi. Editor: Hiroshi Yamada. Fight Choreography: Shohei Miyauchi. Cast: Shintaro Katsu (Zato Ichi), Mikiko Tsubouchi, Chitose Maki, Mieko Kondo, Seizaburo Kawazu. Distribution: Daiei. Release date: March 15, 1963. 91 minutes. Alternate English Titles: *New Tale of Zato Ichi*; *Zato Ichi Enters Again*; *Zato Ichi: The Blind Swordsman's Return*. Video: Home Vision Entertainment.

MASSEUR ICHI, THE FUGITIVE (*Zatoichi Kyojo Tabi*, 1963). Director: Tokuzo Tanaka. Screenplay: Seiji [Kiyoshi] Hoshikawa. Photography: Chishi Makiura [Eastmancolor; DaieiScope]. Lighting: Genken Nakaoka. Art Direction: Seiichi Ota. Music: Akira Ifukube. Sound: Sakae Nagaoka. Editor: Hiroshi Yamada. Fight Choreography: Shohei Miyauchi. Cast: Shintaro Katsu (Zato Ichi), Miwa Takada, Masayo Banri, Junichiro Narita, Katsuhiko Kobayashi, Toru Abe, Jutaro Hojo, Sachiko Murase, Hiroshi Nawa. Distribution: Daiei. Release date: August 10, 1963. 86 minutes. Alternate English Titles: *Zato Ichi, Crazy Journey*. Video: Home Vision Entertainment.

ZATO ICHI (or *ZATO ICHI AND THE SCOUNDRELS* or *ZATO ICHI ON THE ROAD*; *Zatoichi Kenka-Tabi*, 1963). Director: Kimiyoshi Yasuda. Producer: Ikuo Kubodera. Screenplay: Minoru Inuzuka. Photography: Shozo Honda [DaieiScope]. Lighting: Hiroshi Mima. Art Direction: Yoshinobu Nishioka. Music: Akira Ifukube. Sound: Sakae Nagaoka. Editor: Kanji Suganuma. Fight Choreography: Shohei Miyauchi. Cast: Shintaro Katsu (Zato Ichi), Shiho Fujimura (Omitsu), Ryuzo Shimada (Jingoro), Reiko Fujiwara (Ohisa), Matasaburo Niwa (Yamada), Yoshio Yoshida (Tomegoro), Sonosuke Sawamura (Tobei), Shosaku Sugiyama (Hikozo), Yutaka Nakamura (Matsu). Distribution: Daiei. Release date: November 30, 1963. 85 minutes. Video: Home Vision Entertainment.

ZATO ICHI AND A CHEST OF GOLD (*Zatoichi Senryo-Kubi*, 1964). Director: Kazuo Ikehiro. Screenplay: Shozaburo Asai, Akikazu Ota. Photography: Kazuo Miyagawa [DaieiColor; DaieiScope]. Lighting: Genken Nakaoka. Art Direction: Yoshinobu Nishioka. Music: Ichiro Saito. Sound: Iwao Otani. Editor: Takashi Taniguchi. Fight Choreography: Shohei Miyauchi. Cast: Shintaro Katsu (Zato Ichi), Kenzaburo Jo [Tomisaburo Wakayama] (Jushiro), Shogo Shimada (Chuji Kunisada), Mikiko Tsubouchi, Machiko Hasegawa, Tatsuya Ishiguro, Shinjiro Asano, Saburo Date, Hikosaburo Kataoka, Matasaburo Niwa, Toranosuke Tennoji, Koichi Mizuhara, Hiroshi Hayashi, Yusaku Terashima, Ichiro Takakura. Distribution: Daiei. Release date: March 14, 1964. 83 minutes. Video: Home Vision Entertainment.

THE SWORD OF ZATO ICHI (*Zatoichi Abare Dako*, 1964). Director: Kazuo Ikehiro. Screenplay: Shozaburo Asai, Minoru Inuzuka. Photography: Yasukazu Takemura [Eastmancolor; DaieiScope]. Lighting: Hiroya Kato. Art Direction: Yoshinobu Nishioka. Music: Shigeru [Sei] Ikeno. Sound: Masao Osumi. Editor: Takashi Taniguchi. Fight Choreography: Shohei Miyauchi. Cast: Shintaro Katsu (Zato Ichi), Tatsuo Endo, Takashi Edajima, Ryutaro Gomi, Bokuzen Hidari (Kyubei), Naoko Kubo, Mayumi Nagisa, Yutaka Nakamura, Ko Sugita. Distribution: Daiei. Release date: July 11, 1964. 82 minutes. Alternate English title: *Zato Ichi's Flashing Sword*. Video: Home Vision Entertainment.

FIGHT, ZATO ICHI, FIGHT (*Zatoichi Kessho Tabi*, 1964). Director: Kenji Misumi. Screenplay: Seiji [Kiyoshi] Hoshikawa, Tetsuro Yoshida, Masaharu Matsumura. Photography: Chishi Makiura [Eastmancolor; DaieiScope]. Lighting: Reijiro Yamashita. Art Direction: Akira Naito. Music: Akira Ifukube. Sound: Iwao Otani. Editor: Kanji Suganuma. Fight Choreography: Shohei Miyauchi. Cast: Shintaro Katsu (Zato Ichi), Hizuru Takachiho, Nobuo Kaneko, Yoshi Kato, Tatsuya Ishiguro, Jutaro Hojo. Distribution: Daiei. Release date: October 17, 1964. 87 minutes. Video: Home Vision Entertainment.

ADVENTURES OF A BLIND MAN (*Zatoichi Sekisho Yaburi*, 1964). Director: Kimiyoshi Yasuda. Screenplay: Shozaburo Asai. Photography: Shozo Honda [DaieiColor; DaieiScope]. Lighting:

Shintaro Katsu in *Masseur Ichi, the Fugitive*.

Hiroya Kato. Art Direction: Shigeru Kato. Music: Taichiro Kosugi. Sound: Sakae Nagaoka. Editor: Hiroshi Yamada. Fight Choreography: Shohei Miyauchi. Cast: Shintaro Katsu (Zato Ichi), Miwa Takada, Eiko Taki, Mikijiro Hira, Kichijiro Ueda. Distribution: Daiei. Release date: December 30, 1964. 86 minutes. Video: Home Vision Entertainment.

THE BLIND SWORDSMAN'S REVENGE (*Zatoichi Nidan Giri*, 1965). Director: Akira [Sho] Inoue. Screenplay: Minoru Inuzuka. Photography: Fujiro Morita [DaieiScope]. Lighting: Hiroshi Mima. Art Direction: Yoshinobu Nishioka. Music: Akira Ifukube. Sound: Yukio Kaihara. Editor: Hiroshi Yamada. Fight Choreography: Eiichi Kusumoto. Cast: Shintaro Katsu (Zato Ichi), Norihei Miki, Mikiko Tsubouchi (Osayo), Takeshi Kato, Fujio Harumoto, Sanemon Arashi (Hikonoichi). Distribution: Daiei. Release date: April 3, 1965. 84 minutes. Video: Home Vision Entertainment.

ZATO ICHI AND THE DOOMED MAN (*Zatoichi Sakata Giri*, 1965). Director: Kazuo [Issei] Mori. Screenplay: Shozaburo Asai. Photography: Hiroshi Imai [Eastmancolor; DaieiScope]. Lighting: Sadaichi Ito. Art Direction: Seiichi Ota. Music: Seitaro Omori. Sound: Tsuchitaro Hayashi. Editor: Toshio Taniguchi. Fight Choreography: Eiichi Kusumoto. Cast: Shintaro Katsu (Zato Ichi),

Shintaro Katsu in *The Blind Swordsman's Vengeance*.

Kanbi Fujiyama, Eiko Taki, Masako Myojo, Koichi Mizuhara. Distribution: Daiei. Release date: September 18, 1965. 88 minutes. Video: Home Vision Entertainment.

ZATO ICHI'S TRIP INTO HELL (or *SHOWDOWN FOR ZATO ICHI* or *ZATO ICHI AND THE CHESS EXPERT*; *Zatoichi Jigoku-Tabi*, 1965). Director: Kenji Misumi. Screenplay: Daisuke Ito. Photography: Chishi Makiura [DaieiColor; DaieiScope]. Lighting: Kenji Furuya. Art Direction: Akira Naito. Music: Akira Ifukube. Sound: Iwao Otani. Editor: Kanji Suganuma. Cast: Shintaro Katsu (Zato Ichi), Mikio Narita (Jumonji), Chizuru Hayashi (Kume), Kaneko Iwasaki (Otane), Gaku [Manabu] Yamamoto (Tomonoshin), Saburo Date, Takuya Fujioka, Rokko [Mutsuhiro] Toura. Distribution: Daiei. Release date: December 24, 1965. 87 minutes.

THE BLIND SWORDSMAN'S VENGEANCE (*Zatoichi no Uta ga Kikoeru*, 1966). Director: Tokuzo Tanaka. Screenplay: Hajime Takaiwa. Photography: Kazuo Miyagawa [Eastmancolor; DaieiScope]. Lighting: Genken Nakaoka. Art Direction: Yoshinobu Nishioka. Music: Akira Ifukube. Sound: Yukio Kaihara. Editor: Kanji Suganuma. Cast: Shintaru Katsu (Zato Ichi), Shigeru Amachi, Mayumi Ogawa, Kei Sato, Jun Hamamura. Distribution: Daiei. Release date: May 3, 1966. 83 minutes.

ZATO ICHI'S PILGRIMAGE (*Zatoichi Umi o Wataru*, 1966). Director: Kazuo Ikehiro. Screenplay: Kaneto Shindo. Photography: Senkichiro Takeda [DaieiColor; DaieiScope]. Lighting: Reijiro Yamashita. Art Direction: Yoshinobu Nishioka. Music: Ichiro Saito. Sound: Iwao Otani. Editor: Toshio Taniguchi. Cast: Shintaro Katsu (Zato Ichi), Michiyo Yasuda, Kunie Tanaka, Hisashi Igawa, Masao Mishima. Distribution: Daiei. Release date: August 13, 1966. 82 minutes.

THE BLIND SWORDSMAN'S CANE SWORD (*Zatoichi Tekka Tabi*, 1967). Director: Kimiyoshi Yasuda. Producer: Ikuo Kubodera. Screenplay: Ryozo Kasahara. Photography: Senkichiro Takeda [Eastmancolor; DaieiScope]. Lighting: Kenji Furuya. Art Direction: Yoshinobu Nishioka. Music: Ichiro Saito. Sound: Masao Osumi. Editor: Toshio Taniguchi. Cast: Shintaro Katsu (Zato Ichi), Shiho Fujimura (Oshizu), Yoshihiko Aoyama (Seikichi), Makoto Fujita (Umazo), Kiyoko Suizenji (Oharu), Eijiro Tono (Senzo), Masumi Harukawa (Oryu), Junichiro Yamashita (Shinnosuke), Ryutaro Gomi (Ronin), Fujio Suga (Seisuke Kuwayama), Tatsuo Endo (Iwagoro), Ryuji Kita (Genbei), Eigoro Onoe (Zato), Yusaku Terashima (Noodle Shop Owner), Gen Kimura (Hanzo), Yukio Horikita (Mosuke), Kimiko Tachibana (Otane). Distribution: Daiei. Release date: January 3, 1967. 93 minutes.

THE BLIND SWORDSMAN'S RESCUE (*Zatoichi Ro Yaburi*, 1967). Director: Satsuo Yamamoto. Producer: Masaichi Nagata [Katsu Productions]. Screenplay: Takehiro Nakajima, Koji Matsumoto, Kiyokata Saruwaka. Photography: Kazuo Miyagawa [Eastmancolor; DaieiScope]. Lighting: Genken Nakaoka. Art Direction: Yoshinobu Nishioka. Music: Sei [Shigeru] Ikeno. Sound: Tsuchitaro Hayashi. Editor: Kanji Suganuma. Cast: Shintaro Katsu (Zato Ichi), Rentaro Mikuni (Asagoro) Ko [Akira] Nishimura (Uneshiro Suga), Yuko Hamada (Shino), Toshiyuki Hosokawa (Nisaburo), Takuya Fujioka (Zato Sanji), Kenjiro Ishiyama (Tatsugoro). Distribution: Daiei. Release date: August 12, 1967. 96 minutes. Alternate English Titles: *Zatoichi the Outlaw, Zatoichi Breaks Jail*. Video: AnimEigo.

ZATO ICHI CHALLENGED (*Zatoichi Chikemuri Kaido*, 1967). Director: Kenji Misumi. Producer: Ikuo Kubodera. Screenplay: Ryozo Kasahara. Photography: Chishi Makiura [Eastmancolor; DaieiScope]. Lighting: Reijiro Yamashita. Art Direction: Shigenori Shimoishizaka. Music: Akira Ifukube. Sound: Iwao Otani. Editor: Toshio Taniguchi. Fight Choreography: Shohei Miyauchi. Cast: Shintaro Katsu (Zato Ichi), Jushiro Konoe (Tajuro), Miwa Takada (Omitsu), Yukiji Asaoka (Tomoe), Mikiko Tsubouchi (Osen), Mie Nakao (Miyuki), Takao Ito (Shokichi), Asao Koike (Gonzo), Midori Isomura (Omine), Tatsuo Matsumura (Tahei), Eitaro Ozawa [Sakae Ozawa] (Torikoshi), Jotaro Senba, Kojiro Kusanagi, Kenzo Tabu (Manzo of Kanai), Osami Nabe (Hanzo), Akihisa Toda (Shinnosuke

Shintaro Katsu in *The Blind Swordsman's Cane Sword*.

Emi), Koji Fujiyama (Gokichi), Koichi Mizuhara (Sobei), Shosaku Sugiyama (Naruyama), Ikuko Mori (Waitress). Distribution: Daiei. Release date: December 30, 1967. 87 minutes.

THE BLIND SWORDSMAN AND THE FUGITIVES (*Zatoichi Hatashijo*, 1968). Director: Kimiyoshi Yasuda. Producer: Ikuo Kubodera. Screenplay: Kinya Naoi. Photography: Kazuo Miyagawa [Eastmancolor; DaieiScope]. Lighting: Genken Nakaoka. Art Direction: Shigeru Kato. Music: So [Hajime] Kaburagi. Sound: Iwao Otani. Editor: Kanji Suganuma. Cast: Shintaro Katsu (Zato Ichi), Yumiko Nogawa (Oaki), Kayo Mikimoto (Oshizu), Kyosuke Machida, Takashi Shimura (Dr. Junan), Shobun Inoue (Kumeji), Jotaro Senba (Minokichi), Jutaro Hojo (Genta), Hosei Komatsu (Kanzo), Koichi Mizuhara (Sennosuke), Ichiro [Kazuo] Yamamoto (Isuke), Ryuji Funabashi (Ushimatsu), Shozo Nanbu (Tokuzaemon), Yukio Horikita (Inokichi), Seishiro Hara (Sakata), Rieko Oda (Osei), Yukari Mizumachi (Yoshidaya's Maid), Teruko Omi (Osato). Distribution: Daiei. Release date: August 10, 1968. 82 minutes. Alternate English Title: *Zatoichi: A Letter of Challenge*.

THE BLIND SWORDSMAN SAMARITAN (*Zatoichi Kenka-Daiko*, 1968). Director: Kenji Misumi. Producer: Kyuichi Tsuji. Screenplay: Kiyokata Saruwaka, Hisashi Sugiura, Tetsuro Yoshida. Photography: Fujiro Morita [Eastmancolor; DaieiScope]. Lighting: Shunji Kurokawa. Art Direction: Akira Naito. Music: Sei [Shigeru] Ikeno. Sound: Yukio Kaihara. Editor: Toshio Taniguchi. Fight Choreography: Shohei Miyauchi. Cast: Shintaro Katsu (Zato Ichi), Yoshiko Mita (Osode), Makoto Sato (Yasaburo Kashiwazaki), Ko [Akira] Nishimura (Sosuke Saruya), Takuya Fujioka (Shinkichi), Chocho Miyako (Ohaya), Akira Shimizu (Kumakichi), Ryoichi Tamagawa (Chohachi), Machiko Soga (Osen), Ryutaro Gomi (Sashichi), Osamu Okawa (Tokuji), Rokko [Mutsuhiro] Toura (Choji), Kazue Tamaoki, Yukio Horikita (Isokichi), Takeshi Date (Kanzo), Gen Kimura (Daisaku Igawa), Shosaku Sugiyama (Kinsuke), Ichiro [Kazuo] Yamamoto (Dice Player), Akira Moroguchi (Shota), Yuji Hamada (Hyoma Muraki), Jun Katsumura (Rokusuke), Takeshi Yabuuchi (Sakujiro), Teruko Omi (Okatsu). Distribution: Daiei. Release date: December 28, 1968. 84 minutes. Alternate English Title: *Zato Ichi and the Drum*.

ZATO ICHI MEETS YOJIMBO (*Zatoichi to Yojinbo*, 1970). Director: Kihachi Okamoto. Producers: Shintaro Katsu, Hiroyoshi [Kozen] Nishioka [Katsu Productions]. Screenplay: Kihachi Okamoto, Tetsuro Yoshida. Photography: Kazuo Miyagawa [DaieiColor; DaieiScope]. Lighting: Genken Nakaoka. Art Direction: Yoshinobu Nishioka. Music: Akira Ifukube. Editor: Toshio Taniguchi. Sound: Tsuchitaro Hayashi. Fight Choreography: Kentaro Yuasa. Cast: Shintaro Katsu (Zato Ichi), Toshiro Mifune (Daisaku Sasa (Yojimbo)), Ayako Wakao (Umeno), Masakane

270

Yonekura (Masagoro), Osamu Takizawa (Yasuke Eboshiya), Shin Kishida (Kuzuryu), Kanjuro Arashi [Chozaburo Arashi] (Hyoroku), Shigeru Koyama [Kamiyama] (Jinzaburo), Toshiyuki Hosokawa (Sanaemon Goto), Minori Terada, Daigo Kusano, Hideo Sunazuka, Fujio Tokita, Gen Kimura, Hiroshi Tanaka, Ryutaro Gomi, Hirohito Kimura. Distribution: Daiei. Release date: January 15, 1970. 116 minutes. Video: AnimEigo.

THE BLIND SWORDSMAN'S FIRE FESTIVAL (*Zatoichi Abare Himatsuri*, 1970). Director: Kenji Misumi. Producer: Shintaro Katsu [Katsu Productions]. Screenplay: Takayuki Yamada, Shintaro Katsu. Photography: Kazuo Miyagawa [DaieiColor; DaieiScope]. Lighting: Genken Nakaoka. Art Direction: Yoshinobu Nishioka. Music: Isao Tomita. Sound: Masao Osumi. Editor: Toshio Taniguchi. Cast: Shintaro Katsu (Zato Ichi), Tatsuya Nakadai (Ronin), Reiko Ohara (Okiyo), Masayuki Mori (Yamikubo), Peter [Shinnosuke Ikehata] (Umeji), Ko [Akira] Nishimura. Distribution: Daiei. Release date: August 12, 1970. 96 minutes.

THE BLIND SWORDSMAN MEETS HIS EQUAL (Shin *Zatoichi Yabure! Tojin-ken*, 1971). Director: Kimiyoshi Yasuda. Producers: Shintaro Katsu, Hiroyoshi [Kozen] Nishioka [Katsu Productions]. Screenplay: Kimiyoshi Yasuda, Takayuki Yamada. Photography: Chishi Makiura [DaieiColor; DaieiScope]. Lighting: Hiroshi Mima. Art Direction: Yoshinobu Nishioka. Music: Isao Tomita. Sound: Iwao Otani. Editor: Toshio Taniguchi. Cast: Shintaro Katsu (Zato Ichi), "Jimmy" Wang Yu (Kang Wang), Yuko Hama (Osen), Michie Terada (Oyone), Koji Nanbara [Nambara] (Kakuzen). Distribution: Daiei. Release date: January 13, 1971. 94 minutes. Alternate English Title: Zatoichi and the One-Armed Swordsman.

ZATO ICHI AT LARGE (*Zatoichi Goyo-tabi*, 1972). Director: Kazuo [Issei] Mori. Producers: Shintaro Katsu, Hiroyoshi [Kozen] Nishioka [Katsu Productions]. Screenplay: Kinya Naoi. Photography: Fujiro Morita [Fuji Color; TohoScope]. Lighting: Genken Nakaoka. Art Direction: Seiichi Ota. Music: Kunihiko Murai. Sound: Iwao Otani. Editor: Toshio Taniguchi. Cast: Shintaro Katsu (Zato Ichi), Rentaro Mikuni (Tetsugoro), Hisaya Morishige (Tobei), Etsushi Takahashi (Denjuro), Naoko Otani (Yae), Osamu Sakai (Seiji). Distribution: Toho. Release date: January 15, 1972. 88 minutes.

ZATO ICHI IN DESPERATION (Shin *Zatoichi Monogatari Oreta Tsue*, 1972). Director: Shintaro Katsu. Producers: Shintaro Katsu, Hiroyoshi [Kozen] Nishioka [Katsu Productions]. Screenplay: Minoru Inuzuka. Photography: Fujiro Morita [Eastmancolor; TohoScope]. Lighting: Genken Nakaoka. Art Direction: Seiichi Ota. Music: Kunihiko Murai. Sound: Masao Osumi. Editor: Toshio Taniguchi. Cast: Shintaro Katsu (Zato Ichi), Kiwako Taichi (Nishikigi), Kyoko Yoshizawa (Kaede), Yasuhiro Koume (Shinkichi), Katsuo Nakamura, (Ushimatsu), Asao Koike (Mangoro Kagiya), Joji Takagi (Tokiwa), Masumi Harukawa (Ohama). Distribution: Toho. Release date: September 2, 1972. 95 minutes.

ZATO ICHI'S CONSPIRACY (Shin *Zatoichi Monogatari Kasama no Chimatsuri*, 1973). Director: Kimiyoshi Yasuda. Producers: Shintaro Katsu, Hiroyoshi [Kozen] Nishioka [Katsu Productions]. Screenplay: Yoshiko Hattori. Photography: Chishi Makiura [Eastmancolor; TohoScope]. Lighting: Shozo Saito. Art Direction: Seiichi Ota. Music: Akira Ifukube. Sound: Masao Osumi. Editor: Yoshiharu Hayashi. Cast: Shintaro Katsu (Zato Ichi), Yukiyo Toake (Omiyo), Eiji Okada, Kei Sato, Yoshio Tsuchiya, Shiro Kishibe, Rie Yokoyama (Yuri), Tatsuo Endo, Takashi Shimura. Distribution: Toho. Release date: April 21, 1973. 88 minutes.

ZATO ICHI (*Zatoichi*, 1989) Director: Shintaro Katsu. Executive Producers: Shintaro Katsu, June Adams Tsukamoto. Producers: Kiyoshi Tsukamoto, Masanori Sanada [Katsu Productions]. Screenplay: Shintaro Katsu, Tatsumi Ichiyama, Tsutomu Nakamura, based on an adaptation by Kyohei Nakaoka. Photography: Mutsuo [Rokuo] Naganuma (Color). Lighting: Hideo Kumagai. Art Direction: Chiyoo Umeda. Music: Takayuki Watanabe/Edison. Song: "The Loner" by Edison and Mike Dunn, performed by Johnny. Sound: Senji Horiuchi. Editor: Toshio Taniguchi. Fight Choreography: Hiroshi Kuze. Cast: Shintaro Katsu (Zato Ichi), Kanako Higuchi (Ohan), Takanori Jinnai (Inspector), Masahiro Okumura (Goemon), Yuya Uchida (Boss Akabei), Ken Ogata (Ronin), Toyomi Kusano (Oume), Tsurutaro Kataoka, Joe Yamanaka, Norihei Miki. Distribution: Shochiku. Release date: February 4, 1989. 116 Minutes. Video: Samurai Video.

ZATO ICHI (*Zatoichi*, 2003) Director: Takeshi Kitano. Producers: Masayuki Mori, Tsunehisa Saito [Office Kitano Productions]. Screenplay: Kitano based on a story by Kan Shimozawa. Photography: Katsumi Yanagijima. Lighting: Hitoshi Takaya. Art Direction: Norihiro Isoda. Music: Keiichi Suzuki. Sound: Senji Horiuchi. Editors: Yoshinori Ota, Takeshi Kitano. Cast: "Beat" Takeshi [Kitano] (Zato Ichi), Tadanobu Asano (Gennosuke Hattori), Guadalcanal Taka (Shinkichi), Ittoku Kishibe (Ginzo), Michiyo Okusu (Oume), Yuko Daike (Okinu Naruto), Daigoro Tachibana ("Osei" (Seitaro)), Saburo Ishikura (Ogiya), Yui Natsukawa (Oshino, wife of Gennosuke). Distribution: Shochiku. 116 minutes. Video: Buena Vista.

"THE CRIMSON BAT" SERIES (1969-1970)

CRIMSON BAT, THE BLIND SWORDSWOMAN (*Mekura no Oichi Monogatari Makkana Nagaredori*, 1969), Director: Sadatsugu [Teiji] [Sadaji] Matsuda. Producer: Tsugio Saito. Screenplay: Hajime Takaiwa, Ichiro Miyagawa, Ikuro Suzuki, based on the animated story and character by Teruo Tanashita [credited as source material for the entire series]. Photography: Shintaro Kawasaki [Eastmancolor; Shochiku GrandScope]. Lighting: Hiroyoshi Somekawa. Art Direction: Toshitaka Kurahashi. Music: So [Hajime] Kaburagi. Sound: Taro Takahashi. Editor: Katsumi Kawai. Cast: Yoko Matsuyama, (Oichi), Isamu Nagato (Jubei), Akitake Kono (Yasuke), Jun Tatara (Nihei), Bin Amatsu (Denzo), Chizuko Arai (Omon). Distribution: Shochiku. Release date: March 15, 1969. 88 minutes.

TRAPPED, THE CRIMSON BAT (*Mekurano no Oichi Jigokuhada*, 1969). Director: Sadatsugu [Teiji] [Sadaji] Matsuda. Producer: Tsugio Saito. Screenplay: Hiroo Matsuda, Ikuro Suzuki. Photography: Shintaro Kawasaki [Eastmancolor; Shochiku GrandScope]. Lighting: Hiroyoshi Somekawa. Art Direction: Toshitaka Kurahashi. Music: So [Hajime] Kaburagi. Sound: Taro Takahashi. Editor: Katsumi Kawai. Cast: Yoko Matsuyama (Oichi), Kikko Matsuoka (Oen), Yasunori Irikawa (Mosaku), Toru Abe (Bunzo), Jushiro Konoe (Hanbei). Distribution: Shochiku. Release date: June 21, 1969. 87 minutes.

Isamu Nagato and Yoko Matsuyama in *Crimson Bat, the Blind Swordswoman.*

ZATOICHI (2003) Directed by Takeshi Kitaro.

Watch Out, Crimson Bat!

Raizo Ichikawa in *Band of Assassins* (1963).

WATCH OUT, CRIMSON BAT! (*Mekura no Oichi Midaregasa*, 1969). Director: Hirokazu Ichimura. Screenplay: Kinya Naoi, Kei Hattori. Photography: Masao Kosugi [Eastmancolor; Shochiku GrandScope]. Lighting: Shoichi Motohashi. Art Direction: Koji Uno. Music: Takeo Watanabe. Sound: Yoshiomi Hori. Editor: Iwao Ishii. Cast: Yoko Matsuyama (Oichi), Goro Ibuki (Gennosuke), Jun Hamamura (Tessai), Kiyoko Inoue (Kotoe), Asahi Kurizuka (Sakon). Distribution: Shochiku. Release date: October 1, 1969. 87 minutes.

CRIMSON BAT—OICHI, WANTED, DEAD OR ALIVE (*Mekurano no Oichi Inochi Moraimasu*, 1970). Director: Hirokazu Ichimura. Screenplay: Koji Takada. Photography: Masao Kosugi [Eastmancolor; Shochiku GrandScope]. Art Direction: Chiyoo Umeda. Music: Takeo Watanabe. Sound: Tokio Hiramatsu. Editor: Shizu Osawa. Cast: Yoko Matsuyama (Oichi), Yuki Meguro (Sankuro) Shinji Hotta (Jinbei), Hitoshi Omae (Jokai), Jun Tazaki, Meicho Soganoya (Chobei Kamei), Reiko Oshida (Ohan), Tetsuro Tanba [Tamba] (Hyoei). Distribution: Shochiku. Release date: April 8, 1970. 86 minutes.

"BAND OF ASSASSINS" SERIES (1962-1966)

BAND OF ASSASSINS (*Shinobi no Mono*, 1962). Director: Satsuo Yamamoto. Producer: Masaichi Nagata. Screenplay: Hajime Takaiwa, based on an original story by Tomoyoshi Murayama. Photography: Yasukazu Takemura [DaieiScope]. Lighting: Hiroya Kato. Art Direction: Akira Naito. Music: Chumei [Michiaki] [Hiroaki] Watanabe. Sound: Masahiro Okumura. Editor: Mitsuzo Miyata. Fight Choreography: Shohei Miyauchi. Cast: Raizo Ichikawa (Goemon Ishikawa), Kenzaburo Jo [Tomisaburo Wakayama] (Nobunaga Oda), Shiho Fujimura (Maki), Yunosuke Ito (Sandayu Momochi/Nagato Fujibayashi), Reiko Fujiwara (Hata), Kyoko Kishida (Inone), Chitose Maki (Tamo), Yutaka Nakamura. Distribution: Daiei. Release date: December 1, 1962. 105 minutes. Video: Samurai Video.

BAND OF ASSASSINS CONTINUED (or *THE NINJA II*; *Zoku Shinobi no Mono*, 1963). Directors: Satsuo Yamamoto and Eiji Nishizawa. Producer: Masaichi Nagata. Screenplay: Hajime Takaiwa, based on an original story by Tomoyoshi Murayama. Photography: Senkichiro Takeda [DaieiScope]. Lighting: Reijiro Yamashita. Art Direction: Akira Naito. Music: Chumei [Michiaki] [Hiroaki] Watanabe. Sound: Masao Osumi. Editor: Mitsuzo Miyata. Fight Choreography: Eiichi Kusumoto. Cast: Raizo Ichikawa (Goemon Ishikawa), Kenzaburo Jo [Tomisaburo Wakayama] (Nobunaga Oda), So Yamamura (Mitsuhide Akechi),

Shiho Fujimura (Maki), Mikiko Tsubouchi (Tamame), Eijiro Tono (Hideyoshi Toyotomi). Distribution: Daiei. Release date: August 10, 1963. 93 minutes. Video: Samurai Video.

NEW BAND OF ASSASSINS (or *GOEMON WILL NEVER DIE* or *NINJA 3*; *Shin Shinobi no Mono*, 1963). Director: Kazuo [Issei] Mori. Producer: Masaichi Nagata. Producer: Takeo Ito. Screenplay: Hajime Takaiwa, based on an original story by Tomoyoshi Murayama. Photography: Hiroshi Imai [DaieiScope]. Lighting: Sadaichi Ito. Art Direction: Seiichi Ota. Music: Chumei [Michiaki] [Hiroaki] Watanabe. Sound: Tsuchitaro Hayashi. Editor: Takashi Taniguchi. Fight Choreography: Eiichi Kusumoto. Cast: Raizo Ichikawa (Goemon Ishikawa), Ayako Wakao (Yodogimi), Junichiro Narita (Hidetsugu Toyotomi), Yoshiro Kitahara (Mitsunari Ishida), Masao Mishima (Ieyasu Tokugawa), Eijiro Tono (Hideyoshi Toyotomi). Distribution: Daiei. Release date: December 28, 1963. 86 minutes. Video: Samurai Video.

BAND OF ASSASSINS: SAIZO KIRIGAKURE (or *NINJA 4*; *Shinobi no Mono: Kirigakure Saizo*, 1964). Director: Tokuzo Tanaka. Producers: Takeo Ito, Sadao Zaizen. Screenplay: Hajime Takaiwa. Photography: Senkichiro Takeda [DaieiScope]. Lighting: Genken Nakaoka. Art Direction: Akira Naito. Music: Akira Ifukube. Sound: Yukio Kaihara. Editor: Hiroshi Yamada. Fight Choreography: Eiichi Kusumoto. Cast: Raizo Ichikawa (Saizo Kirigakure), Kenzaburo Jo [Tomisaburo Wakayama] (Yukimura Sanada), Ganjiro Nakamura (Ieyasu Tokugawa), Midori Isomura (Akane), Katsuhiko Kobayashi (Daisuke Sanada), Junichiro Narita (Hideyori Toyotomi). Distribution: Daiei. Release date: July 11, 1964. 87 minutes. Video: Samurai Video.

BAND OF ASSASSINS: SAIZO KIRIGAKURE CONTINUED (or *NINJA 5*; *Shinobi no Mono: Zoku Kirigakure Saizo*, 1964). Director: Kazuo Ikehiro. Producer: Takeo Ito. Screenplay: Hajime Takaiwa. Photography: Chishi Makiura [DaieiScope]. Lighting: Reijiro Yamashita. Art Direction: Yoshinobu Nishioka. Music: Sei [Shigeru] Ikeno. Sound: Iwao Otani. Editor: Toshio Taniguchi. Fight Choreography: Eiichi Kusumoto. Cast: Raizo Ichikawa (Saizo Kirigakure), Yukiko Fuji (Akemi), Shiho Fujimura (Shino), Kenzaburo Jo [Tomisaburo Wakayama] (Yukimura Sanada), Saburo Date (Hanzo Hattori), Eitaro Ozawa [Sakae Ozawa] (Ieyasu Tokugawa), Katsuhiko Kobayashi (Daisuke Sanada). Distribution: Daiei. Release date: December 30, 1964. 91 minutes. Video: Samurai Video.

BAND OF ASSASSINS: IGA MANSION (*Shinobi no Mono: Iga Yashiki*, 1965). Director: Kazuo [Issei] Mori. Producer: Takeo Ito. Screenplay: Kinya Naoi, Kei Hattori. Photography: Hiroshi Imai

[DaieiScope]. Lighting: Sadaichi Ito. Art Direction: Seiichi Ota. Music: Chumei [Michiaki] [Hiroaki] Watanabe. Sound: Tsuchitaro Hayashi. Editor: Toshio Taniguchi. Fight Choreography: Eiichi Kusumoto. Cast: Raizo Ichikawa (Saizo Kirigakure/Saisuke Kirigakure), Kaoru Yachigusa (Lady Yuri-hime/Oran), Isao Yamagata (Matsudaira), Mizuho Suzuki (Shosetsu), Kenji Imai (Chuya), Ryuzo Shimada (Lord Kamon), Ryuji Kita (Yorinobu Tokugawa). Distribution: Daiei. Release date: June 12, 1965. 89 minutes. Video: Samurai Video.

BAND OF ASSASSINS: NEW SAIZO KIRIGAKURE (Shinobi no Mono: Shin Kirigakure Saizo, 1966). Director: Kazuo [Issei] Mori. Producers: Sadao Zaizen, Kazumasa Nakano. Screenplay: Hajime Takaiwa. Photography: Hiroshi Imai [DaieiScope]. Lighting: Reijiro Yamashita. Art Direction: Seiichi Ota. Music: Ichiro Saito. Sound: Iwao Otani. Editor: Toshio Taniguchi. Fight Choreography: Eiichi Kusumoto. Cast: Raizo Ichikawa (Saizo Kirigakure), Shiho Fujimura (Akane), Takahiro Tamura, Asao Uchida. Distribution: Daiei. Release date: February 12, 1966. 87 minutes.

ANOTHER VERSION OF BAND OF ASSASSINS (or THREE ENEMIES; Shinsho Shinobi no Mono, 1966). Director: Kazuo Ikehiro. Producer: Hiroaki Fujii. Screenplay: Hajime Takaiwa. Lighting: Hiroya Kato. Art Direction: Seiichi Ota. Music: Takeo Watanabe. Sound: Yukio Kaihara. Editor: Kanji Suganuma. Fight Choreography: Eiichi Kusumoto. Cast: Raizo Ichikawa (Kojiro Kasumi), Manami Fuji, Yunosuke Ito, Kenjiro Ishiyama. Distribution: Daiei. Release date: December 10, 1966. 91 minutes. Video: Samurai Video.

Pre-1950

THE ABE CLAN (Abe Ichizoku, 1938). Director: Hisatora Kumagai. Screenplay: Hisatora Kumagai, Nobuo Adachi, based on a novella by Ogai Mori. Photography: Hiroshi Suzuki. Music: Shiro Kukai. Cast: Chojuro Kawarazaki (Matajuro), Kanemon Nakamura (Yagobe Abe), Masako Tsutsumi (Osaki), Kosaburo Tachibana, Shotaro Ichikawa, Shinzaburo Ichikawa, Yuko Ichinose, Shimajiro Yamazaki. Distribution: Toho. Release date: March 1, 1938. 115 minutes.

AN ACTOR'S REVENGE [Parts I, II, and III](or *YUKINOJO'S DISGUISE* or *THE REVENGE OF UKENO-JO; Yukinojo Henge Dai Ichi-Hen* [I], 1935; *Yukinojo Henge Dai Ni-Hen* [II], 1935; *Yukinojo Henge Kaiketsu-Hen,* [III], 1936). Director: Teinosuke Kinugasa. Screenplay: Daisuke Ito [I]; Teinosuke Kinugasa [II, III], based on the novel by Otokichi Mikami. Cast: Chojiro Hayashi [Kazuo Hasegawa] (Yukinojo). Distribution: Shochiku. Release dates: June 27, 1935 [I]; October 1, 1935 [II]; January 15, 1936 [III]. 97 minutes [I], 97 minutes [II], 111 minutes [III].

BACKWARD CURRENT (Gyakuryu, 1924). Director: Buntaro Futagawa. Screenplay: Rohukei Susukita. Photography: Saichiro Hashimoto. Cast: Tsumasaburo Bando (Nanjo), Kozaburo Kataoka (Genzaburo), Kanzaburo Arashi (Kurahashi), Teruko Makino (Kurahashi's daughter), Reiko Shimizu (Nanjo's sister), Masue Bessho (Nanjo's mother), Michisaburo Segawa (Yamamuro), Manroku Otani (Kuma). Distribution: ToaEiga/Tojien/Makino. Release date: September 26, 1924. 21 minutes.

BLOOD SPLATTERED TAKADANOBABA (Chikemuri Taka-danobaba, 1928). Director/Screenplay: Daisuke Ito. Photography: Hiromitsu Karasawa. Cast: Denjiro Okochi (Yasubei Nakayama), Enichiro Jitsukawa (Yasubei's uncle Rokuroemon Sugano), Harue Ichikawa (maidservant), Kan Togi [Junzaburo Ban] (townsman). Distribution: Nikkatsu Kyoto. Release date: March 15, 1928.

CASTLE OF WIND AND CLOUDS (Fuun Joshi, 1928). Director: Toko Yamazaki. Producer: Teinosuke Kinugasa [Kinugasa Eiga Renmei]. Screenplay: Tetsuro Hoshi. Cast: Chojiro Hayashi [Kazuo

Hasegawa] (Shinpachi), Akiko Chihaya (Chigusa), Ippei Soma (Samonnosuke), Soroku Kazama, Yoshie Nakagawa. Distribution: Shochiku [Shimokamo Studio Kyoto]. Release date: February 10, 1928. 76 minutes.

CHAMPION OF REVENGE (Adauchi Senshu, 1931). Director: Tomu Uchida. Cast: Denjiro Okochi, Isuzu Yamada. Distribution: Nikkatsu. Release date: December 18, 1931.

CHOKON (1926). Director/Screenplay: Daisuke Ito. Photography: Rokuzo Watarai. Cast: Denjiro Okochi, Yuzuru Kume, Utagoro Onoe, Yayoi Kawakami. Distribution: Nikkatsu. Release date: November 15, 1926. 12 minutes [fragment only].

CHUJI FROM KUNISADA [Parts I, II, and III], *I: CHUJI RETURNS HOME (Kunisada Chuji Tabi to Kokyo no Maki,* 1933). Director: Hiroshi Inagaki. Screenplay: Hiroshi Inagaki, based on a story by Kan Shimozawa. Photography: Hideo Ishimoto. Cast: Chiezo Kataoka (Chuji), Takashi Ogawa, Michisaburo Segawa, Ryosuke Kagawa, Seinosuke Hayashi. Distribution: Nikkatsu. Release date: March 15, 1933.

II: CHUJI WANDERS AROUND (Kunisada Chuji Ruro Tenpen no Maki, 1933). Director: Hiroshi Inagaki. Screenplay: Hiroshi Inagaki, based on a story by Kan Shimozawa. Photography: Hideo Ishimoto. Cast: Chiezo Kataoka (Chuji), Michisaburo Segawa, Ryosuke Kagawa, Takeo Yano, Kunitaro Bando. Distribution: Nikkatsu. Release date: June 1, 1933.

III: CHUJI ON MT. AKAGI (Kunisada Chuji Hareru Akagi no Maki, 1933). Director: Hiroshi Inagaki. Screenplay: Itaro Yamagami, based on a story by Kan Shimozawa. Photography: Hideo Ishimoto. Cast: Chiezo Kataoka (Chuji), Michisaburo Segawa, Seinosuke Hayashi, Ryosuke Kagawa, Takeo Yano. Distribution: Nikkatsu. Release date: October 12, 1933.

CHUSHINGURA (Chushingura: Ninjo-Hen, Fukushu-Hen, 1934). Director: Daisuke Ito. Screenplay: Mansaku Itami. Music: Goro Nishi. Cast: Denjiro Okochi, Haruo Tanaka, Togo Yamamoto, Yonosuke Toba. Distribution: Nikkatsu. Release date: May 17, 1934.

CHUSHINGURA: STORY OF HEAVEN, STORY OF EARTH (Chushingura: Ten no Maki, Chi no Maki, 1938). Director: Masahiro Makino. Screenplay: Itaro Yamagami. Photography: Hideo Ishimoto. Music: Goro Nishi. Sound: Toshio Nakamura, Yukio Kaihara. Cast: Chiezo Kataoka, Tsumasaburo Bando, Kanjuro Arashi [Chozaburo Arashi], Ryunosuke Tsukigata, Kikutaro Onoe. Distribution: Nikkatsu. Release date: March 1, 1938.

CHUSHINGURA [Parts I and II] (*Chushingura Zenpen* [I], 1939; *Chushingura Kohen* [II], 1939). Directors: Eisuke Takizawa [I]; Kajiro Yamamoto [II]. Producers: Nobuyoshi Morita [I]; Nobuo Aoyagi [II]. Screenplay: Shintaro Mimura. Photography: Jun Yasumoto [I]; Hiromitsu Karasawa [II]. Music: Nobuo Iida. Art Direction: Kohei Shima. Sound: Kenji Murayama [II]. Cast: Denjiro Okochi (Kuranosuke Oishi), Kazuo Hasegawa [Chojiro Hayashi] (Lord Takumi Asano), Yataro Kurokawa (Kinemon Okano), Ichiro Tsukida (Yogoro Kanzaki), Setsuko Hara (Oteru), Isuzu Yamada (Okaru), Hideko Takamine (Aguri), Hisako Yamane (Ofumi). Distribution: Toho. Release date: Both parts on April 21, 1939. 79 minutes [I], 89 minutes [II].

A COLOR PRINT OF EDO (Nishikie Edo Sugata Hatamoto to Machiyakko, 1939). Director: Kazuo [Issei] Mori. Screenplay: Kenji Hata. Cast: Utaemon Ichikawa, Shinpachiro Asaka, Taisuke Matsumoto. Distribution: Shinko. Release date: March 1, 1939. 68 minutes.

THE CRIMSON BAT [Parts I and II] (*Beni Komori Dai Ichi-Hen* [I], 1931; and *Beni Komori Kohen* [II], 1931). Director: Tsuruhiko Tanaka. Screenplay: Tsuneo Matsumoto, based on the novel by Shin Hasegawa. Photography: Seishi Tanimoto. Cast: Ryuzaburo

Mitsuoka (Chohachiro Tonami), Motoharu Isokawa, Hazaemon Bando, Koichi Katsuragi, Shinpachiro Asaka. Distribution: Nikkatsu. Release dates: March 6, 1931 [I]; May 1, 1931 [II].

DAIBOSATSU PASS PART I (*Daibosatsu Toge Dai Ichi Hen: Kogen Itto Ryu no Maki*, 1935). Director: Hiroshi Inagaki. Screenplay: Shintaro Mimura, Torao Takeda, Hiroshi Inagaki, based on a novel by Kaizan Nakazato. Music: Goro Nishi. Cast: Denjiro Okochi (Ryunosuke Tsukue), Kiyoshi Sawada (Hyoma Utsugi), Kunitaro Sawamura, Kikutaro Onoe, Yonosuke Toba (Yohachi), Reizaburo Yamamoto (Shuzen Kamio), Jushiro Kobayashi, Soji Kiyokawa (Toshizo Hijikita). Distribution: Nikkatsu. Release date: November 15, 1935. 136 minutes.

DAIBOSATSU PASS PART II (*Daibosatsu Toge: Suzuka-Yama no Maki, Mibu Shimabara no Maki*, 1936). Director: Hiroshi Inagaki. Screenplay: Shintaro Mimura, Hiroshi Inagaki, based on a novel by Kaizan Nakazato. Music: Goro Nishi, Shiro Fukai. Cast: Denjiro Okochi (Ryunosuke Tsukue), Kiyoshi Sawada (Hyoma Utsugi), Yataro Kurokawa (Bunnojo Utsugi), Joji Oka (Toranosuke Shimada), Zenichiro Kito, Yonosuke Toba (Yohachi), Kikutaro Onoe, Soji Kiyokawa (Toshizo Hijikita), Kobunji Ichikawa (Kamo Serizawa), Momonosuke Ichikawa, Kichijiro Ueda (Shinbei Tanaka), Jushiro Kobayashi, Koji Nakata (Isami Kondo). Distribution: Nikkatsu. Release date: April 15, 1936. 110 minutes.

DUEL AT TAKADANOBABA (*Chikemuri Takadanobaba*, 1937). Directors: Hiroshi Inagaki, Masahiro Makino. Producer: Masahiro Makino. Screenplay: Tozo Maki. Photography: Hideo Ishimoto, Rokusaburo Mitsui. Music: Nakaba Takahashi. Sound: Yukio Kaihara. Cast: Tsumasaburo Bando (Yasubei Nakayama), Tokumaro Dan (Segawa), Komako Hara (Osai), Shunzaburo Iba (Tengan), Momonosuke Ichikawa (Kumako), Ryosuke Kagawa (Rokuzaemon Sugano), Chiyoko Okura (Otae), Takashi Shimura. Distribution: Nikkatsu. Release date: December 31, 1937. 50 minutes. Alternate English title: *Blood Spattered at Takadanobaba.*

THE 47 RONIN [Parts I and II] (or *THE LOYAL 47 RONIN*; *Chushingura Zenpen: Akokyo no Maki* [I], 1932; *Chushingura Kohen: Edo no Maki* [II], 1932). Director/Screenplay: Teinosuke Kinugasa. Cast: Chojiro Hayashi [Kazuo Hasegawa], Utaemon Ichikawa, Kinuyo Tanaka. Distribution: Shochiku. Release dates: Both parts on December 1, 1932. 109 minutes [I], 103 minutes [II].

THE 47 RONIN [Parts I and II] (or *THE LOYAL 47 RONIN OF THE GENROKU ERA* or *CHUSHINGURA*; *Genroku Chushingura Zenpen* [I], 1941; *Genroku Chushingura Kohen* [II], 1942). Director: Kenji Mizoguchi. Producer: Shintaro Shirai [Koa Eiga]. Screenplay: Kenichiro Hara, Yoshikata Yoda, based on the play by Seika Mayama. Photography: Kohei Sugiyama. Art Direction: Hiroshi Mizutani. Music: Shiro Fukai. Editor: Takako Kuji. Sound: Hidekata Sasaki. Cast: Chojuro Kawarazaki (Kuranosuke Oishi), Kanemon Nakamura (Sukeemon Tomimori), Kunitaro Kawarazaki (Jurozaemon Isogai), Kikunojo Segawa, Kikunosuke Ichikawa, Yoshisaburo Arashi (Lord Takumi Asano), Ryotaro Kawanami, Hiroshi Ouchi, Isamu Kosugi (Denpachiro Okado), Utaemon Ichikawa (Tsunatoyo Tokugawa), Masao Shimizu, Kazutoyo Mimasu (Kozukenosuke Kira), Mitsuko Mirura (Yozeiin, Asano's wife), Choemon Bando (Sozaemon Hara), Joji Kaieda (Yasubei Horibe), Mitsusaburo Ramon (Tokubei Iseki), Shizue Yamagishi (Oriku); [II only] Seizaburo Kawazu (Lord Ecchu Hosokawa), Mieko Takamine (Omino, Isogai's fiancée), Fumiko Yamaji (Okiyo, Tomimori's sister). Distribution: Shochiku. Release dates: December 3, 1941 [I]; February 11, 1942 [II]. 112 minutes [I]; 111 minutes [II]. Video: Home Vision VHS/Image DVD.

THE GAY MASQUERADE (*Benten Kozo*, 1928). Director: Teinosuke Kinugasa. Cast: Chojiro Hayashi [Kazuo Hasegawa] (Benten), Ippei Soma, Akiko Chihaya. Distribution: Shochiku. Release date: January 5, 1928.

GHOST CAT OF NABESHIMA (*Nabeshima Kaibyo-den,* 1949). Director: Kunio Watanabe. Screenplay: Shintaro Mimura. Cast: Denjiro Okochi, Michiyo Kogure, Yataro Kurokawa, Akira Nakamura. Distribution: Toho. Release date: August 23, 1949. 83 minutes.

GHOST STORY OF YOTSUYA [Parts I and II] (*Yotsuya Kaidan Zenpen* [I], 1949; *Yotsuya Kaidan Kohen* [II], 1949). Director: Keisuke Kinoshita. Screenplay: Eijiro Hisaita, based on a novel by Nanboku Tsuruya. Cast: Kinuyo Tanaka, Ken Uehara, Haruko Sugimura, Keiji Sada. Distribution: Shochiku. Release dates: July 5, 1949 [I]; July 16, 1949 [II]. 85 minutes

THE HAWK OF THE NORTH (*Dokuganryu Masamune*, 1942). Director: Hiroshi Inagaki. Screenplay: Hiroshi Inagaki, based on the novel by Yojiro Ishizaka. Photography: Hideo Ishimoto. Music: Goro Nishi. Cast: Chiezo Kataoka, Ryunosuke Tsukigata, Haruyo Ichikawa, Michitaro Mizushima. Distribution: Daiei. Release date: July 2, 1942. 83 minutes.

Kinnosuke Nakamura in *The Hawk of the North*.

THE FAMOUS SWORD BIJOMARU (*Meito Bijomaru*, 1945). Director: Kenji Mizoguchi. Producer: Masahiro Makino. Screenplay: Matsutaro Kawaguchi. Cast: Shotaro Hanayagi (Kiyone Sakurai), Kan Ishii (Kiyotsugu), Eijiro Yanagi (Kiyohide), Ichijiro Oya (Kozaemon Onoda), Isuzu Yamada (Sasae Onoda). Distribution: Shochiku. Release date: February 8, 1945. 67 minutes. Alternate English Titles: *The Famous Sword, The Sword.*

HYAKUMAN RYO HIBUN [Parts I, II and III] (*Hyakuman Ryo Hibun Dai Ichi-Hen* [I], 1927; *Hyakuman Ryo Hibun Dai Ni-Hen* [II], 1927; *Hyakuman Ryo Hibun Dai Saishu-Hen* [III], 1927). Director: Shozo Makino. Cast: Chozaburo Arashi [Kanjuro Arashi]. Release Dates: October 28, 1927 [I]; November 18, 1927 [II]; December 1, 1927 [III]. 124 minutes [all parts].

THE IDLE VASSAL (*Hatamoto Taikutsu Otoko*, 1930). Director/Screenplay: Takuji Furumi, based on a story by Mitsuzo Sasaki. Cast: Utaemon Ichikawa, Michiko Oe, Ryozo Takei. Distribution: Shochiku. Release date: October 17, 1930. 20 minutes.

THE JOBLESS SAMURAI [Parts I, _IIa, IIb, and III] (or STREET OF MASTERLESS SAMURAI or SAMURAI TOWN; Ronin-gai Dai Ichi-Wa: Utsukushiki Emono [I], 1928; Ronin-gai Dai Ni-Wa: Gakuya Buro Dai Ichi-Hen [IIa], 1929; Ronin-gai Dai Ni-Wa: Gakuya Buro Kaiketsu-Hen [IIb], 1929; Ronin-gai Dai San-Wa: Tsukareta Hitobito [III], 1929). Director: Masahiro Makino. Screenplay: Itaro Yamagami. Photography: Minoru [Shigeto] Miki. Cast: Komei Minami, Toichiro Negishi, Umeko Obayashi, Tsuyako Okajima, Juro Tanizaki, Hiroshi Tsumura [II], Toroku Makino [II]. Distribution: Makino. Release dates: October 20, 1928 [I]; January 15, 1929 [IIa]; February 8, 1929 [IIb]; November 15, 1929 [III]. [II] 49 minutes [Part I is lost]

JOURNEY OF A THOUSAND AND ONE NIGHTS (Matatabi Senichiya, 1936). Director: Hiroshi Inagaki. Screenplay: Shintaro Mimura. Photography: Jun Yasumoto. Music: Goro Nishi. Cast: Kanemon Nakamura, Chojuro Kawarazaki, Shizue Yamagishi, Shotaro Ichikawa, Tsuruzo Nakamura. Distribution: Nikkatsu. Release date: October 1, 1936. 87 minutes.

KURAMA TENGU [Parts I and II] (Kurama Tengu [I], 1928; Kurama Tengu Kyofu Jidai [II], 1928). Director: Teppei Yamaguchi. Screenplay: Fujio Kimura, based on a story by Jiro Osaragi. Cast: Kanjuro Arashi [Chozaburo Arashi] (Tengu), Reizaburo Yamamoto (Isami Kondo), Kunie Gomi. Release dates: July 12, 1928 [I]; November 30, 1928 [II]. 75 minutes [both parts].

KURAMA TENGU: STORY OF THE KAKUBEI LION (Kurama Tengu: Kakubei Jishi no Maki, 1938). Directors: Masahiro Makino, Sadatsugu [Teiji] [Sadaji] Matsuda. Screenplay: Yoshitake Hisa, based on a story by Jiro Osaragi. Photography: Kazuo Miyagawa. Music: Nakaba Takahashi. Cast: Kanjuro Arashi [Chozaburo Arashi] (Tengu), Kensaku Hara, Goro Kawabe, Komako Hara, Kunitaro Sawamura, Takashi Shimura. Distribution: Nikkatsu. Release date: March 15, 1938.

KUTSUKAKE TOKIJIRO (1929). Director: Kichiro Tsuji. Screenplay based on a story by Shin Hasegawa. Cast: Denjiro Okochi (Tokijiro), Yoneko Sakai, Koichi Katsuragi. Distribution: Nikkatsu. Release date: June 14, 1929. 63 minutes.

THE LAST DAYS OF EDO (Edo Saigo no Hi, 1941). Director: Hiroshi Inagaki. Screenplay: Shoichi Wada, Hiroshi Inagaki, based on a story by Genjiro Yoshida. Photography: Hideo Ishimoto. Lighting: Kazuo Nishimura. Music: Goro Nishi. Sound: Toshiro Sasaki. Editor: Shigeo Nishida. Cast: Tsumasaburo Bando, Kensaku Hara, Ryosuke Kagawa, Takashi Shimura. Distribution: Nikkatsu. Release date: November 28, 1941. 95 minutes.

THE LIFE OF MATSU THE UNTAMED (Muhomatsu no Issho, 1943). Director: Hiroshi Inagaki. Producer: Yuko Nakaizumi. Screenplay: Mansaku Itami, based on a story by Shunsaku Iwashita. Photography: Kazuo Miyagawa. Lighting: Yasunosuke Okuno. Music: Goro Nishi. Sound: Toshiro Sasaki. Editor: Shigeo Nishida. Cast: Tsumasaburo Bando, Ryunosuke Tsukigata, Kyoji Sugi. Distribution: Daiei. Release date: October 28, 1943. 80 minutes.

MAGISTRATE TATTOO (Irezumi Hangan, 1933). Director: Taizo Fuyushima. Screenplay: Fujio Kimura, based on a story by Shin Hasegawa. Cast: Chojiro Hayashi [Kazuo Hasegawa], Toshiko Iizuka, Hisae Inoue. Distribution: Shochiku. Release date: June 1, 1933. 90 minutes.

MATAEMON, MASTER SWORDSMAN (Kensei Araki Mataemon, 1935). Director: Kumahiko Nishina. Cast: Mitsusaburo Ramon, Saemon Kataoka, Kyoko Sakurai. Distribution: Kyokuto Eiga. Release date: May 30, 1935. 50 minutes.

MITO KOMON: I. THE STORY OF RAIKUNITSUGU; II. THE SECRET LETTER; and III. THE BLOODY SWORDS (Mito Komon Raikunitsugu no Maki [I], 1934; Mito Komon Missho no Maki [II], 1935; Mito Komon Ketsujin no Maki [III], 1935). Directors: Ryohei Arai. Screenplay: Sadao Yamanaka, based on a story by Jiro Osaragi. Cast: Denjiro Okochi (Mitsukuni Mito). Release dates: November 1, 1934 [I]; January 15, 1935 [II]; April 3, 1935 [III]. 179 minutes [all parts].

MIYAMOTO MUSASHI (1944). Director: Kenji Mizoguchi. Producer: Masahiro Makino. Screenplay: Matsutaru Kawaguchi, based on a story by Kan Kikuchi. Photography: Shigeto [Minoru] Miki. Fight Choreography: Hiromasa Takano. Cast: Chojuro Kawarazaki (Miyamoto Musashi), Kanemon Nakamura (Kojiro Sasaki), Kigoro Ikushima (Genichiro Nonomiya), Kinuyo Tanaka (Shinobu Nonomiya). Distribution: Shochiku. Release date: December 28, 1944. 55 minutes. Alternate English Title: The Swordsman.

MIYAMOTO MUSASHI CHI NO MAKI (1936). Director: Eisuke Takizawa. Screenplay: Kinpachi Kajiwara, based on the novel "Miyamoto Musashi" by Eiji Yoshikawa. Cast: Kanjiro Arashi (Musashi Miyamoto), Shosaku Sugiyama (Matahachi Hon'iden), Shizuko Mori (Otsu), Mineko Mori (Akemi). Distribution: Shinko. Release date: May 16, 1936.

MIYAMOTO MUSASHI CHI NO MAKI (1937). Director: Jun Ozaki. Screenplay: Hiroshi Makimoto, based on the novel "Miyamoto Musashi" by Eiji Yoshikawa. Cast: Chiezo Kataoka (Musashi Miyamoto), Kensaku Hara (Matahachi Hon'iden), Yukiko Todoroki (Otsu), Chiyoko Okura (Akemi). Distribution: Nikkatsu. Release date: June 10, 1937.

MIYAMOTO MUSASHI FU NO MAKI (1937). Screenplay: Hiroshi Makimoto, based on the novel "Miyamoto Musashi" by Eiji Yoshikawa. Cast: Yataro Kurokawa (Musashi Miyamoto), Soji Kiyokawa (Matahachi Hon'iden), Mitsuko Takao (Otsu), Senkichi Omura (Jotaro). Distribution: Toho. Release date: June 11, 1937. 78 minutes.

MUSASHI MIYAMOTO: DUEL AT ICHIJOJI TEMPLE (Miyamoto Musashi: Ichijoji no Ketto, 1942). Director: Hiroshi Inagaki. Screenplay: Hiroshi Inagaki, based on the novel "Miyamoto Musashi" by Eiji Yoshikawa. Photography: Hideo Ishimoto. Music: Goro Nishi. Sound: Toshio Nakamura, Toshiro Sasaki. Editor: Shigeo Nishida. Fight Choreography: Reijiro Adachi. Cast: Chiezo Kataoka (Musashi Miyamoto), Tomoemon Otani (Kojiro Sasaki), Chikako Miyagi (Otsu), Sannosuke Fujikawa (Nikkan), Shinpachiro Asaka (Seijuro Yoshioka), Kahoru Futaba, Ryosuke Kagawa, Kajo Onoe, Takashi Shimura, Goro Kawabe, Ikko Okuni, Kichijiro Ueda, Jotaro Togami (Jurozaemon Miike), Saganji Okawara, Tominosuke Hayama, Teruo Shimada (Genjiro Mibu), Hidemichi Ishikawa, Kiyoshi Kasuga, Haruyo Ichikawa (Yoshino Dayu), Otome Tsukimiya. Distribution: Nikkatsu. Release date: March 25, 1942.

THE NAUGHTY ROGUE (Ojo-Kichisa, 1927). Director: Teinosuke Kinugasa. Screenplay: Taizo Fuyushima, based on a story by Nanboku Kema. Photography: Kohei Sugiyama. Cast: Chojiro Hayashi [Kazuo Hasegawa], Sonosuke Azaka, Tetsu Tsuboi. Distribution: Shochiku. Release date: April 1, 1927.

NEW GHOST STORY OF YOTSUYA (Shinpan Yotsuya Kaidan, 1928). Director/Screenplay: Daisuke Ito. Photography: Hiromitsu Karasawa. Cast: Taisuke Matsumoto, Koichi Katsuragi, Naoe Fushimi. Distribution: Nikkatsu. Release date: July 6, 1928.

NEW VERSIONS OF OOKA'S TRIAL [Parts I, II and III] (Shinpan Ooka Seidan Dai Ichi-Hen [I], 1928; Shinpan Ooka Seidan Dai Ni-Hen [II], 1928; Shinpan Ooka Seidan Dai San-Hen Kaiketsu-Hen [III], 1928). Director/Screenplay: Daisuke Ito, based on a novel by Fubo Hayashi [Umitaro Hasegawa]. Cast: Denjiro Okochi (Sazen Tange/Lord Echizen Ooka), Miharu Ito. Distribution: Nikkatsu. Release dates: May 31, 1928 [I]; June 8, 1928 [II]; August 17, 1928 [III].

NEZUMI-KOZO JIROKICHI [Parts I and II] (*Nezumi-Kozo Jirokichi Zenpen* [I], 1931; *Nezumi-Kozo Jirokichi Kohen* [II], 1932). Director/Screenplay: Toichiro Negishi. Cast: Ryutaro Aoyagi, Kunie Gomi, Ayako Chiyoda, Saburo Kumoi. Release dates: December 31, 1931 [I]; January 5, 1932 [II].

THE NOBLE THIEF OF EDO [Parts I and II] (*Edo Kaizokuden Kageboshi Zenpen* [I], 1925; *Edo Kaizokuden Kageboshi Kohen* [II], 1925). Director: Buntaro Futagawa. Screenplay: Rokuhei Susukita. Cast: Tsumasaburo Bando, Shinpei Takagi, Ryunosuke Tsukigata. Release dates: March 6, 1925 [I]; March 13, 1925 [II].

OATSURAE JIROKICHI GOSHI (1931). Director/Screenplay: Daisuke Ito, based on the novel by Eiji Yoshikawa. Photography: Hiromitsu Karasawa. Cast: Denjiro Okochi (Jirokichi), Naoe Fushimi (Osen), Nobuko Fushimi (Okino), Reizaburo Yamamoto, Minoru Takase. Distribution: Nikkatsu. Release Date: December 31, 1931. 59 minutes.

OYUKI THE MADONNA (*Maria no Oyuki*, 1935). Director: Kenji Mizoguchi. Screenplay: Matsutaro Kawaguchi, Tatsunosuke Takashima, based on the story "Boule de Suif" by Guy de Maupassant. Photography: Minoru [Shigeto] Miki. Art Direction: Shichiro Nishi, Gonshiro Saito. Music: Koichi Takagi. Editor: Tokichi Ishimoto. Sound: Junichi Murota. Cast: Isuzu Yamada (Oyuki), Komako Hara (Okin), Yoshisuke Koizumi (Gisuke), Eiji Nakano (Kensuke Sadowara), Daijiro Natsukawa (General Shingo Asakura), Toichiro Negishi (Sobei Gonda), Keiji Oizumi (Yoemon Kurachi, Ochie's father), Shin Shibata (Keishiro Yokoi), Shizuko Takizawa (Osei Gonda), Tadashi Torii (Colonel), Yoko Umemura (Michiko Yokoi), Kinue Utagawa (Ochie). Distribution: Shochiku. Release date: May 30, 1935. 78 minutes.

THE PALANQUIN (*Dochu Sugoroku Kago*, 1927). Director: Teinosuke Kinugasa. Screenplay: Shintaro Mimura. Photography: Kohei Sugiyama. Cast: Soroku Kazama, Tetsu Tsuboi, Misao Seki, Akiko Chihaya. Distribution: Shochiku. Release date: September 15, 1927.

THE PALTRY RONIN FORCES HIS WAY IN (*Suronin Makaritoru*, 1947). Director: Daisuke Ito. Screenplay: Fuji Yahiro. Photography: Shintaro Kawasaki. Music: Goro Nishi. Cast: Tsumasaburo Bando, Ryutaro Otomo, Kusuo Abe, Akihiko Katayama. Distribution: Daiei. Release date: October 28, 1947. 80 minutes.

THE PEERLESS PATRIOT (*Kokushi Muso*, 1932). Director/Screenplay: Mansaku Itami. Producer: Chiezo Kataoka. Photography: Hideo Ishimoto. Cast: Chiezo Kataoka, Isuzu Yamada, Michisaburo Segawa, Ryosuke Kagawa, Junzaburo Ban [Kan Togi]. Distribution: Nikkatsu. Release date: January 14, 1932.

ROKUSUKE OF KEYA VILLAGE (*Keyamura Rokusuke*, 1927). Director: Tamizo Ishida. Photography: Shuichi Otsuka. Cast: Ryuzaburo Mitsuoka, Takeo Kusunoki, Komako Hara. Distribution: ToaEiga. Release date: January 4, 1927. 49 minutes.

THE SAGA OF THE VAGABONDS [Parts I and II] (*Sengoku Gunto-den Zenpen Toraokami* [I], 1937; *Sengoku Gunto-den Kohen Akatsuki no Zenshin* [II], 1937). Director: Eisuke Takizawa. Screenplay: Kinpachi Kajiwara, based on a story by Juro Miyoshi. Photography: Hiromitsu Karasawa. Art Direction: Morio [Takeo] Kita. Music: Kosaku Yamada. Cast: Chojuro Kawarazaki, Shizue Yamagishi, Kanemon Nakamura, Kunitaro Kawarazaki, Tsuruzo Nakamura, Sachiko Chiba. Distribution: Toho Eiga. Release dates: February 11, 1937 [I]; February 20, 1937 [II]. 74 minutes [I], 67 minutes [II].

SAKAMOTO RYOMA (1928). Director: Yoshiro Edamasa. Screenplay: Taizo Fuyushima. Photography: Tatsuo Tomonari. Cast: Tsumasaburo Bando, Shizuko Mori, Kensaku Haruji. Distribution: Shochiku. Release date: May 18, 1928.

SAMURAI PART 1 AND PART 2 (*Miyamoto Musashi Dai Ichibu Kusawake no Hitobito Dai Nibu Eitatsu no Mon*, 1940). Director: Hiroshi Inagaki. Screenplay: Hiroshi Inagaki, Hiroshi Makimoto,

based on the novel *"Miyamoto Musashi"* by Eiji Yoshikawa. Photography: Kazuo Miyagawa. Music: Goro Nishi. Cast: Chiezo Kataoka (Musashi Miyamoto), Ryunosuke Tsukigata (Kojiro Sasaki), Goro Kawabe, Kobunji Ichikawa (Tarozaemon Kobayashi), Chikako Miyagi (Otsu), Chiyoko Okura (Omitsu), Otome Tsukimiya (Akemi), Taeko Hira (Otsuru), Michisaburo Segawa (Juro), Ryosuke Kagawa (Sado Nagaoka), Takashi Shimura (Kakubei Iwama), Shojiro Ichikawa, Kikutaro Onoe (Gonnosuke Muso), Kunitaro Sawamura (Tadatoshi Hosokawa), Kensaku Hara (Matahachi Hon'iden), Kenji Susukida (Tajima Yagyu), Masao Takahashi (Goroji Okatani), Akira Sera, Takashi Ogawa, Kajo Onoe, Kichijiro Ueda (Kumagoro), Katsuhiko Isokawa, Kotaro Nire. Distribution: Nikkatsu. Release date: March 31, 1940.

SAMURAI PART 3 (*Miyamoto Musashi Dai Sanbu Kenshin Ichiro*, 1940). Director: Hiroshi Inagaki. Screenplay: Hiroshi Inagaki, Hiroshi Makimoto, based on the novel *"Miyamoto Musashi"* by Eiji Yoshikawa. Photography: Kazuo Miyagawa. Music: Goro Nishi. Cast: Chiezo Kataoka (Musashi Miyamoto), Goro Kawabe, Kobunji Ichikawa (Tarozaemon Kobayashi), Michisaburo Segawa (Juro), Ryosuke Kagawa (Sado Nagaoka), Takashi Shimura (Kakubei Iwama), Shojiro Ichikawa, Kajo Onoe, Tokumaro Dan (Sasuke), Kichijiro Ueda (Kumagoro), Katsuhiko Isokawa, Sannosuke Fujikawa, Chikako Miyagi (Otsu), Chiyoko Okura (Omitsu), Otome Tsukimiya (Akemi), Ryunosuke Tsukigata (Kojiro Sasaki), Kikutaro Onoe (Gonnosuke Muso), Kunitaro Sawamura (Tadatoshi Hosokawa), Kensaku Hara (Matahachi Hon'iden), Kenji Susukida (Tajima Yagyu), Masao Takahashi (Goroji Okatani), Akira Sera, Takashi Ogawa. Distribution: Nikkatsu. Release date: April 18, 1940. 68 minutes.

A SAMURAI'S CAREER (1929). Director: Hiroshi Inagaki.

THE SERPENT (*Orochi*, 1925). Director: Buntaro Futagawa. Screenplay: Rokuhei Susukita. Photography: Seizo Ishino. Cast: Tsumasaburo Bando (Heizaburo), Shizuko Mori (Ochiyo), Utako Tamaki (Namie). Distribution: Makino. Release date: November 20, 1925.

SHINSENGUMI (1937). Director: Sotoji Kimura. Screenplay by: Tomoyoshi Murayama. Photography: Hiroshi Suzuki. Art Direction: Kazuo Kubo. Sound: Shigeharu Yasue. Editor: Koichi Iwashita. Cast: Chojuro Kawarazaki, Kanemon Nakamura, Yoshisaburo Arashi, Shizue Yamagishi. Release date: October 11, 1937.

THE SURVIVING BAND OF SAMURAI (*Ikinokotta Shinsengumi*, 1932). Director/Screenplay: Teinosuke Kinugasa. Photography: Kohei Sugiyama. Cast: Kotaro Bando, Akiko Chihaya, Masao Hori. Distribution: Shochiku. Release date: May 20, 1932.

A TALE OF ARCHERY FROM SANJUSANGENDO (*Sanjusangendo Toshiya Monogatari*, 1945). Director: Mikio Naruse. Screenplay: Hideo Oguni. Photography: Hiroshi Suzuki. Cast: Kazuo Hasegawa [Chojiro Hayashi], Kinuyo Tanaka, Sensho Ichikawa. Distribution: Toho. Release date: June 28, 1945. 77 minutes.

TANGE SAZEN [Parts I and II] (*Tange Sazen Dai Ichi-Hen* [I], 1933; *Tange Sazen Kengeki no Maki* [II], 1934). Director/Screenplay: Daisuke Ito, based on a novel by Fubo Hayashi [Umitaro Hasegawa]. Cast: Denjiro Okochi (Sazen Tange), Kunitaro Sawamura (Genzaburo Yagyu), Isuzu Yamada. Distribution: Nikkatsu. Release dates: November 15, 1933 [I]; March 29, 1934 [II].

TANGE SAZEN [Parts I, II, and III] (*Tange Sazen Nikko no Maki* [I], 1936; *Tange Sazen Aizo Maken-Hen* [II], 1937; *Tange Sazen Kanketsu Hoko-Hen* [III], 1937). Director: Kunio Watanabe. Screenplay: Itaro Yamagami, based on a novel by Fubo Hayashi [Umitaro Hasegawa]. Music: Yoshinobu Shiraki. Cast: Denjiro Okochi (Sazen Tange/Lord Echizen Ooka), Yataro Kurokawa (Genzaburo Yagyu). Distribution: Nikkatsu. Release dates: December 31, 1936 [I]; April 1, 1937 [II]; April 30, 1937 [III].

TANGE SAZEN AND THE POT WORTH A MILLION RYO (*Tange Sazen Yowa: Hyakuman Ryo no Tsubo*, 1935). Director:

Sadao Yamanaka. Screenplay: Shintaro Mimura, based on a novel by Fubo Hayashi [Umitaro Hasegawa]. Photography: Jun Yasumoto. Cast: Denjiro Okochi (Sazen Tange), Kiyozo (Ofuji), Kunitaro Sawamura (Genzaburo Yagyu), Reizaburo Yamamoto (Yokichi), Minoru Takase (Shigeju), Soji Kiyokawa (Shichibei), Ranko Hanai (Ogino). Distribution: Nikkatsu. Release date: June 15, 1935. 91 minutes.

THE TRAVEL DIARIES OF CHUJI [Parts I, II and III] (*Kunisada Chuji Tabi Nikki Koshu Tate Hen* [I], 1927; *Kunisada Chuji Tabi Nikki Shinshu Kessho Hen* [II], 1927; *Kunisada Chuji Tabi Nikki Goyo Hen* [III], 1927). Director/Screenplay: Daisuke Ito. Photography: Takeo Okusaka [I], Rokuzo Watarai [II], Hiromitsu Karasawa [II]. Cast: Denjiro Okochi (Chuji) [I,II,III], Hideo Nakamura [II], Kichiji Nakamura [II,III], Seinosuke Sakamoto [II,III]; Naoe Fushimi (Oshina) [III], Ranko Sawa [III], Motoharu Isokawa [III], Eiji Murakami [III], Nobuko Akizuki [III], Kajo Onoe [III], Koka Nakamura [III], Mononosuke Ichikawa [III]. Distribution: Nikkatsu. Release dates: March 10, 1927 [I]; August 14, 1927 [II]; December 27, 1927 [III]. 94 minutes [Surviving fragments of II and III].

THE TRUE STORY OF CHUSHINGURA (*Chukon Giretsu Jitsuroku Chushingura*, 1928). Director: Shozo Makino. Screenplay: Itaro Yamagami, Terutaro Saijo. Cast: Ii Yoho, Tsuzuya Moroguchi. Distribution: Makino. Release date: March 14, 1928. 65 minutes.

WANDERLUST (Horo Zanmai, 1928). Director: Hiroshi Inagaki. Screenplay: Mansaku Itami. Photography: Hideo Ishimoto. Cast: Chiezo Kataoka, Kobunji Ichikawa, Mansaku Itami. Release date: August 1, 1928. 60 minutes. Alternate English titles: The Wandering Gambler, Devotion to Wander.

1950-57

THE ADVENTURES OF CHUJI FROM KUNISADA (or *CHUJI KUNISADA; Akagi no Chikemuri: Kunisada Chuji*, 1957). Director: Seiichi Fukuda. Screenplay: Yoshizo Sugiyama, Isamu Nagae, based on a story by Kan Shimozawa. Photography: Kiyoshi Kataoka. Cast: Kokichi Takada, Yunosuke Ito, Michiko Saga. Distribution: Shochiku. Release date: July 1, 1957. 101 minutes.

AKITARO OF THE PAPER STALK (*Orizuru Sandogasa*, 1957). Director: Seiichi Fukuda. Screenplay: Hyogo Suzuki, Tomotaka Motoyama. Cast: Kokichi Takada, Michiko Saga, Michiya Mihashi. Distribution: Shochiku. Release date: May 7, 1957. 100 minutes.

THE BEAUTY AND THE DRAGON (*Kabuki Juhachi-ban Narukami Bijo to Kairyu*, 1955). Director: Kozaburo Yoshimura. Screenplay: Kaneto Shindo. Photography: Yoshio Miyajima. Music:

Akira Ifukube. Cast: Chojuro Karawazaki, Chiyonosuke Azuma, Nobuko Otowa. Distribution: Toei. Release date: October 3, 1955. 106 minutes.

BENI KOMORI (1950). Director/Screenplay: Teinosuke Kinugasa. Photography: Kohei Sugiyama. Music: Yasuji Kiyose. Cast: Kazuo Hasegawa [Chojiro Hayashi], Kentaro Honma, Tokusaburo Arashi. Distribution: Daiei. Release date: December 30, 1950. 91 minutes.

A BLOODY SPEAR ON MOUNT FUJI (*Chiyari Fuji*, 1955). Director: Tomu Uchida. Screenplay: Shintaro Mimura, based on a story by Kintaro Inoue. Photography: Sadaji [Sadatsugu] [Teiji] Yoshida. Cast: Chiezo Kataoka (Gonpachi), Teruo Shimada, Ryunosuke Tsukigata, Daisuke Kato, Motoharu Ueki. Distribution: Toei. Release date: February 27, 1955. 94 minutes.

CHUJI KUNISADA (*Kunisada Chuji*, 1954). Director: Eisuke Takizawa. Screenplay: Ryuzo Kikushima. Cast: Ryutaro Tatsumi (Chuji), Shogo Shimada, Keiko Tsushima, Kogiku Hanayagi. Distribution: Nikkatsu. Release date: June 27, 1954.

THE CURSE OF THE SILVER SNAKE (*Denshichi Torimonocho: Ginda Jumon*, 1957). Director: Seiichi Fukuda. Screenplay: Shigeo Yasuda, Ei Motomochi. Cast: Kokichi Takada, Michiko Saga, Junzaburo Ban [Kan Togi], Kimiko Fukuda. Distribution: Shochiku. Release date: September 22, 1957. 98 minutes.

DAICHI NO SAMURAI (1956). Director: Kiyoshi Saeki. Producer: Hiroshi Okawa. Screenplay: Hajime Takaiwa. Art Direction: Hiroshi Kitagawa. Music: Fumio Hayasaka. Cast: Ryutaru Otomo, Hizuru Takachiho, Akiko Hino. Distribution: Toei. Release date: January 29, 1956.

DISORDER BY THE KURODA CLAN (*Kuroda Sodo*, 1956). Director: Tomu Uchida. Screenplay: Hajime Takaiwa, based on a story by Hideji Hojo. Photography: Sadaji [Sadatsugu] [Teiji] Yoshida. Music: Taichiro Kosugi. Cast: Chiezo Kataoka, Ryutaro Otomo, Mitsuko Miura, Hizuru Takachiho, Shinji Nanbara. Distribution: Toei. Release date: January 8, 1956. 108 minutes.

THE EYE OF HEAVEN (*O-Edo Fusetsu Emaki: Ten no Me*, 1957). Director: Tatsuo Osone. Screenplay: Hyogo Suzuki, based on a story by Shintaro Mimura. Cast: Kokichi Takada, Mieko Takamine, Takahiro Tamura, Michiko Saga, Koshiro Matsumoto. Distribution: Shochiku. Release date: April 16, 1957. 126 minutes.

FREELANCE SAMURAI (*Momotaro Samurai*, 1957). Director: Kenji Misumi. Screenplay: Fuji Yahiro, based on a story by Kiichiro Yamate. Photography: Kohei Sugiyama. Music: Ichiro Saito. Cast: Raizo Ichikawa (Momotaro/Shinnosuke Wakagi), Yoko Uraji (Yuri), Seizaburo Kawazu (Hankuro Iga), Michiyo Kogure (Kosuzu Hanabusa), Shunji Sakai (Inosuke), Toshio Hosokawa (Otaki), Shosaku Sugiyama (Washizuka), Kenjiro Uemura (Takagaki), Yoko Wakasugi (Oume). Distribution: Daiei. Release date: December 15, 1957. 87 minutes.

GAMBLERS ON THE ROAD (*Jirocho Gaiden: Ishimatsu to Oiwake Sangoro*, 1957). Director: Ryosuke Kurahashi. Screenplay: Tomotaka Motoyama, Hiromi Hamakawa. Music: Chuji Kinoshita. Cast: Yataro Kitagami, Hiroshi Nawa, Jushiro Konoe, Toshie Nakajima, Michiko Saga, Hizuru Takachiho. Distribution: Shochiku. Release date: October 23, 1957.

THE GAY REVENGERS [Parts I and II] (*Obozu Tengu Zenpen* [I], 1954; *Obozu Tengu Kohen* [II], 1954). Director: Kunio Watanabe. Screenplay: Toshio Yasumi, based on a story by Kan Shimozawa. Cast: Chiezo Kataoka, Kinnosuke Nakamura [Yorozuya], Kogiku Hanayagi, Ryutaro Otomo. Distribution: Toei. Release dates: September 21, 1954 [I]; October 12, 1954 [II]. 92 minutes [I], 101 minutes [II].

GATE OF HELL (*Jigokumon*, 1953). Director: Teinosuke Kinusaga. Producer: Masaichi Nagata. Screenplay: Teinosuke Kinusaga, based on the play by Kan Kikuchi. Photography: Kohei Sugiyama [Eastmancolor]. Art Direction: Kisaku Ito. Music:

Left, Kazuo Hasegawa as Morito in *Gate of Hell* (1953).

Yasushi Akutagawa. Cast: Kazuo Hasegawa [Chojiro Hayashi] (Morito), Machiko Kyo (Lady Kesa), Isao Yamagata (Wataru Watanabe), Yataro Kurokawa (Shigemori), Kotaro Bando (Rokuro), Jun Tazaki (Kogenta), Koreya Senda (Kiyomori), Masao Shimizu (Nobuyori), Tatsuya Ishiguro (Yachuta), Kenjiro Uemura (Masanaka), Gen Shimizu (Saburosuke), Michiko Araki (Mano), Yoshie Minami (Tone), Kikue Mori (Sawa), Ryosuke Kagawa (Yasutada), Shinobu Araki (Iesada), Kunitaro Sawamura (Moritada), Kanji Koshiba (Munemori), Taiji Tonoyama (Kakisuke), Hiroshi Mizuno (Otoami), Shozo Nanbu (Sadafusa), Shintaro Nanjo (Tanenari), Toshiaki Konoe (Masazumi). Distribution: Daiei. Release date: October 31, 1953. 89 minutes. Video: Home Vision.

GHOST STORY OF BROKEN DISHES AT BANCHO MANSION (*Kaidan Bancho Sara Yashiki,* 1957). Director: Toshikazu Kono. Producer: Yasumasa Omori. Cast: Hibari Misora, Chiyonosuke Azuma, Reiji Tsumura. Distribution: Toei. Release date: July 13, 1957.

GHOST STORY OF YOTSUYA (*Yotsuya Kaidan,* 1956). Director: Masaki Mori. Screenplay: Hideo Oguni, Torao Tanabe. Photography: Hiroshi Suzuki. Cast: Tomisaburo Wakayama [Kenzaburo Jo], Chieko Soma, Akemi Tsukushi. Distribution: Shintoho. Release date: July 12, 1956. 86 minutes.

A HORDE OF DRUNKEN SAMURAI (*Yoidore Hachimanki,* 1951). Director: Masahiro Makino. Screenplay: Masahiro Makino, based on a novel by Itaro Yamagami. Photography: Shigeto [Minoru] Miki. Art Direction: Kazumi Koike. Cast: Kensaku Hara, Chikako Miyagi, Seizaburo Kawazu, Ryunosuke Tsukigata, Kunio Kaga. Distribution: Toei. Release date: October 5, 1951. 101 minutes.

I AM A BODYGUARD (*Ore wa Yojinbo,* 1950). Director: Hiroshi Inagaki. Screenplay: Mansaku Itami. Producer: Mitsuo Makino. Photography: Takeo Ito. Lighting: Tsuruzo Nishikawa. Art Direction: Ippei Saga. Music: Akira Ifukube. Sound: Toshiro Sasaki. Editor: Shintaro Miyamoto. Cast: Chiezo Kataoka, Ryunosuke Tsukigata, Achako Hanabishi, Daisuke Kato, Kunitaro Sawamura, Reiko Kitami, Takashi Shimura. Distribution: Tokyo Eiga. Release date: February 19, 1950. 89 minutes.

KOJIRO SASAKI (*Sasaki Kojiro,* 1950). Director: Hiroshi Inagaki. Screenplay: Hiroshi Inagaki, Kenro Matsuura, Genzo Murakami, based on a story by Genzo Murakami. Producers: Shizuharu Miyagi, Nobuyoshi Morita. Photography: Jun Yasumoto. Lighting: Hyakumi Shima. Art Direction: Morio [Takeo] Kita. Music: Shiro Fukai. Sound: Shoji Kameyama. Editor: Ryoji Bando. Cast: Tomoemon Otani (Kojiro Sasaki), Ryotaro Mizushima, Kamatari Fujiwara, Ryunosuke Tsukigata, Hideko Takamine, Reizaburo Yamamoto, Yoshio Kosugi, Eijiro Tono, Kokuten Kodo, Yuriko Hamada. Distribution: Toho. Release date: December 19, 1950. 116 minutes.

KOJIRO SASAKI II (*Zoku Sasaki Kojiro,* 1951). Director: Hiroshi Inagaki. Technical Credits: Same as Part I. Cast: Tomoemon Otani (Kojiro Sasaki), Kamatari Fujiwara, Ryunosuke Tsukigata, Hideko Takamine, Reizaburo Yamamoto, Yoshio Kosugi, Eijiro Tono, Kokuten Kodo, Yuriko Hamada, Mosaburo Iito, Jotaro Togami, Kichijiro Ueda. Distribution: Toho. Release date: March 31, 1951. 116 minutes.

KOJIRO SASAKI III: DUEL AT GANRYU ISLAND (*Kanketsu Sasaki Kojiro Ganryujima no Ketto,* 1951). Director: Hiroshi Inagaki. Screenplay: Yumi Fujiki, Kenro Matsuura, Genzo Murakami, based on a story by Genzo Murakami. Producers: Hiroshi Inagaki, Shizuharu Miyagi. Photography: Tadashi Iimura. Lighting: Kuichiro Kishida. Art Direction: Morio [Takeo] Kita. Music: Shiro Fukai. Cast: Tomoemon Otani (Kojiro Sasaki), Toshiro Mifune (Musashi Miyamoto), Hisako Yamane, Shin Tokudaiji, Yuriko Hamada, Kamatari Fujiwara, Jun Tazaki, Eijiro Tono, Hisaya Morishige, Toranosuke Ogawa, Tatsuya Ishiguro. Distribution: Toho. Release date: October 26, 1951. 98 minutes.

THE LAST DAY OF THE SAMURAI (or *PLUCKING THE KOTO; Genroku Chushingura Oishi Saigo no Ichitachi Yori: Koto no Tsume,* 1957). Director: Hiromichi Horikawa. Screenplay: Ryuzo Kikushima, Tokuhei Wakao. Photography: Kazuo Yamazaki. Art Direction: Morio [Takeo] Kita. Music: Masaru Sato. Cast: Senjaku Nakamura, Chikage Ogi, Koshiro Matsumoto, Ganjiro Nakamura, Minosuke Yamada, Shiro Tsuchiya, Haruo Tanaka, Akihiko Hirata, Shin Morikawa, Yu Fujiki, Sachio Sakai, Ikio Sawamura. Distribution: Toho. Release date: July 13, 1957.

A MAN VANISHED AT THE FESTIVAL (*Kaito Nezumi Kozo: Matsuri ni Kieta Otoko,* 1956). Director: Ryosuke Kurahashi. Screenplay: Isamu Nagae, Tatsuo Morita. Photography: Mikio Hattori. Cast: Yataro Kitagami, Koji Mitsui, Kyoko Kami, Keiko Yukishira. Distribution: Shochiku. Release date: June 22, 1956.

A MATTER OF VALOR (or *CHUSHINGURA* or *THE LOYAL FORTY SEVEN RONIN; Dai Chushingura,* 1957). Director: Tatsuo Osone. Producer: Kazuo Shirai. Screenplay: Masato Ide. Cast: Ennosuke Ichikawa, Kokichi Takada, Hizuru Takachino. Distribution: Shochiku. Release date: August 10, 1957. 157 minutes.

NINJITSU [or *THE YAGYU SECRET SCROLL; Yagyu Bugeicho,* 1957). Director: Hiroshi Inagaki. Producer: Tomoyuki Tanaka. Screenplay: Takeshi Kimura, Hiroshi Inagaki, based on the novel by Kosuke Gomi. Photography: Tadashi Iimura [AgfaColor; TohoScope]. Lighting: Ichiro Inohara. Art Direction: Morio [Takeo] Kita, Hiroshi Ueda. Music: Akira Ifukube. Sound: Yoshio Nishikawa. Editor: Yoshitami Kuroiwa. Cast: Toshiro Mifune (Tasaburo), Koji Tsuruta (Senshiro), Yoshiko Kuga (Princess Yu), Mariko Okada (Rika), Denjiro Okochi (Tajima Yagyu), Kyoko Kagawa (Oki), Senjaku Nakamura (Matajuro Yagyu), Hanshiro Iwai [Shubo Nishina] (Iemitsu Tokugawa), Jotaro Togami (Jubei Yagyu), Akihiko Hirata (Tomonori Yagyu), Eijiro Tono (Fugetsusai Yamada), Akio Kobori (Izu Matsudaira). Distribution: Toho. Release date: April 14, 1957. 109 minutes.

OKUNI AND GOHEI (*Okuni to Gohei,* 1952). Director: Mikio Naruse. Screenplay: Toshio Yasumi, based on a story by Junichiro Tanizaki. Photography: Kazuo Yamada. Art Direction: Satoshi Chuko. Music: Ichiro Saito. Cast: Michiyo Kogure (Okuni), Tomoemon Otani (Gosuke), So Yamamura (Tomonojo), Jun Tazaki (Iori, Okuni's husband), Eiko Miyoshi (Okuni's mother), Kamatari Fujiwara (Doctor). Distribution: Toho. Release date: April 10, 1952. 91 minutes.

RONIN-GAI (1957). Director: Masahiro Makino. Screenplay: Masahiro Makino, Genzo Murakami, based on a novel by Itaro Yamagami. Photography: Akira Mimura. Art Direction: Shingo Shindo. Music: Seiichi Suzuki. Cast: Jushiro Konoe, Susumu Fujita, Seizaburo Kawazu, Ichiro Ryusaki, Mieko Takamine. Distribution: Shochiku. Release date: April 3, 1957. 91 minutes.

THE ROYALISTS (or *THE FIVE PATRIOTS OF KYOTO; Kyoraku Gonin Otoko,* 1956). Director: Tatsuo Osone. Screenplay: Hideo Oguni. Photography: Hideo Ishimoto. Cast: Kokichi Takada, Takahiro Tamura, Jushiro Konoe, Denjiro Okochi. Distribution: Shochiku. Release date: October 6, 1956. 100 minutes.

SAMURAI [Parts I, II, and III], I: *THE LEGEND OF MUSASHI* (or *MASTER SWORDSMAN* or *MUSASHI MIYAMOTO; Miyamoto Musashi,* 1954). Director: Hiroshi Inagaki. Producer: Kazuo Takimura. Screenplay: Tokuhei Wakao, Hiroshi Inagaki, based on the novel *"Miyamoto Musashi"* by Eiji Yoshikawa. Adaptation: Hideji Hojo. Photography: Jun Yasumoto [Eastmancolor]. Lighting: Shigeru Mori. Art Direction: Kisaku Ito, Makoto Sono. Sound: Choshichiro Mikami. Music: Ikuma Dan. Cast: Toshiro Mifune (Musashi Miyamoto), Rentaro Mikuni (Matahachi Hon'iden), Kaoru Yachigusa (Otsu), Mariko Okada (Akemi), Kuroemon Onoe (Takuan Soho), Mitsuko Mito (Oko), Daisuke Kato (Toji Gion), Eiko Miyoshi (Osugi Hon'iden), Kusuo

Abe (Tenma Tsujikaze), Yoshio Kosugi (Tanzaemon Aoki), Sojin Kamiyama, Kanta Kisaragi, Akihiko Hirata (Seijuro Yoshioka). Distribution: Toho. Release date: September 26, 1954. 94 minutes. Video: Criterion.

II: DUEL AT ICHIJOJI TEMPLE (*Zoku Miyamoto Musashi Ichijoji no Ketto*, 1955). Technical Credits: Same as Part I. Cast: Toshiro Mifune (Musashi Miyamoto), Koji Tsuruta (Sasaki Kojiro), Sachio Sakai (Matahachi Hon'iden), Akihiko Hirata (Seijuro Yoshioka), Yu Fujiki (Denshichiro Yoshioka), Daisuke Kato (Toji Gion), Eijiro Tono (Baiken Shishido), Ko Mihashi (Koetsu Hon'ami), Kokuten Kodo (Priest Nikkan), Kenjin Iida (Jotaro), Kaoru Yachigusa (Otsu), Mariko Okada (Akemi), Mitsuko Mito (Oko), Michiyo Kogure (Yoshino Dayu). Distribution: Toho. Release date: July 12, 1955. 104 minutes.

III: DUEL ON GANRYU ISLAND (or *MUSASHI AND KOJIRO*; *Miyamoto Musashi Kanketsu-Hen Ketto Ganryujima*, 1955). Director: Hiroshi Inagaki. Photography: Kazuo Yamada [Eastmancolor]. Art Direction: Kisaku Ito, Hiroshi Ueda. Lighting: Tsuruzo Nishikawa. Sound: Masanobu Miyazaki. Music: Ikuma Dan. Cast: Toshiro Mifune (Musashi Miyamoto), Koji Tsuruta (Kojiro Sasaki), Kaoru Yachigusa (Otsu), Mariko Okada (Akemi), Michiko Saga (Omitsu), Takashi Shimura (Nagaoka Sado). Distribution: Toho. Release date: January 3, 1956. 105 minutes

SAMURAI OF NIPPON (*Samurai Nippon*, 1957). Director: Tatsuo Osone. Producer: Ginichi Kishimoto. Screenplay: Eijiro Hisaita. Photography: Hideo Ishimoto. Music: Seiichi Suzuki. Cast: Takahiro Tamura, Hizuru Takachiho, Isuzu Yamada, Koshiro Matsumoto. Distribution: Shochiku. Release date: November 19, 1957. 106 minutes.

A SAMURAI'S HONOR AT PAWN (*Aozora Kenpo Yori: Benten Yasha*, 1956). Director: Tatsuo Sakai. Screenplay: Fuji Yahiro, based on a story by Kiichiro Yamate. Cast: Kokichi Takada, Mieko Takamine, Katsuo Nakamura. Distribution: Shochiku. Release date: April 4, 1956.

A SAMURAI'S LOVE (*Bancho Sara Yashiki: Okiku to Harima*, 1954). Director/Screenplay: Daisuke Ito. Photography: Kohei Sugiyama. Music: Akira Ifukube. Cast: Kazuo Hasegawa [Chojiro Hayashi], Keiko Tsushima, Jun Tazaki, Chieko Higashiyama, Michiko Ai. Distribution: Daiei. Release date: March 3, 1954. 94 minutes.

SANSHO THE BAILIFF (*Sansho Dayu*, 1954). Director: Kenji Mizoguchi. Producer: Masaichi Nagata. Screenplay: Yoshikato Yoda, Fuji Yahiro, based on a novel by Ogai Mori. Photography: Kazuo Miyagawa. Art Direction: Kisaku Ito. Music: Fumio Hayasaka. Editor: Mitsuzo Miyata. Cast: Kinuyo Tanaka (Lady Tamaki), Yoshiaki Hanayagi (Zushio), Kyoko Kagawa (Anju), Eitaro Shindo (Sansho Dayu), Akitake Kono (Taro), Masao Shimizu (Masauji Taira), Ken Mitsuda (Prime Minister Fujiwara), Ikko Okuni (Norimura), Yoko Kozono (Kohagi), Kimiko Tachibana (Namiji), Ichiro Sugai (Minister of Justice Nio), Masahiko Kato (Young Zushio), Keiko Enami (Young Anju), Bontaro Miake (Kichiji). Distribution: Daiei. Release date: March 31, 1954. 124 minutes. Video: Home Vision.

SOULS IN THE MOONLIGHT I (*Daibosatsu Toge*, 1957). Director: Tomu Uchida. Cast: Chiezo Kataoka (Ryunosuke Tsukue), Kinnosuke Nakamura [Yorozuya], Yumiko Hasegawa. Distribution: Toei. Release date: July 13, 1957. 119 minutes.

SWORD FOR HIRE (*Sengoku Burai*, 1952). Director: Hiroshi Inagaki. Producer: Tomoyuki Tanaka. Screenplay: Hiroshi Inagaki, Akira Kurosawa, based on a serial novel by Yasushi Inoue. Photography: Tadashi Iimura. Lighting: Tsuruzo Nishikawa. Art Direction: Morio [Takeo] Kita. Sound: Shoji Kameyama. Music: Ikuma Dan. Editor: Shintaro Miyamoto. Cast: Toshiro Mifune (Hayatenosuke Sasa), Rentaro Mikuni (Jurota Tachibana), Danshiro

Ichikawa (Yaheiji Kagami), Yoshiko Yamaguchi (Oryo), Shinobu Asaji (Kano), Takashi Shimura, Eijiro Tono, Ryosuke Kagawa, Kokuten Kodo. Distribution: Toho. Release date: May 22, 1952. 135 minutes.

THE SWORDLESS SAMURAI (*Furyu Ajirogasa*, 1954). Director: Santaro Marune. Screenplay: Fuji Yahiro, based on a story by Genzo Murakami. Cast: Akio Kobori, Sakura Onoe, Yumiko Hasegawa. Distribution: Toho. Release date: May 26, 1954. 87 minutes.

SWORDS AND BROCADE (*Heian Gunto-Den: Hakamadare Yasusuke*, 1951). Director: Eisuke Takizawa. Screenplay: Toshio Yasumi, based on a story by Eiji Yoshikawa. Cast: Ryo Ikebe, Setsuko Wakayama, Hisako Yamane. Distribution: Toho. Release date: June 22, 1951.

TALES OF THE TAIRA CLAN (or *NEW TALES* or *THE LEGEND OF THE TAIRA CLAN* or *THE SACRILEGIOUS HERO*; *Shin Heike Monogatari*, 1955). Director: Kenji Mizoguchi. Producer: Masaichi Nagata. Screenplay: Yoshikata Yoda, Masahige Narusawa, Kyuichi Tsuji, based on a novel by Eiji Yoshikawa. Photography: Kazuo Miyagawa [Eastmancolor]. Music: Fumio Hayasaka, Masaru Sato. Cast: Raizo Ichikawa (Kiyomori Taira), Naritoshi Hayashi (Tokitada Fujiwara), Tatsuya Ishiguro (Tokinobu Fujiwara), Michiko Kogure (Yasuko), Akitake Kono (Heiroku), Yoshiko Kuga (Tokiko), Tamao Nakamura (Shigeko Fujiwara), Shunji Natsume (Emperor Toba), Ichijiro Oya (Tadamori Taira), Mitsusaburo Ramon (Ryokan), Kunitaro Sawamura (Joku), Eitaro Shindo (Banboku), Ichiro Sugai (Carpenter), Eijiro Yanagi (Emperor Shirakawa), Koreya Senda. Distribution: Daiei. Release date: September 21, 1955. 108 minutes.

TANGE SAZEN [Parts I, II, and III] (*Tange Sazen: Kenun no Maki* [I], 1956; *Tange Sazen: Unkon no Maki* [II], 1956; *Tange Sazen: Kanketsu-Hen* [III], 1956). Director: Masahiro Makino. Screenplay: Goro Tanada, based on a novel by Fubo Hayashi [Umitaro Hasegawa]. Music: Seiichi Suzuki. Cast: Michitaro Mizushima, Seizaburo Kawazu, Kunitaro Sawamura, Yoko Minamida, Nobuo Kaneko, Frankie Sakai. Distribution: Nikkatsu. Release dates: January 8, 1956 [I]; January 29, 1956 [II]; February 5, 1956 [III]. 82 minutes [I], 61 minutes [II], 79 minutes [III].

THREE WAYS TO DIE (*Denshichi Torimonocho: Megitsune Kago*, 1956). Director: Seiichi Fukuda. Screenplay: Shigeo Yasuda, Ikuro Kishi. Cast: Kokichi Takada, Junzaburo Ban [Kan Togi], Mitsuko Kusabue, Jushiro Konoe, Chieko Seki. Distribution: Shochiku. Release date: June 1, 1956. 110 minutes.

THE TREASURE OF RYUJIN-MARU (*Denshichi Torimonocho: Bijo Komori*, 1957). Director: Seiichi Fukuda. Screenplay: Isamu Nagae. Cast: Kokichi Takada, Mitsuko Kusabue, Junzaburo Ban [Kan Togi], Michiko Saga. Distribution: Shochiku. Release date: January 29, 1957.

UGETSU (*Ugetsu Monogatari*, 1953). Director: Kenji Mizoguchi. Producer: Masaichi Nagata. Screenplay: Yoshikata Yoda, Matsutaro Kawaguchi, based on the stories "The Inn at Asaji" and "The Smoothness of the Snake" from *Stories of the Pale Moon after the Rain* by Akinari Ueda. Photography: Kazuo Miyagawa. Art Direction: Kisaku Ito. Music: Fumio Hayasaka, Ichiro Saito, Editor: Mitsuzo Miyata. Sound: Iwao Otani. Cast: Masayuki Mori (Genjuro), Machiko Kyo (Lady Wakasa), Kinuyo Tanaka (Miyagi), Sakae Ozawa [Eitaro Ozawa] (Tobei), Mitsuko Mito (Ahama), Kikue Mori (Ukon), Ryosuke Kagawa (Village master), Eigoro Onoe (Knight), Saburo Date (Vassal), Sugisaku Aoyama (Old Priest), Shozo Nanbu (Shinto Priest), Mitsusaburo Ramon, Ichiro Amano (Boatsman), Kichijiro Ueda (Shop Owner), Teruko Omi, Keiko Koyanagi (Prostitutes). Distribution: Daiei. Release date: March 26, 1953. 97 minutes. Alternate English titles: *Tales of Ugetsu*; *Tales of a Pale and Mysterious Moon After the Rain*.

VENDETTA OF SAMURAI (*Araki Mataemon: Ketto Kagiya no Tsuji*, 1952). Director: Kazuo [Issei] Mori. Producer: Sojiro Motoki.

Screenplay: Akira Kurosawa. Photography: Kazuo Yamazaki. Lighting: Kuichiro Kishida. Art Direction: Takashi Matsuyama. Music: Goro Nishi. Sound: Masanobu Miyazaki. Cast: Toshiro Mifune (Mataemon Araki), Yuriko Hamada, Takashi Shimura, Akihiko Katayama, Minoru Chiaki, Daisuke Kato, Shin Tokudaiji, Kokuten Kodo, Bokuzen Hidari, Toranosuke Ogawa. Distribution: Toho. Release date: January 3, 1952. 82 minutes.

THE VENGEANCE TRAIL (Yudachi Kangoro, 1953). Director: Eisuke Takizawa. Screenplay: Kenro Matsuura, Bunta Doi. Cast: Akio Kobori, Kogiku Hanayagi, Torazo Hirosawa. Distribution: Toho. Release date: September 23, 1953.

THE WANDERER (Rindo Garasu, 1957). Director: Seiichi Fukuda. Screenplay: Shigeo Yasuda. Cast: Kokichi Takada, Michiko Saga, Mieko Takamine, Jushiro Konoe, Keiko Yukishiro. Distribution: Shochiku. Release date: January 15, 1957. 99 minutes.

1958

THE ADULTERESS (or THE NIGHT DRUM; Yoru no Tsuzumi). Director: Tadashi Imai. Producer: Tengo Yamada. Screenplay: Shinobu Hashimoto, Kaneto Shindo, based on a play by Monzaemon Chikamatsu. Photography: Shunichiro Nakao. Music: Akira Ifukube. Editor: Akikazu Kono. Cast: Rentaro Mikuni (Hikokuro Ogura), Ineko Arima (Otane), Masayuki Mori (Miyaji), Sumiko Hidaka (Oyura), Nobuo Kaneko (Isobe), Yoshi Kato (Kanze), Kikue Mori (Kiku), Mannosuke Nakamura (Bunroku Ogura), Tomoko Naraoka (Orin), Shizue Natsukawa (Naka), Ichiro Sugai (Ota), Eijiro Tono (Kurokawa), Taiji Tonoyama (Masayama), Eijiro Yanagi (Yonebayashi), Emiko Azuma. Distribution: Shochiku. Release date: April 15, 1958. 95 minutes.

AMBUSH AT IGA PASS (Iga no Suigetsu). Director/Screenplay: Kunio Watanabe. Photography: Takashi Watanabe. Cast: Kazuo Hasegawa [Chojiro Hayashi] (Mataemon Araki), Raizo Ichikawa, Naritoshi Hayashi, Ryuzo Shimada. Distribution: Daiei. Release date: November 15, 1958. 99 minutes.

THE BARBARIAN AND THE GEISHA. Director: John Huston. Producers: Eugene Frenke, Darryl F. Zanuck. Screenplay: Charles Grayson, based on a story by Ellis St. Joseph. Japanese dialog director: Teinosuke Kinugasa. Photography: Charles G. Clarke. Art Direction: Jack Martin Smith, Lyle R. Wheeler. Music: Hugo Friedhofer. Sound: W.D. Flick, Warren B. Delaplain. Editor: Stuart Gilmore. Cast: John Wayne (Townsend Harris), Eiko Ando (Okichi), Sam Jaffe (Henry Heusken), So Yamamura (Governor Tamura), Kodaya Ichikawa (Daimyo), Tokujiro Iketaniuchi (Harusha), Fuji Kasai (Lord Hotta), Takeshi Kumagai (Chamberlain), Hiroshi Yamato (Shogun). Distribution: 20th Century-Fox. Release date: September 30, 1958. 105 minutes.

BATTLE DRUM AT DAWN (Chushingura: Akatsuki no Jindaiko). Director: Ryosuke Kurahashi. Screenplay: Shin Nakazawa, Asami Tanabe. Cast: Miki Mori, Michiko Saga, Jukai Ichikawa, Jushiro Konoe. Distribution: Shochiku. Release date: December 21, 1958. 97 minutes.

THE BLACK-HOODED MAN (Kaiketsu Kurozukin). Director: Shoji Matsumura. Screenplay: Tadashi Ogawa, based on a story by Hitomi Takagaki. Cast: Ryutaro Otomo, Yumiko Hasegawa, Hiroko Sakuramachi, Takashi Shimura. Distribution: Toei. Release date: August 20, 1958. 87 minutes.

BLOODY RIVER (Tenpo Suikoden). Director: Kunio Watanabe. Screenplay: Kunio Watanabe, Hyogo Suzuki, Tomotaka Motoyama. Cast: Kokichi Takada, Michiyo Kogure, Michiko Saga, Jushiro Konoe. Distribution: Shochiku. Release date: May 13, 1958.

BORED SAMURAI (Hatamoto Taikutsu Otoko). Director: Sadatsugu [Teiji] [Sadaji] Matsuda. Screenplay: Yoshitake Hisa, based on a story by Mitsuzo Sasaki. Cast: Utaemon Ichikawa

(Mondonosuke Saotome), Hiroko Sakuramachi, Kinnosuke Nakamura [Yorozuya], Chiezo Kataoka. Distribution: Toei. Release date: August 12, 1958. 108 minutes.

A BULL'S EYE FOR LOVE (Oshidoru Kago). Director: Masahiro Makino. Screenplay: Kota Kanze. Cast: Kinnosuke Nakamura [Yorozuya], Sentaro Fushimi, Hiroko Sakuramachi. Distribution: Toei. Release date: January 15, 1958. 86 minutes.

CHUJI KUNISADA (Kunisada Chuji). Director: Shigehiro Ozawa. Screenplay: Shinji Kessoku, Hajime Takaiwa, based on a story by Rifu Yukitomo. Cast: Chiezo Kataoka (Chuji), Eijiro Yanagi, Soji Kiyokawa, Kotaro Satomi. Distribution: Toei. Release date: August 27, 1958.

THE LOYAL 47 RONIN (Chushingura). Director: Kunio Watanabe. Producer: Masaichi Nagata. Screenplay: Fuji Yahiro, Toshio Tamikado, Masaharu Muramatsu, Kunio Watanabe. Cast: Kazuo Hasegawa [Chojiro Hayashi], Shintaro Katsu, Koji Tsuruta, Raizo Ichikawa, Machiko Kyo. Distribution: Daiei. Release date: April 1, 1958. 166 minutes.

THE DEBUT OF THE SEVEN BLADES (Shichinin Wakashu Tanjo). Director: Ryosuke Kurahashi. Screenplay: Shigeo Yasuda. Cast: Kinshiro Matsumoto, Kimiko Fukuda, Kotobuki Hananomoto, Miki Mori. Distribution: Shochiku. Release date: August 31, 1958. 91 minutes.

THE DRUM AND THE SWORD (Mangetsu Kagura-Daiko). Director: Kokichi Uchide. Screenplay: Shinji Kessoku. Cast: Kotaro Satomi, Hiromi Hanazono, Koinosuke Onoe, Eiko Maruyama. Distribution: Toei. Release date: September 3, 1958. 62 minutes.

FLOWER OF THE PLEASURE QUARTER (Hana no Yukyo-Den). Director: Kimiyoshi Yasuda. Screenplay: Hideo Oguni. Cast: Kazuo Hasegawa [Chojiro Hayashi], Shintaro Katsu, Yoko Uraji, Naritoshi Hayashi. Distribution: Daiei. Release date: August 31, 1958. 98 minutes.

THE GALLANT ON THE HIGHWAY (Tsuma-Koi Dochu). Director: Kunio Matoi. Screenplay: Hiroshi Namie. Cast: Kokichi Takada, Yachiyo Otori, Yataro Kitagami, Michiko Saga. Distribution: Shochiku. Release date: November 23, 1958. 85 minutes.

THE GAY MASQUERADE (Benten Kozo). Director: Daisuke Ito. Screenplay: Fuji Yahiro, based on the Kabuki play by Mokuami Kawatake. Photography: Kazuo Miyagawa [Agfacolor; DaieiScope]. Art Direction: Yoshinobu Nishioka. Music: Ichiro Saito. Cast: Raizo Ichikawa (Benten), Shintaro Katsu (Toyama), Kyoko Aoyama (Ohan), Michiko Ai (Okichi), Mieko Kondo (Osuzu), Yataro Kurokawa, Ryuzo Shimada. Distribution: Daiei. Release date: November 29, 1958. 86 minutes.

THE HAND DRUM OF DEATH (Rakka Kenko-Roku). Director: Ryo Hagiwara. Screenplay: Ippei Hata, Tatsuo Nakata. Cast: Kinshiro Matsumoto, Kimiko Fukuda, Nobu Kawaguchi. Distribution: Shochiku. Release date: November 18, 1958. 90 minutes.

NINJITSU II (or THE YAGYU SECRET SCROLL II; Yagyu Bugeicho Soryu Hiken). Director: Hiroshi Inagaki. Producer: Tomoyuki Tanaka. Screenplay: Hiroshi Inagaki, Tokuhei Wakao, based on the novel by Kosuke Gomi. Photography: Asakazu Nakai [AgfaColor; TohoScope]. Lighting: Choshiro Ishii. Art Direction: Morio [Takeo] Kita, Hiroshi Ueda. Music: Akira Ifukube. Sound: Masao Fujiyoshi. Editor: Yoshitami Kuroiwa. Cast: Koji Tsuruta (Senshiro), Toshiro Mifune (Tasaburo), Nobuko Otowa (Princess Kiyo), Yoshiko Kuga (Princess Yu), Mariko Okada (Rika), Denjiro Okochi (Tajima Yagyu), Eijiro Tono (Fugetsusai Yamada), Senjaku Nakamura (Matajuro Yagyu), Jotaro Togami (Jubei Yagyu), Hanshiro Iwai [Shubo Nishina] (Iemitsu Tokugawa), Akio Kobori (Izu Matsudaira), Koshiro Matsumoto (Hyogonosuke Yagyu). Distribution: Toho. Release date: January 3, 1958. 105 minutes.

NUREGAMI KENPO. Director: Bin Kato. Screenplay: Masaharu Matsumura. Photography: Senkichiro Takeda. Music: Seiichi Suzuki. Cast: Raizo Ichikawa, Kaoru Yachigusa, Tamao Nakamura, Michiko Ai. Distribution: Daiei. Release date: November 8, 1958. 89 minutes.

THE RED BAT (Beni Komori). Director: Santaro Mirune. Photography: Kiyoshi Kataoka. Music: Goro Nishi. Cast: Kinshiro Matsumoto, Akiko Koyama, Ushio Akashi, Ryosuke Kagawa. Distribution: Shochiku. Release date: October 7, 1958. 97 minutes.

A RUFFIAN IN LOVE (Suteuri Kanbei). Director: Masahiro Makino. Photography: Harumi Fujii. Music: Seiichi Suzuki. Cast: Ryutaro Otomo, Kotaro Satomi, Keiko Okawa, Hiromi Hanazono. Distribution: Toei. Release date: November 5, 1958. 94 minutes.

THE SCARLET CLOAK (Akai Jinbaori). Director: Satsuo Yamamoto. Screenplay: Hajime Takaiwa, based on a story by Junji Kinoshita. Cast: Kanzaburo Nakamura, Kyoko Kagawa, Yunosuke Ito. Distribution: Shochiku. Release date: September 23, 1958.

THE SECRET OF THE SCROLL (Ninjutsu Suikoden: Inazuma Kotengu). Director: Shoji Matsumura. Screenplay: Shinji Kessoku, Fumie Sugimura, based on a story by Genzo Murakami. Cast: Chiyonosuke Azuma, Yumiko Hasegawa, Satomi Oka. Distribution: Toei. Release date: January 29, 1958. 83 minutes.

THE SEVEN BLADES RETURN (Shichinin Wakashu Oini Uridasu). Director: Ryosuke Kurahashi. Screenplay: Shigeo Yasuda. Cast: Kinshiro Matsumoto, Kotobuki Hananomoto, Michiko Hamamura. Distribution: Shochiku. Release date: December 21, 1958. 91 minutes.

SOULS IN THE MOONLIGHT II (Daibosatsu Toge Dai Nibu). Director: Tomu Uchida. Cast: Chiezo Kataoka (Ryunosuke Tsukue), Kinnosuke Nakamura [Yorozuya], Yumiko Hasegawa. Distribution: Toei. Release date: April 21, 1958. 105 minutes.

THE SWISHING SWORD (Hitohada Kujaku). Director: Kazuo [Issei] Mori. Screenplay: Masaharu Matsumura. Photography: Soichi Aisaka [Agfacolor; DaieiScope]. Cast: Fujiko Yamamoto, Raizo Ichikawa, Shoji Umewaka, Mieko Kondo, Seizaburo Kawazu. Distribution: Daiei. Release date: August 3, 1958. 99 minutes.

THE SWORDSMAN'S TROUBLE WITH WOMEN (Yagyu Tabi Goyomi: Jonan Itto Ryu). Director: Shoji Matsumura. Screenplay: Shinji Kessoku. Cast: Ryutaro Otomo, Satomi Oka, Keiko Okawa. Distribution: Toei. Release date: October 8, 1958. 88 minutes.

A SWORD AGAINST FATE (Nuretsubame: Kurenai Gonpachi). Director: Kokichi Uchide. Screenplay: Hyogo Suzuki. Cast: Hashizo Okawa, Keiko Okawa, Utaemon Ichikawa. Distribution: Toei. Release date: October 14, 1958. 93 minutes.

A SWORD AND LOVE (Ken wa Shitte Ita: Kogan Muso Ryu). Director: Kokichi Uchide. Screenplay: Hajime Takaiwa, Shinji Kessoku, based on a story by Renzaburo Shibata. Cast: Kinnosuke Nakamura [Yorozuya], Keiko Okawa, Ryunosuke Tsukigata. Distribution: Toei. Release date: September 3, 1958. 104 minutes.

TANGE SAZEN PARTS I to V (*Tange Sazen* [I], 1958; *The Secret Of The Bronze Dragon (Tange Sazen: Doto-Hen)*[II], 1959; *Tange Sazen: Yoto Nuretsubame* [III], 1960; *Tange Sazen: Nuretsubame Itto-Ryu* [IV], 1961; *Tange Sazen: Kenun Unkon no Maki* [V], 1962). Directors: Sadatsugu [Teiji] [Sadaji] Matsuda [I-IV], Tai Kato [V]. Screenplay: Fumio Nakayama [I,II], Hideo Oguni [III], Michihei Muramatsu [IV], Kinya Naoi [IV], Toshiro Ishido [V]. Cast: Ryutaro Otomo (Sazen Tange), Hashizo Okawa. Distribution: Toei. Release dates: March 18, 1958 [I]; January 3, 1959 [II]; January 15, 1960 [III]; May 3, 1961 [IV]; April 17, 1962 [V]. 100 minutes [I], 81 minutes [II], 79 minutes [III], 84 minutes [IV], 86 minutes [V].

THE TOWN HERO (Isshin Tasuke Tenka no Ichidaiji). Director: Tadashi Sawashima. Screenplay: Kazuyoshi Takasawa. Cast: Kinnosuke Nakamura [Yorozuya], Ryunosuke Tsukigata, Hitomi Nakahara. Distribution: Toei. Release date: October 22, 1958. 91 minutes.

THE TOUGH IN A PURPLE HOOD (Murasaki Zukin). Director: Hideaki Onishi. Screenplay: Kiyoyuki Nishikawa, Hajime Takaiwa, based on a story by Rokuhei Susukita. Cast: Chiezo Kataoka, Kotaro Satomi, Hiroko Sakuramachi, Ryunosuke Tsukigata, So Yamamura. Distribution: Toei. Release date: October 29, 1958. 88 minutes.

THE THUNDER KID (Asama no Abarenbo). Director: Toshikazu Kono. Screenplay: Michihei Muramatsu. Cast: Kinnosuke Nakamura [Yorozuya], Satomi Ota, Keiko Okawa. Distribution: Toei. Release date: December 2, 1958. 83 minutes.

THE TRAVELING RUFFIAN (Shimizu Minato no Meibutsu Otoko: Enshu Mori no Ishimatsu). Director: Masahiro Makino. Screenplay: Kota Kanze, based on a story by Genzo Murakami. Photography: Akira Mimura. Music: Seiichi Suzuki. Cast: Kinnosuke Nakamura [Yorozuya], Katsuo Nakamura, Yumiko Hasegawa, Hitomi Nakahara, Takashi Shimura. Distribution: Toei. Release date: June 29, 1958. 98 minutes.

1959

ASAYAKE GUMO NO KETTO. Director: Ryo Hagiwara. Screenplay: Sadao Nakamura, Tatsuo Inada, based on a story by Kan Kikuchi. Cast: Danshiro Ichikawa, Jushiro Konoe, Michiko Saga. Distribution: Shochiku. Release date: January 22, 1959. 91 minutes.

BENI AZAMI. Director: Kimiyoshi Yasuda. Screenplay: Hyogo Suzuki. Cast: Shintaro Katsu, Mieko Kondo, Joji Tsurumi, Kojiro Hongo. Distribution: Daiei. Release date: May 8, 1959. 79 minutes.

THE BLACK-MASKED REFORMER (Kurama Tengu). Director: Masahiro Makino. Screenplay: Shinji Kessoku. Cast: Chiyonosuke Azuma, Hibari Misora, Satomi Oka, Minoru Chiaki. Distribution: Toei. Release date: February 4, 1959. 51 minutes.

EDO YUMIN DEN. Director: Ryo Hagiwara. Screenplay: Shintaro Mimura, Sadao Yamanaka. Cast: Jushiro Konoe, Kinshiro Matsumoto, Michiko Saga, Kyoko Aoyama. Distribution: Shochiku. Release date: March 11, 1959. 106 minutes.

EIGHT BRAVE BROTHERS [Parts I, II, and III] (*Satomi Hakken-Den* [I], *Satomi Hakken-Den: Yokai no Ranbu* [II], *Satomi Hakken-Den: Hakkenshi no Gaika* [III]). Director: Kokichi Uchide. Screenplay: Shinji Kessoku, based on a story by Bakin Takizawa. Cast: Sentaro Fushimi, Kotaro Satomi, Koinosuke Onoe. Distribution: Toei. Release dates: August 11, 1959 [I]; August 19, 1959 [II]; August 26, 1959 [III]. 57 minutes (each part).

AN ESSAY ON CONFLICT (Kodokan ni Hi wa Noboru). Director: Katsuhiko Tasaka. Screenplay: Tetsuro Yoshida. Cast: Kenji Sugawara, Kojiro Hongo, Yoko Uraji. Distribution: Daiei. Release date: April 8, 1959. 82 minutes.

THE FORBIDDEN CASTLE (Binan-Jo). Director: Yasushi Sasaki. Screenplay: Masashige Narusawa, based on a story by Renzaburo Shibata. Cast: Kinnosuke Nakamura [Yorozuya], Keiko Okawa, Satomi Oka. Distribution: Toei. Release date: February 24, 1959. 90 minutes.

THE GAIJIN (Yamada Nagamasa: Oja no Ken). Director: Bin Kato. Screenplay: Hideo Oguni, based on a story by Shofu Muramatsu. Cast: Kazuo Hasegawa [Chojiro Hayashi], Raizo Ichikawa, Yasuko Nakata. Distribution: Daiei. Release date: May 1, 1959. 114 minutes.

282

GHOST STORY OF YOTSUYA (or GHOST STORY OF YOTSUYA IN TOKAIDO; Tokaido Yotsuya Kaidan). Director: Nobuo Nakagawa. Producer: Mitsugu Okura. Screenplay: Masayoshi Onuki, Yoshihiro Ishikawa, based on the play by Nanboku Tsuruya. Photography: Tadashi Nishimoto [Fujicolor, TohoScope]. Art Direction: Haruyasu Kurosawa. Music: Chumei [Michiaki] [Hiroaki] Watanabe. Cast: Shigeru Amachi (Iemon Tamiya), Noriko Kitazawa (Sode), Katsuko Wakasugi (Iwa), Shintaro Emi (Naosuke), Junko Ikeuchi (Ume Ito), Ryozaburo Nakamura, Jun Otomo (Takuetsu). Distribution: Toho. Release: July 1, 1959. 76 minutes.

THE GREAT AVENGERS (Chushingura: Oka no maki, Kikka no maki). Director: Sadatsugu [Teiji] [Sadaji] Matsuda. Screenplay: Yoshitake Hisa. Cast: Chiezo Kataoka, Utaemon Ichikawa, Kinnosuke Nakamura [Yorozuya]. Distribution: Toei. Release date: January 15, 1959. 183 minutes.

THE HAWK OF THE NORTH (Dokuganryu Masamune). Director: Toshikazu Kono. Screenplay: Hajime Takaiwa. Photography: Makoto Tsuboi [Eastmancolor; ToeiScope]. Cast: Kinnosuke Nakamura [Yorozuya] (Masamune), Ryunosuke Tsukigata, Yoshiko Sakuma, Keiko Okawa. Distribution: Toei. Release date: May 25, 1959. 87 minutes.

HEBI-HIME SAMA. Director: Kunio Watanabe. Screenplay: Kunio Watanabe, based on a story by Matsutaro Kawaguchi. Photography: Takashi Watanabe. Cast: Raizo Ichikawa, Michiko Saga, Tamao Nakamura, Yataro Kurokawa, Seizaburo Kawazu. Distribution: Daiei. Release date: February 25, 1959. 96 minutes.

JAN ARIMA NO SHUGEKI. Director/Screenplay: Daisuke Ito. Photography: Hiroshi Imai. Music: Saburo Iida. Cast: Raizo Ichikawa, Junko Kano, Jun Negami. Distribution: Daiei. Release date: July 12, 1959. 114 minutes.

JIROCHO FUJI. Director: Kazuo [Issei] Mori. Screenplay: Fuji Yahiro. Photography: Shozo Honda. Music: Ichiro Saito. Cast: Kazuo Hasegawa [Chojiro Hayashi] (Shimizu no Jirocho), Machiko Kyo (Okatsu), Raizo Ichikawa (Kira no Nikichi), Ayako Wakao (Okiku), Fujiko Yamamoto (Oshin), Eiji Funakoshi, Naritoshi Hayashi, Kojiro Hongo, Shintaro Katsu (Mori no Ishimatsu), Mieko Kondo, Tamao Nakamura, Jun Negami, Ryuji Shinagawa, Osamu Takizawa. Distribution: Daiei. Release date: June 2, 1959. 105 minutes.

KAGERO-GASA. Director: Kenji Misumi. Screenplay: Minoru Inuzuka. Cast: Kazuo Hasegawa [Chojiro Hayashi], Michiyo Aratama, Ganjiro Nakamura. Distribution: Daiei. Release date: January 28, 1959. 87 minutes.

KINOKUNIYA, THE DAUNTLESS MERCHANT (Kinokuniya Bunzaemon). Director: Kunio Watanabe. Screenplay: Kunio Watanabe, Tomotaka Motoyama. Cast: Kokichi Takada, Michiko Saga, Miki Mori, Jushiro Konoe. Distribution: Shochiku. Release date: June 14, 1959.

THE LORD AND THE GAMBLER (Nuregami Sandogasa). Director: Tokuzo Tanaka. Screenplay: Fuji Yahiro. Cast: Raizo Ichikawa, Kojiro Hongo, Keiko Awaji. Distribution: Daiei. Release date: August 1, 1959. 98 minutes.

THE LORD AND THE PIRATES (or SAMURAI VAGABOND; Tono-Sama Yajikita Torimono Dochu). Director: Tadashi Sawashima. Screenplay: Kazuo Kasahara, Kazuyoshi Takasawa. Photography: Makato Tsuboi. Music: Seiichi Suzuki. Cast: Kinnosuke Nakamura [Yorozuya], Katsuo Nakamura, Hitomi Nakahara. Distribution: Toei. Release date: January 3, 1959. 84 minutes.

THE MAN CAME ON THE WIND (Oshidori Dochu). Director: Yasushi Sasaki. Screenplay: Yoshitake Hisa. Cast: Hashizo Okawa, Kyoko Aoyama, Hiroko Sakuramachi. Distribution: Toei. Release date: April 22, 1959. 88 minutes.

MISSION TO HELL (Kogan no Misshi). Director/Screenplay: Tai Kato. Photography: Sadaji [Sadatsugu] [Teiji] Yoshida [Eastmancolor; ToeiScope]. Cast: Hashizo Okawa, Yoshio Yoshida, Jun Tazaki, Sentaro Fushimi. Distribution: Toei. Release date: June 9, 1959. 89 minutes.

NARUTO NO HANAYOME. Director: Katsuhiko Tasaka. Screenplay: Hachiro Nishimura, Masaharu Matsumura. Cast: Shintaro Katsu, Kojiro Hongo, Ryuzo Shimada. Distribution: Daiei. Release date: August 23, 1959. 87 minutes.

THE NAUGHTY ROGUE (Ojo-Kichisa). Director: Tokuzo Tanaka. Screenplay: Minoru Inuzuka. Producer: Nobuo Miura. Photography: Hiroshi Imai. Lighting: Hiroya Kato. Art Direction: Yoshinobu Nishioka. Music: Ichiro Saito. Sound: Yukio Kaihara. Cast: Raizo Ichikawa, Yoko Uraji, Ryuzo Shimada, Yoshiro Kitahara, Tamao Nakamura, Gen Shimizu. Distribution: Daiei. Release date: April 21, 1959. 81 minutes.

NO STRONGER SWORDS (Furyu Shisha: Tenka-Muso no Ken). Director: Sadatsugu [Teiji] [Sadaji] Matsuda. Screenplay: Shinji Kessoku, based on a story by Kosuke Gomi. Cast: Utaemon Ichikawa, Hashizo Okawa, Yumiko Hasegawa. Distribution: Toei. Release date: May 5, 1959. 66 minutes.

NOBUNAGA'S EARLY DAYS (Wakaki Hi no Nobunaga). Director: Kazuo [Issei] Mori. Screenplay: Fuji Yahiro. Cast: Raizo Ichikawa, Atsuko Kindaichi, Kyoko Aoyama. Distribution: Daiei. Release date: March 17, 1959. 97 minutes.

THE ONE-EYED WOLF (Umon Torimonocho: Katame no Okami). Director: Tadashi Sawashima. Screenplay: Hajime Takaiwa, Kazuyoshi Takasawa. Cast: Ryutaro Otomo, Kotaro Satomi, Hiromi Hanazono. Distribution: Toei. Release date: March 3, 1959. 87 minutes.

O-ABARE HAPPYAKUYACHO. Director: Kunio Watanabe. Screenplay: Kunio Watanabe, Taizo Fuyushima. Cast: Kokichi Takada, Michiko Saga, Kyoko Kawaguchi. Distribution: Shochiku. Release date: July 14, 1959. 84 minutes.

THE RAGE (Hayate Monzaburo). Director: Masahiko Izawa. Screenplay: Yuto Nagai. Cast: Tomisaburo Wakayama [Kenzaburo Jo], Keiko Okawa, Yumi Ichijo. Distribution: Toei. Release date: July 22, 1959. 68 minutes.

REVENGE OF THE PRINCESS (Himegimi Itto Ryu). Director: Tomoji Sumida. Music: Hiroya Abe. Cast: Keiko Okawa, Sentaro Fushimi, Eiko Maruyama. Distribution: Toei. Release date: June 16, 1959. 60 minutes.

THE REVENGER IN RED (Beni-Dasuki Kenkajo). Director: Toshikazu Kono. Music: Nakaba Takahashi. Cast: Chiyonosuke Azuma, Hibari Misora, Kotaro Satomi. Distribution: Toei. Release date: April 15, 1959. 74 minutes.

THE RIVER OF FURY (Ketto Suikoden: Doto no Taiketsu). Director: Yasushi Sasaki. Screenplay: Hajime Takaiwa. Cast: Utaemon Ichikawa, Chiezo Kataoka, Kinnosuke Nakamura [Yorozuya], Hashizo Okawa, Chiyonosuke Azuma, Hibari Misora. Distribution: Toei. Release date: August 9, 1959. 114 minutes.

THE SAGA OF THE VAGABONDS (Sengoku Gunto-Den). Director: Toshio Sugie. Producers: Masumi [Sanezumi] Fujimoto, Kazuo Nishino. Screenplay: Sadao Yamanaka, Akira Kurosawa, based on a story by Juro Miyoshi. Photography: Akira Suzuki [Agfacolor; TohoScope]. Art Direction: Morio [Takeo] Kita. Music: Ikuma Dan. Cast: Toshiro Mifune (Rokuro Kai), Koji Tsuruta (Taro), Yoko Tsukasa (Tazu), Misa Uehara (Princess Koyuki), Takashi Shimura (Saemon Toki), Minoru Chiaki (Jibu), Akihiko Hirata (Jiro Hidekuni), Seizaburo Kawazu (Hyoei Yamana), Yoshio Kosugi, Kenzo Tabu, Akira Tani, Sachio Sakai, Yoshifumi Tajima (Jiro's Vassal), Shin Otomo, Tadao Nakamaru. Distribution: Toho. Release date: August 9, 1959. 115 minutes.

SAMURAI SAGA (*Aru Kengo no Shogai*). Director: Hiroshi Inagaki. Producer: Tomoyuki Tanaka. Screenplay: Hiroshi Inagaki, from the play "Cyrano de Bergerac" by Edmond Rostand. Photography: Kazuo Yamada. Lighting: Shoshichi Kojima. Art Direction: Kisaku Ito. Music: Akira Ifukube. Sound: Yoshio Nishikawa, Masanobu Miyazaki. Editor: Kazuji Taira. Cast: Toshiro Mifune (Heihachiro Komaki), Yoko Tsukasa (Lady Ochii aka Princess Chiyo), Akira Takarada (Jurota Karibe), Keiko Awaji (Nanae), Seizaburo Kawazu (Nagashima), Kamatari Fujiwara (Rakuzo the sake seller), Akihiko Hirata (Akaboshi), Eiko Miyoshi (Okuni), Sachio Sakai, Yoshifumi Tajima, Akira Tani, Yutaka Sada, Senkichi Omura, Hideyo [Eisei] Amamoto, Haruo Tanaka, Kichijiro Ueda, Fumindo Matsuo, Chieko Nakakita, Shin Otomo, Akira Sera, Mitsuo Tsuda, Yasuhisa Tsutsumi, Setsuko Wakayama, Ren Yamamoto. Distribution: Toho. Release date: April 28, 1959. 112 minutes.

SAMURAI VENDETTA (*Hakuoki*). Director: Kazuo [Issei] Mori. Screenplay: Daisuke Ito, based on a story by Kosuke Gomi. Photography: Shozo Honda. Music: Ichiro Saito. Cast: Raizo Ichikawa (Tenzen Tange), Shintaro Katsu, Chitose Maki, Tokiko Mita, Yoshiro Kitahara. Distribution: Daiei. Release date: November 22, 1959. 110 minutes. Alternate English Title: *Chronicle of Pale Cherry Blossoms*. Video: Samurai Video.

THE SECRET OF THE BRONZE DRAGON (*Tange Sazen: Doto-Hen* [II], 1959). SEE Tange Sazen (1958).

SENBAZURU HICHO. Director: Kenji Misumi. Screenplay: Fuji Yahiro. Cast: Raizo Ichikawa, Tamao Nakamura, Joji Tsurumi. Distribution: Daiei. Release date: May 20, 1959. 87 minutes.

THE SHOGUN TRAVELS INCOGNITO (*Mito Komon: Tenka no Fuku-Shogun*). Director: Sadatsugu [Teiji] [Sadaji] Matsuda. Screenplay: Hideo Oguni. Cast: Ryunosuke Tsukigata, Kinnosuke Nakamura [Yorozuya], Chiyonosuke Azuma, Kotaro Satomi, Satomi Oka, Tomisaburo Wakayama [Kenzaburo Jo]. Distribution: Toei. Release date: July 12, 1959. 94 minutes.

SHURA ZAKURA. Director: Tatsuo Osone. Screenplay: Hajime Takaiwa. Cast: Kokichi Takada, Miki Mori, Michiko Saga. Distribution: Shochiku. Release date: April 5, 1959.

THE SINGING SWORDSMAN (*Utashigure Senryo Tabi*). Director: Hideaki Onishi. Screenplay: Tadashi Ogawa. Cast: Kotaro Satomi, Hiromi Hanazono, Eiko Maruyama. Distribution: Toei. Release date: February 18, 1959. 61 minutes.

SOULS IN THE MOONLIGHT III (*Daibosatsu Toge Kanketsu-Hen*). Director: Tomu Uchida. Cast: Chiezo Kataoka (Ryunosuke Tsukue), Kinnosuke Nakamura [Yorozuya], Yumiko Hasegawa. Distribution: Toei. Release date: April 28, 1959. 106 minutes.

A SWORD AGAINST INTRIGUE (or *BORED HATAMOTO: RIDDLE OF THE FOREIGN DRUM*; *Hatamoto Taikutsu Otoko: Nazo no Nanban-Daiko*). Director: Yasushi Sasaki. Screenplay: Kaneo Ikegami. Cast: Utaemon Ichikawa, Kinya Kitaoji, Yoshiko Sakuma, Hiroko Sakuramachi. Distribution: Toei. Release date: Januray 9, 1959. 87 minutes

THE SWORD OF THE ITINERANT ACTOR (*Abare Kaido*). Director: Shigehiro Ozawa. Screenplay: Tai Kato, based on a story by Matsutaro Kawaguchi. Cast: Utaemon Ichikawa, Kotaro Satomi, Hiromi Hanazono, Yumiko Hasegawa. Distribution: Toei. Release date: March 25, 1959. 91 minutes.

TAKAMARU AND KIKUMARU (*Takamaru Kikumaru Shippu-Hen*). Director: Santaro Marune. Screenplay: Ryuta Mine. Cast: Kinshiro Matsumoto, Hiroshi Nawa, Kotobuki Hananomoto. Distribution: Shochiku. Release date: March 17, 1959.

THE TEN DUELS OF YOUNG SHINGO [Parts I and II] (*Shingo Juban-Shobu* [I], *Shingo Juban-Shobu Dai Nibu* [II]). Directors: Sadatsugu [Teiji] [Sadaji] Matsuda [I], Shigehiro Ozawa [II]. Screenplay: Matsutaro Kawaguchi. Cast: Hashizo Okawa (Shingo), Ryutaro Otomo, Yumiko Hasegawa. Distribution: Toei. Release dates: March 17, 1959 [I]; August 19, 1959 [II]. 96 minutes [I], 87 minutes [II].

TENRYU NO KARASU. Director: Kimiyoshi Yasuda. Screenplay: Shinichi Yanagawa. Cast: Shintaro Katsu, Shoji Umewaka, Joji Tsurumi. Distribution: Daiei. Release date: January 22, 1959. 83 minutes.

THE THIEF IS SHOGUN'S KINSMAN. Director: Tomu Uchida. Distribution: Toei.

THE THREE TREASURES (*Nippon Tanjo*). Director: Hiroshi Inagaki. Producers: Masumi [Sanezumi] Fujimoto, Tomoyuki Tanaka. Screenplay: Toshio Yasumi, Ryuzo Kikushima, based on legends of the Kojiki and Nihon Shoki. Photography: Kazuo Yamada [AgfaColor, TohoScope]. Lighting: Shoshichi Kojima. Art Direction: Kisaku Ito, Hiroshi Ueda. Music: Akira Ifukube. Sound: Yoshio Nishikawa, Hisashi Shimonaga. Editor: Kazuji Taira. Special Effects: Eiji Tsuburaya, Hidesaburo Araki, Akira Watanabe. Cast: Toshiro Mifune (Prince Yamato Takeru), Yoko Tsukasa (Princess Tachibana), Akihiko Hirata (Takehiko), Kyoko Kagawa (Princess Miyazu), Takashi Shimura (Elder Kumaso), Setsuko Hara (Amaterasu, the Sun Goddess), Kumi Mizuno, Misa Uehara, Kinuyo Tanaka, Akira Kubo, Akira Takarada, Ganjiro Nakamura, Eijiro Tono, Jun Tazaki, Kenichi Enomoto, Hideyo [Eisei] Amamoto (Spectator at Gods' Dance), Kichijiro Ueda, Akira Sera, Minosuke Yamada, Yoshifumi Tajima, Michiyo Tamaki, Akira Tani, Keiko Muramatsu, Haruko Sugimura, Kakuko Murata, Yasuhisa Tsutsumi, Katsumi Tezuka, Chieko Nakakita, Nobuko Otowa, Ikio Sawamura, Shoichi Hirose, Hajime Izu, Bokuzen Hidari, Yu Fujiki, Ichiro Arishima, Junichiro Mukai, Yutaka Sada, Shin Otomo, Tadashi Okabe, Kozo Nomura, Hisaya Ito, Kyoro Sakurai, Fuyuki Murakami, Ko Mishima, Mitsuo Tsuda, Norihei Miki, Ryu Kuze, Yoshio Kosugi, Masayoshi Nagashima, Keiju Kobayashi, Akira Kitano, Shiro Tsuchiya, Nadao Kirino, Fumindo Matsuo, Daisuke Kato, Masao Masuda, Jiro Kumagai, Koji Uemura, Yasuhiro Shigenobu, Haruya Sakamoto, Rinsaku Ogata, Izumi Akimoto, Hiroyoshi Yamaguchi, Akira Yamada, Hiroyuki Wakita, Koji Iwamoto, Yoshiko Ieda, Midori Kishida, Michiko Kawa, Misako Asuka, Toshiko Higuchi, Teruko Mita, Harumi Ueno, Kingoro Yanagiya, Taro Asashio, Koji Tsuruta (Younger Kumaso). Distribution: Toho. Release date: October 25, 1959. 182 minutes. Alternate English titles: *Age of the Gods*, *The Birth of Japan*.

Toshiro Mifune as Prince Yamato in *The Three Treasures*.

284

THE VIOLENT LORD (*Abare Daimyo*). Director: Kokichi Uchide. Screenplay: Hyogo Suzuki. Cast: Utaemon Ichikawa, Keiko Okawa, Kogiku Hanayagi, Satomi Oka. Distribution: Toei. Release date: February 11, 1959. 90 minutes.

THE WOMAN AND THE PIRATE (*Onna to Kaizoku*). Director: Daisuke Ito. Screenplay: Fuji Yahiro, Daisuke Ito. Photography: Kazuo Miyagawa. Lighting: Genken Nakaoka. Art Direction: Yoshinobu Nishioka. Music: Akira Ifukube. Editor: Mitsuzo Miyata. Cast: Kazuo Hasegawa [Chojiro Hayashi] (Shogoro Ozaki), Machiko Kyo (Ayame/Oito), Isao Kimura (Koshichi), Toshio Chiba (Tsune), Saburo Date (Rihei), Yoichi Funaki (Take), Seizaburo Kawazu (Genjiro Kawashima), Mayumi Kurata (Ohyaku), Tokiko Mita, Ikuko Mori (Nishiki), Shunji Sakai (Mamedayu), Jun Tazaki (Yasu), Yoko Wakasugi (Tayu), Keiko Yumi (Kokin). Distribution: Daiei. Release date: April 1, 1959. 90 minutes.

YOTSUYA KAIDAN. Director: Kenji Misumi. Screenplay: Fuji Yahiro. Music: Seiichi Suzuki. Sound: Iwao Otani. Cast: Kazuo Hasegawa [Chojiro Hayashi], Yasuko Nakata, Sanemon Arashi, Joji Tsurumi. Distribution: Daiei. Release date: July 1, 1959. 84 minutes.

THE YOUNG CAVALIERS (*Futari Wakajishi*). Director: Kinnosuke Fukada. Screenplay: Michihei Muramatsu, based on a story by Yukio Namiki. Cast: Chiyonosuke Azuma, Sentaro Fushimi, Shinobu Chihara. Distribution: Toei. Release date: May 19, 1959.

YUTARO KODAN. Director: Katsuhiko Tasaka. Screenplay: Fuji Yahiro, based on a story by Renzaburo Shibata. Photography: Kohei Sugiyama. Art Direction: Yoshinobu Nishioka. Music: Nakaba Takahashi. Cast: Raizo Ichikawa, Yoko Uraji, Masako Kishi, Michiko Ai, Ryosuke Kagawa, Koichi Mizuhara, Tatsuya Ishiguro. Distribution: Daiei. Release date: January 14, 1959. 83 minutes.

1960

ABARE KAGO. Director: Shoji Matsumura. Screenplay: Hyogo Suzuki. Cast: Chiyonosuke Azuma, Tomisaburo Wakayama [Kenzaburo Jo], Eiko Maruyama. Distribution: Toei. Release date: December 6, 1960. 83 minutes.

THE ADVENTURES OF PRINCESS ANMITSU (*Anmitsu-Hime no Mushashugyo*). Director: Tatsuo Osone. Screenplay: Ichiro Sekizawa. Cast: Haruko Wanibuchi, Kanbi Fujiyama, Hiroshi Moriya. Distribution: Shochiku. Release date: December 27, 1960. 86 minutes.

DAYS OF YOUNG JIROCHO: BOSS OF TOKAI (*Wakaki Hi no Jirocho: Tokai no Kaoyaku*). Director: Masahiro Makino. Screenplay: Masahiro Makino, Kazuyoshi Takasawa, Ryunosuke Ono. Cast: Kinnosuke Nakamura [Yorozuya], Satomi Oka, Denjiro Okochi. Distribution: Toei. Release date: December 27, 1960. 88 minutes.

EDO NO ASAKAZE. Director: Hideaki Onishi. Screenplay: Hajime Takaiwa, based on a story by Kiichiro Yamate. Cast: Chiezo Kataoka, Keiko Okawa, Sentaro Fushimi. Distribution: Toei. Release date: November 29, 1960. 92 minutes.

THE GAMBLING SAMURAI (or *CHUJI KUNISADA*; *Kunisada Chuji*). Director: Senkichi Taniguchi. Producer: Masumi [Sanezumi] Fujimoto. Screenplay: Kaneto Shindo. Photography: Rokuro Nishigaki [Agfacolor, TohoScope]. Lighting: Choshiro Ishii. Art Direction: Morio [Takeo] Kita. Music: Masaru Sato. Sound: Wataru Onuma. Cast: Toshiro Mifune (Chuji), Daisuke Kato (Enzo), Tetsuro Tanba [Tamba] (Fumizo), Michiyo Aratama (Toku), Eijiro Tono (Kansuke). Distribution: Toho. Release date: March 29, 1960. 101 minutes.

KAGAMIYAMA KYOENROKU. Director: Masateru Nishiyama. Screenplay: Shinichi Yanagawa. Cast: Katsuhiko Kobayashi, Rieko Sumi, Mieko Kondo. Distribution: Daiei. Release date: December 21, 1960. 80 minutes.

KUROBE-DANI NO DAI-KENKYAKU. Director: Yasushi Sasaki. Screenplay: Shinji Kessoku, based on a story by Ikuo Akita. Cast: Utaemon Ichikawa, Kimiko Fukuda, Ryuji Shinagawa. Distribution: Toei. Release date: August 28, 1960. 86 minutes.

KYOKAKU HARUSAME-GASA. Director/Screenplay: Kunio Watanabe. Producer: Kazuyoshi Takeda. Cast: Kazuo Hasegawa [Chojiro Hayashi], Tamao Nakamura, Misako Uji. Distribution: Daiei. Release date: December 7, 1960. 85 minutes.

THE MASTER FENCER SEES THE WORLD (*Ganbare! Bangaku*). Director: Shue Matsubayashi. Producers: Masumi [Sanezumi] Fujimoto, Hisao Ichikawa. Screenplay: Matsuo Kishi, Kaneto Shindo, based on a story by Kyoji Shirai. Photography: Kozo Okazaki. Lighting: Kazuo Shimomura. Art Direction: Masatoshi Kato. Editor: Shuichi Anbara. Cast: Keiju Kobayashi, Takashi Shimura, Hiroshi Koizumi, Reiko Dan, Yukiko Shimazaki, Toru Abe, Asao Uchida, Shigeki Ishida, Ikio Sawamura. Distribution: Toho. Release date: October 16, 1960. 95 minutes.

MAN'S AMBITION (*Sake to Onna to Yari*). Director: Tomu Uchida. Screenplay: Masato Ide. Cast: Ryutaro Otomo, Chikage Awashima, Hiromi Hanazono. Distribution: Toei. Release date: May 15, 1960. 99 minutes.

THE OGRE ON MOUNT OE (*Oeyama Shuten Doji*). Director: Tokuzo Tanaka. Screenplay: Fuji Yahiro, based on the novel by Matsutaro Kawaguchi. Photography: Hiroshi Imai. Music: Ichiro Saito. Cast: Kazuo Hasegawa [Chojiro Hayashi] (Shuten-doji), Raizo Ichikawa (Minamoto no Yorimitsu), Shintaro Katsu (Watanabe no Tsuna), Kojiro Hongo (Sakata no Kintoki), Ganjiro Nakamura, Yutaka Nakamura, Naritoshi Hayashi (Urabe no Suetake), Ryuzo Shimada (Sadamitsu Usui), Sachiko Hidari (Ibaragi), Fujiko Yamamoto. Distribution: Daiei. Release date: April 27, 1960. 114 minutes.

THE PIRATES (*Kaizoku Bahansen*). Director: Tadashi Sawashima. Screenplay: Kazuyoshi Takasawa. Photography: Takeo Ito. Music: Seiichi Suzuki. Cast: Hashizo Okawa, Satomi Oka, Eiji Okada. Distribution: Toei. Release date: September 18, 1960. 105 minutes.

THE REBEL GENERAL (*Teki wa Hannoji ni Ari*). Director: Tatsuo Osone. Screenplay: Shotaro Ikenami. Cast: Koshiro Matsumoto, Keiko Kishi, Takahiro Tamura, Michiko Saga. Distribution: Shochiku. Release date: September 11, 1960.

THE RIVER FUEFUKI (*Fuefuki-Gawa*). Director/Screenplay: Keisuke Kinoshita, based on a story by Shichiro Fukazawa. Photography: Hiroyuki Kusuda (Color, GrandScope). Art Direction: Kisaku Ito, Kohei Ezaki. Music: Tadashi Kinoshita. Cast: Takahiro Tamura (Sadahei), Hideko Takamine (Okei), Somegoro Ichikawa (Sozo, 1st son), Mannosuke Nakamura (Yasuzo, 2nd son), Shinji Tanaka (Heikichi, 3rd son), Shima Iwashita (Ume). Distribution: Shochiku. Release date: October 19, 1960.

SATAN'S SWORD (or *THE GREAT BUDDHA PASS*; *Daibosatsu Toge*). Director: Kenji Misumi. Producer: Masaichi Nagata. Screenplay: Teinosuke Kinugasa, based on the novel by Kaizan Nakazato. Photography: Hiroshi Imai [Eastmancolor, DaieiScope]. Lighting: Kenichi Okamoto. Art Direction: Akira Naito. Music: Seiichi Suzuki. Sound: Iwao Otani. Cast: Raizo Ichikawa (Ryunosuke Tsukue), Tamao Nakamura (Ohama), Kojiro Hongo (Hyoma Utsugi), Chishu Ryu (old master), Jun Negami, Fujiko Yamamoto (Omatsu), Shogo Shimada, Kenji Sugawara. Distribution: Daiei. Release date: October 18, 1960. 106 minutes. Video: Samurai Video.

SATAN'S SWORD II (or *THE DRAGON GOD*; *Daibosatsu Toge: Ryujin no Maki*). Director: Kenji Misumi. Producer: Masaichi Nagata. Screenplay: Teinosuke Kinugasa, based on the novel by Kaizan Nakazato. Photography: Hiroshi Imai [Eastmancolor, DaieiScope]. Art Direction: Akira Naito. Music: Ichiro Saito. Cast: Raizo Ichikawa (Ryunosuke Tsukue), Tamao Nakamura, Kojiro Hongo, Mieko Kondo, Tokiko Mita, Reiko Fujiwara, Akihiko

Katayama, Fujiko Yamamoto. Distribution: Daiei. Release date: December 27, 1960. 90 minutes. Video: Samurai Video.

SECRETS OF A COURT MASSEUR (*Shiranui Kengyo*). Director: Kazuo [Issei] Mori. Producer: Kazuyoshi Takeda. Screenplay: Minoru Inuzuka, based on a novel by Nobuo Uno. Photography: Soichi Aisaka. Lighting: Genken Nakaoka. Art Direction: Seiichi Ota. Music: Ichiro Saito. Sound: Iwao Otani. Cast: Shintaro Katsu, Tamao Nakamura, Toru Abe, Mieko Kondo, Mayumi Kurata, Joji Tsurumi, Yoko Wakasugi. Distribution: Daiei. Release date: September 1, 1960. 90 minutes.

SORETSU SHINSENGUMI: BAKUMATSU NO DORAN. Director: Yasushi Sasaki. Screenplay: Yoshitake Hisa, based on a story by Kyoji Shirai. Cast: Chiezo Kataoka (Isami Kondo), Tomisaburo Wakayama [Kenzaburo Jo] (Soji [Soshi] Okita), Hashizo Okawa, Ryutaro Otomo, Kokichi Takada, Ryunosuke Tsukigata, Kotaro Satomi, Isao Yamagata, Yataro Kurokawa. Distribution: Toei. Release date: July 10, 1970. 101 minutes.

SWORD OF DESTINY (*Koken wa Orezu: Tsukikage Itto Ryu*). Director: Yasushi Sasaki. Screenplay: Masashige Narusawa. Photography: Motoya Washio. Cast: Koji Tsuruta, Hiroko Sakuramachi, Yoshiko Fujita, Hibari Misora. Distribution: Toei. Release date: December 11, 1960. 89 minutes.

SURONIN HYAKUMAN-GOKU. Director: Shoji Matsumura. Screenplay: Shinji Kessoku, based on a story by Kiichiro Yamate. Cast: Utaemon Ichikawa, Chiyonosuke Azuma, Jushiro Konoe, Keiko Okawa. Distribution: Toei. Release date: November 15, 1960. 85 minutes.

TANGE SAZEN: YOTO NURETSUBAME [III] (1960). SEE *Tange Sazen* (1958).

TENKA GOMEN. Director: Kunio Watanabe. Screenplay: Kunio Watanabe, Tomotaka Motoyama. Cast: Koshiro Matsumoto, Isuzu Yamada, Michiko Saga. Distribution: Shochiku. Release date: December 11, 1960. 85 minutes.

THRONE OF FLAME (*Hono no Shiro*). Director: Tai Kato. Screenplay: Toshio Yasumi, based on the play "Hamlet" by William Shakespeare. Photography: Sadaji [Sadatsugu] [Teiji] Yoshida. Music: Akira Ifukube Cast: Hashizo Okawa, Yoshiko Mita, Denjiro Okochi, Mieko Takamine. Distribution: Toei. Release date: October 30, 1960. 98 minutes.

TSUKINODE NO KETTO. Director: Daisuke Ito. Screenplay: Daisuke Ito, based on a story by Matsutaro Kawaguchi. Cast: Shintaro Katsu, Tamao Nakamura, Yataro Kitagami. Distribution: Daiei. Release date: November 16, 1960. 77 minutes.

WAKASAMA SAMURAI TORIMONOCHO. Director: Yasushi Sasaki. Cast: Hashizo Okawa, Hiroko Sakuramachi, Hiromi Hanazono. Distribution: Toei. Release date: December 27, 1960. 84 minutes.

WANPAKU KOSHI. Director: Mitsuo Hirotsu. Screenplay: Masaharu Matsumura. Cast: Joji Tsurumi, Yoko Uraji, Yutaka Nakamura, Ryuzo Shimada. Distribution: Daiei. Release date: November 22, 1960. 69 minutes.

YOKADEN. Director: Bin Kato. Screenplay: Tetsuro Yoshida, based on a story by Kikuo Tsunoda. Cast: Matasaburo Niwa, Naritoshi Hayashi, Ryuzo Shimada. Distribution: Daiei. Release date: December 21, 1960. 70 minutes.

YOUNG LORD (*Bara Daimyo*). Director: Kazuo Ikehiro. Photography: Heizo Honda. Music: Tetsuo Tsukahara. Cast: Katsuhiko Kobayashi, Yoko Uraji, Raizo Ichikawa. Distribution: Daiei. Release date: December 7, 1960. 68 minutes.

ZOKU JIROCHO FUJI. Director: Kazuo [Issei] Mori. Screenplay: Fuji Yahiro. Music: Hirooki Ogawa. Cast: Kazuo Hasegawa [Chojiro Hayashi] (Shimizu no Jirocho), Raizo Ichikawa, Shintaro Katsu (Mori no Ishimatsu), Kojiro Hongo, Michiko Ai, Tamao Nakamura. Distribution: Daiei. Release date: June 1, 1960. 108 minutes.

1961-62

AKO ROSHI (1961). Director: Sadatsugu [Teiji] [Sadaji] Matsuda. Producer: Hiroshi Okawa. Screenplay: Hideo Oguni, based on a novel by Jiro Osaragi. Photography: Shintaro Kawasaki. Cast: Chiezo Kataoka (Kuranosuke Oishi), Kinnosuke Nakamura [Yorozuya] (Lord Awaji Wakisaka), Chiyonosuke Azuma (Yasubei Horibe), Hashizo Okawa (Lord Takumi Asano), Satomi Oka (Osen), Hiroko Sakuramachi (Osaki), Hiromi Hanazono (Sakura), Keiko Okawa, Katsuo Nakamura (Denkichi), Kotaro Satomi (Tsunanori Uesugi), Hiroki Matsukata (Chikara Oishi), Eijiro Yanagi (Lord Dewa Yanagisawa), Jun Tatara, Koinosuke Onoe (Tadashichi Takebayashi), Ushio Akashi (Soemon Hara), Jotaro Togami (Heihachiro Kobayashi), Kusuo Abe (Katada), Kunio Kaga, Kensaku Hara, Yumiko Hasegawa (Chiyo), Kogiku Hanayagi, Kyoko Aoyama (Kaede), Shinobu Chihara (Ukihashi Dayu), Michiyo Kogure (Osune), Denjiro Okochi (Sakon Tachibana), Jushiro Konoe (Ikkaku Shimizu), Isao Yamagata (Gengoemon Kataoka), Kenji Susukida (Yasubei Horibe), Eitaro Shindo (Denpachiro Okado), Ryunosuke Tsukigata (Kozukenosuke Kira), Ryutaro Otomo (Hotta), Utaemon Ichikawa (Hyobu Chisaka). Distribution: Toei. Release date: March 28, 1961. 150 minutes.

AOI NO ABARENBO (1961). Director: Daisuke Yamazaki. Screenplay: Hideo Oguni. Cast: Kinja Kitaoji, Hiroko Yoshikawa, Midori Isomura. Distribution: Toei. Release date: June 11, 1961. 86 minutes.

ARIGATAYA SANDOGASA (*Moriya Hiroshi no Sandogasa Shiriizu: Arigataya Sandogasa*, 1961). Director: Jun Fukuda. Producers: Reiji Miwa, Shiro Yamamoto. Screenplay: Shinichi Sekizawa. Lighting: Rokuro Ishikawa. Art Direction: Hiroshi Ueda. Music: Kenjiro Hirose. Sound: Norio Tone. Editor: Ryohei Fujii. Fencing Choreography: Ryu Kuze. Cast: Hiroshi Moriya, Makoto Sato, Mie Hama, Sachio Sakai, Fumie Noguchi, Rumiko Sasa, Shoichi Hirose, Takeshi Sakamoto, Tadashi Okabe, Yutaka Nakayama. Distribution: Toho. Release date: August 6, 1961. 71 minutes.

BANDITS ON THE WIND (*Yato Kaze no Naka o Hashiru*, 1961). Director: Hiroshi Inagaki. Producer: Tomoyuki Tanaka. Screenplay: Masato Ide, Hiroshi Inagaki. Photography: Kazuo Yamada [TohoScope]. Lighting: Shoshichi Kojima. Art Direction: Hiroshi Ueda. Music: Kan Ishii. Sound: Yoshio Nishikawa. Cast: Yosuke Natsuki (Taro), Makoto Sato, Somegoro Ichikawa (Gen), Izumi Yukimura (Kayo), Chishu Ryu (Village Priest), Akiko Wakabayashi (Sawa), Mannosuke Nakamura, Jun Tatara, Tadao Nakamaru, Koshiro Matsumoto, Chusha Ichikawa, Akira Tani. Distribution: Toho. Release date: November 22, 1961. 111 minutes.

BISHONEN HENGE (1961). Director: Kimiyoshi Yasuda. Screenplay: Fuji Yahiro, based on a story by Toshio Kitamura. Cast: Junichiro Narita, Misako Uji, Matasaburo Niwa. Distribution: Daiei. Release date: May 31, 1961. 62 minutes.

BISHONEN HENGE: TATSU NO MISAKI NO KETTO (1961). Director: Katsuhiko Tasaka. Screenplay: Fuji Yahiro, based on a story by Toshio Kitamura. Cast: Junichiro Narita, Misako Uji, Matasaburo Niwa. Distribution: Daiei. Release date: June 21, 1961.

CHARINKO KAIDO (1961). Director: Kokichi Uchide. Screenplay: Tadashi Ogawa. Cast: Kokichi Takada, Tomisaburo Wakayama [Kenzaburo Jo], Mari Watanabe. Distribution: Toei. Release date: June 6, 1961. 87 minutes.

CHUSHINGURA—"FORTY-SEVEN RONIN" (*Chushingura: Hana no Maki, Yuki no Maki*, 1962). Director: Hiroshi Inagaki. Producers: Masumi [Sanezumi] Fujimoto, Tomoyuki Tanaka, Hiroshi Inagaki. Screenplay: Toshio Yasumi, based on the play *"Kanadehon Chushingura"* by Shoraku Miyoshi, Senryu Namiki, Izumo Takeda. Photography: Kazuo Yamada [Eastmancolor, TohoScope]. Lighting: Shoshichi Kojima. Art Direction: Kisaku Ito, Hiroshi Ueda. Music: Akira Ifukube. Sound: Yoshio Nishikawa. Editor: Koichi Iwashita. Fight Choreography: Ryu Kuze. Cast: Koshiro Matsumoto (Chamberlain Kuranosuke Oishi), Yuzo

Koshiro Matsumoto as Oishi in Inagaki's *Chushingura*.

Kinnosuke Nakamura in *Conspirator*.

Kayama (Lord Naganori Asano), Tatsuya Mihashi (Yasubei Horibe), Akira Takarada (Gunbei Takada), Yosuke Natsuki (Kinemon Okano), Mannosuke Nakamura (Sanpei Kayano), Chusha Ichikawa (Lord Kozukenosuke Kira), Toshiro Mifune (Genba Tawaraboshi), Makoto Sato (Kazuemon Fuwa), Tadao Takashima (Jujiro Hazama), Seizaburo Kawazu (Chuzaemon Yoshida), Takashi Shimura (Hyobu Chisaka), Daisuke Kato (Kichiemon Terasaka), Keiju Kobayashi (Lord Awaji Wakisaka), Ryo Ikebe (Chikara Tsuchiya), Setsuko Hara (Riku Oishi), Yoko Tsukasa (Aguri Asano), Reiko Dan (Okaru), Yuriko Hoshi (Otsuya), Yumi Shirakawa (Ume), Kumi Mizuno (Saho), Mie Hama (Woman Refugee), Nami Tamura, Yoko Fujiyama (Miyuki the Asano maid), Junko Ikeuchi (Ofumi, of the tea shop), Keiko Awaji (Otoki, Hanbei's wife), Mitsuko Kusabue, Michiyo Aratama, Hisaya Morishige (Hanbei), Frankie Sakai (Heigoro the carpenter), Norihei Miki (Rihei, the male geisha), Kingoro Yanagiya (Otokichi, of the tatami shop), Kiiton Masuda (Tachu Matsubara), Mutoshi Happa (Tokuzo), Toru Yuri (Nonta, Heigoro's cousin), Toshiaki Minami (Denpachi, Heigoro's cousin), Kyu Sazanka (Lord Dewa Yanagisawa), Ichiro Arishima (Lord Denpachiro Okado), Hiroshi Koizumi (Gengo Otaka), Yu Fujiki (Tadashichi Takebayashi), Akira Kubo (Lord Date), Akihiko Hirata (Yasoemon Okajima), Kenji Sahara (Asano Samurai), Hiroshi Tachikawa (Tsunanori Uesugi), Tatsuyoshi Ehara (Daigaku Asano), Tadao Nakamaru (Heihachiro Kobayashi), Sachio Sakai, Yoshio Tsuchiya (Matanojo Ushioda, Saho's brother), Kamatari Fujiwara (Kyubei the innkeeper), Jun Tazaki (Kiken Murakami), Susumu Fujita (Yosobei Kajikawa), Ken Uehara (Seikanji), Jun Funato (Sanburoji Kaizuka), Kiyoshi Kodama, Hisaya Ito (Sezaemon Oishi), Kozo Nomura, Ko Mishima, Kunio Otsuka, Ren Yamamoto (Yogoro Kanzaki), Hideyo [Eisei] Amamoto (Takano), Nadao Kirino (Asano Samurai), Heihachiro Okawa (Kyudayu Mase), Shigeki Ishida (Rishichi), Akira Tani, Yoshifumi Tajima, Ikio Sawamura (Tatami Maker), Yoshio Kosugi (Yahei Horibe, Yasubei's father), Sonomi Nakajima (Otama), Machiko Kitagawa (Okiyo, the bathing guard), Keiko Yanagawa, Mieko Kurenai, Misako Asuka, Hiromi Mineoka, Yaeko Izumo, Haruko Togo (Okyo, Sasaya's wife), Atsuko Ichinomiya (Otomi, Kyubei's wife), Chieko Nakakita (Ofude), Ryosuke Kagawa (Soemon Hara), Soji Kiyokawa (Matazaemon Fujii), Unpei Yokoyama (Matsuemon, Heigoro's uncle), Haruyuki Kato, Yoji Misaki, Gen Shimizu (Gensuke Araga), Jotaro Togami (Ikkaku Shimizu), Sadako Sawamura (Tomiko, Konosuke's wife), Kiyoko Tsuji, Kumeko Otowa, Teruko Mita, Noriko Sakabe, Naoko Sakabe, Shin Otomo, Yutaka Nakayama, Mitsuo Tsuda, Keiichiro

Katsumoto, Hiroshi Akitsu, Haruo Suzuki, Jun Kuroki, Kanzo Uni, Koji Iwamoto, Katsumi Tezuka, Akio Kusama, Kamayuki Tsubono, Koji Uruki, Rinsaku Ogata, Yu Sekita, Hiroyoshi Yamaguchi, Masaki Shinohara, Ryuichi Hosokawa, Saburo Kadowaki, Tadashi Okabe, Akira Yamada, Junpei Natsuki, Koichi Sato, Kenzo Echigo, Jiro Mitsuaki, Ichiro Chiba (Yanagihara), Seiji Ikeda, Junichiro Mukai, Somegoro Ichikawa. Distribution: Toho. Release date: November 3, 1962. 204 minutes. Video: Image.

CONSPIRATOR (*Hangyakuji*, 1961). Director/Screenplay: Daisuke Ito. Photography: Makoto Tsuboi [Eastmancolor; ToeiScope]. Music: Akira Ifukube. Cast: Kinnosuke Nakamura [Yorozuya], Kaneko Iwasaki, Haruko Sugimura, Chiyonosuke Azuma, Hiroko Sakuramachi, Shuji Sano. Distribution: Toei. Release date: November 8, 1961. 110 minutes.

DAREDEVIL IN THE CASTLE (*Osaka-jo Monogatari*, 1961). Director: Hiroshi Inagaki. Producer: Tomoyuki Tanaka. Screenplay: Takeshi Kimura, Hiroshi Inagaki, based on a story by Genzo Murakami. Photography: Kazuo Yamada [Eastmancolor; TohoScope]. Lighting: Shoshichi Kojima. Art Direction: Hiroshi Ueda. Music: Akira Ifukube. Sound: Yoshio Nishikawa, Masanobu Miyazaki. Editor: Koichi Iwashita. Fencing Choreography: Ryu Kuze. Special Effects: Eiji Tsuburaya. Cast: Toshiro Mifune (Mohei), Kyoko Kagawa (Ai), Yuriko Hoshi (Lady Sen), Yoshiko Kuga (Kobue), Isuzu Yamada (Yodogimi), Yosuke Natsuki (Lord Nagato Kimura), Jun Tazaki (Zekaibo Tsutsui), Danko Ichikawa (Saizo Kirigakure), Akihiko Hirata (Hayatonosho 'Hayato' Susukida), Takashi Shimura (Katsumoto Katagiri), Saeko Kuroiwa (Nobuo), Tetsuro Tanba [Tamba] (Sadamasa Ishikawa), Tadao Nakamaru (Hyogo), Ryosuke Kagawa (Itamiya), Yu Fujiki (Danemon Ban), Seizaburo Kawazu (Harunaga Ono), Susumu Fujita (Katsuyasu Sakakibara), Hanshiro Iwai [Shubo Nishina] (Hideyori Toyotomi), Sachio Sakai (Kai), Yoshio Kosugi (Gidayu Morimoto), Kichijiro Ueda (Zenbei, the equipment-shop owner), Ren Yamamoto, Chieko Nakakita (Yae), Haruko Togo (Ono no Otsu), Hideyo [Eisei] Amamoto (Interpreter), Junichiro Mukai (Kumoi), Seiji Ikeda (Chusho Nanjo), Shiro Tsuchiya (Zusho Hotta), Akira Tani (Rice-Shop Owner), Shin Otomo (Itamiya manager), Katsumi Tezuka (Shume Ono), Senkichi Omura, Ikio Sawamura, Koji Uno, Yasuhisa Tsutsumi, Haruo Nakajima, Hans Horneff, Bill Bassman, Toshiko Nakano, Yusef Osman, Shigeki Ishida, Tadashi Okabe, Yu Sekita. Distribution: Toho. Release date: January 3, 1961. 97 minutes.

Toshiro Mifune as Mokei in *Daredevil in the Castle.*

DESTINY'S SON (*Kiru*, 1962). Director: Kenji Misumi. Screenplay: Kaneto Shindo. Photography: Shozo Honda [DaieiColor; DaieiScope]. Cast: Raizo Ichikawa (Shingo Takakura), Shiho Fujimura, Mayumi Nagisa, Junichiro Narita, Masayo Banri, Shigeru Amachi. Distribution: Daiei. Release date: July 1, 1962. 71 minutes. Video: Samurai Video.

DUEL WITHOUT END (or *MIYAMOTO MUSASHI II*; *Miyamoto Musashi Hannyazaka no Ketto*, 1962). Director: Tomu Uchida. Producer: Hiroshi Okawa. Screenplay: Tomu Uchida, Naoyuki Suzuki, based on the novel *"Miyamoto Musashi"* by Eiji Yoshikawa. Photography: Makoto Tsuboi [EastmanColor; ToeiScope]. Lighting: Hiroshi Watada. Art Direction: Takatoshi Suzuki. Music: Taichiro Kosugi. Sound: Hiroo Notsu. Editor: Shintaro Miyamoto. Fight Choreography: Reijiro Adachi. Cast: Kinnosuke Nakamura [Yorozuya] (Musashi Miyamoto), Rentaro Mikuni (Takuan), Satomi Oka (Akemi), Wakaba Irie (Otsu), Shinjiro Ebara (Seijuro Yoshioka), Isao Kimura (Matahachi Hon'iden), Ryunosuke Tsukigata (Nikkan), Michiyo Kogure (Oko), Chieko Naniwa (Osugi), Hiroshi Minami (Toji Gion), Seiji Miyaguchi (Kisuke), Yataro Kurokawa (Inshun). Distribution: Toei. Release date: November 17, 1962. 107 minutes. Alternate English Title: *Showdown at Hannyazaka*. Video: Samurai Video.

EDOKKO BUGYO: TENKA O KIRU OTOKO (1961). Director: Yasushi Sasaki. Photography: Makoto Tsuboi. Music: Taichiro Kosugi. Cast: Kinnosuke Nakamura [Yorozuya], Satomi Oka, Keiko Okawa. Distribution: Toei. Release date: March 12, 1961. 89 minutes.

EDOKKO HADA (1961). Director: Masahiro Makino. Screenplay: Shinji Kessoku, based on a story by Kanji Kunieda. Photography: Sadaji [Sadatsugu] [Teiji] Yoshida [ToeiColor]. Cast: Hashizo Okawa, Yataro Kurokawa, Hiroko Sakuramachi, Chikage Awashima, Isao Yamagata, Ryuji Kita, Tatsuya Ishiguro. Distribution: Toei. Release date: February 7, 1961. 86 minutes.

EDO PROSPERITY (*Edokko Hanjoki*, 1961). Director: Masahiro Makino. Screenplay: Masashige Narusawa. Cast: Kinnosuke Nakamura [Yorozuya], Yumiko Hasegawa, Chitose Kobayashi, Mikijiro Hira. Distribution: Toei. Release date: August 26, 1961. 90 minutes.

EPHEMERAL SAMURAI (*Kagero Samurai*, 1961). Director: Kazuo Ikehiro. Screenplay: Masaharu Matsumura, based on a story

by Daisuke Ito. Cast: Raizo Ichikawa, Yoko Uraji, Tamao Nakamura, Reiko Fujiwara. Release date: November 19, 1961. 89 minutes.

FESTIVAL OF SWORDSMEN (or *GOBLIN FESTIVAL*; *Kengo Tengu Matsuri*, 1961). Director: Shigehiro Ozawa. Screenplay: Hajime Takaiwa, based on a story by Tsuneo Tomita. Cast: Ryutaro Otomo, Keiko Okawa, Satomi Oka, Tomisaburo Wakayama [Kenzaburo Jo], Eiji Okada. Distribution: Toei. Release date: March 21, 1961. 87 minutes.

FUJI NI TATSU WAKAMUSHA (1961). Director: Tadashi Sawashima. Screenplay: Kazuyoshi Takasawa. Music: Seiichi Suzuki. Cast: Hashizo Okawa, Yoshiko Mita, Kunio Kaga, Sonosuke Sawamura. Distribution: Toei. Release date: April 9, 1961. 93 minutes.

FURISODE KOSHO TORIMONOCHO: CHIMONJI HADA (1961). Director: Kinnosuke Fukada. Screenplay: Kaneo Ikegami. Cast: Tossho Sawamura, Sentaro Fushimi, Atsuko Nakazato. Distribution: Toei. Release date: July 2, 1961. 64 minutes.

FURISODE KOSHO TORIMONOCHO: HEBI-HIME BAYASHI (1961). Director: Kinnosuke Fukada. Screenplay: Kaneo Ikegami. Cast: Tossho Sawamura, Sentaro Fushimi, Atsuko Nakazato. Distribution: Toei. Release date: June 6, 1961. 64 minutes.

THE GAMBLER'S CODE (*Kutsukake Tokijiro*, 1961). Director: Kazuo Ikehiro. Screenplay: Masao Uno. Cast: Raizo Ichikawa, Michiyo Aratama, Haruko Sugimura. Distribution: Daiei. Release date: June 14, 1961. 86 minutes.

GHOST STORY OF YOTSUYA: CURSE OF OIWA (*Kaidan Oiwa no Borei*, 1961). Director: Tai Kato. Screenplay: Tai Kato, based on a novel by Nanboku Tsuruya. Photography: Osamu [Osami] [Shin] Furuya. Music: Nakaba Takahashi. Editor: Kozo Horiike. Cast: Tomisaburo Wakayama [Kenzaburo Jo], Tossho Sawamura, Jushiro Konoe, Sentaro Fushimi, Hiroko Sakuramachi, Yumiko Mihara, Yoshiko Fujishiro, Koinosuke Onoe, Atsushi Watanabe. Distribution: Toei. Release date: July 2, 1961. 94 minutes.

GYAKUSHU AMANOHASHIDATE (1961). Director: Kiyoharu Akimoto. Screenplay: Michihei Muramatsu. Cast: Kotaro Satomi, Ryuji Shinagawa, Keiko Ogimachi. Distribution: Toei. Release date: August 1, 1961. 63 minutes.

GOLDEN PEACOCK CASTLE [Parts I, II, III, and IV] (*Shin Shokoku Monogatari: Ogon Kujaku-Jo* [I], 1961; *Shin Shokoku Monogatari: Ogon Kujaku-Jo Dai Nibu* [II], 1961; *Shin Shokoku Monogatari: Ogon Kujaku-Jo Dai Sanbu* [III], 1961; *Shin Shokoku Monogatari: Ogon Kujaku-Jo Kanketsu-Hen* [IV], 1961). Director: Shoji Matsumura. Screenplay: Shinji Kessoku, based on a story by Toshio Kitamura. Cast: Tossho Sawamura, Kotaro Satomi, Choichiro Kawarazaki, Shingo Yamashiro. Distribution: Toei. Release dates: March 28, 1961 [I]; April 9, 1961 [II,III]; April 18, 1961 [IV]. 50 minutes [I], 57 minutes [II], 57 minutes [III], and 55 minutes [IV].

HAKKO RYUKITAI (1961). Director: Eiichi Kudo. Screenplay: Yoshitake Hisa. Music: Eiichi Yamada. Cast: Utaemon Ichikawa, Chiyonosuke Azuma, Choichiro Kawarazaki. Distribution: Toei. Release date: May 11, 1961. 90 minutes.

HANAGASA FUTARI WAKASHU (1961). Director: Yasushi Sasaki. Screenplay: Hideo Oguni. Cast: Kinya Kitaoji, Hiroki Matsukata, Hiromi Hanazomo. Distribution: Toei. Release date: May 17, 1961.

HAREKOSODE (1961). Director: Kimiyoshi Yasuda. Screenplay: Yoshikata Yoda, based on a story by Matsutaro Kawaguchi. Cast: Kazuo Hasegawa [Chojiro Hayashi], Yumeji Tsukioka, Yachiyo Otori, Takashi Shimura. Distribution: Daiei. Release date: January 9, 1961. 84 minutes.

HASHIZO NO WAKASAMA YAKUZA (1961). Director: Toshikazu Kono. Screenplay: Shinji Kessoku, based on story by Kokichi Kitazono. Cast: Hashizo Okawa, Isao Kimura, Keiko Okawa. Distribution: Toei. Release date: June 11, 1961. 90 minutes.

HATAMOTO KENKA-DAKA (1961). Director: Nobuo Nakagawa. Screenplay: Hyogo Suzuki. Photography: Shintaro Kawasaki. Music: Eiichi Yamada. Cast: Utaemon Ichikawa, Yumiko Hasegawa, Ryuji Shinagawa, Atsushi Watanabe. Distribution: Toei. Release date: March 5, 1961. 81 minutes.

HAYABUSA DAIMYO (1961). Director: Shigehiro Ozawa. Screenplay: Fuji Yahiro, based on a story by Rifu Yukitomo. Cast: Chiezo Kataoka, Chiyonosuke Azuma, Keiko Okawa. Distribution: Toei. Release date: June 21, 1961. 87 minutes.

HIZAKURA KOTENGU (1961). Director: Daisuke Yamazaki. Screenplay: Goro Tanada, based on a story by Torao Setoguchi. Cast: Hibari Misora, Keiko Okawa, Ryuji Shinagawa. Distribution: Toei. Release date: April 25, 1961. 77 minutes.

ISOBUSHI GENTA (1961). Director: Kimiyoshi Yasuda. Screenplay: Shozaburo Asai. Cast: Yukio Hashi, Joji Tsurumi, Hajime [Gen] Mitamura. Distribution: Daiei. Release date: July 19, 1961. 64 minutes.

ITAKO-GASA (1961). Director: Akira [Sho] Inoue. Screenplay: Hachiro Nishimura. Cast: Katsuhiko Kobayashi, Yukio Hashi, Mieko Kondo. Distribution: Daiei. Release date: January 27, 1961. 74 minutes.

KAIJU JAKUMA NO MOSHU (1961). Director: Kiyoharu Akimoto. Screenplay: Michihei Muramatsu. Cast: Kotaro Satomi, Ryuji Shinagawa, Keiko Ogimachi. Distribution: Toei. Release date: July 26, 1961. 60 minutes.

KAZE TO KUMO TO TORIDE (1961). Director: Kazuo [Issei] Mori. Screenplay: Toshio Yasumi, based on a story by Yasushi Inoue. Cast: Shintaro Katsu, Kyoko Enami, Hajime [Gen] Mitamura. Distribution: Daiei. Release date: February 22, 1961. 93 minutes.

KENKA FUJI (1961). Director: Kunio Watanabe. Screenplay: Kunio Watanabe, Masaharu Muramatsu. Cast: Shintaro Katsu, Katsuhiko Kobayashi, Yukio Hashi, Yoko Uraji, Keiko Yumi. Distribution: Daiei. Release date: April 26, 1961. 87 minutes.

KIRIMARU KIRIGAKURE (1961). Director: Yasushi Sasaki. Screenplay: Shinji Kessoku. Photography: Motoyo Washio [ToeiColor]. Cast: Hiroki Matsukata, Hiromi Hanazono, Hiroko Yoshikawa. Distribution: Toei. Release date: May 3, 1961. 85 minutes.

KIRIMARU KIRIGAKURE: NANKAI NO OKAMI (1961). Director: Shoji Matsumura. Screenplay: Koji Takada. Cast: Hiroki Matsukata, Hiromi Hanazono, Hiroko Yoshikawa, Mikijiro Hira. Distribution: Toei. Release date: July 9, 1961. 86 minutes.

KISOBUSHI SANDOGASA (1961). Director: Bin Kato. Screenplay: Minoru Inuzuka. Cast: Katsuhiko Kobayashi, Hajime [Gen] Mitamura, Yukio Hashi. Distribution: Daiei. Release date: March 1, 1961. 70 minutes.

KOINA NO GINPEI (1961). Director: Tokuzo Tanaka. Screenplay: Minoru Inuzuka. Cast: Raizo Ichikawa, Tamao Nakamura, Junichiro Narita. Distribution: Daiei. Release date: August 27, 1961. 82 minutes.

KOJIRO TSUBAMEGAESHI (1961). Director: Katsuhiko Tasaka. Screenplay: Kenro Matsuura, based on a story by Kosuke Gomi. Cast: Shintaro Katsu, Tamao Nakamura, Hideo Takamatsu. Distribution: Daiei. Release date: January 9, 1961. 81 minutes.

MANSION OF THE BLOOD CURSE (*Chimonji Yashiki*, 1962). Director: Eiichi Kudo. Screenplay: Shinji Kessoku, based on a story by Fubo Hayashi [Umitaro Hasegawa]. Cast: Ryutaro Otomo, Satomi Oka, Hashizo Okawa. Distribution: Toei. Release date: November 11, 1962. 86 minutes.

MITO KOMON: SUKE-SAN KAKU-SAN O-ABARE (1961). Director: Tadashi Sawashima. Screenplay: Yoshio Shirasaka, Kazuyoshi Takasawa. Music: Masaru Sato. Cast: Hiroki Matsukata, Kinya Kitaoji, Haruo Tanaka, Mari Watanabe. Distribution: Toei. Release date: July 19, 1961. 91 minutes.

MITO KOMON UMI O WATARU (1961). Director: Kunio Watanabe. Screenplay: Kohan Kawauchi, Matsukichi Mori. Photography: Takashi Watanabe. Cast: Kazuo Hasegawa [Chojiro Hayashi], Raizo Ichikawa, Shintaro Katsu, Hitomi Nozoe, Reiko Fujiwara. Distribution: Daiei. Release date: July 12, 1961. 90 minutes.

MIYAMOTO MUSASHI - See *ZEN AND SWORD*, 1961

NAKITO GOZANSU (1961). Director: Jun Fukuda. Producers: Reiji Miwa, Shiro Yamamoto. Screenplay: Shinichi Sekizawa. Lighting: Rokuro Ishikawa. Art Direction: Hiroshi Ueda. Music: Kenjiro Hirose. Cast: Hiroshi Moriya, Mie Hama, Shin Morikawa, Shoichi Hirose, Yutaka Nakayama, Senkichi Omura, Makoto Sato, Sachio Sakai, Masanori Nihei, Fumie Noguchi, Yasuhisa Tsutsumi. Distribution: Toho. Release date: July 23, 1961. 73 minutes.

NARUTO HICHO [Parts I and II] (*Naruto Hicho* [I], 1961; *Naruto Hicho Kanketsu-Hen* [II], 1961). Director: Kokichi Uchide. Screenplay: Hajime Takaiwa. Cast: Koji Tsuruta, Keiko Okawa, Michiyo Kogure. Distribution: Toei. Release dates: January 26, 1961 [I]; February 19, 1961 [II]. 84 minutes [I], 88 minutes [II].

NINGYO SASHICHI TORIMONOCHO: YAMI NI WARAU TEKKAMEN (1961). Director: Junji Kurata. Screenplay: Shinji Kessoku, based on a story by Seishi Yokomizo. Cast: Tomisaburo Wakayama [Kenzaburo Jo], Yumiko Mihara, Atsuko Nakazato. Distribution: Toei. Release date: August 9, 1961. 60 minutes.

NINJA MESSENGER AND THE THREE DAUGHTERS [Parts I and II] (*Ninjutsu-Tsukai to Sannin Musume* [I], 1961; *Ninjutsu-Tsukai to Sannin Musume: Megitsune Henge* [II], 1961). Director: Masahiko Izawa. Screenplay: Yasuro Yokoyama. Cast: Tomisaburo Wakayama [Kenzaburo Jo], Shingo Yamashiro, Hiromi Hanazono. Distribution: Toei. Release dates: May 11, 1961 [I]; July 2, 1961 [II].

OKESA UTAEBA (1961). Director: Kazuo [Issei] Mori. Screenplay: Ryozo Kasahara. Cast: Raizo Ichikawa, Yoshie Mizutani, Yukio Hashi. Distribution: Daiei. Release date: April 5, 1961. 83 minutes.

OTEMOYAN (1961). Director: Shigeru Doi. Producer: Ikuo Kubodera. Screenplay: Hajime Takaiwa. Art Direction: Yoshinobu Nishioka. Music: Hirooki Ogawa. Cast: Joji Tsurumi, Yuko Miki, Hajime [Gen] Mitamura. Distribution: Daiei. Release date: May 3, 1961. 70 minutes.

OWARI NO ABARE-JISHI (1961). Director: Toshikazu Kono. Screenplay: Goro Tanada, based on a story by Kodo Nomura. Cast: Ryutaro Otomo, Tomisaburo Wakayama [Kenzaburo Jo], Satomi Oka. Distribution: Toei. Release date: February 1, 1961. 86 minutes.

THE RED SHADOW (or *REVENGER IN THE SHADOW*; *Akai Kageboshi*, 1961). Director: Shigehiro Ozawa. Screenplay: Yoshitake Hisa, based on a story by Renzaburo Shibata. Cast: Hashizo Okawa (Waka-Kage), Ryutaro Otomo (Jubei Yagyu), Jushiro Konoe (Hanzo Hattori), Yataro Kurokawa (Jiroemon Ono), Denjiro Okochi (Munenori Yagyu), Keiko Okawa (Yuri Endo), Kogiku Hanayagi (Lady Kasuga), Michiyo Kogure (Haha-Kage), Kotaro Satomi (Shintaro Yagyu), Shingo Yamashiro (Shinpachiro Suganuma), Ryuji Shinagawa (Kyutaro Urakata), Tossho Sawamura (Iemitsu Tokugawa). Distribution: Toei. Release date: December 24, 1961. 90 minutes.

SAIKORO BUGYO (1961). Director: Kokichi Uchide. Screenplay: Kenro Matsuura, based on a story by Tatsuro Jinde. Photography: Shigeto [Minoru] Miki. Art Direction: Norimichi Ikawa [Tokumichi Igawa]. Music: Nakaba Takahashi. Cast: Chiezo Kataoka, Eitaro Shindo, Kyoko Aoyama, Satomi Oka, Ryuji Kita, Ryosuke Kagawa, Yataro Kurokawa. Distribution: Toei. Release date: April 18, 1961. 90 minutes.

SAMURAI'S DAUGHTER (*Kodachi o Tsukau Onna*, 1961). Director: Kazuo Ikehiro. Screenplay: Yoshikata Yoda. Cast: Machiko Kyo, Tamao Nakamura, Katsuhiko Kobayashi. Distribution: Daiei. Release date: August 13, 1961. 81 minutes.

SATAN'S SWORD III (*Daibosatsu Toge: Kanketsu-Hen*, 1961). Director: Kazuo [Issei] Mori. Producer: Masaichi Nagata. Screenplay: Teinosuke Kinugasa, based on the novel by Kaizan Nakazato. Photography: Shozo Honda [Eastmancolor, DaieiScope]. Music: Tetsuo Tsukahara. Cast: Raizo Ichikawa, Tamao Nakamura, Katsuhiko Kobayashi, Kojiro Hongo, Mieko Kondo, Hajime [Gen] Mitamura. Distribution: Daiei. Release date: May 17, 1961. 98 minutes. Video: Samurai Video.

SENRYO GARASU (1961). Director: Ryo Hagiwara. Screenplay: Masao Uno, Ikuro Kishi. Cast: Haruo Minami, Michiko Saga, Michiyo Tamaki. Distribution: Shochiku. Release date: May 16, 1961. 81 minutes.

SEVEN KNIGHTS [Parts I, II, and III] (*Shin Ogon Kujaku-Jo: Shichinin no Kishi Dai Ichibu* [I], 1961; *Shin Ogon Kujaku-Jo: Shichinin no Kishi Dai Nibu* [II], 1961; *Shin Ogon Kujaku-Jo: Shichinin no Kishi Kanketsu-Hen* [III], 1961). Director: Kosaku Yamashita. Screenplay: Shinji Kessoku, Koji Takada. Cast: Kotaro Satomi, Shingo Yamashiro, Shintaro Yamanami. Distribution: Toei. Release dates: August 26, 1961 [I,II]; September 6, 1961 [III]. 56 minutes [I], 55 minutes [II], 56 minutes [III].

SHIKAKU YASHIKI (1961). Director: Shin Amano. Screenplay: Tetsuro Yoshida. Cast: Joji Tsurumi, Yoshiko Kamo, Matasaburo Niwa. Distribution: Daiei. Release date: February 22, 1961.

SHINGO'S CHALLENGE [Parts I and II] (*Shingo Nijuban Shobu* [I], 1961; *Shingo Nijuban Shobu Dai Nibu* [II], 1961). Director: Sadatsugu [Teiji] [Sadaji] Matsuda. Screenplay: Matsutaro Kawaguchi, Fumio Nakayama. Cast: Hashizo Okawa, Ryutaro Otomo, Satomi Oka. Distribution: Toei. Release dates: January 3, 1961 [I]; July 9, 1961 [II]. 88 minutes [I], 90 minutes [II].

THE SHOGUN AND THE FISHMONGER (*Iemitsu to Hikoza to Isshin Tasuke*, 1961). Director: Tadashi Sawashima. Screenplay: Hideo Oguni. Cast: Kinnosuke Nakamura [Yorozuya], Eitaro Shindo, Katsuo Nakamura. Distribution: Toei. Release date: January 3, 1961. 93 minutes.

SMUGGLERS IN THE GHOST LAND (*Yurei-jima no Okite*, 1961). Director: Yasushi Sasaki. Screenplay: Shinji Kessoku. Cast: Hashizo Okawa, Hibari Misora, Kinya Kitaoji, Hiroki Matsukata, Satomi Oka. Distribution: Toei. Release date: August 13, 1961. 95 minutes.

THE SWORD FLIES LIKE A SWALLOW (*Tange Sazen: Nuretsubame Itto-Ryu*, 1961). Director: Sadatsugu [Teiji] [Sadaji] Matsuda. Screenplay: Michihei Muramatsu, Kinya Naoi. Cast: Ryutaro Otomo, Hashizo Okawa, Satomi Oka. Distribution: Toei. Release date: May 3, 1961. 84 minutes.

TANGE SAZEN: KENUN UNKON NO MAKI [V] (1962). SEE Tange Sazen (1958).

TANGE SAZEN: NURETSUBAME ITTO-RYU [IV] (1961). SEE Tange Sazen (1958).

TENKA AYATSURI-GUMI (1961). Director: Kazuo Ikehiro. Screenplay: Tetsuro Yoshida, Takuji Umetani, based on story by Norio Nanjo. Cast: Keizo Kawasaki, Ganjiro Nakamura, Yoko Uraji. Distribution: Daiei. Release date: March 15, 1961. 80 minutes.

WAKAKI HI NO JIROCHO: TOKAI-ICHI NO WAKA-OYABUN (1961). Director: Masahiro Makino. Screenplay: Masahiro Makino, Ryunosuke Ono. Cast: Kinnosuke Nakamura [Yorozuya], Satomi Oka, Ryunosuke Tsukigata. Distribution: Toei. Release date: June 21, 1961. 93 minutes.

WAKATONO SENRYO-HADA (1961). Director: Kosaku Yamashita. Photography: Shoji Sugita. Music: Hideo Ozawa. Cast: Tossho Sawamura, Tomisaburo Wakayama [Kenzaburo Jo], Eiko Maruyama. Distribution: Toei. Release date: January 21, 1961. 65 minutes.

YORIKIRI WAKASAMA (1961). Director: Mitsuo Hirotsu. Screenplay: Tetsuro Yoshida. Cast: Hajime [Gen] Mitamura, Joji Tsurumi, Yutaka Nakamura. Distribution: Daiei. Release date: April 2, 1961. 67 minutes.

ZEN AND SWORD (or *UNTAMED FURY* or *MIYAMOTO MUSASHI I*; *Miyamoto Musashi*, 1961). Director: Tomu Uchida. Producer: Hiroshi Okawa. Screenplay: Masahige Narusawa, Naoyuki Suzuki, based on the novel *"Miyamoto Musashi"* by Eiji Yoshikawa. Photography: Makato Tsuboi [Eastmancolor; ToeiScope]. Lighting: Hiroshi Watada. Art Direction: Takatoshi Suzuki. Music: Akira Ifukube. Sound: Hiroo Notsu. Editor: Shintaro Miyamoto. Fight Choreography: Reijiro Adachi. Cast: Kinnosuke Nakamura [Yorozuya] (Takezo Shinmen (Musashi Miyamoto)), Isao Kimura (Matahachi Hon'iden), Michiyo Kogure (Oko), Chieko Naniwa (Osugi), Rentaro Mikuni (Takuan), Wakaba Irie (Otsu), Satomi Oka (Akemi), Minosuke Bando (Terumasa Ikeda), Kunio Kaga (Tenma Tsujikaze), Akiko Kazami (Ogin), Tokue Hanazawa (Tanzaemon Aoki), Kusuo Abe (Gonroku Fuchikawa), Seiji Miyaguchi (Kisuke). Distribution: Toei. Release date: May 27, 1961. 110 minutes. Video: Samurai Video.

See also *DUEL WITHOUT END* (*MIYAMOTO MUSASHI II*; *Miyamoto Musashi Hannyazaka no Ketto*, 1962); *THE WORTHLESS DUEL* (*MIYAMOTO MUSASHI III*; *Miyamoto Musashi Nitoryu Kaigen*, 1963); *DUEL AT ICHIJOJI TEMPLE* (*MIYAMOTO MUSASHI IV*; *Miyamoto Musashi Ichijoji no Ketto*, 1964); *THE LAST DUEL* (*MIYAMOTO MUSASHI V*; *Miyamoto Musashi Ganryujima no Ketto*, 1965); *SWORDS OF DEATH* (*MIYAMOTO MUSASHI VI*; *Shinken Shobu*, 1971).

ZENIGATA HEIJI TORIMONOCHO: YORU NO ENMACHO (1961). Director: Kunio Watanabe. Screenplay: Kunio Watanabe, Kyuichi Tsuji, based on a story by Kodo Nomura. Cast: Kazuo Hasegawa [Chojiro Hayashi], Tamao Nakamura, Hajime Hana. Distribution: Daiei. Release date: March 15, 1961. 87 minutes.

1963-64

AN ACTOR'S REVENGE (or *REVENGE OF A KABUKI ACTOR* or *THE REVENGE OF UKENO-JO*; *Yukinojo Henge*, 1963). Director: Kon Ichikawa. Producer: Masaichi Nagata. Screenplay: Daisuke Ito, Teinosuke Kinugasa, Natto Wada, based on the story by Otokichi Mikami. Photography: Setsuo Kobayashi [DaieScope]. Lighting: Kenichi Okamoto. Art Direction: Yoshinobu Nishioka. Music: Masao Yagi, Yasushi Akutagawa. Sound: Iwao Otani. Editor: Shigeo Nishida. Fight Choreography: Shohei Miyauchi. Cast: Kazuo Hasegawa [Chojiro Hayashi] (Yukinojo Nakamura/Yamitaro the Thief), Fujiko Yamamoto (Ohatsu), Ayako Wakao (Namiji), Eiji Funakoshi (Heima Kadokura), Naritoshi Hayashi, Eijiro Yanagi (Hiromi-ya), Chusha Ichikawa (Kikunojo Nakamura), Ganjiro Nakamura (Sansai Dobe), Saburo Date (Kawaguchi-ya), Jun Hamamura, Kikue Mori (Cruel Old Woman), Masayoshi Kikuno (Yukinojo's Father), Raizo Ichikawa (Hirutaro), Shintaro Katsu (Hojin), Yutaka Nakayama (Townsman), Chitose Maki (Townswoman), Toshio Chiba (Ronin), Koichi Mizuhara (Dobe's

Man), Eigoro Onoe (Shogun), Shiro Otsuji, Tokio Oki (Civil Guardsmen), Musei Tokugawa (Narrator). Distribution: Daiei. Release date: January 13, 1963. 113 minutes. Video: New Yorker.

BLOODY RECORD OF THE SHINSENGUMI (*Shinsengumi Keppuroku: Kondo Isami*, 1963). Director: Shigehiro Ozawa. Screenplay: Kazuo Kasahara, Tai Kato, based on a story by Ryotaro Shiba. Cast: Utaemon Ichikawa (Isami Kondo), Takeshi Kato, Kei Sato. Distribution: Toei. Release date: May 12, 1963. 94 minutes.

BUSHIDO (or *BUSHIDO, SAMURAI SAGA*; *Bushido Zankoku Monogatari*, 1963). Director: Tadashi Imai. Screenplay: Naoyuki Suzuki, Yoshikata Yoda, based on a story by Norio Nanjo. Photography: Makoto Tsuboi [ToeiScope]. Art Direction: Taizo Kawashima. Music: Toshiro Mayuzumi. Cast: Kinnosuke Nakamura [Yorozuya] (Jirozaemon Iikura, Sajiemon Iikura, Kyutaro Iikura, Shuzo Iikura, Shingo Iikura, Osamu Iikura, Susumu Iikura —7 roles), Eijiro Tono (Shikibu-Shosuke Hori), Masayuki Mori (Lord Tanba Munemasa Hori), Kyoko Kishida (Lady Hagi), Shinjiro Ebara (Shikibu-Shosuke Yasutaka Hori), Kikko Matsuoka (Sato, Shuzo's daughter), Yoshiko Mita (Kyoko), Ineko Arima. Distribution: Toei. Release date: April 28, 1963. 123 minutes.

A BRUTAL STORY AT THE FALL OF THE SHOGUNATE (*Bakumatsu Zankoku Monogatari*, 1964). Director: Tai Kato. Screenplay: Takeo [Issei] Kunihiro. Photography: Juhei Suzuki. Music: Hikaru Hayashi. Sound: Shigeji Nakayama. Editor: Katsumi Kawai. Cast: Hashizo Okawa, Choichiro Kawarazaki, Junko Fuji, Isao Kimura, Takeya Nakamura, Ko [Akira] Nishimura, Ryutaro Otomo, Ryohei Uchida. Distribution: Toei. Release date: December 12, 1964. 99 minutes. Video: Samurai Video.

CUT THE SHADOW (*Kage o Kiru*, 1963). Director: Kazuo Ikehiro. Screenplay: Hideo Oguni. Cast: Raizo Ichikawa, Michiko Saga, Mikiko Tsubouchi. Distribution: Daiei. Release date: March 1, 1963. 82 minutes.

DUEL AT ICHIJOJI TEMPLE (*MIYAMOTO MUSASHI IV*; *Miyamoto Musashi Ichijoji no Ketto*, 1964). Director: Tomu Uchida. Producer: Hiroshi Okawa. Screenplay: Naoya Suzuki, Tomu Uchida, based on the novel *"Miyamoto Musashi"* by Eiji Yoshikawa. Photography: Sadaji [Sadatsugu] [Teiji] Yoshida. Lighting: Hiroshi Watada. Art Direction: Takatoshi Suzuki. Music: Taichiro Kosugi. Sound: Yoshio Watabe. Editor: Shintaro Miyamoto. Fight Choreography: Reijiro Adachi. Cast: Kinnosuke Nakamura [Yorozuya] (Musashi Miyamoto), Ken Takakura (Kojiro Sasaki), Shinjiro Ebara (Seijuro Yoshioka), Satomi Oka (Akemi), Wakaba Irie (Otsu), Kaneko Iwasaki (Yoshino-Dayu), Isao Kimura (Matahachi Hon'iden), Choichiro Kawarazaki (Kichijiro Hayashi), Kei Tani (Yasuma Akakabe), Chieko Higashiyama (Myoshu), Mikijiro Hira (Denshichiro Yoshioka), Isao Yamagata (Genzaemon Mibu), Eijiro Tono (Shoyu Haiya), Chieko Higashiyama, Koreya Senda (Koetsu Hon'ami). Distribution: Toei. Release date: January 1, 1964. 128 minutes. Video: Samurai Video.

ESCAPE FROM HELL (*Mushukunin Betsucho*, 1963). Director: Kazuo Inoue. Producer: Masao Shirai. Screenplay: Hideo Oguni, based on a novel by Seicho Matsumoto. Photography: Hiroshi Dowaki. Music: Masayoshi Ikeda. Cast: Keiji Sada (Yajuro), Mariko Okada (Kumi), Takahiro Tamura (Yokouchi), Rentaro Mikuni (Shinpei), Masahiko Tsugawa (Senta), Kiyoshi Atsumi (Ichibei), Junzaburo Ban [Kan Togi] (Chojiro), Sachiko Hidari (Orin), Jiro Kawarazaki (Kyuma), Shinichiro Mikami (Kichisuke), Seiji Miyaguchi (Usuke), Hiroyuki Nagato (Kojuro), Kanemon Nakamura (Seibei), Hiroshi Nihonyanagi (Kisuke), Ko [Akira] Nishimura (Heiroku), Fujio Suga (Sobei), Nakajiro Tomita (Sadagoro). Distribution: Shochiku. Release date: January 27, 1963. 118 minutes.

THE GREAT DUEL (*Dai Satsujin*, 1964). Director: Eiichi Kudo. Screenplay: Kaneo Ikegami. Photography: Osamu [Osami] [Shin] Furuya. Art Direction: Jiro Tomita. Music: Seiichi Suzuki. Cast: Kotaro Satomi, Minoru Oki, Shiro Osaka, Ryutaro Otomo. Distribution: Toei. Release date: June 3, 1964. 119 minutes.

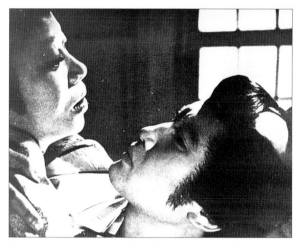

Kinnosuke Nakamura and Yoshiko Mota in *Bushido, Samurai Saga.*

KILL THAT SHADOW! (or *NINJA BREAKUP BY ASSASSINA-TION*; *Ninpo Yaburi Hissatsu*, 1964). Director: Meijiro Umezu. Screenplay: Eibi Motomochi, based on a story by Minoru Inuzuka. Photography: Shozo Kotsuji [GrandScope]. Music: Hiroya Abe. Cast: Isamu Nagato (Magobei), Tetsuro Tanba [Tamba] (Hankuro), Hiroshi Nawa, Kanako Michi, Muga Takewaki. Distribution: Shochiku. Release date: December 26, 1964. 89 minutes.

LEADERSHIP ACCOUNT OF ASSASSIN'S GROUP (*Shinsengumi Shimatsuki*, 1963). Director: Kenji Misumi. Screenplay: Seiji [Kiyoshi] Hoshikawa, based on a story by Kan Shimozawa. Cast: Raizo Ichikawa, Kenzaburo Jo [Tomisaburo Wakayama], Kinshiro Matsumoto, Shiho Fujimura, Shigeru Amachi. Distribution: Daiei. Release date: January 3, 1963. 93 minutes. Alternate English Titles: *Shinsengumi Chronicles, Band of Samurai*. Video: Samurai Video.

ONIBABA (or *WITCH* or *THE HOLE*; *Onibaba*, 1964). Director/Screenplay: Kaneto Shindo. Photography: Kiyomi Kuroda (TohoScope). Art Direction: Kaneto Shindo. Music: Hikaru Hayashi. Editor: Toshio Enoki. Cast: Nobuko Otowa, Jitsuko Yoshimura, Kei Sato, Jukichi Uno, Taiji Tonoyama. Distribution: Toho. Release date: November 21, 1964. 104 minutes.

ORE WA SAMURAI DA! INOCHI O KAKERU SANNIN (1963). Director: Tadashi Sawashima. Screenplay: Shinji Kessoku, based on a story by Renzaburo Shibata. Cast: Ryutaro Otomo, Kotaro Satomi, Shinjiro Ebara. Distribution: Toei. Release date: September 14, 1963. 87 minutes.

RABBLE TACTICS (*Zohyo Monogatari*, 1963). Director: Kazuo Ikehiro. Screenplay: Hideo Oguni, based on a story by Kon Shimizu. Photography: Kazuo Miyagawa. Cast: Shintaro Katsu, Eiji Funakoshi, Shiho Fujimura, Katsuhiko Kobayashi, Kingoro Yanagiya, Shunji Sakai. Distribution: Daiei. Release date: July 13, 1963. 91 minutes. Alternate English Title: *Tale of the Common Soldier.*

THE SAMURAI FROM NOWHERE (*Dojo Yaburi*, 1964). Director: Seiichiro Uchikawa. Producers: Ginichi Kishimoto, Toshio Shimizu. Screenplay: Hideo Oguni, based on a story by Shugoro Yamamoto. Photography: Yoshiharu Ota. Art Direction: Junichi Osumi. Music: Masaru Sato. Cast: Isamu Nagato (Ihei Misawa), Tetsuro Tanba [Tamba] (Gunjuro Oba), Shima Iwashita (Tae), Chieko Baisho (Chigusa), Seiji Miyaguchi (Tatewaki Komuro). Distribution: Shochiku. Release date: January 15, 1964. 93 minutes.

SAMURAI JOKER (*Hana no O-Edo no Musekinin*, 1964). Director: Kajiro Yamamoto. Screenplay: Kajiro Yamamoto, Yasuo Tanami. Producers: Masumi [Sanezumi] Fujimoto, Shin Watanabe. Photography: Seiichi Endo. Lighting: Kiyohisa Hirano. Art Direction:

Hiroshi Ueda. Music: Tessho Hagiwara. Sound: Akira Saito. Editor: Eiji Oi. Cast: Hitoshi Ueki, Kei Tani, Hajime Hana, Mitsuko Kusabue, Reiko Dan, Junko Ikeuchi, Eitaro Shindo, Yoko Fujiyama, Jun Tazaki, Yu Fujiki, Ichiro Arishima, Machiko Kitagawa, Noriko Takahashi, Yaeko Wakamizu, Yoshifumi Tajima, Shin Yasuda, Senri Sakurai, Eitaro Ishibashi, Hiroshi Inuzuka, Shigeki Ishida, Yutaka Sada. Distribution: Toho. Release date: December 20, 1964. 89 minutes.

SAMURAI PIRATE (*Dai Tozoku*, 1963). Director: Senkichi Taniguchi. Producers: Tomoyuki Tanaka, Kenichiro Tsunoda. Screenplay: Takeshi Kimura, Shinichi Sekizawa, based on a story by Toshio Yasumi. Photography: Takao Saito. Art Direction: Morio [Takeo] Kita. Music: Masaru Sato. Sound: Shin Watarai. Editor: Yoshitami Kuroiwa. Fight Choreography: Ryu Kuze. Cast: Toshiro Mifune (Sukezaemon), Tadao Nakamaru (The Premier), Mie Hama (Princess Yaya), Kumi Mizuno (Miwa the Rebel Leader), Ichiro Arishima (Sennin the Wizard), Hideyo [Eisei] Amamoto (Witch in drag), Mitsuko Kusabue (Sobei), Jun Tazaki (Tsuzuka), Akiko Wakabayashi (Yaya's maid), Jun Funato (Prince Ming of Thailand), Makoto Sato (The Black Pirate), Junichiro Mukai (Chief of Royal Guards), Yutaka Nakayama, Eishu Kin (Giant), Takashi Shimura (King Raksha), Rokumaru Furukawa (Niko the Body Guard), Tetsu Nakamura (Chief Archer), Haruo Suzuki (Shiro), Nadao Kirino, Seji Ikeda (Sailors), Yoshio Kosugi (Thai Captain), Yutaka Sada (Governor). Distribution: Toho. Release date: October 26, 1963. 96 minutes. Alternate English Titles: *7th Wonder of Sinbad*, *The Lost World of Sinbad*.

SAMURAI VAGABOND (*Kaze no Bushi*, 1964). Director: Tai Kato. Screenplay: Tatsuo Nogami, based on the novel by Ryotaro Shiba. Art Direction: Taizo Kawashima. Music: Chuji Kinoshita. Sound: Kenjiro Tojo. Cast: Hashizo Okawa (Shinzo Nabari), Hiroko Sakuramachi (Chino), Naoko Kubo (Osei), Sanae Nakahara (Oyumi), Minoru Oki (Denjiro Koriki), Koji Nanbara [Nambara] (Neko), Kazuo Kitamura (Yoroku Nabari), Seiji Miyaguchi, Yoko Nogiwa, Eitaro Shindo. Distribution: Toei. Release date: January 15, 1964. 95 minutes. Alternate English Title: *Samurai on the Wind*.

SASUKE AND HIS COMEDIANS (*Sanada Fuun Roku*, 1963). Director: Tai Kato. Screenplay: Yoshiyuki Fukuda, Fumio Konami, Ryunosuke Ono. Photography: Osamu [Osami] [Shin] Furuya. Music: Hikaru Hayashi. Sound: Shigeji Nakayama. Editor: Shintaro Miyamoto. Fight Choreography: Reijiro Adachi. Cast: Kinnosuke Nakamura [Yorozuya], Mickey Curtis, Jerry Fujio, Choichiro Kawarazaki, Hitoshi Omae, Fujio Tokita, Misako Watanabe. Distribution: Toei. Release date: June 2, 1963. 90 minutes.

THE SEARCHING SWORDSMAN (*Onmitsu Kenshi*, 1964). Director: Sadao Funatoko. Screenplay: Masaru Igami. Music: Hirooki Ogawa. Cast: Koichi Ose (Shintaro Akikusa), Junko Fuji, Fuyukichi Maki (Tonbei), Bin Amatsu, Ryuji Shinagawa. Distribution: Toei. Release date: March 28, 1964. [Feature version of TV series].

THE SEARCHING SWORDSMAN RETURNS (*Zoku Onmitsu Kenshi*, 1964). Director: Sadao Funatoko. Screenplay: Masaru Igami. Music: Hirooki Ogawa. Cast: Koichi Ose (Shintaro Akikusa), Chiyo Okada, Fuyukichi Maki (Tonbei), Kyoko Mikage, Bin Amatsu. Distribution: Toei. Release dates: August 1, 1964. [Feature version of TV series].

SEVENTEEN NINJAS (*Jushichinin no Ninja*, 1963). Director: Yasuto Hasegawa. Screenplay: Kaneo Ikegami. Cast: Kotaro Satomi, Jushiro Konoe, Ryutaro Otomo, Yuriko Mishima. Distribution: Toei. Release date: July 7, 1963. 99 minutes.

TANGE SAZEN (*Tange Sazen*, 1963). Director: Seiichiro Uchikawa. Screenplay: Seiichiro Uchikawa, Yasuhiko Noguchi, based on a novel by Fubo Hayashi [Umitaro Hasegawa]. Music: Seitaro Omori. Cast: Tetsuro Tanba [Tamba] (Sazen Tange/Genzaburo Yagyu), Keisuke Sonoi (Gennojo Yagyu), Haruko Wanibuchi (Hagino), Michiko Saga (Ofuji). Distribution: Shochiku. Release date: November 17, 1963. 95 minutes. Alternate English title: *Return of the Samurai*.

THE THIRD SHADOW (*Daisan no Kagemusha*, 1963). Director: Umetsugu Inoue. Screenplay: Seiji [Kiyoshi] Hoshikawa, based on a story by Norio Nanjo. Cast: Raizo Ichikawa, Hizuru Takachiho, Shigeru Amachi. Distribution: Daiei. Release date: April 21, 1963. 104 minutes.

THIRTEEN ASSASSINS (*Jusan-nin no Shikaku*, 1963). Director: Eiichi Kudo. Screenplay: Kaneo Ikegami. Photography: Juhei Suzuki. Lighting: Yoshiaki Masuda. Art Direction: Norimichi Ikawa [Tokumichi Igawa]. Music: Akira Ifukube. Editor: Shintaro Miyamoto. Fight Choreography: Reijiro Adachi. Cast: Chiezo Kataoka (Shinzaemon Shimada), Kotaro Satomi (Shinrokuro Shimada), Ryohei Uchida (Hanbei Kito), Tetsuro Tanba [Tamba] (Toshitsura Doi), Kanjuro Arashi [Chozaburo Arashi] (Saheita Kuranaga), Ko [Akira] Nishimura (Kujuro Hirayama), Ryunosuke Tsukigata (Yukie Makino), Satomi Oka (Oen), Yuriko Mishima (Chise Makino), Junko Fuji (Kayo), Choichiro Kawarazaki (Uneme Makino), Michitaro Mizushima (Heizo Sawara), Kunio Kaga (Gennai Higuchi), Seishiro Sawamura (Shojiro Ogura), Kusuo Abe (Gunjiro Mitsuhachi), Shingo Yamashiro (Koyata Kiga). Distribution: Toei. Release date: December 7, 1963. 125 minutes.

THE TREASURE OF DEATH CASTLE (*Korera no Shiro*, 1964). Directors: Tetsuro Tanba [Tamba], Yasushi Kikuchi. Screenplay: Kei Tasaka. Cast: Tetsuro Tanba [Tamba], Koji Nanbara [Nambara], Tokue Hanazawa. Distribution: Shochiku. Release date: October 15, 1964.

VENDETTA (*Adauchi*, 1964). Director: Tadashi Imai. Screenplay: Shinobu Hashimoto. Photography: Shunichiro Nakao [ToeiScope]. Cast: Kinnosuke Nakamura [Yorozuya] (Shinpachi), Yoshiko Mita, Tetsuro Tanba [Tamba]. Distribution: Toei. Release date: November 1, 1964. 103 minutes.

YOUNG SAMURAI (*Samurai no Ko*, 1963). Director: Mitsuo Wakasugi. Screenplay: Shohei Imamura, based on a story by Hisashi Yamanaka. Cast: Mitsuo Hamada, Midori Tashiro, Kayo Matsuo. Distribution: Nikkatsu. Release date: February 24, 1963.

YOUNG SWORDSMAN (or *THE SECRET SWORD*; *Hiken*, 1963). Director: Hiroshi Inagaki. Producer: Tomoyuki Tanaka. Screenplay: Hiroshi Inagaki, Takeshi Kimura, based on a story by Kosuke Gomi. Photography: Kazuo Yamada [TohoScope]. Art Direction: Hiroshi Ueda. Music: Kan Ishii. Sound: Yoshio Nishikawa. Editor: Ume Takeda. Cast: Somegoro Ichikawa (Tenzen Hayakawa), Hiroyuki Nagato (Chojuro), Nami Tamura (Sei), Junko Ikeuchi, Susumu Fujita, Ichiro Nakatani [Nakaya], Ryunosuke Tsukigata (Musashi Miyamoto). Distribution: Toho. Release date: August 31, 1963. 108 minutes.

WHIRLWIND (*Shikonmado: Dai Tatsumaki*, 1964). Director: Hiroshi Inagaki. Producer: Tomoyuki Tanaka. Screenplay: Hiroshi Inagaki, Takeshi Kimura, based on the novel *"Shikonmado"* by Norio Nanjo. Photography: Kazuo Yamada [Eastmancolor; TohoScope]. Lighting: Yasuo Konishi. Art Direction: Hiroshi Ueda. Music: Kan Ishii. Sound: Yoshio Nishikawa. Editor: Koichi Iwashita. Fencing Choreography: Ryu Kuze. Cast: Somegoro Ichikawa (Jubei), Yosuke Natsuki, Makoto Sato, Yuriko Hoshi, Kumi Mizuno (Orie, the Witch), Mitsuko Kusabue, Yoshiko Kuga, Akira Kubo, Akihiko Hirata, Sachio Sakai, Yoshio Kosugi, Ren Yamamoto, Akira Tani, Toshiro Mifune (Morishige Akashi). Distribution: Toho. Release date: January 13, 1964. 106 minutes.

WOMEN NINJAS (*Kunoichi Ninpo*, 1964). Director: Sadao Nakajima. Screenplay: So Kuramoto, Sadao Nakajima, based on a novel by Futaro Yamada. Photography: Shigeru Akatsuka. Music: So [Hajime] Kaburagi. Cast: Mari Yoshimura (Omayu), Yumiko Nogawa (Princess Sen), Shigeru Tsuyuguchi (Sakazaki), Sanae Nakahara (Oyui), Yuriko Mishima (Oyo), Michiyo Kogure (Afuku), Minoru Oki (Hayato), Kyosuke Machida (Sutebei), Shingo Yamashiro (Amamaki), Shoichi Ozawa (Usuzumi), Meicho Soganoya (Ieyasu Tokugawa), Yoshio Yoshida (Fuhaku Hannyaji), Mitsuko Aoi (Onami). Distribution: Toei. Release date: October 3, 1964.

THE WORTHLESS DUEL (or *MIYAMOTO MUSASHI III; Miyamoto Musashi Nitoryu Kaigen*, 1963). Director: Tomu Uchida. Screenplay: Tomu Uchida, Naoyuki Suzuki, based on the novel *"Miyamoto Musashi"* by Eiji Yoshikawa. Producer: Hiroshi Okawa. Photography: Sadaji [Sadatsugu] [Teiji] Yoshida [EastmanColor; ToeiScope]. Lighting: Hiroshi Watada. Art Direction: Takatoshi Suzuki. Music: Taichiro Kosugi. Sound: Yoshio Watabe. Editor: Shintaro Miyamoto. Fight Choreography: Reijiro Adachi. Cast: Kinnosuke Nakamura [Yorozuya] (Musashi Miyamoto), Ken Takakura (Kojiro Sasaki), Shinjiro Ebara (Seijuro Yoshioka), Satomi Oka (Akemi), Wakaba Irie (Otsu), Choichiro Kawarazaki (Kichijiro Hayashi), Hiroshi Minami (Toji Gion), Mitsuru Takeuchi (Jotaro), Kei Tani (Yasuma Akakabe), Mikijiro Hira (Denshichiro Yoshioka), Kusuo Abe (Uncle Gon), Isao Kimura (Matahachi Hon'iden), Kenji Susukida (Sekishusai Yagyu), Chieko Naniwa (Osugi), Michiyo Kogure (Oko). Distribution: Toei. Release date: August 14, 1963. 104 minutes. Alternate English Title: *Elevation to the Two-Sword Style*. Video: Samurai Video.

1965-66

THE BETRAYAL (*Dai Satsujin Orochi*, 1966). Director: Tokuzo Tanaka. Producer: Hisashi Okuda. Screenplay: Seiji [Kiyoshi] Hoshikawa, Tsutomu Nakamura, based on a story by Rokuhei Susukita. Photography: Chishi Makiura (DaieiScope). Lighting: Genken Nakaoka. Art Direction: Yoshinobu Nishioka. Music: Akira Ifukube. Sound: Tsuchitaro Hayashi. Editor: Kanji Suganuma. Fight Choreography: Shohei Miyauchi. Cast: Raizo Ichikawa, Kaoru Yachigusa, Shiho Fujimura, Ichiro Nakatani [Nakaya]. Distribution: Daiei. Release date: July 2, 1966. 87 minutes. Video: Samurai Video.

CONQUEST (*Akuto*, 1965). Director: Kaneto Shindo. Screenplay: Kaneto Shindo, based on a story by Junichiro Tanizaki. Music: Hikaru Hayashi. Cast: Eitaro Ozawa [Sakae Ozawa], Kyoko Kishida, Nobuko Otowa, Isao Kimura, Taiji Tonoyama. Distribution: Toho. Release date: November 21, 1965. 119 minutes. Alternate English Title: *A Scoundrel*.

THE GOLDEN COUPLE (*Boken Dai Katsugeki: Ogon no Tozoku*). Director: Tadashi Sawashima. Screenplay: Daisuke Yamazaki, Masahiro Kakefuda, based on a story by Kazuyoshi Takasawa. Photography: Osamu [Osami] [Shin] Furuya [EastmanColor; ToeiScope]. Art Direction: Norimichi Ikawa [Tokumichi Igawa]. Music: Nobuo Hara. Cast: Hiroki Matsukata (Denji), Koichi Ose (Kichizo), Kanbi Fujiyama (Kokichi), Masumi Harukawa (Okiku), Yumiko Nogawa (Kozue). Distribution: Toei. Release date: December 13, 1966. 90 minutes.

THE GRAND DUEL IN MAGIC (*Kairyu Dai Kessen*). Director: Tetsuya Yamanouchi. Screenplay: Masaru Igami. Photography: Motoya Washio [Eastmancolor; ToeiScope]. Art Direction: Seiji Yada. Music: Toshiaki Tsushima. Cast: Hiroki Matsukata (Jiraiya), Tomoko Ogawa (Tsunate), Ryutaro Otomo (Orochimaru), Bin Amatsu. Distribution: Toei. Release date: December 21, 1966. 86 minutes.

ILLUSION OF BLOOD (*Yotsuya Kaidan*, 1965). Director: Shiro Toyoda. Producer: Ichiro Sato. Producers: Ichiro Sato, Hideyuki Shiino. Screenplay: Toshio Yasumi, based on the *Kabuki* play by Nanboku Tsuruya. Photography: Hiroshi Murai [Eastmancolor; TohoScope]. Art Direction: Hiroshi Mizutani. Music: Toru Takemitsu. Cast: Tatsuya Nakadai (Iemon Tamiya), Mariko Okada (Oiwa), Junko Ikeuchi (Osode), Kanzaburo Nakamura (Gonbei Naosuke), Mayumi Ozora (Oume), Yasushi Nagata (Samon Yotsuya), Eitaro Ozawa [Sakae Ozawa] (Kihei Ito), Masao Mishima (Takuetsu), Keiko Awaji (Omaki). Distribution: Toho. Release date: July 25, 1965. 190 minutes [Japan]; 97 minutes [export].

THE LAST DUEL (or *MIYAMOTO MUSASHI V; Miyamoto Musashi Ganryujima no Ketto*, 1965). Director: Tomu Uchida. Producer: Hiroshi Okawa. Screenplay: Naoya Suzuki, Tomu Uchida, based on the novel *"Miyamoto Musashi"* by Eiji Yoshikawa. Photography: Sadaji [Sadatsugu] [Teiji] Yoshida. Lighting: Haruo Nakayama. Art Direction: Takatoshi Suzuki. Music: Taichiro Kosugi. Sound: Yoshio Watabe.

Editor: Shintaro Miyamoto. Fight Choreography: Reijiro Adachi. Cast: Kinnosuke Nakamura [Yorozuya] (Musashi Miyamoto), Ken Takakura (Kojiro Sasaki), Kotaro Satomi (Tadatoshi Hosokawa), Wakaba Irie (Otsu), Satomi Oka (Akemi), Chiezo Kataoka (Sado Nagaoka), Rentaro Mikuni (Takuan), Takahiro Tamura (Tajima Yagyu), Choichiro Kawarazaki (Kichijiro Hayashi), Isao Kimura (Matahachi Hon'iden), Koreya Senda (Koetsu Hon'ami), Asao Uchida (Kakubei Iwama), Gen Shimizu (Tarozaemon Kobayashi), Sumiko Hidaka, Chieko Naniwa (Osugi), Yuriko Mishima (Omitsu). Distribution: Toei. Release date: September 4, 1965. 121 minutes. Alternate English Title: *The Final Duel*. Video: Samurai Video.

MAJIN (*Dai Majin*, 1966). Director: Kimiyoshi Yasuda. Screenplay: Tetsuro Yoshida. Photography: Fujiro Morita. Music: Akira Ifukube. Editor: Hiroshi Yamada. Special Effects: Yoshiyuki Kuroda. Cast: Miwa Takada, Yoshihiko Aoyama, Jun Fujimaki, Ryutaro Gomi, Tatsuo Endo. Distribution: Daiei. Release date: April 17, 1966. 84 minutes.

THE RETURN OF MAJIN (or *THE GREAT DEVIL GROWS ANGRY; Dai Majin Ikaru*, 1966). Director: Kenji Misumi. Screenplay: Tetsuro Yoshida. Photography: Fujiro Morita (Eastmancolor, DaieiScope). Art Direction: Akira Naito. Music: Akira Ifukube. Editors: Kanji Suganuma, Teruo Fujioka. Special Effects: Yoshiyuki Kuroda. Cast: Kojiro Hongo, Asao Uchida, Shiho Fujimura. Distribution: Daiei. Release: August 13, 1966. 79 minutes.

RISE AGAINST THE SWORD (*Abare Goemon*, 1966). Director: Hiroshi Inagaki. Producer: Tomoyuki Tanaka. Screenplay: Masato Ide, Hiroshi Inagaki. Photography: Kazuo Yamada [TohoScope]. Lighting: Shinichi Ono. Art Direction: Hiroshi Ueda. Music: Kan Ishii. Sound: Yoshio Nishikawa. Editor: Koichi Iwashita. Cast: Toshiro Mifune (Goemon), Nobuko Otowa (Osasa), Makoto Sato (Yatota), Ryo Tamura (Hayato), Yuriko Hoshi (Princess Azusa), Ko [Akira] Nishimura, Akihiko Hirata (Asakura), Daisuke Kato (Muteemon Hattori), Gen Shimizu, Takamaru Sasaki (Shirogoro), Ikio Sawamura (Yasubei), Yoshifumi Tajima (Shozaemon), Kichijiro Ueda (Kaniemon), Junichiro Mukai (Kokichi), Susumu Kurobe (Juro Jinbo), Mayumi Ozora (Ayame), Hideyo [Eisei] Amamoto, Yoshio Kosugi (Gonji), Ren Yamamoto (Sukeichi), Yasuo Araki (Heikichi), Naoya Kusakawa (Matahachi), Sachio Sakai (Shigeju), Keiji Sakakida (Sanzo), Wakako Tanabe (Chiyo), Toki Shiozawa, Nakajiro Tomita, Seiji Ikeda (Kaga Senior), Akira Kicchoji (Old Priest). Distribution: Toho. Release date: January 15, 1966. 100 minutes.

SEVENTEEN NINJAS: THE GREAT BATTLE (or *AMMUNITION AND AMBITION; Jushichinin no Ninja: Dai Kessen*, 1966). Director: Motohiro Torii. Screenplay: Kaneo Ikegami, Motohiro Torii. Photography: Shigeru Akatsuka [ToeiScope]. Cast: Hiroki Matsukata, Wakaba Irie, Ryutaro Otomo. Distribution: Toei. Release date: January 26, 1966. 88 minutes.

SHIN KURAMA TENGU (1965). Director: Kimiyoshi Yasuda. Photography: Fujiro Morita. Music: Ichiro Saito. Cast: Raizo Ichikawa (Tengu), Tamao Sato, Jun Fujimaki. Distribution: Daiei. Release date: September 18, 1965. 78 minutes.

SHIN KURAMA TENGU: GOJO-ZAKA NO KETTO (1965). Director: Yoshiyuki Kuroda. Screenplay: Fuji Yahiro. Photography: Senkichiro Takeda [DaieiColor]. Art Direction: Yoshinobu Nishioka. Music: Nakaba Takahashi. Cast: Raizo Ichikawa (Tengu), Ryutaro Gomi, Shosaku Sugiyama. Distribution: Daiei. Release date: November 27, 1965. 75 minutes.

SWORD DEVIL (*Ken Ki*, 1965). Director: Kenji Misumi. Screenplay: Seiji [Kiyoshi] Hoshikawa, based on a story by Renzaburo Shibata. Cast: Raizo Ichikawa, Kei Sato, Michiko Sugata. Distribution: Daiei. Release date: October 16, 1965. 83 minutes. Video: Samurai Video. Video: Samurai Video.

THE THIEVES' WHO'S WHO (*Dorobo Banzuke*, 1966). Director: Kazuo Ikehiro. Screenplay: Daisuke Ito. Cast: Shintaro Katsu, Yoshihiko Aoyama, Tetsuko Kobayashi. Distribution: Daiei. Release date: February 26, 1966.

TOKIJIRO OF KUTSUKAKE (*Kutsukake Tokijiro: Yukyo Ippiki*, 1966). Director: Tai Kato. Screenplay: Naoyuki Suzuki, Masahiro Kakefuda, based on the novel by Shin Hasegawa. Photography: Osamu [Osami] [Shin] Furuya [Color]. Music: Ichiro Saito. Editor: Shintaro Miyamoto. Cast: Kinnosuke Nakamura [Yorozuya], Junko Ikeuchi, Chiyonosuke Azuma, Jiro Okazaki, Keiko Yumi, Nijiko Kiyokawa, Yoko Mihara. Distribution: Toei. Release date: April 1, 1966. 90 minutes.

THE VIRGIN WITNESS (*Shojo ga Mita*, 1966). Director: Kenji Misumi. Screenplay: Kazuo Funabashi, Mitsuo Kodaki. Photography: Chishi Makiura. Art Direction: Shigenori Shimoishizaka. Music: Taichiro Kosugi. Cast: Ayako Wakao, Michiyo Yasuda, Kenzaburo Jo [Tomisaburo Wakayama], Saburo Date, Toru Koyanagi, Shozo Nanbu. Distribution: Daiei. Release date: January 29, 1966. 84 minutes.

WATARI, THE NINJA BOY (*Dai Ninjutsu Eiga: Watari*, 1966). Director: Sadao Funatoko. Producer: Hiroshi Okawa. Screenplay: Masaru Igami, Shunichi Nishimura. Photography: Kunio Kunisada, Shigeru Akatsuka [Eastmancolor; ToeiScope]. Music: Hirooki Ogawa. Cast: Yoshinobu Kaneko, Ryutaro Otomo, Chiyoko Honma, Fuyukichi Maki, Kunio Murai, Asao Uchida. Distribution: Toei. Release date: July 21, 1966. 83 minutes.

1967

BAKUMATSU: TENAMONYA DAI SODO. Director: Kengo Furusawa. Producer: Shin Watanabe. Screenplay: Ryozo Kasahara, Ryuji Sawada, based on a story by Toshio Kagawa. Photography: Senkichi Nagai. Art Direction: Takashi Matsuyama. Music: Naozumi Yamamoto. Cast: Makoto Fujita, Minoru Shiraki, Kei Tani, Yumiko Nogawa, Yukari Ito. Distribution: Toho. Release date: March 12, 1967. 87 minutes.

ELEVEN SAMURAI (*Juichinin no Samurai*). Director: Eiichi Kudo. Screenplay: Kei Tasaka, Takeo [Issei] Kunihiro, Noribumi Suzuki. Music: Akira Ifukube. Cast: Isao Natsuyagi, Ryutaro Otomo, Kotaro Satomi, Ko [Akira] Nishimura, Junko Miyazono. Distribution: Toei. Release date: December 16, 1967. 100 minutes.

THE HOODLUM PRIEST (*Yakuza Bozu*). Director: Kimiyoshi Yasuda. Screenplay: Hajime Takaiwa. Photography: Fujiro Morita. Art Direction: Shigeru Kato. Cast: Shintaro Katsu, Mayumi Ogawa, Mikio Narita, Hosei Komatsu, Naoko Kubo. Distribution: Daiei. Release date: November 15, 1967. 85 minutes.

Watari, Ninja Boy.

Kikunosuke Onoe in *Kojiro* (1967).

KOJIRO (*Sasaki Kojiro*). Director: Hiroshi Inagaki. Producer: Kenichiro Tsunoda. Screenplay: Yoshio Shirasaka, Kenro Matsuura, Hiroshi Inagaki, based on a story by Genzo Murakami. Photography: Takao Saito [Eastmancolor; TohoScope]. Lighting: Hiromitsu Mori. Art Direction: Hiroshi Ueda. Music: Goichi Sakide. Sound: Yoshio Nishikawa. Cast: Kikunosuke Onoe (Kojiro Sasaki), Yoko Tsukasa (Nami), Yuriko Hoshi (Tone), Kenjiro Ishiyama (Lord Tomita), Tatsuya Mihashi (Jubei Minamiya), Isamu Nagato (Shimabei), Tatsuya Nakadai (Musashi Miyamoto), Tadao Nakamaru (Toma Inose), Mayumi Ozora (Hanasode, a harlot), Keiko Sawai (Man), Jotaro Togami (Pirate Nachimaru), Yoshio Tsuchiya (Heisuke Ichinami). Distribution: Toho. Release date: April 1, 1967. 152 minutes.

LIVING BY THE SWORD (*Chichibu Suikoden: Kage o Kiru Ken*). Director: Motomu Ida. Photography: Izumi Hagiwara. Music: Seitaro Omori. Cast: Hideki Takahashi, Yoko Yamamoto, Ryoji Hayama. Distribution: Nikkatsu. Release date: April 8, 1967.

MAJIN STRIKES AGAIN (or *GREAT MAJIN'S COUNTERATTACK*; *Daimajin Gyakushu*). Director: Kazuo [Issei] Mori. Producer: Masaichi Nagata. Screenplay: Tetsuo Yoshida. Photography: Hiroshi Imai, Fujiro Morita (Eastmancolor, DaieScope). Music: Akira Ifukube. Art Direction: Yoshinobu Nishioka, Shigeru Kato. Cast: Hideki Ninomiya, Shinji Horii, Masahide Iizuka. Distribution: Daiei. Release: December 10, 1966. 87 minutes.

THE SHOGUN AND HIS MISTRESSES (*O'oku Maruhi Monogatari*). Director: Sadao Nakajima. Screenplay: Takeo [Issei] Kunihiro, Susumu Saji, Takeo Kaneko, Masahiro Kakefuda. Photography: Sadaji [Sadatsugu] [Teiji] Yoshida [Eastmancolor; ToeiScope]. Art Direction: Taizo Kawashima. Music: So [Hajime] Kaburagi. Cast: Junko Fuji (Omino), Kyoko Kishida (Urao), Tomoko Ogawa (Shinonoi), Yoshiko Sakuma (Ochise), Isuzu Yamada (Matsushima), Masaya Takahashi (Ienobu Tokugawa). Distribution: Toei. Release: July 30, 1967. 95 minutes.

THE WOMEN AROUND THE SHOGUN (or *THE SHOGUN AND HIS MISTRESSES II*; *Zoku O'oku Maruhi Monogatari*). Director: Sadao Nakajima. Screenplay: Takeo [Issei] Kunihiro, Takehiro Nakajima. Photography: Shigeru Akatsuka. Art Direction: Takatoshi Suzuki. Music: Sei [Shigeru] Ikeno. Cast: Tomoko Ogawa (Ochisa), Mako Midori (Okoto), Chieko Higashiyama (Eiho), Takuzo Kawatani, Michiyo Kogure (Otami), Masayo Banri (Ofude), Masao Mishima (Ieharu), Yukari Mishima (Oritsu), Chikako Miyagi (Fujioka), Hiroko Sakuramachi (Oshino). Release: November 1, 1967. Distribution: Toei. 94 minutes.

1968

AMADERA MARUHI MONOGATARI. Director: Sadao Nakajima. Screenplay: Yuko Nishizawa. Photography: Shigeru Akatsuka. Art Direction: Takatoshi Suzuki. Music: So [Hajime] Kaburagi. Cast: Junko Fuji, Masahiko Tsugawa, Tomisaburo Wakayama [Kenzaburo Jo], Yoshiko Mita. Distribution: Toei. Release: February 22, 1968. 89 minutes.

THE BRIDE FROM HADES (*Botandoro*). Director: Satsuo Yamamoto. Producers: Masaichi Nagata. Screenplay: Yoshikata Yoda, based on the novel *"Kaidan Botan-doro"* by Enjo Sanyutei. Photography: Chishi Makiura. Art Direction: Yoshinobu Nishioka. Music: Sei [Shigeru] Ikeno. Sound: Tsuchitaro Hayashi. Cast: Kojiro Hongo (Shinzaburo Hagiwara), Miyoko Akaza (Otsuyu), Mayumi Ogawa (Omine), Michiko Otsuka (Oyone), Takashi Shimura, Atsumi Uda (Kiku). Distribution: Daiei. Release: June 15, 1968. 89 minutes.

CURSE OF THE BLOOD (*Kaidan Zankoku Monogatari*). Director: Kazuo Hase. Screenplay: Masahige Narusawa, Yoshinori Saeki, based on a story by Renzaburo Shibata. Photography: Keiji Maruyama [Shochiku GrandScope]. Art Direction: Kyohei Morita. Music: So [Hajime] Kaburagi. Cast: Rokko [Mutsuhiro] Toura, Nobuo Kaneko, Masakazu Tamura, Yusuke Kawazu, Hiroko Sakurai, Saeda Kawaguchi, Masumi Harukawa. Distribution: Shochiku. Release: May 31, 1968. 88 minutes.

THE DAY THE SUN ROSE (*Gion Matsuri*). Director: Tetsuya Yamanouchi. Producer: Daisuke Ito [Nihon Eiga Fukko Kyoka]. Screenplay: Naoyuki Suzuki, Kunio Shimizu, based on a novel by Katsumi Nishiguchi. Photography: Shintaro Kawasaki. Music: Masaru Sato. Editor: Katsumi Kawai. Cast: Kinnosuke Nakamura [Yorozuya] (Shinkichi), Toshiro Mifune (Kuma), Shima Iwashita (Ayame), Yunosuke Ito (Akamatsu), Takahiro Tamura (Sukematsu), Takashi Shimura (Tsuneemon), Eitaro Ozawa [Sakae Ozawa] (Kadokura), Kunie Tanaka (Gonji), Tomoo Nagai (Matashiro Kawahara), Orie Sato, Hisako Takihana (Ichi), Kamatari Fujiwara, Masami Shimojo, Ryosuke Kagawa, Shinsuke Mikimoto, Tsutomu Shimomoto, Kiyoshi Atsumi, Ken Takakura, Katsuo Nakamura, Eitaro Matsuyama, Kinya Kitaoji, Hibari Misora. Distribution: Shochiku. Release date: November 23, 1968. 168 minutes. Alternate English Title: *Festival of Gion*.

THE EAGLE AND THE WOLF (*Meiji Keppuroku: Taka to Okami*). Director: Akinori Matsuo. Photography: Issen Iwasa. Music: Taichiro Kosugi. Cast: Hideki Takahashi, Hiroko Ogi, Joji Takagi, Kayo Matsuo. Distribution: Nikkatsu. Release date: May 29, 1968. 98 minutes.

THE HUNDRED MONSTERS (or *THE HUNDRED GHOST STORIES*; *Yokai Hyaku Monogatari*). Director: Kimiyoshi Yasuda. Producer: Yamato Yahiro. Screenplay: Tetsuro Yoshida. Photography: Yasukaza Takemura (Eastmancolor). Art Direction: Shigeru Kato, Yoshinobu Nishioka. Music: Chumei [Michiaki] [Hiroaki] Watanabe. Editor: Kanji Suganuma. Cast: Jun Fujimaki (Yasutaro), Ryutaro Gomi (Lord Buzen Hotta), Jun Hamamura (Gohei), Tatsuo Hanabu (Jinbei), Shozo Hayashiya (Storyteller), Sei [Masaru] Hiraizumi (Takichi), Takashi Kanda (Riemon Tajimaya), Hajime Koshikawa, Ikuko Mori (Ronin's Wife), Shozo Nanbu (Old Town Counselor), Koichi Mizuhara (Tobei), Teruko Omi (Otora), Saburo Date (First Ronin), Rookie Shinichi (Shinkichi), Shosaku Sugiyama (Bannai Ibaragi), Miwa Takada (Okiku), Kazue Tamaoki (Village Headman), Mikiko Tsubouchi (Osen), Ichiro [Kazuo] Yamamoto (Second Ronin), Yoshio Yoshida (Jusuke). Distribution: Daiei. Release date: March 20, 1968. 79 minutes.

KURONEKO (*Yabu no Naka no Kuroneko*). Director/Screenplay: Kaneto Shindo. Photography: Kiyomi Kuroda (TohoScope). Art Direction: Takashi Marumo, Norimichi Ikawa [Tokumichi Igawa]. Music: Hikaru Hayashi. Cast: Kichiemon Nakamura (Gintoki), Nobuko Otowa (Mother), Kiwako Taichi (Daughter-in-Law), Kei Sato (Raiko), Taiji Tonoyama (A Farmer), Rokko [Mutsuhiro] Toura (A Samurai), Hideo Kanze (Mikado). Distribution: Toho. Release date: February 24, 1968. 99 minutes. Video: Samurai Video.

THE LONE STALKER (or *THE LONE WOLF*; *Hitori Okami*). Director: Kazuo Ikehiro. Screenplay: Kinya Naoi, based on a story by Genzo Murakami. Cast: Raizo Ichikawa, Isamu Nagato, Mayumi Ogawa. Distribution: Daiei. Release date: April 20, 1968. 84 minutes.

MIYAMOTO MUSASHI. Director: Yasuo Furuhata [Kohata]. Screenplay: Akira [Gyo] Hayasaka, based on a novel by Ryotaro Shiba. Cast: Rentaro Mikuni (Musashi Miyamoto), Jitsuko Yoshimura (Ei), Jun Tatara (Narrator). Distribution: Toei. Release date: April, 1968. 84 minutes. [Originally produced for Television as 4 hour-long episodes].

THE PRIEST AND THE GOLD MINT (*Zoku Yakuza Bozu*). Director: Kazuo Ikehiro. Screenplay: Ryozo Kasahara, Hisashi Sugiura. Photography: Fujiro Morita. Art Direction: Seiichi Oota. Music: Takeo Watanabe. Cast: Shintaro Katsu, Kayo Matsuo, Yukiji Asaoka, Taketoshi Naito, Sonosuke Sawamura. Distribution: Daiei. Release date: July 13, 1968. 80 minutes.

THE SAGA OF TANEGASHIMA (*Tenpo Denraiki*). Director: Kazuo [Issei] Mori. Producer: Masaichi Nagata. Screenplay: Kimiyuki Hasegawa, based on a story by Etsuko Takano. Photography: Fujiro Morita [Eastmancolor; DaieiScope]. Art Direction: Yoshinobu Nishioka. Music: Hikaru Hayashi. Editor: Toshio Taniguchi. Cast: Rick Jason (Captain Pinto), Ayako Wakao (Wakasa), Shiho Fujimura (Otane), Jun Fujimaki (Nobunaga Oda), Eijiro Tono (Kinbei Yaita), Taketoshi Naito (Tokiaki Tanegashima), Saburo Date (Tokunoshin

Nabuko Otawa in *Kuroneko*.

Wakita), Asao Koike (Matasaburo Tachibanaya), Ichiro Nakatani [Nakaya] (Sakuji), Rokko [Mutsuhiro] Toura (Gomine). Distribution: Daiei. Release date: May 18, 1968.

THE SECRET OF THE FYLFOT (*Shinobi no Manji*). Director: Noribumi Suzuki. Screenplay: Susumu Saji, Ryunosuke Ono, based on a story by Futaro Yamada. Cast: Hiroko Sakuramachi, Akemi Mari, Isao Natsuyagi. Distribution: Toei. Release date: January 27, 1968. 89 minutes.

THE TWO BODYGUARDS (*Nihiki no Yojinbo*). Director: Kenji Misumi. Screenplay: Hideo Ando, Hisashi Sugiura. Photography: Hiroshi Imai (Fujicolor). Lighting: Hiroshi Mima. Art Direction: Akira Naito. Music: Taichiro Kosugi. Editor: Hiroshi Yamada. Sound: Masao Osumi. Cast: Kojiro Hongo (Seki), Miwa Takada, Toru Abe, Miyoko Akaza, Machiko Hasegawa (Osumi). Distribution: Daiei. Release date: August 24, 1968. 81 minutes.

YUKIONNA (*Kaidan Yukionna*). Director: Tokuzo Tanaka. Screenplay: Fuji Yahiro. Photography: Chishi Makiura (Eastmancolor). Art Direction: Akira Naito. Music: Akira Ifukube. Editor: Hiroshi Yamada. Cast: Shiho Fujimura (Yuki), Akira Ishihama (Yosaku), Machiko Hasegawa (Lady Mino), Taketoshi Naito (Lord Mino), Mizuho Suzuki (Gyokei), Fujio Suga (Soju), Sachiko Murase (Soyo). Distribution: Daiei. Release date: April 20, 1968. 80 minutes.

1969

ALONG WITH THE GHOSTS (or *JOURNEY WITH GHOSTS ALONG TOKAIDO ROAD*; *Tokaido Obake Dochu*). Directors: Kimiyoshi Yasuda, Yoshiyuki Kuroda. Screenplay: Tetsuo Yoshida, Shozaburo Asai. Photography: Hiroshi Imai, Senkichiro Takeda (Eastmancolor, DaieiScope). Music: Chumei [Michiaki] [Hiroaki] Watanabe. Cast: Kojiro Hongo (Hyakutaro), Pepe Hozumi (Shinta), Masami Furukido (Miyo), Rokko [Mutsuhiro] Toura, Yoshindo Yamaji (Higuruma), Bokuzen Hidari (Jinbei). Distribution: Daiei. Release: March 12, 1969. 78 minutes.

BAND OF ASSASSINS (or *BAND OF SAMURAI*; *Shinsengumi*). Director: Tadashi Sawashima. Producers: Toshiro Mifune, Yoshio Nishikawa, Hiroshi Inagaki [Mifune Productions]. Screenplay: Kenro Matsuura. Photography: Kazuo Yamada [Eastmancolor; TohoScope]. Lighting: Yukio Sato. Art Direction: Hiroshi Ueda. Music: Masaru Sato. Sound: Masamichi Ichikawa. Editor: Yoshihiro Araki. Cast: Toshiro Mifune (Isami Kondo), Keiju Kobayashi (Toshizo Hijikata), Kinya Kitaoji (Soji [Soshi] Okita), Rentaro Mikuni (Kamo Serizawa), Kanemon Nakamura (Lord Awa Katsu), Katsuo Nakamura (Kisaburo Kawai), Umenosuke Nakamura (Keisuke Yamanami), Yoko Tsukasa (Tsune), Junko Ikeuchi (Oyuki), Yuriko Hoshi (Oko), Yumiko Nogawa (Oume). Distribution: Toho. Release date: December 5, 1969. 122 minutes.

BLOOD END (*Tengu-To*). Director: Satsuo Yamamoto. Screenplay: Shun Inagaki, Hajime Takaiwa, based on a story by Juro Miyoshi. Cast: Tatsuya Nakadai (Sentaro), Ayako Wakao (Otsuta), Yukiyo Toake (Otae), Go Kato (Gentaro), Shigeru Koyama [Kamiyama] (Shozaemon Mizuki), Kanemon Nakamura (Jingosa), Ichiro Nakatani [Nakaya] (Chogoro), Mizuho Suzuki (Gunnoshin). Distribution: Daiei. Release date: November 15, 1969. 102 minutes.

THE BODYGUARDS' REVENGE (*Yojinbo Kyojo Tabi*). Director: Akira [Sho] Inoue. Screenplay: Hisashi Sugiura. Cast: Kojiro Hongo, Isamu Nagato, Mitsuyo Kamei. Distribution: Daiei. Release date: May 17, 1969.

BROKEN SWORDS (*Hiken Yaburi*). Director: Kazuo Ikehiro. Screenplay: Daisuke Ito, based on a story by Kosuke Gomi. Photography: Chishi Makiura [Eastmancolor; DaieiScope]. Art Direction: Shigenori Shimoishizaka. Music: Takeo Watanabe. Cast: Hiroki Matsukata (Tenzen Tange), Kojiro Hongo (Yasubei Nakayama), Tomomi Iwai (Chiharu), Shigeru Tsuyuguchi (Ryunoshin Nagao), Yoshi Kato, Tatsuo Matsumura. Distribution: Daiei. Release date: May 31, 1969. 90 minutes.

CURSE OF THE GHOST (or *GHOST OF OIWA* or *GHOST OF YOTSUYA: GHOST OF OIWA* or *CURSE OF THE NIGHT* or *CURSE OF THE GHOST*; *Yotsuya Kaidan: Oiwa no Borei*). Director: Kazuo [Issei] Mori. Producer: Hatsunosuke Fujimoto. Screenplay: Kinya Naoi, based on a story by Nanboku Tsuruya. Photography: Senkichiro Takeda [Fujicolor; DaieiScope]. Art Direction: Seiichi Ota. Music: Ichiro Saito. Cast: Kei Sato (Iemon Tamiya), Kazuko Inano (Oiwa), Yoshihiko Aoyama (Yomoshichi Sato), Akiji Kobayashi (Naosuke), Jun Hamamura (Oiwa's Father), Gen Kimura (Okuda), Kyoko Mikage (Osode), Sonosuke Sawamura (Takuetsu), Chikako Masago (Oure). Distribution: Daiei. Release date: June 28, 1969. 94 minutes.

THE DEVIL'S TEMPLE (*Oni no Sumu Yakata*). Director: Kenji Misumi. Screenplay: Kaneto Shindo, based on a story by Junichiro Tanizaki. Photography: Kazuo Miyagawa, [Eastmancolor; DaieiScope]. Art Direction:

ABOVE: Toshiro Mifune is Isami Kondo of the *shinsengumi* in *Band of Assassins*. BELOW: Kojiro Hongo and Tomomi Iwai in *Broken Swords*.

Akira Naito. Music: Akira Ifukube. Cast: Shintaro Katsu (Mumyo no Taro), Hideko Takamine (Kaede), Michiyo Aratama (Aizen), Kei Sato (high priest). Distribution: Daiei. Release date: May 31, 1969. 76 minutes.

THE FORT OF DEATH (*Gonin no Shokin Kasegi*). Director: Eiichi Kudo. Screenplay: Koji Takada. Photography: Juhei Suzuki [Eastmancolor; ToeiScope]. Music: Toshiaki Tsushima. Cast: Tomisaburo Wakayama [Kenzaburo Jo] (Ichibei Shikoro), Minoru Oki (Yataro Mochizuki), Tomoko Mayama (Kagero), Eizo Kitamura (Onitsuka), Kenji Ushio (Kunai Aoto), Ichiro Nakatani [Nakaya] (Shibaike), Goro Ibuki, Kanjuro Arashi [Chozaburo Arashi] (Tazaemon), Asao Koike (Lord Ozeki). Distribution: Toei. Release date: December 13, 1969. 97 minutes.

THE HAUNTED CASTLE (*Hiroku Kaibyo-den*). Director: Tokuzo Tanaka. Screenplay: Shozaburo Asai. Cast: Kojiro Hongo, Naomi Kobayashi, Mitsuyo Kamei, Rokko [Mutsuhiro] Toura, Koichi Uenoyama, Akane Kawasaki. Distribution: Daiei. Release date: December 20, 1969. 83 minutes.

296

HELL'S TATTOOERS (*Tokugawa Irezumi-shi: Seme Jigoku*). Director: Teruo Ishii. Screenplay: Teruo Ishii, Masahiro Kakefuda. Photography: Motoya Washio [Eastmancolor; ToeiScope]. Music: Masao Yagi. Cast: Teruo Yoshida (Horihide), Masumi Tachibana (Osuzu), Asao Koike (Horitatsu), Yumiko Katayama (Yumi), Mieko Fujimoto (Oryu), Haruo Tanaka (Samejima), Reiichi Hatanaka, Yukie Kagawa, Miki Obana. Distribution: Toei. Release date: May 2, 1969. 95 minutes.

THE KILLER'S MISSION (or HITMAN; *Shokin Kasegi*) Director: Shigehiro Ozawa. Screenplay: Koji Takada, Masaru Igami. Photography: Nagaki Yamagishi (Eastmancolor, ToeiScope). Art Direction: Seiji Yada. Music: Masao Yagi. Cast: Tomisaburo Wakayama [Kenzaburo Jo] (Ichibei Shikoro), Yumiko Nogawa (Kagero), Tomoko Mayama (Akane), Chiezo Kataoka, Bin Amatsu. Distribution: Toei. Release date: August 13, 1969. 90 minutes.

THE LEFTY FENCER (*Onna Sazen: Nuretsubame Katate Giri*). Director: Kimiyoshi Yasuda. Screenplay: Fuji Yahiro. Cast: Michiyo Yasuda, Kojiro Hongo, Isamu Nagato. Distribution: Daiei. Release date: June 14, 1969.

THE MAGOICHI SAGA (*Shirikurae Magoichi*). Director: Kenji Misumi. Screenplay: Ryuzo Kikushima, based on a story by Ryotaro Shiba. Photography: Kazuo Miyagawa [Eastmancolor; DaieiScope]. Art Direction: Yoshinobu Nishioka. Music: Masaru Sato. Cast: Kinnosuke Nakamura [Yorozuya] (Magoichi Saika), Komaki Kurihara (Komichi), Kojiro Hongo, Katsuo Nakamura (Tokichiro Kinoshita), Shintaro Katsu (Nobunaga Oda), Eiko Azusa, Yoko Namikawa (Princess Kano). Distribution: Daiei. Release date: September 13, 1969. 95 minutes.

MITO KOMON MANYU-KI. Director: Yasuki Chiba. Producer: Ichiro Sato. Screenplay: Ryozo Kasahara. Photography: Kiyoshi Hasegawa. Lighting: Tsuruzo Nishikawa. Art Direction: Satoshi Chuko. Music: Masaru Sato. Sound: Norio Tone. Editor: Ume Takeda. Cast: Hisaya Morishige (Mito), Akira Takarada, Tadao Takashima, Junko Ikeuchi, Norihei Miki, Kinichi Hagimoto, Jiro Sakagami. Distribution: Toho. Release date: November 1, 1969.

NINJA SCOPE (*Tobidasu Boken Eiga: Akakage*). Directors: Junji Kurata, Tetsuya Yamanouchi. Music: Hirooki Ogawa. Cast: Toru Sakaguchi, Yoshinobu Kaneko, Fuyukichi Maki, Kotaro Satomi. Distribution: Toei. Release date: July 20, 1969. 52 minutes.

PORTRAIT OF HELL (*Jigokuhen*). Director: Shiro Toyoda. Producer: Tomoyuki Tanaka. Screenplay: Toshio Yasumi, based on a story by Ryunosuke Akutagawa. Photography: Kazuo Yamada [Eastmancolor; Panavision]. Art Direction: Shinobu Muraki. Music: Yasushi Akutagawa. Sound: Norio Tone. Cast: Kinnosuke Nakamura [Yorozuya] (Lord Hosokawa), Tatsuya Nakadai (Yoshihide), Yoko Naito (Yoshika), Shun Oide, Hideyo [Eisei] Amamoto. Distribution: Toho. Release date: September 20, 1969. 95 minutes. Video: Samurai Video.

Masumi Tachibana is menaced in *Hell's Tattooers.*

QUICK DRAW OKATSU (*Yoen Dokufu-Den: Hitokiri Okatsu*). Director: Nobuo Nakagawa. Screenplay: Koji Takada. Photography: Masahiko Iimura. Music: Koichi Kawabe. Cast: Junko Miyazono (Okatsu), Reiko Oshida, Ko [Akira] Nishimura, Kenji Imai, Yuriko Mishima. Distribution: Toei. Release date: April 10, 1969. 89 minutes.

UNDER THE BANNER OF THE SAMURAI (or SAMURAI BANNERS; *Furin Kazan*). Director: Hiroshi Inagaki. Producers: Toshiro Mifune, Tomoyuki Tanaka, Yoshio Nishikawa, Hiroshi Inagaki, [Mifune Productions]. Screenplay: Shinobu Hashimoto, Takeo [Issei] Kunihiro, based on a story by Yasushi Inoue. Photography: Kazuo Yamada [Eastmancolor; TohoScope]. Lighting: Yukio Sato. Art Direction: Hiroshi Ueda. Music: Masaru Sato. Sound: Shoichi Fujinawa. Editor: Yoshihiro Araki. Fencing Choreography: Ryu Kuze. Cast: Toshiro Mifune (Kansuke Yamamoto), Yoshiko Sakuma (Princess Yu), Kinnosuke Nakamura [Yorozuya] (Shingen Takeda), Yujiro Ishihara (Kenshin Uesugi), Katsuo Nakamura (Nobusato Itagaki), Kankuro Nakamura (Katsuyori Takeda), Kanemon Nakamura (Nobukato Itagaki), Masakazu Tamura (Nobushige Takeda), Mayumi Ozora (Princess Okoto), Ken Ogata, Takashi Shimura. Distribution: Toho. Release date: March 1, 1969. 166 minutes.

1970

THE AMBITIOUS (*Bakumatsu*). Director/Screenplay: Daisuke Ito, based on a novel by Ryotaro Shiba. Producers: Kinichiro Ogawa, Kinnosuke Nakamura [Yorozuya] (Nakamura Productions). Photography: Kazuo Yamada (Eastmancolor; Panavision). Lighting: Haruo Nakayama. Art Direction: Juichi Ito. Music: Masaru Sato. Sound: Hiroo Notsu. Cast: Kinnosuke Nakamura [Yorozuya] (Ryunosuke Sakamoto), Toshiro Mifune (Shojiro Goto), Tatsuya Nakadai (Shintaro Nakaoka), Sayuri Yoshinaga (Oryo), Noboru Nakaya (Hanpeita Takechi), Katsuo Nakamura (Chojiro Kondo), Eitaro Matsuyama (Umanosuke Niimya), Shigeru Koyama [Kamiyama] (Kaishu Katsu), Keiju Kobayashi (Kichinosuke Saigo), Shinsuke Mikimoto (Kogoro Katsura), Akihiko Katayama (Toranosuke Nakahira), Terumi Niki (Mitsukazu Nakadaira), Isao Yamagata (Hiroe Yamada), Ryuichi Nagashima (Tabun Iegami), Kentaro Osato (Unosuke Urashima), Hiroshi Aoyama (Bensai), Shogen Nitta (Shoji Sawaki), Gaku [Manabu] Yamamoto (Ukichi Sensa), Jo Okuda (Hidemi Shinda), Hiroshi Tanaka (Kisuke Deishi), Isamu Fukumoto (Denjiro Jodo), Senzo Hashimoto (Kinba Yasuoka), Hiroyuki Ota (Mikami), Shinnosuke Ogata (Jutaro Chiba), Tayoko Ueda (Mari), Toshiaki Amada (Yataro Shinagawa), Yoshitaro Asawaka (Muta), Takashi Yasuda (Kuo), Akira Nairai (Ikuhisa), Shintaro Ebara (Shinzo Sankichi), Shiro Otsuji, Chiemi Eri, Keiko Akata (Ofuku), Hiromi Takano (Ochiyo), Atsushi Watanabe (Kan), Saburo Sawai (Ichinojo Fuse), Tokinosuke Nakamura (Koshitaro Ito), Ryosuke Kagawa (Fujikichi), Keiko Kagawa (Otome). Distribution: Toho. Release date: February 14, 1970. 120 minutes. Alternate English Title: *The Restoration of Meiji*. Video: Samurai Video.

THE AMBUSH (or INCIDENT AT BLOOD PASS; *Machibuse*). Director: Hiroshi Inagaki. Producers: Toshiro Mifune, Yoshio Nishikawa [Mifune Productions]. Screenplay: Yumi Fujiki, Hideo Oguni, Hajime Takaiwa, Ichiro Miyagawa. Photography: Kazuo Yamada [Eastmancolor; TohoScope]. Lighting: Yukio Sato. Art Direction: Hiroshi Ueda. Music: Masaru Sato. Sound: Masamichi Ichikawa. Cast: Toshiro Mifune (Yojimbo), Shintaro Katsu (Gentetsu), Kinnosuke Nakamura [Yorozuya] (Hyoma Ibuki), Ruriko Asaoka (Okuni), Yujiro Ishihara (Yataro), Mika Kitagawa (Oyuki), Ichiro Arishima (Tokubei), Yoshio Tsuchiya (Itahachi), Ryunosuke Yamazaki (Tatsu), Jotaro Togami (Gonji), Chusha Ichikawa (Unknown Samurai). Distribution: Toho. Release date: March 21, 1970. 118 minutes.

DUEL AT EZO (or FORT EZO; *Ezo Yakata no Ketto*). Director: Kengo Furusawa. Producers: Masumi [Sanezumi] Fujimoto, Yorihiko Yamada [Tokyo Eiga]. Screenplay: Ryozo Kasahara, based on a story by Renzaburo Shibata. Photography: Hiroshi Murai

Under the Banner of the Samurai.

[Eastmancolor; TohoScope]. Art Direction: Motoji Kojima. Music: Kenjiro Hirose. Cast: Yuzo Kayama (Saburota Edo), Tatsuya Nakadai (Lord Daizen Honjo), Rentaro Mikuni (Shinbei Usa), Toru Abe (the ronin), Kunie Tanaka (Kurobei), Toshio Kurosawa (Kyuma), Shogo Shimada (Jirozaemon Ezo), Mitsuko Baisho. Distribution: Toho. Release date: February 8, 1970. 131 minutes.

THE HAUNTED SAMURAI (or THE HUNTED SAMURAI or SUPERMAN ON THE GALE; Tsuchinin-ki: Kaze no Tengu). Director: Keiichi Ozawa. Producers: Eiichi Imado, Kunifumi Tokieda. Screenplay: Seiji [Kiyoshi] Hoshikawa, based on a story by Goseki Kojima. Photography: Minoru Yokoyama. Art Direction: Toshiyuki Matsui. Music: So [Hajime] Kaburagi. Editor: Shinya Inoue. Cast: Hideki Takahashi (Roppeita), Isao Natsuyagi (Kyonosuke), Seiichiro Kameishi (Tarao), Masako Izumi (Toki), Yoshiro Aoki (Aochi), Shoki Fukae (Nachi). Distribution: Nikkatsu. Release date: November 14, 1970. 81 minutes.

THE INVISIBLE SWORDSMAN (Tomei Kenshi). Director: Yoshiyuki Kuroda. Screenplay: Tetsuro Yoshida. Photography: Hiroshi Imai. Art Direction: Shigeru Kato. Music: Takeo Watanabe. Cast: Osamu Sakai, Hachiro Oka, Yasushi Yokoyama, Kiyoshi Nishikawa. Distribution: Daiei. Release date: March 21, 1970. 79 minutes.

THE MASSEUR'S CURSE (Kaidan Kasanegafuchi). Director: Kimiyoshi Yasuda. Screenplay: Shozaburo Asai, based on the novel "Shinkei Kasanegafuchi" by Enjo Sanyutei. Photography: Chishi Makiura [Eastmancolor; DaieiScope]. Art Direction: Akira Naito. Music: So [Hajime] Kaburagi. Sound: Tsuchitaro Hayashi. Cast: Ritsuo Ishiyama, Kenjiro Ishiyama (Soetsu), Maya Kitajima, Reiko Kasahara, Akane Kawasaki, Natsuko Oka (Osono), Takumi Shinjo, Saburo Date (Fukami), Mitsuko Tanaka (Sawano). Distribution: Daiei. Release date: June 20, 1970. 83 minutes.

MISSION: IRON CASTLE (or LAST IGA SPY or BAND OF NINJA; Shinobi no Shu). Director: Kazuo [Issei] Mori. Screenplay: Takayuki Yamada, based on a story by Ryotaro Shiba. Photography: Fujio Morita [DaieiScope]. Lighting: Reijiro Yamashita. Art Direction: Shigenori Shimoishizaka. Music: So [Hajime] Kaburagi. Sound: Iwao Otani. Editor: Toshio Taniguchi. Fight Choreography: Eiichi Kusumoto. Cast: Hiroki Matsukata (Yoshiro), Ryunosuke Minegishi (Onikobu), Kojiro Hongo (Sukedayu), Michiyo Yasuda (Orin), Shiho Fujimura (Lady Oichi), Yoko Namikawa, Taketoshi Naito, Rokko [Mutsuhiro] Toura, Tomu Uchida. Distribution: Daiei. Release date: February 7, 1970. 79 minutes. Video: Samurai Video.

NAKED AMBITION (Onna Gokuaku-cho). Director: Kazuo Ikehiro. Screenplay: Seiji [Kiyoshi] Hoshikawa. Cast: Michiyo Yasuda, Masakazu Tamura, Akiko Koyama. Distribution: Daiei. Release date: April 4, 1970.

WILL TO CONQUER (Shokon Ichidai: Tenka no Abarenbo). Director: Seiji Maruyama. Producers: Masayuki Sato, Tomoyuki Tanaka. Screenplay: Toshio Yasumi. Photography: Rokuro Nishigaki [Eastmancolor; TohoScope]. Art Director: Satoshi Chuko. Music: Akira Ifukube. Cast: Kinnosuke Nakamura [Yorozuya] (Yataro Iwasaki), Tatsuya Nakadai (Toyo Yoshida), Yoshiko Sakuma (Ritsu), Isao Kimura (Hanpeita Takechi), Eijiro Tono (Sezaemon), Ichiro Nakatani [Nakaya] (Shojiro Goto), Takahiro Tamura, Kinya Kitaoji. Distribution: Toho. Release date: October 17, 1970. 113 minutes.

1971-79

THE ASSASSINATION OF RYOMA (Ryoma Ansatsu, 1974). Director: Kazuo Kuroki. Producers: Seitaro Kuroda, Kinshiro Kuzui, Takayoshi Miyagawa, Mikio Tomita. Screenplay: Kunio Shimizu, Yasushi Tanabe. Photography: Masaki Tamura. Art Direction: Hiroshi Yamashita. Music: Teizo Matsumura. Editor: Hiroshi Asai. Cast: Yoshio Harada (Ryoma Sakamoto), Renji Ishibashi (Nakaoka), Rie Nakagawa (Cho), Yusaku Matsuda (Yuta), Kaori Momoi (Tae), Keisuke Noro (Tokichi), Ryo Tamura (Okubo), Go Awazu (Tomita). Distribution: Art Theatre Guild. Release date: August 3, 1974. 118 minutes.

ASSASSIN'S QUARRY (Hissatsu Shikake-nin: Baian Ari Jigoku, 1973). Director: Yusuke Watanabe. Producer: Akira Oda. Screenplay: Ichiro Miyagawa, Yusuke Watanabe. Photography: Masao Kosugi. Art Direction: Kyohei Morita. Music: So [Hajime] Kaburagi. Cast: Ken Ogata, Yoichi Hayashi, So Yamamura, Kayo Matsuo, Asao Koike, Kei Sato, Kyoko Tsuda. Distribution: Shochiku. Release date: September 29, 1973. 91 minutes.

BLOODSHED (or DEMONS or PANDEMONIUM; Shura, 1971). Director: Toshio Matsumoto. Screenplay: Toshio Matsumoto, based on the play by Nanboku Tsuruya. Photography: Tatsuo Suzuki. Cast: Katsuo Nakamura (Gengo), Yasuko Sanjo (Koman), Juro Kara (Sangoro), Masao Imafuku (Hachiemon). Distribution: Shochiku. Release date: February 13, 1971. 134 minutes.

THE BUSHIDO BLADE (or THE BLOODY BUSHIDO BLADE, 1979). Director: Tom Kotani. Producer: Arthur Rankin Jr. Screenplay: William Overgard. Photography: Shoji [Masaharu] Ueda. Lighting: Kazuo Shimomura. Art Direction: Toyokazu Ohashi. Music: Maury Laws. Sound: Yuji Miyoshi. Editors: Yoshitami Kuroiwa, Anne V. Coates (consultant). Fencing Choreography: Ryu Kuze. Cast: Richard Boone (Commodore Matthew Perry), Tetsuro Tanba [Tamba] (Lord Yamato), Frank Converse (Captain Lawrence Hawk), Shinichi

The Masseur's Curse.

"Sonny" Chiba (Prince Ido), Toshiro Mifune (Shogun's Commander Hayasi), Laura Gemser (Tomoe), Mako (Enjiro), James Earl Jones (The Prisoner), Timothy Murphy (Midshipman Robin Burr), Mayumi Asano (Yuki). Distribution: Aquarius. 94 minutes. Video: Wellspring.

CHIMIMORYU: A SOUL OF DEMONS (Yami no Naka no Chimimoryo, 1971). Director/Producer: Ko Nakahira. Screenplay: Kaneto Shindo. Photography: Aguri Sugita. Music: Toshiro Mayuzumi. Cast: Akaji Maro, Kazuko Inano, Mariko Kaga, Hiroko Ogi, Eiji Okada. Distribution: Toho. Release date: June 19, 1971. 107 minutes.

DEATH OF A SHOGUN (or SHOGUN ASSASSINS or RENE-GADE NINJAS; Sanada Yukimura no Boryaku, 1979). Director: Sadao Nakajima. Producers: Tan Takaiwa, Goro Kusakabe, Norimichi Matsudaira, Keizo Mimura. Screenplay: Kazuo Kasahara, Isao Matsumoto, Yozo Tanaka, Sadao Nakajima. Photography: Shigeru Akatsuka (Eastmancolor). Music: Masaru Sato. Cast: Hiroki Matsukata (Yukimura Sanada), Kinnosuke Yorozuya [Nakamura] (Ieyasu Tokugawa), Teruhiko Aoi, Kensaku Morita, Yoko Akino, Fujita Okamoto, Shohei Hino, Ichiro Ogura, Hiroyuki Sanada, Minori Terada, Tetsuro Tanba [Tamba], Tatsuo Umemiya. Distribution: Toei. Release date: September 1, 1979. 148 minutes.

FEMALE NINJA MAGIC: 100 TRAMPLED FLOWERS (or FEMALE NINJAS; Kunoichi Inpo: Hyakka Manji Garami, 1974). Director: Chusei Sone. Screenplay: Masaru Takesue. Photography: Masaru Mori. Art Direction: Yoshie Kikukawa. Cast: Junko Miyashita (Tsukinojo), Kyoko Kano, Hitomi Kozue, Yuko Katagiri, Hyoei Enoki (Kamekubi), Tatsuya Hamaguchi (Konoe), Maya Hiromi (Okaru), Setsuko Oyama (Koyuki), Nahomi Oka (Lady Oren), Nagatoshi Sakamoto (Kuroiwa), Kenji Shimamura, Hajime Tanimoto (Wakasa), Yuri Yamashina. Distribution: Nikkatsu. Release date: August 3, 1974. 76 minutes.

FEMALE NINJAS: IN BED WITH THE ENEMY (Kunoichi Ninpo: Kannon Biraki, 1976). Director: Takayuki Minagawa. Screenplay: Isao Matsumoto, Seiko Shimura. Cast: Maki Tachibana, Keiko Kinugasa, Megumi Hori, Jiro Okazaki, Hiroshi Nawa, Akira Shioji, Tadashi Naruse. Distribution: Toei. Release date: February 14, 1976. 66 minutes. Alternate English Titles: Magic Female Ninjas: Open Altar Doors; In Bed with the Enemy.

47 SWORDS OF VENGEANCE: FALL OF AKO CASTLE (Ako-jo Danzetsu, 1978). Director: Kinji Fukasaku. Screenplay: Koji Takada. Photography: Yoshio Miyajima. Music: Toshiaki Tsushima. Cast: Kinnosuke Yorozuya [Nakamura], Shinichi "Sonny" Chiba, Hiroki Matsukata, Toshiro Mifune, Teruhiko Saigo, Tsunehiko Watase, Tetsuro Tanba [Tamba], Nobuo Kaneko, Shinsuke Ashida, Yoshiko Mita, Mariko Okada, Takuya Fujioka, Masaomi Kondo, Mieko Harada, Mikio Narita. Distribution: Toei. Release date: October 28, 1978. 140 minutes.

LADY SNOWBLOOD (Shurayukihime, 1973). Director: Toshiya Fujita. Producer: Kikumaru Okuda. Screenplay: Norio Osada, based on a story by Kazuo Koike and Kazuo Kamimura. Photography: Masaki Tamura (Eastmancolor, TohoScope). Lighting: Choshiro Ishii. Art Director: Kazuo Satsuya. Music: Masaaki Hirao. Sound: Noboru Kamikura. Editing: Osamu Inoue. Fight Choreography: Kunishiro Hayashi. Cast: Meiko Kaji (Yuki), Toshio Kurosawa, Masaaki Daimon, Miyoko Akaza, Takeo Chii, Noboru Nakaya, Yoshiko Nakada, Akemi Negishi, Kaoru Kusuda, Sanae Nakahara. Distribution: Toho. Release date: December 1, 1973. 97 minutes. Video: AnimEigo

LADY SNOWBLOOD: LOVE SONG OF VENGEANCE (Shurayukihime: Urami Koiuta, 1974). Director: Toshiya Fujita. Producer: Kikumaru Okuda. Screenplay: Kiyohide Ohara, Norio Osada, based on a story by Kazuo Koike and Kazuo Kamimura. Photography: Tatsuo Suzuki (Eastmancolor, TohoScope). Editing: Osamu Inoue. Music: Kenjiro Hirose. Cast: Meiko Kaji (Yuki), Yoshio Harada, Kazuko Yoshiyuki, Shin Kishida, Koji Nanbara [Nambara], Rinichi Yamamoto, Juzo Itami. Distribution: Toho. Release date: June 15, 1974. 89 minutes. Video: AnimEigo

THE LAST SAMURAI (Okami yo Rakujitsu o kire: Fuun-Hen, Gekijo-Hen, Doto-Hen, 1974). Director: Kenji Misumi. Producer: Yoshiharu Mishima. Screenplay: Kenji Misumi, Takeo [Issei] Kunihiro, based on a novel by Shotaro Ikenami. Photography: Masao Kosugi. Art Direction: Chiyo Umeda. Music: Akira Ifukube. Sound: Hideo Kobayashi. Cast: Hideki Takahashi (Toranosuke Sugi), Ken Ogata (Hanjiro Nakamura/Toshiaki Kirino), Keiko Matsuzaka (Reiko), Kiwako Daichi (Ohide/Oshuni the Nun), Asao Sano (Kingoro), Takahiro Tamura (Ikemoto) Ryutaro Tatsumi (Saigo), Ryunosuke Minegishi (Aizawa), Masaomi Kondo (Hachiro Iba), Teruhiko Saigo (Soji [Soshi] Okita). Distribution: Shochiku. Release date: September 21, 1974. 159 minutes. Alternate English Titles: Wolf, Chop the Setting Sun! or Last Day Of The Wolf Cat.

THE LAST SWORDSMAN (or SAMURAI OKITA SOSHI; Okita Soji [Soshi], 1974). Director: Masanobu Deme. Screenplay: Yasuko Ono. Photography: Kazutami Hara. Music: Riichiro Manabe. Editor: Yoshitami Kuroiwa. Cast: Masao Kusakari (Soji [Soshi] Okita), Koji Takahashi, Masahane Yonekura, Kyoko Maya [Mano], Jiro Kawarazaki, Shigeru Koyama [Kamiyama]. Distribution: Toho. Release date: November 2, 1974. 92 minutes.

MIYAMOTO MUSASHI (or SWORD OF FURY 1 & 2; Miyamoto Musashi, 1973). Director: Tai Kato. Producer: Yoshiharu Mishima. Screenplay: Yoshitaro Nomura, Kiyomoto Yamashita, based on the novel "Miyamoto Musashi" by Eiji Yoshikawa. Photography: Keiji Maruyama. Music: So [Hajime] Kaburagi. Cast: Hideki Takahashi (Musashi Miyamoto), Jiro Tamiya (Kojiro Sasaki), Keiko Matsuzaka (Otsu), Mitsuko Baisho (Akemi), Frankie Sakai (Matahachi Hon'iden), Chishu Ryu (Takuan), Toshiyuki Hosokawa (Seijuro Yoshioka), Yoshi Kato (Sado Nagaoka). Distribution: Shochiku. Release date: July 14, 1973. 148 minutes.

SAMURAI ADVISOR (or LORD INCOGNITO; Mito Komon, 1978). Director: Tetsuya Yamanouchi. Photography: Toshio Masuda. Art Direction: Yoshikazu Sano. Music: Chuji Kinoshita. Cast: Eijiro Tono (Mito), Kotaro Satomi, Ichiro Nakatani [Nakaya], Toru Abe, Toshiro Mifune, Gentaro Takahashi, Hajime Hana, Kei Tani. Distribution: Toei. Release date: December 23, 1978. 88 minutes.

SWORD OF JUSTICE (Goyokiba, 1972) Director: Kenji Misumi. Producers: Shintaro Katsu, Hiroyoshi [Kozen] Nishioka [Katsu Productions]. Screenplay: Kazuo Koike, based on the manga by Kazuo Koike and Takeshi Konda. Photography: Chishi Makiura [Daieicolor; DaieiScope]. Lighting: Shozo Saito. Art Direction: Seiichi Ota. Music: Kunihiko Murai. Sound: Masao Osumi. Editor: Yoshiharu Hayashi. Fight Choreography: Jun Katsumura. Cast: Shintaro Katsu (Hanzo the "Razor" Itami), Yukiji Asaoka, Mari Atsumi, Ko [Akira] Nishimura (Magobei Onishi), Kamatari Fujiwara, Akira Yamauchi, Zenpei Saga, Akiji Kobayashi, Daigo Kusano, Keizo Kanie, Renji Ishibashi. Distribution: Daiei. Release date: December 30, 1972. 88 minutes. Video: AnimEigo.

SWORD OF JUSTICE 2: THE SNARE (Goyokiba: Kamisori Hanzo Jigoku-Zeme, 1973) Director: Yasuzo Masamura. Producers: Shintaro Katsu, Hiroyoshi [Kozen] Nishioka [Katsu Productions]. Screenplay: Yasuzo Masamura, based on the manga by Kazuo Koike and Takeshi Konda. Photography: Kazuo Miyagawa [Daieicolor; DaieiScope]. Lighting: Genken Nakaoka. Art Direction: Seiichi Ota. Music: Isao Tomita. Sound: Iwao Otani. Editor: Toshio Taniguchi. Fight Choreography: Jun Arimura. Cast: Shintaro Katsu (Hanzo the "Razor" Itami), Ko [Akira] Nishimura (Magobei Onishi), Keiko Aikawa, Kazuko Inano, Keizo Kanie, Shin Kishida, Hosei Komatsu, Toshio Kurosawa, Daigo Kusano, Kei Sato. Distribution: Daiei. Release date: August 11, 1973. 89 minutes. Video: AnimEigo.

SWORD OF JUSTICE 3: WHO'S GOT THE GOLD (Goyokiba: Oni no Hanzo Yawahada Koban, 1974) Director: Yoshio Inoue. Producers: Shintaro Katsu, Hiroyoshi [Kozen] Nishioka [Katsu Productions]. Screenplay: Yasuzo Masamura, based on the manga by Kazuo Koike and Takeshi Konda. Music: Hideaki Sakurai. Cast: Shintaro Katsu (Hanzo the "Razor" Itami), Ko [Akira] Nishimura

(Magobei Onishi), Mako Midori (Yumi), Mikio Narita (Bansaku Tonami), Asao Koike (Ishiyama), Etsushi Takahashi (Sugino), Daigo Kusano (Onibi), Keizo Kanie (Mamushi). Distribution: Daiei. Release date: February 9, 1974. 84 minutes. Video: AnimEigo.

SWORD OF VENGEANCE; SWORD OF VENGEANCE II: BABY CART AT THE RIVER STYX; SWORD OF VENGEANCE III: BABY CART TO HADES (*Kozure Okami: Ko wo Kashi Ude Kashi Tsukamatsuru* [I], 1972; *Kozure Okami: Sanzu no Kawa no Ubaguruma* [II], 1972; *Kozure Okami: Shi ni Kaze ni Mukau Ubaguruma* [III], 1972). Director: Kenji Misumi. Producers: Shintaro Katsu, Hisaharu Matsubara [Katsu Productions]. Screenplay: Kazuo Koike, based on the *manga* by Kazuo Koike and Goseki Kojima. Photography: Chishi Makiura [Eastmancolor, TohoScope]. Lighting: Hiroshi Mima. Art Direction: Akira Naito [I,II], Yoshinobu Nishioka [III]. Music: Hideaki Sakurai. Editor: Toshio Taniguchi. Sound: Tsuchitaro Hayashi. Fight Choreography: Eiichi Kusumoto. Cast: Tomisaburo Wakayama [Kenzaburo Jo] (Itto Ogami), Akihiro Tomikawa (Daigoro Ogami), Yunosuke Ito (Retsudo Yagyu) [I], Fumio Watanabe (Bizen Yagyu) [I], Tomoko Mayama (Osen) [I], Shigeru Tsuyuguchi (Kurando Yagyu) [I], Asao Uchida (Sugito) [I], Taketoshi Naito [I], Yoshi Kato [I], Yoshiko Fujita (Azami Ogami) [I], Reiko Kasahara [I], Kayo Matsuo (Sayaka Yagyu) [II], Akiji Kobayashi (Ozunu Kurokuwa) [II], Minoru Oki (Benma Hidari, Master of Death #1) [II], Shin Kishida (Kuruma Hidari, Master of Death #2) [II], Shogen Nitta (Tenma Hidari, Master of Death #3) [II], Kappei Matsumoto (Ichirobei Hirano) [II], Kanji Ebata (Sanji) [II], Go Kato (Kanbei Magomura) [III], Yuko Hama (Torizo) [III], Isao Yamagata (Genba Miura) [III], Michitaro Mizushima [III], Ichiro Nakatani [Nakaya] (Yagyu Samurai) [III], Sayoko Kato (Omatsu) [III], Jun Hamamura (Tatewaki Miura) [III]. Distribution: Toho. Release dates: January 15, 1972 [I]; April 22, 1972 [II]; September 2, 1972 [III]. 83 minutes [I], 81 minutes [II], 89 minutes [III]. Alternate English Titles: *Lone Wolf and Cub: Child and Expertise For Rent* [I]; *Lone Wolf and Cub: Sword of Vengeance* [I]; *Lone Wolf and Cub: Perambulator of the River of Sanzu* [II]; *Lone Wolf and Cub II: Baby Cart at the River Styx*; *Lone Wolf and Cub: Perambulator Against the Winds of Death* [III]; *Lone Wolf and Cub III: Baby Cart to Hades*. Video: AnimEigo.

SWORD OF VENGEANCE IV (*Kozure Okami: Oya no Kokoro Ko no Kokoro*, 1972). Director: Buichi Saito. Producers: Tomisaburo Wakayama [Kenzaburo Jo], Hisaharu Matsubara [Katsu Productions]. Screenplay: Kazuo Koike, based on the *manga* by Kazuo Koike and Goseki Kojima. Photography: Kazuo Miyagawa (Eastmancolor, TohoScope). Lighting: Genken Nakaoka. Art Direction: Shigenori Shimoishizaka. Music: Hideaki Sakurai. Editor: Toshio Taniguchi. Sound: Tsuchitaro Hayashi. Fight Choreography: Eiichi Kusumoto. Cast: Tomisaburo Wakayama [Kenzaburo Jo] (Itto Ogami), Akihiro Tomikawa (Daigoro), Yoichi Hayashi (Gunbei Yagyu), Michi Azuma (Oyuki), So Yamamura (Gomune Jindaiyu), Asao Koike (Yoshinao Tokugawa), Hiroshi Tanaka (Juzaemon Kashiwagi), Tatsuo Endo (Retsudo Yagyu), Asao Uchida, Shin Kishida (Enki Kozuka), Koji Sekiyama, Gakuya Morita, Hiroshi Hasegawa, Riki Harada, Michimaro Otabe, Seishiro Hara. Distribution: Toho. Release date: December 30, 1972. 81 minutes. Alternate English Titles: *Lone Wolf and Cub: Heart of the Parent, Heart of the Child*; *Lone Wolf and Cub IV: Baby Cart in Peril*. Video: AnimEigo.

SWORD OF VENGEANCE V (*Kozure Okami: Meifumado*, 1973). Director: Kenji Misumi. Producers: Tomisaburo Wakayama [Kenzaburo Jo], Masanori Sanada [Katsu Productions]. Screenplay: Kazuo Koike, Tsutomu Nakamura, based on the *manga* by Kazuo Koike and Goseki Kojima. Photography: Fujiro Morita (Eastmancolor, TohoScope). Art Direction: Shigenori Shimoishizaka. Music: Hideaki Sakurai. Editor: Toshio Taniguchi. Fight Choreographer: Eiichi Kusumoto. Cast: Tomisaburo Wakayama [Kenzaburo Jo] (Itto Ogami), Akihiro Tomikawa (Daigoro), Michiyo Yasuda (Shiranui), Minoru Oki (Retsudo Yagyu), Shingo Yamashiro (Kanbei), Tomomi Sato (Quick Change Oyo), Akira Yamauchi (Insp. Senzo), Eiji Okada (Shogen Wakita), Hideji Otaki, Fujio Suga, Taketoshi Naito, Rokko [Mutsuhiro]

The Last Samurai.

Toura (Ukon Ayabe), Ritsu Ishiyama (Shusuke Mogami), Yoshi Kato, Hiroshi Tanaka (Koyata Murao), Koji Fujiyama, Michimaro Otabe, Kazuyo Sumida, Bin Amatsu (Yamon Kikuchi), Kenji Ushio (Tomekichi the moll), Gakuya Morita (Saburobei Tsunekawa). Distribution: Toho. Release date: August 11, 1973. 89 minutes. Alternate English Titles: *Lone Wolf and Cub: The Crossroads to Hell*; *Lone Wolf and Cub V: Baby Cart in the Land of Demons*. Video: AnimEigo.

SWORD OF VENGEANCE VI (*Kozure Okami: Jigoku e Ikuzo! Daigoro*, 1974). Director: Yoshiyuki Kuroda. Producers: Tomisaburo Wakayama [Kenzaburo Jo], Masanori Sanada [Katsu Productions]. Screenplay: Tsutomu Nakamura, based on the *manga* by Kazuo Koike and Goseki Kojima. Photography: Chishi Makiura (Eastmancolor, TohoScope). Art Direction: Akira Naito. Music: Kunihiko Murai. Editor: Toshio Taniguchi. Cast: Tomisaburo Wakayama [Kenzaburo Jo] (Itto Ogami), Akihiro Tomikawa (Daigoro), Junko Hitomi (Kaori Yagyu), Minoru Oki (Retsudo Yagyu), Isao Kimura (Hyoei), Goro Mutsumi (Ozuru Ishine), Daigo Kusano, Jiro Miyaguchi, Renji Ishibashi, Ritsuo Ishiyama (Shogun), Chie Kobayashi (Azusa), Gakuya Morita, Koji Fujiyama (Tatewaki Tomita), Kyoichi Sato. Distribution: Toho. Release date: April 24, 1974. 83 minutes. Alternate English Titles: *Lone Wolf and Cub: We're Off to Hell!*; *Lone Wolf and Cub VI: White Heaven in Hell*. Video: AnimEigo.

SWORD OF VENGENCE 7 see LONE WOLF WITH CHILD: AN ASSASSIN ON THE ROAD TO HELL (1989)

SWORDS OF DEATH (or *MIYAMOTO MUSASHI VI; Shinken Shobu*, 1971). Director: Tomu Uchida. Producers: Hideyuki Shiino, Shunji Oki. Screenplay: Daisuke Ito, based on the novel *"Miyamoto Musashi"* by Eiji Yoshikawa. Photography: Tokuzo Kuroda [Eastmancolor; TohoScope]. Music: Taichiro Kosugi. Cast: Kinnosuke Nakamura [Yorozuya] (Musashi Miyamoto), Rentaro

Mikuni (Baiken Shishido), Hideko Okiyama (Omaki), Hiroshi Tanaka, Koji Iwamoto. Distribution: Toho. Release date: February 20, 1971. 79 minutes. Alternate English Titles: *Miyamoto Musashi VI*; *Death Match*; *Samurai, Part 6*.

TRAIL OF BLOOD [Parts I, II, and III] (*Mushukunin Mikogami no Jokichi: Kiba wa Hiki Saita* [I], 1972; *Mushukunin Mikogami no Jokichi: Kawakaze ni Kako wa Nagareta* [II], 1972; *Mushukunin Mikogami no Jokichi: Ko Kai ni Senko ga Hinda* [III], 1973). Director: Kazuo Ikehiro. Screenplay: Yoshihiro Ishimatsu [I,II], Kazuo Ikehiro [II,III], Shuichi Nagahara [III], based on a story by Saho Sasazawa. Photography: Kazuo Miyagawa [I,II], Yasuyuki Ichihara [I], Kozo Okazaki [III]. Art Direction: Motoji Kojima. Music: Takeo Watanabe. Editor: Michio Suwa. Cast: Yoshio Harada (Jokichi), Atsuo Nakamura, Ryunosuke Minegishi. Distribution: Toho. Release dates: June 10, 1972 [I]; October 10, 1972 [II]; June 9, 1973 [III]. 88 minutes [I], 80 minutes [II], 83 minutes [III].

THE YAGYU CONSPIRACY (or *SHOGUN'S SAMURAI* or *CONSPIRACY OF THE YAGYU CLAN*; *Yagyu Ichizoku no Inbo*, 1978). Director: Kinji Fukasaku. Screenplay: Tatsuo Nogami, Hiroo Matsuda, Kinji Fukasaku. Photography: Toru Nakajima. Music: Toshiaki Tsushima. Cast: Kinnosuke Yorozuya [Nakamura] (Tajima Yagyu), Shinichi "Sonny" Chiba (Jubei Yagyu), Hiroki Matsukata (Iemitsu Tokugawa), Toshiro Mifune (Yoshinao Tokugawa), Teruhiko Saigo (Tadanaga Tokugawa), Tetsuro Tanba [Tamba] (Genshinsai Ogasawara), Reiko Ohara (Okuni), Yoshio Harada (Sanzaburo Nagoya), Shinsuke Ashida (Toshikatsu Doi), Isuzu Yamada (Oeyo), Etsushi Takahashi (Izu Matsudaira), Isao Natsuyagi (Shozaemon Bekki), Etsuko Shihomi (Akane Yagyu), Kentaro Kudo (Matajuro Yagyu), Jiro Yabuki (Samon Yagyu), Mikio Narita (Ayamaro Karasuma), Sanae Nakahara (Lady Kasuga), Nobuo Kaneko (Michifusa Kujo), Hideo Murota (Sagenta Negoro), Hiroyuki Sanada (Hayate), Mayumi Asano (Man), Ichiro Nakatani [Nakaya] (Gyobu Amano). Distribution: Toei. Release date: January 21, 1978. 130 minutes.

1980s

THE DEATH OF A TEA MASTER (*Sen no Rikyu: Honkakubo Ibun*, 1989). Director: Kei Kumai. Producer: Kazunobu Yamaguchi. Screenplay: Yoshitaka Yoda, based a novel by Yashushi Inoue. Photography: Masao Tochizawa. Art Direction: Takeo Kimura. Music: Teizo Matsumura. Editor: Osamu Inoue. Cast: Eiji Okuda (Honkakubo), Toshiro Mifune (Sen no Rikyu), Kinnosuke Nakamura [Yorozuya] (Urakusai Oda), Go Kato (Oribe Furuta), Shinsuke Ashida (Hideyoshi Toyotomi), Eijiro Tono (Kokei), Tsunehiko Kamijo (Soji Yamagami), Taro Kawano (Sen no Sotan), Teizo Muta (Daitokuya), Taketoshi Naito (Toyobo), Distribution: Toho. Release date: October 7, 1989. 107 minutes.

EIJANAIKA (*Eejanaika*, 1980). Director/Producer: Shohei Imamura. Producers: Shoichi Ozawa, Jiro Tomoda, Shigemi Sugisaki. Screenplay: Shohei Imamura, Ken Miyamoto. Photography: Shinsaku Himeda. Editor: Shinichiro Ikebe. Editor: Keiichi Uraoka. Cast: Kaori Momoi (Ine), Shigeru Izumiya (Genji), Ken Ogata (Furukawa), Shigeru Tsuyuguchi (Kinzo), Yohei Kono (Hara), Minori Terada (Ijuin), Tsutomu Hiura (Sanji), Masao Kusakari, Shohei Hino, Masahiro Noguchi, Mitsuko Baisho, Yuko Tanaka, Yasuaki Kurata. Distribution: Shochiku. Release date: March 14, 1981. 151 minutes. Alternate English Title: *Why Not?*

GHOST STORY OF YOTSUYA: HAUNTED SUMMER (*Masho no Natsu: Yotsuya Kaidan Yori*, 1981). Director: Yukio Ninagawa. Producer: Hideshi [Shuji] [Hideji] Miyajima. Screenplay: Eiichi Uchida, based on a novel by Nanboku Tsuruya. Photography: Noritaka Sakamoto. Music: Shuichi Chino. Cast: Kenichi Hagiwara (Iemon Tamiya), Keiko Sekine [Takahashi] (Oiwa), Masako Natsume (Osode), Aiko Morishita (Oume), Miyoko Akaza, Renji Ishibashi. Distribution: Shochiku. Release date: May 23, 1981. 96 minutes.

LEGEND OF THE EIGHT SAMURAI (or *THE LEGEND OF EIGHT FROM SATOMI*; *Satomi Hakken-den*, 1983). Director: Kinji Fukasaku. Executive Producer: Haruki Kadokawa. Producers: Masao Sato, Hiroshi Sugawara, Izumi Toyoshima. Screenplay: Toshio Kamata, Kinji Fukasaku, based on the novel by Toshio Kamata. Photography: Seizo Sengen [Color; Panavision]. Lighting: Mitsuo Watanabe. Art Direction: Tsutomu Imamura. Music: Masahide Sakuma, Hiroyuki Nanba. Sound: Teruhiko Arakawa. Editor: Isamu Ichida. Fight Choreography: Toshio Sugawara. Special Effects: Nobuo Yajima. Cast: Hiroko Yakushimaru (Shizu-Hime), Hiroyuki Sanada (Shinbei Inue), Shinichi "Sonny" Chiba (Dosetsu Inuyama), Etsuko Shihomi (Keno Inusaka), Mari Natsuki (Tamazusa), Minori Terada (Daikaku Inumura), Yuki Meguro (Motofuji Hikita), Nana Okada (Hamaji), Masaki Kyomoto (Shino Inuzuka), Kenji Oba (Genpachi Inukai), Ryoichi Takayanagi (Masaharu Ota), Shunsuke Kariya (Kobungo Inuta), Takuya Fukuhara (Sosuke Inugawa), Nagare Hagiwara (Yonosuke), Akira Hamada (Akushiro), Mikio Narita (Sukemasa Ota), Tatsuo Endo (Hikiroku), Keiko Matsuzaka (voice of Fuse-Hime). Distribution: Toei. Release date: December 10, 1983. 136 minutes.

LONE WOLF WITH CHILD: AN ASSASSIN ON THE ROAD TO HELL (or *LONE WOLF AND CUB 7*; *Kozure Okami: Meifumado no Shikaku-nin*, 1989). Director: Tokuzo Tanaka. Screenplay: Seiko Shimura, based on the *manga* by Kazuo Koike and Goseki Kojima. Cast: Hideki Takahashi (Itto Ogami), Tomisaburo Wakayama [Kenzaburo Jo] (Retsudo Yagyu), Meiko Kaji (Torizo), Mari Natsuki (Otoshi), Yoko Nagayama (Osato), Koji Aeba (Daigoro Ogami), Saori Yuki (Azami Ogami), Kiyoshi Nakajo (Shogun Ietsuna Tokugawa), Guts Ishimatsu. Distribution: TV Asahi/Toei. Release date: October 5, 1989. 139 minutes. [TV Movie]

THE MAN WHO ASSASSINATED RYOMA (*Ryoma o Kitta Otoko*, 1987). Director: Kosaku Yamashita. Screenplay: Tsutomu Nakamura, based on a story by Mitsugu Saotome. Photography: Fujiro Morita. Music: Shuichi Chino. Cast: Kenichi Hagiwara, Jinpachi Nezu, Yoko Shimada. Distribution: Shochiku. Release date: October 17, 1987. 109 minutes.

NINJA WARS (*Iga Ninpo-Cho*, 1982). Director: Kosei [Mitsumasa] Saito. Executive Producer: Haruki Kadokawa. Producers: Masao Sato, Izumi Toyoshima. Screenplay: Ei Ogawa, based on the novel by Futaro Yamada. Photography: Fujiro Morita. Lighting: Yoshiaki Masuda. Art Direction: Norimichi Ikawa [Tokumichi Igawa], Kazuyoshi Sonoda. Music: Toshiaki Yokota. Sound: Fumio Hashimoto. Editor: Isamu Ichida. Fight Choreography: Toshio Sugawara. Special Effects: Hideo Suzuki. Cast: Hiroyuki Sanada (Flute player Jotaro), Noriko Watanabe (Kagaribi/Ukyodayu/Onibi), Shinichi "Sonny" Chiba (Shinzaemon Yagyu), Akira Nakao (Danjo Matsunaga), Mikio Narita (Kashin-Koji), Jun Miho (Isaribi), Yuki Kazamatsuri (Rasetsubo (Chidori)), Strong Kongo (Kongobo), Gajiro Sato (Suijubo), Noboru Matsuhashi (Yoshioki Miyoshi), Akira Hamada (Hagunbo), Seizo Fukumoto (Kokubo), Nodoka Kawai, Sanji Kojima, Hiroshi Tanaka (Hanzo Hattori). Distribution: Toei. Release date: December 18, 1982. 100 minutes.

RIKYU (*Rikyu*, 1989). Director: Hiroshi Teshigahara. Producers: Shizuo Yamanouchi, Hisao Minemura, Kazuo Watanabe. Screenplay: Genpei Akasegawa, Hiroshi Teshigahara, based on the novel by Yaeko Nogami. Photography: Fujiro Morita. Lighting: Gen Nakaoka. Art Direction: Yoshinobu Nishioka, Shigemori Shigeta. Music: Toru Takemitsu. Editor: Toshio Taniguchi. Sound: Hideo Nishizaki. Cast: Rentaro Mikuni (Rikyu), Yoshiko Mita (Riki), Tsutomu Yamazaki (Hideyoshi Toyotomi), Kyoko Kishida (Hideyoshi's wife), Tanie Kitabayashi (Hideyoshi's mother), Sayoko Yamaguchi, Ryo Tamura (Lord Hidenaga), Koshiro Matsumoto (Nobunaga Oda), Kichiemon Nakamura (Ieyasu Tokugawa), Yasosuke Bando (Mitsunari), Akira Kubo (Geni), Keishi Arashi (Oribe), Hisashi Igawa (Soji), Ichiro Zaitsu (Abbott Kokei), Hideo Kanze (Rikyu's brother-in-law), Masao Imafuku (Ceramist), Ruis

Marques (Stefano), Donald Richie (Priest). Distribution: Shochiku. Release date: September 15, 1989. 135 minutes. *Release date*: September 15, 1989. VIDEO: Capital Home /Slingshot DVD

SAMURAI REINCARNATION (*Makai Tensho*, 1981). Director: Kinji Fukasaku. Executive Producer: Haruki Kadokawa. Producers: Masao Sato, Tatsuo Honda, Seiji Inaba. Screenplay: Tatsuo Nogami, Takato Ishikawa, Kinji Fukasaku, based on the novel by Futaro Yamada. Photography: Kiyoshi Hasegawa, Shozo Sakane (ToeiColor, Panavision). Lighting: Yoshiaki Masuda. Art Direction: Norimichi Ikawa [Tokumichi Igawa], Yoshikazu Sano. Music: Hozan Yamamoto, Mitsuaki Kanno. Sound: Shigeji Nakayama. Editor: Isamu Ichida. Fight Choreography: Toshio Sugawara. Special Effects: Nobuo Yajima. Cast: Shinichi "Sonny" Chiba (Jubei Yagyu), Kenji Sawada (Shiro Amakusa), Tomisaburo Wakayama [Kenzaburo Jo] (Tajima Yagyu), Ken Ogata (Musashi Miyamoto), Akiko Kana (Garacia Hosokawa/Otama), Hiroyuki Sanada (Kirimaru), Tetsuro Tanba [Tamba] (Muramasa), Ai Kanzaki (Otsu), Hideo Murota (Inshun Hozoin), Noboru Matsuhashi (Tadaoki Hosokawa/Ietsuna Tokugawa), Yuko Kikuchi (Omitsu), Naoko Kubo (Lady Yajima), Mikio Narita (Izu Matsudaira), Hiroshi Inuzuka (Sogoro), Asao Uchida (Uta Sakai), Jun Oba (Samon Yagyu), Tadashi Naruse (Genjuro Koga), Etsuo Shima (Matajuro Yagyu), Yuko Asuka (Koga Female Ninja), Jun Hamamura (Mozaemon), Noboru Mitani (Traveling Priest), Aoi Nakajima (Female Farmer), Mizuho Suzuki (Shosai Ogasawara). Distribution: Toei. Release date: June 6, 1981. 122 minutes. Video: Arena Home Video. Alternate English Titles: *Darkside Reborn*; *Reincarnation of the Devil's World*.

SHADOW WARRIORS (*Kage no Gundan: Hattori Hanzo*, 1980). Director: Eiichi Kudo. Screenplay: Koji Takada, Seiko Shimura, Takayuki Yamada. Photography: Toru Nakajima. Art Direction: Norimichi Ikawa [Tokumichi Igawa]. Cast: Tsunehiko Watase, Teruhiko Saigo, Ken Ogata, Aiko Morishita, Emi Harada, So Yamamura, Mikio Narita, Nobuo Kaneko, Noboru Nakaya, Makoto Fujita, Yoichi Miura, Yutaka Nakajima. Distribution: Toei. Release date: February 23, 1980. 133 minutes.

SHOGUN'S DESTINY (*Tokugawa Ichizoku no Hokai*, 1980). Dir: Kosaku Yamashita. Screenplay: Hiroo Matsuda. Music: Toshiro Mayuzumi. Cast: Kinnosuke Yorozuya [Nakamura], Hiroki Matsukata, Mikijiro Hira. Distribution: Toei. Release date: May 24, 1980. 139 minutes.

SHOGUN'S NINJA (*Ninja Bugeicho Momochi Sandayu*, 1980). Director: Noribumi Suzuki. Producers: Goro Kusakabe, Tatsuo Honda. Screenplay: Takato Ishikawa, Fumio Konami, Ichiro Otsu. Photography: Toru Nakajima, Shin Ogawahara. Lighting: Sakae Umiji. Art Direction: Yoshikazu Sano. Music: Masakatsu Suzuki. Sound: Kiyoshige Hirai. Editor: Isamu Ichida. Fight Choreography: Ryuzo Ueno, Shinichi "Sonny" Chiba. Cast: Hiroyuki Sanada (Takamaru Momochi), Shinichi "Sonny" Chiba (Shogen Shiranui), Etsuko Shihomi (Ai Lin), Isao Natsuki (Hanzo Hattori), Yuki Ninagawa (Otsu), Tetsuro Tanba [Tamba] (Hakuunsai Tozawa), Shohei Hino (Gosuke), Kazuma Hase (Ishime), Go Awazu (Monta), Kumiko Hidaka (Kikunojo), Maki Tachibana (Otsuya), Katsumasa Uchida (Gennosuke Shiranui), Asao Koike (Hideyoshi Hashiba), Makoto Sato (Yatoji), Akira Shioji (Iguchi), Masashi Ishibashi (Sandayu Momochi), Masaharu Arikawa (Terunosuke Manji), Masataka Iwao (Heiroku), Akira Hamada (Mitsuhide Akechi), Yoko Nogiwa (Chiyo Momochi), Masumi Harukawa (Yodogimi). Distribution: Toei. Release date: November 15, 1980. 117 minutes.

SHOGUN'S SHADOW (*Shogun Iemitsu no Ranshin: Gekitotsu*, 1989). Director: Yasuo Furuhata [Kohata]. Producers: Tatsu Honda, Toshio Zushi, Masahisa Nakayama. Screenplay: Sadao Nakajima, Hiroo Matsuda. Photography: Kiyoshi Kitasaka. Lighting by: Yoshikazu Watanabe. Art Direction by: Norimichi Ikawa [Tokumichi Igawa], Kazuyoshi Sonoda. Music: Masaru Sato. Sound: Yoshio Horiike. Editor: Eifu Tamaki. Fight Choreography: Akinori Tani, Shinichi

"Sonny" Chiba. Cast: Ken Ogata (Gyobu Igo), Shinichi "Sonny" Chiba (Shozaemon Iba), Miyuki Kano (Lady Yajima), Hiroki Matsukata (Shigeji Abe), Sayoko Ninomiya (Lady Oman), Tetsuro Tanba [Tamba] (Masamori Hotta), Masaki Kyomoto (Iemitsu Tokugawa), Takeshi Maya (Masatoshi Hotta), Yuji Oda (Saheiji Tobe), Toshihiro Asari (Iori Sobue), Norihito Arai (Den'emon Kori), Masataka Naruse (Genzaburo Domon), Hiroyuki Nagato (Rokubei Tagaya), Ippei Shigeyama (Takechiyo Tokugawa), Chien-Chiang Hu (Jingoemon Shishi, the mute). Distribution: Toei. Release date: January 14, 1989. 110 minutes. Alternate English Titles: *Attack! Shogun Iemitsu is Crazy* or *Geki Totsu: The Insanity of Emperor Iemitsu*.

SURE DEATH! (*Hissatsu!*, 1984). Director: Masahisa Sadanaga. Producers: Hisashi Yamauchi, Yozo Sakurai, Yoshiki Nomura. Screenplay: Tatsuo Nogami, Takeshi [Go] Yoshida. Photography: Shigeru [Ko] Ishihara. Music: Masaaki Hirao. Editor: Koichi Sonoi. Cast: Makoto Fujita (Mondo Nakamura), Kunihiko Mitamura (Hide), Izumi Ayukawa (Kayo), Kiyoshi Nakajo (Yuji), Isuzu Yamada (Oriku), Mari Shiraki (Ritsu), Gannosuke Ashiya (Masa), Takao Kataoka. Distribution: Shochiku. Release date: June 16, 1984. 124 minutes. VIDEO: AnimEigo. [Feature version of television series].

SURE DEATH 2: BROWN, YOU BOUNDER! (*Hissatsu! Buraun-Kan no Kaibutsu-Tachi*, 1985). Director: Jo Hirose. Producers: Hisashi Yamauchi, Yozo Sakurai. Screenplay: Takeshi [Go] Yoshida. Photography: Shigeru [Ko] Ishihara. Music: Masaaki Hirao. Editor: Koichi Sonoi. Cast: Makoto Fujita (Mondo Nakamura), Izumi Ayukawa (Kayo), Masaki Kyomoto (Ryu), Hiroaki Murakami (Masa), Ippei Hikaru (Junnosuke Nishi), Toshio Yamauchi (Tanaka), Sakai Umezu (Tamasuke), Kin Sugai (Sen), Mari Shiraki (Ritsu). Distribution: Shochiku. Release date: June 29, 1985. 122 minutes. Alternate English Titles: *Sure Death: The Monsters in Brown's Mansion* or *Hissatsu II* or *Sure Death: Stop the Conspiracy*. VIDEO: AnimEigo. [Feature version of television series].

SURE DEATH 3, 4, and 5 (*Hissatsu! III: Ura ka Omote ka*, 1986; *Hissatsu! 4: Urami Harashimasu*, 1987; *Hissatsu! 5: Ogon no Chi*, 1991). Directors: Eiichi Kudo [3], Kinji Fukasaku [4], Toshio Masuda [5]. Screenplay: Tatsuo Nogami [3], Yoshiki Hori [3], Katsuyuki Nakamura [3], Kinji Fukasaku [4], Akira Nakahara [4], Tatsuo Nogami [4], Takeshi [Go] Yoshida [5]. Cast: Makoto Fujita (Mondo Nakamura), Kunihiko Mitamura (Hide), Hiroaki Murakami (Masa), Kin Sugai (Sen), Shinichi "Sonny" Chiba (Bunshichi) [4], Hiroyuki Sanada (Ukyonosuke) [4], Mitsuko Baisho (Ofuku) [4], Ippei Hikaru (Junnosuke) [4], Renji Ishibashi (Yasuda) [4], Keizo Kanie (Kyuzo) [4], Kazuko Kato (Otama) [4], Kyoko Kishida (Benten) [4], Hitomi Kobayashi (Okiku) [4], Hideo Murota (Yahei) [4], Mikio Narita (Sakai) [4], Haruko Sagara (Omitsu) [4], Daijiro Tsutsumi (Jinbo) [4]. Distribution: Shochiku. Release dates: May 24, 1986 [3]; June 6, 1987 [4]; December 23, 1991 [5]. 126 minutes [3], 131 minutes [4], 104 minutes [5]. Alternate English Titles: *Sure-Fire Death 4: We Will Avenge You*; *Sure Death Revenge* [4]. [Feature versions of television series].

1990S

BAKUMATSU JYUNJYODEN (*Bakumatsu Junjoden*, 1991). Director: Mitsuyuki Yakushiji. Producers: Haruki Kadokawa, Kazuyoshi Okuyama. Screenplay: Mitsuyuki Yakushiji, based on the novel by Kohei Tsuka. Photography: Takeshi Hamada. Art Direction: Hisao Inagaki. Music: Ryoichi Kuniyoshi. Sound: Yutaka Tsurumaki. Editor: Shizuo Arakawa. Fight Choreography: Takami Morioka. Cast: Ken Watanabe (Ryoma Sakamoto), Riho Makise (Soji [Soshi] Okita), Tetta Sugimoto (Toshizo Hijikata), Masato Ibu (Isami Kondo), Kazuya Kimura (Izo Okada), Binpachi [Toshiya] Ito (Hanjiro Nakamura), Yoneko Matsukane (Otose), Kenjiro Ishimaru (Toshimichi Okubo), Kinzo Sakura (Takamori Saigo), Umitaro Nozaki (Sanosuke Harada), Takuya Goto (Shinpachi Nagakura), Satoshi Sadanaga (Keisuke Yamanami), Tatsuhiko Tomoi (Heisuke

Todo), Eisuke Tsunoda (Genzaburo Inoue), Naomi Zaizen (Miyuki), Takaaki Enoki (Katamori Matsudaira), Akira Emoto (Kogoro Katsura), Masahiko Tsugawa (Tomomi Iwakura). Distribution: Shochiku. Release: July 6, 1991. 105 minutes.

FEMALE NINJAS MAGIC CHRONICLES [Parts I to VI] (*Kunoichi Ninpo-Cho*, 1991; *Kunoichi Ninpo-Cho II: Seishojo no Hiho*, 1992; *Kunoichi Ninpo-Cho III: Higi Densetsu no Kai*, 1993; *Kunoichi Ninpo-Cho IV: Chushingura Hisho*, 1994; *Kunoichi Ninpo-Cho: Jiraiya Hisho* [V], 1995; *Kunoichi Ninpo-Cho: Ninja Tsukikage Sho* [VI], 1996). Director: Masaru Tsushima. Cast: Yasuyo Shirashima [I], Reiko Hayama [I], Hitomi Okazaki [I], Yuki Sumida [II], Kenji Yamaguchi [II], Yumiko Itaya [II], Miki Mizuno [II], Mieko Arai [II], Shiho Wakabayashi [III], Kunihiko Ida [III], Miyuki Komatsu [III], Marino Hase [III], Mika Okamoto [III], Yuki Ohashi [III], Makiko Ueno [IV], Toshihide Wakamatsu [IV], Megumi Sakita [IV], Sayoko Yoda [IV], Michiyo Nakajima [V], Takanori Kikuchi [V], Yuka Onishi [VI], Tetsuo Kurata [VI], Rina Kitahara [VI], Miho Nomoto [VI], Chisato Naruse [VI]. Release dates: October 21, 1991 [I]; August 21, 1992 [II]; May 21, 1993 [III]; March 24, 1994 [IV]; May 6, 1995 [V]; April 13, 1996 [VI]. 80 minutes [I], 80 minutes [II], 73 minutes [III], 79 minutes [IV], 93 minutes [V], 80 minutes [VI].

FEMALES NINJAS YAGYU STORY [Parts I and II] (*Kunoichi Ninpo-Cho Yagyu Gaiden: Edo Bana Jigoku-hen* [I], 1998; *Kunoichi Ninpo-Cho Yagyu Gaiden: Aizu Yuki Jigoku-hen* [II], 1998). Director: Hitoshi Ozawa. Screenplay: Junichi Inoue, Hitoshi Ozawa, based on the novel *"Yagyu Ninpo-Cho"* by Futaro Yamada. Cast: Hitoshi Ozawa (Jubei Yagyu), Yuko Moriyama. 98 minutes [I], 81 minutes [II].

THE 47 RONIN- GHOST OF YOTSUYA (or *CREST OF BETRAYAL* or *GHOST OF YOTSUYA: CHUSHINGURA VERSION*; *Chushingura Gaiden Yotsuya Kaidan*, 1994). Director: Kinji Fukasaku. Producers: Yozo Sakurai, Tetsuo Sasho, Ryuta Saito. Screenplay: Kinji Fukasaku, Motomu Furuta. Photography: Shigeru [Ko] Ishihara. Music: Kaoru Wada. Cast: Koichi Sato (Iemon Tamiya), Saki Takaoka (Oiwa), Keiko Oginome (Oume), Tsunehiko Watase (Yasubei Horibe), Eriko Watanabe (Omaki), Renji Ishibashi (Kihei Ito), Keizo Kanie (Ichigaku Shimizu), Masahiko Tsugawa (Kuranosuke Oishi), Takahiro Tamura (Kozukenosuke Kira), Shohei Hino, Hiroyuki Sanada (Lord Takumi Asano). Distribution: Shochiku. Release: October 22, 1994. 106 minutes.

THE 47 KILLERS (or *THE 47 RONIN* or *47 ASSASSINS*; *Shijushichinin no Shikaku*, 1994). Director: Kon Ichikawa. Screenplay: Kon Ichikawa, Kaneo Ikegami, Yo Takiyama, based on the play by Shoichiro Ikemiya. Photography: Yukio Isohata. Art Direction: Yoshiro Muraki. Music: Kensaku Tanigawa. Editor: Chizuko Nagata. Cast: Ken Takakura (Kuranosuke Oishi), Kiichi Nakai (Matashiro Irobe), Rie Miyazawa (Karu), Ruriko Asaoka (Riku), Hisashi Igawa (Okuda), Renji Ishibashi (Heihachiro), Koji Ishizaka (Yoshiyasu Yanagisawa), Tatsuo Matsumura (Yahei), Hisaya Morishige (Hyobu Chisaka), Ko [Akira] Nishimura (Kozukenosuke Kira), Misa Shimizu (Hori), Ryudo Uzaki (Yasubei). Distribution: Toho. Release: October 22, 1994. 129 minutes.

THE GREAT SHOGUNATE BATTLE (or *GREAT BATTLE AT EDO CASTLE* or *EDO CASTLE REBELLION*; *Edo-jo Tairan*, 1991). Director: Toshio Masuda. Screenplay: Koji Takada. Photography: Kiyoshi Kitasaka. Music: Shinichiro Ikebe. Editor: Isamu Ichida. Cast: Hiroki Matsukata, Yukiyo Toake, Tomokazu Miura, Shinobu Sakagami, Takeshi Kato, Tetsuro Tanba [Tamba], Nobuo Kaneko, Masaki Kanda, Mami Nomura. Distribution: Toei. Release date: December 14, 1991. 113 minutes.

HEAVEN AND EARTH (*Ten to Chi to*, 1990). Director: Haruki Kadokawa. Producer: Yutaka Okada. Screenplay: Haruki Kadokawa, Toshio Kamata, Isao Yoshihara, based on a story by Chogoro Kaionji. Photography: Yonezo Maeda (Panavision). Art Direction: Hiroshi Tokuda. Music: Tetsuya Komuro. Editors: Akira Suzuki, Robert C. Jones. Fight Choreography: Hiroshi Kuze. Cast: Takaaki Enoki

(Nagao Kagetora), Masahiko Tsugawa (Shingen Takeda), Atsuko Asano (Nami), Tsunehiko Watase (Usami), Naomi Zaizen (Yae), Binpachi [Toshiya] Ito (Kakizaki), Isao Natsuyagi (Katsuke), Akira Hamada (Naoe). Distribution: Toei (Japan)/Triton Pictures (North America). Release date: June 23, 1990. 118 minutes. Video: Live.

JOURNEY OF HONOR (or *KABUTO* or *SHOGUN MAYEDA* or *SHOGUN WARRIOR*, 1991). Director: Gordon Hessler. Producer: Sho Kosugi. Executive Producers: Hiroshi Tsuchiya, Toshiaki Hayashi. Screenplay: Nelson Gidding, based on a story by Sho Kosugi. Photography: John Connor. Music: John Scott. Fight Choreography: Hiroshi Kuze. Cast: Sho Kosugi (Daigoro Mayeda), David Essex (Don Pedro), Kane Kosugi (Yorimune Tokugawa), Toshiro Mifune (Ieyasu Tokugawa), Christopher Lee (King Phillip III), Norman Lloyd (Father Vasco), Ronald Pickup (Captain Crawford), John Rhys-Davies (El Zaidan), Polly Walker (Lady Cecilia), Dylan Kussman (Smitty), Miwa Takada (Lady Yodogimi), Nijiko Kiyokawa (Councellor), Yuki Sugimura (Chiyo Mayeda). Distribution: Toho-Towa (Japan)/MCA Universal (North America). 106 minutes. Video: Universal.

LONE WOLF AND CUB: A HANDFUL OF SAND (or *LONE WOLF AND CUB: FINAL CONFLICT*; *Kozure Okami: Sono Chisaki Teni*, 1993). Director: Akira [Sho] Inoue. Screenplay: Tsutomu Nakamura, based on the *manga* by Kazuo Koike and Goseki Kojima. Cast: Masakazu Tamura (Itto Ogami), Tatsuya Nakadai (Retsudo Yagyu), Yuko Kotegawa (Azami Ogami), Yushi Shoda (Daigoro Ogami), Mayumi Wakamura (Nanao Yagyu), Isao Hashizume, , Renji Ishibashi, Kimiko Ikegami, Shima Iwashita, Kunie Tanaka. Distribution: Shochiku. Release date: February 6, 1993. 119 minutes.

THE PASSAGE TO JAPAN (*Fukuzawa Yukichi*, 1991). Director: Shinichiro Sawai. Screenplay: Kazuo Kasahara, Chiho Katsura. Photography: Seizo Sengen. Music: Jo Hisaishi. Cast: Kyohei Shibata (Yukichi Fukuzawa), Takaaki Enoki, Toru Nakamura, Yoko Minamino, Mayumi Wakamura, Sho Aikawa, Hiroshi Katsuno. Distribution: Toei. Release date: August 24, 1991. 123 minutes.

REBORN FROM HELL: SAMURAI ARMAGEDDON (or *DARK-SIDE REBORN*; *Makai Tensho*, 1996). Director: Masakazu Shirai. Screenplay: Akinori Kikuchi, based on the novel by Futaro Yamada. Photography: Yoshihiro Ito [Color]. Music: Takashi Nakagawa, Sachi Sakamoto. Cast: Hiroyuki Watanabe (Jubei Yagyu), Tomorowo Taguchi (Shosetsu Yui), Yuko Moriyama (Ohiro), Hitomi Shimizu (Lady Kasuga), Shunya [Toshiya] Wazaki (Tajima Yagyu), Hiroshi Miyauchi (Musashi Miyamoto), Kotaro Yoshida (Shiro Amakusa), Nobuyuki Ishida (Izu Matsudaira), Shohei Yamamoto (Inshun Hozoin). Distribution: Gaga Communications. Release date: April 26, 1996. 85 minutes. Video: Tokyo Shock/Media Blasters.

REBORN FROM HELL II: JUBEI'S REVENGE (or *DARKSIDE REBORN: PATH TO HELL*; *Makai Tensho: Mado-hen*, 1996). Director: Masakazu Shirai. Screenplay: Akinori Kikuchi, based on the novel by Futaro Yamada. Photography: Yoshihiro Ito [Color]. Music: Takashi Nakagawa, Sachi Sakamoto. Cast: Hiroyuki Watanabe (Jubei Yagyu), Tomorowo Taguchi (Shosetsu Yui), Yuko Moriyama (Ohiro), Hitomi Shimizu (Lady Kasuga), Hiroshi Miyauchi (Musashi Miyamoto), Kotaro Yoshida (Shiro Amakusa), Shunya [Toshiya] Wazaki (Tajima Yagyu), Nobuyuki Ishida (Izu Matsudaira), Hozumi Goda. Distribution: Gaga Communications. Release date: October 4, 1996. 83 minutes. Video: Tokyo Shock/Media Blasters

RONIN-GAI (1990). Director: Kazuo Kuroki. Producers: Yoshito Yamazaki, Yoshiki Nomura, Yasutaka Tarumi. Screenplay: Kazuo Kasahara, based on a story by Itaro Yamagami. Photography: Hitoshi Takaiwa. Music: Teizo Matsumura. Cast: Yoshio Harada (Gennai Aramaki), Kanako Higuchi (Oshin), Shintaro Katsu ("Bull" Goemon), Renji Ishibashi (Gonbei), Moeko Ezawa (Otoku), Hiroko Isayama (Oyo), Michitaro Mizushima (Tahei), Hiroyuki Nagato, Tatsu Nakamura (Onaka), Akira Nakao, Kei Sato (Iseya), Kaoru Sugita (Obun), Kunie Tanaka (Magohachiro). Distribution: Shochiku. Release date: August 18, 1990. 117 minutes.

A FILM BY HIROYUKI NAKANO
SAMURAI FICTION
MORIO KAZAMA, TOMOYASU HOTEI, MITSURU FUKIKOSHI, TAMAKI OGAWA, AND MARI NATSUKI

SAMURAI FICTION (SF Samurai Fiction: Episode One, 1998). Director: Hiroyuki Nakano. Screenplay: Hiroshi Saito. Producers: Takaaki Ezaki, Hiroto Kimura, Kaoru Hayashi, Tsuyoshi Takashiro, Hiroyuki Nakano (Nikko Edomura Satsueisyo). Photography: Yujiro Yajima. Lighting: Kazutaka Shiihara. Art Direction: Masasteru Moshizuki, Hiroshi Fujita. Music: Tomoyasu Hotei. Sound: Ichiro Hoshi. Editor: Kiyoharu Miyazaki. Fight Choreography: Eiji Takakura, Keiji Yamada. Cast: Morio Kazama (Hanbei Mizoguchi), Mitsuru Fukikoshi (Heishiro Inukai), Tomoyasu Hotei (Rannosuke Kazamatsuri), Tamaki Ogawa (Koharu Mizoguchi), Mari Natsuki (Okatsu), Taketoshi Naito (Kanzen Inukai), Kei Tani (Kagemaru), Fumiya Fujii (Ryunosuke Kuzumi), Naoyuki Fujii (Shintaro Suzuki), Ken Osawa (Tadasuke Kurosawa), Hiroshi Kanbe (Gosuke), Ryoichi Yuki (Ninja Hayabusa), Akiko Mono (Ninja Akakage), Taro Maruse (Sakyonosuke Kajii), Yuji Nakamura (Samejima), Kitaro (Surveying Samurai), Ramo Nakajima (Denbei Kimura), Ryo Iwamatsu (Muroto), Shogo Suzuki (Yagi), Pierre Taki (Bad Ronin Juzo Araki), Yutaka Tadokoro (Onimatsu), Utaroku Miyakoya (Kuma-San), Yoshiaki Umegaki (Rascal Baba), Masahiro Sato (Rascal Ooka), Kazuhide Motooka (Rascal Toyama), Norikazu Kobayashi (Massage-Oichi), Nagine Hoshikawa (Yukie Kimura), Yasuto Hida (Bad Ronin Kuroiwa), Hideaki Yoshioka (Sakichi), Ryuji Takasaki (Ushimatsu). Distribution: Pony Canyon. Release date: August 1, 1998. 111 minutes. Video: Samurai Video.

TABOO (Gohatto, 1999). Director: Nagisa Oshima. Producers: Eiko Oshima, Shigehiro Nakagawa, Kazuo Shimizu [Bac/Canal/Recorded Picture]. Executive Producers: Nobuyoshi Otani, Jean Labadie, Jeremy Thomas. Screenplay: Nagisa Oshima, based on the stories "With a Lock of Hair Over His Forehead" and "The Revolt of the Mountain from Tales of the Shinsengumi" by Ryotaro Shiba. Photography: Toyomichi Kurita (Color). Lighting: Hiroshi Takehisha. Art Direction: Yoshinobu Nishioka. Music: Ryuichi Sakamoto. Sound: Kunio Ando. Editor: Tomoyo Oshima. Cast: "Beat" Takeshi [Kitano] (Lt. Commander Toshizo Hijikata), Ryuhei Matsuda (Sozaburo Kano), Shinji Takeda (Lt. Soji [Soshi] Okita), Tadanobu Asano (Hyozo Tashiro), Yoichi Sai (Commander Isami Kondo), Koji Matoba (Heibei Sugano), Tommys' Masa (Inspector Yamazaki), Masato Ibu (Officer Koshitaro Ito), Uno Kanda (Nishikigi-Dayu), Kazuko Yoshiyuki (Omatsu), Tomorowo Taguchi (Tojiro Yuzawa), Jiro Sakagami (Lt. Genzaburo Inoue), Zakoba Katsura (Wachigaiya), Yoji Tanaka (Seijuro Muto), Susumu Terajima (Shinsengumi spy), Kei Sato (Narrator). Distribution: Shochiku. Release date: December 18, 1999. 100 minutes. VIDEO: New Yorker.

ZIPANG (or THE LEGEND OF ZIPANG; Jipangu, 1992). Director: Kaizo Hayashi. Producers: Koji Tsutsumi, Kosuke Kuri. Screenplay: Kaizo Hayashi, Noriyuki Kurita. Photography: Masaki Tamura. Art Direction: Takeo Kimura, Yuji Maruyama. Music: Hidehiko Urayama, Yoko Kumagai. Sound: Hisayuki Miyamoto. Fight Choreography: Kanta Ina. Cast: Masahiro Takashima, Mikijiro Hira, Narumi Yasuda, Haruko Wanibuchi, Mikio Narita, Kipp Hamilton. Distribution: Toho. Release date: January 27, 1990.

AFTER THE RAIN (Ame Agaru, 2000). Director: Takashi Koizumi. Producers: Masato Hara, Hisao Kurosawa. Screenplay: Akira Kurosawa, based on the novel by Shugoro Yamamoto. Photography: Shoji [Masaharu] Ueda. Art Direction: Yoshiro Muraki. Music: Masaru Sato. Sound: Kenichi Benitana. Editor: Hideto Aga. Cast: Akira Terao (Ihei Misawa), Yoshiko Miyazaki (Tayo Misawa), Shiro Mifune (Lord Shigeaki), Mieko Harada (Okin), Fumi Dan (Okugata), Hisashi Igawa (Kihei Ishiyama), Hidetaka Yoshioka (Gonnojo Sakakibara), Tatsuya Nakadai (Gettan Tsuji) Takayuki Kato (Hayato Naito), Tatsuo Matsumura (Old Preacher). Distribution: Asmik Ace/Toho. Release date: January 22, 2000. 91 minutes. Video: Samurai Video.

AZUMI (2003). Director: Ryuhei Kitamura, Producers: Mataichiro Yamamoto, Toshiaki Nakazawa. Screenplay: Isao Kiriyama, based on the comic book by Yu Koyama. Art Direction: Yuji Hayashida. Fight Choreography: Yuta Morokaji. Cast: Aya Ueto (Azumi), Yoshio Harada (Master Gessai), Jo Odagiri (Bijomaru), Aya Okamoto (Yae), Kenji Kohashi (Hyuga), Minoru Matsumoto (Saru), Kazuki Kitamura (Kanbei), Naoto Takenaka (Lord Kiyomasa), Masato Ibu (Nagamasa Asano). Distribution: Toho. Release date: May 10, 2003. 142 minutes.

AZUMI 2: DEATH OR LOVE (2005) Director: Shusuke Kaneko. Producer: Mataichiro Yamamoto. Screenplay: Rikiya Mizushima, Yoshiaki Kawajiri, based on the comic book by Yu Koyama. Photography: Yoshitaka Sakamoto. Sound Recording: Yoshiya Obara. Cast: Aya Ueto (Azumi), Yuma Ishigaki (Nagara), Chiaki Kuriyama (Kozue), Shun Oguri (Nachi), Kenichi Endo, Kai Shishido (Hanzo), Eugene Nomura (Samurai Z), Tak Sakaguchi (Tsuchi-gumo), Shoichiro Matsumoto (Saburota), Kenji Takechi (Kiheita), Ai Maeda (Chiyo), Toshie Negishi (Yone), Toshiya Nagasawa (Yukimura Sanada), Shigeru Koyama [Kamiyama] (Priest Tenkai), Kazuki Kitamura (Kanbei Inoue), Mikijiro Hira (Masayuki Sanada), Reiko Takashima, Shun Ito (Kijimaru). Distribution: Toho.

BLOOD GETS IN YOUR EYES (aka ASHURA; Ashura-jo no Hitomi, 2005) Director: Yojiro Takita. Screenplay: Masashi Todayama, Hal Kawaguchi._Photography: Katsumi Yanagijima. Art Direction: Yuji Hayashida. Music: Isao Tomita. Cast: Somegoro Ichikawa (Izumo), Rie Miyazawa (Tsubaki), Atsuro Watabe, Takashi Naito, Kanako Higuchi. Distribution: Shochiku.

DORA HEITA (or PLAYBOY HEITA; Dora Heita, 2000). Director: Kon Ichikawa. Producer: Yoshinobu Nishioka. Screenplay: Kon Ichikawa, Masaki Kobayashi, Akira Kurosawa, Keisuke Kinoshita, based on the novel Diary of a Town Magistrate by Shugoro Yamamoto. Photography: Yukio Isohata. Art Direction: Yoshinobu Nishioka. Music: Kensaku Tanigawa. Fight Choreography: Tang Te Hsiang. Cast: Koji Yakusho (Koheita Mochizuki), Yuko Asano (Kosei), Ryudo Uzaki (Senba), Tsurutaro Kataoka (Yasukawa), Bunta Sugawara (Nadahachi), Renji Ishibashi (Saibei), Tsuyoshi Ujiki, Isao Bito, Nekohachi Edoya, Saburo Ishikura, Takeshi Kato, Kyoko Kishida, Shigeru Koyama [Kamiyama], Noboru Mitani. Distribution: Toho. Release: May 13, 2000. 111 minutes. Video: Samurai Video.

GANRYUJIMA (2003) Screenplay/Director: Seiji Chiba. Photography: Akira Sako. Music: Naoki Otsubo. Editor: Yoshiyuki Okuhara. Cast: Masahiro Motoki (Musashi Miyamoto), Masahiko Nishimura (Kojiro Sasaki), Atsushi Tamura (Sukezo), Miho Yoshioka (Kame), Noboru Kaneko (Shintaro Yoshimoto), Toshio Kakei (Kennosuke Imai), Shunji Fujimura (Todoroki), Tsuyoshi Nakagawake (Todoroki's assistant), Reiji Nakagawake (Samurai), Kenji Haga (Samurai). Distribution: Toho. 77 minutes.

GOJOE (Gojo Reisenki, 2000). Director: Sogo Ishii. Producer: Takenori Sento. Screenplay: Sogo Ishii, Goro Nakajima. Photography: Makoto Watanabe. Music: Hiroyuki Onogawa. Editor: Shuichi Kakesu. Cast: Tadanobu Asano, Masatoshi Nagase, Daisuke Ryu, Masakatsu Funaki. Distribution: Toho. Release: October 7, 2000. 137 minutes. Video: Samurai Video.

304

THE HIDDEN BLADE (*Kakushi ken oni no tsume*, 2004) Director: Yoji Yamada. Producer: Hiroshi Fukazawa. Screenplay: Yoshitaka Asama, Yoji Yamada, based on stories by Shuhei Fujisawa. Photography: Mutsuo [Rokuo] Naganuma. Art Direction: Mitsuo Degawa. Music: Isao Tomita. Editor: Iwao Ishii. Cast: Masatoshi Nagase (Munezo Katagiri), Takako Matsu (Kie), Hidetaka Yoshioka (Samon Shimada), Yukiyoshi Ozawa (Yaichiro Hazama), Min Tanaka (Kansai Toda), Tomoko Tabata (Shino), Ken Ogata (Shogen Hori), Nenji Kobayashi, Reiko Takashima (Yaichiro's wife), Sachiko Mitsumoto, Kunie Tanaka, Chieko Baisho. Distribution: Shochiku. 132 minutes.

THE LAST SAMURAI (2003). Director: Edward Zwick. Screenplay: John Logan, Marshall Herskovitz, Edward Zwick. Producers: Edward Zwick, Marshall Herskovitz, Tom Cruise, Paula Wagner, Scott Kroopf, Tom Engelman. Screenplay: Marshall Herskovitz, John Logan, Edward Zwick. Photography: John Toll. Art Direction: Lily Kilvert. Music: Hans Zimmer. Editors: Steven Rosenblum, Victor du Bois. Fight Choreography: Lauro Chartrand. Cast: Tom Cruise (Capt. Nathan Algren), Ken Watanabe (Katsumoto), Koyuki (Taka), Masao Harada (Omura), Hiroyuki Sanada (Ujio), Tony Goldwyn (Col. Benjamin Bagly), Shin Koyamada (Nobutada), Shichinosuke Nakamura (Emperor), Seizo Fukumoto ("Bob," the silent samurai), Billy Connolly (Sgt. Zebulah Gant), Togo Igawa (Hasegawa), Sosuke Ikematsu, John Koyama (Omura's Bodyguard), William Atherton. Distribution: Warner Bros. Release date: December 5, 2003. 154 minutes. Video: Warner Bros.

PEASANT UPRISINGS IN GUJO (*Gujo Ikki*, 2000). Director: Seijiro Koyama. Producers: Yutaka Oike, Yoshiyuki Sakamoto, Seijiro Koyama. Screenplay: Nobuyo Kato, Seijiro Koyama, based on a story by Hiroshi Kobayashi. Photography: Fuminori Minami. Music: Kaoru Wada. Cast: Naoto Ogata (Sadajiro), Ryuzo Hayashi (Shirozaemon), Go Kato (Sukezaemon). Release: December 23, 2000. 112 min.

RED SHADOW (*Akakage*, 2001). Director: Hiroyuki Nakano. Screenplay: Hiroshi Saito, Masatoshi Kimura, based on the television series created by Mitsuteru Yokoyama. Photography: Hideo Yamamoto. Art Direction: Akira Naito, Kinya Uchida. Music: Toshiyuki Kishi. Cast: Masanobu Ando (Akakage), Megumi Okina (Koto-Hime), Jun Murakami (Aokage), Naoto Takenaka (Shirokage), Kumiko Aso (Asuka), Fumiya Fujii (Ranmaru), Shuhei Mainoumi (Rikimaru), Masahiko Tsugawa (Lord Togo), Takanori Jinnai. Distribution: Toei. Release date: August 11, 2001. 108 minutes. Video: Samurai Video.

SAKUYA: SLAYER OF DEMONS (*Sakuya Yokaiden*, 2000). Director: Tomoo Haraguchi. Screenplay: Kimihide Mitsuyasu. Cast: Nozomi Ando (Sakuya), Shuichi Yamauchi, Kyusaku Shimada, Keiichiro Sakagi, Yuki Kuroda, Tetsuro Tanba [Tamba], Hiroshi Fujioka, Keiko Matsuzaka. Distribution: Warner Bros. Release date: August 12, 2000. 88 minutes.

TALES OF THE UNUSUAL: SAMURAI CELLULAR (*Yonimo Kimyo na Monogatari Eiga Tokubetsuhen: Keitai Chushingura*, 2000). Director: Masayuki Suzuki. Screenplay: Ryoichi Kimizuka. Photography: Hiroshi Takase. Music: Kunaiki Haishima. Cast: Kiichi Nakai (Kuranosuke Oishi), Megumi Okina (Karu), Keiko Toda (Riku). Distribution: Toho. Release date: November 3, 2000. 131 minutes.

TANGE SAZEN (*Tange Sazen: Hyakuman Ryo no Tsubo*, 2004) Director, Photography, Editor: Toyoshi Tsuda. Screenplay: Jun Edoki, based on the original screenplay by Shintaro Mimura, based on a story by Fubo Hayashi. Cast: Etsushi Toyokawa (Sazen Tange), Emi Wakui (Ofuji), Hironobu Nomura (Genzaburo Yagyu), Kumiko Aso (Hagino), Akashi Takei, Akio Kaneda, Nagatoshi Sakamoto (Yahei), Shigeru Araki, Katsumi & Sayuri, Hiroyuki Watanabe (Shichibei), Kosuke Toyohara (Yojinbo). Distribution: Eden. 115 minutes.

THE TWILIGHT SAMURAI (*Tasogare Seibei*, 2002). Director: Yoji Yamada. Producers: Shigehiro Nakagawa, Hiroshi Fukazawa, Ichiro Yamamoto. Screenplay: Yoji Yamada, Yoshitaka Asama, based on stories by Shuhei Fujisawa. Photography: Mutsuo [Rokuo] Naganuma.

Lighting: Genken Nakaoka. Art Direction: Yoshinobu Nishioka, Mitsuo Degawa. Sound: Kazumi Kishida. Editor: Iwao Ishii. Fight Choreography: Hiroshi Kuze. Cast: Hiroyuki Sanada (Seibei Iguchi), Rie Miyazawa (Tomoe Iinuma), Min Tanaka (Zenemon), Nenji Kobayashi (Chobei Kusaka), Ren Osugi (Toyotaro Koda), Mitsuro Fukikoshi (Michinojo Iinuma), Hiroshi Kanbe (Naota), Erina Hashiguchi (Ito Iguchi, age five), Miki Ito (Kayana Iguchi), Tetsuro Tanba [Tamba] (Great Uncle), Keiko Kishi (Mother). Distribution: Shochiku. Release date: November 2, 2002. 129 minutes. Video: Samurai Video; Empire.

WHEN THE LAST SWORD IS DRAWN (*Mibu Gishi-Den*, 2003). Director: Yojiro Takita. Producers: Hideshi [Shuji] [Hideji] Miyajima, Nozomu Enoki. Screenplay: Takehiro Nakajima, based on a story by Jiro Asada. Photography: Takeshi Hamada. Lighting: Tatsuya Osada. Art Direction: Kyoko Heya. Music: Jo Hisaishi. Sound: Osamu Onadera. Editor: Isao Tomita, Nobuko Tomita. Cast: Kiichi Nakai (Kanichiro Yoshimura), Koichi Sato (Hajime Saito), Yui Natsukawa (Shizu), Takehiro Murata (Chiaki Ono), Miki Nakatani (Nui), Yuji Miyake (Jiroemon Ono), Ayumi Saito. Distribution: Shochiku. Release date: January 18, 2003. 137 minutes. Video: Samurai Video.

YEAR ONE IN THE NORTH (*Kita no zeronen*, 2005) Director: Isao Yukisada. Screenplay: Machiko Nasu. Executive Producers: Hiroshi Hayakawa, Sunao Sakagami. Photography: Nobuyasa Kita. Lighting: Yuki Nakamura. Art Direction: Kyoko Heya. Music: Michiru Oshima. Editor Tsuyoshi Imai. Cast: Sayuri Yoshinaga (Shino Komatsubara), Ken Watanabe (Hideaki Komatsubara), Etsushi Toyokawa (Ashirika), Toshiro Yanagiba (Denzo Mamiya), Yuriko Ishida (Kayo Mamiya), Teruyuki Kagawa (Kurazo Mochida), Satomi Ishihara (Tae Komatsubara), Sadao Abe (Matajuro Nakano), Yu Fujiki (Kamejiro Nakano), Mitsuru Fukikoshi (Keiichiro Hase), Mitsuru Hirata (Eita Kawakubo), Renji Ishibashi (Kahei Horibe), Haruko Mabuchi (Sue Hase), Moro Morooka, Takeo Nakahara (Uchida), Kaoru Okunuki (Sato Hase), Susumu Terajima (Kanji Hanamura), Mayu Tsuruta (Otsuru). Distribution: Toei. 170 minutes.

CREDITS FOR THE SAME PERSON APPEARING UNDER TWO DIFFERENT BUT VALID NAMES

Hideyo [Eisei] Amamoto
Chozaburo/Kanjuro Arashi
Junzaburo Ban/Kan Togi
Kazuo Hasegawa [Chojiro Hayashi]
Umitaro Hasegawa/Fubo Hayashi
Chojiro Hayashi/Kazuo Hasegawa
Fubo Hayashi/Umitaro Hasegawa
Shinnosuke Ikehata/Peter
Sei/Shigeru Ikeno
Hanshiro Iwai/Shubo Nishina
Kenzaburo Jo/Tomisaburo Wakayama]
Minoru/Shigeto Miki
Kinnosuke Nakamura/Yorozuya
Shubo Nishina/Hanshiro Iwai
Peter/Shinnosuke Ikehata
Sakae/Eitaro Ozawa
Keiko Sekine/Takahashi
Keiko Takahashi/Sekine
Kan Togi/Junzaburo Ban
Tomisaburo Wakayama/Kenzaburo Jo
Kinnosuke Yorozuya/Nakamura

CREDITS FOR THE SAME PERSON APPEARING UNDER A VALID NAMES AND AOFTEN USED BUT INCORRECT ROMAJI

Masumi [Sanezumi] Fujimoto
Yasuo Furuhata [Kohata]
Akira [Gyo] Hayasaka
Sei [Masaru] Hiraizumi
Seiji [Kiyoshi] Hoshikawa
Norimichi Ikawa [Tokumichi Igawa]
Akira [Sho] Inoue
Shigeru [Ko] Ishihara
Binpachi [Toshiya] Ito
So [Hajime] Kaburagi
Morio [Takeo] Kita
Shigeru Koyama [Kamiyama]
Takeo [Issei] Kunihiro
Kyoko Maya [Mano]
Sadatsugu [Teiji] [Sadaji] Matsuda
Hajime [Gen] Mitamura
Hideshi [Shuji] [Hideji] Miyajima
Kazuo [Issei] Mori
Mutsuo [Rokuo] Naganuma
Ichiro Nakatani [Nakaya]
Koji Nanbara [Nambara]
Ko [Akira] Nishimura
Hiroyoshi [Kozen] Nishioka
Soji [Soshi] Okita
Tetsuro Tanba [Tamba]
Shigemasa [Jusho] Toda
Rokko [Mutsuhiro] Toura
Shoji [Masaharu] Ueda
Chumei [Michiaki] [Hiroaki] Watanabe
Shunya [Toshiya] Wazaki
Gaku [Manabu] Yamamoto
Ichiro [Kazuo] Yamamoto

Sadaji [Sadatsugu] [Teiji] Yoshida
Takeshi [Go] Yoshida

VIDEO DISTRIBUTORS

The Distributors listed in the Filmography are for VHS and Region 1 (US/Canada) DVDs. Many titles are also available for other Regions. For those with multi-region players many newer Japanese (Region 2) NTSC DVDs have English sub-titles encoded. In addition, many Hong Kong NTSC (Region 3) DVDs of samurai films have both Chinese and English-language sub-titles, although many are inferior transfers and/or have problematic sub-titles (poor grammar and characters given Chinese names in the English sub-titles).

Samurai Video
PO Box 372
Suffern, NY 10901
TEL: (845) 357-5141
FAX: (845) 357-0780
www.samuraiflix.com

DVDAsian.Com
Omni Video, Inc
13340 E. Firestone Blvd Unit H
Santa Fe Springs CA 90670
TEL: (562) 921-0581
FAX: (562) 921-0582
Email: dvdasian2@covad.net
www.dvdasian.com

1-World Films
1worldfilms.com/SAMURAIFILMS.htm

Artsmagic Ltd.
PO Box 25
Ebbw Vale
Blaenau Gwent NP23 5YG, UK
FAX: 44 (0)1495 307343
www.artsmagic.co.uk/Samurai/

AnimEigo
P.O. Box 989
Wilmington, NC 28402-0989.
TEL: (800) 242-6463
FAX: (910) 763-2376
www.animeigo.com

Home Vision Entertainment
4423 N. Ravenswood Ave.
Chicago, Illinois 60640-5802
www.homevision.com [No direct sales]

VHS/DVD RENTAL OUTLETS

CineFile Video
11280 Santa Monica Boulevard
Los Angeles, CA 90025
TEL: (310) 312-8836
www.cinefilevideo.com/

Vidiots
302 Pico Blvd.
Santa Monica, CA 90405
TEL: (310) 392 8508
FAX: (310) 392 0099
www.vidiotsvideo.com

BIBLIOGRAPHY

BOOKS (GENERAL)

Anderson, Joseph L. and Richie, Donald. *The Japanese Film: Art and Industry*. New Jersey: Princeton University Press, 1983. [Kurosawa, Kobayashi, and Inagaki]

Beasley, W.G. *The Modern History of Japan*. New York: Praeger, 1963.

Bock, Audie. *Japanese Film Directors*. Tokyo: Kodansha, 1978.

Brinkley, F. *Samurai*. Burbank, California: Ohara Publications, 1975.

Burch, Noël. *Form and Meaning in the Japanese Cinema*. London: Scholar Press, 1979.

Charensol, Georges. *Le Cinema*. Paris: Librairie Larousse, 1966. [Kurosawa and Kobayashi]

Collis,, Maurice. *The Land of the Great Image*. New York: New Directions, 1958.

Cowie, Peter, editor. *A Concise History of the Cinema*. New York: A.S. Barnes, 1971. [Kurosawa and Kobayashi]

Davis, Darrell William. *Picturing Japaneseness*. New York: Columbia University Press, 1996.

Dorson, Richard M. *Folk Legends of Japan*. Rutland, Vermont: Charles B. Tuttle, 1962.

Dures, Peter. *Feudalism in Japan*. New York: Knopf, 1969.

Fenellosa, Ernest and Pound, Ezra. *The Chinese Written Character as a Medium for Poetry*. San Francisco: City Light Books, 1968.

Galbraith, Stuart, IV. *The Emperor and the Wolf: The Lives of Akira Kurosawa and Toshiro Mifune*. New York and London: Faber and Faber, 2001.

____. *The Japanese Filmography: 1900 Through 1994*. North Carolina and London: McFarland & Company, 1996.

Grilli, Peter, editor. *Japan In Film*. New York: Japan Society, 1984.

Gubern, Roman. *Historia del Cine*. Madrid: Ediciones Danae, 1969. [Kurosawa and Kobayashi]

Harris, Victor, translator. *A Book of Five Rings: Miyamoto Musashi*. Woodstock, New York: Overlook Press, 1974.

Hearn, Lafeadio. *Japan: An Attempt at Interpretation*. Rutland, Vermont: Charles E. Tuttle, 1955. [Reprint of MacMillan 1906 Edition]

High, Peter B. *The Imperial Screen: Japanese Film Culture in the Fifteen Years' War, 1931–1945*. Madison: University of Wisconsin Press, 2003.

Hornung, Clarence P. *Handbook of Designs and Devices*. New York: Harper, 1932.

Houston, Penelope. *The Contemporary Cinema*. London: Penguin, 1963. [Kurosawa and Kobayashi]

Isobe, Yaichiro. *Tales from the Kojiki*. Tokyo: San Kaku Sha, 1928.

Jacobs, Lewis. *The Movies as Medium*. New York: Strauss and Giroux, 1970. [Kurosawa and Kobayashi]

Jarvie, Ian C. *Movies and Society*. New York: Basic Books. 1970. [Kurosawa and Kobayashi]

Keene, Donald, editor. *An Anthology of Japanese Literature*. New York: Grove Press, 1960.

____, translator. *Chushingura: A Treasury of Loyal Retainers*. New York: Columbia University Press. 1971.

King, Winston L. *Zen and the Way of the Sword: Arming the Samurai Psyche*. Oxford: Oxford University Press, 1994.

Livingston, John; Moore, Joel; and Oldfather, Felicia, editors. *Imperial Japan*: 1800-1945. New York: Random House, 1963.

Macias, Patrick. *Tokyoscope: The Japanese Cult Film Companion*. Canada: Cadence Books, 2001.

Mellen, Joan. *The Wave at Genji's Door: Japan through Its Cinema*. New York: Pantheon Books, 1976.

Mintz, Marilyn. *Martial Arts Movies*. Cranbury, New Jersey: A.S. Barnes, 1978.

Mitford, A.B. *Tales of Old Japan*. Cambridge, Massachusetts: Wordsworth, 2001. [Reprint of 1871 MacMillan Edition]

Munsterberg, Hugo. *The Arts of Japan*. Rutland, Vermont: Charles E. Tuttle, 1957.

Nitobe, Inazo. *Bushido, The Soul of Japan*. Rutland, Vermont: Charles E. Tuttle, 1969. [Reprint of 1905 Edition]

Nolletti, Arthur and Desser, David, editors. *Reframing Japanese Cinema: Authorship, Genre, History*. Bloomington: Indiana University Press, 1992.

Piggott, Julia. *Japanese Mythology*. London: Paul Hamlyn, 1972.

Piña, Francisco. *El Cine Japonés*. Mexico City: Madero, 1965. [Kurosawa, Kobayashi, Inagaki, and Ito]

Quandt, James. *Kon Ichikawa*. Toronto: Toronto International Film Festival Group, 2001.

Ratti, Oscar and Westbrook, Adele. *Secrets of the Samurai*. Rutland, Vermont: Charles B. Tuttle, 1973.

Reischauer, Edwin O. *Japan*. New York: Aldfred A. Knopf, 1964.

Richie, Donald. *Japanese Movies*. Tokyo: Japan Travel Bureau, 1961. [Kurosawa, Kobayashi, and Inagaki]

____. *The Japanese Movie, An Illustrated History*. Tokyo: Kodansha, 1966. [Kutosawa and Kobayashi]

____. *Japanese Cinema*. New York: Doubleday, 1971. [Kurosawa, Kobayashi, Inagaki, Shinoda, Okamoto]

____. *A Hundred Years of Japanese Film*. Tokyo: Kodansha, 2001.

Sadoul, Georges. *Histoire du Cinéma Mondial*. Paris: Flammarion, 1966. [Kurosawa and Kobayashi]

Sanson, George A. *A History of Japan, 1615 To 1867*. Stanford, California: Stanford University Press, 1963.

Sato, Hiroaki. *The Legends of the Samurai*. Woodstock, New York: Overlook Press, 1995.

____. *Japan: A Short Cultural History*. New York: Appleton-Century-Crofts, 1962.

Sato, Tadao. *Currents in Japanese Cinema*. Tokyo: Kodansha, 1982. Gregory Barrett, translator.

Seward, Jack. *Hara-Kiri: Japanese Ritual Suicide*. Rutland, Vermont: Charles E. Tuttle, 1968.

Singer, Kurt. *Mirror, Sword, and Jewel*. New York: George Braziller, 1973.

Smith, Bradley. *Japan: A History in Art*. Garden City, New Jersey: Doubleday, 1964.

Souyri, Pierre Francois. *The World Turned Upside Down: Medieval Japanese Society*. Kathe Roth, translator. New York: Columbia University Press, 2001.

Suzuki, Daisetz. T. *Zen and Japanese Culture*. New Jersey: Princeton University Press, 1970.

Sword of Doom (1966). Starring Tatsuya Nakadai (center) as the evil swordsman Trukue. See page 264

308

Svensson, Arne. *Japan: An Illustrated Guide*. London: Zwemmer, 1971. [Kurosawa, Kobayashi, Inagaki, Ito, and Shinoda]

Takeo, Yataki. *Social Change and the City in Japan*. Tokyo: Japan Publications, 1968.

Tessier, Max. *Images du Cinéma Japonais*. Paris: Henri Veyrier, 1981.

Tucker, Richard B. *Japan: Film Image*. London: Studio Vista, 1973. [Kurosawa, Kobayashig and Shinoda]

Turim, Maureen. *The Films of Nagisa Oshima: Images of a Japanese Iconoclast*. Berkeley: University of California Press, 1998.

Turnbull, Stephen. *The Book of the Samurai*. New York: Arco, 1982.

____. *Samurai Sourcebook*. London: Arms & Armour, 2000.

____. *Samurai Warfare*. London: Arms & Armour, 1997.

Varley, H. Paul with Morris, Ivan and Nobuko. *Samurai*. London: Weidenfeld and Nicholson, 1970.

Varley, H. Paul. *A Syllabus of Japanese Civilization*. New York: Columbia University Press, 1972.

____. *Japanese Culture*, New York: Praeger, 1973.

Waley, Arthur, translator. *The No Plays of Japan*. New York: Grove Press, 1957.

____. *The Way and Its Power: A Study of The Tao Te Ching and Its Place in Chinese Thought*. New York: Grove Press, 1958.

Weisser, Thomas and Weisser, Yuko Mihara. *Japanese Cinema Essential Handbook*. Florida: Vital Books, 1996/1998 (revised).

Wilson, William Scott, translator. *Hakagure: the Book of the Samurai*. Rutland, Vermont: Charles E. Tuttle, 1992. [Translation of 18th Century work by Tsunetomo Yamamoto]

Yoshimoto, Mitsuhiro. *Kurosawa: Film Studies and Japanese Cinema*. North Carolina: Duke University Press, 2000.

Yumoto, John M. *The Samurai Sword*. Rutland, Vermont: Charles S.Tuttle, 1958.

Yuzan [Yusan], Daidoji. *Code of the Samurai: A Modern Translation of the Bushido Shoshinsu*. Rutland, Vermont: Charles S.Tuttle, 1999. Thomas Cleary, translator.

PERIODICALS (GENERAL)

Anderson, Joseph L. "Japanese Swordfighters and American Gunfighters," *Cinema Journal* (Spring, 1973), pp. 1-21.

Boudreau, Chad. "An Abriged History of *Manga*," *Comicbookreaders.com*, p. mangacolumns_mangabeginners-history.shtml.

Ciment, Michel. "Approaches du Cinéma Japonais." *Positif*, Number 73, p. 69f. [Kurosawa and Kobayashi]

Desjardins, Chris. "Samurai Films: A Neglected Genre" [Four part article], *Cult Movies*, Issues 12, 13, 15, 16 (1994-1995).

Desser, David. "Toward a Structural Analysis of the Postwar Samurai Film," *Quarterly Review of Film Studies*, Volume VIII, number 1 (Winter 1983), pp. 25-41.

The Film Journal, Number 11 (October, 1958). [Issue on Japanese Cinema]

Frazer, Robert. "The Psychology of the Samurai," *Psychology Today*, Volume II, number 8 (January, 1969), pp. 49-53, 68.

Kaminsky, Stuart. "The Samurai Film and the Weatern," *The Journal of Popular Film* (Fall, 1972), p. 312f.

Niogret, Hubert; Tessier, Max; Bourguignon, Thomas. "Memoires du Japan," *Positif*, Number 369 (November, 1991), pp. 80-104.

Richie, Donald. "The Face of 1963," *Films and Filming* (July, 1963), pp. 15-18, 35-36. [Kurosawa and Kobayashi]

____. "Honour All Round," *Films and Filming* (December, 1964).

____. "Japan—the Younger Talents," *Sight and Sound* (Spring, 1960).

____. "The Unexceptional Japanese Films," *Films in Review* (June-July, 1955), p. 273f. [Kurosawa and Kobayashi]

Silver, Alain. "Samurai," *Film Comment*, Volume XI, number 5 (September-October 1975), pp. 10-15.

____. "Miyamoto Musashi: The Ultimate Swordsman," *Martial Arts Movies* (January, 1982), pp. 34-39.

Stephens, Chuck. "Deadly Youth," *Film Comment*, Volume XXXVI, Number 6 (November-December, 2000), pp 22-26.

Strick, Philip. "Love, Honour and Obey," *Sight and Sound*, Volume IX, Number 8 (August, 2001), pp. 38-39, 44.

Tada, M. "The Destiny of Samurai Films," *East-West Film Journal*, Volume I, number 1 (December, 1986), pp. 48-58.

Tessier, Max, editor. "Le Cinéma Japonias au Present," *Cinéna d'Aujourd'hui*, Number 15 (Winter, 1979).

Ward, Elizabeth and Silver, Alain. "Tatsuya Nakadai: The Intellectual Tiger of *Chambara*," *Martial Arts Movies* (December, 1981), pp. 33-38.

White, Allen. "A Man, a Blade, an Empty Road: Postwar Samurai Film to 1970," *GreenCine.com* (March 28, 2003).

MASAKI KOBAYASHI - PERIODICALS

Cinema (USA). "Hara-kiri, Kobayashi, Humanism," (April-May, 1962) p. 32 f. [Includes Interview]

Iwabutchi, M. "Japan's Idealists," *Films and Filming* (January, 1960), p. 31.

Strick, Philip. "Rebellion," *Sight and Sound* (Spring, 1968), pp. 97-98.

Tessier, Max. "Cinq Japonais en quete de films: Masaki Kobayashi," *Écran* (March, 1972), pp. 19-24.

AKIRA KUROSAWA - BOOKS

Blumenthal, J. *Renaissance of the Film*. London: Collier, 1970. [*Throne of Blood*]

Desser, David. *The Samurai Films of Akira Kurosawa*. Ann Arbor, Michigan: UMI Research Press, 1983.

Dickinson, Thorold. *A Discovery of Cinema*. London: Oxford University Press, 1971.

Erens, Patricia. *Akira Kurosawa: A Guide to References and Resources*. Boston: G.K. Hall, 1979.

Études Cinématographiques. *Akira Kurosawa*. Paris: 1964.

Ezratty, Sacha. *Kurosawa*. Paris: Editions Universitaire, 1964.

Geduld, Harry, editor. *Filmmakers On Filmmaking*. Bloomington: Indiana University Press, 1970. [Interview]

Goodwin, James. *Akira Kurosawa and Intertextual Cinema*. Baltimore and London: John Hopkins University Press, 1994.

____, editor. *Perspectives on Akira Kurosawa*. Boston: G.K. Hall, 1994. [includes a reprint of Chapter Three from the second edition of this book]

Kurosawa, Akira. *Something Like an Autobiography*. New York: Random House, 1983. Audie E. Bock, translator.

Kurosawa, Akira and Richie, Donald, editor. *Rutgers Films in Print #6: Rashomon*. New Jersey: Rutgers University Press, 1987.

Manvell, Roger. *Shakespeare and the Film*. London: I.M. Dent, 1971. [*Throne of Blood*]

Prince, Stephen. *The Warrior's Camera: The Cinema of Akira Kurosawa*. New Jersey: Princeton University Press, 1991 & 1999 (revised).

Richie, Donald. *The Films of Akira Kurosawa*. 'Berkeley: University of California Press, 1965.

____, editor. *Focus on Rashomon*. Englewood Cliffs, New Jersey: Prentice-Hall, 1972. [Collection of Essays and Reviews]

____, editor. *Seven Samurai*. London: Lorimer, 1970. [Introduction and Screenplay]

____, editor. *Ikuru*. New York: Simon and Schuster, 1968. [Introduction and Screenplay]

____, editor. *Rashomon*. New York: Grove Press, 1969. [Essays, source material, and screenplay]

Sarris, Andrew. *Interviews with Film Directors*. New York: Bobbs-Merrill, 1967. [Interview]

Tyler, Parker. *Rashomon as Modern Art*. New York: Cinema 16, 1952. [Pamphlet]

PERIODICALS

Agel, Henri. "La Liturgie du Desespoir," *Positif*, Number 2.

Amengual, Barthelemy. "Dossier Akira Kurosawa," *Positif*, Number 296 (October, 1985), pp. 41-62.

Anderson, Joseph L. "The History of Japanese Moviest" *Films in Review* (June-July, 1955), p. 273f.

Anderson, Lindsay. "Two Inches Off the Ground," *Sight and Sound* (Spring, 1955), pp. 202-205.

Barbarow, G. "Rashomon and the Fifth Witness," *The Hudson Review* (Autumn, 1952).

Blumenthal, J. "'Macbeth' into *Throne of Blood*," *Sight and Sound* (Autumn, 1965), pp. 191-195.

Cinema (USA). "*Dodeskaden* Spectrum—Akira Kurosawa," Volume

7, Number 2, pp. 14-23. [Interview and articles by Masahiro Ogi and Joan Mellen]

Falk, Ray. "Introducing Japan's Top Director," *New York Times* (January 6, 1952)

____. "Interview with Kurosawa," *New York Times* (June-1, 1952).

Franklyn, A. Fredric. "Kurosawa: Ethnic Directors," *International Press Bulletin*, Volume I, number 4.

Gaffary, F. "Les Deux Visages d'Akira, Kurosawa," *Positif*, Number 22.

Gerlacht, John. "Shakespeare, Kurosawa, and Macbeth: A Response to J. Blumenthal." *Literature/Film Quarterly*, Volume I, number 4 (Fall, 1973), PP. 352-359.

Harrington, Curtis. "Rashomon et le Cinema, Japonais," *Cahiers du Cinéma*, Number 12 (May, 1952).

Higham, Charles. "Kurosawa's Humanism," *The Kenyon Review* (Autumn, 1965). pp. 737-742.

Iida, Shinbi. "Akira Kurosawa," *Cinema* (USA) (August-September, 1963), pp. 27-31-

Iwabutchi, M. "1954 in Japan," *Sight and Sound* (Spring, 1955), pp. 202-205.

____. "Japanese Cinema, 1961," *Film Culture* (Spring, 1962), pp. 85-88.

Iwasaki, A. "Japants New Screen Art—More Real than *Rashomon*," *Nation* (May 12, 1956), pp. 398-401.

____. "The Japanese Cinemas" *Film* (GB) (November-December, 1956), pp. 6-10.

____. "Kurosawa, and His Work," *Japan Quarterly* (January/ March, 1965), pp. 59-64.

Kael, Pauline. "Body and Soul," *Partisan Review* (Summer, 1963).

Kerr, D. "Samurai Lear," *American Film*, Volume X, number 10 (September, 1985), pp. 20-26.

Kirby,, Gordon. "An Index to the Films of Akira, Kurosawa," *Film Journal* (October, 1958), pp. 22-28.

Knight, Arthur. "Season in the Sun," *Saturday Review* (February 13, 1960).

Koichi, Yamada. "Destin de Samourai," *Cahiers du Cinéma*, Number 182 (September, 1966). [Interview and Filmography]

Leyda, Jay. "The Films of Akira Kurosawa," *Sight and Sound* (October-December, 1954), pp. ?4-78.

McVay, Douglas. "The Rebel in a Kimono," *Films and Filming* (July, 1961), pp. 9-10, 34.

____. "Samurai and Small Beer," *Films and Filming* (August, 1961), pp. 15-16.

Mellen, Joan. "The Epic Cinema of Akira Kurosawa," *Take One* (June, 1972), pp. 16-19.

Mercier, Pierre. "*Rashomon* et le Pedantisme," *Cahiers du Cinéma*, Number 24 (June, 1953).

Miller, Marilyn A. "Akira Kurosawa—the Man and His Movies," *Screen Education* (July-August, 1967), pp. 42-55.

Ortolani, Benito. "The Films and Faces of Akira Kurosawa," *America* (October 2, 1965), pp. 368-371.

Richardson, Tony. "*The Seven Samurai*," *Sight and Sound* (Spring, 1955), pp. 195-196.

Richie, Donald. "Where the Silver Screen has turned to Gold," *Theater Arts* (March, 1954), pp. 81-83, 87.

____. "Japanese Cinema versus Television," *Film Journal* (February, 1959), pp. 3-6.

____. "The Clashing Twain," *Film Journal* (November, 1959), pp. 19-21.

____. "Akira Kurosawa," *Orient-West* (Summer, 1962).

____. "Dostoievski with a Camera," *Horizon* (July, 1962), pp. 42-47.

____ "Kurosawa on Kurosawa," *Sight and Sound* (I: Summer, 1964; II: Autumn, 1964).

Roemer, Michael. "Kurosawa's Way of Seeing'" *The New York Reporter* (March 17, 1960). pp. 36-38.

Sadoul, Georges. "Existe-t-il un Neo-realism Japonais?" *Cahiers du Cinéma*, Number 28 (November, 1953).

Seton, Marie. "Japanese Cinema," *The Living Cinema*, Volume I, number 4, pp. 189-195.

Show business illustrated. "Kurosawa, Japan's Poet Laureate of Film," (April, 1962), pp. 28-29.

Silver, Alain and Ward, Elizabeth. "The Warrior's Way to Wisdom: Akira Kuraswa's Martial Arts Epics," *Martial Arts Movies* (September, 1981), pp. 22-30.

Silverstein, Norman. "Kurosawa's Detective Story Parables," *Japan Quarterly* (July-September, 1965), pp. 351-354.

Stanbrook, Alan. "Break with the Past," *Films and Filming* (March, 1960), pp. 9-11, 30.

____. "Oriental Talent," *Films and Filming* (April, 1960), pp. 13-14t 30.

Strauss, Harold. "My Affair with Japanese Movies," *Harper's Magazine* (July, 1955). pp. 54-59.

Thomas, Kevin. "Kurosawa: Founder of Japanese Film Dynasty," *Los Angeles Times* (August 4, 1963).

Time. "A Japanese Apocalypse," (September 21, 1962).

West, Anthony. "The Art of Akira Kurosawa," *Show* (July, 1962), pp. 58-62.

Wolf, Barbara. "Detectives and Doctors," *Japan Quarterly* (January-March, 1972), pp. 83-87-

Young, Vernon. "*The Hidden Fortress*: Kurosawa's Comic Mode," *The Hudson Review* (Summer, 1961), pp. 2?0-2?5.

SHINODA MASAHIRO - PERIODICALS

Johnston, Claire. "Double Suicide," *Focus on Film* (March-April, 1970), pp. 3-6.

Johnston, Claire and Svensson, Arne. "Masahiro Shinoda—Biography and Filmography," *Focus on Film* (March-April, 1970).

World Cinema. "Masahiro Shinoda—Biography and Interview," (December 10, 1971) .

GLOSSARY

akindo — the commercial class, lowest of the four major classes.

aragoto — "rough style" of acting in *Kabuki* tradition, an abbreviation of *aramushogato* or "reckless warrior matter."

ashigaru — a foot-soldier.

bakufu — a military government; used to refer to various eras of rule by a *shogun*.

bakumatsu — the fall of a military regime; used to designate the restoration to power of the Meiji dynasty in 1867.

bidanshi — "handsome man."

bishojo/bishonen — "beautiful youths"; somewhat androgenous depictions of young women (*jo*) and men (*nen*) in *anime*.

bokken or *bo-ken* — a wooden sword.

budo — "the martial path"; the martial arts, methods of fighting with and without arms in which the samurai was rigorously instructed.

bujutsu — "the martial art"; synonymous with *budo*. The alternate spelling "*jitsu*" is also used, sometimes more generally, as in *jujitsu*.

buke — the warrior class or samurai

buke-sho-hatto — a code of military conduct, often cited as first formalization of some of the unwritten tenets of *bushido* initially drafted written in 1615 by the first Tokugawa shogun, Ieyasu. The actual rules for the samurai, the *Shoshi Hatto* [see below], were promulgated in 1632.

buke-zukuri — a relatively modern type of sword mounting with a cross-taped handle.

bunraku — a style of theater using puppets rather than human actors as primary performers.

bushi — a warrior; *bu*: "martial"; *shi*: "knight."

bushido — "the way of the warrior," an unwritten ethical code of to be followed by all samurai. See also *budo* and *shido*.

bushi no-ichi gon — the word of a warrior, a solemn oath given by a Samurai to support an assertion or promise.

butsudo — the way of Buddha; Buddhism in Japan.

chambara — a realistically staged display of sword-fighting in a *Jidai-geki* or period drama; in motion pictures, a generic designation for a samurai film.

chanoyu — a formal tea ceremony which became part of samurai training and discipline.

chori — outcasts; a substrata of persons who did not hereditarily belong to any of the four major classes and who were isolated in ghetto-like communities.

chi-bara — a suicide out of loyalty, performed by a vassal order to admonish or follow his master in death.

dai-sho — a matched pair of long and medium length swords which could legally be worn only by the samurai class.

daito — literally "long saber," a sword with a blade length of at least two and one-half feet (measured in *shaku*—see below) but possibly over three feet, traditionally associated with the samurai, who was the only person privileged to carry it. Modern *daitos* have 40-inch blades. See also *tachi* and *katana*.

Dan-o-ura — the scene of the final battle between the Minamoto (victors) and Taira clans in 1185.

dojo — a gymnasium or place of religious meditation.

doshin — a constable.

fukushu — a "blood feud."

funshi — suicide out of righteous indignation.

geku-kujo — overthrow by underlings; an upset of the feudal hierarchy though armed rebellion; "the world turning upside down."

gendai-geki — a contemporary dramas in motion pictures, stories set from the Meiji restoration onward.

geta — open-toed wooden clogs with two raised feet on the underside, the wearing of which was a privilege of rank.

giri — "right reason"; the dutiful service which bushido directs the warrior to give to his family, clans and lord.

gokenin — "men of the house"; feudal vassals.

haniwa — clay statues of warriors, some small, some half life-size, found in graves of the Kara period.

hara-kiri — "stomach-cut," a reversal of the ideographs for *seppuku*; a common or vulgar term for ritual-suicide.

hatamoto — the highest rank of samurai retainer; literally "banner men."

heimin — a commoner; a non-samurai.

higeki — sorrowful drama; Japanese term for tragedy.

hinin — "non-man"; part of the populace not legally considered to be human beings.

isagi-yoku — without regrets; dying after all obligations have been fulfilled.

ishin shishi — "men of high purpose," young, low-ranking samurai from the outside provinces who supported the *bakumatsu*.

issho-kemmei — "all going together"; striving to advance in feudal status, the individual striving to earn distinction in order to enhance the social position of himself and his family.

ikko-ikki — "warrior monks"; partcipants in pre-Tokugawa conflicts from the 10th century onward who were ultimately repressed by Oda Nobunaga.

jindachi-zukuri — a relatively older type of sword mounting in which the scabbard is tied around the waist with a sash cord.

jitsuaku — villainous samurai.

jizamurai — a land-owning or farming samurai.

junshi — suicide performed to follow one's master in death.

kabuki — a style of theater which originated at the end of the 16th Century, combining dialogue with interludes of singing and dancing to musical accompaniment. Early forms include *yujo* (all female), *wakashu* (all young men), and *yaro* (all adult men).

kachi — Lower ranking members of a samurai clan.

kaishaku — the second in *hara-kiri*, the man who decapitates the performer after he stomach-cut has been accomplished.

kanshi — suicide to admonish an overlord for his unseemly or erratic behavior.

karoku — the stipend (room, board, and/or a monetary allowance) paid to a clan retainer.

kataki-uchi. — a vendetta; the securing of revenge for an insult or murder by surviving relatives or retainers.

katana — originally designating a medium sword blade, between about two shaku long and shorter than a *daito*. Only samurai could carry blades longer than two *shaku*. Modern *katanas* have up to 30-inch blades. Alternate: *uchigatana* or "inside sword" in the *otoshi-zashi*.

kendo — "the way of the sword," the art and technique of swordplay. Variants: *kenjutsu* and *kenjitsu*.

ken-geki — "sword theater"; dramas centering on or containing much swordplay.

kenin — "men of the house"; feudal vassals.

kikenshiso — "dangerous thoughts"; expressions of doubt about fealty or the caste system.

kirisutogomen,—- the right to kill a man of lower caste; a privilege reserved for the samurai class.

kodan — prose tales of warriors and heroes.

kojiki — the record of ancient matters; quasi-mythical history compiled in the first millennium.

koku — five bushels of rice which was deemed sufficient to feed a person for one year. This was also a land measure, in that one acre of land would produce about 10,000 bushels a year or 2,000 *koku*. Coinage was similarly based. The thin, oval gold coin or *ryo* often seen as a prop in *chambara* equaled 4 *koku*; one *bu* or *ichibukin* equaled a single *koku*, while one *shu* equaled 1/4th and one *mon* equaled 1/12th of a *koku*.

kokugaku, literally "nation study," the attempt during the Tokugawa era by scholars called *kokugakushu* to isolate and define Japanese culture.

kozuka — a small knife or dart kept in a special compartment of the scabbard.

kufu — discipline; de-localizing the mind to guard against over concentration.

kurogo — black-clad figures who "invisibly" change the scenery in *kabuki* and manipulate the puppets In *bunraku*.

kyokaku — a sword-carrying commoner.

kyunin — higher ranking members of a clan.

manji — "ten thousand"; the ideograph is written either as a crosssaltire or a swastika, and the number ten thousand connotes infinity or wholeness.

manyoshu — literally "book of ten thousand leaves"; the earliest collection of Japanese poetry containing 4,500 poems and published around 770 C.E. at the end of the Nara period.

metsuke — roving eyes; a term for professional spies.

munen-bara — see *funshi*.

musha-shugyo — training in hardship acquisition of skill in the martial arts through practical experience.

mushin no shin — "no-mindedness"; the mind capable of movement from unconscious thought to action; de-concentration.

naginata — a halberd-like weapon.

nakago — the tang or portion of the sword to which the hilt is fastened.

naniwa-bushi — poetic recitals of warrior exploits.

nihon-ji — chronical of Japan; companion volume to the *kojiki*.

ninaime — a *kabuki* actor who performs in the *wagoto*-style of Tojuro Sakata.

ninjo — man's will; the personal or conscientious inclination which is often opposed or constrained by *giri* or duty.

niten-ryu — "two-sword style"; a method of fighting simultaneously with both swords developed by Miyamoto Musashi.

noh — a style of theater employing chanted dialogue, carefully modulated dance, masks, and male actors exclusively.

oibara — see *junshi*

osho — an instuctor of *budo*; a monk.

otoko no michl — "the manly way"; for the samurai, living according to the demands of *giri* and *bushido*.

otoshi-zashi — method of wearing a *dai-sho* or matched pair so that the scabbards are tucked into the kimono sash.

oyabun — title for the head or boss of a group of *yakuza*.

ronin — "man on the wave"; a disenfranchised or masterless samurai; variant from the late Tokugawa era: *roshi* or "wave knight."

ryobu-Shinto — the two ways of the gods; merging of Shinto and Buddhist beliefs.

ryo-sebai — double guilt; concept by which a lord or magistrate may arbitrate a quarrel without declaring either party in the right.

312

sankin-kotai — alternate duty; the requirement that a *damiyo* attened the shogun six months out of the year or alternate years, often having to leave or substitute his heir for himself when not present.

samurai — literally a "servant"; warriors retained in the service of a clan.

sanzuku — bandits; feudal highwaymen who preyed on travelers and lsolated villages.

satori — "enlightenment"; in Buddhist thought, coming to understand the true nature of reality.

Sekigahora — scene of a decisive battle between the forces of Ieyasu Tokugawa (victor) and Hideyoshi Toyotomi for control of the *shogunate*, in 1600; beginning of the Tokugawa era.

sensei — a master, a term of respect for a teacher.

seppuku — "cutting the stomach"; reversal of the ideographs in *hara-kiri*; formal term for ritual suicide.

shaku — a unit of linear measure. A modern *shaku* is 30cm or just under 12 inches (11.96).

shido — "the knight's path"; sometimes used to refer to the non-martial code of the samurai.

shikomi-zue — a cane sword.

Shin Buddhism — Japanese variant in which the Amida Buddha welcomes anyone who will take the vow and invoke his name, ultimately transporting them to the Pure Land.

shinju — double suicide.

shin-ken — "new sword"; the period of sword-making after 1500. Also *shinto*—see below.

shi-no-ko-sho — the four major classes of feudal Japan: warriors, farmers, artisans, and businessmen.

shinogi-zukuri — a long sword blade tempered with a ridge line.

shinsengumi — "new group of select [men]"; citizen militia, quasi-unofficial police and vigilantes for the Tokugawa in Kyoto during the *bakumatsu*.

Shinto — "the way of the gods" or *shin tao* in Chinese; Japan's indigenous religion. Also *shinto*, literally "new saber" designating sword made during the Tokugawa era.

shizoku — descendants of the samurai who lost their privileges in 1876.

shogun — a generalissimo or field-marshal; the office held by the non-Imperial, hereditary rulers of feudal Japan.

shogunate — period of *de facto* rule by a shogun.

shokin kasegi — "reward earnings" used as a term for bounty hunting or a bounty hunter.

shoji — the painted wall and door panels of period rooms.

shoshi hatto — "rules for gentry," the official code of behavior established by the Tokugawa regime in 1632. The core version was established by Iemitsu Tokugawa four years later.

shoto — see *daito*

shushi — ethics; a moral system based on religious belief.

shushigaku — Sino-Japanese belief that a person's life is governed by the circumstances of his or her birth.

soka sensei — founding master of a school.

sokutsu-shi — suicide in honorable expiation for a crime.

sonno-joi — "restore the emperor, expel the foreigners," a slogan of the *bakumatsu* (revived in the 1930s by those who favored the Showa restoration).

suki — the space between which something can enter; a fatal inattention engendered by self-consciousness.

sunyata — emptiness voiding the body of conscious thoughts which in swordsmanship guards against over-concentration.

sumi — ink used to paint on rice paper; *sumi-e*, "ink painting."

tachi — a *daito* hung from sash or slung over the back.

tanto — a very short sword or dagger with a blade length of less than one foot or *shaku*.

tateyaku — the male protagonist in *kabuki* who, unlike the *ninaime*, behaves in a forceful and masculine manner.

tozama — the outside *daimyos*; traditionally a reference to the eighty-six clan lords who rank below the *go-sanke* (three exalted families) and the eighteen *kokushu* or lords of provinces.

ukiyo — the floating world; a *Shinto* conception of creation.

uji — the clan; among the samurai the group of families which constituted the ruling clan in a; province.

ujigami — familial gods; ancestral spirits to sacred to a particular clan.

ushin no shin — the mind conscious of itself; the opposite of *mushin-no shin,* over-concentration.

wagoto — refined style of acting in Kabuki tradition.

wakizashi — a medium sword with a 19 or 20-inch blade (between one and two *shaku*), the second sword of a "two-sword man." See *daito* and *katana* above.

wakon yosai — literally "Japanese ethos, Western technology"; a term from the early Meiji era concerning how Japanese should embrace modernization, that is usually translated as "Japanese spirit, Western things."

yakuza — literally "8-9-3" from a losing card combination; in feudal society a member of a roving group of gamblers (*bakuto*) or pimps (*ponbiki*).

yamato-damashi — the soul of Yamato; a soul disposed towards deification at the time of death.

yari — a lance.

yojimbo — a bodyguard.

yugen — "mystery"; the harmonious combination of visual and aural expressions in art.

yukaku — brothel districts precincts of the *hinin* or non-men.

zankanjo — a note of explanation left at the eight of an assassination.

zanshin — "remaining mind"; a principle by which one stays alert and ready before and after any moment of actual combat.

zen — "meditation"; Japanese form of Buddhism.

NOTES

INTRODUCTION

1. From *The Noh Plays of Japan* translated by Arthur Waley.

2. The exact date of the introduction of Buddhism to Japan by Korean missionaries is uncertain. Lafcadio Hearn sets the date at 552 A.D.; but the earliest estimate is the end of the 4th century, around the same time as the influx of Chinese culture and Confucianism. Buddhism's influence was not strongly felt until the 9th Century, by which time Japanese language as well as social customs has already been revised according to a Chinese/Confucian model.

3. The short document consists of 13 articles:

1. Literature, arms, archery and horsemanship are, systematically, to be the favourite pursuits.

2. Drinking parties and gaming amusements must be kept within due bounds.

3. Offenders against the law are not to be harbored in the domains.

4. Throughout the domains whether of the greater or lesser barons (*daimyo* and *shomyo*) or of the holders of minor benefices, if any of the gentry or soldiers (*shi* and *sotsu*) in their service be guilty of rebellion or murder, such offenders must be at once expelled from their domain.

5. Henceforth no social intercourse is to be permitted outside of one's own domain, with the people of another domain.

6. The residential castles in the domains may be repaired; but the matter must invariably be reported. Still more imperative is it that the planning of structural innovations of any kind must be absolutely avoided.

7. If in a neighboring domain innovations are being hatched or cliques being formed the fact is to be reported without delay.

8. Marriages must not be contracted at private convenience.

9. As to the rule that the *Daimyos* shall come (to the Shogun's Court at Edo) to do service.

10. There must be no confusion in respect of dress uniforms, as regards the materials thereof.

11. Miscellaneous persons are not at their own pleasure to ride in palanquins.

12. The samurai throughout the provinces are to practice frugality.

13. The lords of the great domains must select men of capacity for office.

4. Translated by D.T. Suzuki in *Zen and Japanese Culture*. See bibliography for a newer translation.

5. Translated by A.B. Mitford in *Tales of Old Japan*.

6. According to Jack Seward in *Hara-Kiri: Japanese Ritual Suicide*, the progressive penalties for samurai misbehavior instituted by the Tokugawa shogunate were: (1) *Hissoku*, penitential seclusion; (2) *Heimon*, house arrest for either 50 or 100 days; (3) *Chikkyo*, solitary confinement, temporary retirement, or permanent retirement with reinstatement to the samurai rolls after death; (4) *Kai-eki*, attainder or permanent removal of the individual or family name from the samurai rolls; (5) *Seppuku*.

7. Although it continued as a fairly common practice until the end of World War II and received renewed attention in 1970 when the novelist Yukio Mishima performed it, *seppuku* lost formal recognition as a social institution shortly after the Meiji restoration. Despite the overwhelming defeat of a law aimed at abolishing it outright in 1869, with defenders claiming it was a pious deed and a "shrine of the national spirit," *seppuku* was degraded and eliminated from the legal statutes four years later.

8. Monzaemon Chikamatsu, who is often dubbed Japan's Shakespeare, wrote two plays loosely inspired by the then-recent events: *Keisei mitsu no kuruma*, a *kabuki* piece performed the year of the 47 *ronins*' suicide and *Goban Taheiki* (1710), a puppet play. The films are discussed in the next chapter. The Fuji networks made-for-television movie, *Chushingura 1/47*, was broadcast in 2001.

9. According to H. Paul Varley in *Samurai*, the latter sword acquired its name because, when used to decapitate a man, its edge was so keen that it could slice through not just the neck but the beard and knees also.

10. Translated by D. T. Suzuki.

11. Idem

CHAPTER ONE

1. Translated by Ryusaku Tsunoda and Donald Keene in *Anthology of Japanese Literature*.

2. Tezuka quoted in Chad Boudreau, "An Abriged History of Manga," *Comicbookreaders.com*.

3. Ernest Fenellosa, *The Chinese Written Character as a Medium for Poetry*.

CHAPTER TWO

1. The sequence shot or an entire scene photographed in a single take adds both a literal visual unity and a dynamic visual tension to the normal shot. The latter effect depends on the viewer's awareness (conscious or unconscious) that a "standard" sequence is usually constructed from a number of different angles edited together. There is also a consequent tension in anticipation of the visual break or cut which the director is withholding.

CHAPTER THREE

1. Translated by David Wright.

2. The historical figure, Ryoma Sakamoto (1835-1867), was born in Tosa *han* and is buried near Kiyomozu Temple in Kyoto. The son of a wealthy merchant who purchased the privileges of a low-ranking samurai, Sakamoto was initially a rabid follower of *sonno-joi* who planned to assassinate Rintaro Katsu, a shogunate official charged with normalizing relations with Western powers. Meeting Katsu changed Sakamoto, and he became a proponent of opening the country to trade, building a commercial fleet, and ultimately "restoring" Emperor Meiji as a precursor to parliamentary rule. In 1864 Sakamoto established a trading company in Nagasaki. Shortly thereafter he approached the Choshu clan, ostracized since attacking the Dutch ships. By early 1866 he had helped forge a "secret" pact between Tosa, Satsuma, and Choshu. The day after the pact was signed in Kyoto, the shogunate sent *shinsengumi* to kill Sakamoto. Using a pistol to fight them off, he was wounded but escaped. Late in 1867, a month after the shogun's abdication, he was assassinated. In fall of 2003, Sakamoto became the first individual in Japan to have an airport named after him.

Chapter Four

1. From Chapter V, *The Way and Its Power, A Study of Tao Te Ching* by Arthur Waley.

2. Katsu Productions then began a Zato Ichi television series which aired over a hundred episodes.

3. Although there were three earlier Toho Productions starring Koji Tsurata and also two final films in the Daiei series starring Hiroki Matsukata (see filmography for details), in terms of sustained popularity with film audiences the Nemuri character died with Ichikawa in 1969.

4. *Currents in Japanese Cinema*, p. 39.

5. See filmography for individual titles beginning with *Zen and Sword* (*Miyamoto Musashi!*, 1960). Before his death Uchida produced a sixth title, *Swords of Death* (*Shinken Shobu*, 1970), released by Toho. Both the Inagaki and Uchida multi-part versions are based on a novel by Eiji Yoshikawa. The Ryotaro Shiba novel *The True Story of Miyamoto Musashi* (*Shisetsu Miyamoto Musashi*) was used in the 1968 *Musashi*.

6. From *Zen and Japanese Culture*.

Chapter Five

1. Bokuden (1489-1571), the founding master of Kashima Shinto-ryu, undertook the first "sword pilgrimage" and wrote the *Bokuden Ikun Sho*, 100 *waka* or short poems about the art of the sword. This one is translated by Ryusaku Tsunoda and Donald Keene in *Anthology of Japanese Literature*.

2. From *The Book of Five Rings* translated by Victor Harris.

3. A popular series which preceded any feature film work and first brought Gosha some name recognition in the Japanese entertainment industry. Given the prominence of Gosha's work as a director in this study, a few biographical details are appropriate. After studying business at Meiji University, Gosha began working in television in 1952 and became a producer for Fuji TV in 1959. After the premiere of the *Three Outlaw Samurai* series in 1963, Shochiku commissioned a feature version.

4. A term I am using to designate a zoom-shot which not only moves into a detail or goes "in a straight-line" but also pans or tilts while zooming, so that the shot is more fully recomposed.

5. A situation which requires only a glance at a bibliography still devoid of any studies of Gosha's films for confirmation. At this writing a Google® search for Akira Kurosawa returns 795,000 hits, still considerably more than comtemporary filmmaker Takeshi Kitano at 278,000. Masaki Kobayashi receives 15,300; Shinobu Hashimoto, 4,710; Masahiro Shinoda, 5,630; and Kihachi Okamoto, 10,200. Thanks to the availability of several Zato Ichi titles on DVD, even Kenji Misumi has 15 times as many hits as Gosha's 781; and many of those pages are lists of "most wanted films" posted by *chambara* fans desperate to see *Tenchu*.

6. The historical Izo Okada (c.1838-1865) was a Tosa assassin reputedly of the Kyoushin Meichi-Ryu school of swordmanship.

Chapter Six

1. A work with which a Western film-viewer may be familiar as the puppet play which inspires the double suicide of the American non-com and his Japanese wife in *Sayonara* (1957).

Chapter Seven

1. Suburbs of Kyoto where the Boshin War began in January, 1868 when shogunate and *shinsengumi* fighters lost to a smaller *ishin shishi* force equipped with more firearms and cannon.

2. In the actual creation myth two divine beings, the male Izanagi and the female Izanami, stand on the Floating Bridge of Heaven, and Izanagi thrusts through the viscous waters with the *Ama-no-Nuboko*, a jeweled spear. When he draws it back he drops that fall from the tip coagulate into the island of Onokoro. The couple settle on the island and ultimately Izanami gives birth to the rest of the islands and sundry gods of the sea and wind. In one variant, all the islands of Japan are formed from the drops that fall from the *Ama-no-Nuboko*.

3. Takamori Saigo was one of the *ishin shishi* from Satsuma who helped bring about the *bakumatsu*. After leading the Imperial forces during most of the Boshin War, he was appointed minister of the Army in the first cabinets of Prince Mutsuhito/Emperor Meiji and acted as head of the Imperial Guard. Rebuffed in 1873 over his plan to invade Korea, Saigo resigned and returned to Satsuma where he founded a private academy. When some of his followers attacked a government arsenal, he was forced into open rebellion. In the actual climactic battle of Tabura-zaka hill, which ended the Satsuma Rebellion of 1876-77, Saigo was indeed wounded and did commit suicide with his own sword. While Katsumoto's force is depicted as a small band of mountain samurai armed only with swords, lances, bows and arrows, and a cavalry unit, Saigo's rebel army numbered 10,000 men, who wore uniforms not samurai armor, carried muzzle-loading rifles, had no cavalry, but did field a couple of artillery pieces. They faced a better equipped force more than twice their size in a battle that left over 7,000 dead. After death, Takamori was pardoned by the Emperor, valorized as an example of the warrior ideal, and a statue (ironically in Western garb) erected in his honor in Satsuma. "Ujio" would appear to be based on Hanjiro Nakamoto, a key character in Kenji Misumi's *The Last Samurai*, who died in the battle. "Omura" is actually Okubo Toshimitsu, a wealthy Satsuma samurai who worked with Takamori during the *Bakumatsu* but opposed the war with Korea. He was assassinated in 1878 by six Satsuma clansmen seeking revenge for his "betrayal" of Saigo.

4. The attribution of emotion to the neutral expression of an actor through montage, based on the "Mozhukin Experiments" of 1919 in which director Lev Kuleshov intercut an identical, archival "reaction" shot of prominent stage actor Ivan Mozhukin with very different point-of-view shots (food, an infant, a dead woman) and "tricked" the spectator into believing Mozhukin had been directed to alter his facial expression and register different emotions (hunger, paternity, sorrow).

Filmography

1. It has been asserted, initially by David Desser and frequently since the release of *Last Man Standing* in 1996, that *Yojimbo* is an uncredited adaptation of Dashiell Hammett's 1928 novel *Red Harvest*. The fact that Walter Hill was one of several directors to attempt an adaptation of the Hammett novel long before acquiring the rights to remake *Yojimbo* has muddied the waters. While there is a narrative resemblance between the Kurosawa and Hammett works in that a main character plays two corrupt factions against each other, there is not much else to connect them. Plot points cross-over from fiction and between films and one writer/director may inspire another—for example the plot point of a police detective who looses his gun drives both Kurosawa's *Stray Dog* and Walter Hill's *48 Hrs.*, but that hardly makes one an uncredited adaptation of the other.

Works in italics are films unless otherwise indicated. Page numbers in italics indicate illustrations. Page numbers after the semi-colon refer to entries in the filmography, bibliography, and/or glossary.